HOW THE TALMUD WORKS

THE BRILL REFERENCE LIBRARY
OF
ANCIENT JUDAISM

Editors

J. NEUSNER *(Bard College)* — H. BASSER *(Queens University)*

A.J. AVERY-PECK *(College of the Holy Cross)* — Wm.S. GREEN *(University of Rochester)* — G. STEMBERGER *(University of Vienna)* — I. GRUENWALD *(Tel Aviv University)* — M. GRUBER *(Ben-Gurion University of the Negev)*

G.G. PORTON *(University of Illinois)* — J. FAUR *(Bar Ilan University)*

VOLUME 9

HOW THE TALMUD WORKS

BY

JACOB NEUSNER

BRILL
LEIDEN · BOSTON · KÖLN
2002

This book is printed on acid-free paper.

Cover design: Robert Nix, Badhoevedorp, The Netherlands

Die Deutsche Bibliothek - CIP-Einheitsaufnahme

Neusner, Jacob:
How the Talmud works / by Jacob Neusner. – Leiden ; Boston ; Köln :
Brill, 2002
(The Brill reference library of ancient Judaism ; Vol. 9)
ISBN 90–04–12796-8

Library of Congress Cataloging-in-Publication Data

Library of Congress Cataloging-in-Publication Data is also available

ISSN   1566-1237
ISBN   90 04 12796 8

CONTENTS

PART ONE

THE INTELLECTUAL PROGRAM

PREFACE

The Bavli, or Talmud of Babylonia, the foundation-document of Judaism, sets forth an orderly world, resting on reason and tested by rationality, all in accord with consistent principles. The document in its coherent intellectual program of inquiry and in its modes of formal cogency embodies that same passion for order, proportion, and rationality that, animates its concrete discussions. In this two-part recapitulation of some of my monographs on how the Bavli works—the problem of the Bavli's intellectual cogency and formal coherence—I spell out in exemplary detail the evidence that sustains that characterization of the writing.

A commentary to the Mishnah, a philosophical law-code made up of sixty-two topical expositions or tractates compiled in the Roman-ruled Land of Israel by ca. 200 C.E., the Bavli, produced at about 600 C.E. in the Iranian satrapy of Babylonia, in the vicinity of present-day Baghdad, takes up the Hebrew Scriptures (a.k.a., the Old Testament). The Talmud translates Pentateuchal narratives and laws into a systematic account of its "Israel's" entire social order. In its thirty-seven topical presentations of Mishnah-tractates, the Talmud portrays not so much how people are supposed to live—this the Mishnah does—as how they ought to think, the right way of analyzing circumstance and tradition alike. That is what makes encounter with the Bavli urgent for the contemporary situation. To a world such as ours, engaged as it is, at the dawn of a new century by standard reckoning, in a massive enterprise of reconstruction after history's most destructive century, old systems having given way, new ones yet to show their merit and their mettle, the Talmud presents a considerable resource.

The Talmud embodies applied reason and practical logic in quest of the holy society. That model of criticism and reason in the encounter with social reform of which I spoke is unique. The kind of writing that the Talmud represents has serviceable analogues but no known counterpart in the literature of world history and philosophy, theology, religion, and law. That is because the Talmud sets forth not only decisions and other wise and valuable information, but the choices that face reasonable persons and the bases for de-

ciding matters in one way rather than in some other. And the Talmud records the argument, the constant, contentious, uncompro-
mising argument, that endows with vitality the otherwise merely
informative corpus of useful insight. "Let logic pierce the mountain"—that is what sages say. Not many have attained the purity of
intellect characteristic of this writing. With the back-and-forth argument, the Talmud enlightens and engages. How so? The Talmud
sets forth not so much a record of what was said as a set of notes
that permit the engaged reader to reconstruct thought and recapitulate reason and criticism. Indeed, the Talmud treats coming generations the way composers treat unborn musicians: they provide the
notes for the musicians to reconstruct the music. In the Talmudic
framework, then everything is in the moving, or dialectical argument,
the give and take of unsparing rationality, by which, through our
own capacity to reason, we are expected to reconstitute the issues,
the argument, the prevailing rationality. The Bavli makes enormous
demands upon its future. It pays a massive compliment to its heirs.

In this part of the account, I summarize research that shows the
formal cogency of the Bavli. First of all, I demonstrate that a single
plan of organization governs. The Bavli is exquisitely organized, once
one discerns the principles of order and recognizes the problems the
sages solved in adopting those principles. Just as the Bavli as a whole
is cogent, doing some few things over and over again, so it follows
a simple program, start to finish. Second, I turn to the one important challenge to that view, the massive miscellanies we find here
and there, which disrupt the flow of discourse. I explain the contribution that these make to the document and account for their po-
sitioning. Pursuing the same question, I turn in the third study to
the substantive result of the insertion of a miscellany, dealing with
entire tractates. I show that the intrusion of a miscellany represents
a constructive initiative, an intended reshaping of the exposition
altogether. When we ask, what has this to do with that, and when
we attempt a response, we find time and again that at the foundations of the jarring juxtaposition or not-to-be-predicted connection
is a self-evident proposition. Fourth, pursuing this same inquiry into
evidence that contradicts my basic theory, I turn to the other-than-
Mishnah-exegetical compositions and composites that the Bavli
utilizes but that the Bavli's primary framers and compilers did not
produce in their work of Talmud-making. I ask this kind of composition and composite to tell us where that part of the document comes

from, outside of the circles of its primary writers and compilers, the Mishnah-exegetes who composed the Talmud from beginning to end. I seek to identify the building blocks of Talmudic discourse that advance a redactional program other than that of the Talmud overall, in its paramount components. Once we know how to identify the irreducible minima of discourse other than that that sets the norm in the Talmud, we can take up the analysis of the Talmud's extra-talmudic component. Finally, at the end, I explain the reference-system that I have devised for the Talmud (and, by extension, for the rest of the Rabbinic documents of late antiquity).

All of the research epitomized here was carried on at the University of South Florida and Bard College, in the years from my appointment in 1990 at USF to 2000, and in 1994 at Bard College to the present. Both centers of higher learning provided generous research grants, and, more important, through the professorships that I held, they afford on-going support, so that I was able to do this work. Since 1990 I have taken up problems of a far more demanding and weighty character than I was able to consider in the twenty-one years prior in a less fortunate, because slothful and intellectually inert, academic setting. I am inclined to credit my colleagues at USF and Bard for the shift. Their rigorous challenge, their sustained interest in the response to their questions, and their cordial collegiality have made a huge difference in my life, all to the good.

JACOB NEUSNER
BARD COLLEGE

BIBLIOGRAPHY

Each chapter of this book summarizes and condenses a sizable monograph. Readers who wish to see my full exposition of the Bavli and its traits, with complete texts, on which each point is based may refer to the items listed here.

THE TORAH IN THE TALMUD:
The Torah in the Talmud. A Taxonomy of the Uses of Scripture in the Talmuds. Tractate Qiddushin in the Talmud of Babylonia and the Talmud of the Land of Israel. I. *Bavli Qiddushin Chapter One.* Atlanta, 1993: Scholars Press for South Florida Studies in the History of Judaism.
The Torah in the Talmud. A Taxonomy of the Uses of Scripture in the Talmuds. Tractate Qiddushin in the Talmud of Babylonia and the Talmud of the Land of Israel. II. *Yerushalmi Qiddushin Chapter One. And a Comparison of the Uses of Scripture by the Two Talmuds.* Atlanta, 1993: Scholars Press for South Florida Studies in the History of Judaism.

THE QUESTION OF TRADITION:
Sources and Traditions. Types of Composition in the Talmud of Babylonia. Atlanta, 1992: Scholars Press for South Florida Studies in the History of Judaism.
The Bavli and its Sources: The Question of Tradition in the Case of Tractate Sukkah. Atlanta, 1987: Scholars Press for Brown Judaic Studies.

WHERE THE TALMUD DOES NOT COME FROM
Where the Talmud Comes From: A Talmudic Phenomenology. Identifying the Free-Standing Building Blocks of Talmudic Discourse. Atlanta, 1995: Scholars Press for South Florida Studies in the History of Judaism.
The Bavli That Might Have Been: The Tosefta's Theory of Mishnah-Commentary Compared with That of the Babylonian Talmud. Atlanta, 1990: Scholars Press for South Florida Studies in the History of Judaism.
Tradition and Selectivity
Tradition as Selectivity: Scripture, Mishnah, Tosefta, and Midrash in the Talmud of Babylonia. The Case of Tractate Arakhin. Atlanta, 1990: Scholars Press for South Florida Studies in the History of Judaism.
The Initial Phases of the Talmud's Judaism. Atlanta, 1995: Scholars Press for South Florida Studies in the History of Judaism. I. *Exegesis of Scripture.*
The Initial Phases of the Talmud's Judaism. Atlanta, 1995: Scholars Press for South Florida Studies in the History of Judaism. II. *Exemplary Virtue.*
The Initial Phases of the Talmud's Judaism. Atlanta, 1995: Scholars Press for South Florida Studies in the History of Judaism. III. *Social Ethics.*
The Initial Phases of the Talmud's Judaism. Atlanta, 1995: Scholars Press for South Florida Studies in the History of Judaism. IV. *Theology.*
The Talmud's Intellectual Character.
The Bavli's Intellectual Character. The Generative Problematic in Bavli Baba Qamma Chapter One and Bavli Shabbat Chapter One. Atlanta, 1992: Scholars Press for South Florida Studies in the History of Judaism.

Decoding the Talmud's Exegetical Program: From Detail to Principle in the Bavli's Quest for Generalization. Tractate Shabbat. Atlanta, 1992: Scholars Press for South Florida Studies in the History of Judaism.

TALMUDIC DIALECTICS
Talmudic Dialectics: Types and Forms. Atlanta, 1995: Scholars Press for South Florida Studies in the History of Judaism. I. *Introduction. Tractate Berakhot and the Divisions of Appointed Times and Women.*
Talmudic Dialectics: Types and Forms. Atlanta, 1995: Scholars Press for South Florida Studies in the History of Judaism. II. *The Divisions of Damages and Holy Things and Tractate Niddah.*

THE TALMUD'S STRUCTURE AND ITS RATIONALITY
Rationality and Structure: The Bavli's Anomalous Juxtapositions. Atlanta, 1997: Scholars Press for South Florida Studies in the History of Judaism.
The Theological Grammar of the Oral Torah. Binghamton, 1998: Dowling College Press/Global Publications of Binghamton University [SUNY]. II. *Syntax: Connections and Constructions*

THE LANGUAGES OF THE BAVLI
Language as Taxonomy. The Rules for Using Hebrew and Aramaic in the Babylonian Talmud. Atlanta, 1990: Scholars Press for South Florida Studies in the History of Judaism.

THE BAVLI'S ONE VOICE
The Bavli's One Voice: Types and Forms of Analytical Discourse and their Fixed Order of Appearance. Atlanta, 1991: Scholars Press for South Florida Studies in the History of Judaism.

THE BAVLI'S UNIQUE VOICE
The Bavli's Unique Voice. A Systematic Comparison of the Talmud of Babylonia and the Talmud of the Land of Israel. Volume One. *Bavli and Yerushalmi Qiddushin Chapter One Compared and Contrasted.* Atlanta, 1993: Scholars Press for South Florida Studies in the History of Judaism.
The Bavli's Unique Voice. A Systematic Comparison of the Talmud of Babylonia and the Talmud of the Land of Israel. Volume Two. *Yerushalmi's, Bavli's, and Other Canonical Documents' Treatment of the Program of Mishnah-Tractate Sukkah Chapters One, Two, and Four Compared and Contrasted. A Reprise and Revision of* The Bavli and its Sources. Atlanta, 1993: Scholars Press for South Florida Studies in the History of Judaism.
The Bavli's Unique Voice. A Systematic Comparison of the Talmud of Babylonia and the Talmud of the Land of Israel. Volume Three. *Bavli and Yerushalmi to Selected Mishnah-Chapters in the Division of Moed. Erubin Chapter One, and Moed Qatan Chapter Three.* Atlanta, 1993: Scholars Press for South Florida Studies in the History of Judaism.
The Bavli's Unique Voice. A Systematic Comparison of the Talmud of Babylonia and the Talmud of the Land of Israel. Volume Four. *Bavli and Yerushalmi to Selected Mishnah-Chapters in the Division of Nashim. Gittin Chapter Five and Nedarim Chapter One. And Niddah Chapter One.* Atlanta, 1993: Scholars Press for South Florida Studies in the History of Judaism.
The Bavli's Unique Voice. A Systematic Comparison of the Talmud of Babylonia and the Talmud

of the Land of Israel. Volume Five. *Bavli and Yerushalmi to Selected Mishnah-Chapters in the Division of Neziqin. Baba Mesia Chapter One and Makkot Chapters One and Two.* Atlanta, 1993: Scholars Press for South Florida Studies in the History of Judaism.

The Bavli's Unique Voice. A Systematic Comparison of the Talmud of Babylonia and the Talmud of the Land of Israel. Volume Six. *Bavli and Yerushalmi to a Miscellany of Mishnah-Chapters. Gittin Chapter One, Qiddushin Chapter Two, and Hagigah Chapter Three.* Atlanta, 1993: Scholars Press for South Florida Studies in the History of Judaism.

The Bavli's Unique Voice. Volume Seven. *What Is Unique about the Bavli in Context? An Answer Based on Inductive Description, Analysis, and Comparison.* Atlanta, 1993: Scholars Press for South Florida Studies in the History of Judaism.

How the Bavli is Organized
The Rules of Composition of the Talmud of Babylonia. The Cogency of the Bavli's Composite. Atlanta, 1991: Scholars Press for South Florida Studies in the History of Judaism.

The Principal Parts of the Bavli's Discourse: A Final Taxonomy. Mishnah-Commentary, Sources, Traditions, and Agglutinative Miscellanies. Atlanta, 1992: Scholars Press for South Florida Studies in the History of Judaism.

The Composition and the Composite
How the Bavli Shaped Rabbinic Discourse. Atlanta, 1991: Scholars Press for South Florida Studies in the History of Judaism.

The Bavli's Massive Miscellanies
The Bavli's Massive Miscellanies. The Problem of Agglutinative Discourse in the Talmud of Babylonia. Atlanta, 1992: Scholars Press for South Florida Studies in the History of Judaism.

The Talmud's One Statement
The Bavli's One Statement. The Metapropositional Program of Babylonian Talmud Tractate Zebahim Chapters One and Five. Atlanta, 1991: Scholars Press for South Florida Studies in the History of Judaism.

The Talmud's Exegetical Program
The Bavli's Primary Discourse. Mishnah Commentary, its Rhetorical Paradigms and their Theological Implications in the Talmud of Babylonia Tractate Moed Qatan. Atlanta, 1992: Scholars Press for South Florida Studies in the History of Judaism.

The Talmud's Essential Discourse: The Law behind the Laws
The Law Behind the Laws. The Bavli's Essential Discourse. Atlanta, 1992: Scholars Press for South Florida Studies in the History of Judaism.

This is not the first reprise of diverse research-projects that I have published. I may also note that I produced a volume of summaries at the end of some sustained research half a decade ago, in the following:

How to Study the Bavli: The Languages, Literatures, and Lessons of the Talmud of Babylonia. Atlanta, 1992: Scholars Press for South Florida Studies in the History of Judaism.

I have tried also to publish in article-form reprises of a number of works, the sheer volume of which creates difficulties for those interested in following my solutions to some of the principal problems of the Rabbinic literature.

My translations, outlines, and academic commentaries of both Talmuds are as follows:

The Talmud of Babylonia. An Academic Commentary. Atlanta, 1994-6: Scholars Press for *USF Academic Commentary Series.*

I.	*Bavli Tractate Berakhot*
II.A	*Bavli Tractate Shabbat. Chapters One through Twelve*
II.B	*Bavli Tractate Shabbat. Chapters Thirteen through Twenty-Four*
III.A	*Bavli Tractate Erubin. Chapters One through Five*
III.B	*Bavli Tractate Erubin. Chapters Six through Eleven*
IV.A	*Bavli Tractate Pesahim. Chapters One through Seven.*
IV.B	*Bavli Tractate Pesahim. Chapters Eight through Eleven.*
V.	*Bavli Tractate Yoma*
VI.	*Bavli Tractate Sukkah*
VII.	*Bavli Tractate Besah*
VIII.	*Bavli Tractate Rosh Hashanah*
IX.	*Bavli Tractate Taanit* [1999]
X.	*Bavli Tractate Megillah*
XI.	*Bavli Tractate Moed Qatan*
XII.	*Bavli Tractate Hagigah*
XIII.A	*Bavli Tractate Yebamot. Chapters One through Eight*
XIII.B	*Bavli Tractate Yebamot. Chapters Nine through Seventeen*
XIV.A	*Bavli Tractate Ketubot. Chapters One through Six*
XIV.B	*Bavli Tractate Ketubot. Chapters Seven through Fourteen*
XV.	*Bavli Tractate Nedarim*
XVI.	*Bavli Tractate Nazir* [1999]
XVII.	*Bavli Tractate Sotah*
XVIII.	*Bavli Tractate Gittin*
XIX.	*Bavli Tractate Qiddushin*
XX.	*Bavli Tractate Baba Qamma*
XXI.A	*Bavli Tractate Baba Mesia. Chapters One through Six*
XXI.B	*Bavli Tractate Baba Mesia. Chapters Seven through Eleven*
XXII.A	*Bavli Tractate Baba Batra. Chapters One through Six*
XXII.B	*Bavli Tractate Baba Batra. Chapters Seven through Eleven*
XXIII.A	*Bavli Tractate Sanhedrin. Chapters One through Seven*
XXIII.B	*Bavli Tractate Sanhedrin. Chapters Eight through Twelve*
XXIV.	*Bavli Tractate Makkot*
XXV.	*Bavli Tractate Abodah Zarah*
XXVI.	*Bavli Tractate Horayot*
XXVII.	*Bavli Tractate Shebuot*
XXVIII.A	*Bavli Tractate Zebahim. Chapters One through Seven*
XXVIII.B	*Bavli Tractate Zebahim. Chapters Eight through Fifteen*
XXIX.A	*Bavli Tractate Menahot. Chapters One through Six*
XXIX.B	*Bavli Tractate Menahot. Chapters Seven through Fourteen*
XXX.	*Bavli Tractate Hullin*
XXXI.	*Bavli Tractate Bekhorot*
XXXII.	*Bavli Tractate Arakhin*
XXXIII	*Bavli Tractate Temurah*

XXXIV.   *Bavli Tractate Keritot*
XXXV.   *Bavli Tractate Meilah and Tamid*
XXXVI.   *Bavli Tractate Niddah*

The Talmud of Babylonia. A Complete Outline. Atlanta, 1995-6: Scholars Press for *USF Academic Commentary Series.*
I.A   *Tractate Berakhot and the Division of Appointed Times. Berakhot, Shabbat, and Erubin.*
I.B   *Tractate Berakhot and the Division of Appointed Times. Pesahim through Hagigah.*
II.A.   *The Division of Women. Yebamot through Ketubot*
II.B.   *The Division of Women. Nedarim through Qiddushin*
III.A   *The Division of Damages. Baba Qamma through Baba Batra*
III.B   *The Division of Damages. Sanhedrin through Horayot*
IV.A   *The Division of Holy Things and Tractate Niddah. Zebahim through Hullin*
IV.B   *The Division of Holy Things and Tractate Niddah. Bekhorot through Niddah*

The Talmud of the Land of Israel. An Academic Commentary to the Second, Third, and Fourth Divisions. Atlanta, 1998-9: Scholars Press for *USF Academic Commentary Series.*
I.   *Yerushalmi Tractate Berakhot*
II.A   *Yerushalmi Tractate Shabbat. Chapters One through Ten*
II.B   *Yerushalmi Tractate Shabbat. Chapters Eleven through Twenty-Four. And the Structure of Yerushalmi Shabbat*
III.   *Yerushalmi Tractate Erubin*
IV.   *Yerushalmi Tractate Yoma*
V.A   *Yerushalmi Tractate Pesahim. Chapters One through Six.*
V.B   *Yerushalmi Tractate Pesahim. Chapters Seven through Ten. And the Structure of Yerushalmi Pesahim*
VI.   *Yerushalmi Tractate Sukkah*
VII.   *Yerushalmi Tractate Besah*
VIII.   *Yerushalmi Tractate Taanit*
IX.   *Yerushalmi Tractate Megillah*
X.   *Yerushalmi Tractate Rosh Hashanah*
XI.   *Yerushalmi Tractate Hagigah*
XII.   *Yerushalmi Tractate Moed Qatan*
XIII.A.   *Yerushalmi Tractate Yebamot. Chapters One through Ten*
XIII.B   *Yerushalmi Tractate Yebamot. Chapters Eleven through Seventeen. And the Structure of Yerushalmi Yebamot*
XIV.   *Yerushalmi Tractate Ketubot*
XV.   *Yerushalmi Tractate Nedarim*
XVI.   *Yerushalmi Tractate Nazir*
XVII.   *Yerushalmi Tractate Gittin*
XVIII.   *Yerushalmi Tractate Qiddushin*
XIX.   *Yerushalmi Tractate Sotah*
XX.   *Yerushalmi Tractate Baba Qamma*
XXI.   *Yerushalmi Tractate Baba Mesia*
XXII.   *Yerushalmi Tractate Baba Batra*
XXIII.   *Yerushalmi Tractate Sanhedrin*
XXIV.   *Yerushalmi Tractate Makkot*
XXV.   *Yerushalmi Tractate Shebuot*
XXVI.   *Yerushalmi Tractate Abodah Zarah*

XXVII.   *Yerushalmi Tractate Horayot*
XXVIII.   *Yerushalmi Tractate Niddah*

The Talmud of The Land of Israel.. An Outline of the Second, Third, and Fourth Divisions.
Atlanta, 1995-6: Scholars Press for for USF Academic Commentary Series.
I.A   *Tractate Berakhot and the Division of Appointed Times. Berakhot and Shabbat*
I.B   *Tractate Berakhot and the Division of Appointed Times. Erubin, Yoma, and Besah*
I.C   *Tractate Berakhot and the Division of Appointed Times. Pesahim and Sukkah*
I.D   *Tractate Berakhot and the Division of Appointed Times. Taanit, Megillah, Rosh Hashanah, Hagigah, and Moed Qatan*
II.A.   *The Division of Women. Yebamot to Nedarim*
II.B.   *The Division of Women. Nazir to Sotah*
III.A   *The Division of Damages and Tractate Niddah. Baba Qamma, Baba Mesia, Baba Batra, Horayot, and Niddah*
III.B   *The Division of Damages and Tractate Niddah. Sanhedrin, Makkot, Shebuot, and Abodah Zarah*

The Two Talmuds Compared. Atlanta, 1995-6: Scholars Press for USF Academic Commentary Series.
I.A   *Tractate Berakhot and the Division of Appointed Times in the Talmud of the Land of Israel and the Talmud of Babylonia. Yerushalmi Tractate Berakhot*
I.B   *Tractate Berakhot and the Division of Appointed Times in the Talmud of the Land of Israel and the Talmud of Babylonia. Tractate Shabbat.*
I.C   *Tractate Berakhot and the Division of Appointed Times in the Talmud of the Land of Israel and the Talmud of Babylonia. Tractate Erubin*
I.D   *Tractate Berakhot and the Division of Appointed Times in the Talmud of the Land of Israel and the Talmud of Babylonia. Tractates Yoma and Sukkah*
I.E   *Tractate Berakhot and the Division of Appointed Times in the Talmud of the Land of Israel and the Talmud of Babylonia. Tractate Pesahim*
I.F   *Tractate Berakhot and the Division of Appointed Times in the Talmud of the Land of Israel and the Talmud of Babylonia. Tractates Besah, Taanit, and Megillah*
I.G   *Tractate Berakhot and the Division of Appointed Times in the Talmud of the Land of Israel and the Talmud of Babylonia. Tractates Rosh Hashanah, Hagigah, and Moed Qatan*
II.A   *The Division of Women in the Talmud of the Land of Israel and the Talmud of Babylonia. Tractates Yebamot and Ketubot.*
II.B   *The Division of Women in the Talmud of the Land of Israel and the Talmud of Babylonia. Tractates Nedarim, Nazir, and Sotah.*
II.C   *The Division of Women in the Talmud of the Land of Israel and the Talmud of Babylonia. Tractates Qiddushin and Gittin.*
III.A   *The Division of Damages and Tractate Niddah in the Talmud of the Land of Israel and the Talmud of Babylonia. Tractates Baba Qamma and Baba Mesia*
III.B   *The Division of Damages and Tractate Niddah in the Talmud of the Land of Israel and the Talmud of Babylonia. Baba Batra and Niddah.*
III.C   *The Division of Damages and Tractate Niddah. Sanhedrin and Makkot.*
III.D   *The Division of Damages and Tractate Niddah. Shebuot, Abodah Zarah, and Horayot.*

In addition, my general introduction to the entire subject of Rabbinic literature is contained in the following:

Introduction to Rabbinic Literature. N.Y., 1994: Doubleday. The Doubleday Anchor
Reference Library. Religious Book Club Selection, 1994.

Finally, I call attention to the counterpart of the present work, where I present my main results concerning the history of the religion of Rabbinic Judaism in its formative age:

The Mind of Classical Judaism. I. *The Philosophy and Political Economy of Formative Judaism. The Mishnah's System of the Social Order.* Atlanta, 1997: Scholars Press for
South Florida Studies in the History of Judaism.

The Mind of Classical Judaism. II. *Modes of Thought: Making Connections and Drawing Conclusions.* Atlanta, 1997: Scholars Press for South Florida Studies in the History
of Judaism.

The Mind of Classical Judaism. III. *From Philosophy to Religion.* Atlanta, 1997: Scholars Press for South Florida Studies in the History of Judaism.

The Mind of Classical Judaism. IV. *What is "Israel"? Social Thought in the Formative Age.* Atlanta, 1997: Scholars Press for South Florida Studies in the History of Judaism.

Scholars Press titles are now distributed by University Press of America, 4720 Boston
way, Lanham, MD 20706 USA.

CHAPTER ONE

THE BAVLI'S ONE STATEMENT

I. *Saying the Same Thing about Many Things*

When a document says the same thing about many things, it presents not only propositions but a metaproposition, which frames the teleology of its recurrent propositions. Since—as we see in the companion volume of this set—the Talmud of Babylonia says a great many things in only a single manner, everywhere appealing to a severely restricted rhetorical repertoire that serves throughout, we come at the end to ask the question, how are we to know whether, in saying in one way a great many things, the document's authors propose also to say one thing about a great many things? The Bavli forms a vast, anonymous, collective, politically-authoritative writing, from its closure has served as the principal statement of the canonical theology and law of Judaism. Reaching conclusion by the end of the seventh century, on the eve of the birth of Islam, the document together with its commentaries, codes of its laws, and compilations of ad hoc decisions ("responsa"), defined Judaism. So if we want to know how to define Judaism, we had best teach ourselves to find out what one thing the foundation-document of that faith has to say about many things.

How do we know? We know that we have identified the metapropositional program ("the same thing about many things") of a writing when we can say what we think is at stake, in the most general terms, in a variety of specific syllogisms and turn out to be saying the same thing again and again. We may test our hypothetical metaproposition by asking whether, in those many things, we may identify any other proposition to define the stakes of a demonstration; or whether some other encompassing proposition may serve as well as the one we propose over as broad a range of data as we examine. Where may we expect to find not only propositions but a statement that coheres throughout: a statement in behalf of all propositions? A coherent legal system, for one example, not only sets forth rules for diverse circumstances but, through the rules, also may lay out a philosophy of the social order, an account of what is always fair and just; then all of the cases, each with its generalization, turn out to repeat in different ways a single encompassing statement.

So too, while the author of a document makes statements about a great many subjects, a well-crafted document by a strong-minded writer will find the author saying much the same thing about all things. Then the key to good writing will be the power to make the same point again and again without boring the reader or belaboring the obvious. Indeed, an important and truly well-conceived piece of writing addressed to a long future will precipitate productive debates about not only details but what that some one thing said in many ways is meant to propose. Great writing leaves ample space for readers. That is the mark of a strong argument, a well-crafted formulation of a considered viewpoint, the expression of a deeply-reflected-upon attitude, or, in intellectual matters, a rigorously-presented proposition. To find out what we might imagine some one thing a writer may say about many things, we ask simply, "What is at stake if this point is validated?" or simply, "if so, so what?" If time and again we find that treatment of a given subject yields as its final and most general and abstract point a proposition that turns out also to emerge from an unrelated treatment of some other subject, altogether, then we have what I call a metaproposition, meaning, a proposition that transcends a variety of propositions and that occurs in all of them.

Obviously, defining the metapropositional statement that an author repeatedly sets forth involves an element of eisegesis—and even subjectivity. That is invariably a starting point. On the one side, others may see some other metaproposition that circulates throughout a piece of writing, different from one that I might propose. On the other, still others may perceive no metaproposition at all. How to test a thesis on the metaproposition of a diverse piece of writing? One irrefutable demonstration is that a single rhetoric prevails, for that legitimates asking whether saying everything in some one way, writers also say one thing about many things. To define that some one thing, and to find out whether or not a proposed metaproposition in fact circulates throughout such a writing, first of all, a massive survey must show where, how, and why one proposes that one and same proposition that—according to a proposed metaproposition—an author persists in setting forth in the context of a great many diverse discussions. If it can be shown that most, or even all, of a large and various corpus of writing turns out to be saying that one thing through its treatment of a great many things, then one is justified in claiming to have set forth that proposition beyond the propositions that animates a document. It is the one that the authors have composed the document to set forth and in a vast number of ways to demonstrate. But let me forthwith turn to the two problems just now noted. What about the possibility that another metaproposition may be shown to inhere, different from the one that as a matter of hypothesis is set forth at the outset? Or what if a proposed metaproposition not to be present at all? Then the experiment has failed. And how are we going to test the validity of two or more proposed metapropositions, and so to know whether or not the metaproposition that is suggested is the right one? The answer lies in a detailed demonstration that the proposed metaproposition is the best one possible one, in the context of a variety of possibilities, to encompass the data at hand. And God lives in the details.

II. *How the Mishnah Says the Same Thing about Many Things: The Case of Hierarchical Ontology*

Before turning to the Bavli, we take up the Mishnah, where, it is easy to demonstrate, a determinate and economical set of propositions governs the exposition of nearly all topics—and we can define those propositions with great precision. We address an example of a metapropositional statement set forth in a single, public, anonymous, and authoritative writings, and can define the contents of one such statement.

We shall examine the remarkably cogent and simple metaproposition, the recurrent statement that defines what is at stake in detailed syllogistic argument, which inheres in the Mishnah and proves paramount throughout. The pervasive telos of thought in the Mishnah is such that many things are made to say one thing, which concerns the nature of being. Specifically, the Mishnah's authority repeatedly demonstrates that that all things are not only orderly, but are ordered in such wise that many things fall into one classification. So one thing may hold together many things of a diverse classifications. These two matched and complementary propositions—[1] many things are one, [2] one thing encompasses many—complement each other. In forming matched opposites, the two provide a single, complete and final judgment of the whole of being, social, natural, supernatural alike. Nearly the whole of the document's tractates in one way or another repeat that simple point. The metaproposition is never expressed but it is everywhere demonstrated by showing, in whatever subject is treated, the possibility always of effecting the hierarchical classification of all things: each thing in its taxon, all taxa in correct sequence, from least to greatest.

Showing that all things can be ordered, and that all orders can be set into relationship with one another, we of course transform method into message. The message of hierarchical classification is that many things really form a single thing, the many species a single genus, the many genera an encompassing and well-crafted, cogent whole. Every time we speciate, we affirm that position. Each successful labor of forming relationships among species, e.g., making them into a genus, or identifying the hierarchy of the species, proves it again. Not only so, but when we can show that many things are really one, or that one thing yields many (the reverse and confirmation of the former), we say in a fresh way a single immutable truth, the one of this philosophy concerning the unity of all being in an orderly composition of all things within a single taxon. Exegesis always is repetitive—and a sound exegesis of the systemic exegesis must then be equally so, everywhere explaining the same thing in the same way.

To state with emphasis what I conceive to be that one large argument—the metaproposition—that the Mishnah's authorship sets forth in countless small ways: *the very artifacts that* appear *multiple in fact form classes of things, and, moreover, these classes themselves are subject to a reasoned ordering, by appeal to this-worldly characteristics signified by properties and indicative traits.* Monotheism hence is to be demonstrated by appeal to those very same data that for paganism prove the opposite. The way to one God, ground of being and ontological unity of the world, lies through "rational reflection on themselves and on the world," this world, which yields a living unity encompassing the whole. That claim, conducted in an argument covering overwhelming detail in the Mishnah, directly faces the issue as framed by paganism. Immanent in its medium, it is transcendent in its message.

To show how the metaproposition is stated through the treatment of a wide range of subjects, concrete recapitulations of this abstract statement are now required. So I turn to the sustained effort to demonstrate how many classes of things—actions, relationships, circumstances, persons, places—are demonstrated really to form one class. Just as God, in creation, ordered all things, each in its class under its name, so in the Mishnah classification works its way through the potentialities of chaos to explicit order. The issue concerns nature, not supernature, and sorts out and sifts the everyday data of the here and the now. It will prove its points, therefore, by appeal to the palpable facts of creation, which everyone knows and can test. So recognition that one thing may fall into several categories and many things into a single one comes to expression, for the authorship of the Mishnah, in secular ways. One of the interesting ones is the analysis of the several taxa into which a single action may fall, with an account of the multiple consequences, e.g., as to sanctions that are called into play, for a single action. The right taxonomy of persons, actions, and things will show the unity of all being by finding many things in one thing, and that forms the first of the two components of what I take to be the philosophy's teleology.

Mishnah-tractate Keritot 3:9

A. There is one who ploughs a single furrow and is liable on eight counts of violating a negative commandment:

B. [specifically, it is] he who (1) ploughs with an ox and an ass [Deut. 22:10], which are (2,3) both Holy Things, in the case of (4) [ploughing] Mixed Seeds in a vineyard [Deut. 22:9], (5) in the Seventh Year [Lev. 25:4], (6) on a festival [Lev. 23:7] and who was both a (7) priest [Lev. 21:1] and (8) a Nazirite [Num. 6:6] [ploughing] in a grave-yard.

C. Hanania b. Hakhinai says, "Also: He is [ploughing while] wearing a garment of diverse kinds" [Lev. 19:19, Deut. 22:11).

D. They said to him, "This is not within the same class."

E. He said to them, "Also the Nazir [B8] is not within the same class [as the other transgressions]."

Here is a case in which more than a single set of flogging is called for. B's felon is liable to 312 stripes, on the listed counts. The ox is sanctified to the altar, the ass to the Temple upkeep (B2,3).

Hanania's contribution is rejected since it has nothing to do with ploughing, and sages' position is equally flawed. The main point, for our inquiry, is simple. The one action draws in its wake multiple consequences. Classifying a single thing as a mixture of many things then forms a part of the larger intellectual address to the nature of mixtures. But it yields a result that, in the analysis of an action, far transcends the metaphysical problem of mixtures, because it moves us toward the ontological solution of the unity of being.

So much for actions. How about substances? Can we say that diverse things, each in its own classification, form a single thing? Indeed so. Here is one example, among a great many candidates, taken from Mishnah-tractate Hallah. The tractate takes as its theme the dough-offering to which the framers assume Num. 15:17-21 refers: "of the first of your coarse meal you shall present a cake as an offering." The tractate deals with the definition of dough liable to the dough offering, defining the bread, the process of separating dough-offering, and the liability of mixtures.

MISHNAH-TRACTATE HALLAH 1:1, 3

1:1 A. [Loaves of bread made from] five types [of grain] are subject to dough offering:

B. (1) wheat, (2) barley, (3) spelt, (4) oats, and (5) rye;

C. lo, [loaves of bread made from] these [species] are subject to dough offering,

D. and combine with each other [for the purpose of reckoning whether or not a batch of dough comprises the minimum volume subject to dough offering (M. Hal. 1:4, 2:6, M. Ed. 1:2)].

E. and products of these species are forbidden for common use until Passover under the category of new produce [produce harvested before the waving of the first sheaf (Lev. 23:14)].

F. And grasses of these species may not be reaped until the reaping of the first sheaf.

G. And if they took root prior to the waving of the first sheaf, the waving of the first sheaf releases them for common use;

H. but if they did not take root prior to the waving of the omer, they are forbidden for common use until the next omer.

1:3 A. Grain in the following categories is liable to dough-offering when made into dough but exempt from tithes:

B. Gleanings, forgotten sheaves, produce in the corner of a field, that which has been abandoned, first tithe from which heave offering of the tithe has been removed, second tithe, and that which is dedicated to the temple which has been redeemed, the left over portion of grain which was harvested for the offering of the first sheaf, and grain which has not reached a third of its anticipated growth.

C. R. Eliezer says, "Grain which has not reached one third of its growth is exempt from dough offering when made into dough."

M. Hal. 1:1 addresses the issuing of whether or not five species of grain join together to produce dough of sufficient volume to incur liability to the dough-offering. Since they share in common the trait that they are capable of being leavened, they do. So the genus encompasses all of the species, with the result that the classification-process is neatly illustrated. "Joining together" or connection then forms a statement that these many things are one thing. M. 1:2 makes the same point about the five species. The interstitial cases at M. Hal. 1:3 are subject to ownership other than that of the farmer. But that fact does not change their status as to dough offering. We take no account of the status with regard to ownership, past or present use as another type of offering, or the stage of growth of the grain whence the dough derives. This then forms the other side of the taxonomic labor: indicators that do not register distinguish. The upshot is as I said: many things are one thing; one rule applies to a variety of classes of grains.

In Mishnah-tractate Keritot the governing purpose is to work out how many things are really one thing. This is accomplished by showing that the end or consequence of diverse actions to be always one and the same. The issue of the tractate is the definition of occasions on which one is obligated to bring a sin-offering and a suspensive guilt-offering. The tractate lists those sins that are classified together by the differentiating criterion of intention. If one deliberately commits those sins, he is punished through extirpation. If it is done inadvertently, he brings a sin-offering. In case of doubt as to whether or not a sin has been committed (hence: inadvertently), he brings a suspensive guilt offering. Lev. 5:17-19 specifies that if one sins but does not know it, he brings a sin-offering or a guilt offering. Then if he does, a different penalty is invoked, with the suspensive guilt offering at stake as well. While we have a sustained exposition of implications of facts that Scripture has provided, the tractate also covers problems of classification of many things as one thing, in the form of a single-sin-offering for multiple sins, and that problem fills the bulk of the tractate. Here is a sizable sample that goes over that point.

Mishnah-tractate Keritot 1:1, 2, 7, 3:2, 4

1:1 A. Thirty-six transgressions subject to extirpation are in the To-rah...

1:2 A. For those [transgressions] are people liable, for deliberately doing them, to the punishment of extirpation,

B. and for accidentally doing them, to the bringing of a sin offering,

C. and for not being certain of whether or not one has done them, to a suspensive guilt offering [Lev. 5:17]—

D. "except for the one who imparts uncleanness to the sanctuary and its Holy Things,

E. "because he is subject to bringing a sliding scale offering (Lev. 5:6-7, 11)," the words of R. Meir.

F. And sages say, "Also: [except for] the one who blasphemes, as it is said, 'You shall have one law for him that does anything unwittingly' (Num. 15:29)—excluding the blasphemer, who does no concrete deed."

1:7 A. The woman who is subject to a doubt concerning [the appear-ance of] five fluxes,

B. or the one who is subject to a doubt concerning five miscarriages

C. brings a single offering.

D. And she [then is deemed clean so that she] eats animal sacrifices.

E. And the remainder [of the offerings, A, B] are not an obligation for her.

F. [If she is subject to] five confirmed miscarriages,

G. or five confirmed fluxes,

H. she brings a single offering.

1. And she eats animal sacrifices.

J. But the rest [of the offerings, the other four] remain as an obliga-tion for her [to bring at some later time]—

K. M'SH S: A pair of birds in Jerusalem went up in price to a golden denar.

L. Said Rabban Simeon b. Gamaliel, "By this sanctuary! I shall not rest tonight until they shall be at [silver] denars."

M. He entered the court and taught [the following law]:

N. "The woman who is subject to five confirmed miscarriages [or] five confirmed fluxes brings a single offering.

0. "And she eats animal sacrifices.

P "And the rest [of the offerings] do not remain as an obligation for her."

0. And pairs of birds stood on that very day at a quarter-denar each [one one-hundredth of the former price].

3:2 A. [If] he ate [forbidden] fat and [again ate] fat in a single spell of inadvertence, he is liable only for a single sin offering,

B. [If] he ate forbidden fat and blood and remnant and refuse [of an offering] in a single spell of inadvertence, he is liable for each and every one of them.

C. This rule is more strict in the case of many kinds [of forbidden food] than of one kind.

D. And more strict is the rule in [the case of] one kind than in many kinds:

E. For if he ate a half—olive's bulk and went and ate a half—olive's bulk of a single kind, he is liable.

F. [But if he ate two half-olive's bulks] of two [different] kinds, he is exempt.

3:4 A. There is he who carries out a single act of eating and is liable on its account for four sin offerings and one guilt offering:

B. An unclean [lay] person who ate (1) forbidden fat, and it was (2) remnant (3) of Holy Things, and (4) it was on the Day of Atonement.

C. R. Meir says, "If it was the Sabbath and he took it out [from one domain to another] in his mouth, he is liable [for another sin offering]."

D. They said to him, "That is not of the same sort [of transgression of which we have spoken heretofore since it is not caused by eating (A)]."

M. Ker. 1:7 introduces the case of classifying several incidents within a single taxon, so that one incident encompasses a variety of cases and therefore one penalty or sanction covers a variety of instances. That same conception is much more amply set forth in Chapter Two. There we have lists of five who bring a single offering for many transgressions, five who bring a sliding scale offering for many incidents, and the like, so M. 2:3-6. Then M. 3:1-3 we deal with diverse situations in which a man is accused of having eaten forbidden fat and therefore of owing a sin-offering. At M. 3:1 the issue is one of disjoined testimony. Do we treat as one the evidence of two witnesses. The debate concerns whether two cases form a single category. Sages hold that the case are hardly the same, because there are differentiating traits. M. 3:2-3 show us how we differentiate or unify several acts. We have several acts of transgression in a single spell of inadvertence; we classify them all as one action for purposes of the penalty. That at stake is the problem of classification and how we invoke diverse taxic indicators is shown vividly at M. 3:2 in particular. Along these same lines are the issues of M. Ker. 3:3, 4-6: "There is he who carries out a single act of eating and is liable on its account for four sin-offerings and one guilt-offering; there is he who carries out a single act of sexual intercourse and becomes liable on its account for six sin-offerings," with the first shown at M. 3:4.

Showing that many things are really of one kind because they produce a single consequence—the same offering—proves inad-

equate. The reason is that that mode of argument by appeal to
outcome or consequence ignores the traits of things, which the
Mishnah's system, so it seems, deems paramount. So the approach
provides a demonstration that bears three negative traits. It is
formal, not substantive. It is static, not dynamic, and so fails to
deal with movement and change, which is where diversity takes
place. And it addresses consequence, not essence; and that teleo-
logical proof leaves open the question of whether or not being
as it is, not only as they are meant to be, really forms a unity.
For proving (or, at least, illustrating) that proposition, which demands a far more important place in the philosophical program
meaning to state the unity of ontology, we have to find a different sort of proof altogether. It is one that appeals—not surprisingly!—to processes of classification of things *as they are,* not as to
their consequences but as to their essence or very being. And this
draws us—as is our way—to ask whether there is a complete tractate that is devoted to showing the unity of *phenomena.* And indeed
there is, and an odd one at that. The intrinsic and inherent traits
of things on their own prove the besought proposition.

So much for the impalpable and invisible realm of classification and status. There we can conjure, but cannot touch or feel
or see, the lines of structure and division. Order is imputed and
imagined. What about the visible world of space? Here we can
frame a question that permits a highly tangible representation of
the complexity of unity and diversity, the demonstration that one
thing encompasses many things, so many things form one thing.
The question is asked in this way: When is a field a field, and
when is it two or ten fields? That taxonomic problem of how many
are one, or how one is deemed many, is addressed at Mishnah-
tractate Peah, which concerns itself with giving to the poor produce abandoned at the corner of a field. Then we have to know
what constitutes a field, hence the question of when one thing is
many things, or when many things are one thing, framed in terms
of spatial relations:

MISHNAH-TRACTATE PEAH 2:1, 5; 3:5

2:1 A. And these [landmarks] establish [the boundaries of a field] for
[purposes of designating] peah:
B. (1) a river, (2) pond, (3) private road, (4) public road, (5) public path,

(6) private path that is in use in the hot season and in the rainy season, (7) uncultivated land, (8) newly broken land, (9) and [an area sown with] a different [type of] seed.

C. "And [as regards] one who harvests young grain [for use as fodder—the area he harvests] establishes [the boundaries of a field] ," the words of R. Meir.

D. But sages say, "[The area he harvests] does not establish [the boundaries of a field], unless he has also ploughed [the stubble] under."

2:5 A. One who sows his field with [only] one type [of seed], even if he harvests [the produce] in two lots

B. designates one [portion of produce as] peah [from the entire crop].

C. If he sowed [his field] with two types [of seeds], even if he harvests [the produce] in only one lot,

D. he designates two [separate portions of produce as] peah, [one from each type of produce].

E. He who sows his field with two types of wheat—

F [if] he harvests [the wheat] in one lot, [he] designates one [portion of produce as] peah.

G. [But if he harvests the wheat in] two lots, [he] designates two [portions of produce as] peah.

3:5 A. [Two] brothers who divided [ownership of a field which previously they had jointly owned]

B. give two [separate portions of produce] as peah [each designates peah on behalf of the produce of his half of the field].

C. [If] they return to joint ownership [of the field]

D. [together] they designate one [portion of produce] as peah [on behalf of the entire field].

E. Two [men] who [jointly] purchased a tree [together] designate one [portion of produce] as peah [on behalf of the entire tree]—

F. But if one purchased the northern [half of the tree], and the other purchased the southern [half of the tree],

G. the former designates peah by himself, and the latter designates peah by himself.

The principle of division rests upon the farmer's attitude and actions toward a field. If the farmer harvests an area as a single entity, that action indicates his attitude or intentionality in regard to that area and serves to mark it as a field. For each patch of grain the householder reaps separately a peah-share must be designated; the action indicates the intentionality to treat the area as a single field. But natural barriers intervene; rivers or hills also may mark off a fields boundaries, whatever the farmer's action and therefore a priori intentionality or attitude. So in classifying an area of ground as a field, there is an interplay between the givens of the physical traits and the attitude, confirmed by action, of the farmer.

M. Peah 2:5-8 provide excellent cases for the application of these operative principles. A farmer might harvest a single field delimited by physical barriers, or how may harvest two fields in one lot.[1] In both cases we ask: do the physical barriers define matters? Or does the attitude of the farmer confirmed by his action dictate the field's boundary? And a further issue is whether or not a field produces a single crop. If it does, then a single portion is designated, even if the produce is harvested on a number of different occasions. So much for the many and the one. Readers will surely stipulate that any number of other examples of the same proposition, proved in the same manner, can be adduced. The ones in hand seem to me to suffice to demonstrate that, reading the Mishnah as philosophy, the document really does say some few things in a great many ways, in the analogy to the hedgehog, not the fox, offered at the outset.

If then many things become one thing, how about the one thing that yields the many? If we can show that a single classification may be *subdivided*, then the unity of the many in the one is demonstrated from a fresh angle. If so, the systemic contention concerning the fundamental and essential unity of all being finds reenforcement. That the question is faced may be shown, as usual in so coherent a piece of writing as the Mishnah, at a variety of passages. To take only a single instance, M. Makkot 3:5, 7-9 raise a question familiar to us from Mishnah-tractate Horayot: when are many actions classified as a single action, or a single action as many. But, more to the point, let us turn immediately to a very concrete reflection on the nature of actions and differentiating among them.

MISHNAH-TRACTATE NAZIR 6:4-5

6:4 A. A Nazir who was drinking wine all day long is liable only on one count.

B. [If] they said to him, "Don't drink it!" "Don't drink it!" and he continues drinking, he is liable on each and every count [of drinking].

C. [If] he was cutting his hair all day long, he is liable only on a single count.

---

[1] Roger Brooks, *Support for the Poor in the Mishnaic Law of Agriculture: Tractate Peah* (Chico, 1983: Scholars Press), p. 53.

D. [If] they said to him, "Don't cut it!" "Don't cut it!" and he continued to cut his hair, he is liable for each and every count [of cutting].

E. [If] he was contracting corpse uncleanness all day long, he is liable
on only one count.

F. If they said to him, "Don't contract corpse uncleanness!" "Don't
contract corpse uncleanness!" and he continued to contract corpse
uncleanness, he is liable for each and every count.

6:5 A. Three things are prohibited to a Nazir: [corpse] uncleanness,
cutting the hair, and anything which goes forth from the grapevine.

B. A more strict rule applies to corpse uncleanness and haircutting than
applies to that which comes forth from the grapevine.

C. For corpse uncleanness and haircutting cause the loss of the days
already observed, but [violating the prohibition against] that which goes
forth from the vine does not cause the loss of the days already observed.

D. A more strict rule applies to that which goes forth from the vine
than applies to corpse uncleanness and haircutting.

E. For that which goes forth from the vine allows for no exception,
but corpse uncleanness and haircutting allow for exceptions,

F. in the case of [cutting the hair for] a religious duty and in the case
of finding a neglected corpse [with no one else to provide for burial,
in which case, the Nazir is absolutely required to bury the corpse].

G. A more strict rule applies to corpse uncleanness than to haircutting.

H. For corpse uncleanness causes the loss of all the days previously
observed and imposes the liability for an offering.

I. But haircutting causes the loss of only thirty days and does not impose liability for an offering.

At M. Naz. 6:4 we take up the issue of disjoined actions, for each
of which one is liable, when these actions are of a single species.
What distinguishes one action from another, when all are of the
same species, is that one is made aware each time he does the
prohibited action that he is forbidden to do so. Then each action
is individual. But if not, then all of the actions form a single sustained action, for which one is liable on only one count. This
interesting conception then imposes upon the differentiation of
actions the consideration of intentionality: the man now knows
that the particular action he is about to undertake is prohibited.
Hence it seems to me a case in which we invoke intentionality in
the work of the classification of actions (=counts of culpability).
What is at stake in the issue? It is the application of hierarchical
classification, which as we know forms the goal of the philosophy's
method of classification. So we see the unity of philosophical

medium and philosophical message. For M. Naz. 6:5 takes the facts of Scripture and forms of them a composition of hierarchical classification, in which the taxic indicators are laid out in accord with a single program.

I have repeatedly claimed that the recognition that one thing becomes many does not challenge the philosophy of the unity of all being, but confirms the main point. Why do I insist on that proposition? The reason is simple. If we can show that differentiation flows from within what is differentiated,—that is, from the intrinsic or inherent traits of things—then we confirm that at the heart of things is a fundamental ontological being, single, cogent, simple, that is capable of diversification, yielding complexity and diversity. The upshot is to be stated with emphasis. *That diversity in species or diversification in actions follows orderly lines confirms the claim that there is that single point from which many lines come forth.* Carried out in proper order—[1] the many form one thing, and [2] one thing yields many—the demonstration then leaves no doubt as to the truth of the matter. Ideally, therefore, we shall argue from the simple to the complex, showing that the one yields the many, one thing, many things, two, four.

Mishnah-tractate Shabbat 1:1

1:1 A. [Acts of] transporting objects from one domain to another, [which violate] the Sabbath, (1) are two, which [indeed] are four [for one who is] inside, (2) and two which are four [for one who is] outside,
B. How so?
C. [If on the Sabbath] the beggar stands outside and the householder inside,
D. [and] the beggar stuck his hand inside and put [a beggar's bowl] into the hand of the householder,
E. or if he took [something] from inside it and brought it out,
F. the beggar is liable, the householder is exempt.
G. [If] the householder stuck his hand outside and put [something] into the hand of the beggar,
H. or if he took [something] from it and brought it inside,
I. the householder is liable, and the beggar is exempt.
J. [If] the beggar stuck his hand inside, and the householder took [something] from it,
K. or if [the householder] put something in it and he [the beggar] removed
L. both of them are exempt.
M. [If] the householder put his hand outside and the beggar took [something] from it,

N. or if [the beggar] put something into it and [the householder] brought it back inside,

0. both of them are exempt.

M. Shab. 1:1 classifies diverse circumstances of transporting objects from private to public domain. The purpose is to assess the rules that classify as culpable or exempt from culpability diverse arrangements. The operative point is that a prohibited action is culpable only if one and the same person commits the whole of the violation of the law. If two or more people share in the single action, neither of them is subject to punishment. At stake therefore is the conception that one thing may be many things, and if that is the case, then culpability is not incurred by any one actor.

The consequence of showing that one thing is many things is set forth with great clarity in the consideration not of the actor but of the action. One class of actions is formed by those that violate the sanctity of the Sabbath. Do these form many subdivisions, and, if so, what difference does it make? Here is a famous passage that shows how a single class of actions yields multiple and complex speciation, while remaining one:

Mishnah-tractate Shabbat 7:1-2

7:1 A. A general rule did they state concerning the Sabbath:

B. Whoever forgets the basic principle of the Sabbath and performed many acts of labor on many different Sabbath days is liable only for a single sin offering.

C. He who knows the principle of the Sabbath and performed many acts of labor on many different Sabbaths is liable for the violation of each and every Sabbath.

D. He who knows that it is the Sabbath and performed many acts of labor on many different Sabbaths is liable for the violation of each and every generative category of labor.

E. He who performs many acts of labor of a single type is liable only for a single sin offering.

7:2 A. The generative categories of acts of labor [prohibited on the Sabbath] are forty less one:

B. (1) he who sews, (2) ploughs, (3) reaps, (4) binds sheaves, (5) threshes, (6) winnows, (7) selects [fit from unfit produce or crops], (8) grinds, (9) sifts, (10) kneads, (11) bakes;

C. (12) he who shears wool, (13) washes it, (14) beats it, (15) dyes it;

D. (16) spins, (17) weaves,

E. (18) makes two loops, (19) weaves two threads, (20) separates two threads;

F (21) ties, (22) unties,

G. (23) sews two stitches, (24) tears in order to sew two stitches;

.H. (25) he who traps a deer, (26) slaughters it, (27) flays it, (28) salts it, (29) cures its hide, (30) scrapes it, and (31) cuts it up;

I. (32) he who writes two letters, (33) erases two letters in order to write two letters;

J. (34) he who builds, (35) tears down;

K. (36) he who puts out a fire, (37) kindles a fire;

L. (38) he who hits with a hammer; (39) he who transports an object from

one domain to another—

M. lo, these are the forty generative acts of labor less one.

Now we see how the fact that one thing yields many things confirms the philosophy of the unity of all being. For the many things all really are one thing, here, the intrusion into sacred time of actions that do not belong there. M. Shab. 7:1-2 presents a parallel to the discussion, in Mishnah-tractate Sanhedrin, of how many things can be shown to be one thing and to fall under a single rule, and how one thing may be shown to be many things and to invoke multiple consequences. It is that interest at M. 7:1 which accounts for the inclusion of M. 7:2, and the exposition of M. 7:2 occupies much of the tractate that follows. Accordingly, just as at Mishnah-tractate Sanhedrin the specification of the many and diverse sins or felonies that are penalized in a given way shows us how many things are one thing and then draws in its wake the specification of those many things, so here we find a similar exercise. It is one of classification, working in two ways, then: the power of a unifying taxon, the force of a differentiating and divisive one. The list of the acts of labor then gives us the categories of work, and performing any one of these constitutes a single action in violation of the Sabbath.

How, exactly, do these things work themselves out? If one does not know that the Sabbath is incumbent upon him, then whatever he does falls into a single taxon. If he knows that the Sabbath exists and violates several Sabbath days in succession, what he does falls into another taxon. If one knows that the Sabbath exists in principle and violates it in diverse ways, e.g., through different types of prohibited acts of labor, then many things become still more differentiated. The consideration throughout, then, is how to assess whether something is a single or multiple action as to the reckoning of the consequence.

I have repeatedly pointed to the philosophical unity of mode of argument, medium of expression, and fundamental proposition. In this connection let us turn back to our consideration of the rules of speciation. These form the methodological counterpart to the proposition that one thing yields many things. Here is the consequence, in the context of the exposition of the one and the many, of the rule of sub- and super-speciation:

Mishnah-tractate Shabbat 10:6

10:6 A. He who pares his fingernails with one another, or with his teeth,
B. so too [if he pulled out the hair of] his (1) head, (2) moustache, or (3) beard—
C. and so she who (1) dresses her hair, (2) puts on eye shadow, or (3) rouges her face—
D. R. Eliezer declares liable [for doing so on the Sabbath].
E. And sages prohibit [doing so] because of [the principle of] Sabbath rest.
F. He who picks [something] from a pot which has a hole [in the bottom] is liable.
G. [If he picks something from a pot] which has no hole [in the bottom], he is exempt.
H. And R. Simeon exempts him on this account and on that account.

The interest in the classification of acts of labor draws attention, at M. 10:6, to the lesson of super-speciation. We make a distinction between a derivative of the generative categories of prohibited acts, commission of which invokes a penalty, and an act which is not to be done by reason of the general principle of "Sabbath rest," but which is not culpable under the list of thirty-nine specifically prohibited acts of labor. From super-speciation—acts that cannot be speciated but that fall into the genus of prohibited deeds—we move, in Chapters Twelve through Sixteen, to the subspecies of the thirty-nine categories of prohibited acts of labor. Here we ask about the extent to which one must perform a prohibited act of labor in order to be subject to liability; Chapter Twelve addresses building, ploughing, writing; in Chapter Thirteen, we proceed to weaving and hunting (one who completes an action is liable, one who does not is exempt; one who does not intend by his action to violate the Sabbath is not liable and one who does intend to violate the Sabbath is liable; if two people together do a single act of prohibited labor, neither is liable); Chapter Fifteen moves on to knot-tying; Chapter Sixteen, to saving things from the fire even though that involves moving objects across the boundary between private and public domain.

I asked at the outset how we might know whether our proposed metaproposition if right or wrong. The evidence in behalf of my reading of the Mishnah covers nearly the entirety of the document. It is not episodic but structural, in that entire tractates can be demonstrated to take shape around issues of hierarchical classification and the principles that guide correct classification. It does not seem to me plausible that it is merely by accident that these sustained efforts, covering the vast surface of the writing—sixty-one usable tractates (omitting reference to tractates Eduyyot and Abot) and more than five hundred and fifty chapters—go through the same process time and again. Hierarchization defines the problematic throughout, as I have shown in *Judaism as Philosophy. The Method and Message of the Mishnah*. Columbia, 1991: University of South Carolina Press. It is certainly possible to propose a variety of recurrent concerns that animate the document, for example, the inquiry into the power of human intentionality, as I have suggested. But these can be shown to find a subordinated position within the overriding interest, since the purpose of intentionality is taxonomic, and the goal of taxonomy of course, hierarchical classification. To this point no one has met the challenge of suggesting some other metaproposition that circulates throughout a piece of writing, different from one that I proposed. Whether or not others may perceive no metaproposition at all is not equivalently obvious; for a sustained effort at showing that what I see is simply not there has yet to be undertaken. So to review my opening questions: what about the possibility that another metaproposition may be shown to inhere, different from the one that as a matter of hypothesis is set forth at the outset? Or what if a proposed metaproposition not to be present at all? My detailed demonstration that the proposed metaproposition is not only the best, but the only possible one is in hand. More than that I cannot contribute.

It is therefore the incontrovertible fact that the framers of the Mishnah set forth not only cases, examples, propositions as to fact, but also, through the particulars, a set of generalizations about classification and the relationships of the classes of things that yield a metaproposition. The whole composition of thought is set forth, in the correct intellectual manner, through the patient classification of things by appeal to the traits that they share, with comparison and contrast among points of difference then yielding the governing rule for a given classification. And the goal was through proper classification of things to demonstrate the hierarchical order of being, culminating in the proposition that all things derive from, and join within, (in secular language) one thing or (in the language of philosophy of religion) the One. If the Mishnah establishes the science of lists, then, as we turn to the Bavli, we find a continuation of the labor: the transformation of the list into a series, as I shall now show for a very particular, logical problem.

III. *Analogical-Contrastive Thinking and the Problem of Dialectical Thought*

Having shown that diverse topics of the Mishnah are so represented as to make a single set of cogent points about hierarchical classification, I turn directly to the problem of the Bavli: can the same claim be made of the Mishnah's greatest single commentary, that it too says one thing about many things? The answer to the "can" lies in rhetoric: do the people talk in the same way about many subjects? The answer is that they do. But before proceeding, we have to address the two methodological premises of all that follows. First, it is legitimate to ask our question about uniformities of thought because of the demonstrated uniformities of rhetoric that characterize the writings. If as we now realize, the Bavli's writers manage to say a great many things in some one way, then, through that one voice, do they state one message? Second, when we listen to the Bavli, we must pay attention to not the details but the main point, and the main point is presented in the composite, which is made up, in the nature of things, of diverse compositions; the compositions that comprise the composite are selected and inserted for the purposes of the framers of the composite. That is to say, the Bavli is not run-on, disorganized, disconnected, a mere compendium of this and that, but it is cogent, coherent, well-organized, purposive, above all, intended in its principal whole expositions to make points and to set forth propositions. But only when we know how the composite does its work, that is to say, how it defines the arena of discourse, shall we learn how to listen to the composite, even while attending to the compositions that are utilized in the exposition of the point of the composite.

It is one thing to observe that implicit in the program of issues and problems that precipitate the Bavli's exegesis of the Mishnah are premises that constitute, also, metapropositions: premises present throughout, which, forming the grounds of inquiry, also find confirmation in the detailed results of that inquiry. It is quite another to demonstrate that entire chapters of the Bavli work in detail on accumulating evidence in behalf of a single, unarticulated but always stipulated, proposition. That demonstration draws our attention to a metapropositional statement of a different order from the utterly abstract ones that we have turned out in our random-sample of a single chapter. And it presents us with the possibility that a great many chapters of the Bavli work out presentations, in acute detail alone, of metapropositions of a quite concrete order. Here I shall show that, for the chapter under discussion, the point of the sustained discussion, never expressed, is everywhere paramount. That is the important trait of discourse, since what it means is that the framers of the chapter before us have brought to the Mishnah-chapters on which they proposed to work a well-considered point they wished to make, demonstrate, and confirm—but never specify. They obviously took the view that they did not have to state their point in the form of a generalization and an abstract principle, because what was implicit would be fully realized by a careful reader—a disciple, really—of their writing. And they were, of course, correct, for their presentation can leave no vacuum of implicit meaning and message. Since their method was inductive, their result gained only through sifting of a mass of data, so our reading will conform to the rules their writing set for us: we read the way they wrote. I add, as before, what I gain out of what they say, pointing up uniformities of proposition, evidence, and argument. By the end, it will prove superfluous to state what uniform point inheres throughout.[2]

Readers will note that the Talmud for Mishnah-Zebahim 5:1-2 is nearly uniform in serving as primary discourse, with only a few secondary amplifications requiring indentation. The rest of this chapter, by contrast, which I have not reproduced, follows

---

[2] References to "Freedman" in this chapter allude to *Hebrew-English Edition of the Babylonian Talmud. The Babylonian Talmud. Zebahim. Translated into English with notes, glossary, and indices by* H. Freedman. *Under the editorship of* Rabbi Dr. I. Epstein (London, 1989: The Soncino Press).

the more familiar pattern of inserting footnotes and appendices in the body of the text, highlighted by me in the method of indentation and double indentation. From M. 5:3 onward, the indentations become common. That fact underlines the aptness of my proposition, that the composite of M. 5:1-2 in the main is a single composition, which in a systematic and amazingly orderly way sets forth principles of not exegesis of Scripture but logic of comparison and contrast within the discipline of dialectical thinking—matters I shall explain as they require our attention. I should regard the Talmud for M. Zebahim 5:1-2 as the single most remarkable achievement of this amazing document.

MISHNAH/BAVLI TRACTATE ZEBAHIM 5:1-2
5:1

A. **What is the place [in which the act of sacrifice] of animal offerings [takes place]?**

B. **Most Holy Things [the whole offering, sin offering, and guilt offering]—the act of slaughtering them is carried out at the north [side of the altar].**

C. **The bullock and the he-goat of the Day of Atonement— the act slaughtering them is at the north.**

D. **And the receiving of their blood is carried out in a utensil of service, at the north [side of the altar].**

E. **And their blood requires sprinkling over the space between the bars [of the ark], and on the veil, and on the golden altar.**

F. **One act of placing of their [blood] [if improperly done] impairs [atonement].**

G. **And the remnants of the blood did one pour out at the western base of the outer altar.**

H. **[But] if he did not place [the remnants of their blood at the stated location], he did not impair [atonement].**

5:2

A. **Bullocks which are to be burned and he-goats which are to be burned—**

B. **the act of slaughtering them is at the north [side of the altar].**

C. **And the receiving of their blood is in a utensil of service at the north.**

D. **And their blood requires sprinkling on the veil and on the golden altar.**

E. **[47B] [The improper sprinkling of] one act of placing of their [blood] impairs [atonement].**

F   **The remnants of their blood did one pour out on the west-
     ern base of the outer altar.**

G.   **If he did not place [the remnants of the blood at the stat-
     ed location], he did not impair [atonement].**

H.   **These and those are burned in the ash pit.**

I.1

A.   *But why should the Tannaite author of the passage not state in the opening clause
     [A-B] as he does later on [Cff.]:* **And the receiving of their blood is
     carried out in a utensil of service, at the north [side of the
     altar]**/

B.   *Since there is the matter of the guilt offering presented by the person healed of the
     skin ailment [which is classified also as Most Holy Things], the blood of which is
     received in the hand [not in a utensil of service], he leaves out that item.*

C.   *But is the blood not received in a utensil of service? And lo, it is taught later on,*
     **The peace offerings of the congregation and the guilt offer-
     ings—What are the guilt offerings? (1) The guilt offering
     for false dealing, and (2) the guilt offering for acts of sac-
     rilege, and (3) the guilt offering [because of intercourse with]
     a betrothed bondwoman, and (4) the guilt offering of a Nazir,
     and the (5) guilt offering of the person healed of the skin
     ailment , and (6) the suspensive guilt offering—the act of
     slaughtering them is at the north [side of the altar]. And
     the receiving of their blood is with a utensil of service at
     the north {M. 5:5}**/

D.   *To begin with he took the position that the receiving of the blood was to be done by
     hand. So he omitted reference to the item here [just as has been explained]. But
     when he realized that the collection of the blood cannot be done unless a utensil is
     used, he included it later on. For it has been taught on Tannaite authority:*

E.   "And the priest shall take of the blood of the guilt offering"—might
     one think that this is done with a utensil?

F.   Scripture states, "and the priest shall put it" (Lev. 14:14)—just as the
     putting on of the blood is to be done by the priest's hand itself, so
     the taking of the blood also should be done by the priest's hand it-
     self.

G.   Might one suppose that that is the same for the altar [so that blood
     to be sprinkled on the altar is received not in a utensil but in the
     hand]?

H.   Scripture states, "For as the sin offering so is the guilt offering" (Lev.
     14:13)—just as the sin offering requires a utensil for receiving the
     blood, so the guilt offering requires a utensil for receiving the blood.

I.   You must then draw the conclusion that two priests received the blood
     of the guilt offering of the one healed of the skin ailment, one in his
     hand, the other in a utensil. The one who received the blood in a
     utensil went to the altar and put the blood there, and the one who
     received it in his hand went to the person who had been healed of
     the skin ailment and put it on the specified parts of his body.

II.1

A. [48A] **Bullocks which are to be burned and he-goats which are to be burned—the act of slaughtering them is carried out at the north side of the altar. And the receiving of their blood is in a utensil of service at the north. And their blood requires sprinkling on the veil and on the golden altar:**

B. *Now take note that the requirement that the rite be carried out at the north side of the altar is written in regard to the burnt offering, so let the framer of the passage formulate the rule by making reference first of all to the burnt offering.*

C. *[The reason that he treats the sin offering first is that] since the rule covering the sin offering derives from exegesis of Scripture [rather than being stated explicitly therein], it is regarded by him as of greater value.*

D. *But then let him present the rules governing the sin offerings that are offered on the outer altar!*

E. *Since the blood of those listed first is taken into the inner sanctum, t is regarded by him as of greater value.*

We open with two entirely conventional questions, namely, analysis of the formulation of the Mishnah's rule, within the premise that the wording in all of its patterns yields meaning. The solution of the initial problem, in appeal to a verse of Scripture, provides only a routine demonstration of the metaproposition that Scripture forms the court of final appeal. The second entry follows suit. Now begins the chapters great, sustained project.

2. A. *Where in Scripture is reference made to the rule governing the burnt offering?*

B. "And he shall kill it on the side of the altar at the north" (Lev. 1:11).

C. *So we have found the explicit rule that treats a beast deriving from the flock. How do we know that the same rule governs what comes of the herd?*

D. Scripture states, ""And if his offering be of the flock," and the word "and" continues the preceding statement, with the result that the subject that is prior may be deduced from the one given following. [Freedman: when a passage commences with 'and' the conjunction links it with the previous portion, and a law stated in one applies to the other too. Here the subject above is the burnt offering of the herd and the subject below is the flock.]

E. *That answer is satisfactory for him who takes the view that one may indeed derive a rule governing a prior subject from one that is given later on, but from the perspective of him who denies that fact, what is to be said?*

The question before us is startling. In the prior chapter, and in the materials just now examined, no one has told us that there are rules of exegesis, which provide sign posts on the road from Scripture to the Mishnah, or from Scripture to the law. Now we encounter the first of the chapter's sustained and systematic discussions of rules of reading Scripture.

F. *For it has been taught on Tannaite authority:*

G. "'And if any one [commits a breach of faith and sins unwittingly in any of the holy things of the Lord]' (Lev. 5:15)—this ["and if"] serves to impose liability for a suspensive guilt-offering in the case of an act of sacrilege that is subject to doubt," the words of R. Aqiba.

H. And sages declare him exempt.

I. *May not one say that this is what is subject to dispute: R. Aqiba takes the view that we derive the rule for a prior matter from one that is mentioned later on, and rabbis maintain that we do not derive the rule governing a prior matter from a matter that is mentioned later on.* [The prior matter is the one regarding sacrilege, the one that follows deals with the suspensive guilt offering, so Lev. 5:17: If any one sins, doing any of the things that the Lord has commanded not to be done, though he does not know it, yet he is guilty and shall bear his iniquity." Aqiba then derives the rule governing the case of an act of sacrilege that is subject to doubt from the rule governing unwitting sins that are subject to doubt, and consequently requires a suspensive guilt offering, and that explains his position: **R. Aqiba declares [a person] liable to a suspensive guilt offering in the case of a matter of doubt regarding acts of sacrilege**. Sages do not read the rule of the latter passage into the definition of the former.]

J. Said R. Pappa, *"All parties concur that we derive the rule for a prior topic from one that comes later on,* [B. Ker. 22B adds:] *for otherwise we should have no basis for the law that the bullock has to be slaughtered on the north side of the altar* [for that rule derives from the fact that while the rule on the bullock offerings, Lev. 1:3-4, comes prior to the rule on offering small cattle, Lev. 1:10f., and only the latter requires the slaughter to take place on the north side of the altar, we do indeed slaughter the bullock offerings on the north side of the altar as well]. *But this is the reason for the position of rabbis, who declare one exempt [from having to present a suspensive guilt offering in the case of a matter of doubt regarding acts of sacrilege]: they derive an verbal analogy to a sin offering based on the appearance of the word 'commandments' with reference to both matters.* There [at Lev. 4:27, with reference to a sin offering] there is an offense for which one is liable to extirpation in the case of a deliberate violation of the law, and to a sin offering in the case of an inadvertent violation of the law, and to a suspensive guilt offering in the case of doubt. So in every case, for which one is liable to extirpation in the case of a deliberate violation of the law, and to a sin offering in the case of an inadvertent violation of the law, and to a suspensive guilt offering in the case of doubt, the same rule applies; *but this excludes sacrilege, for in that case,* a deliberate violation of the law does not bring on the penalty of extirpation." [B. Ker. 22B adds: *For it has been taught on Tannaite authority,* He who deliberately committed an act of sacrilege—Rabbi says, "He is subject to the death penalty." And sages say, "He is subject to an admonition."]

K. And how about the position of R. Aqiba?

L. *He maintains that when we draw an a verbal analogy between the reference here to "commandments" and the reference to "commandments" with regard to the sin offering [thus yielding the position outlined at E], it serves for the eating of prohibited fat, and accomplishes the following purpose:* just as in that matter, reference is made to a sacrifice of fixed value, so all of the sacrifices must be of fixed value, *thus excluding sacrifices of variable value [such as those listed at Lev. 5:1-13], e.g., a sin offering brought on account of imparting uncleanness to the sanctuary and its Holy Things, which is expiated by an offering of variable value.*

M. *And rabbis?*

N. They take the view that one may not derive from an argument by analogy established through the use of a word in common only a limited repertoire of conclusions [but once the analogy is drawn, then all of the traits of one case apply to the other].

Now we find something that captures our attention, which is evidence of a sustained and systematic inquiry. First we have introduced our guide-line on moving from Scripture to law. Then, second and by consequence, we have introduced a refinement on the guide line. At stake is the limits of analogy: is something like something else in one way analogous in all other ways, so that every rule pertaining to the one thing applies also to the other? Or is an analogy limited, determinate only for itself? That seems to me a question of sufficient abstraction to impress the thinkers behind the propositions we gained in Chapter One of this same tractate, since it has to do with, not the rules of argument or guidelines in an exegetical venture, but the rules of thought and guidelines on right reason. Once people think in a deep system of analogy and contrast, the issue before us becomes urgent and unavoidable.

O. *Then does it follow that* R. Aqiba holds that one may derive from an argument by analogy established through the use of a word in common only a limited repertoire of conclusions? [Not at all.] *All parties concur that* one may not derive from an argument by analogy established through the use of a word in common only a limited repertoire of conclusions [but once the analogy is drawn, then all of the traits of one case apply to the other].

P. *And this is the operative consideration for the position of R. Aqiba:* Scripture has said, "And if any one," with the result that the use of the "if" serves to complement the matter that is treated first and to impose upon that matter a rule that is presented only later on. [thus: "'And if any one [commits a breach of faith and sins unwittingly in any of the holy things of the Lord]' (Lev. 5:15)—this 'and if' serves to impose liability for a suspensive guilt-offering in the case of an act of sacrilege that is subject to doubt," the words of R. Aqiba.]

Q. *Now surely rabbis have to take account of the fact that* Scripture has said, "And if any one," [with the result that the use of the "if" serves to complement the matter that is treated first and to impose upon that matter a rule that is presented only later on].

R. *May one propose that it is in the following point that they differ:*

S. *One authority maintains that proof supplied by analogy [here: the analogy sustained by the use of "and" to join the two subjects] takes priority, and the other party maintains that the proof supplied by the demonstration of a totality of congruence among salient traits takes precedence. Rabbis prefer the latter, Aqiba the former position.]*

T. *Not at all! All parties concur that proof supplied by analogy [here: the analogy sustained by the use of "and" to join the two subjects] takes priority. But rabbis in this context will say to you that the rule governing the subject treated below derives from the rule governing the subject treated above, so that the guilt offering must be worth a least two silver sheqels. This is established so that you should not argue that the doubt cannot be more stringent than the matter of certainty, and just as where there is certainty of having committed a sin, one has to present a sin offering that may be worth even so little as a sixth of a zuz in value, so if there is a matter of doubt, the guilt offering worth only a sixth of a zuz would suffice.*

What I said a moment ago pertains here as well. The same issue is now restated and refined. Do we have to show that things that are alike are alike in all respects, or is it sufficient to show likeness in only salient, therefore indicative and determinative, ones?

U. *And how does R. Aqiba derive that same theory?*

V. *He derives it from the verse,* "And this is the Torah of the guilt offering" (Lev. 7:1), meaning, there is a single Torah that covers all guilt offerings.

W. *You may then leave off considering the issue from the view of him who maintains that "Torah" is to be interpreted in that way, but on the view of him who maintains that "Torah" is not to be interpreted in that way, what is to be said?*

Y. *Such a one derives the matter from the use of* "according to your valuation" *at Lev. 5:15 and Lev. 5:18 [and that yields a verbal analogy based on congruence of shared traits].*

Z. *That poses no problems in the context in which* "according to your valuation" *occurs, but what about the guilt offering that is presented in the case of the violation of a maidservant who has been promised in marriage [Lev. 19:20-22], in which no reference is made to* "according to your valuation"?

AA. *There we find the repetition of* "with the lamb" (Lev. 5:16 and 19:22) [which yields the same rule on the minimum value of the beast offered for this purpose].

It suffices at this point to observe that this rather long and complex inquiry is cogent, and the cogency is both on the surface and underneath. The sustained sequence of moving questions and answers ("dialectic"), with a question's answer raising its own question, carries the surface-discourse from point to point, beginning to end. But at the deep structure is also a program of inquiry, exemplified at the surface, and the inquiry concerns principles of the reading of Scripture, which can obviously serve for the reading of any other writing to which the standing and stylistic power of Scripture are imputed, within a logic of comparison and contrast. What we want to know in the sub-text (if that is the right term for the here-articulated program exemplified by the text) is that logic: if we find similarity, what conclusions do we draw from that similarity?

III.1

A. [Supply: **Most Holy Things (...sin offering...)—the act of slaughtering them is carried out at the north side of the altar:**]

B. *How on the basis of Scripture do we know that the sin offering has to be prepared at the north side of the altar?*

C. As it is written, "And he shall kill the sin offering in the place of the burnt offering" (Lev. 4:24).

D. *So we have found that the act of slaughter must take place in the designated place, but how on the basis of Scripture do we know that the same rule applies to the act of receiving the blood?*

E. As it is written, "And the priest shall take of the blood of the sin offering" (Lev. 4:25). ["...take"means to receive the blood, and the "and" joins this to the immediately-preceding verse (Freedman)].

F. *What about the rule governing the location of the priest himself who receives the blood? How on the basis of Scripture do we know that rule?*

G. Said Scripture, "And he shall take to himself" [in the place where the blood is received, that is, at the north of the altar].

H. *So we have found the manner in which the religious duty is optimally carried out. But how do we know that these rules are absolutely indispensable to the rite [so that if they are not observed, the offering is ruined]?*

I. *A further verse of Scripture states,* "And he shall kill it for a sin offering in the place where they kill the burnt offering" (Lev. 4:33), *and it has been taught on Tannaite authority:*

J. Where is the burnt offering slaughtered? It is in the north. This too [the sin offering] also is slaughtered in the north.

K. **[48B]** Now is it from this verse that the rule is to be derived? Is it not in point of fact stated, "In the place where the burnt offering is killed shall the sin offering be killed" (Lev. 6:18) [referring to all

sin offerings]? So why is this [sin offering presented by a ruler] singled out? It is to establish the place in which it is to be killed, so to
prove that if one did not slaughter it in the north, it is invalid [and
that repetition teaches the rule just now stated, yielding the fact that
the keeping these rules is indispensable to the valid performance of
the rite].

L.   You maintain that that is the reason that the matter has been singled out. But perhaps it is not the case, but rather to indicate that
this offering alone [the ruler's sin offering] is the only one that
requires the north, but no other sin offering has to be killed at the
north side of the altar? Therefore Scripture states, "And he shall
kill the sin offering in the place of the burnt offering," so stating an
encompassing rule in regard to all sin offerings: all have to be slaughtered in the north.

M.   *So we have found the rule governing the sin offering presented by the ruler: it is*
both described as properly carried out in this way and also prescribed as indis-
pensably carried out in this way. And we also know that other sin offerings are
properly carried out in this way. But how do we know that it is necessary to carry
out other sin offerings in this way [so that if they are not slaughtered at the north,
they are invalid]?

N.   Because the same requirement is specified in Scripture in regard to
both the lamb (Lev. 4:33) and the she-goat (Lev. 4:29).

Here is a model of the familiar inquiry into the linkage between
Scripture and the law presented in the Mishnah. What we now
are beginning to perceive is that our entire chapter is going to
tell us the answer to the one question: what is the scriptural basis
for the rule before us? Why the subject-matter of this chapter of
the Mishnah persuades the framers of the Talmud to the chapter
of the Mishnah that the issue of scriptural sources of the law in
the Mishnah is a compelling and dominant theme is clear: the
question can be asked, because, on this subject, Scripture is prolix and abundant, rich in rules, prolix in their formulation. Consequently, where the question can be asked, it is asked; our authors
would have had a very difficult time pursuing the same question
in connection with, e.g., writs of divorce, where a couple of verses
of Scripture pertain, all the more so the many Mishnah-tractates
to which no verses of Scripture allude at all. It is because the
subject-matter of the Mishnah-chapter coincides with numerous
and well-articulated verses of Scripture that we are able to address what I claim to be the deeper issues throughout: not only
exegesis or rules of exegesis, but rather, analogical-contrastive
thinking and the rules of the logic of comparison and contrast. It

is the point at which these deeper issues of thought are articulated that the Talmud moves away from the obvious program of linking law to Scripture; and that same point, moreover, concerns not rules of exegesis at all, but rules of right thinking.

2.   A.   [As to the verse, "And he shall kill *it* for a sin offering in the place where they kill the burnt offering" (Lev. 4:33),] what is the purpose of the word "it"?

     B.   *It is required in line with that which has been taught on Tannaite authority:*

     C.   "...it..." is slaughtered at the north side of the altar, but the goat presented by Nahshon is not slaughtered at the north side of the altar [that is, the goats brought as a sin offering at the consecration of the altar, Num. 7:.. These are not really sin offerings at all.].

     D.   *And it has been taught on Tannaite authority:*

     E.   "'And he shall lay his hand upon the head of the goat' (Lev. 4:24 [the goat brought by the ruler]—this encompasses the goat brought by Nahshon under the rule of the laying on of hands," the words of R. Judah.

     F.   R. Simeon says, "It serves to encompass under the rule of laying on of hands the goats brought on account of inadvertent idolatry."

     G.   [Reverting to the question of A,] *You might have supposed that since they are encompassed under the rule of laying on of hands, they also are encompassed under the rule of being slaughtered in the north. So we are informed to the contrary.*

     H.   *To this proposition Rabina objected, "That conclusion serves full well for R. Judah, but from R. Simeon's perspective, what is there to be said?"* [Freedman: he does not include it in respect of laying hands, so a text is not required to show that the north does not apply to it].

What follows is of special interest, because it articulates another (rather obvious) rule of analogical thinking, which is, rules can be derived not only by appeal to Scripture but also by reference to analogy not made explicit by the verbal formulations of Scripture. The main point here is that, once an analogy serves, it serves everywhere an analogy can be drawn; there is no a priori that limits the power of an analogy to govern all like cases.

     I.   *Said Mar Zutra b. R. Mari to Rabina, "And does that conclusion serve so well for R. Judah anyhow? Where it is included under the law, it is included under the law, where not, not [so no verse of Scripture is required]. And should you say that if Scripture had not included the matter, we should have reached the same conclusion by argument for analogy, then if that is the case, we can infer by analogy also the rule on laying on of hands. So you must answer that a temporary sacrifice [done once, as with Nahshon's] cannot derive its law by inference from a permanent one, and so here too, a sacrifice brought only on a special occasion cannot find its rule by analogy to the rule governing a sacrifice that is permanent. [There is no reason to suppose that the sin offering of Nahshon, which was for an occasion, had to be done at the north, and therefore why is a text needed to exclude it? So we do not know the answer to our question, As to the verse, "And he shall kill it for a sin offering in the place where they kill the burnt offering" (Lev. 4:33), what is the purpose of the word "it"?]*

J. "Rather: 'it' is slaughtered in the north, but the one who does the slaughtering does not have to stand in the north."

K. *But the law on the slaughterer derives from what R. Ahia said. For it has been taught on Tannaite authority:*

L. R. Ahia says, "'And he shall kill it on the side of the altar at the north:' why is this stated? It is because we find that the priest who receives the blood must stand in the north and also must receive the blood in the north. If he stood in the south and received the blood in the north, the offering is invalid. So you might have thought that the same rule governs slaughtering the animal. Scripture says, 'And he shall kill it,' meaning, 'it' must be in the north, while the one who does the act of slaughter need not be in the north."

M. [Reverting again to the question of A,] "it" must be killed in the north, but a bird does not have to be killed in the north [when the neck of the bird is wrung to kill it as a sacrifice]. *For it has been taught on Tannaite authority:*

N. Might one suppose that killing a bird offering must be done in the north?

O. That conclusion, after all, stands to reason, for if killing a lamb, which does not have to be done by a priest, must be done in the north, killing a bird, which does have to be done by a priest, surely should be done in the north!

P. Accordingly, it is necessary to specify "it," to bear the meaning, "it" must be killed in the north, but a bird does not have to be killed in the north.

Q. No, what is particular to the lamb is that Scripture has required the use of a utensil in killing it [while no knife is required for a bird]!

R. Rather, [reverting again to the question of A,] "it" must be killed in the north, but a Passover offering does not have to be slaughtered in the north. *For it has been taught on Tannaite authority:*

S. R. Eliezer b. Jacob says, "Might one suppose that slaughtering the Passover offering must take place in the north? For it stands to reason. If Scripture required that the burnt offering be slaughtered at the north, though it did not specify a fixed time for slaughtering the burnt offering, surely the Passover offering, for which Scripture did prescribed a fixed time for slaughter, surely should have to be slaughtered in the north.

T. "Accordingly, it is necessary to specify 'it,' to bear the meaning, 'it' must be killed in the north, but a Passover offering does not have to be killed in the north."

U. Not at all. The distinctive trait of the burnt offering is that it is wholly burned up.

V. Then derive the matter from the sin offering [which is not wholly burnt up but yields meat to the priest].

W. What is distinctive about the sin offering is that it achieves atonement for those who are liable to the penalty of extirpation.

X. Then derive the matter from the guilt offering.

Y. What is distinctive about the guilt offering is that it falls into the classification of Most Holy Things, and, as a matter of fact, you cannot derive the rule from the cases of the burnt offering, guilt offering or sin offerings, for all of them are in the classification of Most Holy Things.

Z. *So, in the end, it must be as we originally said:*

AA. "it" is slaughtered in the north, but the one who does the slaughtering does not have to stand in the north."

BB. *And as to the question that you raised based on what R. Ahia said* [R. Ahia says, "'And he shall kill it on the side of the altar at the north:' why is this stated? It is because we find that the priest who receives the blood must stand in the north and also must receive the blood in the north. If he stood in the south and received the blood in the north, the offering is invalid. So you might have thought that the same rule governs slaughtering the animal. Scripture says, 'And he shall kill it,' meaning, 'it' must be in the north, while the one who does the act of slaughter need not be in the north."]—*the answer is, the sense is not to exclude the slaughterer from the requirement that the rite be done in the north, but rather,* "While the one who does the slaughtering need not be in the north, the one who receives the blood must be in the north."

CC. *The receiver? But surely that is deduced from the language,* "and he shall take," meaning, "let him take himself to the north"!

DD. The authority at hand does not accept the sense, "and he shall take," meaning, "let him take himself to the north."

It is hardly necessary to remind ourselves that we are dealing with a sustained and continuous exposition, once that holds together from start to finish: the same question, addressed in sequence to successive statements of the same base-text (the Mishnah's paragraph), and answered in a consistent way throughout.

3. A. *So we have found that, so far as fulfilling the religious duty, the act of slaughtering of the burnt offering must be done in the north, and the act of receiving, so far as fulfilling the religious duty, must be done in the north. How do we know that it is indispensable that the act of slaughtering and receiving the blood be done in the north [and if not, the offering is invalid]?*

B. Said R. Adda b. Ahbah—others say, Rabbah b. Shila, "It is an argument a fortiori: if slaughtering and receiving the blood at the north form an indispensable part of the rite of offering the sin offering, the rule of which in any event is derived from the rule governing the burnt offering, then surely it is reasonable to suppose that these same procedures' being done in the north are indispensable in the case of the burnt offering, from which the rules governing the sin offering derive!"

C. But the distinctive trait of the sin offering is that it effects atonement for those who are liable to extirpation.

D. *Said Rabina, "[The reason that nonetheless Adda utilizes the argument a fortiori is as follows: this is what R. Adda bar Ahbah found troubling: do we ever find the rule governing a derivative matter more stringent than the rule governing the primary matter?"* [The sin offering here is secondary to the burnt offering, since the requirement of offering the sacrifice at the northern side of the altar occurs primarily in connection with the burnt offering (Freedman].

E. Said Mar Zutra b. R. Mari to Rabina, "Do we not find such a case? **[49A]** Lo, there is the matter of second tithe, which itself can be redeemed, while what is purchased with money exchanged for produce in the status of second tithe cannot be redeemed. *For we have learned in the Mishnah:* **[Produce] purchased with coins [in the status] of second tithe, which becomes unclean [and therefore may not be eaten as second tithe]—let it be redeemed. R. Judah says, "Let it be buried." They said to R. Judah, "If it is the case that when produce which is designated as second tithe itself becomes unclean, lo, it must be redeemed, is it not logical that produce purchased with coins in the status of second tithe which becomes unclean also should be redeemed?" He said to them, "No! If you say this in regard to [produce designated as] second tithe itself, which, if in a state of cleanness, may be redeemed when it is outside Jerusalem, can you say so as regards produce purchased with coins [in the status of second tithe which, when it is [in a state of] cleanness, may not be redeemed when outside Jerusalem?" [M. M.S. 3:10].**

F. *In that case the power of the sanctification is insufficient to govern its redemption.* [Freedman: An object must possess a certain degree of sanctity before the sanctity can be transferred to something else, while the sanctity of this is too light to permit such a transfer. Hence Judah's ruling arises out of the lesser, not the greater, sanctity of what has been purchased.]

G. *And lo, there is the case of a beast declared as a substitute for a consecrated beast, for while an act of consecration does not affect a beast that is permanently blemished, an act of substitution does affect a beast that is permanently blemished!*

H. *The consecration of the beast declared as a substitute derives from the consecration of the consecrated beast itself, while the sanctification of a consecrated animal for its part derives from its originally-unconsecrated status. [Another ani-*

mal already has been sanctified.]

I. *And lo, there is the case of the Passover, which itself does not require the laying on of hands, drink offerings, and the waving of the breast and shoulder, while a beast purchased with the remainder of funds set aside for the purchase of a Passover offering, when it is offered up on that occasion, does require the laying on of hands, drink offerings, and the waving of the breast and shoulder.*

J. *But the animal purchased with the remainder of funds set aside for the purchase of a Passover offering during the rest of the year is classified simply as a peace offering [and it is not a Passover offering at all; it is a different sacrifice, subject to its own rules (Freedman)].*

K. *If you prefer, I shall say,* Scripture has said, "the burnt offerings," meaning, "it must be in its appointed place." [That means doing so in the northern area is essential to the rite, not merely recommended.[

IV.1

A. [Supply: **Most Holy Things (...guilt offering)—the act of slaughtering them is carried out at the north side of the altar].**

Here we go again: how on the basis of Scripture do we know the law that the Mishnah has stated without a proof-text.

B. *How on the basis of Scripture do we know that the guilt offering has to be prepared at the north side of the altar?*

C. *As it is written,* "In the place in which they kill the burnt offering shall they kill the guilt offering" (Lev. 7:1).

D. *So we have found that the act of slaughter of the guilt offering must take place at the northern side of the altar. How on the basis of Scripture do we know that the collecting of the blood also must take place there?*

E. "And the blood thereof shall be dashed" (Lev. 7:2).

F. *So the receiving of the blood must also be in the north. How about the location of the one who receives the blood?*

G. *That is indicated by the use of the accusative particle et [which extends the law to the one who receives the blood] in the verse,* "And the blood thereof shall be dashed" (Lev. 7:2).

H. *So we have found that that is the recommended manner of carrying out the rite. But how do we know that it is indispensable to the proper performance of the rite that matters be done in this way?*

I. *There is another verse that is written in this same connection:* "And he shall kill the he lamb in the place where they kill the sin offering and the burnt offering" (Lev. 14:13) [repeating the rule in regard to another guilt offering shows that it is indispensable to the proper carrying out of the rite].

2. A. *But does the cited verse really serve the stated purpose in particular? Surely it serves another purpose altogether, as has been taught on Tannaite authority:*

B. If a matter was covered by an encompassing rule but then was sin-

gled out for some innovative purpose, you have not got the right
to restore the matter to the rubric of the encompassing rule unless
Scripture itself explicitly does so.

C. How so?

D. "And he shall kill the lamb in the place where they kill the sin offering and the burnt offering, in the holy place; for the guilt offering, like the sin offering, belongs to the priest; it is most holy" (Lev.
14:13)—

E. Now what need does Scripture have to state, "for the guilt offering, like the sin offering"? [Freedman: for if it is to teach that it is
slaughtered in the north, that follows from the first half of the verse;
if it teaches that sprinkling of the blood and eating the meat follow
the rules of the sin offering, that is superfluous, since it is covered
by the general regulations on guilt offerings given at Lev. 7:1-10].
And why does Scripture state, "for the guilt offering, like the sin offering"?

F. The reason is that the guilt offering presented by the person healed
of the skin ailment was singled out for the innovative purpose of indicating the following:

G. in regard to the thumb of the hand, big toe of the foot, and right
ear, you might have thought that the rite does not require the presentation of the blood of the offering and the parts to be burned
up on the altar. Scripture therefore states, "for the guilt offering,
like the sin offering," to show that just as the sin offering's blood and
sacrificial parts have to be presented on the altar, so the blood and
sacrificial parts of the guilt offering presented by the person healed
of the skin ailment have to be presented on the altar.

H. *If [you claim that the purpose of the verse is as stated and not to teach that doing
the rite at the north is indispensable, as originally proposed,] then Scripture should
have stated only the rule governing the rite for the one healed from the skin ailment but not the earlier version of the rule.*

I. *Quite so—if we take the view that when something becomes the subject of a new
law, it cannot then be covered by an encompassing rule that otherwise would apply,* **[49B]** *while the encompassing rule still can be derived from that special case.
But if we take the view that when something becomes the subject of a new law,
then it cannot be covered by an encompassing rule that otherwise would apply,
and the encompassing rule also cannot be derived from that special place, then the
law [Lev. 7:1-10, indicating that the guilt offering must be killed in the north]
is needed for its own purpose!*

J. *Since Scripture has restored the matter to the rubric of the encompassing rule explicitly, that restoration has taken place.*

K. *Said Mar Zutra b. R. Mari to Rabina, "But why not say, when Scripture restored the matter to the rubric of the encompassing rule, that was solely in regard
to having to present the blood and the sacrificial parts on the altar, since the priest
is necessary to perform that rite. But as to slaughtering the animal, which does
not have to be done by a priest, that does not have to be done at the northern side
of the altar?"*

L. *[He said to him,] "If so, Scripture should say simply, 'for it is like the sin offering.' Why say, 'or the guilt offering, like the sin offering'? It is to teach, let it be like other guilt offerings [that must be slaughtered at the northern side of the altar]."*

3. A. *Why must a verbal analogy [for the burnt offering] be drawn to both a sin offering and also a guilt offering?*

    B. *Said Rabina, "Both are necessary. If a verbal analogy had been drawn to a sin offering but not to a burnt offering, I should have reached this conclusion: from what source did we derive the rule that a sin offering is slaughtered at the north side of the altar? It is on the basis of the analogy to the burnt offering. The consequence is that a rule that has been derived by analogy in turn generates another rule through analogy [so to avoid such a circularity, Scripture adds the matter of the burnt offering, to prove that that is not the case]."*

    C. *Said Mar Zutra b. R. Mari to Rabina, "Then draw the analogy to the burnt offering and omit reference to a verbal analogy to the sin offering altogether!"*

What are the limits of the verbal analogy? Now we come to one of the great moments of our chapter: the truly dialectical question, that is generated by the dialectical mode of thought. What we want to know, stated narrowly, is the limits of verbal analogy. To explain what is at issue, we have to proceed in a moving argument, hence, the issue is the dialectics of analogy. Specifically: I have two items, A and B. I claim that B is like A, therefore the rule governing A applies also to B. Now I turn forward, to C. C is not analogous to A; there are no points of congruence or (in the exegetical formulation that our authors use) verbal intersection. But C is like B. It is like B because there is an analogy by reason of verbal intersection (the same word being used in reference to C and B.) The question is, may I apply to C, by reason of the verbal intersection between C and B, the lesson that I have learned in regard to B only by reason of B's similarity by reason of congruence, not verbal intersection, to A? This is formulated (as best as I can translate the Hebrew/Aramaic) as, "can a conclusion that is derived on the basis of a verbal analogy go and impart a lesson by reason of analogy to a third item?" This issue is going to occupy us for quite some time. It is the one thing said about many things that imparts to the chapter as a whole its remarkable cogency.

D. *[He said to him,] "Then I might reach the conclusion that [elsewhere] what is derived on the basis of a verbal analogy turns around and imparts a lesson by means of a verbal analogy [and there would be nothing in the text to show the contrary (Freedman)]. And if you should say, then draw the analogy to a sin offering, I would reply: Scripture prefers to draw the analogy to what is primary rather than to what is secondary [and the sin offering is the primary source of the law, since that is where the requirement that the rite take place at the north is specified, and the sin offering is derivative of he burnt offering]. That is why the analogy is drawn to the sin offering and also to the burnt offering, bearing the sense that that which is derived on the basis of a verbal analogy does not in turn go and impart a lesson by means of a verbal analogy."*

4. A. *Raba said, "[The proposition that that which is derived on the basis of a verbal analogy does not in turn go and impart a lesson by means of a verbal analogy] derives from the following proof:*

    B. "It is written, 'As is taken off from the ox of the sacrifice of peace offerings' (Lev. 4:10) [namely, the sacrificial parts of the anointed priest's bullock brought for a sin offering]—*now for what purpose is this detail given? hat the lobe of the liver and the two kidneys are to be burned on the altar [as is the case with those of the sin offering], that fact is specified in the body of the verse itself. But the purpose is to intimate that the burning of the lobe of the liver and the two kidneys of the he goats brought as sin offerings for idolatry are to be derived by analogy from the bullock of the community brought on account of an inadvertent sin. That law is not explicitly stated in the passage on the bullock that is brought for an inadvertent sin, but is derived from the rule governing the bullock of the anointed priest. 'As is taken off' is required so that it might be treated as something written in that very passage [on the bullock of inadvertence, being superfluous in its own context], not as something derived on the basis of a verbal analogy does not in turn go and impart a lesson by means of a verbal analogy."*

    C. *Said R. Pappa to Raba, "Then let Scripture inscribe the rule in that very passage, and not trouble to draw a verbal analogy to the bullock of the anointed priest at all."*

    D. *"If the rule had been inscribed in its own context and not been presented by means of a verbal analogy to the bullock of the anointed priest, I might have said that that which is derived on the basis of a verbal analogy does in turn go and impart a lesson by means of a verbal analogy. And if you should object, 'Then let Scripture present the rule by analogy without making it explicit,' I could answer that Scripture prefers to make an explicit statement in the proper context rather than to present a law through a verbal analogy. Scripture therefore inscribed the matter in the passage dealing with the anointed priest and established the analogy so as to demonstrate that that which is derived on the basis of a verbal analogy does not in turn go and impart a lesson by means of a verbal analogy."*

My claim that this chapter is systematic and orderly, composed with a broader program in mind and not narrowly limited to the exegesis of phrases of the Mishnah read in sequence, is now demonstrated by what is to follow. We have proven one point. It bears a consequence. We go on to the consequence. The mode of thought is dialectical not only in form, but also in substance: if A, then B. If B, then what about C? But we see that matters are not only continued, but also refined. It is one thing to have shown that if B is like A, and C, unlike A, is rendered comparable to B by a verbal analogy, then may I take the next step and draw into the framework of B and C, joined by verbal analogy and assigned a common rule by B's congruent-analogy to A, also D, E, F, and G, that is, other classes of things joined to C by verbal analogy—but not necessarily the same verbal analogy that has joined C to B? That indeed is the obvious next step to be taken, and it is now taken.

5. A. Now it is a fact that that which is derived on the basis of a verbal analogy does in turn go and impart a lesson by means of a verbal analogy, *demonstrated whether in the manner of Raba or in the manner of Rabina.*

   B. Is it the rule, however, that *that which is derived on the basis of a verbal analogy may in turn go and impart a lesson by means of an argument on the basis of congruence?* [Freedman: Thus the law stated in A is applied to B by analogy. Can that law then be applied to C because of congruence between B and C?]

   C. [Indeed it can.] *Come and take note:* R. Nathan b. Abetolomos says, "How on the basis of Scripture do we know that when there is a spreading of disease-signs [of Lev. 13-14] in clothing, [if it covers the entire garment], it is ruled to be clean? The words 'baldness on the back of the head' and 'baldness on the front of the head' are stated in respect to man, and 'baldness on the back' and 'baldness on the front' are mentioned in connection with clothing. Just as is in the former case, if the baldness spread throughout the whole, the man is clean, so here too, if the baldness spread throughout the whole, the garment is clean."

   D. And in that context how do we know the rule [that that which spreads and covers the whole head is clean, since Lev. 13:12-13 refers to what is on the skin, not the head? And furthermore, the symptoms differ (Freedman)]? Because it is written, "And if the skin ailment...cover all the skin...from his head even to his feet" (Lev. 13:12)—so the head is treated as analogous to the feet. Just as if the feet have all turned white, the ailment have spread over the whole of the body, the man is clean, so here too when it spreads over the whole of the head and beard, he is clean. [Thus we derive the rule by a verbal analogy that the specified marks covering the whole head are clean, and then the same rule is applied to the garments by the argument resting on congruence, as stated at C (Freedman)].

   E. [To the contrary,] said R. Yohanan, "Throughout the Torah we infer one rule from another that has itself been derived by inference, except for the matter of consecration, in which we do not derive a rule from another that has itself been inferred."

   F. *Now if it were the fact that we did so, then let the reference to "north" not be stated*

in the context of the guilt offering at all, and it could be inferred from the rule
governing sin offerings, by means of the argument based on the congruence of the
language, "It is most Holy" [which is stated in the setting of the sin offering at
Lev. 7:18 and the built offering at Lev. 7:1]! Does that not bear the implica-
tion that that which is derived on the basis of a verbal analogy may not in turn
go and impart a lesson by means of an argument on the basis of congruence?

G. *But perhaps the reason that we do not learn the lesson at that passage is that there*
is an ample refutation: the reason that the sin offering has to be offered in the north
is that it achieves atonement for those who are liable to the penalty of extirpation?

H. *Still, in context, there is nonetheless a superfluous reference to* "most Holy"[at
Num. 18:9]. [Freedman: Since this is superfluous, an argument from
congruence is plausible, even though the guilt offering is dissimilar
to the sin offering; the that that we do not do so proves that in the
case of sacrifices that which is derived on the basis of a verbal analogy may not in turn go and impart a lesson by means of an argument on the basis of congruence.]

What follows simply proceeds to the logically next question: we
have now linked B to C via a verbal analogy. C stands in relationship to other classes of things, but not for the same reason
that it stands in relationship to B, that is, through other than verbal analogical relationships. It forms a relationship a fortiori, for
instance, with D, E, and F. If something applies to C, the lesser,
it surely should apply to D, the greater. So now we want to know
the permissible grounds for drawing relationships—comparisons
and contrasts—of classes of things. The deeper issue of compara-
tive-contrasting thinking is now right on the surface: what constitutes the proper basis for establishing the plausibility of comparison
and contrast anyhow? We obviously do not want to compare things
that do not bear comparison because they are not species of the
same genus, but distinct genera. But then on what basis do we
move from species to species and uncover the genera of which
they form a part (if they do form a part)? Is it only verbal correspondence or intersection, as has been implicit to this point? Or
are there more abstract bases for the same work of genus-construction (in our language: category-formation and re-formation)?
This simple issue is going to keep us busy from here to nearly
the end of the chapter, because there is a rich repertoire of principles that establish of discrete data classes of data and that then
link one class to another. The first was, we recall, deriving a rule
by analogy and then moving on to transmit the rule to classes
linked by not analogy but rather verbal intersection. We proceed
to the next problem, which is, whether or not a rule shown to

apply to two or more classes of things linked by verbal analogy may then be applied to further classes of things that relate to the foregoing by not verbal analogy but a relationship a fortiori.

6. A. That which is learned by a verbal analogy may in turn go and impart a rule by an argument *a fortiori* .
   B. **[50A]** That is in line with that which the Tannaite authority of the household of R. Ishmael set forth.
7. A. Can that which is learned by verbal analogy in turn go and impart a rule by an analogy based on the congruence of other shared traits [but not verbal ones in context]? [This mode of argument depends not on verbal analogy supplied by Scripture but an analogy drawn from similarity of the traits of two subjects.]
   B. *Said R. Jeremiah, "Let Scripture omit reference to slaughtering the guilt offering at the north of the altar, and that rule can have been inferred by appeal to an analogy based on the congruence of other shared traits [but not verbal ones in context] from the rule governing a sin offering. [Both offerings expiate sin. So the rule governing the one will pertain to the other.]*
   C. *"So why has Scripture stated that law? Is it not to indicate that* that which is learned by verbal analogy established may not in turn go and impart a rule by an analogy based on the congruence of other shared traits [but not verbal ones in context]??"
   D. *But in accord with your reasoning, let the rule be inferred by an analogy based on the congruence of other shared traits [but not verbal ones in context] from the one governing a burnt offering!* [The rule is explicitly stated in that context, and the intermediate analogy based on verbal similarities is not required at all (Freedman).]
   E. *So why is it not inferred in that way?*
   F. *It is because one may present the following challenge:* the distinguishing trait of the burnt offering is indeed that it is turned to ashes on the altar! [That is not the case of the guilt offering.]
   G. *In reference to the sin offering, one may also present a challenge, namely:* the distinguishing trait of the sin offering is that it expiates sins that bear the sanction of extirpation.
   H. *While, therefore, admittedly one cannot learn the rule on a one to one basis, why not derive the rule by imputing to the third classification the law governing two other classifications of sacrifice [so that Scripture can have intimated that slaughter at the north is required for two of the three classifications, and by an argument based on the congruent of other shared traits, we should derive the rule governing the third of the three]?*
   I. *From which two of the three can the rule have been derived for the third? If Scripture had not written the rule in connection with the burnt offering, you might have derived the rule for that classification from the one covering the sin offering and the guilt offering.*
   J. *Not at all, for the distinguishing trait of these is that they effect atonement [which is not accomplished by the burnt offering].*

K. *Then let Scripture not state the rule in connection with the sin offering, and de-rive it from the other two.*

L. *Not at all, for the distinguishing trait of these is that they require male animals [which is not the case of the sin offering, which is a female].*

M. *Then let Scripture not state the rule in connection with the guilt offering, and derive it from the other two.*

N. *Not at all, for the distinguishing trait of these is that they may be brought as much in behalf of the community as in behalf of an individual. [A guilt offering is presented only by an individual.]*

Not surprisingly, we now move forward once more—but by taking a step backward. We have shown that we may move from a class of things joined to another through analogy based on congruence, that is, from A to B, onward to other classes of things joined to the foregoing by verbal analogy or intersection, that is, from B to C and beyond. But can we then move from C, linked to B via verbal analogy, to D, linked to C, but not to A or B, by congruence, e.g., comparable and shared traits of a salient order? The issue then, is may we move forward to further classes of things by moving "backward," to a principle of linkage of classes that has served to bring us to this point, in other words, reversing the course of principles of linkage? What our framers then want to know is a very logical question: are there fixed rules that govern the order or sequence by which we move from one class of things to another, so that, if we propose to link classes of things, we can move only from A to B by one principle (comparison and contrast of salient traits), and from B to C by a necessarily consequent and always second principle (verbal intersection); then we may move (by this theory) from C to D only by verbal intersection but not by appeal to congruence. Why not? Because, after all, if C is linked to B only by verbal intersection but not by congruence, bearing no relationship to A at all, then how claim that D stands in a series begun at A, if it has neither verbal connection, nor, as a matter of fact, congruence to link it to anything in the series. Is then a series substantive, in that we ask that there be some "natural logic" holding the parts together, a "natural logic" that derives from the sequence of operative principles of comparison and contrast? Or is a series merely formal, in that if we can link D to C in one way but D to A in no ways, D still has been shown, in the course of argument but not by the reason or internal logic of the argument, to relate to A at all? This enormously engaging question dictates everything that is coming, and I do not have to repeat the point, since there is no grasping a line from here to nearly the end of the chapter if we do not understand that what our sages are trying to find out is whether a series is a series because of its external form alone or because of its internal, inherent traits as well. If I were a mathematician, I could appeal to the issue of whether the symbolic representation of, e.g., spatial relations is limited by tests out there, as Euclid supposed, so that we move from data to symbol, or may there be a symbolic representation of "things" for which there is no "out there" there, as non-Euclidean geometries claim. But I am not a mathematician.

8. A. Can a rule that is derived by analogy based on the congruence of other shared traits [but not verbal ones in context] turn around and teach a lesson through an analogy based on verbal analogy?

B. *Said R. Pappa, "'This is the law of the sacrifice of peace offerings…if he offers it for a thanksgiving offering' (Lev. 7:11ff.): in this verse we learn the rule that funds for the purchase of an animal offered for a thanksgiving offering may derive from money exchanged for produce in the status of second tithe, since we find, in point of fact, that peace offerings themselves [into the class of which the cited verse assimilates thanksgiving offerings] may be purchased from money exchanged for produce in the status of second tithe."*

C. *And how do we know, as a matter of fact, that that peace offerings themselves [into the class of which the cited verse assimilates thanksgiving offerings] may be purchased from money exchanged for produce in the status of second tithe?*

D. *The reason is that the word* "there" *is written in the context of both a beast purchased for use as a peace offering and also second tithe, [at Dt. 27:7 and Dt. 14:23, respectively].* [It follows that the rule governing the peace offering derives from an argument based on an analogy established through verbal congruence, and that rule is then applied to a thanksgiving offering by an analogy based on other than verbal congruence.]

E. *Said Mar Zutra b. R. Mari to Rabina, "But tithe of grain is in the status of unconsecrated food in general [but the issue at hand addresses tithe of the corral, which is in the status of Holy Things]!"*

F. *He said to him, "Who has claimed that* that to which a rule is transferred [by means of the exegetical principle at hand] must be in the class of Holy Things and that that from which a rule is transferred likewise must be in the class of Holy Things?"

9. A. Can a rule that is derived by an analogy based on the congruence of other shared traits [but not verbal ones in context] turn around and teach a lesson through an analogy based on the congruence of [other] shared traits?

B. *Said Rami bar Hama, "It has been taught on Tannaite authority:*

C.   """"Of fine flour soaked" (Lev. 7:12)—this teaches that the soaked cake [one that is made of boiled flour] must be made of fine flour.

D.   "'How do we know the rule that applies to the ordinary unleavened cakes [*hallot*]?

E.   "'Scripture in both contexts [speaking of the cakes that are soaked as well as the unleavened ones] speaks of *hallot*.

F.   "'How do we know that the same rule applies to thin wafers?

G.   "'Because Scripture in both contexts speaks of unleavened bread.'" [Freedman: Thus we first learn by an analogy based on shared traits that the ordinary unleavened cakes must be made of fine flour, and then by a further such argument we learn from the ordinary unleavened cakes that the thin wafers likewise must be of fine flour.]

H.   *Said to him Rabina, "How do you know that he derives the rule governing unleavened cakes from the one governing ordinary unleavened cakes? Perhaps he derives the rule from the law governing oven baked cakes [Lev. 2:4] [without appeal to the analogy that has been drawn here]?"*

I.   Rather, said Raba, "It has been taught on Tannaite authority:

J.   """"And its innards and its dung, even the whole bullock shall he carry forth outside of the camp" (Lev. 4:11)—this teaches that they carry it out whole.

K.   "'Might one suppose that they burn it whole?

L.   "'Here we find a reference to "its head and its legs," and elsewhere [Lev. 1:8-9, 12-13] we find reference also to "its head and its legs." Just as in that other case, this is done only after cutting up the beast, so here too it means only after cutting up the beast.

M.   "'If so, then just as there this is after flaying the hide, so here too is it to be after flaying the hide? Scripture states, "and its innards and its dung."'"

N.   *What conclusion is supposed to be drawn here?*

O.   Said R. Pappa, "Just as its dung is kept within the innards, so the meat must be held within the hide."

P.   *And so too it has been taught on Tannaite authority:*

Q.   Rabbi says, "Here [with reference to the bullock and he goat of the Day of Atonement] we find a reference to 'hide and meat and dung,' **[50B]** and elsewhere, we find a reference to hide and meat and dung [in connection with the bullock of the anointed priest]. Just as there, the beast was burned only after being cut up, but without flaying the hide, so here too the beast was burned only after being cut up, but without flaying the hide." [Thus the result of one such argument is transferred to another case by another such argument (Freedman)].

10. A.   Can a rule that is derived by an analogy based on the congruence of other shared traits [but not verbal ones in context] go and teach a lesson through an argument a fortiori?

B.   Indeed so, by reason of an argument a fortiori:

C.   If an argument deriving from an analogy based on verbal congruence, which cannot go and, by an argument based on verbal congruence, impart its rule to some other class—*as has been shown by either Raba's or Rabina's demonstration*—nonetheless can go and by an argument a fortiori impart its rule to some other class—*as has been shown by the Tannaite authority of the household of R. Ishmael*—then a rule that is derived by an argument based on analogy based on other than verbal congruence, which can for its part go and impart its lesson by an argument based on an analogy resting on verbal congruity— *as has been shown by R. Pappa*—surely can in turn teach its lesson by an argument a fortiori to yet another case!

D. *That position poses no problems to one who takes the view that R. Pappa's case has been made. But for one who takes the view that R. Pappa's case has not been made, what is to be said?*

E. *Rather, this is an argument a fortiori in favor of the same point:*

F. If an argument deriving from an analogy based on verbal congruence, which cannot go and, by an argument based on verbal congruence, impart its rule to some other class—*as has been shown by either Raba's or Rabina's demonstration*—nonetheless can go and by an argument a fortiori impart its rule to some other class—*as has been shown by the Tannaite authority of the household of R. Ishmael*—then a rule that is derived by an argument based on analogy based on other than verbal congruence, which can for its part go and impart its lesson by an argument based on an analogy resting on verbal congruity which is like itself— *as has been shown by Rami bar Hama*—surely can in turn teach its lesson by an argument a fortiori to yet another case!

11. A. Can a rule that is derived by an analogy based on the congruence of other shared traits [but not verbal ones in context] go and teach a lesson through an argument constructed by analogy based on the congruence of other shared traits among two or more classifications of things?

B. *That question must stand.*

12. A. Can a rule derived by an argument a fortiori go and teach a rule established through analogy of verbal usage?

B. The affirmative derives from an argument a fortiori:

C. If an argument deriving from an analogy based on points of other than verbal congruence, which cannot go and, by an argument based on verbal congruence, impart its rule to some other class— *as has been shown by either R. Pappa's demonstration,*—then a rule that is derived by an argument a fortiori, which can be derived by an argument based on the shared verbal traits of two things,—*as has been shown by the Tannaite authority of the house of R. Ishmael*—surely should be able to impart its rule to another classification of things by reason of an argument based on a verbal analogy!

D. *That position poses no problems to one who takes the view that R. Pappa's case has been made. But for one who takes the view that R. Pappa's case has not been made, what is to be said?*

E. *The question then must stand.*

13. A. Can a rule that is derived by an argument a fortiori go and teach

a lesson through an argument based on the congruence of other shared traits [but not verbal ones in context]?

B. The affirmative derives from an argument a fortiori:

C. If an argument deriving from an analogy based on points of other than verbal congruence, which cannot be derived from an argument based on verbal congruence, impart its rule to some other class— *as has been shown by R. Yohanan's demonstration,*—can go and teach a lesson by an argument based on an analogy established through other than verbal traits, *as has been shown by Rami bar Hama*—a rule based on an argument a fortiori, which can be derived by an argument based on an analogy resting on verbal coincidence, surely should be able to impart its rule to another classification of things by reason of an argument based on an other than verbal analogy!

14. A. Can a rule based on an argument a fortiori turn around and teach a lesson through an argument based on an argument a fortiori?

B. Indeed so, and the affirmative derives from an argument a fortiori:

C. If an argument deriving from an analogy based on points of other than verbal congruence, which cannot be derived from an argument based on verbal congruence, impart its rule to some other class— *as has been shown by R. Yohanan's demonstration,*—can go and teach a lesson by an argument a fortiori, as we have just pointed out, then an argument that can be derived from an analogy based on verbal congruence—*as has been shown by the Tannaite authority of the household of R. Ishmael*—surely should be able to impart its rule by an argument a fortiori!

D. But would this then would represent what we are talking about, namely, a rule deriving from an argument a fortiori that has been applied to another case by means of an argument a fortiori? Surely this is nothing more than a secondary derivation produced by an argument a fortiori!

E. Rather, argue in the following way:

F. Indeed so, and the affirmative derives from an argument a fortiori:

G. if an argument based on an analogy of a verbal character cannot be derived from another such argument based on an analogy between two classes of things that rests upon a verbal congruence— *in accordance with the proofs of either Raba or Rabina*—nonetheless can then go and impart its lesson by an argument a fortiori—*in accordance with the proof of the Tannaite authority of the household of R. Ishmael*—then an argument a fortiori, which can serve to transfer a lesson originally learned through an argument based upon verbal congruence, *in accordance with the proof of the Tannaite authority of the household of R. Ishmael*— surely should be able to impart its lesson to yet another classification of things through an argument a fortiori.

H. And this does represent what we are talking about, namely, a rule deriving from an argument a fortiori that has been applied to another case by means of an argument a fortiori.

15. A. Can a rule based on an argument a fortiori turn around and teach
        a rule through an argument constructed on the basis of shared traits
        of an other-than-verbal character among two classifications of
        things?

    B. *Said R. Jeremiah, "Come and take note:* **[If] one pinched off the neck
        and [the bird] turned out to be terefah—R. Meir says,
        "It does not impart uncleanness of the gullet [since
        slaughtering a beast is wholly equivalent to pinching the
        neck of a bird]." R. Judah says, "It does impart unclean-
        ness of the gullet." [Birds and beasts in no way are com-
        parable; neither slaughtering an unconsecrated clean bird
        nor pinching the neck of a consecrated one will exempt
        from uncleanness a bird which turns out to be terefah.]
        Said R. Meir, "It is an argument a fortiori: now if in the
        case of the carrion of a beast, which imparts unclean-
        ness through contact and through carrying, proper slaugh-
        ter renders clean from its uncleanness that which was
        terefah, [in the case of] the carrion of fowl, which to
        begin with does not impart uncleanness through contact
        and through carrying, it should logically follow that its
        proper slaughter should render clean from its unclean-
        ness that which was terefah. Just as we find that its
        proper slaughter [in the case of a bird or beast] renders
        it valid for eating [51A] and renders it clean from its un-
        cleanness in the case of terefah, so proper pinching of
        the neck, which renders it valid for eating, should ren-
        der it clean from its uncleanness in the case of terefah."
        R. Yosé says, "It is sufficient that it [the slaughtering
        of the bird] be equivalent to the carrion of a beast: its
        [a beast's or a bird's] slaughtering renders clean [what
        is terefah], but the pinching of the neck [of a bird does]
        not [render clean what is terefah]" [M. Zeb. 7:6].** [The
        language **"Just as we find"** then represents an argument based
        on shared traits of two distinct classifications of things, and so we
        see that a rule derived by an argument a fortiori then through such
        an argument based on shared traits is transferred to another class
        of things altogether.]"

    C. *But that is not so. For even if we concede that that is the case there, then still the
        rule derives from the act of slaughter of unconsecrated beasts [Freedman].*

16. A. Can a rule derived by an argument based on shared traits of an
        other than verbal character shared among two classes of things then
        turn around and teach a lesson by an argument based on an anal-
        ogy of a verbal character, an analogy not of a verbal character, an
        argument a fortiori, or an argument based on shared traits?

    B. *Solve at least one of those problems by appeal to the following:*

    C. On what account have they said that if blood of an offering is left overnight on the altar, it is fit? Because if the sacrificial parts are kept overnight on the altar, they are fit. And why if the sacrificial parts are kept overnight on the altar are they fit? Because if the meat of the offering is kept overnight on the altar it is fit. [Freedman: thus the rule governing the sacrificial parts is derived by an appeal to an argument based on shared traits of an other than verbal character shared among two classes of things, and that rule in turn is applied to the case of the blood by another such argument based on shared traits of an other than verbal character shared among two classes of things].

D.   What about the rule governing meat that is taken outside of the Temple court? [If such meat is put up on the altar, it is not removed therefrom. Why so?]

E.   Because meat that has been taken out of the holy place is suitable for a high place.

F.   What about the rule governing unclean meat? [If such meat is put up on the altar, it is not removed therefrom. Why so?]

G.   Since meat that is unclean is subject to a remission of the prohibition affecting it in the case of an offering made in behalf of the entire community.

H.   What about the rule governing the sacrificial parts of a burnt offering that the officiating priest subjected to the intention of being burned after the proper time? [If such meat is put up on the altar, it is not removed therefrom. Why so?]

I.   Since the sprinkling of the blood is effective and propitiates in making such meat refuse by reason of the improper intentionality [we leave the sacrificial portions on the altar once they have been put there].

J.   What about the rule governing the sacrificial parts of a burnt offering that the officiating priest subjected to the intention of being eaten outside of the proper place? [If such meat is put up on the altar, it is not removed therefrom. Why so?]

K.   Since sacrificial meat in that class is treated as analogous to sacrificial meat that has been subjected to an improper intentionality in respect to eating the meat outside of the proper time.

L.   What about the rule governing the sacrificial parts of a burnt offering the blood of which unfit priests have received and tossed, when such unfit persons are eligible for an act of service in behalf of the community...? [This question is not answered.]

M.   [Reverting to C-E:] Now can an analogy be drawn concerning something that has been disposed of in the proper manner for something that has not been disposed of in the proper manner? [If the sacrificial parts are kept over night, they are not taken off the altar, and therefore the meat kept overnight is fit; but the meat may be kept overnight, while the sacrificial parts may not. So too when the Temple stood, the flesh might not be taken outside, but where there was no Temple and only high places, the case is scarcely analogous!]

N.   *The Tannaite authority for this rule derives it from the augmentative sense, extending the rule, deriving from the formulation,* "This is the Torah of the burnt offering" (Lev. 6:2). [Freedman: the verse teaches that all burnt offerings, even with the defects catalogued here, are subject to the same rule and do not get removed from the altar once they have been put there; the arguments given cannot be sustained but still support that proposition.]

The simple order of the whole, the allows the answer to one question to precipitate the consequent and necessary next question. I need hardly review what our authors have made so clear through their own exposition. I cannot imagine anybody's not seeing that a sustained methodological inquiry is taking place at the very surface of discourse on the bloody rite of the Temple!

V.1

A.   **The remnants of their blood did one pour out on the western base of the outer altar. If he did not place [the remnants of the blood at the stated location], he did not impair [atonement]:**
B.   *What is the Scripture basis for this rule?*
C.   Scripture has said, "And all the remaining blood of the bullock shall he pour out at the base of the altar of the burnt offering which is at the door of the tent of meeting" (Lev. 4:7).
D.   *That speaks of the first altar that one meets [as you enter from the door, and that is the western base].*

What needs to be said once does not have to be repeated: the work of the framers of the Talmud is sometimes thought about thinking, but always inquiry into the relations between Scripture and law (in the Mishnah, as elsewhere). The former must be done once, it serves then throughout; but the latter has to be repeated many times. It would therefore vastly misrepresent the Talmud were I to present only parts I-IV or to claim that the deep structure of discourse of parts I-IV is present throughout; that is contrary to fact. The reason is that the Talmud's authorship remains bound within the limits of the medium it has chosen for the expression of its ideas, which is the form of a commentary to the Mishnah. And that means, the Mishnah will be commented upon! Now that commentary proves quite cogent, pursuing a few and limited questions over and over again. And one of these is, we recall very well, the scriptural basis for the Mishnah's law. That

question overrides any intent to expound the principles of comparison and contrast among genera, the linkage between genus
and genus, let alone to set forth the deep structure of abstract
thought on the nature of the series, that is, on the movement of
an argument from point to point. All of that wonderful thought,
shown in Part IV, now subsides, as we revert to our work. Once
we have finished one job, we now undertake the same job, in
the setting of another statement of the Mishnah. The competition between the wonders of sheer thought, at which our sages
excel, and exegesis always is won by exegesis. These geniuses of
ours were very modest men.

2. A. *Our rabbis have taught on Tannaite authority* [Freedman: there are five
        passages that deal with the sin offering, Lev. 4: the sin offering of
        the anointed priest, Lev. 4:1-12; the sin offering of the entire con-
        gregation, Lev. 4:13-22, the sin offering of a rule, Lev. 4:22-26, the
        female goat of an ordinary person, Lev. 4:27-32, and the lamb of
        an ordinary person, Lev. 4:32-35. The first two were offered on the
        inner altar, the other three on the outer. In regard to the first three
        Scripture states that the residue of the blood is to be poured out
        "...at the base of the altar of the burnt offering..." (Lev. 4:7, 18,
        25), and in connection with the other two there is an allusion to the
        base of the altar without reference to "of the sin offering." Here
        rabbis explain why Scripture specifies the altar of the burnt offer-
        ing in the first three cases. The first teaches that the residue is
        poured out at the base of the outer altar, the altar of the burnt
        offering, but not at the base of the inner altar, even though the
        blood was sprinkled on the horns of the inner altar. The second is
        superfluous, and it teaches that only the outer altar had such a base,
        not the inner altar. The third reference intimates that the residue
        of the blood of all sacrifices whose blood is sprinkled on the altar
        of burnt offering must be poured out at its base. thus:]:
    B. "...at the base of the altar of the burnt offering..." (Lev. 4:7)—and
        not at the base of the inner altar.
    C. "...at the base of the altar of the burnt offering..." (Lev. 4:18)—
        the inner altar has no base anyhow.
    D. "...at the base of the altar of the burnt offering..." (Lev. 4:25)—
        apply the laws governing the base to the altar of the burnt offer-
        ing.
    E. But perhaps that is not the sense, but rather, let there be a base
        around the altar of the burnt offering? [Freedman: perhaps the
        verse says nothing about the residue of the blood but indicates that
        the two sprinklings of the blood of the burnt offering must be made
        at that part of the altar that had a special base, excluding the south-
        eastern horn, which did not have a special base.]

F. Said R. Ishmael, "The proposition can be shown to derive from an argument a fortiori: if the residue of the blood of the sin offering, which does not make atonement, has to be poured out at the base, then the sprinkling of the blood of the burnt offering itself, which does make atonement, surely would require the base [meaning, it must be a corner of the altar at which the horn has been provided with a base]." [Then a verse is not required to make that point, if the teaching is as proposed. Hence the proposed proof is null.]

G. Said R. Aqiba, "[Along the same lines,] the proposition can be shown to derive from an argument a fortiori: if the residue of the blood of the sin offering, which does not make atonement and which is not presented for the purposes of atonement in any way, has to be poured out at the base, then the sprinkling of the blood of the burnt offering itself, which does make atonement, and which is presented for the purposes of atonement, surely would require the base [meaning, it must be a corner of the altar at which the horn has been provided with a base]. So why does Scripture state, 'at the base of the altar of burnt offering'? It is to indicate that the laws of the base should pertain to the altar of the burnt offering."

3. A. A master has said, "'…at the base of the altar of the burnt offering…' (Lev. 4:7)—and not at the base of the inner altar:"

B. *Surely that clause is required to make its own point [and not to prove the derivative, "and not…," point]!*

C. That point itself derives from the language, "which is at the door of the tent of meeting" [indicating that the outer altar is what is required, so the specification "of the burnt offering" is superfluous and serves the specified purpose].

4. A. [Supply: a master has said,] "'…at the base of the altar of the burnt offering…' (Lev. 4:25)—**[51B]** apply the laws governing the base to the altar of the burnt offering:"

B. *For if it should enter your mind that the passage is to be read literally as written, then what need do I have for a verse of Scripture dealing with the residue, since pouring out the residue was an act done in the outer courtyard and not in the inner sanctum?*

C. *And if you should say that without that verse, I might have concluded that it is indeed to be reversed, **[52A]** with the residue of the inner offering to be poured at the outer altar and the residue of the outer altar to be performed at the inner altar, in point of fact, the inner altar had no base [so the interpretation is possible only as given].*

5. A. [Supply: a master has said,] "But perhaps that is not the sense, but rather, let there be a base around the altar of the burnt offering:" [Freedman: perhaps the verse says nothing about the residue of the blood but indicates that the two sprinklings of the blood of the burnt offering must be made at that part of the altar that had a special base, excluding the southeastern horn, which did not have a special base.]

B. But is it not written, "at the base of the altar of burnt offering"?

[Freedman: if the verse intimated that the sprinkling itself must be performed on that part of the altar that has a base, it could not refer to sin offerings, the blood of which was sprinkled on all the horns of the altar, including the southeast. Hence it would have to refer to the burnt offering alone. But in that case, Scripture should write, "at the base of the burnt offering," which would intimate that the blood of the burnt offering must be sprinkled over against the base. The word "altar" then becomes redundant.]

C. *If the verse stated, "at the base of the burnt offering," I might have supposed that the sense was, on the top of the base [right up by the altar itself]. But since it is written, "at the base of the altar of burnt offering," the meaning is, "at the top of the base."*

D. Said R. Ishmael, "What need do I have for a verse to tell me that it is to be spilled out at the top of the base? It would follow through an argument a fortiori: if the residue of the blood of the sin offering, which does not make atonement, has to be poured out at the top of the base, then the sprinkling of the blood of the burnt offering itself, which does make atonement, surely would require the top of the base."

E. Said R. Aqiba, "[Along the same lines,] the proposition can be shown to derive from an argument a fortiori: if the residue of the blood of the sin offering, which does not make atonement and which is not presented for the purposes of atonement in any way, has to be poured out at the top of the base, then the sprinkling of the blood of the burnt offering itself, which does make atonement, and which is presented for the purposes of atonement, surely would require the top of the base. So why does Scripture state, 'at the base of the altar of burnt offering'? It is to indicate that the laws of the base should pertain to the altar of the burnt offering."

6. A. *In what regard do the two authorities differ?*

    B. *Said R. Adda b. Ahbah, "At issue between them is whether or not the pouring out of the residue of the blood is indispensable to the rite. One authority maintains that pouring out of the residue of the blood is indispensable to the rite. The author takes the view that pouring out of the residue of the blood is not indispensable to the rite."*

    C. *R. Pappa said, "All parties maintain that pouring out of the residue of the blood is not indispensable to the rite. But here what is at issue is whether or not the draining out of the blood of a bird that has been presented as a sin offering is indispensable to the rite. One authority takes the view that it is, the other, that it is not, indispensable to the rite."*

    D. *There is a Tannaite formulation in accord with the theory of R. Pappa:*

    E. "'And all the remaining blood of the bullock [of the offering of the anointed priest] shall he pour out at the base of the altar:' (Lev. 4:7)—Why does Scripture make reference to 'the bullock' [since the context makes clear that that is what is at issue]? It teaches concerning the bullock that is offered on the Day of Atonement that the blood has to be poured out at the base of the altar," the words of R. [Aqiba].

F.   Said R. Ishmael, "It is an argument a fortiori [that that is the case, and a proof-text is not required]. If the blood of an offering that is not obligatory [the bullock presented by a sin offering by the anointed priest, which is not an obligatory offering in that the man does not have to have said], presented on the inner altar, has to be poured out at the base, the blood of an offering that is obligatory, [the bullock presented on the Day of Atonement, which is required, whether or not the high priest has sinned], presented on the inner altar, surely should have to be poured out at the base!"

H.   Said R. Aqiba, "If an offering that is neither obligatory nor even a matter of a mere religious duty, the blood of which is not brought into the inner sanctum [the Holy of Holies], has to be poured out onto the base of the altar, an offering that is a statutory obligation, the blood of which is taken into the inner sanctum, surely should require a base!"

I.   "Now you might have supposed that the pouring out of the residue is indispensable for the rite [of the bullock on the Day of Atonement], and therefore Scripture states, 'And he shall make an end of atoning' (Lev. 16:20), meaning, all of the rites of atonement are now complete," the words of R. Ishmael.

J.   [Reverting to the claim of D:] Now it is an argument a fortiori in regard to the bullock of the anointed priest, namely, if the blood of an offering that is neither obligatory nor even a matter of religious duty which is not taken to the inner altar but still has to be poured out at the base of the altar, surely the blood of an offering whether obligatory or a matter of religious duty surely should have to be poured out at the base of the altar!

K.   Might one suppose that it is indispensable to the rite?

L.   Scripture states, "And all the remaining blood of the bullock he shall pour out," and in this way Scripture turns the matter the residual aspect of a religious duty, indicating that pouring out the residue is not indispensable to the correct carrying out of the rite.

7. A.   *But does R. Ishmael really take the position [as Pappa has claimed] that* draining out of the blood of a bird that has been presented as a sin offering is indispensable to the rite? And has it not been set forth as a Tannaite rule by the Tannaite authority of the household of R. Ishmael, "'And the rest of the blood shall be drained out:'—what is left is to be drained out, **[52B]** but what is not left is not drained out "? [Freedman: all the blood may be used in sprinkling, so that nothing is left for draining, hence draining cannot be indispensable.]

    B.   *There is a conflict among Tannaite versions of the opinions of R. Ishmael.*

8. A.   *Said Rami bar Hama, "The following Tannaite authority takes the view that pouring out the residue of the blood is indispensable. For it has been taught on Tannaite authority:"*

B. "This is the law of the sin offering...the priest who offers it for sin [having correctly carried out the rite in every detail] shall eat it" (Lev. 6:18-19)—"it" meaning, the one, the blood of which has been tossed above the red line around the altar, and not the one the blood of which was tossed below the red line around the altar.

C. Now explain [why might you have supposed that even though the blood was not properly sprinkled, the meat nonetheless still may be eaten, absent a proof-text to the contrary]!

D. It is a conclusion that can have been implied by the following verse, "and the blood of your sacrifices shall be poured out...and you shall eat the meat" (Dt. 12:27)—thereby we have learned concerning a case in which it is required to toss the blood four times, that if one has tossed the blood in a single action, he has achieved atonement.

E. Might one therefore suppose that if the blood that was supposed to be sprinkled above the red line was sprinkled below, the offering might also have achieved atonement for the donor?

F. For it is a matter of logic: there is blood that is to be tossed above the red line [a sin offering made of a beast], and there is blood that is to be tossed below the red line [a sin offering of a bird], so, just as the blood that is supposed to be tossed below the red line does not atone if it is tossed above, so blood that is supposed to be tossed above the red line will not atone if it is sprinkled below it.

G. Not at all. If you invoke that rule in the case of blood that is supposed to be sprinkled below the red line, it is because in the end it will not be above at all, but will you say the same of blood that is to be sprinkled above the red line, which ultimately will be located down below [in the form of the residue]. [Freedman: hence when he sprinkles the blood below the line, he is putting it where it will eventually be located and so effects atonement.]

H. Let blood that is to be tossed on the inner altar prove the case, for it is going in the end to be brought outside [where the residue is poured out around the base of the outer altar], and yet if the blood that is to be tossed on the inner altar to begin with is tossed on the outer altar, the priest has not effected atonement.

I. Not at all, for if you raise the issue of blood to be tossed on the inner altar, that is because the rite performed on the inner altar does not complete the ritual attached to the entire liturgy [since after the blood is sprinkled on the inner altar, the residue has to be poured out at the base of the outer altar]. But can you say the same of the tossing of the blood on the upper part of the altar, in which case putting the blood on the horns complete the rite [and no further action is indispensable once the blood has been sprinkled on the horns of the altar]. Since sprinkling the blood on the horns of the altar complete the rite, if the priest sprinkled below the red line, the rite also is fit.

J. [Because of the possibility of composing such an argument,] Scripture states, "This is the law of the sin offering...the priest who offers it for sin [having correctly carried out the rite in every detail] shall eat it" (Lev. 6:18-19)—"it" meaning, the one, the blood of which has been tossed above the red line around the altar, and not the one the blood of which was tossed below the red line around the altar.

K. *What is the meaning of the phrase*, the rite performed on the inner altar does not complete the ritual attached to the entire liturgy? *Surely this refers to the residue of the blood [and that proves that pouring out the residue of the blood is an indispensable part of the rite].*

L. *Said Raba to him, "If so, then you may prove the point through an argument a fortiori:* if to begin with blood of an offering performed on the inner altar which is poured out on the outer altar does not make atonement, even though in the end it will be obligatory to pour out that blood on the outer altar, then as to blood that is to be sprinkled above the red line, which in the end is not subject to the obligation of being poured out below the line for the sacrifice to achieve its goal of atonement, if to begin with one sprinkled such blood below the red line, the offering should not secure atonement [Freedman: the sacrifice is invalid, and the meat may not be eaten. So why is a verse of Scripture required to prove the point? Hence the premise of this argument, that pouring out of the residue is essential, must be false.]

M. Rather, this is the sense: it is not tossing the blood on the altar alone that completes the rite, but tossing the blood on the veil as well.

9. A. *Our rabbis have taught on Tannaite authority:*

B. "'And he shall make an end of atoning for the holy place and the tent of meeting and the altar' (Lev. 16:20)—if he atoned [by carrying out the rites required for atonement in other matters, e.g., the four sprinklings on the altar, the seven before the vil (Freedman)], he has completed the rite, but if he has not atoned, he has not completed the rite," the words of R. Aqiba.

C. Said to him R. Judah, "Why should we not say, 'if he made an end to the rite, he has atoned, and if not, he did not atone'? [So the rites, including the four applications, are necessary, and it is on that basis that that fact is to be demonstrated]."

D. *What is at issue between them?*

E. R. Yohanan and R. Joshua b. Levi:

F. *One said, "At issue is the correct interpretation of Scripture."* [Freedman: but not in law. Both hold that all four applications of blood are indispensable, and that pouring out the residue is not. Aqiba holds that the conclusion, atoning, illumines the beginning, make an end, so completion depends on atonement, on the four applications. Judah maintains that 'atoning' might merely refer to a single application of blood, and therefore the interpretation must be revised, and the beginning of the verse illuminates the end; only when he completely

G. *The other said, "At issue is whether or not pouring out the residue of the blood at the base is indispensable to the rite."*

H. *Now you may draw the conclusion that it is R. Joshua b. Levi who took the position that at issue is whether or not pouring out the residue of the blood at the base is indispensable to the rite.* For said R. Joshua b. Levi, "In the opinion of the one who said that the pouring out the residue of the blood is an indispensable part of the rite, one must bring another bullock and begin the rite on the inner altar." [Freedman: if the residue of the blood was spilled after the four applications, another bullock must be slaughtered and its blood first sprinkled at the inner altar, and then the residue poured out at the base of the outer altar. But the priest cannot simply pour out all the blood at the base, for then it is not a residue, and it is indispensable that a residue be poured out. Thus Joshua b. Levi holds that there is a view that pouring out of the residue is indispensable.]

I. *But does R. Yohanan not maintain this same theory of matters? And has not R. Yohanan said,* "R. Nehemiah taught as a Tannaite authority in accord with the opinion of one who maintains that the pouring out of the residue of the blood is indispensable to the rite"?

J. *Rather, you have to say, In accord with the words of him who says...," but not, "in accords with those of these Tannaite authorities in particular [Aqiba and Judah], and so too here [in the matter of Joshua b. Levi,], In accord with the words of him who says...," but not, "in accords with those of these Tannaite authorities in particular.*

Part Four is the important component of this astonishingly coherent piece of writing. Nos. 5-16 build on No. 4, systematically and patiently working through the entire repertoire of possibilities on the exegetical rules for deriving lessons from Scripture. The range of exegetical principles—argument a fortiori, argument based on analogy established through shared verbal choices, argument based on analogy established through other than shared verbal choices, analogy based on the congruence of other shared traits [but not verbal ones in context]—is entirely systematic, with each exegetical technique compared to all of the others. The unified and accumulative effect of the whole is demonstrated by No. 10, which appeals to foregoing materials to make its point. Obviously this beautifully articulated composition—not a mere composite—has been worked out prior to insertion here; but the relevance to our chapter's rules and interests is obvious, and we have been prepared to anticipate just such a theoretical exercise.

IV. *Listening for the Bavli's Own Statement*

Monotonously set forth in the treatment of Mishnah-tractate Zebahim 5:3ff. to the end, which I have not reproduced, nearly the entire chapter addresses the question of the connection between rules recorded in the Mishnah and rules presented in Scripture. The metaproposition that encompasses the numerous specific propositions is simple: how do we make connections between rules and their point of origin. Every time we ask, "what is the source [in Scripture] for this statement," we find an answer that is left to stand. So one fundamental and ubiquitous metaproposition of the Bavli may be set forth in this language:

1. it is important to link laws that occur in one source to those that occur in another;
2. among the compilations [components of "the one whole Torah of Moses, our rabbi," in later mythic language] that enjoy canonical status [in our language], the premier is Scripture;
3. so whenever we find a statement of a rule in the Mishnah and ask for its source, the implicit criterion of success will be, "the rule is founded on language of Scripture, properly construed;"
4. so, consequently, the proposition implicit in numerous propositions, common to them all and holding them all together, is this: *all rules cohere, and the point of origin of nearly all of them is the written part of the Torah revealed by God to Moses at Sinai.*

The particular document in which the rules now circulate does not place into a hierarchy of importance the various rules, because they all are one; but the reason they all are one is that nearly all of them find a point of origin in the written part of the Torah; and every single one of them is harmonious in principle with each of the others—once we identify the principle implicit in the cases that make up the law. Now if we asked the framers of the Mishnah their judgment upon these allegations of one of the metapropositional planks of the platform of the Bavli, they will have found surprising only our inquiry. For, while not common or characteristic of Mishnaic discourse, each of these traits can be located therein. The Mishnah's framers sometimes explicitly cite a verse of Scripture in support of the law; they occasionally undertake the exegesis of a verse of Scripture in order to discover the law; they know the distinction between rulings of the Torah and rulings of scribes, the latter standing a cut below the former; and their heirs, in undertaking vast exercises of linkage of the

Mishnah to Scripture in such documents as Sifra to Leviticus and
Sifré to Deuteronomy, engage in a persistent and compelling
demonstration of the same metapropositional program, point by
point.

And yet—

And yet we cannot then assign to the authorship of our chapter and the numerous other chapters in which a principal, recurrent concern and point of generative tension is the link of the law
(contained in the Mishnah or other Tannaite compilations) to the
law (contained in Scripture) and its particular wording merely the
task of saying explicitly what the framers of the Mishnah occasionally said and commonly implied. For there is a second
metaproposition in our chapter, and it does not pertain to so
general an issue as the ubiquitous one now well represented. It
is the issue of the nature and structure of thought, and when we
understand that issue, we shall see the remarkable intellectual
achievement of the authorship of the Bavli's reading of Mishnah-
tractate Zebahim 5:1-2. At stake in this appreciation of what they
have accomplished is the demonstration that metapropositions in
the Bavli are not only particular to the problem of the documentary provenance of rules—Scripture forms the basis of nearly all
rules; all rules harmonize, at their foundations in abstract principles, with all other rules. The metapropositional program turns
out, as I shall now show through a reprise of the pertinent propositions of the Bavli's reading of Mishnah-tractate Zebahim 5:1-2,
to be so abstract as vastly to transcend rules and their generalizations and harmonies, rising to the height of principles of thought
that guide the intellect in contemplation of all being and all reality.

V. *Thinking about Thought*

To grasp the metapropositional program that, in my view, defines
the stakes of discourse, let me specify what I conceive to be the
counterpart program, pertaining to not connecting rules to Scripture, but rather, connecting principle to (consequent) principle:
how thought really takes place, which is, not in a stationary pool
but in a moving stream. To state the result up front: the Mishnah
portrays all things at rest, a beautifully composed set in stasis, a
stage on which nothing happens. The Bavli portrays all things in

motion, a world of action, in which one thing leads to some other, and nothing stands still. All of this is accomplished in a shift in the received mode of thought, and the shift is set forth in the metaproposition, fully exposed, in the reading of two paragraphs of the Mishnah. We now consider what I conceive to be the counterpart program to the one that, in my view, the Bavli's sages inherited from the Mishnah and spelled out in tedious and unending particulars. To understand what is fresh and important in the Bavli's metapropositional program concerning the nature of thought, we have to call to mind what they inherited, for what they did was to impose the stamp of their own intellect upon the intellectual heritage that the Mishnah had provided for them.

To set forth the basic theory of the framers of the Mishnah on how thought takes place, which is to say, how we may understand things and know them, we must recall a simple fact. The Mishnah teaches the age-old method of scientific thought through comparison and contrast. Like things follow like rules, unlike things, the opposite rules, and the task of thought is to show what is like something else and therefore follows the rule that governs that something else; or what is unlike something else and therefore follows the opposite of the rule that governs that something else. So the Mishnah's mode of thought establishes connections between and among things and does so, as is clear, through the method of taxonomy, comparison and contrast, list-making of like things, yielding the rule that governs all items on the list.

List-making places on display the data of the like and the unlike and implicitly (ordinarily, not explicitly) then conveys the rule. The Mishnah is then a book of lists, with the implicit order, the nomothetic traits of a monothetic order, dictating the ordinarily unstated general and encompassing rule. And all this why? It is in order to make a single statement, endless times over, and to repeat in a mass of tangled detail precisely the same fundamental judgment. The framers of the Mishnah appeal solely to the traits of things. List-making then defines way of proving propositions through classification, so establishing a set of shared traits that form a rule which compels us to reach a given conclusion. Probative facts derive from the classification of data, all of which point in one direction and not in another. A catalogue of facts, for example, may be so composed that, through the regularities and indicative traits of the entries, the catalogue yields a propo-

sition. A list of parallel items all together point to a simple conclusion; the conclusion may or may not be given at the end of
the catalogue, but the catalogue—by definition—is pointed. All
of the catalogued facts are taken to bear self-evident connections
to one another, established by those pertinent shared traits implicit in the composition of the list, therefore also bearing meaning and pointing through the weight of evidence to an inescapable
conclusion. The discrete facts then join together because of some
trait common to them all. This is a mode of classification of facts
to lead to an identification of what the facts have in common and—
it goes without saying, an explanation of their meaning.

If I had to specify a single mode of thought that established
connections between one fact and another, it is in the search for
points in common and therefore also points of contrast. We seek
connection between fact and fact, sentence and sentence in the
subtle and balanced rhetoric of the Mishnah, by comparing and
contrasting two things that are like and not alike. At the logical
level, too, the Mishnah falls into the category of familiar philosophical thought. Once we seek regularities, we propose rules.
What is like another thing falls under its rule, and what is not
like the other falls under the opposite rule. Accordingly, as to the
species of the genus, so far as they are alike, they share the same
rule. So far as they are not alike, each follows a rule contrary to
that governing the other. So the work of analysis is what produces
connection, and therefore the drawing of conclusions derives from
comparison and contrast: the *and*, the *equal*. The proposition then
that forms the conclusion concerns the essential likeness of the
two offices, except where they are different, but the subterranean
premise is that we can explain both likeness and difference by
appeal to a principle of fundamental order and unity. To make
these observations concrete, we turn to the case at hand. The
important contrast comes at the outset. The high priest and king
fall into a single genus, but speciation, based on traits particular
to the king, then distinguishes the one from the other. Now if I
had to specify the deepest conviction at the most profound layers
of thought, it is that things set in relationship always stand in that
same relationship. The work of making connections and drawing
conclusions produces results that are fixed and final. If we establish a connection between one set of things and another, that
connection forms the end of matters—that, and not a series, by

which the connection between A and B serves as a guide to a movement from C to A via B, that is, as we shall now see, the formation of not a connection but a series of things that are connected only to one another, but not to other components of the same series—which is to say, a series. To put matters very simply, if A is like B, and B is like C, then is C like A? And if we entertain the possibility of a series, then, *what are the rules of connection that form the links of the results of comparison and contrast?* In other words, in the aftermath of classification comes not hierarchization but movement, this thing in relationship to that, that in relationship to the other, all things in movement, nothing at rest. So, if a series is possible, then how is a series composed? That is the question answered by the Bavli, the question on one in the Mishnah asked, because the Mishnah's framers contemplated a world at rest, and the Bavli's, a world in motion.

In so stating, I have leapt over each of the necessary stages of my exposition, So let us begin from the beginning. Now that the Mishnah's position is in hand, we revert to my claim that the Bavli's own statement in the chapter under discussion concerns the nature of thought. Let us first of all review the points that are made, and the sequence in which they are set forth. We begin with the point of intersection:

1. it is important to know how to connect rules to Scripture;
2. the principles that governing the making of connections to Scripture are those that govern making connections not between words and words ("the hermeneutical principles") but rather between one thing and something else, that is, defining a genus and its species; so when we know how to compare and contrast, find what is like something else and what is different from something else, we know how to conduct the passage from rules to Scripture;
3. exegetical rules tell us how to form classes of things in relationship to Scripture;
4. dialectical rules tell us how to move from one class of things to another class of things.

No. 2 then marks the point of departure, and Nos. 3 and 4, the remarkable shift in the passage. We go not only from rule to generalization, or from case to principle. That, to be sure, takes place and forms an everywhere-present metaproposition, as the tedium of the remainder of the chapter showed us. Rather, we go from thinking about things and their connections (comparison and contrast) to thinking about thought itself. So what I have

represented as the rules of dialectical thinking—not merely argument!—turn out to tell us how thought happens; the Bavli's reading
of Mishnah-tractate Zebahim 5:1-2 forms a fundamental exercise
of thought about thinking. For, when we review the principal steps
in the sustained and unfolding inquiry, we realize that, in particulars and in detail, the framers of the passage have set forth a
profound essay on thought. In the terms just now given, if A=B,
and B=C, then does C=A? Is a series possible? Are there limits
to the extension of a series? And on what basis do we construct a
series? Do the media of linkage between A and B, that is, A=B,
have to be the same as those that link B to C, for C to stand in
the series that A has begun? These abstract questions have to
become concrete before the sense of matters will emerge. So let
us now review the sequence of points that represent the inquiry
into the making of connections, which is to say, the Bavli's
metapropositional statement on the character of a series. For it is
the series, first this, then that, finally the third thing, and the rules
that govern the movement from this, to that, to the third thing,
that defines what is the center of deep thought in the Bavli's reading
of the specified Mishnah-paragraphs.

I cite the pertinent language, reviewing what has already been
given, and then provide my comments that specify what I conceive to be the metapropositional issues under discussion. The
stages in the argument of the Talmud are now marked by bold
face capital letters at the reference system, thus A, B, C, and so
on at the outer margin of the indented abstract.

> **A.**   II.2.   E.   That answer is satisfactory for him who takes the view
> that one may indeed derive a rule governing a prior subject from one
> that is given later on, but from the perspective of him who denies that
> fact, what is to be said?

The opening question contains the entirety of what is to follow:
the conviction that anterior to conclusions and debates on fixed
propositions is a premise, and the premise concerns not issues but
thought itself. For what is before us is not a hermeneutical principle that guides the exegesis of Scripture, the movement from a
rule back to a scriptural formulation deemed to pertain. It is a
rule of how to think. And the issue is explicit: does thought flow,
or does it stand still? Does it flow backward from conclusion to a
conclusion already reached? In the context of the document at
hand, the issue is one of arrangements of words, that is, a liter-

ary and therefore an exegetical question. That is, then, the proposition. But the metaproposition is otherwise, though that is not yet explicit.

> **B.** II.2. J.   But this is the reason for the position of rabbis, who declare one exempt [from having to present a suspensive guilt offering in the case of a matter of doubt regarding acts of sacrilege]: they derive an verbal analogy to a sin offering based on the appearance of the word 'commandments' with reference to both matters.
>
> N.   They take the view that one may not derive from an argument by analogy established through the use of a word in common only a limited repertoire of conclusions [but once the analogy is drawn, then all of the traits of one case apply to the other].

Here is an issue not of exegesis, therefore of hermeneutics, but of the rules of right thinking: thinking about thought. And what is concerns, as I have suggested in context, is how we establish not classes of things but linkage between and among classes of things. Let me state the centerpiece in simple words but with heavy emphasis: *since I make connections through analogy and contrast, may I proceed to make connections beyond the limits of the original connection? And the answer is, I must proceed, because thought does not come to rest. Comparison and contrast yield connections, which then govern.*

In the language before us, once I draw an analogy, do all traits of the two classes of things that have been linked through analogy—of necessity only partial, since were the analogy entire, both classes would constitute a single class!—pertain to each class? In the present context, what we establish is the anonymous, therefore the governing rule. The norm is that once we draw an analogy, the connection established by the (mere) analogy takes over, so that we treat as analogous traits not covered by the analogy at all. The analogy establishes the connection; but then the movement of thought is such that the connection is deemed to have established a new class of things, all of them subject to one rule. The movement—the dialectic—therefore is not a mere trait of argument, "if you say this, I say that," but a trait of thought: if this is the result of step A, then step B is to be taken—out from, without regard to, the limitations of step A. Thought then is continuous, always in motion, and that metaproposition states in the most abstract terms possible the prior and generative metaproposition that, when we compare classes of things, the comparison initiates a process that transcends the limits of comparison.

That is to say, again with emphasis, *we can effect a series.*

> **C.**   II.2   S.   *One authority maintains that proof supplied by analogy [here: the analogy sustained by the use of "and" to join the two subjects] takes priority, and the other party maintains that the proof supplied by the demonstration of a totality of congruence among salient traits takes precedence. Rabbis prefer the latter, Aqiba the former position.]*
>
> T.   *Not at all! All parties concur that proof supplied by analogy [here: the analogy sustained by the use of "and" to join the two subjects] takes priority. But rabbis in this context will say to you that the rule governing the subject treated below derives from the rule governing the subject treated above, so that the guilt offering must be worth a least two silver sheqels. This is established so that you should not argue that the doubt cannot be more stringent than the matter of certainty, and just as where there is certainty of having committed a sin, one has to present a sin offering that may be worth even so little as a sixth of a zuz in value, so if there is a matter of doubt, the guilt offering worth only a sixth of a zuz would suffice.*

Once the connection is made, linking an earlier rule (in Scripture's orderly exposition) to a later one, then the connection is such that movement is not only forward but backward. We have established not a connection between one thing and something else, but a series that can encompass a third thing and a fourth thing, on-ward—but with, or without, formal limit? This principle of right thinking that the hypothesis of the series requires is revealed by Scripture, as is made explicit once more in the following:

> **D.**   III.1   I.   *…And should you say that if Scripture had not included the mat-ter, we should have reached the same conclusion by argument for analogy, then if that is the case, we can infer by analogy also the rule on laying on of hands…*The main point here is that, once an analogy serves, it serves everywhere an analogy can be drawn; there is no a priori that limits the power of an analogy to govern all like cases.

A series is possible once the work of thought moves beyond con-trast and analogy. And it is the rule of right thought that, once we have established a comparison and a contrast, that fact vali-dates drawing conclusions on other aspects of the classes of things that have been connected through the comparison and contrast—analogical-contrastive thinking is then not static but in motion. Is the motion perpetual? Not at all, for Scripture, for its part, has the power to place limits on a series.

> **E.**   IV.2.   B.   If a matter was covered by an encompassing rule but then was singled out for some innovative purpose, you have not got the right to restore the matter to the rubric of the encompassing rule unless Scripture itself explicitly does so. [That means that the encom-passing rule does not apply to an item that Scripture, for its own pur-

poses, has singled out. The upshot is that the identified item is now exceptional in some aspect, so it is no longer subject to a common rule governing all other items in context; then the limits of analogy are set by Scripture's treatment of the items of a series. It is worth while reviewing the pertinent example:]

The series is subjected to limits, if an item in the sequence of connections that forms the series proves exceptional: this is connected to that, that to the other thing, but the other thing is other in some other way, so there the series ends.

C.   How so?

D.   "And he shall kill the lamb in the place where they kill the sin offering and the burnt offering, in the holy place; for the guilt offering, like the sin offering, belongs to the priest; it is most holy" (Lev. 14:13)—

E.   Now what need does Scripture have to state, "for the guilt offering, like the sin offering"? [Freedman: for if it is to teach that it is slaughtered in the north, that follows from the first half of the verse; if it teaches that sprinkling of the blood and eating the meat follow the rules of the sin offering, that is superfluous, since it is covered by the general regulations on guilt offerings given at Lev. 7:1-10]. And why does Scripture state, "for the guilt offering, like the sin offering"?

F.   The reason is that the guilt offering presented by the person healed of the skin ailment was singled out for the innovative purpose of indicating the following:

G.   in regard to the thumb of the hand, big toe of the foot, and right ear, you might have thought that the rite does not require the presentation of the blood of the offering and the parts to be burned up on the altar. Scripture therefore states, "for the guilt offering, like the sin offering," to show that just as the sin offering's blood and sacrificial parts have to be presented on the altar, so the blood and sacrificial parts of the guilt offering presented by the person healed of the skin ailment have to be presented on the altar.

H.   *If [you claim that the purpose of the verse is as stated and not to teach that doing the rite at the north is indispensable, as originally proposed,] then Scripture should have stated only the rule governing the rite for the one healed from the skin ailment but not the earlier version of the rule.*

I.   *Quite so—if we take the view that when something becomes the subject of a new law, it cannot then be covered by an encompassing rule that otherwise would apply, while the encompassing rule still can be derived from that special case. But if we take the view that when something becomes the subject of a new law, then it cannot be covered by an encompassing rule that otherwise would apply, and the encompassing rule also cannot be derived from that special place, then the law [Lev. 7:1-10, indicating that the guilt offering must be killed in the north] is needed for its own purpose!*

     J.   *Since Scripture has restored the matter to the rubric of the encompassing rule explicitly, that restoration has taken place.*

     K.   *Said Mar Zutra b. R. Mari to Rabina, "But why not say, when Scripture restored the matter to the rubric of the encompassing rule, that was solely in regard to having to present the blood and the sacrificial parts on the altar, since the priest is necessary to perform that rite. But as to slaughtering the animal, which does not have to be done by a priest, that does not have to be done at the northern side of the altar?"*

     L.   *[He said to him,] "If so, Scripture should say simply, 'for it is like* the sin offering.' *Why say,* 'or the guilt offering, like the sin offering'? *It is to teach, let it be like other guilt offerings [that must be slaughtered at the northern side of the altar]."* Here again, therefore, the issue is the limits of analogy, how these are determined.

  F.   IV.4. A.   *Raba said, "[The proposition that that which is derived on the basis of a verbal analogy does not in turn go and impart a lesson by means of a verbal analogy] derives from the following proof:*

We go over familiar ground. Raba takes the view that a series is simply not possible. Others allege that if we connect one class of things to some other by means, e.g., of a verbal analogy, then making that same connection once again, where another verbal analogy connects the second class of things to yet a third, is not correct. Scripture shows that verbal analogies do not validate the making of series.

     B.   "It is written, 'As is taken off from the ox of the sacrifice of peace offerings' (Lev. 4:10) [namely, the sacrificial parts of the anointed priest's bullock brought for a sin offering]—*now for what purpose is this detail given? That the lobe of the liver and the two kidneys are to be burned on the altar [as is the case with those of the sin offering], that fact is specified in the body of the verse itself. But the purpose is to intimate that the burning of the lobe of the liver and the two kidneys of the he goats brought as sin offerings for idolatry are to be derived by analogy from the bullock of the community brought on account of an inadvertent sin. That law is not explicitly stated in the passage on the bullock that is brought for an inadvertent sin, but is derived from the rule governing the bullock of the anointed priest. 'As is taken off' is required so that it might be treated as something written in that very passage [on the bullock of inadvertence, being superfluous in its own context], not as something derived on the basis of a verbal analogy does not in turn go and impart a lesson by means of a verbal analogy."*

To repeat my exposition of this matter: I have two items, A and B. I claim that B is like A, therefore the rule governing A applies also to B. Now I turn forward, to C. C is not analogous to A; there are no points of congruence or (in the exegetical formulation that our authors use) verbal intersection. But C is like B. It is like be because there is an analogy by reason of verbal intersection (the same word being used in reference to C and B.) The question is, may I apply to C, by reason of the verbal intersection between C and B, the lesson that I have learned in regard to B only by reason of B's similarity by reason of congruence, not verbal intersection, to A? Can a conclusion that is derived on the basis of a verbal analogy go and impart a lesson by reason of analogy to a third item? Raba now maintains that that is not the case. But the matter has gone in the other direction: a series is possible. But if a series is possible, then what limits are to be placed on the media by which a series is effected?

G. IV.5. A. Now it is a fact that that which is derived on the basis of a verbal analogy does in turn go and impart a lesson by means of a verbal analogy, *demonstrated whether in the manner of Raba or in the manner of Rabina.*

Now we revert to our basic issue: the validity of a series. Here we move into as yet unexplored ground, which is the basis for my claim that the order of problems is dictated by an interest in a systematic presentation of the rules of right thinking. We have been exposed to the case in favor of a series: once the analogy makes the connection, then all traits of the things connected are brought into relationship with all other such traits. Scripture then provides one limit to the length of a series: a series cannot be infinite. But there is another limit proposed, and it is not scriptural but substantive, in the nature of things, a trait of thought itself. Here is the point at which I find this sustained exposition of thinking about thought simply remarkable.

B. Is it the rule, however, that *that which is derived on the basis of a verbal analogy may in turn go and impart a lesson by means of an argument on the basis of congruence?* [Freedman: Thus the law stated in A is applied to B by analogy. Can that law then be applied to C because of congruence between B and C?]

We have proven one point. It bears a consequence. We go on to the consequence. The mode of thought is dialectical not only in form, but also in substance: if A, then B. If B, then what about C? It is one thing to have shown that if B is like A, and C, unlike A, is rendered comparable to B by a verbal analogy. But then may I take the next step and draw into the framework of B and C, joined by verbal analogy and assigned a common rule by B's congruent-analogy to A, also D, E, F, and G, that is, other classes of things joined to C by verbal analogy—but not necessarily the same verbal analogy that has joined C to B? That indeed is the obvious next step to be taken, and it is now taken. It is taken in the simple words just now given, and the same point is now going to be made, in a systematic way, for each medium by which classes of things are formed and then connected to one another. Analogical contrastive thinking therefore is not static but always in motion, since, once a connection is made, other connections made follow. If we make a connection between A and B on the basis of one set of shared traits, we may proceed to make a connection between C and A, via B, on the basis of traits shared by B and C but not by A and C. Not only so, but the same mode of thought extends to the media of connection. If I connect A to B by verbal analogy, I may connect B to other classes of things, e.g., C, D, E, by other media of connection, e.g., verbal analogy connects A to B, and an argument based on congruent connects B to C, and backward to A; and an argument a fortiori may connect C to D, and backward to A and B—series without end, or series that end only in the dictates of revelation, the ultimate arbiter of the classification and hierarchy of all things. What is truly impressive in what follows is the rigorous order by which each possibility is raised in its turn, the connections fore and aft, such that the framer of the whole not only makes his point in words, but also illustrates it in his own representation of matters: a series is not only possible, it is also compelling. So we see as we move forward, now with no need for further exposition, from H to M.

H. IV.6. A. That which is learned by a verbal analogy may in turn go and impart a rule by an argument *a fortiori* .

I. IV.7. A. Can that which is learned by verbal analogy established may in turn go and impart a rule by an analogy based on the congruence of other shared traits [but not verbal ones in context]? Once more to review: we have now linked B to C via a verbal analogy. C stands in relationship to other classes of things, but not for the same reason that it stands in relationship to B, that is, through other than verbal analogical relationships. It forms a relationship a fortiori, for instance, with D, E, and F. If something applies to C, the lesser, it surely should apply to D, the greater. So now we want to know the permissible grounds for drawing relationships—comparisons and contrasts—of classes of things. So on what basis do we move from species to species and uncover the genera of which they form a part (if they do form a part)? Is it only verbal correspondence or intersection, as has been implicit to this point? Or are there more abstract bases for the same work of genus-construction (in our language: category-formation and re-formation)?

J. IV.8. A. Can a rule that is derived by analogy based on the congruence of other shared traits [but not verbal ones in context] turn around and teach a lesson through an analogy based on verbal analogy?

K. IV.9. A. Can a rule that is derived by an analogy based on the congruence of other shared traits [but not verbal ones in context] turn around and teach a lesson through an must be held within the hide."

L. IV.10. A. Can a rule that is derived by an analogy based on the congruence of other shared traits [but not verbal ones in context] go and teach a lesson through an argument a fortiori?

M. IV.10 F. If an argument deriving from an analogy based on verbal congruence, which cannot go and, by an argument based on verbal congruence, impart its rule to some other class—*as has been shown by either Raba's or Rabina's demonstration*—nonetheless can go and by an argument a fortiori impart its rule to some other class—*as has been shown by the Tannaite authority of the household of R. Ishmael*—then a rule that is derived by an argument based on analogy based on other than verbal congruence, which can for its part go and impart its lesson by an argument based on an analogy resting on verbal congruity which is like itself— *as has been shown by Rami bar Hama*—surely can in turn teach its lesson by an argument a fortiori to yet another case!

So at stake throughout is the question of how a series is composed: the media for the making of connections between one thing and something else (that is, one class of things and some other class of things, in such wise that the rules governing the one are shown by the analogy to govern the other as well). We want to know not only that a connection is made, but how it is made. And some maintain that if the connection is made between one thing and something else by means, e.g., of a verbal analogy dictated by Scripture's wording, then a connection between that something else and a third thing must also be made in a manner consistent with the initial medium of connection, verbal analogy. It cannot be made by means of some other medium of connection. But the paramount position is otherwise: dialectics affect not only argument but thought itself, because connections are made through all media by which connections are made. We now reach the end of the matter, in a set of ultimately-theoretical issues:

N. IV.11. A. Can a rule that is derived by an analogy based on the congruence of other shared traits [but not verbal ones in context] go and teach a lesson through an argument constructed by analogy based

on the congruence of other shared traits among two or more classifications of things?

B.   *That question must stand.*

O.   IV.12. A.   Can a rule derived by an argument a fortiori go and
teach a rule established through analogy of verbal usage?

B.   The affirmative derives from an argument a fortiori:

C.   If an argument deriving from an analogy based on points
of other than verbal congruence, which cannot go and, by an argument based on verbal congruence, impart its rule to some other class—
as has been shown by either R. Pappa's demonstration,—then a rule that is derived
by an argument a fortiori, which can be derived by an argument based
on the shared verbal traits of two things,—*as has been shown by the Tannaite
authority of the house of R. Ishmael*—surely should be able to impart its rule
to another classification of things by reason of an argument based on
a verbal analogy!

D.   *That position poses no problems to one who takes the view that R.
Pappa's case has been made. But for one who takes the view that R. Pappa's case has
not been made, what is to be said?*

E.   *The question then must stand.*

P.   IV.13. A.   Can a rule that is derived by an argument a fortiori
go and teach a lesson through an argument based on the congruence
of other shared traits [but not verbal ones in context]?

B.   The affirmative derives from an argument a fortiori:

C.   If an argument deriving from an analogy based on points
of other than verbal congruence, which cannot be derived from an
argument based on verbal congruence, impart its rule to some other
class—*as has been shown by R. Yohanan's demonstration,*—can go and teach
a lesson by an argument based on an analogy established through other
than verbal traits, *as has been shown by Rami bar Hama*—a rule based on
an argument a fortiori, which can be derived by an argument based
on an analogy resting on verbal coincidence, surely should be able to
impart its rule to another classification of things by reason of an argument based on an other than verbal analogy!

Q.   IV.14. A.   Can a rule based on an argument a fortiori turn around
and teach a lesson through an argument based on an argument a fortiori?

B.   Indeed so, and the affirmative derives from an argument a
fortiori:

C.   If an argument deriving from an analogy based on points
of other than verbal congruence, which cannot be derived from an
argument based on verbal congruence, impart its rule to some other
class—*as has been shown by R. Yohanan's demonstration,*—can go and teach
a lesson by an argument a fortiori, as we have just pointed out, then
an argument that can be derived from an analogy based on verbal
congruence—*as has been shown by the Tannaite authority of the household of R.
Ishmael*—surely should be able to impart its rule by an argument a fortiori!

D.   But would this then would represent what we are talking about, namely, a rule deriving from an argument a fortiori that has been applied to another case by means of an argument a fortiori? Surely this is nothing more than a secondary derivation produced by an argument a fortiori!

E.   Rather, argue in the following way:

F.   Indeed so, and the affirmative derives from an argument a fortiori:

G.   if an argument based on an analogy of a verbal character cannot be derived from another such argument based on an analogy between two classes of things that rests upon a verbal congruence—*in accordance with the proofs of either Raba or Rabina*—nonetheless can then go and impart its lesson by an argument a fortiori—*in accordance with the proof of the Tannaite authority of the household of R. Ishmael*—then an argument a fortiori, which can serve to transfer a lesson originally learned through an argument based upon verbal congruence, *in accordance with the proof of the Tannaite authority of the household of R. Ishmael*— surely should be able to impart its lesson to yet another classification of things through an argument a fortiori.

H.   And this does represent what we are talking about, namely, a rule deriving from an argument a fortiori that has been applied to another case by means of an argument a fortiori.

R. IV.15. A.   Can a rule based on an argument a fortiori turn around and teach a rule through an argument constructed on the basis of shared traits of an other-than-verbal character among two classifications of things?

C.   *But that is not so. For even if we concede that that is the case there, then still the rule derives from the act of slaughter of unconsecrated beasts [Freedman].*

S. IV.16. A.   Can a rule derived by an argument based on shared traits of an other than verbal character shared among two classes of things then turn around and teach a lesson by an argument based on an analogy of a verbal character, an analogy not of a verbal character, an argument a fortiori, or an argument based on shared traits?

B.   *Solve at least one of those problems by appeal to the following:*

C.   On what account have they said that if blood of an offering is left overnight on the altar, it is fit? Because if the sacrificial parts are kept overnight on the altar, they are fit. And why if the sacrificial parts are kept overnight on the altar are they fit? Because if the meat of the offering is kept overnight on the altar it is fit. [Freedman: thus the rule governing the sacrificial parts is derived by an appeal to an argument based on shared traits of an other than verbal character shared among two classes of things, and that rule in turn is applied to the case of the blood by another such argument based on shared traits of an other than verbal character shared among two classes of things].

D.   What about the rule governing meat that is taken outside

of the Temple court? [If such meat is put up on the altar, it is not removed therefrom. Why so?]

E.   Because meat that has been taken out of the holy place is
suitable for a high place.

M.   [Reverting to C-E:] Now can an analogy be drawn concerning something that has been disposed of in the proper manner for
something that has not been disposed of in the proper manner? [If the
sacrificial parts are kept over night, they are not taken off the altar,
and therefore the meat kept overnight is fit; but the meat may be kept
overnight, while the sacrificial parts may not. So too when the Temple
stood, the flesh might not be taken outside, but where there was no
Temple and only high places, the case is scarcely analogous!]

N.   *The Tannaite authority for this rule derives it from the augmentative
sense, extending the rule, deriving from the formulation,* "This is the Torah of
the burnt offering" (Lev. 6:2). [Freedman: the verse teaches that all
burnt offerings, even with the defects catalogued here, are subject to
the same rule and do not get removed from the altar once they have
been put there; the arguments given cannot be sustained but still support that proposition.].

The movement from point to point, first things first, second things
in sequence, is so stunning in the precise logic of the order of
issues—we must know **A** before we can contemplate asking about
B—, that only a brief review is called for. We have shown that
we may move from a class of things joined to another through
analogy based on congruence, that is, from A to B, onward to
other classes of things joined to the foregoing by verbal analogy
or intersection, that is, from B to C and beyond. But can we then
move from C, linked to be via verbal analogy, to D, linked to C,
but not to A or B, by congruence, e.g., comparable and shared
traits of a salient order? The issue then, is may we move forward
to further classes of things by moving "backward," to a principle
of linkage of classes that has served to bring us to this point, in
other words, reversing the course of principles of linkage? What
our framers then want to know is a very logical question: are there
fixed rules that govern the order or sequence by which we move
from one class of things to another, so that, if we propose to link
classes of things, we can move only from A to B by one principle
(comparison and contrast of salient traits), and from B to C by a
necessarily consequent and always second principle (verbal intersection); then we may move (by this theory) from C to D only by
verbal intersection but not by appeal to congruence. Why not?
Because, after all, if C is linked to B only by verbal intersection

but not by congruence, bearing no relationship to A at all, then how claim that D stands in a series begun at A, if it has neither verbal connection, nor, as a matter of fact, congruence to link it to anything in the series. What is clear in this reprise is that the issue is drawn systematically, beginning to end. By simply seeing the sequence of questions, we grasp the whole: the program, the method, the order, all dictated by the inner requirements of sustained inquiry into the logic of comparison and contrast, read as a dialectical problem.

The metapropositional program contributed by the Bavli's framers concerns how series are made, which is to say, whether connections yield static or dynamic results, which is to say, at the deepest layers of intellect, how thought happens. Now, at the end, we ask the framers of the Mishnah to address the question before us. And in answer, they give us silence. So we know that here we hear what is distinctive to, and the remarkable discovery of, the authorship of the Bavli. Since, it is clear, that discovery has taken place within the words of the written Torah, and, since their deepest metaproposition maintained that the words of the written Torah are the words of God to Moses, our rabbi, at Sinai,— the words, not just the gist—we have to conclude with what I conceive to be the bed-rock of the metapropositional program before us: the Torah teaches us not only what God said, but how God thinks. When we understand the Torah rightly, we engage in thinking about thought. And that is how we know God: through thought. So on this point, if not on others, Spinoza was not so heretical after all.

CHAPTER TWO

THE BAVLI'S EXEGETICAL PROGRAM

I. *What, Exactly, Does the Talmud Want to Know about the Mishnah*

The Bavli in form and substance presents a commentary to the Mishnah, and, to markedly lesser degree, Scripture as well. From 80% to 99% of the composites of the tractates of the Bavli—depending on the tractate—focus upon the work of Mishnah-exegesis. Exegesis stands for many kinds of inquiry, as many as the hermeneutics that animate the exegesis. Therefore, to form a general theory of what the Talmud says, we classify the types of exegetical compositions and composites that accomplish the paramount goal of explaining the sense and meaning of the Mishnah. I treat in particular the manner in which the Talmud of Babylonia proposes, in Bavli-tractate Moed Qatan, to read Mishnah-tractate Moed Qatan. Defining in detail what the sages of the Bavli did, and how they did it, imparts immediacy and concreteness to the general description of their writing as "a commentary to the Mishnah." Not only so, but by showing how most of the Bavli's composites, as well as the larger part of the composites formed into those composites, form a commentary to the Mishnah or a secondary expansion of commentary to the Mishnah, I provide in highly graphic form a clear picture of the structure of the document as a commentary, covering also secondary elaboration of its own commentaries. At the end I shall identify the principal parts of the Bavli's exegetical program for the Mishnah and specify what I conceive to be the theological propositions set forth through the exposition of details in the same way again and again.

The Mishnah's exegetical program may be summed up in the following way. At the end of this chapter, when readers will have seen the data for themselves, I spell out the theological issues implicit in the hermeneutics that animate these specific questions:

An purposive program guides the articulation of the Talmud's
entire exegesis of the Mishnah: following a prescribed order of
inquiry, as set forth above, in a severely truncated repertoire of
rhetorical paradigms, the sages of the Talmud systematically investigate an economical and focused set of questions to prove a
single theological proposition. What emerges from the Bavli's
reading of the Mishnah is a statement on the character of the
Mishnah, which is presented as a supernatural writing. So the point
of the Talmud is to demonstrate the perfection of the Mishnah.
Now let me show that that is so.

II. *How To Define the Bavli's Mishnah-Commentary*

For the most part, the Talmud of Babylonia is a commentary to
the Mishnah. Let me start by giving a simple example of what
characterizes the initial phase of nearly every sustained composite of the Bavli: a commentary to the Mishnah. This is what I
mean by Mishnah-commentary: I mark Mishnah-citation in bold
face type, Aramaic in italics, Hebrew in regular type.

MISHNAH-TRACTATE BABA QAMMA
3:1

A.   He who leaves a jug in the public domain,

**B.   and someone else came along and stumbled on it and
broke it—**

C.   [the one who broke it] is exempt.

**D.   And if [the one who broke it] was injured by it, the owner
of the barrel is liable [to pay damages for] his injury.**

I.1

A. *How come the framer of the passage refers to begin with to a* **jug** *but then concludes with reference to a* **barrel***? And so too we have learned in another passage in the Mishnah:* **This one comes along with his barrel , and that one comes along with his beam—[if] the jar of this one was broken by the beam of that one, [the owner of the beam] is exempt.** *How come the framer of the passage refers to begin with to a* **barrel** *but then concludes with reference to a* **jug***? And so too we have learned in the Mishnah:* **This one is coming along with his barrel of wine, and that one is coming along with his jug of honey—the jug of honey cracked, and this one poured out his wine and saved the honey in his jar—he has a claim only for his wages [M. B.Q. 10:4A-E].** *How come the framer of the passage refers to begin with to a* **barrel** *but then concludes with reference to a* **jug***?*

B. Said R. Hisda, "Well, as a matter of fact, there really is no difference between a jar and a barrel.'

C. *So what is the practical difference between the usages?*

D. It has to do with buying and selling.

E. *How can we imagine such a case? If it is in a place in which a jug is not called a barrel, nor a barrel a jug, for in such a case, the two terms are kept distinct!*

F. *The distinction is required for a place in which most of the people call a jug a jug and a barrel a barrel, but some call a barrel and jug and some call a jug a barrel. What might you then have supposed? That we follow the majority usage?* **[27B]** *So we are informed that that is not the case, for in disputes over monetary transactions, we do not follow the majority usage.*

All that we have here is an investigation of the linguistic properties of the Mishnah-paragraph that is cited. The framer of the anonymous writing notes that a variety of other passages seem to vary word choices in a somewhat odd way. The point of insistence—the document is carefully drafted, the writers do not forget what they were talking about, so when they change words in the middle of a stream of thought, it is purposeful—constitutes a exegetical point, pure and simple.

The foregoing exemplifies Mishnah-commentary as a process of clarification. But commentators in the Bavli stand not only within the framework of the Mishnah, aiming at the explanation of what it says. They also take a stance outside of that framework, and propose to challenge its statements or their implications. To understand precisely what the Bavli means by a commentary to the Mishnah, we have therefore begin with the clear picture that the Bavli asks the questions of not only the teacher, standing inside of the document and looking outward, but also of the reader, located outside of the document and looking inward. In what follows, then, the stance of the commentator now is external to the text, and the commentator wants to know why the Mishnah finds self-evident what is not necessarily obvious to all parties:

1:7-8/I.1

A. *So if it's* **an occasion of rejoicing for the groom,** *what's so bad about that?*

B. Said R. Judah said Samuel, and so said R. Eleazar said R. Oshaia, and some say, said R. Eleazar said R. Hanina, "The consideration is that one occasion of rejoicing should not be joined with another such occasion."

C. Rabbah bar R. Huna said, "It is because he neglects the rejoicing of the festival to engage in rejoicing over his wife."

D. Said Abbayye to R. Joseph, "This statement that has been said by Rabbah bar R. Huna belongs to Rab, for said R. Daniel bar Qattina said Rab, 'How on the basis of Scripture do we know that people may not take wives on the intermediate days of the festival? As it is said, "You shall rejoice in your feast" (Dt. 16:14), meaning, in your feast—not in your new wife.'"

E. Ulla said, "It is because it is excess trouble."

F. R. Isaac Nappaha said, "It is because one will neglect the requirement of being fruitful and multiplying" [if people postponed weddings until festivals, they might somehow diminish the occasion for procreation, which is the first obligation]."

G. *An objection was raised:* All those of whom they have said that they are forbidden to wed on the festival **[9A]** are permitted to wed on the eve of the festival. *Now this poses a problem to the explanations of all the cited authorities!*

H. *There is no problem from the perspective of him who has said,* "The consideration is that one occasion of rejoicing should not be joined with another such occasion," *for the main rejoicing of the wedding is only a single day.*

I. *And from the perspective of him who has said,* "It is because it is excess trouble," *the principal bother lasts only one day.*

J. *And from the perspective of him who has said,* "It is because one will neglect the requirement of being fruitful and multiplying," *for merely one day someone will not postpone the obligation for any considerable length of time.*

What is important in understanding the nature of commentary in the Bavli is the dual stance of the commentator: inside and outside.

Now to generalize on the basis of the cases before us: what I mean by a commentary is a piece of writing that depends for its program—topics to be treated, coherence and cogency, alike—upon some other writing. We know the difference between a base-text and a commentary because the base-text will be cogent in its own terms, and the commentary will make sense only in relationship to the base-text. And we know the difference between the one and the other because a commentary's author will always signal the text, e.g., by citing a phrase or by a clear allusion, and will further identify what he then proposes to contribute. Commentaries in this context may take a variety of forms, but the mark of them all will be the same: they make sense only by appeal to, in the context of, some piece of writing outside of themselves. But that common trait among them all scarcely exhausts the program that a commentary will undertake—or even define it. One type of commentary will follow a quite well-defined program of questions, another will promiscuously comment on this, that, and the other thing, without ever suggesting that the commentator has a systematic inquiry in mind. And, it goes without saying, the range of issues subject to comment—philological, historical, aesthetic, not to mention theological—can be limited only by the number of texts deemed by an author or compiler to deserve a commentary.

These somewhat abstract and general remarks may forthwith be given concrete exemplification in a passage that, in my view, forms an archetype of the Bavli's commentary to the Mishnah. Let us rapidly examine it and identify its paramount traits, then turning to the question of how we shall then define, for the Bavli overall the repertoire and program that dictated to its authors of compositions and compilers of composites precisely the task they were to undertake. Since our initial exercise in definition and classification pertains to Bavli tractate Moed Qatan, I take my exemplary definition from the opening lines of that tractate. To explain what follows: the Mishnah paragraphs are cited in bold face type, and whenever they recur, it is in the same form.

Mishnah/Bavli tractate Moed Qatan 1:1

A. They water an irrigated field on the intermediate days of a festival and in the Seventh Year,

B. whether from a spring that first flows at that time, or

from a spring that does not first flow at that time.

I.1

A. [**They water an irrigated field on the intermediate days of a festival and in the Seventh Year, whether from a spring that first flows at that time, or from a spring that does not first flow at that time**:] *since it is explicitly stated that they may water from a spring that flows for the first time, which may damage the soil by erosion [making necessary immediate repair of the damage during the intermediate days of the festival], is it necessary to specify that they may water from a spring that does not first flow at that time, which is not going to cause erosion?*

The question that our commentary asks at the outset concerns the language of the Mishnah, and the specific issue is whether the Mishnah's framer has repeated himself or has told us something that, absent his articulation of the point, we might not have discerned on our own. That is what precipitates the question before us.

B. *One may say that it is necessary to include both the latter and the former, for if the Tannaite framer had given the rule only covering a spring that first flows on the intermediate days of the festival, it is in that case in particular in which it is permitted to work on an irrigated field, but not for a rain-watered field, because the water is going to cause erosion, but in the case of a spring that does not first flow on the intermediate days, which is unlikely to cause erosion, I might have said that even a rain-watered field may be watered. So he tells us that there is no distinction between a spring that flows for the first time and one that does not flow for the first time. The rule is the same for both: an irrigated plot may be watered from it, but a rain-watered plot may not be watered from [either a new or an available spring].*

The second comment on the Mishnah is equally interested in the formulation of the Mishnah, but it is now concerned with the meanings of words and phrases.

2. A. *And on what basis is it inferred that the meaning of the words "irrigated field" is, a thirsty field [which has to be irrigated]?*

B. *It is in line with that which is written:* "When you were faint and weary" (Dt. 25:18), *and the Hebrew word for weary is represented in Aramaic by the word that means, "exhausted."*

C. *And how do we know that the words translated rain-watered field refers to a fucked field?*

D. "For as a man has sexual relations with a maiden, so shall your sons be as husbands unto you" (Is. 62:5), *and the word in Aramaic is rendered,*

"Behold, as a boy fucks a girl, so your sons shall get laid in your midst."

Our third comment wishes to identify the authority behind the rule of our Mishnah, which is to say, who stands behind a premise that is implicit and formative?

3.   A.   *Who is the Tannaite authority who takes the position that work on the interme-diate days of a festival is permitted if it is to prevent loss, but if it is to add to gain it is not permitted, and, further, even to prevent loss, really heavy labor is forbidden?*

     B.   *Said R. Huna, "It is R. Eliezer b. Jacob, for we have learned in the Mishnah:* **R. Eliezer b. Jacob says, 'They lead water from one tree to another, on condition that one not water the entire field. Seeds which have not been watered before the fes-tival one should not water on the intermediate days of the festival' [M. 1:3].** *"*

     C.   *Well, I might concede that there is a representation of R. Eliezer's position that he prohibits work to add to one's gain, but have you heard a tradition that he dis-allows work in a situation in which otherwise loss will result?*

     D.   *Rather, said R. Pappa, "Who is the authority behind this rule? It is R. Judah, for it has been taught on Tannaite authority:* **'From a spring that first flows on the intermediate days of a festival they irrigate even a rain watered field,' the words of R. Meir. And sages say, 'They irrigate from it only a field that depends upon irrigation, which has gone dry.' R. Eleazar b. Aza-riah says, "Not this nor that, [[but they do not irrigate a field from it [namely, a field the spring of which has gone dry] even in the case of an irrigated field]' [T. Moed 1:1A-C].** *Even further, said R. Judah, 'A person should not clean out a water channel and with the dredging on the intermediate days of a festival water his garden or seed bed.'"*

     E.   *Now what is the meaning of* "that has gone dry"? *If you say that it really has dried up, then what is going to be accomplished by watering it?*

     F.   *Said Abbayye, "The point is that this former water source has gone dry and an-other has just emerged."*

     G.   **R. Eleazar b. Azariah says, "Not this nor that:"** *there is no difference between the case of an old spring that has gone dry or that has not gone dry, in any event a spring that has just flowed may not be utilized on the inter-mediate days of the festival.*

     H.   *And how to you know [that it is Judah in particular who takes the position that work on the intermediate days of a festival is permitted if it is to prevent loss, but if it is to add to gain it is not permitted, and, further, even to prevent loss, really heavy labor is forbidden]? Perhaps R. Judah takes the position that he does, that is, that it is permitted to use the water for an irrigated field but not for a field that depends on rain, only in the case of a spring that has just now begun to flow,* **[2B]** *since it may cause erosion, but in the case of a spring that has not just*

> *now begun to flow and will not cause erosion might be permitted for use even on a field that depends on rain?*
>
> I.   *If so, then in accord with which authority will you assign our Mishnah-paragraph? For in fact, in R. Judah's view, there is no distinction between a spring that has just now flowed and one that has not just now flowed; in either case, an irrigated field may be watered, one that depends on rain may not. And the reason that the passage specifies the spring that has just now flowed is only to show the extent to which R. Meir was prepared to go, even a spring that has just now flowed may be used, and that is, even for a field that depends upon rain.*

With these three comments, the work of Mishnah-commentary has come to a conclusion. We have already noted that, where the full exegetical program is undertaken for a given Mishnah-paragraph, the order of topics that is followed here is exemplary. At this point I need hardly underscore the regularity that prevails or repeat how logical and orderly the procedure shows itself to be.

Enough has been said to define the work before us. We now work our way through a single tractate and ask, line by line, about the purpose of a given statement, meaning, a whole and complete unit of thought. Since, the very form of the document dictates, the initial, and precipitating, purpose of all compositions and many composites is the exegesis of the Mishnah, on the strength of our survey, we catalogue the types of Mishnah-commentary set forth by the authors of the Bavli's tractate, Moed Qatan, organized around the Mishnah's tractate of the same name.

III. *The Exegetical Program of Bavli-Tractate Moed Qatan for Mishnah-Tractate Moed Qatan*

Since I claim that the Bavli is a commentary to the Mishnah, I also account, systematically, for compositions and even entire composites that are not written in response to the statements of the Mishnah but that stand on their own, forming coherent statements out of all relationship to the Mishnah. I indent what I conceive to be secondary expansions of prior materials. Indented material is not Mishnah-commentary; but it is always tacked on to complement Mishnah-commentary, or to supplement a theme introduced by the Mishnah's statement or by the Bavli's Mishnah-commentary. Not uncommonly I refer to a passage as (a) talmud; by this I mean a sustained, rigorous exegesis of a given text. Thus "a talmud to a Tosefta-passage" is not much different from "a

talmud to a Mishnah-passage," namely, a sustained exegesis of
the prior text, amplifying detail, proposing propositions and testing them. I reproduce, with my annotations, all of Chapter One
but abbreviate from that point onward. A sufficient sample of the
whole is given to validate the generalizations presented in part
iv of this chapter.

Mishnah/Bavli-tractate Moed Qatan 1:1-2
1:1

A. **They water an irrigated field on the intermediate days
of a festival and in the Seventh Year,**

B. **whether from a spring that first flows at that time, or
from a spring that does not first flow at that time.**

C. **But they do not water [an irrigated field] with (1) collected rainwater, or (2) water from a swape well.**

D. **And they do not dig channels around vines.**

1:2

A. **R. Eleazar b. Azariah says, "They do not make a new water channel on the intermediate days of a festival or in
the Seventh Year."**

B. **And sages say, "They make a new water channel in the
Seventh Year, and they repair damaged ones on the intermediate days of a festival."**

C. **They repair damaged waterways in the public domain and
dig them out.**

D. **They repair roads, streets, and water pools.**

E. **And they (1) do all public needs, (2) mark off graves, and
(3) go forth [to give warning] against Diverse Kinds.**

We commence with a proof that, while the Mishnah covers a
variety of cases, it is not verbose or repetitious, because each case
makes its own point and therefore has to be set forth in its own
terms.

I.1

A. **[They water an irrigated field on the intermediate days
of a festival and in the Seventh Year, whether from a
spring that first flows at that time, or from a spring that
does not first flow at that time:]** *since it is explicitly stated that they
may water from a spring that flows for the first time, which may damage the soil
by erosion [making necessary immediate repair of the damage during the intermediate days of the festival], is it necessary to specify that they may water from*

> *a spring that does not first flow at that time, which is not going to cause erosion?*
>
> B.   *One may say that it is necessary to include both the latter and the former, for if the Tannaite framer had given the rule only covering a spring that first flows on the intermediate days of the festival, it is in that case in particular in which it is permitted to work on an irrigated field, but not for a rain-watered field, because the water is going to cause erosion, but in the case of a spring that does not first flow on the intermediate days, which is unlikely to cause erosion, I might have said that even a rain-watered field may be watered. So he tells us that there is no distinction between a spring that flows for the first time and one that does not flow for the first time. The rule is the same for both: an irrigated plot may be watered from it, but a rain-watered plot may not be watered from [either a new or an available spring].*

The comment is to be classified as criticism of the formulation of the Mishnah, with the intent of proving that the Mishnah does not repeat itself. We now proceed to another Mishnah-commentary, this one on the language of the Mishnah, the meanings of its word-choices:

2.   A.   *And on what basis is it inferred that the meaning of the words "irrigated field" is, a thirsty field [which has to be irrigated]?*
>
> B.   *It is in line with that which is written:* "When you were faint and weary" (Dt. 25:18), *and the Hebrew word for weary is represented in Aramaic by the word that means, "exhausted."*
>
> C.   *And how do we know that the words translated rain-watered field refers to a fucked field?*
>
> D.   "For as a man has sexual relations with a maiden, so shall your sons be as husbands unto you" (Is. 62:5), *and the word in Aramaic is rendered,* "Behold, as a boy fucks a girl, so your sons shall get laid in your midst."

The foregoing forms a standard talmudic inquiry: what do words mean? The answer will ordinarily derive from the lexical evidence of Scripture.

3.   A.   *Who is the Tannaite authority who takes the position that work on the intermediate days of a festival is permitted if it is to prevent loss, but if it is to add to gain it is not permitted, and, further, even to prevent loss, really heavy labor is forbidden?*
>
> B.   *Said R. Huna, "It is R. Eliezer b. Jacob, for we have learned in the Mishnah:* **R. Eliezer b. Jacob says, 'They lead water from one tree to another, on condition that one not water the entire field. Seeds which have not been watered before the festival one should not water on the intermediate days of the festival' [M. 1:3].**"
>
> C.   *Well, I might concede that there is a representation of R. Eliezer's position that*

he prohibits work to add to one's gain, but have you heard a tradition that he disallows work in a situation in which otherwise loss will result?

D. *Rather, said R. Pappa, "Who is the authority behind this rule? It is R. Judah, for it has been taught on Tannaite authority:* **'From a spring that first flows on the intermediate days of a festival they irrigate even a rain watered field,' the words of R. Meir. And sages say, 'They irrigate from it only a field that depends upon irrigation, which has gone dry.' R. Eleazar b. Azariah says, "Not this nor that, [[but they do not irrigate a field from it [namely, a field the spring of which has gone dry] even in the case of an irrigated field]' [T. Moed 1:1A-C].** Even further, said R. Judah, 'A person should not clean out a water channel and with the dredging on the intermediate days of a festival water his garden or seed bed.'"

E. *Now what is the meaning of "that has gone dry"? If you say that it really has dried up, then what is going to be accomplished by watering it?*

F. *Said Abbayye, "The point is that this former water source has gone dry and another has just emerged."*

G. **R. Eleazar b. Azariah says, "Not this nor that:"** *there is no difference between the case of an old spring that has gone dry or that has not gone dry, in any event a spring that has just flowed may not be utilized on the intermediate days of the festival.*

H. *And how to you know [that it is Judah in particular who takes the position that work on the intermediate days of a festival is permitted if it is to prevent loss, but if it is to add to gain it is not permitted, and, further, even to prevent loss, really heavy labor is forbidden]? Perhaps R. Judah takes the position that he does, that is, that it is permitted to use the water for an irrigated field but not for a field that depends on rain, only in the case of a spring that has just now begun to flow,* **[2B]** *since it may cause erosion, but in the case of a spring that has not just now begun to flow and will not cause erosion might be permitted for use even on a field that depends on rain?*

I. *If so, then in accord with which authority will you assign our Mishnah-paragraph? For in fact, in R. Judah's view, there is no distinction between a spring that has just now flowed and one that has not just now flowed; in either case, an irrigated field may be watered, one that depends on rain may not. And the reason that the passage specifies the spring that has just now flowed is only to show the extend to which R. Meir was prepared to go, even a spring that has just now flowed may be used, and that is, even for a field that depends upon rain.*

Yet another standard inquiry raises the question of authority: who stands behind a rule, or who does not concur with a rule? is the authority behind the rule consistent in applying the same principle to other cases? and similar matters.

What follows is not Mishnah-commentary in particular, but the rule of the Mishnah is refined through the presentation of secondary and derivative questions. I indent this passage and what follows to show that it is not Mishnah-commentary in the simple sense operative until this point, but it also is not utterly unrelated to the exposition of the rule of the Mishnah. I do not catalogue as Mishnah-commentary entries that address the theme and principle of the Mishnah, but that stand entirely on their own foundations and do not require for intelligibility an allusion to or citation of the Mishnah's language. In my *Bavli's One Voice*, I classified such items as amplification of the Mishnah, which they are, but I do not regard them as commentary in the same way as the foregoing items form commentaries to a prior document.

4. A. *It has been stated:*
   B. He who on the Sabbath weeds a field or waters his seedlings—*on what count is he to be admonished [not to do so]?*
   C. Rabbah said, "On the count of ploughing."
   D. R. Joseph said, "On the count of sowing."
   E. *Said Rabbah, "It is more reasonable to see matters as I do. For what is the purpose of ploughing, if not to loosen the soil, and, here too, he loosens the soil."*
   F. *Said R. Joseph, "It is more reasonable to see matters as I do. For what is the purpose of sowing? It is to make produce sprout up. And here too, he makes produce sprout up."*
   G. *Said Abbayye to Rabbah, "There is a problem in your position, and there also is a problem in the position of R. Joseph.*
   H. *"There is a problem in your position: does this act come only under the classification of ploughing and not sowing?*
   I. *"And there also is a problem in the position of R. Joseph: does this act come only under the classification of sowing and not ploughing?*
   J. *"And should you say that in any place in which an act may be classified under two taxa, one is subject to liability on only one count, has not* R. Kahana said, 'If one pruned his tree but requires the wood for fuel, he is liable on two counts, one on the count of planting, the other on the count of harvesting'?"
   K. *That's a problem.*
5. A. Objected R. Joseph to Rabbah, "**He who weeds or covers with dirt diverse seeds is flogged. R. Aqiba says, 'Also one who preserves them'** [T. Kil. 1:15A-B]. *Now from my perspective, in that I hold that one is liable on the count of sowing, that explains the penalty, since sowing is forbidden in connection with mixed seeds in the vineyard; but from your perspective, in that you say that the count is ploughing, is there any prohibition of ploughing in connection with mixed seeds?"*
   B. *He said to him, "The count is that he has preserved them."*
   C. *"But lo, since the concluding clause states,* **R. Aqiba says, 'Also one who preserves them,'** *it must follow that the initial Tannaite authority maintains that the count for sanction is not that of preserving the crop of mixed seeds!"*

D. *"The whole of the statement represents the position of R. Aqiba, and the sense of the passage is to explain the operative consideration, specifically: what is the reason that* **he who weeds or covers with dirt diverse seeds is flogged***? It is because one is thereby preserving them, since* **R. Aqiba says, 'Also one who preserves them.'** *"*

E. *What is the basis in Scripture for the position of R. Aqiba?*

F. *It is in line with that which has been taught on Tannaite authority:*

G. "You shall not sow your field with two kinds of seed" (Lev. 19:19)—

H. I know only that sowing is forbidden. How do we know that preserving the sown seed is forbidden?

I. Scripture says, "Mixed seeds in your field not....," [meaning: it is the mixing of seeds that is emphatically forbidden, and you may have no share by your action in producing such a situation (Lazarus)].

II.1

A. *We have learned in the Mishnah:* **They water an irrigated field on the intermediate days of a festival and in the Seventh Year:**

B. [With respect to the inclusion of **in the Seventh Year**:] *Now there is no difficulty understanding the rule concerning the intermediate days of the festival, which pertains to a situation in which there is substantial loss, on account of which rabbis have permitted irrigation. But as to the Seventh Year, whether one holds that watering is classified as sowing or that watering is classified as ploughing, is it permitted either to sow or to plough in the Sabbatical Year [that it should be permitted to water the field]?*

C. Said Abbayye, "It is concerning the Seventh Year at this time that the rule speaks, and the rule represents the position of Rabbi."

D. *For it has been taught on Tannaite authority:*

E. Rabbi says, "'This is the manner of release: release [by every creditor of that which he has lent his neighbor' (Dt. 15:2)—it is of two different acts of release that Scripture speaks, one, the release of lands, the other, the release of debts. When you release lands you release debts, and when you do not release lands, you do not release debts." [The prohibition of agricultural labor in the Seventh Year now that the Temple is destroyed is merely by reason of rabbinical authority, and that prohibition is not enforced where loss is involved (Lazarus).]

F. *Raba said, "You may even maintain that the rule before us represents the position of rabbis [vis à vis Rabbi].* It is the generative categories of labor that the All-Merciful has prohibited, **[3A]** but the subsidiary classes of labor have not been forbidden. For it is written, 'But in the seventh year shall be a Sabbath of solemn rest for the land...you shall neither sow your field nor prune your vineyard. That which grows of itself of your harvest you shall not reap and the grapes of your undressed vine you shall not gather' (Lev. 25:4-5). *Since pruning falls within the generative category of sowing, and grape gathering falls within the generative category of reaping, for what concrete legal purpose did the All-Merciful make written reference to these items? It is to present the inference that it is to these particular derivative classes of generative categories of labor that liability pertains, but to all others, there is no liability."*

G.   *So they don't, don't they? But has it not been taught on Tannaite authority:*

H.   [**"The Lord said to Moses on Mount Sinai, Say to the people of Israel, When you come into the land which I give you, the land shall keep a Sabbath to the Lord. Six years you shall sow your field, and six years you shall prune your vineyard and gather in its fruits; but in the seventh year there shall be a Sabbath of solemn rest for the land, a Sabbath to the Lord; you shall not sow your field or prune your vineyard. What grows of itself in your harvest you shall not reap, and the grapes of your undressed vine you shall not gather; it shall be a year of solemn rest for the land. The Sabbath of the land shall provide food for you, for yourself and for your male and female slaves and for your hired servant and the sojourner who lives with you; for your cattle also and for the beasts that are in your land all its yield shall be for food" (Lev. 25:1-7):] "you shall not sow your field or prune your vineyard:"**

I.   **the Torah forbids me only to sow or prune,**

J.   **And how do we know that farmers may not fertilize, prune trees, smoke the leaves or cover over with powder for fertilizer?**

K.   **Scripture says, "your field you shall not...."—no manner of work in your field, no manner of work in your vineyard, shall you do.**

L.   **And how do we know that farmers may not trim trees, nip off dry shoots, trim trees?**

M.   **Scripture says, "your field you shall not...."—no manner of work in your field, no manner of work in your vineyard, shall you do.**

N.   **And how do we know that one may not manure, remove stones, dust the flower of sulphur, or fumigate?**

O.   **Scripture says, "your field you shall not...."—no manner of work in your field, no manner of work in your vineyard, shall you do.**

P.   **Since Scripture says, "you shall not sow your field or prune your vineyard,"**

Q.   **might one suppose that the farmer also may not hoe under the olive trees, fill in the holes under the olives trees, or dig between one tree and the next?**

R.   **Scripture says, "you shall not sow your field or prune your vineyard"—**

S.   **sowing and pruning were subject to the general prohibition of field labor. Whey then were they singled out?**

T.   **It was to build an analogy through them, as follows:**

U.   **what is distinctive in sowing and pruning is that they are forms of labor carried on on the ground or on a tree.**

V.   **So I know that subject to the prohibition are also other forms of labor that are carried on on the ground or on a tree, [excluding from the prohibition, therefore, the types of labor listed] [Sifra CCXLV:I.3-6].**

W.   *What we have here is a rule made by rabbinical authority, for which support is adduced from Scripture.*

Here is an instance in which scriptural bases for the rules of the Mishnah are set forth; there are many forms in which this exegetical staple will be set forth. What follows sets forth a secondary exposition of the foregoing, and for that reason is indented here.

2.   A.   *And is it permitted to sir the soil under an olive tree in the Seventh Year? Has it not been taught on Tannaite authority:*

B.   Now it is permitted to hoe [in the Seventh Year]?

C.   And has it not been taught on Tannaite authority:

D.   "But the seventh year you shall let [the land] rest and lie still" (Ex. 23:11).

E.   "You shall let it rest" from hoeing,

F.   "and lie still" from having stones removed.

G.   Said R. Uqba bar Hama, "There are two kinds of hoeing. In one kind one closes up the holes [around the roots of a tree], and in the other, he aerates the soil [around the roots of a tree].

H.   "Aerating the soil is forbidden, closing up the holes is permitted [since the former serves the roots of the tree, the latter merely protects the tree]."

The next entry forms a secondary-development of the foregoing, so is further indented. This allows us to see how the Mishnah forms the principal element of the Bavli's program, with secondary expansion and tertiary amplification of Mishnah-commentary making up an important part of the whole. At the same time, we also note that the Bavli's composites, as we have seen them to this point, simply explain the Mishnah or explain the explanation.

3.   A.   *It has been stated:*

B.   He who ploughs in the Seventh Year—

C.   R. Yohanan and R. Eleazar—

D.   One said, "He is flogged."

E.   The other said, "He is not flogged."

F.   *May we say that the dispute concerns that which R. Abin said R. Ilaa said, for*
said R. Abin said R. Ilaa, "In any passage in which you find a generalization concerning an affirmative action, followed by a qualification expressing a negative commandment, people are not to
construct on that basis an argument resting on the notion of a
general proposition followed by a concrete exemplification only
the substance of the concrete exemplification." [Freedman, *Sanhedrin,* p. 777-8, n. 8: The rule in such a case is: the general proposition includes only what is enumerated in the particular specification. But when one is thrown into the form of a positive
command and the other stated as a negative injunction this does
not apply.]

G.   *By this theory of what is at issue, one who says he is flogged does not concur
with what R. Abin said R. Ilai said, and one who said, "He is not flogged,"
concurs with what R. Abin said.* [Lazarus: The general rule in positive
terms: "The land shall keep a Sabbath..." (Lev. 25:2-5); the particulars in negative terms, "You shall neither sow..." (Lev. 25:4-5);
the general rule again in positive form, "It shall be a year of solemn rest...." Then the particulars are considered typical as illustrations, serving to include in the general rule all such items as are
similar to the particulars. If the particulars are typical of the general
rule, one who does any of these would break the law. In the case
of the former, he takes sowing, pruning, reaping, and gleaning as
typical illustrative instances, and ploughing is covered and is punishable. In the case of the latter, ploughing is not included among
the forbidden processes and is not punishable.]

H.   *No, all parties reject the position stated by R. Abin in R. Ilai's name. One who
says he is flogged has no problems anyhow.*

I.   *The one who says he is not flogged may reply in this way:*

J.   *Since pruning falls within the generative category of sowing, and grape gathering falls within the generative category of reaping, for what concrete legal purpose did the All-Merciful make written reference to these items? It is to present
the inference that it is to these particular derivative classes of generative categories of labor that liability pertains, but to all others, there is no liability."*

K.   *So they don't, don't they? But has it not been taught on Tannaite authority:*

L.   **["The Lord said to Moses on Mount Sinai, Say to the
people of Israel, When you come into the land which I
give you, the land shall keep a Sabbath to the Lord. Six
years you shall sow your field, and six years you shall
prune your vineyard and gather in its fruits; but in the
seventh year there shall be a Sabbath of solemn rest
for the land, a Sabbath to the Lord; you shall not sow
your field or prune your vineyard. What grows of itself**

in your harvest you shall not reap, and the grapes of your undressed vine you shall not gather; it shall be a year of solemn rest for the land. The Sabbath of the land shall provide food for you, for yourself and for your male and female slaves and for your hired servant and the sojourner who lives with you; for your cattle also and for the beasts that are in your land all its yield shall be for food" (Lev. 25:1-7):] "you shall not sow your field or prune your vineyard:"

M. the Torah forbids me only to sow or prune,

N. And how do we know that farmers may not fertilize, prune trees, smoke the leaves or cover over with powder for fertilizer?

O. Scripture says, "your field you shall not...."—no manner of work in your field, no manner of work in your vineyard, shall you do.

P. And how do we know that farmers may not trim trees, nip off dry shoots, trim trees?

Q. Scripture says, "your field you shall not...."—no manner of work in your field, no manner of work in your vineyard, shall you do.

R. And how do we know that one may not manure, remove stones, dust the flower of sulphur, or fumigate?

S. Scripture says, "your field you shall not...."—no manner of work in your field, no manner of work in your vineyard, shall you do.

T. Since Scripture says, "you shall not sow your field or prune your vineyard,"

U. might one suppose that the farmer also may not hoe under the olive trees, fill in the holes under the olives trees, or dig between one tree and the next?

V. Scripture says, "you shall not sow your field or prune your vineyard"—

W. sowing and pruning were subject to the general prohibition of field labor. Whey then were they singled out?

X. It was to build an analogy through them, as follows:

Y. what is distinctive in sowing and pruning is that they are forms of labor carried on on the ground or on a tree.

Z. So I know that subject to the prohibition are also other forms of labor that are carried on on the ground or on a tree, [excluding from the prohibition, therefore, the types of labor listed] [Sifra CCXLV:I.3-6].

AA. *What we have here is a rule made by rabbinical authority, for which support is adduced from Scripture.*

What follows carries forward the prior item.

4. A. **[3B]** *When R. Dimi came, he said, "Might one suppose that one is flogged even for doing so during the additional time that has been added to the Seventh Year [fore and aft]? But the discussion resolved in favor of exempting one who worked during the addition to the Seventh Year."*

    B. *But I don't know what is this "discussion" and to what reference is made under the category, "addition"!*

    C. *R. Eleazar said, "Reference is made to ploughing, and this is the sense of the statement: might one suppose that one is flogged on account of ploughing in the Seventh Year? For that conclusion would derive from a reading of the relevant verses under the principle of a generalization followed by a particularization of the foregoing followed by another generalization. And the discussion resolved in favor of exempting one who worked during the addition to the Seventh Year in the following way: if the flogging were in order, then what is the sense of the many particularizations that the text contains?"*

    D. *R. Yohanan said, "Reference is made to* the days that sages added to the Seventh Year prior to the advent of the New Year that marks the commencement of the Seventh Year proper, *and this is the sense of the statement: might one suppose that one is flogged on account of ploughing on the days that sages added to the Seventh Year prior to the advent of the New Year that marks the commencement of the Seventh Year proper? For that conclusion would derive from the following:* 'In ploughing time and in reaping time you shall rest' (Ex. 34:21). *And the discussion resolved in favor of exempting one who did so,"* as we shall have to explain below.

I have omitted two further components, which carry forward the purpose and program already established. Now we return to the amplification of the Mishnah, starting a new clause; there is no continuity between the foregoing and what follows. What holds the whole together is the Mishnah, only that. That fact once more underlines the character of the Bavli as Mishnah-commentary, however wide-ranging and even meandering; and it further shows us how the Bavli holds together all of its materials only by referring back to a prior, exterior document, not by an effort—however contrived—at showing the linkage between one principal unit of discourse and those that come fore and aft. We further note that, once we do turn to the Mishnah, we start all over again; nothing from the foregoing compositions and composites is required to grasp a single line of what now follows.

III.1

    A. **But they do not water [an irrigated field] with (1) collected rain water, or (2) water from a swape well:**

    B. *There is no trouble in understanding why water from a swape well should not be used, since watering in that way involves heavy labor. But what objection can there be to using collected rain water, since what heavy labor can possibly be involved in irrigating with rain water?*

C.   Said R. Ilaa said R. Yohanan, *"It is a precautionary decree, on account of the possibility of the farmer's going on to make use of water from a swape well."*

D.   R. Ashi said, "Rain water itself can be as hard to draw as the water of a swape well."

E.   *At issue between them is what R. Zira said. For* said R. Zira said Rabbah bar Jeremiah said Samuel, "From irrigation streams that draw water from ponds it is permitted to irrigate on the intermediate days of the festival." *One authority [Ashi} concurs with the position of R. Zira, and the other authority does not concur with the position of R. Zira.*

The foregoing represents an explanation of how the Mishnah's several examples cohere; we explain an unanticipated ruling.

2. A.   Reverting to the body of the foregoing: said R. Zira said Rabbah bar Jeremiah said Samuel, "From irrigation streams that draw water from ponds it is permitted to irrigate on the intermediate days of the festival."

B.   *Objected R. Jeremiah to R. Zira,* "**But they do not water [an irrigated field] with collected rain water, or water from a swape well.**"

C.   *He said to him, "Jeremiah my son, the pools in Babylonia are like water that never languishes."*

For the purpose of the present inquiry into the characteristics of the Bavli's Mishnah-commentary, we shall not deal with Tannaite complements to the Mishnah, e.g., originating in the Tosefta, that, on their own, do not fall into the category of commentary. My definition of commentary then limits our interest to what clearly cites or alludes to the Mishnah's statements and clarifies them in some important way. Topically-relevant materials formulated on Tannaite authority but not clearly serving as amplification of the Mishnah in particular in a broad and maximalist definition may be seen as Mishnah-commentary, and in my earlier discussion of the Mishnah's one voice I do regard Toseftan and other Tannaite restatement of rules pertinent to the Mishnah's rules as Mishnah-exegesis. But for the present purpose, a parallel Tannaite formulation of a rule must be bypassed, unless it clearly relates to, and means to expand and refine, a rule of the Mishnah or the secondary implications thereof, e.g., a more complex case, clarification of how a rule of the Mishnah applies (or does not apply) and

similar matters. So while the following is of interest in study of
the law of the Mishnah, it is not Mishnah-commentary. I indent
the item, to indicate that it is attached to the foregoing but not
continuous with it. Most of the Tosefta serves to amplify statements in the Mishnah, whether the Mishnah's language is quoted
or merely alluded to; only a small proportion of the Tosefta is
fully and exhaustively understood without reference to the
Mishnah's counterpart statements. We now see that other materials formulated like Tosefta's statements, and marked with the
same sigla (e.g., "it has been taught on Tannaite authority" and
the like) stand in the same relationship of dependency.

3. A. *Our rabbis have taught on Tannaite authority:*
    B. Ditches and pools that were filled with water on the eve of the
        festival may not be used for irrigation on the intermediate days of
        the festival. But if an irrigation ditch passes between them, they
        may be used.
    C. Said R. Pappa, "But that is so only if the greater part of that field
        derives its water from that irrigation ditch."
    D. R. Ashi said, "Even though the greater part of that field does not
        derive its water from that irrigation ditch, *since the water flows con-
        tinuously, the owner concludes, the the field does not get enough water one day,
        it will get enough two or three days later [and he will not undertake heavy labor
        during the intermediate days of the festival]."*

4. A. *Our rabbis have taught on Tannaite authority:*
    B. **A pool that gets a trickle of water from an irrigated field
        higher up may be used for watering another field. [R.
        Simeon b. Menassia says, "Two pools,. one above the
        other—one should not draw water from the lower to
        water the upper, but he may draw water from the up-
        per to water the lower one. R. Simeon b. Eleazar says,
        "A furrow, part of which is low and part high—one should
        not draw water from the lower part for the upper part
        and irrigate it. But he may draw water from the upper
        part for the lower part and irrigate by that means" [T.
        Moed 1:1F-I].**
    C. [With reference to the statement, **A pool that gets a trickle
        of water from an irrigated field higher up may be used
        for watering another field,**] *but lo, will it not give out?*
    D. Said R. Jeremiah, "In any event at this moment it is still trickling."
    E. Said Abbayye, "The rule applies only so long as the first spring has
        not languished." [Lazarus: but once the trickling has ceased, the
        pool has lost its supply and becomes like a swape well or stored
        rain likely to entail exertion.]

5. A. *It has been taught on Tannaite authority:*

B.   **R. Simeon b. Menassia says, "Two pools,. one above the other—one should not draw water from the lower to water the upper, but he may draw water from the upper to water the lower one.**

C.   **R. Simeon b. Eleazar says, "A furrow, part of which is low and part high—one should not draw water from the lower part for the upper part and irrigate it. But he may draw water from the upper part for the lower part and irrigate by that means" [T. Moed 1:1F-I].**

6.   A.   *Our rabbis have taught on Tannaite authority:*

    B.   They may raise up water by buckets from a well during the festival week for vegetables so as to eat them. But if it is only to improve their appearance, it is forbidden to do so.

7.   A.   *Rabina and Rabbah Tosefaah were going along the way. They saw somebody who was drawing buckets of water during the intermediate days of the festival. Said Rabbah Tosefaah to Rabina, "So let's go and excommunicate theat man."*

    B.   *He said to him, "But has it not been taught on Tannaite authority* They may raise up water by buckets from a well during the festival week for vegetables so as to eat them. But if it is only to improve their appearance, it is forbidden to do so.?"

    C.   *He said to him, "Do you really think that the meaning of 'raise up' means raise up water? What is the real meaning of 'raise up'?* **[4B]** *it is to pull out vegetables. That meaning of the word is in line with what we have learned in the Mishnah:* **"He who thins [using the word at hand] grape vines, just as he [is allowed] to thin his own [produce, the normal clusters], so may he thin [the defective clusters] which belong to the poor," the words of R. Judah. R. Meir says, "He is permitted to thin his own [produce], but he is not permitted [to thin produce] which belongs to the poor" [M. Peah 7:5].***

    D.   *He said to him, "But has it not been taught on Tannaite authority: They may raise up water by buckets from a well during the festival week for vegetables so as to eat them?"*

    E.   *He said to him, "So if that has been taught on Tannaite authority, that is what has been taught [and no more discussion]."*

Once more we revert to the Mishnah, and once more we commence afresh, now with the explanation of the meanings of words and phrases.

IV.1

A.   **And they do not dig channels around vines:**

    B.   *What are "channels"?*

    C.   *Said R. Judah, "They are little hollows."*

    D.   *So too it has been taught on Tannaite authority:*

E. **What are channels dug around a tree? These are ditch-es dug around the roots of trees [T. Moed 1:2B-C].** They hoe lightly around the roots of olives and vines.

F. *Is that so? But did not R. Judah permit the sons of Bar Zittai to make little hollows in their vineyards?*

G. *That's no problem, the statement of our Mishnah speaks of fresh ones, R. Judah's to established ones.*

V.1

A. **R. Eleazar b. Azariah says, "They do not make a new water channel on the intermediate days of a festival or in the Seventh Year." And sages say, "They make a new water channel in the Seventh Year, and they repair damaged ones on the intermediate days of a festival:"**

B. *There is no problem with respect to the prohibition concerning the intermediate days of a festival, since the operative consideration is that this is heavy labor, but why ever not make a channel in the Seventh Year?*

C. R. Zira and R. Abba b. Mamel differ on the matter—

D. One said, "The reason is that the one who digs appears to be hoeing."

E. And the other said, "The reason is that he looks as though he is preparing the banks for sowing."

F. *So what's at stake?*

G. *At issue is when water comes along immediately. From the perspective of him who has said,* "The reason is that he looks as though he is preparing the banks for sowing," *it is still objectionable. But from the perspective of him who has said,* "The reason is that the one who digs appears to be hoeing," *there is no objection.*

H. *But should not the one who objects for the reason that it looks as though he is spading also object that he looks as though he is preparing the bank for seed?*

I. *Rather, this is what's at stake between the two explanations: it would involve a case in which he takes what is in the trench and tosses it out. From the perspective of him who says,* "The reason is that he looks as though he is preparing the banks for sowing," *there is no objection; but from the perspective of him who says,* "The reason is that the one who digs appears to be hoeing," *it is still subject to an objection.*

J. *But from the perspective of him who says that he appears to be preparing the sides for seed, would he not also admit that he seems to be hoeing?*

K. *Not really, for one who hoes, as soon as he takes up a spadeful, he puts it down again in place.*

We proceed to a secondary expansion of the foregoing.

2. A. *Amemar repeated the Mishnah's law along with the reason,* The reason is that the one who digs appears to be hoeing, *but this presented a problem to him because of a contradiction between two statements of R. Eleazar b. Azariah: "And has* R. Eleazar b. Azariah taken the position that any act

that looks as if he is hoeing is forbidden? *And in contradiction to that position:* **A person places [all] the manure in his possession in [one large] pile. R. Meir forbids [the farmer from doing this] unless he either deepens [the ground by] three [handbreadths] or raises [the ground by] three [handbreadths] . If one had a small amount [of manure already piled up in the field], he continually adds to it. R. Eleazar b. Azariah forbids [the farmer from doing so] unless he either deepens [the ground by] three [handbreadths] or raises [the ground by] three [handbreadths] or unless he places [the manure] on rocky ground [M. Shebiit 3:3D-G].** [Lazarus: here Eleazar permits digging in the field in the sabbatical year to prepare a place for the manure store without concern about giving a wrong impression, such as he had in mind when he prohibited making a water channel.]

B.   R. Zira and R. Abba b. Mamel differ on the matter—

C.   One said, "The cited passage speaks of a case in which he had the place excavated."

D.   And the other said, "The operative consideration is that the manure heap itself shows what his real intention is."

What follows contains no surprises: reversion to a clause of the Mishnah, repetition of an established exegetical program, here: meanings of words and phrases.

VI.1

A.   **and they repair damaged ones on the intermediate days of a festival:**

B.   *What is the meaning of* "damaged ones"?

C.   Said R. Abba, "If one was only a handbreadth deep, he may restore it to a depth of six handbreadths."

2.   A.   *It is obvious that restoring the channel from a half handbreadth to three, since there was to begin with hardly any flow of water, is null [and work that is useless]' to deepen it from two handbreadths to the original twelve involves heavy labor and that is not permitted. But what about deepening it from two to seven? Here he deepens it by five handbreadths, from one to six, so here too he deepens it by five, two to seven? Or perhaps what is going on here is that he is actually deepening it by an extra handbreadth, so that involves heavy and needless labor and is forbidden?*

B.   *The question stands.*

The next entry carries forward the foregoing and draws upon it:

3.   A.   *Abbayye permitted the people of Harmakh [during the intermediate days of the festival] to clear away the growths obstructing the irrigation ditch.*

B. *R. Jeremiah permitted the people of Sacuta [during the intermediate days of the festival] to dredge a ditch that had been blocked.*

C. *R. Ashi permitted the people of Mata Mehasia to clear obstructions from the Barnis canal, saying, "Since people get their water from it, it is as public domain, and we have learned in the Mishnah:* **And they do all public needs.**

The clarification of the Mishnah now requires us to investigate the implications, for law and principle, of the language of the Mishnah. The close reading of the Mishnah's formulation is what generates the problem that will be discussed.

VII.1

A. [5A] **They repair damaged waterways in the public domain and dig them out:**

B. *Repairing is all right, but not digging afresh.*

C. Said R. Jacob said R. Yohanan, "They have taught this rule only when the public has no need of the waterways, but if the public needs them, then it is permitted even to dig afresh."

D. *But if the public needs them, is it permitted to do that work? And has it not been taught on Tannaite authority:* Cisterns, pits, and caverns that belong to private property may be cleaned out, and, it goes without saying, those that belong to the public; but cisterns, pits, and caverns belonging to the public may not be dug, and all the more so those of a private person? *Does this not address a case in which the public has need of these facilities?*

E. *No, it addresses a case in which the public has no need of those facilities.*

F. *Along these same lines with respect to a private party, where the private person has no need of the facility, is repairing allowed? And has it not been taught on Tannaite authority:* As to cisterns, pits, and caverns of a private person, they collect water in them but they may not be cleaned out, nor may their cracks be plastered; but as to those belonging to the public, they may be cleaned out and their cracks may be plastered?

G. *Now what is the point here? It is when a private person has need of the facility. And in that case, in regard to what is required for public use, where the public has need of it the same rule pertains? And where the public has need of the facility, is it forbidden to dig? Has it not been taught on Tannaite authority:* As to cisterns, pits, and caverns belonging to a private person, they collect water in them and clean them out, but they may not plaster their cracks nor put scourings into them to fill cracks; as to those serving the public, they may dig them to begin with and plaster them with cement?

H. *So the initial formulation poses a contradiction.*

I. *This is how to iron out the difficulty:* They may clean out wells, ditches or caverns of a private person, when the private party requires the facility, and, it goes without saying, those that belong to the public *when the public require use of the facility, in which case even digging them out is permitted.* But they may not dig out wells, ditches, or caverns belonging to the public when the public does not require use of the facility, and, it goes without saying, those belonging to a private party. *When the private party does not require using them, then even cleaning them out is forbidden.*

J. *Said R. Ashi, "A close reading of our Mishnah-paragraph yields the same result:* **And they do all public needs.** *Now what is encompassed within the augmentative formulation,* **all***? Is it not to encompass, also, digging?"*

K. *Not at all, it is to encompass what is covered in that which has been taught on Tannaite authority:* **On the fifteenth day of Adar agents of the court go forth and dig cisterns, wells, and caves. And they repair immersion pools and water channels. Every immersion pool that contains forty seahs of water is suitable for receiving further drawn water if need be, and to every immersion pool that does not contain forty seahs of water they lead a water course and s complete its volume to the measure of forty seahs of water that has not been drawn so that it is suitable to receive further drawn water if need be [T. Sheq. 1:1].** And how on the basis of Scripture do we know that if they did not go forth and carry out all these duties, that any blood that is shed there is credited by Scripture as though they had shed it? Scripture states, "And so blood be upon you" (Dt. 19:10).

L. *Lo, in point of fact the framer of the Mishnah has covered these matters explicitly:* **They repair roads, streets, and water pools. And they do all public needs***! what is encompassed within the augmentative formulation,* **all***? Is it not to encompass, also, digging?*

M. *Yes, that's the proof!*

The following item cites further language of the Mishnah and adduces scriptural foundations for the Mishnah's rule:

VIII.1

A. **mark off graves:**

B. Said R. Simeon b. Pazzi, "Whence do we find an indication in Scripture that it is required to mark off graves? Scripture states, 'And when they pass through the land and one sees a man's bone, then shall he set up a sign by it' (Ez. 29:15)."

C. *Said Rabina to R. Ashi, "So before Ezekiel made that point, how did we know it?"*

H. *Said R. Ashi to Rabina, "So until Ezekiel came along and made that statement, how did we know the correct rule?"*

I. *"According to your reasoning, when R. Hisda made his statement,* 'This matter we have not learned from the Torah of our lord, Moses, but from the teachings of Ezekiel b. Buzi we have learned it, "No alien, uncircumcised in heart and uncircumcised in flesh, shall enter my sanctuary" (Ez. 44:9),'—*until Ezekiel came along and made that statement, how did we know the correct rule? Rather, it is a tradition that was handed on, and Ezekiel came along and supplied it with support from Scripture. Here too, it is a tradition that was handed on, and Ezekiel came along and supplied it with support from Scripture."*

2. A.   R. Abbahu said, "It derives from the following: 'And he shall cry, unclean, unclean' (Lev. 13:45)—the uncleanness affecting him cries out for him and says, 'Keep away.'"

    B.   And so said R. Uzziel, grandson of Rabbah, "'...the uncleanness affecting him cries out for him and says, 'Keep away.'"

    C.   *But does that verse serve the specified purpose? It is in point of fact required in line with that which has been taught on Tannaite authority:*

    D.   "And he shall cry, unclean, unclean" (Lev. 13:45)—one has to publicize his pain in public, so that the public may seek for mercy on his behalf.

    E.   *If that were the case, then Scripture can as well have written,* "Unclean he shall cry out." *Why say,* "Unclean, unclean"? *It is to yield both points.*

3. A.   *Abbayye said, "It derives from the following:* 'And do not put a stumbling block before the blind' (Lev. 19:14)."

    B.   *R. Pappa said, "It derives from the following:* 'And he will say,m Cast you up, cast you up, clear the way' (Is. 57:14)."

    C.   *R. Hinena said, "It derives from the following:* 'Take up the stumbling block out of the way of my people' (Is. 57:14)."

    D.   *R. Joshua b. R. Idi said, "It derives from the following:* 'And you shall show them the way in which they must walk' (Ex. 18:20)."

    E.   *Mar Zutra said, "It derives from the following:* 'And you shall separate the children of Israel from their uncleanness' (Lev. 15:31)."

    F.   *R. Ashi said, "It derives from the following:* 'And they shall have charge of my charge' (Lev. 22:9), meaning, protect my charge [the priesthood]."

    G.   *Rabina said, "It derives from the following:* 'And to him who orders his way will I show the salvation of God' (Ps. 50:23)."

4. A.   And R. Joshua b. Levi said, "Whoever properly sets his ways in this world will have the merit of witnessing the salvation of the Holy One, blessed be he,

    B.   "as it is said, 'To him who orders his way I will show the salvation of God' (Ps. 50:23).

    C.   "Do not read 'orders' but 'properly sets' [his] way" [Cohen, *Sotah*, p. 21, n. 6: He calculates the loss incurred in fulfilling a precept against the reward it will bring him.]

5. A.   *R. Yannai had a disciple who day by day raised tough questions, but on the Sabbaths of Festivals did not raise tough questions.*

    B.   **[5B]** *In his regard he recited the verse,* "And to him who orders his way will I show the salvation of God" (Ps. 50:23).

The next item is already familiar: amplification of the Mishnah by citation and analysis of the Tosefta's counterpart materials.

6. A. *Our rabbis have taught on Tannaite authority:*
    B. They do not may a mark to indicate the presence of corpse matter that is not bigger in volume than an olive's bulk, nor a human bone that is not bigger than a barley seed, nor any human remains that would not convey uncleanness when under a tent. But they do make a marking to indicate the presence of a spine, skull, or major limb of a skeleton, or the larger part of the small bones.
    C. They make markings not when the matter is certainly known, but only when it is uncertain.
    D. What are cases of uncertainty?
    E. leafy bowers, jutting ledges, and a grave-area.
    F. And they do not make a mark right on the spot of the source of uncleanness, so as not to waste what is unaffected, nor is a mark placed far from the spot, so as not to waste space in the Land of Israel [cf. T. Sheq. 1:5].
    G. *But will an olive's bulk of human flesh not convey uncleanness in a tent? Lo, we have learned in the Mishnah:* **These contaminate in the Tent: (1) the corpse, and (2) an olive's bulk [of flesh] from the corpse, [and (3) an olive's bulk of corpse dregs, and (4) a ladleful of corpse mould; (5) the backbone, and the skull, and (6) a limb from the corpse, and (7) a limb from the living person on which is an appropriate amount of flesh; (8) a quarter-qab of bones from the larger part of the frame [of the skeleton] or (9) from the larger number; and (10) the larger part of the frame or (11) the larger number of the corpse, even though there is not among them a quarter-qab, are unclean. How much is the "larger number"? One hundred twenty-five] [M. Oh. 2:1]**/
    H. *Said R. Pappa, "Here we deal with a piece of flesh precisely an olive's bulk in size, since ultimately it will be found lacking. It is better that on its account food in the status of priestly rations and Holy Things should be burned on its account for a little while, but not for all time."*
7. A. **What are cases of uncertainty? Leafy bowers, jutting ledges, and a grave-area:**
    B. **leafy bowers:** a tree that overshadows the ground near a cemetery.
    C. **jutting ledges: Protruding stones that project from a wall [T. Oh. 9:2].**
    D. **and a grave-area:** *that is in line with that which we have learned in the Mishnah:* **He who ploughs up the grave—lo, he makes [the field into] a grave area. How much [space] does he make? The length of a furrow of a hundred cubits,**

[over] a space of four seahs [M. Oh. 17:1A-B].

8.   A.   *So does dirt deriving from a grave-area convey uncleanness through over-*
           shadowing by a common tent? But did not R. Judah say Samuel said,
           "One [who wants to remain uncontaminated by corpse mat-
           ter] in a *beth haperas [a grave area, an area possibly contaminated by*
           corpse matter] blows away the earth and goes along his way."

     B.   R. Judah bar Ammi in the name of R. Judah said, "A *beth haperas*
           [a grave area, an area possibly contaminated by corpse matter] that has
           been trodden down is no longer a source of uncleanness."

     C.   Said R. Pappa, "There is no contradiction. The one statement
           speaks of a field in which the location of a grave has been lost"
           [so the whole field is a source of uncleanness], and the other
           speaks of a field in which a grave has been turned up by a
           plough [which crushes the bones so that they are no longer
           a source of uncleanness]."

     D.   *But is a field in which a grave has been ploughed up even classified as a*
           grave area?

     E.   *Yes indeed, for we have learned in the Mishnah:* **There are three**
           kinds of grave areas: [1] He who ploughs up the
           grave—it may be planted with any kind of tree, but
           it may not be sown with any kind of seed, except
           for seed [the plants of which] are cut. And if one
           uprooted it, one heaps up the threshing floor in it,
           and sifts—"the grain through two sieves," the words
           of R. Meir. And sages say, "The grain with two
           sieves, and the pulse through three sieves." And one
           burns the stubble and the stalks [in the grave area].
           And it renders unclean through contact and through
           carrying, and it does not render unclean through the
           Tent. [2] A field in the midst of which a grave has
           been lost is sown with any kind of seed but is not
           planted with any kind of tree. And they do not pre-
           serve trees in it, except for a barren tree, which does
           not produce fruits. And it renders unclean through
           contact and through carrying and through the Tent.
           [3] A field of mourners/tomb niches is not plant-
           ed, and is not sown, but its dust is clean. And they
           make from it ovens for holy [use] [M. Oh. 18:2-4].

What now follows is a talmud to the Tosefta's and other Tannaite complements to the Mishnah; much of the Bavli is made
up of this kind of talmud—sustained amplification, analysis, secondary inquiry of various other sorts—to its own Mishnah-commentary. I continue to indent what is an expansion of amplifica-
tory material.

9.   A.   *What is the definition of* **A field of mourners***?*

     B.   R. Joshua bar Abba in the name of Ulla said, "It is a field in which they take leave of the dead."

     C.   *And how come [it is classified as a grave area, imparting uncleanness]?*

     D.   Said Abimi, "It is because of the contingency of abandonment by the owners [of the limbs that may have been dropped there when collection was made for secondary burial]."

10. A.   *And is it not necessary to mark off a field in which a grave has been dug up by a plough? Has it not been taught on Tannaite authority:*

     B.   If one found a field that is marked off as having corpse matter in its midst, and the nature of the uncleanness is not known, if there is a tree in it, one may be sure that a grave has been ploughed up in it. If there is no tree in it, one may be sure that a grave has been lost in it.

     C.   Said R. Judah, "Under what circumstances? When there is available a sage or a disciple, for not everybody is going to be expert in this matter" [T. Ahilot 17:12].

     D.   *Said R. Pappa, "When that passage was repeated on Tannaite authority, it made reference to a field in which a grave had been lost and which therefore had been marked. If, then, there are trees in the field, that means that a grave had been ploughed up by a plough thereafter; if there are no trees in it, it means a grave has been lost in it."*

     E.   *But should we not take account of the possibility that trees are located in the field but the grave lies outside of it? For that would be in line with what Ulla said,* "We speak of a case in which trees are located at the edges of the field," *so here too,* "We speak of a case in which trees are located at the edges of the field."

     F.   **[6A]** *But perhaps the uncleanness is located inside the field and trees are situated outside* [Lazarus: and since corpses are not buried on the road, the grave must be located among the trees and it must have been run over by the plough when the field was tilled for the sake of the trees].

     G.   *We deal with a case in which the trees were planted irregularly.*

     H.   *If you prefer, I shall say,* "It is in line with what we said earlier: **nor is a mark placed far from the spot, so as not to waste space in the Land of Israel**."

11. A.   **Said R. Judah, "Under what circumstances? When there is available a sage or a disciple, for not everybody is going to be expert in this matter:"**

     B.   *Said Abbayye, "That proves that, when a neophyte rabbi is located in a place, all affairs of the place are assigned to his authority."*

12. A.   Said R. Judah, "If one found a stone with a marking, the space under it is deemed to be unclean [with corpse uncleanness]. If there were two such stones, then if there is lime between them, the space between them is deemed unclean. If there is

no lime between them, then the space between them is
deemed clean."

B.   *But is that the case even if there is no mark of ploughing there? And has it not
been taught on Tannaite authority:*

C.   If one found a single stone marked off, even though it is not to
be kept in that way, he who overshadows it is clean. If one found
two of them, if there is a mark of ploughing between them, the
space between them is clean, if not, it is unclean [T. Sheq. 1:5D-
E].

D.   Said R. Pappa, "Here we deal with a case in which the lime was
poured on top of the stones and then spread down on either side.
If there is a mark of ploughing between them, the space is clean,
*for we assume that the lime that splashed was peeled off by the ploughing; if there
is no mark of ploughing, the lime is clearly intended to mark the space between
and that space is held to be unclean.*"

13. A.   Said R. Assi, "If there is a marking on one side, that side is unclean,
the rest of the whole field is clean. it there is marking on two sides,
those are unclean, the whole rest of the field is clean; if there was
marking on three sides, those are unclean, but the whole rest of
the field is clean. If there is a marking on four boundaries, they
are then held to be the marks of what is clean, but the entire field
inside is unclean."

B.   "For a master has said, **nor is a mark placed far from the
spot, so as not to waste space in the Land of Israel.**"

We now compare a rule of the Mishnah with an intersecting one,
showing that the two do not contradict one another.

IX.1

A.   **and go forth [to give warning] against Diverse Kinds:**

B.   *But in fact in the intermediate days of a festival do we go about to inspect whether
or not there are mixed seeds in a field? But there is the following contradiction:*
**On the first day of Adar they make public announce-
ment concerning [payment of] sheqel dues and concerning the sowing of mixed seeds [Lev. 19:19, Dt. 22:9].
On the fifteenth day of that month they read the
Megillah [Scroll of Esther] in walled cities. And they
repair the paths, roads, and immersion pools. And they
carry out all public needs. And they mark off the graves.
And they go forth [to inspect the fields] on account of
mixed seeds [M. Sheq. 1:1]***!***

C.   R. Eleazar and R. Yosé bar Hanina—

D.   One said, "The latter refers to the crops that ripen earlier [in mid-
Adar], the other, of late-ripening crops [and our Mishnah-paragraph has a further inspection, now in mid-Nisan, during the intermediate days of the festival of Passover]."

E.   And the other said, "In the one case [in Adar] they go out to inspect the condition of grain fields, in the other, vegetable patches."

F.   Said R. Assi said R. Yohanan, "The rule pertains only in a case in which the sprouts are not yet recognizable [earlier on]; but where it is possible to discern the character of the sprouts early on, they went forth to inspect the situation earlier."

We proceed to a talmud for the foregoing.

2.   A.   *What makes the festival week special that we go out at that time for the purpose at hand?*

      B.   *Said R. Jacob said R. Yohanan, "It is at that time labor is cheap with us [since there is no demand for labor during the intermediate days of the festival]."*

      C.   *Said R. Zebid, and some say, R. Mesharshayya, "That leads to the inference that, when we pay them, we pay them out of the heave offering taken up from the sheqel-chamber. For if you should imagine that the owners of the fields are paid, what difference does it make to us? Pay whatever the workers ask [and don't try to hire workers at a time when wages are low, since the householders are going to have to shell out]!"*

3.   A.   How much [constitutes a mixture of seeds]?

      B.   Said R. Samuel bar Isaac, "It is in line with that which we have learned in the Mishnah: **[Concerning] every seah [of one kind of seeds] which contains** [6B] **a quarter [-qab] of another kind—he shall lessen [the quantity of seeds of the other kind, so that those seeds form less than a quarter-qab] [M. Kil. 2:1A]**."

      C.   *But has it not been taught on Tannaite authority:* They ordained that they should declare ownerless the crop of the entire field?

      D.   *There is no contradiction, the Mishnah-rule describes how things were done before the ordinance, the latter tells us how things were done afterward, in line with what has been taught on Tannaite authority:* .At first they would uproot the crops and throw them in front of their cattle, but the householders were delighted on two counts, first, that they weeded their fields for them, second, they threw the crop to the cattle. So they ordained that they should uproot the forbidden crop and throw it in the road. So the householders were still delighted, because the court then took care of weeding their field. So in the end they ordained that they should declare ownerless the crop of the entire field.

Now to review the entirety of the foregoing. **I.1** raises a fundamental question of Mishnah-exegesis. No. 2 proceeds to explain the meanings of words. No. 3 asks a third routine question of Mishnah-exegesis. Nos. 4-5 pursue their own interests, and the composite is included here because of the point of intersection with our Mishnah; this is then an appendix. **II.1** raises the obvious exegetical question concerning a detail of the Mishnah. No. 2 footnotes the foregoing. No. 3 then provides a further composition for this thematic anthology on the general theme of work done or not done in the Seventh Year. Nos. 4-6 continue No. 3. **III.1** asks an obvious question in clarifying the principle of the Mishnah's rule. No. 2 footnotes the foregoing. Nos. 3, 4, 5, 6+7 provide an anthological supplement, principally deriving from the Tosefta, to the theme of the Mishnah. **IV.1** engages in a simple exercise of Mishnah-exegesis. **V.1** asks a question invited by the point of the Mishnah's rule. No. 2 clarifies the foregoing explanation. **VI.1** explains the meaning of the language of the Mishnah, and No. 2 then builds on the facts given in No. 1. No. 3 then provides case reports on how the law at hand is applied. **VII.1** investigates the implications of the rule of the Mishnah in light of other Tannaite formulations on the subject. **VIII.1, 2, 3** ask the familiar question of the scriptural basis for a rule of the Mishnah. No. 4 is tacked on to the foregoing by reason of the shared proof-text. No. 5 is present for the same reason. The Mishnah's theme then accounts for the inclusion of the Tannaite appendix that follows, Nos. 6, 7-13, which is hardly required except for a complete presentation of the topic. **IX.1** investigates the implications of the framing of the Mishnah's rule and harmonizes them with other rulings. No. 2 continues the exposition of the Mishnah's rule. No. 3 then turns to the theme at hand.

MISHNAH/BAVLI TRACTATE MOED QATAN 1:3

A. R. Eliezer b. Jacob says, "They lead water from one tree to another,

B. "on condition that one not water the entire field.

C. "Seeds which have not been watered before the festival one should not water on the intermediate days of the festival."

D. And sages permit in this case and in that.

We begin with an example of how the Bavli will ask about the way in which the law is realized, here meaning, the conditions under which the Mishnah's statement applies:

I.1

A.   [**on condition that one not water the entire field**:] said R. Judah, "If the field's soil is clay, he may water it."

B.   *So too it has been taught on Tannaite authority:*

C.   When they made the rule that it is forbidden to irrigate on the intermediate days of a festival, they made that statement only concerning seed that had not drunk before the festival; but as to seed that had been watered before the festival, they may be watered during the intermediate days of the festival; and if the soil of the field was clay, it is permitted to water it. And a bare field [without a crop at that time] is not watered during the festival week. But sages permit doing so in both cases [where seeds were not watered, watering a bare field].

D.   *Said Rabina, "That statement leads to the inference that it is permitted to hand-sprinkle a vegetable patch during the intermediate days of a festival. For in the case of a bare field, why is it permitted to do so? It is because that renders the soil fit to be sown or planted, and here too, that is permitted."*

Next comes a Tannaite complement to the Mishnah's rule. This will be investigated in the same way in which that of the Mishnah is worked out. We want to know how two Tannaite formulations cohere, and whether or not they contradict; if they do, then we shall try to show the rational basis for the conflict, e.g., two different authorities; two conflicting principles, each brought into play under circumstances particular to itself; and the like.

2.   A.   *Our rabbis have taught on Tannaite authority:*

B.   They sprinkle water on a field of grain in the Seventh Year but not during the intermediate days of a festival.

C.   *But lo, it has been taught on Tannaite authority:*

D.   It is permitted to sprinkle a grain field both in the Seventh Year and in the intermediate days of the festival?

E.   *Said R. Huna, "There is no contradiction, the one speaks for R. Eliezer b. Jacob* [**R. Eliezer b. Jacob says, "They lead water from one tree to another, on condition that one not water the entire field. Seeds which have not been watered before the festival one should not water on the intermediate days of the festival"**], *the other, rabbis."*

3.   A.   *It has been further taught on Tannaite authority:*

B.   A field of grain may be sprinkled on the even of the Seventh Year so that the greens may sprout in the Seventh Year; and not only so, but they may sprinkle a field of grain in the Seventh Year so that the greens may sprout in the year after the Seventh Year.

I.1 clarifies the application of the Mishnah's rule. Nos. 2, 3 deal with the subsidiary issue of the Seventh Year, which is not addressed in our Mishnah-paragraph.

Mishnah/Bavli tractate Moed Qatan 1:4

A. **They hunt moles and mice in a tree-planted field and in a field of grain,**
B . **in the usual manner,**
C. **on the intermediate days of a festival and in the Seventh Year.**
D. **And sages say [R. Judah], "[They do so] in a tree-planted field in the normal manner, and in a grain field not in the normal manner."**
E. **They [may only] block up a breach in the intermediate days of a festival.**
F. **And in the seventh year, one builds it in the normal way.**

Our starting point presents no surprises: explaining the words used in the Mishnah. Where the Bavli proposes to investigate the language or sources (e.g., in the written Torah) of the Scripture, that inquiry will always stand at the head of the presentation of the Mishnah-paragraph at hand. There is a clear order of business, first, language and sources and authorities, second, inquiry into issues of conflict and harmonization, and, third, investigation of secondary issues raised by the Mishnah's rule but not required for the clear re-presentation of that rule. As to the items of the first of the three categories of Mishnah-commentary, I see no fixed order, though, in general, we shall expect the matter of the source of the Mishnah, in Scripture, to come first; then the clarification of the Mishnah's language; then any other items on the order of business for a given paragraph of the Mishnah; and, finally, Tannaite amplification of the Mishnah's rule or extension of its theme to other matters altogether. After translating all thirty-seven Bavli-tractates, I cannot point to a single passage in which the Mishnah is first complemented with Tannaite materials and only then analyzed as to its language and sources and authority. But, I hasten to add, in a document of the dimensions of this one, it is easier to say what we find than what we do not find.

I.1

   A.   *What is the definition of* **moles***?*

   B.   Said R. Judah, "It is a creature without eyes."

   C.   *Said Raba bar Ishmael, and some say, R. Yemar bar Shelamayya, "What is the pertinent verse of Scripture?* 'Let them be as a snail that melts and passes away, like the young mole that has not seen the sun' (Ps. 58:9).*"*

Now comes the Tannaite complement, this one adding to the Mishnah's rule, then itself amplified in exactly the same manner as is the Mishnah itself.

2.   A.   *Our rabbis have taught on Tannaite authority:*

   B.   **Moles and mice may be trapped in a grain field and in an orchard in the ordinary way, and ants' holes may be destroyed. How are they destroyed? Rabban Simeon b. Gamaliel says, "They get earth from one hole and put it into another and the ants strangle each other" [T. Moed 1:5].**

   C.   *Said R. Yemar bar Shelamayya in the name of Abbayye, "And that is the case only if the nests are located on opposite sides of the river, if there is no bridge, if these is not even a plank, if there is not even a rope."*

   B.   **[7A]** How far apart must they be?

   C.   Up to a parasang.

The next clause of the Mishnah is amplified by Tannaite complements; these are not merely congruent to the Mishnah but allude to and explain its language.

II.1

   A.   **And R. Judah says, "[They do so] in a tree-planted field in the normal manner, and in a grain field not in the normal manner:"**

   B.   *Our rabbis have taught on Tannaite authority:*

   C.   **What is the usual way? He digs a hole and suspends a trap in it. What is the unusual way? He drives in a stake or strikes it with a pick and crushes the dirt underneath [T. Moed 1:4A-B].**

2.   A.   *It has been taught on Tannaite authority:*

   B.   **R. Simeon b. Eleazar says, "When they spoke of a grain field in which it was not to be done in the normal manner, reference was made to a grain field near town. But as to a grain field near an orchard, even doing it in the normal way is permitted, lest the pests come out of the grain field and destroy the orchard" [T. Moed 1:4C-D].**

Another form of explanation of the Mishnah, and the simplest, will be to answer a question left open by the Mishnah and urgent for the explanation of the Mishnah's rule: commentary in its simplest form.

III.1

- A. **They block up a breach in the intermediate days of a festival. And in the seventh year, one builds it in the normal way:**
- B. How is the breach blocked up?
- C. *Said R. Joseph, "With [Lazarus:] a hurdle made of twigs and daphne stakes."*
- D. *In a Tannaite statement it was set forth:* one piles up pebbles but does not hold them down with mortar.
- 2. A. Said R. Hisda, "This rule has been taught only of a wall around a vegetable patch, but as to a wall around a courtyard, one may build it up in the normal way."
  - B. *May we say that the following supports his position:* **As to a wall that is hanging over into public domain, they may tear it down and rebuild it in the usual way, because it is a public nuisance [T. 1:7A-B]***?*
  - C. *Well, that does not necessarily sustain the proposition, for that case bears a stated reason, namely,* **because it is a public nuisance.**
  - D. *And there are those who present matters in this way:*
  - E. *Come and take note:* **As to a wall that is hanging over into public domain, they may tear it down and rebuild it in the usual way, because it is a public nuisance [T. 1:7A-B]**, *so if it is a public nuisance, that may be done, but if not, it may not be done. Then may we say that this forms a refutation of the position of R. Hisda?*
  - F. *R. Hisda may say to you, "There one may both tear down the wall and rebuild it, here one may build the wall but not tear it down."*
  - G. *So in that case, too, maybe one should tear down the wall but not rebuild it?*
  - H. *If so, one will just give up and not tear it down at all!*
  - I. *Said R. Ashi, "A careful reading of the Mishnah yields that same result:* **And in the seventh year, one builds it in the normal way. Now what is the point of saying he may block up the breach**. *If it is the wall of his courtyard, this hardly requires explicit articulation. So it can only be a breach in his garden wall, even though it might appear that he is doing it to safeguard his crop."*
  - J. *That leads to the proposed inference.*

I.1 clarifies a word-choice in the Mishnah. No. 2 then complements the Mishnah with a Tannaite addition. **II.1, 2** do the same. **III.1** answers a question of Mishnah-exegesis. No. 2 explains the application of the Mishnah's rule.

MISHNAH/BAVLI TRACTATE MOED QATAN 1:5A-B

A. **R. Meir says, "They examine marks of the presence of the skin ailment [to begin with] to provide a lenient ruling but not to provide a strict ruling."**

B. **And sages say, "Neither to provide a lenient ruling nor to provide a strict ruling."**

The Tannaite complement to the Mishnah-paragraph in fact forms a commentary upon it. We have a restatement of matters in the Mishnah, now with a consideration of how matters are to be worked out in practice: Rabbi's statement of his judgment.

I.1

A. *It has been taught on Tannaite authority:*

B. **R. Meir says, "They examine marks of the presence of the skin ailment [to begin with] to provide a lenient ruling but not to provide a strict ruling."**

C. **R. Yosé says, "Neither to provide a lenient ruling nor to provide a strict ruling, for if you undertake a ruling in his case so as to present a lenient ruling, you will have also to provide the stringent ruling if it is called for."**

D. **Said Rabbi, "The opinion of R. Meir makes more sense in the case of one who is merely shut up for inspection, and the opinion of R. Yosé makes more sense in the case of one who is certified as unclean" [T. Moed 1:8].**

A secondary expansion of the Tannaite complement to the Mishnah now gets underway:

2. A. *Said Raba, "In the case of someone who is now assumed to be clean, all parties concur that he is not subject to an examination at all during the intermediate days of the festival. In the case of someone who has been shut up for the first week, all parties concur that he is examined. Where there is a disagreement, it concerns* **[7B]** *one who has been shut up for a second span of time.*

B. *"One authority [Meir] takes the view that we leave the decision to the priest's discretion, so that if the person is clean, he declares him clean, but if he looks unclean, the priest shuts his mouth, while the other authority invokes the verse,* 'this is the law of the plague and the skin ailment, to make a pronouncement of clean or unclean' (Lev. 13:59), [meaning, without dissimulation]."

3. A. The master has said: **"The opinion of R. Meir makes more sense in the case of one who is merely shut up for inspection, and the opinion of R. Yosé makes more sense in the case of one who is certified as unclean:"**

B. *But has not the opposite between taught on Tannaite authority?*

C.   *It represents a conflict of Tannaite statements in respect to the position of Rabbi.*
     One authority takes the view that having company is preferable to the victim,
     the other, having the company of his wife is preferable to him. [Lazarus: Meir
     has confirmed patient in mind and holds, "Inspect him now to
     mitigate his plight; if he is still a leper, he loses nothing; if he is
     found cured, he can at once get back to town, even though he
     has to part from his wife for seven days, he does not mind, since
     he wants to get back to his buddies. Yosé has in mind a second
     shutting up and says there should be no inspection, for if he is
     found a leper, he is then confirmed as such and isolated from
     everybody except his wife.]

D.   *Is that to say that sexual relations [in Rabbi's view] are permitted to a per-*
     son who is confirmed unclean with the skin ailment?

E.   *Yes indeed, for so it has been taught on Tannaite authority:*

F.   **"And he will dwell outside his tent" (Lev. 14:8)—**

G.   **he is prohibited from having sexual relations, for "His**
     tent" (Lev. 14:8)—his tent means only his wife, as it
     is said, "Return to your tents" (II Kings 15:1) [Sifra
     CL:I.4].

H.   **R. Judah says, "'And after he is cleaned they shall**
     reckon for him seven days' (Ez. 44:26)—that is while
     he is counting seven clean days, but not while he is
     confirmed as unclean with the skin ailment."

I.   **R. Yosé b. R. Judah says, "If he is prohibited during**
     the days of his counting, all the more so is he to be
     prohibited during the days when he is completely
     unclean."

J.   **Said R. Hiyya, "I said before Rabbi, 'You have taught**
     us, our lord, that Jothan was born to Uzziah [2 Kgs.
     15:5] only during the days when he was certified
     unclean'" [T. Neg. 8:6].

K.   He said to him, "Yeah, that's just what I said."

L.   *What is at issue between them?*

M.   *R. Yosé b. R. Judah takes the view that the All-Merciful has made it explic-*
     it that during the days of his counting out [clean days] ["shall dwell
     outside his tent,"] and all the more so should he not have sexual relations
     when he is confirmed as unclean with the skin ailment.

N.   *Rabbi takes the position is that what Scripture has articulated is to be taken*
     as fact, and what has not to be explicitly articulated is not to be imputed.

4.   A.   *Does that position of Raba stated earlier [In the case of someone who is now*
          assumed to be clean, all parties concur that he is not subject to an examina-
          tion at all during the intermediate days of the festival. In the case of some-
          one who has been shut up for the first week, all parties concur that he is
          examined. Where there is a disagreement, it concerns One authority [Meir]
          takes the view that we leave the decision to the priest's discretion, so that if
          the person is clean, he declares him clean, but if he looks unclean, the priest
          shuts his mouth, while the other authority invokes the verse, 'this is the law

of the plague and the skin ailment, to make a pronouncement of clean or unclean' (Lev. 13:59),] *bear the implication that the postponement of a decision on the cultic status of the person depends on the priest's discretion?*

B. *Yes indeed, for so it has been taught on Tannaite authority:*

C. "And on the day" (Lev. 13:14)—there is a day on which you inspect him, and there is a day on which you do not inspect him.

D. In this connection they have said: **A bridegroom on whom a plague appeared—they give him the seven days of the marriage feast [before inspecting him], him, and his house, and his garment. And so with respect to the festival: they give him all the seven days of the festival [M. Neg. 3:2],** the words of R. Judah.

E. **Rabbi says, "Lo it says, 'And the priest will command that they empty the house before the priest goes in to see the plague, that all that is in the house not be made unclean' (Lev. 14:36).**

F. **"If they wait for an optional matter, should they not wait for a required matter?" [Sifra CXXXIV:I.1-2]**

G. *What is at issue between them?*

H. Said Abbayye, "The implications of the exegesis of Scripture is what is at issue between them."

I. *And Raba said, "The disposition of an optional matter is what is at issue between them. And R. Judah does not derive the rule from the verse cited by Rabbi [Lev. 14:36], because that is an anomaly, for, in any event,* **[8A]** *wood and stone in general do not contract uncleanness, while here they contract uncleanness. Rabbi for his part says that the verse is required [not for the purpose cited by Judah but for another purpose,] for had Scripture written,* 'and on the day when raw flesh shall be seen in him' *alone, I might have supposed that one may postpone inspection only in connection with carrying out a religious duty but not in the case of an optional matter, so the All-Merciful has already said,* 'And the priest shall command.' *And if the All-Merciful had said only,* 'And the priest shall command that they empty the house,' *I might have supposed that that is in the case of these matters because uncleanness does not affect a human being, but in a case in which the uncleanness affects a human being, I might have supposed that the priest has to inspect him without delay. So both verses are required."*

5. A. *The master has said:* "And on the day" (Lev. 13:14)—there is a day on which you inspect him, and there is a day on which you do not inspect him. *How does the cited verse yield this conclusion?*

B. *Said Abbayye, "If the verse yielded no such conclusion, the All-Merciful could as well have written,* 'on the day.' *Why say,* 'and on the day'? *That yields the conclusion that there is a day on which you inspect him, and there is a day on which you do not inspect him."*

C. *Raba said, "The whole of the verse is redundant, for otherwise Scripture could have said,* 'and when raw flesh is seen in him.' *Why add,* 'and on a day'? *That yields the conclusion that there is a day on which you* inspect him, and there is a day on which you do not inspect him."

D. *And Abbayye?*

E. *That is required to indicate,* by day and not by night.

F. *And how does Raba know that it is to be* by day and not by night?

G. *He derives that fact from the following:* "According to everything that the priest sees" (Lev. 13:12) [which is to say, by day, when people can see properly].

H. *And Abbayye?*

I. *That is required to exclude from the inspection process a priest who is blind in one eye.*

J. *And does not Raba require the verse to make this point as well?*

K. *True enough.*

L. *Then how does he know that it is to be* by day but not by night?

M. *He derives it from the verse,* "Like as a plague was seen by me in the house" (Lev. 14:35)—by me, not with the help of a lamp.

N. *And Abbayye?*

O. *If the rule derived from there, I might have supposed that the restriction applies when the uncleanness does not affect a person's body, but where uncleanness affects the body, I might have supposed that one may inspect it by a lamp. So the original proof-text is the better one.*

I.1 complements the Mishnah's ruling with further relevant data, and Nos. 2, 3, 4 (reverting to No. 2), and 5 form a talmud to the foregoing.

Mishnah/Bavli tractate Moed Qatan 1:5C–G

C. **And further did R. Meir say, "[On the intermediate days of the festival] a man may go out and gather the bones of his father and his mother,**

D. **"because it is a time of rejoicing for him."**

E. **R. Yosé says, "It is a time of mourning for him."**

F. **A person may not call for mourning for his deceased,**

G. **or make a lamentation for him thirty days before a festival.**

Our first inquiry concerns the harmony of the law. We see here that the intersecting rule need not occur in another Mishnah-paragraph. The item before us is in the same Hebrew as the Mishnah's rule, but does not bear an explicit indicator of Tannaite origin or formulation; the language forms the taxic indicator.

I.1

A. **"because it is a time of rejoicing for him:"**

B. *An objection was raised on the basis of the following:*

C. He who collects the bones of his mother and father for secondary burial—lo, one observes mourning for them all that day. But in the evening he no longer observes mourning for them. And in that connection said R. Hisda, "Even if he had them tied up in a sheet."

D. *Said Abbaye, "Say the rule as follows: 'because the rejoicing of the festival affects him.'"*

Clarification of the Mishnah's language forms the purpose of the treatment of the next clause of the Mishnah:

II.1

A. **A person may not call for mourning for his deceased:**

B. *What is the sense of* **may not call for mourning for his deceased***?*

C. *Said Rab, "In the West, when a professional lamenter comes around, people say, 'Let everybody of mournful spirit weep with him.'"*

III.1

A. **or make a lamentation for him thirty days before a festival:**

B. *What distinguishes the spell of* **thirty days***?*

C. Said R. Kahana said R. Judah said Rab, "There was the case of someone who saved money to go up to Jerusalem for the festival, and the professional mourner came along and stood at the door of his house, and his wife took the money and handed it over to him, so he never got to go up. At that moment they said, a **person may not call for mourning for his deceased, or make a lamentation for him thirty days before a festival**."

D. And Samuel said, **[8B]** "It is because for at least thirty days, the deceased is not put out of mind."

E. What is at issue between them?

F. At issue between them is where the professional mourner does it for nothing.

I.1 harmonizes Tannaite rules on the same subject. **II.1** clarifies the facts to which the Mishnah's rule makes reference. **III.1** explains what is at issue in the rule of the Mishnah.

MISHNAH/BAVLI TRACTATE MOED QATAN 1:6

A. **They do not hew out a tomb niche or tombs on the intermediate days of a festival.**

B. **But they refashion tomb niches on the intermediate days of a festival.**
C. **They dig a grave on the intermediate days of a festival,**
D. **and make a coffin,**
E. **while the corpse is in the same courtyard.**
F. **R. Judah prohibits, unless there were boards [already sawn and made ready in advance].**

Not surprisingly, we commence with the explanation of the language of the Mishnah:

I.1

A. *What are* **tomb niches** *and what are* **tombs***?*
B. Said R. Judah, "Tomb niches are formed by digging, and tombs are formed by building."
C. *So too it has been taught on Tannaite authority:*
D. What are tomb niches and what are tombs? Tomb niches are formed by digging, and tombs are formed by building.

We proceed to a secondary amplification of the Mishnah's rule: information required for full comprehension of the Mishnah's statement.

II.1

A. **But they refashion tomb niches on the intermediate days of a festival:**
B. How do they refashion them?
C. Said R. Judah, "If it was too long, they may shorten it."
D. *In a Tannaite formulation it is set forth:* **One makes it broader or longer [T. Moed 1:8A-B].**

Once more we address the word-choices of the Mishnah.

III.1

A. **They dig a grave on the intermediate days of a festival:**
B. *What is* **a grave***?*
C. Said R. Judah, "It is a small hollow creek" [Lazarus].
D. But has it not been taught on Tannaite authority: **...a grave and a small hollow... [cf. T. Moed 1:8C].**
E. {That does not mean they are the same thing, for] said Abbayye, and some say, R. Kahana, *"They relate as do a [Lazarus:] trough and a little trough."*

The next clause of the Mishnah is amplified by appeal to a Tannaite formulation, external to the Mishnah and entirely cogent with it:

IV.1

    A.   **and make a coffin, while the corpse is in the same court-yard:**

    B.   *We have a Tannaite formulation along these same lines in that which our rabbis have taught on Tannaite authority:*

    C.   They do all that is needed for the deceased, cutting the hair, washing his garment, making a box of boards out of boards that had been cut prior to the festival.

    D.   Rabban Simeon b. Gamaliel says, "They may even bring lumber and, in the privacy of one's house, cut it to size."

I.1 explains the meaning of words in the Mishnah. **II.1** amplifies the sense of the Mishnah's statement. **III.1** produces a relevant Tannaite complement.

MISHNAH/BAVLI TRACTATE MOED QATAN 1:7-8

1:7

    A.   **They do not take wives on the intermediate days of a festival,**

    B.   **whether virgins or widows.**

    C.   **Nor do they enter into levirate marriage,**

    D.   **for it is an occasion of rejoicing for the groom.**

    E.   **But one may remarry his divorced wife.**

    F.   **And a woman may prepare her wedding adornments on the intermediate days of a festival.**

    G.   **R. Judah says, "She should not use lime, since this makes her ugly."**

MISHNAH/BAVLI TRACTATE MOED QATAN 1:8

    A.   **An unskilled person sews in the usual way.**

    B.   **But an expert craftsman sews with irregular stitches.**

    C.   **They weave the ropes for beds.**

    D.   **R. Yosé says, "They [only] tighten them."**

Here, the clarification of the Mishnah's rule is substantive, not linguistic. That is to say, the stance of the commentator now is external to the text, and the commentator wants to know why the Mishnah finds self-evident what is not necessarily obvious to all parties:

I.1

    A.   *So if it's* **an occasion of rejoicing for the groom,** *what's so bad about that?*

    B.   Said R. Judah said Samuel, and so said R. Eleazar said R. Oshaia, and some say, said R. Eleazar said R. Hanina, "The consideration is that one occasion of rejoicing should not be joined with another such occasion."

    C.   Rabbah bar R. Huna said, "It is because he neglects the rejoicing of the festival to engage in rejoicing over his wife."

    D.   Said Abbayye to R. Joseph, "This statement that has been said by Rabbah bar R. Huna belongs to Rab, for said R. Daniel bar Qattina said Rab, 'How on the basis of Scripture do we know that people may not take wives on the intermediate days of the festival? As it is said, "You shall rejoice in your feast" (Dt. 16:14), meaning, in your feast—not in your new wife.'"

    E.   Ulla said, "It is because it is excess trouble."

    F.   R. Isaac Nappaha said, "It is because one will neglect the requirement of being fruitful and multiplying" [if people postponed weddings until festivals, they might somehow diminish the occasion for procreation, which is the first obligation]."

    G.   *An objection was raised:* All those of whom they have said that they are forbidden to wed on the festival **[9A]** are permitted to wed on the eve of the festival. *Now this poses a problem to the explanations of all the cited authorities!*

    H.   *There is no problem from the perspective of him who has said,* "The consideration is that one occasion of rejoicing should not be joined with another such occasion," *for the main rejoicing of the wedding is only a single day.*

    I.   *And from the perspective of him who has said,* "It is because it is excess trouble," *the principal bother lasts only one day.*

    J.   *And from the perspective of him who has said,* "It is because one will neglect the requirement of being fruitful and multiplying," *for merely one day someone will not postpone the obligation for any considerable length of time.*

The foregoing has taken for granted a principle not contained in the Mishnah, and we now find a scriptural basis for not the Mishnah but that ancillary principle:

2.   A.   *And how on the basis of Scripture do we know that* one occasion of rejoicing should not be joined with another such occasion?

    B.   *It is in line with that which has been written:* "So Solomon made the feast at that time and all Israel with him, a great congregation from the entrance of Hamath to the Brook of Egypt, before the Lord our God seven days and seven days, even fourteen days" (1 Kgs. 8:65). *Now if it were permitted to join one occasion of rejoicing with another such occasion, he should have postpone the celebration of the consecration of the Temple until the Festival and should then have held it for seven days concurrently, for both the Festival and the consecration [rather than celebrating the occasions sequentially].*

C. *Well, maybe the rule means only that one should not deliberately postpone a wedding until the festival, but where it just happens to work out that way, we may nonetheless hold the wedding on the festival?*

D. *Well, if that were the case, then he should have left unfinished some small detail of the building of the house of the sanctuary?*

E. *We do not leave over some small detail in the building of the Temple!*

F. *He could have left off a cubit of the scarecrow's parapet!*

G. The scarecrow's parapet was an essential part of the Temple.

H. *Rather, in point of fact the cited formulation of Scripture leaves a redundancy.* For it says "fourteen days," so why go and say also, "Seven days and seven days"? *That yields the simple fact that the two sets of seven days were kept distinct from one another [each marking its own occasion for rejoicing].*

What follows stands on its own feet and can be fully understood without reference to the foregoing. The sole issue is why it has been inserted at all, and the answer is clear as soon as the question is asked, so we have a composition that is used to provide a talmud to a talmud:

3. A. Said R. Parnakh said R. Yohanan, "In that year, the Israelites did not observe the Day of Atonement, so they worried, saying, 'Perhaps Israel has become subject to extinction. An echo came forth and said to them, 'You all are singled out for the life of the world to come.'"

B. *What was the exegesis that led them to that concern?*

C. They thought along these lines: "It is a matter a fortiori. For if in the case of the tabernacle, which was sanctified not for all time [but only for an interval], the offering of an individual [presented on the occasion of the consecration of the tabernacle, Num. 7] overrode the restriction of the Sabbath, which ordinarily represents a prohibition the violation of which is penalized by stoning, then in the case of the sanctuary, the sanctification of which is for all time, all the more so should it be permitted to present an offering in behalf of the community and the Day of Atonement, which are subject to the penalty merely of extirpation, all the more so [should it be permitted to present offerings in behalf of the individual]!" *So what were they worried about?*

D. *[Reference is made to the private offerings presented by the heads of the tribes as individuals, Num. 7:] there, in that earlier case, the offerings were presented to meet the requirements of the Most High [since the burnt offerings and sin offerings yielded no meat for the people, and the sin offerings yielded meat only to the male priests], while here the offerings were presented to meet the requirements of common folk [since there were peace offerings for everybody's pleasure].*

E. *Well, here too, they could have made the offering, without eating the meat or drinking.*

F. There is no such thing as celebration without eating and drinking.

4. A. *And how do we know that the consecration of the tabernacle overrode the restrictions of the Sabbath? Should I say because it is written, "On the first day...on the seventh day so and so offered...," [at at Num. 7:12, 18, 42? But maybe that means only, the seventh day in sequence of offerings [but not the Sabbath]!*

B. Said R. Nahman bar Isaac, "Said Scripture, 'On the day of the eleventh day' (Num. 7:72)—just as a day is consecutive, so all the eleven days were consecutive [encompassing the Sabbath, without skipping]."

C. *But perhaps reference is made to days that ordinarily were suitable for such private offerings?*

D. *There is yet another verse of Scripture that pertains:* "On the day of the twelfth day" (Num. 7:78)— just as a day is consecutive, so all the twelve days were consecutive [encompassing the Sabbath, without skipping].

E. *But perhaps here too reference is made to days that ordinarily were suitable for such private offerings?*

F. *If that were the sense, why do I need two distinct verses to make the same point?*

5. A. *And how do we know that the consecration of the tabernacle overrode the restrictions of the Day of Atonement? Should I say because it is written, "...even fourteen days"?*

B. *But perhaps reference is made to days that ordinarily were suitable for such private offerings?*

C. *We draw a verbal analogy based on the common usage of "day" in that other context.*

6. A. "An echo came forth and said to them, 'You all are singled out for the life of the world to come:'"

B. How do we know that they were forgiven?

C. *It is in line with what Tahalipa taught as a Tannaite statement:*

D. "'On the eighth day he sent the people home and they blessed the king and went to their own tents joyful and glad of heart for all the goodness that the Lord had shown to David his servant and to Israel his people' (1 Kgs. 8:66)—

E. "'to their own tents;' they went and found their wives in a state of cleanness suitable for sexual relations.

F. "'joyful:' for they had feasted on the splendor of God's presence;

G. "'and glad of heart:' for the wife of every one of them became pregnant with a male child.

H. "'for all the goodness:' for an echo came forth and said to them, 'You all are singled out for the life of the world to come.'"

7. A. "to David his servant and to Israel his people:"

B. *Now there is no problem understanding the reference to Israel, his people, since the sin of violating the Day of Atonement was forgiven them. But what is the meaning of the reference to David his servant?*

C. Said R. Judah said Rab, "When Solomon had built the house of the sanctuary, he tried to bring the ark into the house of the Holy of Holies. The gates cleaved to one another. He recited twenty-four prayers [Freedman, p. 734, n. 4: in 2 Chr. 6 words for prayer, supplication and hymn occur twenty-four times], but was not answered.

D. "He said, 'Lift up your head, O you gates, and be lifted up, you everlasting doors, and the King of glory shall come in. Who is this King of glory? The Lord strong and might, the Lord mighty in battle' (Ps. 24:7ff.).

E. "And it is further said, 'Lift up your heads, O you gates even lift them up, you everlasting doors/ (Ps. 24:7).

F. "But he was not answered.

G. "When he said, 'Lord God, turn not away the face of your anointed, remember the mercies of David, your servant'(2 Chr. 6:42), forthwith he was answered.

H. "At that moment the faces of David's enemies turned as black as the bottom of a pot, for all Israel knew that the Holy One, blessed be he, had forgiven him for that sin."

8. A. *R. Jonathan b. Asemai and R. Judah, son of proselytes, repeated the Tannaite presentation of the laws of vows at the household of R. Simeon b. Yohai and took their leave of him by night, but the next morning they came, and again they took their leave of him. He said to them, "But did you not take leave of me last night?"*

B. *They said to him, "But did you not take leave of me last night?"*

C. They said to him, "You have taught us, our lord: 'A disciple who takes leave of his master but spends the night in that town has to take leave from him once again, in line with this verse: "On the eighth day he sent the people home and they blessed the king and went to their own tents joyful and glad of heart for all the goodness that the Lord had shown to David his servant and to Israel his people" (1 Kgs. 8:66); and then it is written, "And on the twenty-third day of the seventh month he sent the people away" (2 Chr. 7:10). Thus we learn that a disciple who takes leave of his master but spends the night in that town has to take leave from him once again.'"

9. A. *He said to his son, "My son, these men are men of standing. Go to them so that they will bestow their blessing on you."*

B.   *He went and found them contrasting verses one against the next, in
     the following way:* "It is written, 'Balance the path of your
     feet and let all your ways be established' (Prov. 4:26), and,
     by contrast, 'Lest you should balance the path of life'
     (Prov. 5:5). But there is no conflict between the advice of
     these two verses. The one speaks to a case in which a
     religious obligation can be carried out through someone
     else, the latter, a case in which the religious obligation can
     be carried out only by oneself."

C.   *They again went into session and raised questions along these lines:*
     "It is written, 'Wisdom is more precious than rubies, and all
     things you can desire are not to be compared to her'
     (Prov. 3:10), meaning that what Heaven wants of you are
     comparable to Wisdom [Lazarus: your own affairs and
     wishes are not comparable to the study of the Torah, but
     such pursuits as please Heaven are comparable to it], but
     it is written, 'And all things desirable are not to be com-
     pared with Wisdom' (Prov. 8:11), which means that what
     Heaven demands of you is comparable with her. And
     again, 'And all things desirable are not to be compared to
     her' (Prov. 8:12), meaning that even things that Heaven
     wants of you are not comparable to her [so study of Torah
     is supreme over all]. But there is no conflict between the
     advice of these two verses. The one speaks to a case in
     which a religious obligation can be carried out through
     someone else, the latter, a case in which the religious
     obligation can be carried out only by oneself."

D.   *They said to him, "What did you want here?"*

E.   *He said to them, "Father said to me, 'Go to them so that they may
     bestow their blessing on you.'"*

F.   *They said to him, "May it please God that you sow and not harvest,
     go in but not go out, go out but not go in; that your house be empty
     but your inn filled; that your table be upset and you not see a new
     year."*

G.   *When he got home, he said to his father, he said to him, "Not only
     did they not bless me, but they called down pain upon me!"*

H.   *He said to him, "So what did they say to you?"*

I.   *"Thus and so did they say to me!"*

J.   He said to him, "But all of their statements were blessings:

K.   *"'that you sow and not harvest:' that you father children and they not
     die;*

L.   *"'go in but not go out:' that you bring home daughters in law and
     your sons not die so that the wives do not have to depart from you;*

M.   *"'go out but not go in:' that you give your daughters in marriage and
     their husbands not die so that your daughters do not have to come back;*

N.   *"'that your house be empty but your inn filled:' this world is your inn,
     the other world is home, 'Their grave is their house for ever'*

(Ps. 49:12), reading not 'their inward thought' but 'their grave is their house for ever, and their dwelling places be for generations.'

O. *"'that your table be upset:' by sons and daughters;*

P. *"'and you not see a new year:' your wife should not die so you do not have to take a new wife."*

10. A. *R. Simeon b. Halapta took his leave of Rabbi. Said Rabbi to his son, "Go to him that he may bless you."*

B. *He said to him, "May it please God that you not put anybody to shame nor feel ashamed."*

C. *He came back to his father, who said to him, "What did he say to you?"*

D. *He said to him, "Oh, nothing out of the ordinary."*

E. *He said to him, "What he gave to you was the blessing that the Holy One, blessed be he, bestowed upon Israel two times: 'And you shall eat in plenty and be satisfied and shall praise the name of the Lord your God...and my people shall never be ashamed. And you shall know that I am in the midst of Israel, and that I am the Lord your God, and there is none else, and my people shall never be ashamed' (Joel 2:26-27)."*

We have completed our journey through one of those massive miscellanies that makes the Talmud appear to be run-on and aimless. We return to the Mishnah, and once more begin with a Tannaite complement to the Mishnah's statement. This one explicitly refers to the Mishnah and is formulated as an explanation of its rule.

II.1

A. **And a woman may prepare her wedding adornments on the intermediate days of a festival:**

B. *Our rabbis have taught on Tannaite authority:*

C. What are women's adornments: she may blue her eyes, curl her hair, trim her hair and nails, put on rouge, and some say, shave her sexual organs.

The next entry forms a case in illustration of the foregoing:

2. A. R. Hisda's wife made herself up in front of her daughter in law.

B. *In session before R. Hisda, R. Hina bar Hinnena said, "That rule applies only in the base of a girl. But as to a mature woman, that is not so."*

C.   He said to him, "By God! Even your mother, and even your mother's mother, and even if she is ready to fall into the grave!' *For people say, 'At sixty, at six,* [Lazarus:] *the sound of the timbrel makes her nimble.'"*

The treatment of the next clause of the Mishnah follows the plan of the foregoing. We note that a given Mishnah-paragraph may be split up into two or more clauses, and then the treatment of each clause in form will be identical with the presentation of the others, e.g., if we have a scriptural proof serving clause A, we shall have the same in sequence for clauses B, C, and D of the same Mishnah-paragraph; if we have a Tannaite complement to clause A, then the same will be given to the successive clauses. Not only so, but each of these will then be analyzed along the same formal lines, so that a single plan and program will dictate the treatment of successive clauses of the Mishnah-paragraph.

III.1

A.   **R. Judah says, "She should not use lime, since this makes her ugly:"**

B.   *It has been taught on Tannaite authority:*

C.   R. Judah says, "A woman should not put lime on her face on the intermediate days of a festival, since it makes her ugly." But R. Judah concedes that if the lime can be scraped off during the intermediate days of the festival, she may put it on during those same intermediate days, for **even though it is distressing to her now, she will be happy about it later**." [There is therefore a contradiction between the two rulings in Judah's name.]

D.   *But does R. Judah hold this view? And have we not learned in the Mishnah:* **Before the festivals of gentiles for three days it is forbidden to do business with them: (1) to lend anything to them or to borrow anything from them; (2) to lend money to them or to borrow money from them.; (3) to repay them or to be repaid by them. R. Judah says, "They accept repayment from them, because it is distressing to him." They said to him, "Even though it is distressing to him now, he will be happy about it later" [M. A.Z. 1:1]**?

E.   Said R. Nahman bar Isaac, "Forget about the laws of the intermediate days of the festival, for all of them fall into the category, '**Even though it is distressing to him now, he will be happy about it later**.'"

F.   *Rabina said, "As to a gentile, so far as getting repaid is concerned, it is always a source of anguish."*

2. A. Said R. Judah, "Israelite girls who reached puberty before they reach the normal age of maturity in years [twelve years and a day], if they are poor, may put on a lime-concoction; if they are rich, they put on fine flour; princesses put on oil of myrrh, as it is said, 'Six months with oil of myrrh' (Est. 2:12)."

3. A. "Six months with oil of myrrh" (Est. 2:12):

   B. *What is oil of myrrh?*

   C. R. Huna bar Hiyya said, "It is stacte."

   D. R. Jeremiah bar Abba said, "It is oil derived from olives not yet a third grown."

4. A. *It has been taught on Tannaite authority:*

   B. R. Judah says, "**[Olives for olive oil] from a manured field** refers to olives that are not a third grown. And why is it used for smearing? Because it serves as a depilatory and skin-softener."

   C. Why do they apply it? Because it removes hair and softens the skin.

5. A. *R. Bibi had a daughter with dark skin, on which he put that ointment limb by limb, and this produced for her a husband who had four hundred zuz.*

   B. *A gentile neighbor also had a daughter with dark skin, on which he put that ointment all at once, so she died.*

   C. *He said, "Bibi killed my daughter."*

   D. *Said R. Nahman, "R. Bibi drank beer, so his daughters needed ointments, but we don't drink beer, so our daughters don't need ointments."*

Now come several citations and amplifications of the language of the Mishnah, illustrating the point that a single plan and program, involving even a single formal construction, will address successive, free-standing phrases or clauses or sentences of the Mishnah:

IV.1

A. [10A] **An unskilled person sews in the usual way:**

B. *What is the definition of* **an unskilled person?**

C. At the household of R. Yannai they said, "It is anyone who cannot draw a needleful of stitches all at once."

D. R. Yosé bar Hanina said, "It is any that cannot sew an even seam on the hem of his shirt."

V.1

A. **But an expert craftsman sews with irregular stitches:**

B. *What does it mean to* **sew with irregular stitches?**

C. R. Yohanan said, "Overstepping."

D. *Rabbah bar Samuel said, "Dogs' teeth."*

VI.1

A. **They weave the ropes for beds. R. Yosé says, "They [only] tighten them:"**

B. *What defines* **weaving and tightening***?*

C. *When R. Dimi came, he said, "There was a dispute on this matter between R. Hiyya bar Abba and R. Assi, both of them speaking in the name of Hezekiah and R. Yohanan.*

D. "One said, 'Interlacing means interlacing warp and woof, and tightening means putting in the warp but not the woof.'

E. "And the other said, 'Interlacing means putting in the warp without the woof, and tightening means he tightens a girth cord if it becomes loose.'"

A talmud to the foregoing now commences:

F. *Is that so? But lo, R. Tahalipa bar Saul taught, "And they concur that they may not insert new cords to begin with." Now that poses no problem to him who maintains that the interlacing that is permitted is,* interlacing warp and woof, and tightening means putting in the warp but not the woof. *In line with that view, R. Tahalipa could say,* "And they concur that they may not insert new cords to begin with." *But from the perspective of him who has said,* Interlacing means putting in the warp without the woof, and tightening means he tightens a girth cord if it becomes loose, *what sense does R. Tahalipa b. Saul's statement make? If you maintain that* interlacing the warp and woof is forbidden, *is there any need to add that* they may not insert new cords to begin with?

G. *That's a problem.*

H. *Said R. Nahman bar Isaac to R. Hiyya bar Abin, "But is there anybody who takes the view that 'interlacing' means inserting a warp without the woof? Have we not learned in the Mishnah:* **R. Meir says, "The bed [becomes susceptible to uncleanness] when one will have knit together on it three rows [of the mesh of the underwebbing]" [M. Kel. 16:1F]***?"*

I. *Rather, when Rabin came, he said, "All concur that* interlacing involves both warp and woof. *Where there is a dispute, it concerns tightening. One master takes the view that* the tightening that is permitted means inserting the warp without the woof, *and the other master maintains that what is permitted is* tightening a cord that became loose."

J. *An objection was raised:*

K. "During the intermediate days of a festival they may interlace bed frames, and, it goes without say, they may be tightened," the words of R. Meir.

L. R. Yosé says, "They may be tightened but not interlaced."

M. Some say, "They may not tighten at all."

N.   *Now from the perspective of him who has said, "Tightening means inserting the warp without the woof,"* then there is a place for "some say" to dissent. *But from the perspective of him who says that tightening means tightening the cord that has become slack, then in the view of some say, will even this simple improvement not be allowed?*

O.   *Well, yes! For since it is possible to fill up the sag with bedding, we don't have to go to any more trouble than that during the intermediate days of the festival.*

I.1 provides a reason for the Mishnah's rule, and No. 2 then derives from Scripture the consideration that explains the Mishnah's rule. Nos. 3-6+7, 8-10, supplement No. 2, a run-on thematic anthology, each item tied to the foregoing. **II.1** complements the Mishnah with a Tannaite extension, and No. 2 follows suit. **III.1** harmonizes two rulings of the cited authority. No. 2, supplemented by Nos. 3, 4, 5, adds a thematic complement. **IV.1, V.1, VI.1** explain references in the Mishnah.

Mishnah/Bavli tractate Moed Qatan 1:9

A.   They set up an oven or double stove or a hand mill on the intermediate days of a festival.

B.   R. Judah says, "They do not rough the millstones [which are smooth and so not now usable for grinding grain] for the first time."

We begin once more with the analysis of words and phrases, then secondary development of the proposed lexical entry:

I.1

A.   *What is the meaning of* **rough***?*

B.   R. Judah said, "It means chiselling holes into the millstones [so that the grain may be milled]."

C.   R. Yehiel said, "It means fixing an eye hole [on the upper stone, through which the grain is poured in (Lazarus)]."

D.   *An objection was raised:* **"They set up an oven or double stove or a hand mill on the intermediate days of a festival,** on condition that the work is not completely finished," the words of R. Eliezer.

E.   And sages say, "It may even be finished."

F.   R. Judah says in his [Eliezer's] name, "They may set up a new one and roughen an old one."

G.   And some say, "They may not do any roughening at all."

H.   *Now from the perspective of him who says that "rough" means scoring the*

> *millstones, that explains why the process pertains also to an old mill [which*
> *has been smoothed through use], but from the perspective of him who says*
> *that it means fixing an eye hole, how does a used mill require fixing an*
> *eye hole [since it already has one]?*

I.   *It would involve, for example, one that requires widening a bit more.*

2.   A.   *R. Huna heard somebody scraping millstones during the intermediate days*
          of a festival . He said, "May the person of him who profanes the inter-
          mediate days of the festival be profaned."

     B.   *He then takes the position of* "some say [They may not do any
          roughening at all]."

3.   A.   R. Hama presented this exposition: "On the intermediate days
          of the festival, people may roughen millstones."

     B.   In the name of R. Meir one said, "On the intermediate days
          of the festival one may even trim the hooves of a horse on
          which he rides or an ass on which he rides, **[10B]** *but one may*
          not do so to the ass who turns the mill."

     C.   *R. Judah permitted trimming the hooves of the ass that turns the mill, setting*
          up a mill, building a mill, constructing a base for the mill, and building
          a stable for horses.

     D.   *Rab permitted currying horses, constructing a bed, or making a mattress*
          box.

4.   A.   *During the intermediate days of a festival Raba permitted bleeding cattle.*

     B.   *Said to him Abbayye, "In support of your position it has been taught on*
          Tannaite authority: During the intermediate days of a festival they
          may bleed cattle and they do not withhold any means of heal-
          ing from an animal."

5.   A.   *Raba permitted softening carded sheets of cloth.*

     B.   *How come?*

     C.   *It is a process that can be carried out by unskilled labor.*

     D.   *Said R. Isaac bar Ammi said R. Hisda, "It is forbidden to pleat sleeve ends*
          [Lazarus]. *How come? Because that is a process that can be carried out*
          only by skilled labor."

What follows is a set of rules in the name of a single authority,
all of them complementary to the rule of the Mishnah-paragraph
before us; and all of them are understood in their own terms. The
composition has been worked out for its own purpose, then inserted here because it serves the purpose of the framers of the
document. In this context, the composition functions as does a
Tannaite complement to the Mishnah: it is not analytical, but it
also is not paraphrastic. It both stands on its own and also enriches our grasp of the law of the Mishnah. In our catalogue of
types of Mishnah-commentary, this item finds no place; but in
our grasp of how the Bavli overall constitutes a commentary to

the Mishnah, this item is of exemplary value and critical importance:

6. A. *Said Raba, "One who levels the ground, if it is with the purpose in mind of evening the slope of the threshing floor, that is permitted; if it is with the purpose in mind of leveling the soil, it is forbidden.*

   B. *"How so? If he takes up the heaped up soil to heap on soil, or hard soil to lay on hard soil, that indicates that the purpose is to improve the threshing floor. But if he takes heaped up soil and puts it on hard soil, that shows it is to improve the ground."*

7. A. *And said Raba, "Someone who collects chips of wood in his field, if it is with gathering fire wood in mind, it is permitted; if it is with clearing the ground in mind, it is forbidden.*

   B. *"How so? If he picks up big pieces and leaves little ones, that shows that it is with the purpose of gathering fire wood; if he picks up both the big and little pieces, this shows that he has in mind to clear the field."*

8. A. *And said Raba, "Someone who opens sluices to let water run off into the field, if it be with the purpose in mind of collecting the fish, it is permitted; if it is to irrigate the field, it is forbidden.*

   B. *"How so? If he opens two flood gates, one above, the other below, that proves it is to collect the fish; but if it is only one gate, that is with the purpose in mind of irrigating the field."*

9. A. *And said Raba, "Someone who trims his palm, if it is with the purpose of getting food for his animals, it is permitted. If it is to benefit the palm, it is forbidden.*

   B. *"How so? If he trims only one side, this shows that it is with the need of his cattle that he trims the palm; if he trims both sides, it is to benefit the palm and the act is forbidden on the intermediate dates of the festival."*

10. A. *And said Raba, "Unripe tuhalani-dates may be picked but not pressed."*

    B. *R. Pappa said, "But if they were getting rotten, then it is like a business deal that would involve a loss if one does not carry it out on the intermediate days of a festival and they may be pressed during the intermediate days of a festival."*

11. A. *And said Raba, "Any sort of business deal is forbidden [on the intermediate days of a festival."*

    B. Said R. Yosé bar Abin, "But with regard to a deal that, if not carried out right away, may go sour, it is permitted."

When we come to a set of cases, e.g., practical decisions or illustrations of the rule by appeal to actions of a major authority, we know we near the end of the composite assigned to a given clause of the Mishnah. Here is a fine instance:

12. A. *Rabina had a deal that would have produced six thousand zuz; he put it off until after the festival and sold the same at twelve thousand.*

13. A. *Rabina lent some money to people from Aqra deShanuta. He asked R. Ashi and said, "What about going over there now [during the intermediate days*

of the festival]?"

B.   *He said to him, "Since just now they have the ready cash but some other day they may not put their hands on it, it falls into the category of* a deal that, if not carried out right away, may go sour, *so it is permitted."*

C.   *It has been taught on Tannaite authority along these same lines with regard to dealing with idolators:* **[Israelites] may go** [11A] **to a fair of gentiles and buy from them beasts, slave-boys and slave-girls, houses, fields, and vineyards, and write deeds and deposit them in their archives, because thereby what one does is rescue [property] from their hands.**

14. A.   *Rab permitted Hiyya bar Ashi to repair basket traps during the intermediate days of a festival.*

B.   *How come?*

C.   This is unskilled work.

D.   *But mending mesh nets if forbidden.*

E.   *How come?*

F.   This is skilled work.

15. A.   *R. Judah permitted Ammi the oven maker to build up ovens, and Rabbah bar Ashbi to plait sieves.*

B.   *Is that so? But did not Rabbah bar Samuel repeat as a Tannaite formulation,* "And they concur that they do not build up an oven to begin with"*?*

C.   There is no contradiction, the former ruling applies during the dry season, the latter during the rainy season [Passover, Tabernacles, respectively; in the former period the clay dries quickly and the oven can be used right away, but in the latter festival the rain delays the hardening process, so the oven will not be available right away (Lazarus)].

I.1 defines the principal word of a Mishnah-sentence. No. 2 provides a case illustrative of the rule. Nos. 3-15 supplement the foregoing composite.

Mishnah/Bavli tractate Moed Qatan 1:10

A.   They make a parapet for a roof or a porch in an unskilled manner,

B.   but not in the manner of a skilled craftsman.

C.   They plaster cracks and smooth them down with a roller, by hand, or by foot, but not with a trowel.

D.   A hinge, socket, roof beam, lock, or key, [any of] which broke

E.   do they repair on the intermediate days of the festival,

F.   so long as one had not [earlier on] had the intention to [postpone the work so as to] do work on it on the intermediate days of the festival.

G.   And all pickled foods which a man can eat during the intermediate days of a festival he also may pickle.

The starting-point, predictably, is explanation of words and phrases:

I.1

A.   [**They make a parapet for a roof or a porch in an unskilled manner, but not in the manner of a skilled craftsman**:] *What is the definition of* **an unskilled manner?**

B.   *Said R. Joseph, "With* [Lazarus:] *a hurdle made of twigs and daphne stakes."*

D.   *In a Tannaite statement it was set forth:* one piles up pebbles but does not hold them down with mortar.

Mishnah-criticism moves forward, in the following, with a reductio ad absurdum, yielding a clarification of the sense of the Mishnah's language:

II.1

A.   **They plaster cracks and smooth them down with a roller, by hand, or by foot, but not with a trowel:**

B.   *Now if it is permitted to use a roller to flatten it down, is there any question that one may do so by hand or by foot?*

C.   *This is the sense of the statement:* They may plaster crevices and flatten down the plaster as with a roller, by hand or by foot, but not with ramming tools.

Words and phrases having been clarified, we proceed to the contradiction between our rule and an intersecting one, and of course the harmonization of the conflict; then the item bears in its wake a talmud of its own.

III.1

A.   **A hinge, socket, roof beam, lock, or key, [any of] which broke do they repair on the intermediate days of the festival, so long as one had not [earlier on] had the intention to [postpone the work so as to] do work on it on the intermediate days of the festival:**

B.   *An objection was raised:* **Yohanan the High Priest [John Hyrcanus]: until his time, hammers would pound [work was done] in Jerusalem [during the intermediate days of**

Passover and Sukkot] [M. M.S. 5:15C]. *The meaning then is,* **until his time** *but not afterward!*

C.   *There is no contradiction. There reference is made to the hammer of a smith, here, it is to the joiner's mallet [which is permitted].*

     D.   *Objected R. Hisda, "Then some will say that a loud noise is forbidden, but a soft one permitted."*

     E.   *Rather, said R. Hisda, "There still is no contradiction: The tool that may be used is a bill hook, the other is an adze"* [Lazarus's translations of the substantives].

     F.   R. Pappa said, "The one speaks of the period prior to the decree, the other, afterward."

     G.   *R. Ashi said, "The one represents the position of R. Judah, the other R. Yosé. For said R. Isaac bar Abdimi, 'Who is the Tannaite authority who takes the view that one has to perform in an extraordinary manner an act that is permitted in a matter in which considerable loss is going to be incurred by postponement? It is not in accord with R. Yosé.'"*

     H.   *Said Rabina, "In accord with whom do we these days deem permitted in the intermediate days of a festival the raising of [Lazarus:] pivot cups of doors? It is in accord with R. Yosé."*

Where, as in the following, we are given a case illustrative of the Mishnah's rule, there will be no prior clarification of the Mishnah, e.g., a commentary on its sources, language, or authorities:

IV.1

     A.   **And all pickled foods which a man can eat during the intermediate days of a festival he also may pickle:**

     B.   *At Luba on the Badita Canal everybody went fishing and caught some [at Passover, when fish are abundant], and Raba permitted them to salt them.*

     C.   *Said to him Abbayye, "But lo, we have learned in the Mishnah:* **And all pickled foods which a man can eat during the intermediate days of a festival he also may pickle***!"*

     D.   *He said to him, "Since to begin with they caught them with eating them in mind, and if they leave them, they will rot, it falls into the category of* a deal that, if not carried out right away, may go sour, *so it is permitted."*

     E.   *There are those who report the case in this way:*

     F.   *Raba permitted them to go trapping. They went and brought in the fish and salted them.*

     G.   *Said to him Abbayye, "But lo, we have learned in the Mishnah:* **And all pickled foods which a man can eat during the intermediate days of a festival he also may pickle***!"*

     H.   *He said to him, "These too may be eaten if they are pressed."*

     I.   That is in line with the case of Samuel, when they pressed fish in salt sixty times, and he ate it.

2.   A.   *Raba visited the household of the exilarch. They made for him fish pressed sixty times, and he ate it.*

3.   A.   *Rab visited Bar Shappir, and they set before him a fish that was boiled a third, salted a third, and broiled a third. Said Rab, "Adda the fisherman told me that a fish is best just when it is going to turn putrid."*

        B.   *And said Raba, "Said to me Adda the Fisherman, 'Broil the fish with its brother [salt], put it into its father [water], eat it with its son [sauce], and wash it down with its father [water].'"*

        C.   *And said Raba, "Said to me Adda the Fisherman, 'After eating fish, fill our belly with cress and milk, don't lie down.'"*

        D.   *And said Raba, "Said to me Adda the Fisherman, 'After eating fish, cress and milk, drink water not fermented date-juice, or that but not wine.'"*

I.1, II.1 clarifies the sense of the Mishnah's statements, and **III.1** then harmonizes the implications of this Mishnah's rule with those of another. **IV.1** refines the application of the law, and Nos. 2, 3 then provide an appendix to the foregoing. I discern nothing new in Bavli Moed Qatan Chapter Two, so proceed directly to Chapter Three. Here my cuts are fairly drastic, but the main points make their appearance.

MISHNAH/BAVLI TRACTATE MOED QATAN 3:1-2
3:1

A. Who are they who may get a hair cut on the intermediate days of a festival?

B. (1) he who comes from overseas or from captivity;

C. (2) and he who goes forth from prison;

D. (3) and he whose excommunication has been lifted by sages.

E. (4) And so too: he who sought absolution from a sage [for release from a vow not to get a haircut] and was released;

F. and the Nazirite [Num. 6:5] or a person afflicted with the skin ailment [Lev. 14:8-9] who emerges from his state of uncleanness to his state of cleanness.

3:2

A. And who are they who may wash their clothes on the intermediate days of a festival?

B. (1) he who comes from overseas or from captivity;

C. (2) and he who goes forth from prison;

D. [14A] (3) and he whose excommunication has been lifted by sages.

E. (4) And so too: he who sought absolution from a sage [for release from a vow not to wash clothes] and was released.

F. (1) Hand towels, (2) barber's towels, and (3) bath towels [may be washed].

G. (1) Male and (2) female Zabs, (3) women in their men-
    strual period, (4) women after childbirth, and all who go
    up from a state of uncleanness to cleanness,
H. lo, these are permitted [to wash their clothes].
I. But all other people are prohibited.

Here is another Mishnah-commentary that asks about the operative considerations that dictate the rule of the Mishnah. The case
at hand invokes a rule in another passage of the Mishnah to explain the one at hand:

I.1

A. *What is the reason that all other classifications of persons are forbidden to do so?*
B. *It is in line with that which we have learned in the Mishnah:* **Members of
    the priestly watch and members of the public delegation
    [presence] are prohibited to get a haircut and to wash
    their clothes. But on Thursday they are permitted to do
    so, because of the honor owing to the Sabbath [M. Taanit
    2:7B-C].**
C. *And said Rabbah bar bar Hanna said R. Eleazar, "What is the operative con-
    sideration that allows them to do on Thursday?* It is so that they should not
    enter in a condition of slovenliness their membership on the priestly
    watch. *Here too, the operative consideration is that* they not enter the
    festival in a slovenly condition."

The free-standing theoretical inquiry that follows is utilized for
the extension of the principle set forth by the Mishnah's rule:

2. A. *R. Zira raised this question: "If someone lost something on the eve of a festival,
        [what is the law about getting a haircut or washing clothes on the intermediate
        days of the festival]? Since it was under constraint that he could not have done
        so prior to the festival, he may get a haircut or wash clothes on the festival? Or
        perhaps, since the reason is not compelling, he may not do so?"*
    B. Said Abbayye, "Well, people would say, 'While all Syrian loaves are
        forbidden, Syrian loaves of Boethus are permitted' [so we'd better
        not discriminate, lest people get the wrong idea]."
    C. *Yeah, well, from your reasoning, lo,* said R. Assi said R. Yohanan, "Any-
        one who has only a single garment may wash it during the festival
        week,"—there too, won't people say, "While all Syrian loaves are
        forbidden, Syrian loans of Boethus are permitted"?
    D. *Well, in fact it has been stated in this connection:* said Mar bar R. Ashi, "The
        man's loin cloth shows the facts of the matter [that is, that's all he's
        got]."
3. A. *R. Ashi repeated the same matter in this way: 'R. Zira raised this ques-*

tion: "If a craftsman lost something on the eve of the festival, do we say that, since he is a craftsman, the reason that, on the festival, he is permitted to get a haircut or wash his clothes is self-evident, or since the reason is not going to be so self-evident as in the cases mentioned in the Mishnah, he may not get a haircut or wash his clothes during the intermediate days of the festival?""

B.   *In that form, the question must stand.*

The harmonization of conflict will take the form of the comparison of rules of diverse authorities on the same matter. In what follows, the Mishnah's rule is set side by side with a rule in the name of a given authority, and then the conflict is underlined and explained.

3:1-2/II.1

A.   **Who are they who may get a hair cut on the intermediate days of a festival? (1) he who comes from overseas or from captivity…:**

B.   *Our Mishnah-paragraph's rule is not in accord with the position of R. Judah. For it has been taught on Tannaite authority:* **R. Judah says, "One who comes home from overseas may not get haircuts during the intermediate days of the festival, because he went abroad at such a season without the permission of sages [who would have told him to go after the festival, so as to avoid this situation]"** [T. Moed 2:2G].

C.   Said Raba, "If he went out merely to sightsee, all parties concur that he is forbidden. If he went out to make a living, all parties concur that he is permitted. They differ only if he made the trip just to make money. *One authority invokes the analogy of going sight seeing, the other, of going to make a living."*

D.   An objection was raised: **Said Rabbi, "The opinion of R. Judah makes more sense to me in a case in which one has not gotten permission from sages to go abroad, and that of sages makes more sense in a case in which he has gotten permission from sages to go abroad"** [T. Moed 2:2I]. *Now what does* **in which one has not gotten permission from sages** *mean? If I should say that it means to go sightseeing, have you not said,* all parties concur that he is forbidden? *And could it then mean to make a living? But have you not said,* all parties concur that he is permitted? *So it is obvious that it means just to make money.*

E.   *But then I invoke the concluding clause:* **and that of sages makes more sense in a case in which he has gotten permission from sages to go abroad!** *Now what could "with permission" mean here? If I should say that it means to make a living, have you not said,* all parties concur that he is permitted? *And might it be just to make money? But have you* *not said,* **The opinion of R. Judah makes more sense to me in a case in which one has not gotten permission from sages to go abroad**?

F.   *This is the sense of the statement at hand:* The opinion of R. Judah makes more sense than that of rabbis when he went forth without permission, *and what circumstance might that involve? It is for sightseeing. For sages only differed from R. Judah when it comes to making money. But as to merely sightseeing, they concur with R. Judah.* And the opinion of rabbis seems to make more sense than R. Judah's when he went forth with permission, *and what might that involve? It would be for making a living, for even R. Judah differed with rabbis only when it was to make money. But as to going abroad to make a living, he concurs with them.*

A secondary issue is attached to the Mishnah, showing applications of the rule to unanticipated cases:

2.   A.   Said Samuel, "A baby born on the intermediate days of the festival is it permitted to shave on the festival, for you have no more authentic a prison than that!"

   B.   *That rule then applies only if it was born during the intermediate days of the festival week, but if it was born prior to the week, it is then forbidden to shave it during the intermediate days of the festival [since that should have been done beforehand].*

   C.   Objected R. Phineas, "**As to all those for whom they have ruled that they may cut their hair on the intermediate days of a festival, it is permitted to get a haircut within [thirty days of] the occurrence of a bereavement [T. Moed. 2:1A-B].** Lo, all those who are forbidden to get a haircut during the intermediate days of the festival also are forbidden to get a hair cut during the thirty days of mourning. **[14B]** *But if you say that there is a difference in the case of the infant at hand, you also are implying that observing mourning pertains to a minor, while it has been taught on Tannaite authority,* 'A minor does not tear his clothing as an expression of grief'?"

   D.   *Said R. Ashi, and some say, R. Shisha b. R. Idi, "Is the correct inference,* 'but those who are forbidden' [Lazarus: to get a haircut in the intermediate days of a festival are also forbidden to do it during the days of mourning]? *Perhaps this is the sense:* 'there are some who are forbidden and others who are permitted [meaning, minors].'"

3.   A.   Amemar, and there are those who say, R. Shisha b. R. Idi, repeated as a Tannaite formulation the following: "Said Samuel, 'It is permitted to give a haircut to a minor on the intermediate days of the festival. *There is no differentiation between whether he was born during the festival week and whether he was born prior.*'"

   B.   *Said R. Phineas, "We too have learned the same rule from the following Tannaite formulation:* **As to all those for whom they have**

**ruled that they may cut their hair on the interme-
diate days of a festival, it is permitted to get a haircut within [thirty days of] the occurrence of a bereavement [T. Moed. 2:1A-B].** Lo, if they are forbidden
to get a hair cut on the intermediate days of the festival, they
also are forbidden to get a hair cut during the time of bereavement. And if you say that an infant is forbidden, you turn out
to maintain that the rules of bereavement apply to a minor,
and yet it has been taught on Tannaite authority, 'A minor does not
tear his clothing as an expression of grief.'"

C. Said R. Ashi, "*Said R. Ashi,* "*Is the correct inference,* 'but those who
are forbidden'? *Perhaps this is the sense:* 'there are some who are
forbidden and others who are permitted [meaning, minors].'"

Now we have a set of free-standing rules, which, in the aggregate, tell us more about the theme introduced by the Mishnah.
Once more we deal with materials that on their own are not formulated as comments upon the Mishnah, but that are set forth
in such a way as to amplify the Mishnah's rule.

4. A. A mourner does not observe the rules of mourning on the festival,
as it is said, "And you shall rejoice in your feast" (Dt. 16:14).

  B. *If the period of bereavement commenced prior to the festival, then the affirmative
action that pertains to the community at large comes along and overrides the af-
firmation action required of an individual. And if it is a bereavement that has begun
now, on the festival, the affirmative action required of an individual does not come
along and override the affirmative action that pertains to the community at large.*

5. A. As to a person subjected to excommunication, what is the law on
his being required to observe on the intermediate days of the festival the rules covering his excommunication?

  B. Said R. Joseph, "*Come and take note:* **They judge capital cases,
property, cases, and cases involving fines [T. Moed. 2:11I].**
*Now if the guilty party does not pay attention to the decision of the court, we are
going to have to excommunicate him. Now if you should maintain that a person
subjected to excommunication does not observe on the intermediate days of the
festival the rules covering his excommunication, then if in the case of one has already
been subjected to excommunication, the festival comes and suspends the excommunication, are we going to declare that, to begin with, on the intermediate days
of a festival, a person is subject to the decree of excommunication? [Obviously not,
and therefore, it must follow, a person subjected to excommunication does observe
on the intermediate days of the festival the rules covering his excommunication].*"

  C. *Said to him Abbayye, "But perhaps the purpose of the court process is only to
consider the charge against him [but not to judge the case]. For if you do not take
that view, then how in the world can we interpret the reference to capital cases?
Do you maintain that, here too, we should actually put the man to death? And
would that not keep the judges themselves from truly rejoicing in the festival? For*

it has been taught on Tannaite authority: R. Aqiba says, 'How do we know that a sanhedrin that put someone to death should not taste any food all that day? Scripture says, "You shall not eat anything with bloodshed" (Lev. 19:26)'? *So in that matter, the purpose of the court process is only to consider the charge against him [but not to judge the case], and here too, the purpose of the court process is only to consider the charge against him [but not to judge the case]."*

D. *He said to him, "Well then you turn out to postpone judgment and turn the trial into an ordeal. But what happens is that they come early in the morning, examine the charges, go home and eat and drink all day, and come back at sunset, reach a final decision, and put him to death."*

E. *Said to him Abbayye, "Come and take note:* **and he whose excommunication has been lifted by sages**.*"* [Such a person is automatically released from the restrictions of excommunication.]

F. *Said Raba, "Does the formulation read,* 'whom sages have released'? *What is says is,* **whose excommunication has been lifted by sages**, *meaning, a case in which the person has gone and made things good with the plaintiff, and then he came before our rabbis, who then released him from the prior restraints [but if that did not happen, he would remain subject to them on the festival]."*

The enormous composite, given in part, has drawn to a close; clearly, it has been framed for its own purpose, holding together around its own interests, and only then been inserted whole into the talmud to our Mishnah-paragraph. If the bulk of the Bavli consisted of materials of this kind, then we could hardly characterize the document as a commentary to the Mishnah. It would require an altogether different characterization. But, we realize in the context of our tractate, the bulk of the Bavli is not made up of free-standing composites, intersecting only formally with a theme that occurs, in other terms altogether, in the document upon which said composites are suspended.

What follows is equally remote from the Mishnah's rules and their principles; we have information on a topic that, in a rather general way, is congruent with our Mishnah-paragraph's topic.

23. A. *Our rabbis have taught on Tannaite authority:*

    B. No decree of excommunication may be for a spell of less than thirty days, and no rebuke takes effect for a spell of less than seven days. Even though there is no explicit proof for that proposition, there is at least an indication for it in this verse: "If her father had only spit in her face, should she not hide in shame for seven days? Let her be shut up outside of the camp for seven days and afterward she shall be brought in again" (Num. 12:14).

24. A.   Said R. Hisda, "Our decree of excommunication is equivalent to their rebuke."

    B.   *But is their rebuke only for seven days and no longer? And Lo, R. Simeon bar Rabbi [Judah the Patriarch] and Bar Qappara were in session and engaged in review of traditions and had difficulty with a given tradition, so said R. Simeon to Bar Qappara, "This matter requires Rabbi."*

    C.   Said Bar Qappara to R. Simeon, "So what does Rabbi say in this matter?"

    D.   *He went and told his father, who took offense. Bar Qappara went to appear before Rabbi, who said to him,* "Bar Qappara, [who is it that you say you are?] I have never known you."

    E.   *He knew that Rabbi had taken the matter seriously and treated himself as subject to rebuke for thirty days.*

The further large composite, given only in part, having drawn to a close, we return to our Mishnah-paragraph. What is interesting once more is that what follows entirely ignores what precedes and reverts to an established program of Mishnah-exegesis, pure and simple. In the case at hand, the exegesis addresses the substance of the law and raises a necessary question of explanation:

III.1

    A.   **and the Nazirite [Num. 6:5] or a person afflicted with the skin ailment [Lev. 14:8-9] who emerges from his state of uncleanness to his state of cleanness:**

    B.   *Asked R. Jeremiah of R. Zira, "Is this concession permitted only where they had not earlier had a chance to get a haircut, or is that the rule even if they could have done it earlier?"*

    C.   *He said to him, "We have learned it as a Tannaite rule:* All those whom they have said are permitted to get a haircut on the intermediate days of the festival are those who had no opportunity to do so earlier, but if they had an opportunity, they are forbidden. A Nazirite and one with the skin ailment, even though they had the opportunity, are permitted, so that they will not delay offering their purification-sacrifices."

2. A.   *A Tannaite statement:* A priest and a mourner are permitted to shave during the festival week."

    B.   *As to the mourner, what sort of case can be in mind? If we say that the eighth day of mourning coincided with the day prior to the festival, then he should have gotten a haircut then, on the day prior to the festival? If the eighth day of his mourning coincided with the Sabbath that came immediately prior to the festival, he should then have gotten a haircut on Friday, in line with what* R. Hisda said Rabina bar Shila said: "The decided law is in accord with Abba Saul, and Sages concur with Abba Saul that when the eighth day of the mourning period coincides with the Sabbath that is the eve of a festival, it is permitted to get a haircut on the eve of the Sabbath."

C. *The rule is required to cover a case in which the seventh day of the mourning period coincided with the Sabbath that was the eve of the festival. This extrinsic Tannaite authority concurs with the position of* Abba Saul, who says, "Part of a day is classified as the whole of the day." *Consequently, the seventh day of his mourning period is counted both with the preceding and the following period, and since that coincides with the Sabbath, the mourned could not get a haircut on the eve of the festival* [not negligence but circumstances explains the fact, and he may then get his haircut in the festival week itself (Lazarus)]. *[Since the formulation of the Mishnah omits reference to the priest and the mourner,] the framer of our Mishnah-passage concurs with sages, who say,* "Part of a day is not classified as the entire day," *so the mourner has not yet completed the seven days of mourning prior to the festival [and the rest of the period is to be fulfilled afterward, and he cannot get a haircut during the intermediate days of the festival].*

D. *And as to the case of the priest [who can get a haircut in the intermediate days of the festival], what sort of case can be in mind? If we say that the concluding day of his priestly watch [during which he could not get a haircut or wash clothes] came to an end on the eve of the festival, then he should have gotten a haircut on the eve of the festival.*

E. *The rule is required to cover a case in which his priestly watch came to an end on the festival day itself [so he could not get a haircut at that time and had to wait until the intermediate days of the festival]. [Since the formulation of the Mishnah omits reference to the priest and the mourner,] the framer of our Mishnah-passage that since we have learned in the Mishnah,* **Three times a year all the priestly watches shared equally in the offerings of the feasts and in the division of the Show Bread. At Pentecost they would say to him, "Here you have unleavened bread, here is leavened bread for you." The priestly watch whose time of service is scheduled [for that week] is the one which offers the daily whole-offerings, offerings brought by reason of vows, freewill offerings, and other public offerings [M. Suk. 5:17A-D], it is as though his priestly watch had not come to an end** *The framer of the other passage takes the position that even though he belongs to the other watches, still, his own ward has actually completed its watch [so he may get a haircut].*

3. A. *Our rabbis have taught on Tannaite authority:*

    B. **As to all those for whom they have ruled that they may cut their hair on the intermediate days of a festival, it is permitted to get a haircut within [thirty days of] the occurrence of a bereavement [T. Moed. 2:1A-B].**

    C. *But has it not been taught on Tannaite authority: they are forbidden?*

    D. Said R. Hisda said R. Shila, *"When that Tannaite formulation was set forth that they are allowed to do so, it speaks only of* those who have suffered bereavements that are immediately sequential."

    E. *If it is the fact that* it speaks only of those who have suffered bereavements that are immediately sequential, *then why frame the rule as* **As to all those for whom they have ruled that they may cut their hair on the intermediate days of a festival**? *It would apply to everybody anyhow. For it has been taught on Tannaite authority:* If there were immediately sequential bereavements, so that one's hair got very heavy, he may trim it with a razer and wash his clothing in water.

F.   Lo, it has been stated in that regard: said R. Hisda, "That means he may do so with a razer and not with scissors, with water and not with soap or lye."

G.   Said R. Hisda, "What this shows is that otherwise a mourner may not wash his clothes."

4. A.   *Our rabbis have taught on Tannaite authority:*

B.   "Just as they have said that it is forbidden to get a haircut on the intermediate days of the festival, so it is forbidden to cut one's fingernails on the intermediate days of the festival," the words of R. Judah.

C.   And R. Yosé permits doing so.

D.   "And just as they have said that a mourner is forbidden to get a haircut during his time of bereavement, so he is forbidden to cut his fingernails during his time of bereavement," the words of R. Judah.

E.   And R. Yosé permits doing so.

F.   Said Ulla, "The decided law is in accord with R. Judah in regard to a mourner, and the decided law is in accord with R. Yosé in respect to the intermediate days of the festival."

G.   Samuel said, **[18A]** "The decided law is in accord with R. Yosé in respect to both the intermediate days of the festival and also a bereavement."

H.   For said Samuel, "The decided law accords with the lenient ruling in matters having to do with bereavement."

5. A.   *Phineas, the brother of Mar Samuel, had a bereavement. Samuel went to see him to ask him why it had happened. He saw that his fingernails were long, so he said to him, "Why didn't you take them off?"*

B.   *He said to him, "If this had happened to you, would you have reacted so casually to the loss?"*

C.   *It was* "like an error that proceeds from a ruler" (Qoh. 10:5), *and Samuel for his part suffered a bereavement. Phineas, the brother of Samuel, went to see him to ask why it had happened. Samuel cut his nails and threw them in his face. He said to him, "Don't you concur that* 'a covenant has been made with the lips [so that how you say something may predict what will come about]?'"

D.   For said R. Yohanan, "How on the basis of Scripture do we know that a covenant is made with the lips? As it is said, 'And Abraham said to his young men, Stay here with the ass, and I and the boy will go up yonder, and we will worship and we will come back to you' (Gen. 22:5), *and that is what happened, for both of them came back."*

6.   A.   *On the basis of the cited incident, some drew the conclusion that it is permitted for a mourner to cut the fingernails but not the toenails. Said R. Anan b. Tahalipa, "To me was it explained explicitly by Samuel: there is no difference between the fingernails and the toenails."*

     B.   Said R. Hiyya bar Ashi said Rab, "But it is forbidden to cut them with a nail cutter."

7.   A.   *Said R. Shemen bar Abba, "I was standing before R. Yohanan at the house of study on the intermediate days of the festival, [and I saw that] he bit off his nails and threw them out. Three lessons are to be inferred from this incident.*

     B.   *"It is to be inferred that* it is permitted to pare the nails on the intermediate days of the festival.

     C.   *"It is to be inferred that* it is not regarded as disgusting to bite one's nails.

     D.   *"It is to be inferred that* it it is permitted to throw them away."

     E.   *Well is that so? And has it not been taught on Tannaite authority:* Three statements were made with reference to the disposal of fingernails: one who burns them is pious, who buries them is righteous, who simply tosses them away is wicked?

     F.   *What is the operative consideration?* A pregnant woman might step over them and suffer a miscarriage. *But women are not frequently located in the house of study.*

     G.   *And should you say that sometimes nails are collected and thrown out, the fact is that, once they have been moved about, they have been moved about [and their condition is thereby transformed].*

8.   A.   Said R. Judah said Rab, "A pair of masters came from Hamatan before Rabbi..."

     B.   And Mar Zutra repeated it in this way: "A pair of masters came from Hamatan before Rabbi..."

     C.   "...and they asked him about paring the nails [during a bereavement], and he permitted them to do so."

     D.   And Samuel said, "They also asked him about the moustache, and he permitted them."

The comment on the cited sentence of the Mishnah consists in a secondary extension of the rule.

IV.1

    A.   **And who are they who may wash their clothes on the intermediate days of a festival? (1) he who comes from overseas or from captivity; (2) and he who goes forth from prison; (3) and he whose excommunication has been lifted by sages. (4) And so too: he who sought absolution from a sage [for release from a vow not to wash clothes] and** was released. **(1) Hand towels, (2) barber's towels, and (3) bath towels [may be washed].** **(1) Male and (2) female Zabs, (3) women in their menstrual period, (4) women after childbirth, and all who go up from a state of uncleanness to cleanness, lo, these are permitted [to wash their clothes]. But all other people are prohibited:**

B. Said R. Assi said R. Yohanan, "He who had only a single shirt is permitted to launder it during the intermediate days of a festival."

C. *Objected R. Jeremiah,* "**And who are they who may wash their clothes on the intermediate days of a festival? (1) he who comes from overseas or from captivity; (2) and he who goes forth from prison; (3) and he whose excommunication has been lifted by sages. (4) And so too: he who sought absolution from a sage [for release from a vow not to wash clothes] and was released.** *These are permitted, but he who had only a single shirt is not."*

D. *Said R. Jacob to R. Jeremiah, "I will explain the wording of the rule to you: our Mishnah-paragraph permits one to wash his clothes even if he had two, if they are dirty [but if he has only one, he may wash it without restriction]."*

2. A. R. Isaac bar Jacob bar Giyuri in the name of R. Yohanan sent word, "It is permitted to launder linen garments on the intermediate days of a festival."

B. *Objected Raba,* "**Hand towels, (2) barber's** [18B] **towels, and (3) bath towels [may be washed].** *These may be wished, but linen items may not."*

C. *Said to him Abbayye, "Our Mishnah-rule extends even to other kinds of material [but there are no restrictions on linen ones]."*

D. *Said Bar Hedayya, "I personally have seen at the Sea of Galilee people bringing laundry baskets full of linen garments and washing them during the intermediate days of the festival."*

E. *[Said Abbayye,] "Yeah, will how do you know that they did it with sages' approval? They might have been doing it without the sages' approval!"*

I.1 asks an obvious exegetical question. No. 2 raises a secondary question in amplification of the principle of the Mishnah. **II.1** proceeds to another familiar exercise in Mishnah-exegesis, the identification of the authority behind an anonymous rule. Nos. 2, 3 add further, relevant rules together with their talmuds. No. 4 adds a rule thematically pertinent to the Mishnah, and that leads to the refinement proposed at Nos. 5, 6, in which the Mishnah's own language and rule play a role. No. 7 stands at the head of a vast thematic anthology on the rules of mourning, attached here because of the general comparison of the application, on the intermediate days of the festival, of the rules of mourning and the rules governing persons of the classifications listed in the Mish-

nah. This anthology extends through Nos. 8-19. No. 20 is tacked
on to No. 19 because of the intersecting theme of sending things,
so it seems to me. No. 21, then continues No. 20, with special
attention to its closing entry. Nos. 22, 23-24+25-49, resume the
general theme of Raba's long account of court procedure, now
shading over into an anthology on excommunication as a sanction of the court, a vast appendix tacked on for obvious reasons.
III.1 clarifies the application of the Mishnah's rule. Nos. 2, 3, 4,
each with a rich talmud of its own, complement the foregoing.
No. 5 is tacked on to No. 4, and Nos. 6-7 serve No. 5. Nos. 8, 9
pursue the established theme. No. 10 is tacked on to No. 9 because of the name of the authority at 10.A. **IV.1, 2** propose a
stipulation in the application of the Mishnah's rule and otherwise
amplify the rule.

MISHNAH/BAVLI TRACTATE MOED QATAN 3:5-6
3:5

    A. **He who buries his dead three days before the festival—
the requirement of the seven days of mourning is nullified for him.**

    B. **[He who buries his dead] eight days [before the festi-
val]—the requirement of the thirty days of mourning is
nullified for him.**

    C. **For they have said, "The Sabbath counts [in the days of
mourning] but does not interrupt [the period of mourn-
ing], [while] the festivals interrupt [the period of mourn-
ing] and do not count [in the days of mourning]."**

3:6

    A. **R. Eliezer says, "After the Temple was destroyed, Pen-
tecost is deemed equivalent to the Sabbath."**

    B. **Rabban Gamaliel says, "The New Year and the Day of
Atonement are deemed equivalent to festivals."**

    C. **And sages say, "The rule is in accord with the opinion
neither of this one nor of that one.**

    D. **"But Pentecost is deemed equivalent to a festival, and
the New Year and the Day of Atonement are deemed
equivalent to the Sabbath."**

We begin with an extension of the law of the Mishnah, in which
the rule of the Mishnah is qualified and made more precise as to
its application.

I.1

A. [**the requirement of the seven days of mourning is nullified for him**:] Said Rab, "The restrictions are nullified, but the days of mourning are not nullified [but deferred until after the festival]."

B. And so said R. Huna, "The restrictions are nullified, but the days of mourning are not nullified [but deferred until after the festival]."

C. *But R. Sheshet said, "Even the days of mourning also are nullified."* [Lazarus: they are not to be compensated after the festival to the number of days during which the mourning formalities were suspended.]

Now comes a talmud to the foregoing.

2. A. *What is the meaning of* but the days of mourning are not nullified?

B. If one did not get a haircut on the day prior to the festival, he is forbidden to get a haircut after the festival.

C. *[19B] For has it not been taught on Tannaite authority:*

D. He who buries his dead three days before the festival—the requirement of the seven days of mourning is nullified for him. [He who buries his dead] eight days [before the festival]—the requirement of the thirty days of mourning is nullified for him. And he should get a hair cut on the eve of the festival. If he did not get a haircut on the eve of the festival, it is forbidden to get a haircut after the festival.

E. Abba Saul says, "It is permitted to get a haircut after the festival, for just as the religious duty of observing three days vitiates the religious duty of observing seven [which, after the festival, are null], so the religious duty of observing seven days vitiates the religious duty of observing thirty."

F. "Seven"? *But lo, we have learned in the Mishnah* **eight**!

G. *Abba Saul takes the view that* part of a day is classified as the whole of the day, and here the seventh day of mourning counts in both directions [Lazarus: after part has been observed for the seventh day, the rest counts as the eighth day, with its easier rules].

H. Said R. Hisda said Rabina bar Shila, "The decided law is in accord with the view of Abba Saul."

I. And sages concede to Abba Saul that, when the eighth day of one's bereavement coincides with the Sabbath that is also the eve of a festival, he may get a haircut on Friday.

The talmud now gets its own talmud:

3. A. *In accord with which authority is that which* R. Amram said Rab

said, "Once the comforters have arisen to leave a mourner, he is permitted to bathe"?

B. In accord with whom? It is in accord with Abba Saul.

We return to the talmud itself:

4. A. Said Abbayye, "The decided law is in accord with the view of Abba Saul with respect to the seventh day of mourning, and sages concede the position of Abba Saul in respect to the thirtieth day of mourning that, in that regard, *we do maintain that* part of a day is classified as the whole of the day."

B. Raba said, "The decided law accords with the view of Abba Saul in regard to the thirtieth day, but the decided law is not in accord with Abba Saul in regard to the seventh day."

C. And the Nehardeans say, "The decided law accords with Abba Saul in both cases, for said Samuel, 'The decided law accords with the opinion of the more lenient authority in matters having to do with bereavement.'"

What follows is not Mishnah-amplification in particular, but a proof from Scripture for a fact that is taken for granted (also) in the Mishnah. This is in fact a gloss on the foregoing, and accordingly is indented.

5. A. *How on the basis of Scripture do we know that the span of thirty days is required for mourning?*

B. *It derives from a verbal analogy based on the presence of the word "disheveled" that occurs with regard to mourning [at Lev. 10:6] and with regard to the Nazirite [at Num. 6:5].*

C. Here: "Let not the hair of your heads become disheveled" (Lev. 10:6) and there: "He shall let the locks of the hair of his head become disheveled" (Num. 6:5). Just as in the latter case, the period of observance is thirty days, so in the former it is thirty days.

D. *And how do we derive that span of time in the latter case?*

E. Said R. Mattena, "Where there is a Nazirite vow without a specified limit, it is for thirty days."

F. *What is the Scriptural basis?*

G. *The word "shall be holy" is used there, and the numerical value of the letters for "shall be" is thirty.*

We resume the talmud interrupted for the foregoing gloss:

6. A. Said R. Huna b. R. Joshua, "All parties [even Abba Saul] concur that, when the third day of one's bereavement coincides

with the eve of a festival, it is forbidden to wash until evening."

B.   *Said R. Nehemiah b. R. Joshua, "I came across R. Pappi and R. Pappa who were in session and stating, 'The decided law is in accord with the statement of R. Huna b. R. Joshua.'"*

C.   *Some say it in this version:*

D.   *Said R. Nehemiah b. R. Joseph, "I came across R. Pappi, R. Pappa, and R. Huna b. R. Joshua, who in session stated, 'All parties [even Abba Saul] concur that, when the third day of one's bereavement coincides with the eve of a festival, it is forbidden to wash until evening.'"*

We now turn to a theoretical question, which is settled by appeal to a Tosefta-passage pertinent to our Mishnah-passage. The whole—Mishnah, Tosefta, Bavli-composition—holds together because a single theme is under discussion, and the Bavli predictably presents the discussion at the point at which the Mishnah's treatment of that theme is at hand. We cannot call the composition that follows a Mishnah-commentary, but we also cannot regard it as utterly free-standing and out of phase with the Mishnah. A well-crafted talmud, such as the Bavli, aiming at the formation of a Mishnah-commentary, can be relied upon to situate a discussion of this kind in precisely the right place.

7.   A.   *Abbayye raised this question of Rabbah:* "If the burial took place on the festival, does the festival count in the thirty days or does the festival not count in the thirty days? *As to whether or not it counts in the seven, I am not troubled, for the observance of the religious duty involving the seven days does not apply during the festival at all. What I am asking about is the period of thirty days, since the fulfillment of the religious duty involving the thirty does does pertain during the festival.* [Lazarus: for then too as during the thirty days, it is forbidden to wash clothes and get a haircut]. *What is the rule?"*

B.   He said to him, "It does not count."

C.   *He raised an objection based on the following:* "**He who buries his dead two days before the festival interrupts his mourning rites for the festival and counts five supplementary days of mourning after the festival, and the public takes care of him, and his work is done by other people. His male slaves and female slaves work in private at home. And the public does not get involved with him [in consoling him]** [20A] **for they have already done so on the festival itself. The operative principle is this: whatever concerns the mourner himself [formal mourning by him] is suspended by the festival, but whatever is on account of the**

obligations of the community at large is not suspected by the festival. If he buried his dead with three days left of the festival week itself, he counts seven days of mourning after the festival. For the first four, the public takes care of him. For the other three, the public does not take care of him. For they have already done so on the festival. And the festival counts. [For they have said that the days of mourning that took place on the festival so affect him that the public must take care of him. And his work is done by others. His male slaves and female slaves work in private for other people] [cf. T. Moed. 2:6-7]. *Does the sentence,* **And the festival counts,** *not refer to the latter part [if one buried the dead three days prior..., the festival days count, and Rabbah has said they do not count]?"*

D. *"No, it refers to the opening clause."*

E. *He raised an objection based on the following:* "How does the festival count within the thirty days? If they buried the deceased at the beginning of the festival, he counts seven days after the festival, and his work is done by others, and his male and female slaves work in private in his own house, and the public does not get involved with condoling him, for they have already done so on the festival, and the festival counts."

F. *That is a solid refutation.*

8. A. *When Rabin came,* he said R. Yohanan said, "Even if one buried his dead during the festival [that part of the festival counts in the thirty days]."

   B. *So to R. Eleazar instructed his son R. Pedat,* "Even if one buried his dead during the festival [that part of the festival counts in the thirty days]."

We again revert to the amplification of a Tannaite statement pertinent to our Mishnah's rule:

9. A. *Our rabbis have taught on Tannaite authority:*

   B. **He who fulfilled the rite of turning over the bed for three days before the festival does not have to turn over the bed after the festival,"** the words of R. Eliezer.

   C. **And sages say, "Even if he did so one day or even one hour."**

   D. **Said R. Simeon b. Eleazar, "This represents precisely what the House of Shammai and the House of Hillel said.**

   E. **"For the House of Shammai say, 'Three days.'**

   F. **"And the House of Hillel say, 'Even one day'"** [T. Moed 2;(A-D].

   10. A. *Said R. Huna said R. Hiyya bar Abba said R. Yohanan, and some say, said R. Yohanan to R. Hiyya bar Abba and to R. Huna,* "Even one

day, even one hour."

B. *Raba said, "The decided law accords with the position of our Tannaite authority, who said,* 'three days.' [That is the minimum observance of mourning prior to the festival, on account of which the advent of the festival remits the rest.]"

11. A. *Rabina came to Sura on the Euphrates. Said R. Habiba to Rabina, "What is the decided law?"*

    B. *He said to him, "Even one day, even one hour."*

        12. A. *In session R. Hiyya bar Abba and R. Ammi and R. Isaac Nappaha under the awning of R. Isaac b. Eleazar. This matter came up among them:* "How do we know on the basis of Scripture that mourning is for a period of seven days? As it is written, 'And I shall turn your feasts into mourning, and I will make it as the mourning for an only son' (Amos 8:10)—just as the Feast [that is, Tabernacles] is for seven days, so the mourning is for seven days."

            B. *Well, why not invoke the analogy of Pentecost [which is one day]?*

            C. *That analogy is required for the matter explained by R. Simeon for Laqish, for said* R. Simeon b. Laqish in the name of R. Judah the Patriarch, "How on the basis of Scripture do we know that mourning on account of news of a bereavement that has come from a great distance applies only for a single day? As it is written, 'And I shall turn your feasts into mourning, and I will make it as the mourning for an only son' (Amos 8:10)—*just as the Pentecost is a feast that lasts one day [so here too the mourning is for only one day]."*

Once more we turn to a Tannaite treatment of the established subject. At this point, we realize, our particular passage of the Bavli proposes to provide a rather substantial composite, formed around thematic interests, and only then given its present location; this cannot be seen as Mishnah-commentary in any meaningful sense; but the Bavli has presented the composite in the context of the Mishnah and given the composite its legitimate place within the larger document only in relationship to the Mishnah's introduction of the theme at hand.

The treatment of the Mishnah-sentence is narrowly exegetical. We now ask precisely the interstitial question that is required by the rule of the Mishnah: something is classified in two contradictory ways, so we propose to resolve the ambiguity.

II.1

A. **For they have said, "The Sabbath counts [in the days of mourning] but does not interrupt [the period of mourning], [while] the festivals interrupt [the period of mourning] and do not count [in the days of mourning]:"**

B. *Judeans and Galilaeans—*

C. *These say,* **[23B]** "Mourning pertains to the Sabbath."

D. *And those say,* "Mourning does not pertain to the Sabbath."

E. *The one who says,* "Mourning pertains to the Sabbath," *cites the Mishnah's statement,* **The Sabbath counts [in the days of mourning].**

F. *The one who says,* "Mourning does not pertain to the Sabbath," *cites the Mishnah's statement,* **but does not interrupt [the period of mourning]**. *Now if you take the view that mourning applies to the Sabbath, if mourning were observed, would there be any question of its interrupting the counting of the days of mourning?*

G. *Well, as a matter of fact, the same passage does say* **The Sabbath counts [in the days of mourning]***!*

H. *The inclusion of that phrase is on account of what is coming, namely,* **[while] the festivals interrupt [the period of mourning] and do not count [in the days of mourning]**, *so the Tannaite formulation to balance matters also stated,* **The Sabbath counts [in the days of mourning].**

I. *And as to the position of him who says,* "Mourning pertains to the Sabbath," *does the passage not say,* **but does not interrupt [the period of mourning]***?*

J. *That is because the framer of the passage wishes to include,* **the festivals interrupt [the period of mourning]**, *so for the sake of balance he stated as well,* **The Sabbath...does not interrupt [the period of mourning].**

Now that we have laid out the issue at hand, which involves a close reading of the language of the Mishnah, we proceed to ask whether the same issue divides Tannaite opinion on other, parallel matters; this then provides a talmud to the foregoing:

2. A. *May we say that at issue is what is under debate in among the Tannaite authorities in the following:*

B. As to one whose deceased [actually] lies before him, he eats in a different room. If he does not have another room, he eats in the room of his fellow. If he has no access to the room of his fellow, he makes a partition and eats [separate from the corpse]. If he has nothing with which to make a partition, he turns his face away and eats.

C. He does not recline and eat, he does not eat meat, he does not drink wine, he does not say a blessing before the meal, he does not serve to form a quorum, and people do not say a blessing for him or include him in a quorum.

D. He is exempt from the requirement to recite the *Shema* and from the Prayer and from the requirement of wearing phylacteries and from all of the religious duties that are listed in the Torah.

E. But on the Sabbath he does recline and eat, he does eat meat, he does drink wine, he does say a blessing before the meal, he does serve to form a quorum and people do say a blessing for him and include him in a quorum. And he is liable to carry out all of the religious duties that are listed in the Torah.

F. Rabban Simeon b. Gamaliel says, "Since he is liable for these [religious duties], he is liable to carry out all of them."

G. And [in connection with the dispute just now recorded], R. Yohanan said, *"What is at issue between [Simeon and the anonymous authority]? At issue is the matter of having sexual relations.* [Simeon maintains that the mourner on the Sabbath has the religious obligation to have sexual relations with his wife, and the anonymous authority does not include that requirement, since during the mourning period it does not apply.]"

H. Is now this what is at stake between them, namely, one authority [Simeon b. Gamaliel] maintains, "Mourning pertains to the Sabbath," and the other takes the view, "Mourning does not pertain to the Sabbath"?

I. *What compels that conclusion? Perhaps the initial Tannaite authority takes the view that he does there only because of the simple consideration that the deceased is lying there awaiting burial, but in the present case, in which the deceased is not lying there awaiting burial, he would not take the position that he does. And, further, perhaps Rabban Simeon b. Gamaliel takes the position that he does in that case because, at that point [prior to burial] the restrictions of mourning do not pertain, but, here, where the restrictions of mourning do pertain, he would concur [that the mourning does pertain to the Sabbath].*

Yet a tertiary level of inquiry into the same issue, precipitated by the framing of the Mishnah's rule, now follows:

3. A. **[24A]** *R. Yohanan asked Samuel,* "Does mourning pertain to the Sabbath or does mourning not pertain to the Sabbath?"

B. He said to him, "Mourning does not pertain to the Sabbath."

The next items are tacked on for thematic reasons; I do not see any connection to the program of Mishnah-exegesis that has now come to an end. Rather, what commences here appears to me rather miscellaneous.

4.   A.   *Rabbis in session before R. Pappa stated in the name of Samuel, "A*
          mourner who had sexual relations during his time of bereave-
          ment is liable to the death penalty."
     B.   *Said to them R. Pappa, "It is forbidden is what has been stated in the*
          name of R. Yohanan, and if you have heard the tradition in the name of
          Samuel, this is what you have heard: said R. Tahalipa bar Abimi said
          Samuel, 'A mourner who did not let his hair get disheveled
          and did not tear his clothing is liable to the death penalty, for
          it has been said, "Do not let the hair of your heads become
          disheveled and do not tear your clothing, that you do not die"
          (Lev. 10:6), which bears the implication that if any other
          mourner did not let the hair of his head become disheveled
          or did not tear his clothing, he is subject to the death penalty.'"
5.   A.   Said Rafram bar Pappa, "A Tannaite formulation in the
          Major Compilation on Mourning: A mourner may not have
          sexual relations during the days of mourning.
     B.   "'There was the case of someone who had sexual relations
          during the days of mourning, and pigs dragged off his corpse."
6.   A.   Said Samuel, "On the Sabbath, unveiling the head, turning
          the torn side of the garment from front to back, and upright-
          ing the couch, are obligatory; putting on sandals, sexual re-
          lations, and washing the hands and feet with warm water on
          the eve of the Sabbath are optional."
     B.   And Rab said, "Unveiling the head also is optional."
     C.   *And how come Samuel identifies putting on the sandal as optional? It is*
          because not everybody ordinarily wears sandals. So it should be the same
          with unveiling the head, as not everybody goes around with head unveiled!
     D.   *Well, Samuel is entirely consistent with positions he holds in general, for*
          said Samuel, "Any tear that is not made at the very moment
          of grief is no tearing, and any covering of the face which is
          not done the way the Ishmaelites do it is not classified as a
          proper covering up."
     E.   *R. Nahman showed how to do it, right up to the sides of the beard.*
     F.   [As to the difference of opinion between Rab and Samuel
          about uncovering the head,] said R. Jacob said R. Yohanan,
          "That was taught only in the case of one who has no sandals
          on his feet, but if he had sandals on his feet [on the Sabbath],
          the sandals testify to his circumstance [which is that he does
          not observe mourning on the Sabbath]."

One form of Mishnah-commentary is the presentation of a final
decision on a matter subject to dispute in the Mishnah itself.

3:5-6/\III.1

A. **R. Eliezer says, "After the Temple was destroyed, Pentecost is deemed equivalent to the Sabbath." Rabban Gamaliel says, "The New Year and the Day of Atonement are deemed equivalent to festivals." And sages say, "The rule is in accord with the opinion neither of this one nor of that one. But Pentecost is deemed equivalent to a festival, and the New Year and the Day of Atonement are deemed equivalent to the Sabbath:"**

B. Said R. Giddal bar Menassia said Samuel, "The decided law accords with the position of Rabban Gamaliel."

C. *There are those who repeat this statement of R. Giddal bar Menassia in connection with the following:* "Any infant who died within thirty days of birth is carried out for burial in one's arms and is buried by one woman and two men, but not by one man and two women.

D. **[24B]** "Abba Saul says, 'Even by one man and two women.'

E. "They do not form a line of mourners on his account, and they do not say on his account the blessing of mourners or the consolation addressed to mourners.

F. "As to an infant who died after thirty days of life, he is carried out in a box .

G. "R. Judah says, 'Not a box that is carried on the shoulder, but one that is taken in the arms.'

H. "They do form a line of mourners on his account, and they do say on his account the blessing of mourners and the consolation addressed to mourners.

I. "As to an infant who died after twelve months of life, he is taken out for burial on a bier.

J. "R. Aqiba says, 'If he is a year old, but her limbs were like those of a two year old, then it is classified as a two year old; if it was two years old but the limbs were those of a year old, he is taken out on a bier.'

K. "R. Simeon b. Eleazar says, 'In the case of anyone who is carried out on a bier, the community shows public signs of distress, and on account of any that is not carried out on a bier, the community does not show public signs of distress.'

L. "R. Eleazar b. Azariah says, 'If he is publicly known, then the public engages in his rites, but if he is not known to the public, the public does not engage with his rites.'

M. "And what about a lamentation?

N. "R. Meir in the name of R. Ishmael says, 'In the case of the poor, they make a lamentation for a child of three, in the case of the rich, for one of five.'

O. "R. Judah in his name says, 'For a child of the poor [which is all poor people have as pleasure in their lives (Rashi)], they make a lament for a five year old, for a child of the rich, six.'

P.   "And as for the children of the sages, they are classified as are the children of the poor.

Q.   "Said R. Giddal bar Menassia said Rab, 'The decided law accords with the position of R. Judah in the name of R. Ishmael.'"

The amplification of the Mishnah's rule in the following is not ambitious:

IV.1

A.   [**But Pentecost is deemed equivalent to a festival**:] *R. Annani bar Sasson gave this exposition at the door of the house of the patriarch:* "One day of mourning prior to Pentecost and Pentecost itself count as fourteen days [out of the thirty]."

B.   *R. Ammi heard this and was disgusted. He said, "Does this belong to him alone? It belongs to R. Eleazar speaking in the name of R. Oshaia."*

2.   A.   R. Isaac bar Nappaha gave this exposition under the awning of the exilarch's house: "One day of mourning prior to Pentecost and Pentecost itself count as fourteen days [out of the thirty]."

B.   *R. Sheshet heard this and was disgusted. He said, "Does this belong to him alone? It belongs to R. Eleazar speaking in the name of R. Oshaia."*

C.   For said R. Eleazar said R. Oshaia, "How on the basis of Scripture do we know that Pentecost is counted as the equivalent of a full seven days toward the completion of thirty days of mourning [like Tabernacles and Passover]? 'Three times a year shall all your males appear before the Lord your God in the place he shall choose, on the feast of unleavened bread, and on the feast of weeks, and on the feast of tabernacles, and they shall not appear before the Lord your God empty handed' (Dt. 16:16). Just as the festival of unleavened bread is counted as the equivalent of a full seven days toward the completion of thirty days of mourning, so the feast of weeks [Pentecost] is counted as the equivalent of a full seven days toward the completion of thirty days of mourning."

The exposition now moves outward from the case to the principle and its problem:

3.   A.   *R. Pappa appointed R. Avia the Elder to serve as his loud-speaker and then gave this exposition:* "One day prior to the New Year and the New Year itself add up to fourteen days of the thirty days of bereavement."

B.   Said Rabina, "Therefore one day prior to the Festival of Tabernacles, and the Festival of Tabernacles, and the Eighth Day of Solemn Assembly that pertains to it—lo, we have here twenty-one of the thirty days of the bereavement period."

4.   A.   Rabina came to Sura on the Euphrates. Said R. Habiba of Sura on the Euphrates to Rabina, "Did the master say, 'One day prior to the

New Year and the New Year itself add up to fourteen days of the thirty days of bereavement'?"

B.   *He said to him, "I said it, reasoning from Rabban Gamaliel's position."*

I.1 amplifies the rule of the Mishnah. No. 2 glosses the foregoing. Nos. 3, 4, continued at No. 6 then supplement No. 2. No. 5 then stands at the head of a miscellaneous anthology on the general theme of the Mishnah-paragraph. The further entries are Nos. 7-8, 9-11+12, 13-42, a protracted presentation and gloss of a quite coherent composite. **II.1+2, 3**—a coherent composite indeed!— appeal to the Mishnah's rule to settle a tangential question, thereby also clarifying the Mishnah's sense as well. The composite is enriched by entirely cogent materials at Nos. 4, 5, 6-10. **III.1** begins with a judgment of the final decision on the dispute of the Mishnah, another familiar form of Mishnah-exegesis, but obviously rather elaborate space-filler, like much that has gone before. **IV.1-2** amplifies the Mishnah's rule. No. 3, 4 continue the same program.

Mishnah/Bavli tractate Moed Qatan 3:7A-B

A.   **They tear their clothing, bare the shoulder, or provide food for mourners, only in the case of the near relatives of the deceased.**

B.   **And they provide mourners food only on an upright couch.**

We begin by contrasting the rule of the Mishnah with an intersecting one:

I.1

A.   **[25A] [They tear their clothing, bare the shoulder, or provide food for mourners, only in the case of the near relatives of the deceased:]** Even in the case of a sage? *But has it not been taught on Tannaite authority:* When a sage dies, everybody is regarded as related to him?

B.   *Do you really think that the rule is,* When a sage dies, everybody is regarded as related to him? *Rather,* When a sage dies, everybody is regarded as if he were related to him!

C.   [In consequence:] all tear their clothing on his account, all bare their shoulders on his account, and all provide a meal for those who mourn on his account in the public space.

D. *Our Mishnah-paragraph's ruling is required to deal with the case of one who was not classified as a sage.*

E. *Still, even if it was merely a worthy person, people are obligated to tear their clothes on that account, as it is stated on Tannaite authority:* How come someone's sons and daughters died young? It is so that a person should weep and mourn for a worthy person.

    F. *Are weeping and mourning obligations to be carried out in advance* [that is, is it the rule that one is given a cause to weep anticipating some worthy person may die and not be fittingly mourned by the person whose sons or daughters have died in infancy (Lazarus)]?

    G. Rather, [How come someone's sons and daughters died young?] It is because one did not weep and mourn for a worthy person.

    H. Then is it the fact that for anyone who weeps and mourns for a worthy person is forgiven for all his sins on account of the honor that he has paid to him?!

    I. [The statement of the Mishnah-paragraph is required to cover the case] in which the deceased is not a particularly virtuous person.

    J. *But if someone is standing right there at the time that the soul goes forth, he still is obligated, for it has been taught on Tannaite authority:* R. Simeon b. Eleazar says, "He who is standing at the side of the deceased at the very moment that the soul comes forth is obligated to tear his garment. To what is this comparable? To a scroll of the Torah that catches fire. For one is liable on that account to tear his clothing."

    K. *[The statement of the Mishnah-paragraph is required to cover the case] in which someone is not standing right there at the time that the soul goes forth,*

We now leave behind the explanation of the Mishnah's rule and turn toward a long sequence of tales, formed within the framework of mourning rites for sages, only afterward assigned a place in the sequence commencing with the foregoing composition. Since I cannot regard what follows as in any way related to the preceding, I mark the autonomy of the set by indenting it at both margins. I give only a small part of the whole.

  2. A. *When R. Safra's soul came to rest, our rabbis did not tear their clothes on his account, saying, "We learned nothing from him."*

    B. Said to them Abbayye, *"Has it been taught on Tannaite authority, 'When a rabbi [meaning, one's own master] dies...'? It is, 'when a sage dies [meaning, an acknowledged, public authority], all are classified as his relations.' And furthermore, every day his traditions are in the mouths of those who are in the house of study."*

    C. *They supposed that what happened happened [without consequence.]*

D. *Said to them Abbayye, "We have learned as a Tannaite statement:* As to a sage that died, so long as they are engaged in his obsequies, people are liable to tear their clothing."

E. *They supposed that they should make the tear on the spot.*

F. *Said to them Abbayye, "We have learned as a Tannaite statement:* As to a sage, the mode of paying honor to him is by a proper eulogy [and that is when the rites are performed]."

3. A. *When R. Huna's soul came to rest, they considered putting a scroll of the Torah on his bier. Said to them R. Hisda, "Something that in his lifetime he never considered proper are we now going to go and do to him? For said R. Tahalipa, 'I saw R. Huna, when he wanted to sit down on his couch, he saw a scroll of the Torah lying there, so he put an inverted jar on the ground and put the scroll of the Torah into it. So he took for granted that* it is forbidden to sit on a sofa on which a scroll of the Torah was lying.'"

B. *His bier would not go through the doorway. They considered letting it down from the roof. Said R. Hisda, "I learned the following tradition from him himself:* As to a deceased sage, the correct manner of paying respect to him is to take out his bier through the door."

C. *They then considered moving him into another [narrower] bier for the same purpose. Said R. Hisda, "I learned the following tradition from him himself:* As to a deceased sage, the correct manner of paying respect to him is to make use of the initial bier into which his corpse has been placed. For said R. Judah said Rab, 'How do we know on the basis of Scripture that as to a deceased sage, the correct manner of paying respect to him is to make use of the initial bier into which his corpse has been placed? As it is said, 'And they set the ark of God on a new cart and brought it out of the house of Abinadab that was on the hill' (2 Sam. 6:3)."

D. *So they cut a hole in the door and brought out the bier that way.*

We return to the Tannaite complements to our Mishnah's rule:

15. A. *Our rabbis have taught on Tannaite authority:*

B. **[26A]** These tears on the garments are not to be sewn up again: he who makes a tear for his father or his mother, his master who taught him wisdom, a patriarch, a principal of the court, for having bad news, for having heard blasphemy, when a scroll of the Torah has been burned, for seeing the ruined cities of Judea, the holy house, or Jerusalem. One makes a tear first for the Temple and then enlarges it for Jerusalem.

Now commences a talmud to the foregoing:

16. A. "he who makes a tear for his father or his mother, his master who taught him wisdom:" how on the basis of Scripture do we know this fact?

B.   As it is written, "And Elisha saw it and cried, My father, my father, the chariots of Israel and the horsemen thereof" (2 Kings
2:12)—

C.   "My father, my father:" this means to tear one's garment on
the death of a father or mother.

D.   "the chariots of Israel and the horsemen thereof:" this means
that one tears one's garment on the death of his master who
taught him wisdom

E.   *And what is the sense?*

F.   *It is in line with the Aramaic version given by R. Joseph, "My master, my
master, who protected Israel with his prayer better than chariots and horsemen could."*

17.   A.   And how on the basis of Scripture do we know that these tears
are not to be sewn up again?

B.   "And he took hold of his own clothes and tore them into two
pieces" (2 Kgs. 2:12)—having said "and tore them," do I not
know that it was "into two pieces"? But it teaches that they remain torn into two parts for all time."

C.   Said R. Simeon b. Laqish to R. Yohanan, "Elijah yet lives [so
how can a rite performed at his disappearance prove exemplary]?"

D.   *He said to him, "Since it is written, 'and he saw him no more,' he
was as dead to Elisha."*

19.   A.   "for having heard blasphemy:" how on the basis of Scripture
do we know this fact?

B.   As it is written, "Then came Eliakim son of Hilkiah who was
in charge of the household and Shebna the scribe and Joah
son of Asaph recorder to Hezekiah, with their clothes torn,
and told him the blasphemous words of Rabshakeh" (2 Kgs.
18:37).

Now comes a Tannaite treatment of the theme of the immediately-foregoing, which is to say, a composition made into a comment:

20.   A.   *Our rabbis have taught on Tannaite authority:*

B.   All the same are the one who actually hears [the blasphemy] and the one who hears it from the one who heard it.
Both are liable to tear their garments.

C.   But the witnesses are not liable to tear their garments, for
they already did so at the moment when they heard the
original blasphemy.

D.   But if they did so at the moment when they heard the
original blasphemy, *what difference does that make? Lo, they are
now hearing it again!*

E.   *Do not let that argument enter your mind, for it is written,* "And it came to pass, when King Hezekiah heard it, that *he* tore his clothes? (2 Kgs. 18:37).

F. King Hezekiah tore his clothes, but they did not tear their clothes.

We revert to our talmud:

21. A. "are not to be sewn up again:" how do we know this fact?
    B. It derives from the analogy to be drawn between the act of tearing done by King Hezekiah and acts of tearing done elsewhere [2 Kgs. 2:12].
22. A. "when a scroll of the Torah has been burned:" how on the basis of Scripture do we know this fact?
    B. As it is written, "And it came to pass that when Jehudi had read three or four columns that he cut it with a pen knife and cast it into the fire that was in the brazier" (Jer. 36:23f.).
    C. *What is the point of saying* "three or four columns"?
    D. *They said to Jehoiakim that Jeremiah had written the book of Lamentations. He said to them, "What is written in it?"*
    E. "How does the city sit solitary" (Lam. 1:1).
    F. *He said to them, "I am king!"*
    G. "She sweeps sore in the night" (Lam. 1:2).
    H. *He said to them, "I am king!"*
    I. "Judah has gone into exile before of affliction" (Lam. 1:3).
    J. *He said to them, "I am king!"*
    K. "The ways of Zion mourn" (Lam. 1:4).
    L. *He said to them, "I am king!"*
    M. "Her adversaries are become the head" (Lam. 1:5).
    N. *"Who said that!"*
    O. "For the Lord has afflicted her for the multitude of her transgressions" (Lam. 1:5).
    P. Forthwith he cut out all the instances in which the name of god is written therein and he burned the rest in fire, so it is written, "Yet they were not afraid nor tore their garments, neither the king nor any of his servants who heard all these words" (Jer. 36:24), *implying that they ought to have done so.*
    Q. *Said R. Pappa to Abbayye, "But maybe they did so because of the bad news?"*
    R. *He said to him, "But had any bad news actually come to them as yet?"*

Once more, back to the Tannaite complement to the Mishnah's theme:

27. A. *Our rabbis have taught on Tannaite authority:*
    B. And all of these tears may be tacked together, basted together,

picked up by the grayed edges or with a ladder stitch, but they may not be reunited by a sewn seam along the edges [following Lazarus's translation].

C. Said R. Hisda, **[26B]** "Or with Alexandrian mending."

28. A. *Our rabbis have taught on Tannaite authority:*

B. He who makes the tear on a part of the garment that was tacked, basted together or where edges are picked up by a cross or ladderstitch has not carried out his obligation. If it was a part that had been rejoined in a seam, he has carried out his obligation" [following Lazarus's translation].

C. Said R. Hisda, "Or with Alexandrian mending."

29. A. *Our rabbis have taught on Tannaite authority:*

B. A person has the right to turn the garment inside out and to mend the tear.

C. R. Simeon b. Eleazar forbids completely mending the tear.

D. And just as the seller may not reunite the tear completely, so the buyer is forbidden to reunite it, so the seller has to tell the buyer why the tear has been made.

30. A. *Our rabbis have taught on Tannaite authority:*

B. "The tear to begin with is to be a handbreadth, and an addition to it is to be of three fingers breadth," the words of R. Meir.

C. R. Judah says, "The tear to begin with is to be three fingerbreadths and the addition may be of any length at all."

D. Said Ulla, "The decided law accords with the position of R. Meir as to the initial tear, and the decided law accords with R. Judah as to the additional tear."

The foregoing pattern—citation of a clause of the Mishnah, addition of Tannaite complements of a thematic character—now continues.

II.1

A. **And they provide mourners food only on an upright couch:**

B. *Our rabbis have taught on Tannaite authority:*

C. He who goes to a house of mourning, if he is an old friend and does not stand on ceremony, serves the meal for him on overturned touches. If not, he serves it on couches set upright.

2. A. *Raba had a bereavement. Abba bar Marta, that is, Abba bar Mihyumi, came to him. Raba sat on a couch right side up, and Abba bar Marta sat on one upside down.*

B. *Said Raba, "That neophyte rabbi has no sense!"*

3. A. *Our rabbis have taught on Tannaite authority:*

B. He who is on a trip [and suffered a bereavement], **[27A]** if he can cut down on business, he should d so, and if not, then let him proceed with his affairs.

4. A. *Our rabbis have taught on Tannaite authority:*

    B. "At what point do they turn over the couches? When the bier has left the door of the house," the words of R. Eliezer.

    C. R. Joshua says, "When the rolling stone has closed the mouth of the sepulchre."

    D. There was the case, when Rabban Gamaliel the Elder died, and as soon as the corpse was taken out the door of the house, said to them R. Eliezer, "Turn over your beds." But as soon as the rolling stone had closed the mouth of the sepulchre, said to them R. Joshua, "Turn over your beds."

    E. They said to him, "We already turned them over on the instructions of the other elder."

5. A. *Our rabbis have taught on Tannaite authority:*

    B. When do they set the beds upright on the eve of the Sabbath? From the time of the offering at dusk and onwards.

    C. Said Rabbah bar Huna, "Even so, he may sit on the upright bed only after dark."

    D. And at the end of the Sabbath, even though he has only a single day more of mourning, he turns the bed over once more.

6. A. *Our rabbis have taught on Tannaite authority:*

    B. He who turns over his bed does not, in fact, turn over only his own bed, but he turns over all the beds that he has in the house, even if he has ten located in two places, he turns over all of them.

    C. And even if there are five brothers, and one of them died, all of the others turn over the beds.

    D. If he had a bed designated for clothing, that one is not necessarily overturned.

    E. A *dargesh*-bed is not overturned but is tilted up.

    F. Rabban Simeon b. Gamaliel says, As to a *dargesh*-bed, it suffices to loosen the bolster-frame and let it drop on its own."

    7. A. *What is the definition of a dargesh-bed?*

        B. *Said Ulla, "It is a small couch* [Shachter, *Sanhedrin*, p. 106, n. 3: not used for rest but placed in the home merely as an omen of good fortune]."

        C. *Said to him Rabbah, "But what about the rule that is stated with regard to the king, which we have learned in the Mishnah:* **And when they provide him with the funeral meal, all the people sit on the ground while he sits on a couch [M. San. 2:3F].** *Now is there something on which, up to that time, he had never sat, and now we seat him on that object?"*

        D. *R. Ashi objected to this argument, "What sort of problem is this? Perhaps it may be compared to the matter of eating and drinking, for up to this point we gave him nothing to eat or drink, while now we bring him food and drink.*

        E. *"But if there is a question, this is the question: As to a couch* [of the present sort], *it is not necessary to lower it but it is stood up* [6.E above]. *Now if you think that the couch under discussion is a small couch [such as was described above], why is it not necessary to lower it? Has it not been taught on Tannaite authority:* He who lowers beds [in the house of mourning] does not lower the mourner's bed alone but all of the beds in the house.' *[So why not lower the one under discussion?]."*

F. *But what is the problem? Perhaps it falls into the category of a bed set aside for the storage of utensils, concerning which it has been taught on Tannaite authority:* If it was a bed set aside for storing utensils, it is not necessary to lower it.

G. *Rather, if there is a problem, this is the problem:* R. Simeon b. Gamaliel says, "As to a small couch, one loosens the loops, and it will fall on its own." *Now if you maintain that it is a small couch [such as was described above], are there any loops?*

H. *Rather, when Rabin came, he said,* "One of the rabbis told me, and it was R. Tahalipa by name, that he would frequent the leather-workers market, and he asked one of them, 'What is a couch?' And he was told, 'It is the name of a bed of skins.'" [Shachter, p. 107, n. 2: Its strapping consisted of leather instead of ropes. Not being supported by long legs, it stood very low, and therefore on practical grounds, the first Tannaite authority maintains that is must not be undone and lowered, as the leather will be spoiled through the damp earth, while Rabban Simeon b. Gamaliel holds that there is no fear of this.]

I. *So too it has been stated:* Said R. Jeremiah, "A couch has its webbing affixed on the inside, while a bed has its webbing affixed on the outside."

J. Said R. Jacob bar Aha said R. Joshua b. Levi, "The decided law accords with the opinion of Rabban Simeon b. Gamaliel."

K. Said R. Jacob bar Aha said R. Assi, "In the case of a bed the poles of which protrude, it is enough to set it up [on one side] [Shachter, p. 107, n. 8: because if actually lowered, it may appear to be standing in its usual position, since then the poles protrude upwards]."

8. A. *Our rabbis have taught on Tannaite authority:*

B. If a mourner sat on a bed, chair, or stall for urns, or even sleeps on the bare ground, he has not carried out his duty."

C. Said R. Yohanan, "He has not in doing these actions carried out the obligation of turning the bed over"?

9. A. *Our rabbis have taught on Tannaite authority:*

B. They may sweep or through straw in the room of a mourner and wash the plates and dishes and glasses and flagons in the household of a bereaved person, but they do not bring perfumes or spices into a house of mourning.

C. Is that so? But did not Bar Qappara teach, "They do not say a blessing over perfume or spices used in a house of mourning," *yielding the premise that while we do not say a blessing, we may take them into the house of mourning!*

D.   *There is no contradiction, the one speaks of a house of mourning, the other, the house filled with comforters.*

I.1 clarifies the situation to which our Mishnah's rule pertains. No. 2 is tacked on because it is directly relevant to the forgoing, and then Nos. 3-5+6 are a set joined to the foregoing because of their direct intersection on details of rules, and the rest, Nos. 7-14 are joined because of a general thematic relevance, namely, death-scenes of masters. Obviously, the principle of agglutination of these compositions into a quite coherent composite has no bearing on Mishnah-exegesis but derived from a program of compiling exemplary accounts of critical moments in sages' lives. Of these, we see, how they died was found of special interest. No. 15, with its own talmud at Nos. 16-27, provides a Tannaite complement to our Mishnah's general theme. Nos. 28-34 set forth a variety of other Tannaite rules on the same theme, many of them given further amplification. **II.1** glosses the Mishnah with a Tannaite refinement, itself glossed at No. 2, and Nos. 3-6+7, 8-9 move forward with the same exercise.

Mishnah/Bavli tractate Moed Qatan 3:7C-E

C.   **They do not bring [food] to a house of mourning on a tray, salver, or flat basket, but in plain baskets.**

D.   **And they do not [in Grace after meals] say the blessing for mourners during the intermediate days of the festival.**

E.   **But [the mourners] do stand in a line and offer consolation and dismiss those that have gathered together.**

Mishnah/Bavli tractate Moed Qatan 3:8A-C

A.   **They do not set the bier down in the street,**

B.   **so as not to give occasion for a lamentation.**

C.   **And under no circumstances do they set down the bier of women in the street, on account of respect.**

No analytical program pertinent to the Mishnah makes an appearance in the present sequence of Mishnah-paragraphs. All we have is a compilation of Tannaite treatments of the theme to which the Mishnah's rule, for its part, is devoted. This is not a talmud, but it is one way in which the Bavli organizes its materials, and, we

see, a very common way: a collection of treatments of a theme
presented in the Mishnah, set forth in the context of that Mishnah-paragraph.

I.1

    A.   *Our rabbis have taught on Tannaite authority:*

    B.   In times of old they would bring food to the house of mourning,
the rich in silver and gold baskets, the poor in wicker-baskets of
peeled willow twigs, so the poor were embarrassed. They ordained
that everybody should bring the food in wicket baskets of peeled
willow twigs out of respect for the poor.

2. A.   *Our rabbis have taught on Tannaite authority:*

    B.   **In times of old they would serve drinks in a house of
mourning, the rich in white glass, the poor in colored,
so the poor were embarrassed. They ordained that everybody should serve drinks in colored glass, out of respect for the poor.**

    C.   **At first they would leave the faces of the well-to-do ex-
posed on the bier but cover over the faces of the poor,
because their faces would be blackened by years of
drought, so the poor were embarrassed. They ordained
that everybody should be covered over, out of respect
for the poor.**

    D.   **At first they would bring out the rich on a woven bed
and the poor [27B] on a plain bier, so the poor were
embarrassed. They ordained that everybody should be
brought out on a plain bier, out of respect for the poor.**

    E.   **At first they would put out a pan of incense under the
bed of those who had died of stomach trouble, so those
yet alive who had stomach trouble were embarrassed.
They ordained that incense should be set out under everybody, out of respect for the living who had stomach
trouble.**

    F.   **At first they would immerse all utensils used by men-
struants who had died, and the living women who were
menstruating were embarrassed, so they ordained that
they should do the same to utensils used by all dying
women, out of respect for the menstruants yet alive.**

    G.   **At first they would immerse all utensils used by those
suffering from flux-uncleanness when they were dying,
and the living who had the same form of uncleanness
were embarrassed, so they ordained that they should
immerse all utensils out of respect for the living who were
unclean with flux-uncleanness.**

    H.   **At first the expense of taking out the dead fell harder**

on the relatives than did the death itself, so the kin fled from the corpse, until in the end Rabban Gamaliel came forward and, ignoring the honor owing to him, he came out for burial in clothing made of flax, and so afterward everybody followed suit and was buried in linen [T. Nid. 9:16-17].

I.   Said R. Pappa, "Nowadays everybody comes out even in a cheap shroud that costs a mere penny."

II.1.

A.   **They do not set the bier down in the street, so as not to give occasion for a lamentation:**

B.   Said R. Pappa, "The consideration of the intermediate days of the festival does not stand in the face of the burial of a disciple of a sage, all the more so the consideration of Hanukkah and Purim. *But that ruling concerns only the location where the corpse is situated, but elsewhere, that is not the case [and it is forbidden to mourn on those days]."*

C.   *Is that so? And lo, R. Kahana lamented R. Zebid of Nehardea at the town of Pum-Nahara [where the corpse was not located]!*

D.   *Said R. Pappi, "That was the day on which the bad news came, and it was as though he were present at the bier of the corpse."*

2.   A.   Said Ulla, "'A lamentation' involves striking the breast: 'Tremble, strip, and put on sackcloth on your loins, striking upon the breast' (Is. 32:11-12)."

3.   A.   *Our rabbis have taught on Tannaite authority:*

B.   He who stamps the foot [as a sign of mourning] should stamp wearing not a sandal or a boot, because it is dangerous [to the foot itself].

4.   A.   Said R. Yohanan, "As soon as a mourner has nodded his head, the comforters are no longer permitted to sit with him."

B.   And said R. Yohanan, "All are obligated to rise before the patriarch except for a mourner and a sick person."

C.   And said R. Yohanan, "To every classification of person is said, 'Take your seat,' except for a mourner and a sick person."

5.   A.   Said R. Judah said Rab, "On the first day of bereavement a mourner is forbidden to eat his own bread, in line with what the All-Merciful said to Ezekiel, 'And you should not eat bread belonging to other people' (Ez. 24:17)."

B.   *Rabbah and R. Joseph traded meals with one another.*

C.   And said R. Judah said Rab, "When someone dies in a town, everybody in town is forbidden to work."

D.   *R. Hamnuna came to Daru-Mata. He heard the sound of a ram's horn announcing a death. He saw people doing their work. He said to them, "These people are to be excommunicated, has someone not died in town?"*

E.   *They said to him, "There is an association in town [assigned to care for the burial of the deceased]."*

F. *He said to them, "Then it's o.k."*

G. And said R. Judah said Rab, "Whoever grieves excessively for his deceased will weep for yet another death."

H. *There was a woman in the neighborhood of R. Huna who had seven sons. One of them died, and she wept excessively for him. R. Huna sent word to her, "Don't do this." She paid no attention to him.*

I. *He sent word to her, "If you pay attention, well and good, and if not, then you'd better prepare [shrouds] for another!" The next son died, and then the rest. In the end he said to her, "Are you making provision [of shrouds] for yourself ['cause you should]?" And she died.*

6. A. *Our rabbis have taught on Tannaite authority:*

B. "Weep not for the dead, nor bemoan him" (Jer. 22:10)—

C. "Weep not for the dead" excessively.

D. "nor bemoan him" beyond what is reasonable.

E. How so?

F. Three days are for weeping, seven for lamenting, thirty for not getting a hair cut and not wearing meticulously groomed clothing.

G. After that point, the Holy One, blessed be he, says, "Are you going to be more compassionate towards him than I was [towards Moses]?"

7. A. "Weep bitterly for the one who goes away" (Jer. 22:10)—

B. Said R. Judah, "This refers to the one who goes away leaving no children."

C. R. Joshua b. Levi would go to a house of mourning only in the case of someone who had gone off without children, in line with the verse, 'Weep bitterly for the one who goes away, for he shall return no more nor see his native country' (Jer. 22:10)."

8. A. "'Weep bitterly for the one who goes away, for he shall return no more nor see his native country" (Jer. 22:10):

B. R. Huna said, "This refers to someone who committed a transgression and repeated it."

C. *R. Huna is consisted with views stated elsewhere, for* said R. Huna, ""Once a person has committed a transgression and done it again, it is permitted to him."

D. "It is <u>permitted</u> to him" do you say?

E. Rather, I should say, It is transformed for him so that it appears to be permitted.

9. A. Said R. Levi, "On the first three days of bereavement a mourner should see himself as though a sword were hanging over him between his shoulders; from the third to the seventh day, it is as if it stands in the corner opposite; afterward it is as though it were moving alongside in the market place."

After citing another clause of the Mishnah, we revert to one of our established exegetical programs: the limits of the application of the Mishnah's rule.

III.1

A. **And under no circumstances do they set down the bier of women in the street, on account of respect:**

B. *Said the Nehardeans*, "They have taught this rule only **[28A]** in connection with a woman who had died in childbirth, but other women's corpses may be set down."

C. R. Eleazar said, "Even other women [are subject to this restriction]: 'And there Miriam died, and there she was buried' (Num. 20:1)—burial closely followed her death."

What is now tacked on to the amplification of the Mishnah is a composite on the theme tangentially mentioned in the foregoing, in this case, Miriam. This is a kind of talmud, but not a very analytical kind:

2. A. And said R. Eleazar, "Miriam too died by a kiss. That is shown by a verbal analogy formed of the use of the word 'there' in both her case and in the case of Moses.

B. "And how come Scripture does not say 'by the mouth of the Lord' as in the case of Moses [Dt. 34:5]?

C. "Because saying such a thing would be inappropriate [in the case of a woman]."

3. A. Said R. Ammi, "How come the story of the death of Miriam is situated adjacent to the passage that deals with the burning of the red cow?

B. "It is to teach you that just as the ashes of the red cow effect atonement, so the death of the righteous effects atonement."

4. A. Said R. Eleazar, "How come the story of the death of Aaron is situated adjacent to the passage on the priestly garments [Num. 20:26, 28]?

B. "It is to teach you that just as the priest's garments serve to effect atonement, so the death of the righteous effects atonement."

5. A. *Our rabbis have taught on Tannaite authority:*

B. If someone died suddenly, that is classified as "being caught up."

C. If someone died after an illness of one day, that is classified as "being rushed out."

D. R. Hanania b. Gamaliel says, "That is death by a stroke: 'Son of man, behold I take away from you the desire of your eyes with a pestilential stroke' (Ez. 24:16), and then, 'So I spoke to the people in the morning, and at evening my wife died' (Ez. 24:18)."

E. If someone lingered for two days and then died, this is classified as a precipitous death.

F. After three—this is classified as a death of reproof.

G. After four—this is classified as a death of rebuff.

H. After five—this is classified as a routine death.

    I. *Said R. Hanina, "What verse of Scripture indicates it?* 'Lo, your days are approaching that you must die' (Dt. 31:14). 'Behold' *is one,* 'your days,' *two more,* 'are approaching' *represents two more."*

    J. "Behold" makes one because the Greek word for one is *hen* [which is the Hebrew word for "behold"].

K. [Continuing from H:] If one died at under fifty years of age—this is classified as death by extirpation.

L. If one died at fifty-two—this is classified as the death of Samuel of Ramah.

M. If one died at sixty—this is classified as death at the hand of Heaven.

    N. *Said Mar Zutra, "What verse of Scripture indicates it?* 'You shall come to your grave in ripe age' (Job 5:26), *and the numerical value of the word for in ripe age is sixty."*

O. If one died at the age of seventy—this is classified as the hoary head.

P. If one died at the age of eighty—this is classified as the vigorous old man: "The days of our years are three score and ten, or even by reason of strength, four score" (Ps. 90:10).

R. Said Rabbah, "If one died from age fifty to age sixty, that is classified as death by extirpation, *and the reason that is not stated explicitly is out of respect to Samuel of Ramah."*

6. A. *When R. Joseph reached the age of sixty, he made for the rabbis a festival day, saying, "I have now emerged from the age at which my death would have marked punishment by extirpation."*

    B. *Said to him Abbayye, "Granted that you have now passed the limit of the age at which extirpation would have been the case, have you escaped the limit at which death would mark dying out of a sudden illness on a single day?"* [That is, If someone died suddenly, that is classified as "being caught up."]

    C. *He said to him, "Anyhow, grab half of whatever you can get."*

7. A. *R. Huna died suddenly. The rabbis were worried about it. Zoga of Adiabene repeated to them the following Tannaite statement:* "What we learned as the rule pertains only if one has not attained eighty years of age, but if one has attained the age of eighty, sudden death is the same as dying by a kiss."

I.1, 2 complement the Mishnah with Tannaite amplifications. **II.1** clarifies the relationship between the Mishnah's rule and the larger theme of our tractate, the intermediate days of the festival. Nos. 2-9 form an anthology on the general theme of mourning, not clearly connected to the rule of the Mishnah in particular. **III.1** works out the limits of the application of the law of the Mishnah.

Nos. 2, 3, 4 form a thematic appendix to 1.C. Then Nos. 5-15 are tacked on as a further, somewhat run-on, thematic anthology.

MISHNAH/BAVLI TRACTATE MOED QATAN 3:8D-E, 3:9
3:8D-E

D.   [28B] **Women on the intermediate days of a festival wail but do not clap their hands.**

E.   **R. Ishmael says, "Those who are near the bier clap their hands."**

3:9

A.   **On the new moons, Hanukkah, and Purim they wail and clap their hands.**

B.   **On none of them do they sing a dirge.**

C.   **Once the deceased has been buried, they do not wail or clap their hands.**

D.   **What is a wail?**

E.   **When all sing together.**

F.   **What is a dirge?**

G.   **When one starts, and then all join in with her,**

H.   **as it is said, "Teach your daughters wailing, and every one her neighbor a dirge" (Jer. 9:19).**

I.   **But in the time which is coming, it says, "He has swallowed up death forever, and the Lord God win wipe away tears from off all faces, and the reproach of his people he shall take away from off all the whole earth, for the Lord has spoken it" (Is. 25:8).**

We begin with a more conventional kind of Mishnah-commentary: answering a question invited by the Mishnah, filling in a detail required by the Mishnah. But only in the most formal sense is what follows "Mishnah-commentary," since each entry, e.g., B, C, D, and so on, stands on its own and makes a complete and comprehensible statement without appeal, for context and meaning, to the Mishnah's rule or language.

I.1

A.   *What do they say?*

B.   Said Rab:
     [Lazarus:] Cry over him who is departing!
     Cry over his wounds and smarting.

C.   *Said Raba, "This is what the women of Shoken-Seb say:*
     [Lazarus:] Withdraw the bone from out the pot,

And the kettles fill with water hot.

D. *And said Raba, "This is what the women of Shoken-Seb say:*
[Lazarus:] Be muffled, you high mountains,
Clouds covering your head;
Of high lineage and grand ancestry
Came he who is dead.

The Mishnah-commentary having been completed, we now go on to Tannaite treatments of the theme introduced by the Mishnah:

2. A. *It has been taught on Tannaite authority:*
   B. R. Meir would say, "'It is better to go to the house of mourning than to go to the house of celebration, for that is the end of all men and the living will lay it to heart' (Qoh. 7:2)."
   C. *What is the meaning of and the living will lay it to heart?*
   D. *One who laments—others will lament for him; one who assists at a burial—others will bury him. One who bears the bier—others will bear him. One who raises his voice—others will raise their voice for him.*
   E. *Others say, "And he who does not raise himself with pride," others will raise him:* "Glorify not yourself in the presence of the king and do not stand in the place of great men, for it is better that he said to you, 'Come up hither,' than that you be put low down in the presence of the prince' (Prov. 25:6-7)."

I.1 amplifies the Mishnah's theme. Nos. 2, 3+4-5 provide further examples of words of lamentation and comfort. No. 6 then resumes our sequence of rules governing conduct in bereavement. This miscellany continues through Nos. 7-12.

IV. *The Bavli's Primary Discourse*

"Primary discourse," it is now clear, refers to the main lines of expression of a coherent document. When the Bavli's authorship, having cited a passage of the Mishnah, begins its statement, it always begins with attention to the cited passage. When further materials, not those of Mishnah-commentary follow, these relate to the initial discussion. So while many compositions, and even some very large composites, take shape in their own terms and stand independent of the Mishnah, when they find a place in the Bavli, it is ordinarily in the framework of Mishnah-commentary, very often as a secondary expansion of what is set forth to begin with for the exegesis of what is in the Mishnah. The part of the tractate that we have examined leaves no doubt about the coherence, with a cited passage of the Mishnah, of nearly everything in the Bavli. Materials that do not cohere either with Mishnah-exegesis, or with secondary amplification of that exegesis, prove sparse indeed. When we recall that sizable components of the Bavli—numerous compositions—stand on their own and not as Mishnah-commentary, we realize how much the authorship of the Bavli has done in reframing matters to serve its distinctive purpose: nearly everything that they utilized, they presented in the framework of Mishnah-commentary and amplification. Let us now review the types of Mishnah-commentary that, over all, forms the Bavli's primary discourse.

I. *Its Rhetorical Paradigms*

1. *Scriptural Foundations of the Laws of the Mishnah*

The single most commonplace and characteristic inquiry of the Bavli is framed in the question: what is the source of the rule of the Mishnah? Conventionally, this inquiry occurs in simple language, e.g., "What is the source of this rule," always with the implication, "in Scripture"? Here is one common way of asking and answering the question:

BAVLI BERAKHOT 1:1

A. From what time do they recite the Shema in the evening?
B. From the hour that the priests [who had immersed after uncleanness and awaited sunset to complete the process of purification] enter [a state of cleanness, the sun having set, so as] to eat their heave offering—

I.1

A. On what basis does the Tannaite authority stand when he begins by teaching the rule, "From what time...," [in the assumption that the religious duty to recite the <u>Shema</u> has somewhere been established? In point of fact, it has not been established that people have to recite the <u>Shema</u> at all.]
B. Furthermore, on what account does he teach the rule concerning the evening at the beginning? Why not start with the morning?
C. The Tannaite authority stands upon the authority of Scripture, [both in requiring the recitation of the <u>Shema</u> and in beginning with the evening], for it is written, "When you lie down and when you rise up" (Deut. 6:7).

D. And this is the sense of the passage: When is the time for the rec-
    itation of the <u>Shema</u> when one lies down? It is **from the hour
    that the priests enter [a state of cleanness so as] to eat
    their heave-offering [M. 1:1B].**
E. And if you prefer, I may propose that the usage derives from the
    order of the description of creation, for it is said, "And there was
    evening, and there was morning, one day" (Gen. 1:5).

2. Authorities behind the Laws of the Mishnah

A primary exegetical question concerns whether or not a law stands
for an individual's opinion or a consensus of sages. The inquiry
takes a variety of forms. The simplest is, "Who is the authority
behind the Mishnah's [anonymous] rule?" This allows us to find
out whether we have a schismatic (individual) or normative (con-
sensual) opinion; we may further ask whether the cited authority
is consistent, testing the principle behind the rule at hand against
the evidence of his rulings in other cases in which the same principle determines matters.

1:1-2/3.

A. *Who is the Tannaite authority who takes the position that work on the interme-
    diate days of a festival is permitted if it is to prevent loss, but if it is to add to
    gain it is not permitted, and, further, even to prevent loss, really heavy labor is
    forbidden?*
B. *Said R. Huna, "It is R. Eliezer b. Jacob, for we have learned in the Mishnah:*
    **R. Eliezer b. Jacob says, 'They lead water from one tree
    to another, on condition that one not water the entire
    field. Seeds which have not been watered before the fes-
    tival one should not water on the intermediate days of
    the festival' [M. 1:3].***"
C. *Well, I might concede that there is a representation of R. Eliezer's position that
    he prohibits work to add to one's gain, but have you heard a tradition that he
    disallows work in a situation in which otherwise loss will result?*
D. *Rather, said R. Pappa, "Who is the authority behind this rule? It is R. Judah,
    for it has been taught on Tannaite authority:* **'From a spring that first
    flows on the intermediate days of a festival they irrigate
    even a rain watered field,' the words of R. Meir. And
    sages say, 'They irrigate from it only a field that depends
    upon irrigation, which has gone dry.' R. Eleazar b. Aza-
    riah says, "Not this nor that, [[but they do not irrigate
    a field from it [namely, a field the spring of which has
    gone dry] even in the case of an irrigated field]' [T. Moed
    1:1A-C].** Even further, said R. Judah, 'A person should not clean
    out a water channel and with the dredging on the intermediate days
    of a festival water his garden or seed bed.'"

E. *Now what is the meaning of "that has gone dry"? If you say that it really has dried up, then what is going to be accomplished by watering it?*

F. *Said Abbayye, "The point is that this former water source has gone dry and another has just emerged."*

G. **R. Eleazar b. Azariah says, "Not this nor that:"** *there is no difference between the case of an old spring that has gone dry or that has not gone dry, in any event a spring that has just flowed may not be utilized on the intermediate days of the festival.*

H. *And how to you know [that it is Judah in particular who takes the position that work on the intermediate days of a festival is permitted if it is to prevent loss, but if it is to add to gain it is not permitted, and, further, even to prevent loss, really heavy labor is forbidden]? Perhaps R. Judah takes the position that he does, that is, that it is permitted to use the water for an irrigated field but not for a field that depends on rain, only in the case of a spring that has just now begun to flow,* **[2B]** *since it may cause erosion, but in the case of a spring that has not just now begun to flow and will not cause erosion might be permitted for use even on a field that depends on rain?*

I. *If so, then in accord with which authority will you assign our Mishnah-paragraph? For in fact, in R. Judah's view, there is no distinction between a spring that has just now flowed and one that has not just now flowed; in either case, an irrigated field may be watered, one that depends on rain may not. And the reason that the passage specifies the spring that has just now flowed is only to show the extend to which R. Meir was prepared to go, even a spring that has just now flowed may be used, and that is, even for a field that depends upon rain.*

The harmonization of conflict will take the form of the comparison of rules of diverse authorities on the same matter. In what follows, the Mishnah's rule is set side by side with a rule in the name of a given authority, and then the conflict is underlined and explained.

3:1-2/II.1

A. **Who are they who may get a hair cut on the intermediate days of a festival? (1) he who comes from overseas or from captivity…:**

B. *Our Mishnah-paragraph's rule is not in accord with the position of R. Judah. For it has been taught on Tannaite authority:* **R. Judah says, "One who comes home from overseas may not get haircuts during the intermediate days of the festival, because he went abroad at such a season without the permission of sages [who would have told him to go after the festival, so as to avoid this situation]"** [T. Moed 2:2G].

C. Said Raba, "If he went out merely to sightsee, all parties concur that he is forbidden. If he went out to make a living, all parties concur that he is permitted. They differ only if he made the trip just to make money. *One authority invokes the analogy of going sight seeing, the other, of going to make a living.*"

D. An objection was raised: **Said Rabbi, "The opinion of R. Judah makes more sense to me in a case in which one has not gotten permission from sages to go abroad, and that of sages makes more sense in a case in which he has gotten permission from sages to go abroad" [T. Moed 2:2I].** *Now what does* **in which one has not gotten permission from sages** *mean? If I should say that it means to go sightseeing, have you not said,* all parties concur that he is forbidden? *And could it then mean to make a living? But have you not said,* all parties concur that he is permitted? *So it is obvious that it means just to make money.*

E. *But then I invoke the concluding clause:* **and that of sages makes more sense in a case in which he has gotten permission from sages to go abroad!** *Now what could "with permission" mean here? If I should say that it means to make a living, have you not said,* all parties concur that he is permitted? *And might it be just to make money? But have you not said,* **The opinion of R. Judah makes more sense to me in a case in which one has not gotten permission from sages to go abroad?**

F. *This is the sense of the statement at hand:* The opinion of R. Judah makes more sense than that of rabbis when he went forth without permission, *and what circumstance might that involve? It is for sightseeing. For sages only differed from R. Judah when it comes to making money. But as to merely sightseeing, they concur with R. Judah.* And the opinion of rabbis seems to make more sense than R. Judah's when he went forth with permission, *and what might that involve? It would be for making a living, for even R. Judah differed with rabbis only when it was to make money. But as to going abroad to make a living, he concurs with them.*

3. Meanings of Words and Phrases

We come to Mishnah-commentary of the most conventional kind: explanation of the meanings of words and phrases of the Mishnah, appealing for scriptural parallels to set forth lexical evidence, on the one side, inquiry into the sense and meaning of sentences of the Mishnah, on the other.

1:1-2/2.

A. *And on what basis is it inferred that the meaning of the words "irrigated field" is, a thirsty field [which has to be irrigated]?*

B. *It is in line with that which is written:* "When you were faint and weary" (Dt. 25:18), *and the Hebrew word for weary is represented in Aramaic by the word that means, "exhausted."*

C. *And how do we know that the words translated rain-watered field refers to a fucked field?*

D.   "For as a man has sexual relations with a maiden, so shall your sons
     be as husbands unto you" (Is. 62:5), *and the word in Aramaic is rendered,*
     "Behold, as a boy fucks a girl, so your sons shall get laid in your midst."

Another form of explanation of the Mishnah, and the simplest,
will be to answer a question left open by the Mishnah and urgent for the explanation of the Mishnah's rule: commentary in
its simplest form.

1:4/III.1

A.   **They block up a breach in the intermediate days of a**
     festival. And in the seventh year, one builds it in the
     normal way:
B.   How is the breach blocked up?
C.   *Said R. Joseph, "With* [Lazarus:] *a hurdle made of twigs and daphne stakes."*
D.   *In a Tannaite statement it was set forth:* one piles up pebbles but does not
     hold them down with mortar.

A third form of Mishnah-explanation will carry us into the criticism of the language of the Mishnah. In what follows, we ask why
the Mishnah-paragraph under discussion changes the subject. At
stake then is the issue of whether or not the framer of a passage
forgets by the end where he started—that is, the issue of the perfection of the verbatim formulation of the document:

2:1/I.1

A.   *While the passage commences by discussing mourning, it concludes solely with*
     advice on how to press oil!
B.   Said R. Shisha b. R. Idi, "That bears the implication that what one
     may do during the intermediate days of a festival one may not do
     during the week of mourning." [Lazarus: one may do these things
     now only in the intermediate days of the festival but not during the
     mourning week].
C.   *R. Ashi said, "The formulation is meant to yield the reading, 'it goes without*
     saying,' in this way: it is not necessary to give the rule governing the time of
     mourning, which is in any event based on the authority of rabbis and so such acts
     of labor are permitted, but even during the intermediate days of a festival, during
     which, on the authority of the Torah, acts of supererogatory labor are forbidden,
     still, where there may be a great loss, rabbis have permitted such an act of labor."

4. Text-Criticism. The Issue of Repetition
The matter of text-criticism covers a variety of distinct inquiries.
In the first sort, we want to know why the Mishnah frames mat-

ters as it does, with the generative issue being whether or not the document repeats itself. The type of Mishnah-commentary is signalled by a single word, "it is necessary," and what will follow is an implicit justification of presenting more than a single rule or case. This form is not limited to Mishnah-criticism; on the contrary, it is commonly used for any formulation—Tannaite or other—of a variety of cases that illustrate the same principle, and the form, brief though it is, suitably sets forth the exegetical problem to be solved.

1.1-2/I.1

A. [**They water an irrigated field on the intermediate days of a festival and in the Seventh Year, whether from a spring that first flows at that time, or from a spring that does not first flow at that time**:] *since it is explicitly stated that they may water from a spring that flows for the first time, which may damage the soil by erosion [making necessary immediate repair of the damage during the intermediate days of the festival], is it necessary to specify that they may water from a spring that does not first flow at that time, which is not going to cause erosion?*

B. *One may say that it is necessary to include both the latter and the former, for if the Tannaite framer had given the rule only covering a spring that first flows on the intermediate days of the festival, it is in that case in particular in which it is permitted to work on an irrigated field, but not for a rain-watered field, because the water is going to cause erosion, but in the case of a spring that does not first flow on the intermediate days, which is unlikely to cause erosion, I might have said that even a rain-watered field may be watered. So he tells us that there is no distinction between a spring that flows for the first time and one that does not flow for the first time. The rule is the same for both: an irrigated plot may be watered from it, but a rain-watered plot may not be watered from [either a new or an available spring].*

The key-word is simply "necessary," whether introducing a question or a declarative statement. Then the rest follows.

Another kind of text-criticism involves the explanation of how a variety of examples hold together; the Mishnah may present three or more examples, and what we want to know is whether a stringency or leniency is conveyed by setting forth examples that do not really cohere. Here is an example of this other sort of analysis of the formulation of the Mishnah:

III.1

A. **But they do not water [an irrigated field] with (1) collected rain water, or (2) water from a swape well:**

B. *There is no trouble in understanding why water from a swape well should not be used, since watering in that way involves heavy labor. But what objection can there be to using collected rain water, since what heavy labor can possibly be involved in irrigating with rain water?*

C. *Said R. Ilaa said R. Yohanan, "It is a precautionary decree, on account of the possibility of the farmer's going on to make use of water from a swape well."*

D. R. Ashi said, "Rain water itself can be as hard to draw as the water of a swape well."

E. *At issue between them is what R. Zira said. For said R. Zira said Rabbah bar Jeremiah said Samuel, "From irrigation streams that draw water from ponds it is permitted to irrigate on the intermediate days of the festival." One authority [Ashi] concurs with the position of R. Zira, and the other authority does not concur with the position of R. Zira.*

5. *Conflict of Principles Implicit in the Mishnah's Rules*

One important issue in the Bavli's Mishnah-commentary is whether or not two rules, intersecting in detail or in fundamental principle, cohere. A sustained effort characterizes the Bavli's inquiry into the harmony of the law of the Mishnah, the object of which invariably is to demonstrate that the Mishnah's law form a single, wholly cogent law, perfect in their harmony. Here is an example of how that interest is expressed:

IX.1

A. **and go forth [to give warning] against Diverse Kinds:**

B. *But in fact in the intermediate days of a festival do we go about to inspect whether or not there are mixed seeds in a field? But there is the following contradiction:* **On the first day of Adar they make public announcement concerning [payment of] sheqel dues and concerning the sowing of mixed seeds [Lev. 19:19, Dt. 22:9]. On the fifteenth day of that month they read the Megillah [Scroll of Esther] in walled cities. And they repair the paths, roads, and immersion pools. And they carry out all public needs. And they mark off the graves. And they go forth [to inspect the fields] on account of mixed seeds [M. Sheq. 1:1]**/

C. R. Eleazar and R. Yosé bar Hanina—

D. One said, "The latter refers to the crops that ripen earlier [in mid-Adar], the other, of late-ripening crops [and our Mishnah-paragraph has a further inspection, now in mid-Nisan, during the intermediate days of the festival of Passover]."

E.   And the other said, "In the one case [in Adar] they go out to in-
     spect the condition of grain fields, in the other, vegetable patches."
F.   Said R. Assi said R. Yohanan, "The rule pertains only in a case in
     which the sprouts are not yet recognizable [earlier on]; but where
     it is possible to discern the character of the sprouts early on, they
     went forth to inspect the situation earlier."

There are various solutions to the problem of conflict between
rules, of which the foregoing is one common sort: distinguishing
the point of reference of two or more rules, showing that each
bears its own distinctive considerations.

We see in what follows that the intersecting rule need not occur in another Mishnah-paragraph. The item before us is in the
same Hebrew as the Mishnah's rule, but does not bear an explicit indicator of Tannaite origin or formulation; the language
forms the taxic indicator.

1:5C-G/I.1

A.   **"because it is a time of rejoicing for him:"**
B.   *An objection was raised on the basis of the following:*
C.   He who collects the bones of his mother and father for secondary
     burial—lo, one observes mourning for them all that day. But in the
     evening he no longer observes mourning for them. And in that
     connection said R. Hisda, "Even if he had them tied up in a sheet."
D.   *Said Abbayye, "Say the rule as follows:* 'because the rejoicing of the fes-
     tival affects him.'"

6. Execution of the Law of the Mishnah
Here is an example of how the Bavli will ask about the way in
which the law is realized, here meaning, the conditions under
which the Mishnah's statement applies:

1:3/I.1

A.   [**on condition that one not water the entire field**:] said R.
     Judah, "If the field's soil is clay, he may water it."
B.   *So too it has been taught on Tannaite authority:*
C.   When they made the rule that it is forbidden to irrigate on the
     intermediate days of a festival, they made that statement only con-
     cerning seed that had not drunk before the festival; but as to seed
     that had been watered before the festival, they may be watered
     during the intermediate days of the festival; and if the soil of the
     field was clay, it is permitted to water it. And a bare field [without
     a crop at that time] is not watered during the festival week. But sages

permit doing so in both cases [where seeds were not watered, watering a bare field].

D. *Said Rabina, "That statement leads to the inference that it is permitted to hand-sprinkle a vegetable patch during the intermediate days of a festival. For in the case of a bare field, why is it permitted to do so? It is because that renders the soil fit to be sown or planted, and here too, that is permitted."*

At stake is where and how the simple rule of the Mishnah pertains; a Tannaite formulation of the same conclusion then reenforces the proposed reading of the Mishnah's rule.

7. *The Operative Consideration behind the Law of the Mishnah*

One of the exegetically-productive initiatives of the Bavli will raise the question of the operative consideration that has led to a given rule in the Mishnah. That inquiry will lead us deep into the principles that are given expression in concrete rules, and we often see how entirely abstract conceptions are conceived to stand behind rather commonplace laws.

V.1

A. **R. Eleazar b. Azariah says, "They do not make a new water channel on the intermediate days of a festival or in the Seventh Year." And sages say, "They make a new water channel in the Seventh Year, and they repair damaged ones on the intermediate days of a festival:"**

B. *There is no problem with respect to the prohibition concerning the intermediate days of a festival, since the operative consideration is that this is heavy labor, but why ever not make a channel in the Seventh Year?*

C. R. Zira and R. Abba b. Mamel differ on the matter—

D. One said, "The reason is that the one who digs appears to be hoeing."

E. And the other said, "The reason is that he looks as though he is preparing the banks for sowing."

F. *So what's at stake?*

G. *At issue is when water comes along immediately. From the perspective of him who has said, "The reason is that he looks as though he is preparing the banks for sowing," it is still objectionable. But from the perspective of him who has said, "The reason is that the one who digs appears to be hoeing," there is no objection.*

H. *But should not the one who objects for the reason that it looks as though he is spading also object that he looks as though he is preparing the bank for seed?*

I. *Rather, this is what's at stake between the two explanations: it would involve a case in which he takes what is in the trench and tosses it out. From the perspective of him who says, "The reason is that he looks as though he is pre-*

paring the banks for sowing," *there is no objection; but from the perspective of him who says,* "The reason is that the one who digs appears to
be hoeing," *it is still subject to an objection.*

J. *But from the perspective of him who says that he appears to be preparing the sides
for seed, would he not also admit that he seems to be hoeing?*

K. *Not really, for one who hoes, as soon as he takes up a spadeful, he puts it down
again in place.*

What we want to know here is the reason behind the rule, a very
familiar inquiry of the Bavli's Mishnah-exegetes.

8. *The Implications, for the Law in General, of the Mishnah's Particular
Formulation*
In the following what generates the sustained discussion of the
Talmud is a close reading of the Mishnah's language. This careful analysis produces an inference that has to be investigated in
its own terms. Since there is no understanding the sustained discussion apart from the Mishnah's own statement, the entire composition falls into the classification of Mishnah-commentary.

VII.1

A. [5A] **They repair damaged waterways in the public domain and dig them out:**

B. *Repairing is all right, but not digging afresh.*

C. Said R. Jacob said R. Yohanan, "They have taught this rule only
when the public has no need of the waterways, but if the public
needs them, then it is permitted even to dig afresh."

D. *But if the public needs them, is it permitted to do that work? And has it not been
taught on Tannaite authority:* Cisterns, pits, and caverns that belong to
private property may be cleaned out, and, it goes without saying,
those that belong to the public; but cisterns, pits, and caverns belonging to the public may not be dug, and all the more so those of
a private person? *Does this not address a case in which the public has need
of these facilities?*

E. *No, it addresses a case in which the public has no need of those facilities.*

F. *Along these same lines with respect to a private party, where the private person
has no need of the facility, is repairing allowed? And has it not been taught on
Tannaite authority:* As to cisterns, pits, and caverns of a private person, they collect water in them but they may not be cleaned out,
nor may their cracks be plastered; but as to those belonging to the
public, they may be cleaned out and their cracks may be plastered?

G. *Now what is the point here? It is when a private person has need of the facility.
And in that case, in regard to what is required for public use, where the public
has need of it the same rule pertains? And where the public has need of the facil-*

ity, is it forbidden to dig? Has it not been taught on Tannaite authority: As to cisterns, pits, and caverns belonging to a private person, they collect water in them and clean them out, but they may not plaster their cracks nor put scourings into them to fill cracks; as to those serving the public, they may dig them to begin with and plaster them with cement.*

H. *So the initial formulation poses a contradiction.*

I. *This is how to iron out the difficulty:* They may clean out wells, ditches or caverns of a private person, when the private party requires the facility, and, it goes without saying, those that belong to the public *when the public require use of the facility, in which case even digging them out is permitted.* But they may not dig out wells, ditches, or caverns belonging to the public when the public does not require use of the facility, and, it goes without saying, those belonging to a private party. *When the private party does not require using them, then even cleaning them out is forbidden.*

J. *Said R. Ashi, "A close reading of our Mishnah-paragraph yields the same result:* **And they do all public needs.** *Now what is encompassed within the augmentative formulation,* **all***? Is it not to encompass, also, digging?"*

K. *Not at all, it is to encompass what is covered in that which has been taught on Tannaite authority:* **On the fifteenth day of Adar agents of the court go forth and dig cisterns, wells, and caves. And they repair immersion pools and water channels. Every immersion pool that contains forty seahs of water is suitable for receiving further drawn water if need be, and to every immersion pool that does not contain forty seahs of water they lead a water course and s complete its volume to the measure of forty seahs of water that has not been drawn so that it is suitable to receive further drawn water if need be [T. Sheq. 1:1].** And how on the basis of Scripture do we know that if they did not go forth and carry out all these duties, that any blood that is shed there is credited by Scripture as though they had shed it? Scripture states, "And so blood be upon you" (Dt. 19:10).

L. *Lo, in point of fact the framer of the Mishnah has covered these matters explicitly:* **They repair roads, streets, and water pools. And they do all public needs***! what is encompassed within the augmentative formulation,* **all***? Is it not to encompass, also, digging?*

M. *Yes, that's the proof!*

Another mode of commentary, in the inquiry into the implications of the Mishnah's rule for law in general, involves presenting a theoretical possibility that is subject to confirmation, or refutation, by a statement of a Mishnah-paragraph. That theorizing in response to a rule of the Mishnah then explores the implications of a rule of the Mishnah.

I.1

A. [**writs of betrothal for women**:] Said Samuel, "It is permitted for a man to betroth a woman on the intermediate days of the festival, lest someone else get there first."

B. *May we say that the following supports his thesis:* **And these do they write on the intermediate days of a festival: writs of betrothal for women***? Does this not mean that one quite literally may draw up a writ of betrothal?*

C. *Not at all, it refers, rather, to drawing up preliminary terms, in line with what R. Giddal said Rab said [in defining such an agreement].*

D. For said R. Giddal said Rab, "'How much are you going to give to your son?' 'Thus and so.' 'How much are you going to give to your daughter?' 'Thus and so.' If they then arose and declared the formula of sanctification, they have effected the right of ownership. These statements represent matters in which the right of ownership is transferred verbally."

E. *May one propose, then, that the following supports [Samuel's] thesis:* **They do not take wives on the intermediate days of a festival, whether virgins or widows. Nor do they enter into levirate marriage, for it is an occasion of rejoicing for the groom.** *Lo, it is permitted then to betroth a woman!*

F. *No, the matter is formulated in terms of "it goes without saying," in this manner: not only may not one betroth a woman, in which case one is not in any event carrying out a religious duty, but even marrying a woman, in which case one is carrying out a religious duty, is forbidden on that occasion. Come and take note of what has been repeated as a Tannaite formulation in the household of Samuel:* They may betroth, but they may not bring the bride home, and they may not make a feast of betrothal, **Nor do they enter into levirate marriage, for it is an occasion of rejoicing for the groom.**

G. *Well, that proves it.*

9. *Settling the Point Subject to Dispute in the Mishnah*

While not a principal focus of exegetical interest, some attention is given to settling the dispute presented in the Mishnah by a statement of the decided law. Here is an example of that form of Mishnah-exegesis:

3:5-6/III.1

A. **R. Eliezer says, "After the Temple was destroyed, Pentecost is deemed equivalent to the Sabbath." Rabban Gamaliel says, "The New Year and the Day of Atonement are deemed equivalent to festivals." And sages say, "The rule is in accord with the opinion neither of this one nor**

of that one. But Pentecost is deemed equivalent to a festival, and the New Year and the Day of Atonement are deemed equivalent to the Sabbath:"

B. Said R. Giddal bar Menassia said Samuel, "The decided law accords with the position of Rabban Gamaliel."

C. *There are those who repeat this statement of R. Giddal bar Menassia in connection with the following:* "Any infant who died within thirty days of birth is carried out for burial in one's arms and is buried by one woman and two men, but not by one man and two women.

D. **[24B]** "Abba Saul says, 'Even by one man and two women.'

E. "They do not form a line of mourners on his account, and they do not say on his account the blessing of mourners or the consolation addressed to mourners.

F. "As to an infant who died after thirty days of life, he is carried out in a box .

G. "R. Judah says, 'Not a box that is carried on the shoulder, but one that is taken in the arms.'

H. "They do form a line of mourners on his account, and they do say on his account the blessing of mourners and the consolation addressed to mourners.

I. "As to an infant who died after twelve months of life, he is taken out for burial on a bier.

J. "R. Aqiba says, 'If he is a year old, but her limbs were like those of a two year old, then it is classified as a two year old; if it was two years old but the limbs were those of a year old, he is taken out on a bier.'

K. "R. Simeon b. Eleazar says, 'In the case of anyone who is carried out on a bier, the community shows public signs of distress, and on account of any that is not carried out on a bier, the community does not show public signs of distress.'

L. "R. Eleazar b. Azariah says, 'If he is publicly known, then the public engages in his rites, but if he is not known to the public, the public does not engage with his rites.'

M. "And what about a lamentation?

N. "R. Meir in the name of R. Ishmael says, 'In the case of the poor, they make a lamentation for a child of three, in the case of the rich, for one of five.'

O. "R. Judah in his name says, 'For a child of the poor [which is all poor people have as pleasure in their lives (Rashi)], they make a lament for a five year old, for a child of the rich, six.'

P. "And as for the children of the sages, they are classified as are the children of the poor.

Q. "Said R. Giddal bar Menassia said Rab, 'The decided law accords with the position of R. Judah in the name of R. Ishmael.'"

II. *Theological Implications*

Since a survey of any other tractate will yield the same repertoire, and so far as I know, no tractate will vastly expand the number of issues treated in providing the Mishnah with a sustained talmud, we legitimately ask whether a theological program animates the formation of the Bavli as a Mishnah-commentary. A brief statement of the upshot of each of our repeated initiatives in Mishnah-exegesis provides the outline of an answer, though a complete answer obviously will emerge only from a survey of not a single tractate but all thirty-seven tractates. What follows, therefore, must be regarded as only a preliminary hypothesis of the theological implications of the Bavli's exegetical program. The sole unproved premise is what follows is that people do not ask questions unless they know in advance they will produce not merely answers, but answers that conform to a larger systemic program.

1) *Scriptural Foundations of the Laws of the Mishnah*

The premise of this question is that every statement of the Mishnah (to which the question is addressed) can indeed be shown to rest on scriptural foundations. Hence, it must follow, the Mishnah overall states what Scripture has already said, spelling out in its details principles or conceptions that the written Torah has laid forth.

2) *Authorities behind the Laws of the Mishnah*

The intent of the question, "this passage is/is not in accord with Rabbi X," ordinarily is to demonstrate that the consensus of the sages, not a private individual, stands behind an anonymous statement of the Mishnah. Where an individual is identified, a further issue will be whether his rule here is consistent in its underlying principle with a rule elsewhere that rests on exactly the same principle or its opposite. The intent is to show that sages are consistent in their rulings.

3) *Meanings of Words and Phrases*

Scripture or common speech ordinarily provides the meaning of otherwise unfamiliar words and phrases.

4) *Text-Criticism*

The purpose of text-criticism is to identify flaws in the formulation of the Mishnah and generally to show that the wording of the document is flawless. This will cover proofs that the framers of the document do not repeat themselves and demonstrations that, where the Mishnah seems to say something obvious, it is indeed necessary to make that point, since, if not made explicit, the purpose of the Mishnah's statement will otherwise be lost.

5) *Conflict of Principles Implicit in the Mishnah's Rules*
The Mishnah's rules give expression, in concrete and exemplary form, to underlying principles. A few weighty principles underlie, and come to realization, in numerous rules. Can we show that the various cases' implicit principles are uniform and harmonious? Always.

6) *Execution of the Law of the Mishnah*
I see no theological issue inherent in this approach to the explanation of the Mishnah.

7) *The Operative Consideration behind the Law of the Mishnah*
The Mishnah's rules, when understood in the setting of the considerations at stake in making them up, prove weighty and consequential; the stakes are always high; the operative considerations are always entirely rational and accessible, also, to our reason.

8) *The Implications, for the Law in General, of the Mishnah's Particular Formulation*
When we understand what is at issue in the Mishnah's exemplary case, we are able to settle a great many more, and larger, questions than those at hand in that case in particular. So the Mishnah addresses weightier questions than its concrete cases apparently suggest, and when we have mastered its law, we may use what we know in a broad exploration of rules not at all set forth in the Mishnah in particular.

9) *Settling the Point Subject to Dispute in the Mishnah*
Where the Mishnah contains disputes, the sages of the Torah can settle those disputes; the purpose of disputes is not process but proposition, and a decision can always be made upon the conflicted proposition of the Mishnah.

III. *A Supernatural Writing: The Perfection of the Mishnah*

If, therefore, we had to state in a single sentence the exegetical proposition, indeed the hermeneutical principle, that animates the Bavli's reading of the Mishnah, it may be stated very simply:

the Mishnah is a supernatural writing, because it can be shown to be flawless in its language and formulation, never repetitious, never slovenly in any detail, always and everywhere the model of perfection in word and thought; the Mishnah is moreover utterly rational in its principles; and of course, the Mishnah is wholly formed upon the solid foundations of the written Torah of Sinai.

No mere human being can have achieved such perfection of language and of thought in conformity with the Torah. That is the point made, over and over again, in the Bavli's primary discourse.

CHAPTER THREE

TRADITION AND SELECTIVITY

I. *Deliberate Choice or a Process of Tradition*

Some maintain that the Talmud came into being through a long, incremental process of accumulation, as each generation added its bits and pieces to the growing document. Then the Talmud begins "way back," and no governing pattern, determined by a single intellect or shared opinion at some one time, accounts for the traits of the writing. Here I argue that the Talmud results from acts of choice, exercises in taste and judgment, by a determinate group of sages. That theory, I maintain, best accounts for the characteristics of the Talmud. One important test for the conflicting theories—and both cannot be right—is readily devised. It concerns how the final statement of the Talmud, the document as we know it, relates to its sources. Does its authorship—the collectivity of authors, compilers, and editors who did the work that yielded the writing we have—merely take over and hand on what prior writings dictated? Or does that authorship impose the stamp of its intellect, the traits of its editorial purpose and program, upon whatever writings came into its hands? If the former, then the Talmud exhibits traits of a document that emerges from the tradition of the ages, subordinated at the end to choices made much earlier. Accordingly, its final editors simply polished the detritus of the past. If the latter, then the Talmud shows itself to be the work of a commanding generation of decisive thinkers, writers, compilers, and editors.

That is why I ask, how does the Bavli (the Talmud of Babylonia), as exemplified in one tractate, relate to its sources, by which I mean, materials it shares with other and (by definition) earlier-redacted documents? In this instance what I want to know is how Bavli Arakhin deals with the topic and facts set forth at [1] Lev. 27:1-7, 16-25, the prior reading of [2] Sifra to those verses, [3] the received version of those same facts set forth by [3] Mishnah-

tractate Arakhin, and the exegesis of Mishnah-tractate Arakhin by
[4] Tosefta Arakhin. What is at stake is an account of just how
"traditional" the Bavli is. The question that defines the problem
is how the Bavli has formed of available writings (redacted in
documents now in hand) a single, cogent, and coherent statement
presented by the Bavli's authorship as summary and authoritative: a canonical statement on a given subject. In what ways does
a Bavli-tractate frame such a (theologically-canonical) statement
out of what (as attested in extant writings) its authorship has in
hand? My indicative choice for the prior sources are the Tosefta
and Sifra. That is because all parties concur, the Tosefta and Sifra,
works that allude to, and therefore derive from the period after
the closure of, the Mishnah, were generally available by ca. 300
C.E., long before the Bavli took shape.

The Talmud of Babylonia, ca. 600, comes at the end of a set
of writings produced by sages of Judaism over a period of four
hundred years, starting with the Mishnah in ca. 200. In various
ways, these writings produced over a period of four centuries
related both to Scripture and to the Mishnah, as well as to one
another. Consequently, the formation of the Judaic system attested
by the Talmud of Babylonia is described as a traditional process,
in the sense that later sages received from earlier ones traditions
to be preserved, refined, and handed on, in an on-going and
continuous process of a linear, harmonious, and one dimensional,
connected manner. The Judaism that came to expression in the
Talmud of Babylonia therefore is portrayed as a traditional religion, the result of a sustained process of tradition. That view of
the formation of Judaism is not sustained by the character of the
Talmud of Babylonia and, it follows, the Judaic system set forth,
in written form, by that Talmud is to be classified as not tradition or the result of a process of tradition but as autonomous, free-
standing, and fully autocephalic—the result of a process of
selection. But the literary form given to that system was indeed
traditional, hence the long-standing misreading of the matter by
people familiar with the classical writings of that Judaism.

Through the analysis of the qualities of literary evidence in
Tosefta, Sifra, and the Talmud of Babylonia, the first two highly
traditional in form and intent, the third quite different from the
others, for the case at hand, halakhah-tractate Arakhin/Lev.
Chapter Twenty-Seven, I propose to show that the Bavli took

shape through a process of not tradition but selectivity. If Tosefta in relationship to the Mishnah, and Sifra in relationship to Scripture, prove both formally and programmatically quite traditional, then the Bavli in relationship to the entire inherited corpus of writing is not at all traditional. Its authorship, moreover, scarcely pretended to do more than select and recast whatever they wished out of a received body of writings in such a way as to make the statement that they, for their part, chose to make.

What happens if I can show, however, that in treating a given topic the prior Torah—Scripture, the Mishnah, the Tosefta, the Midrash-compilation—has set forth a fair number of facts, propositions, and conceptions, that prove of no consequence to the framers of the Talmud in their formulation of their statement about that same topic? Then it turns out that the Talmud in fact does not deal with "the nature of all things according to the Torah," but, rather, the framers of the Talmud formulate a given topic in line with what they think important, and they set forth that topic in line with the facts that suit their framing of matters, and, finally, they then select from the inherited holy books—Scripture, Midrash, Tosefta, and Midrash alike—whatever suits their purpose. They simply neglect the rest. If I can show that that process of selectivity characterizes the Babylonian Talmud's authors' reading of the prior writings, then I can show that it is false to describe the Talmud as an account of "all things according to the Torah."

The test undertaken in this chapter can have taken any tractate among the thirty-seven that make up the Talmud of Babylonia. But if we wish to know how the framers of the Babylonian Talmud's treatment of a given topic in relationship to Scripture works itself out, then to begin with we had better select a tractate that rests upon solid foundations in Scripture (and many do not). I have chosen tractate Arakhin because it does, indeed, call upon Scripture, and, moreover, the scriptural books that supply its topic and rules are subjected to not one but two very important Midrash-exercises, contained in Sifra and Leviticus Rabbah. Hence if those responsible for the Bavli's materials—authors of compositions, editors of composites alike—do exhibit the traits that people commonly assign to them, it is in a tractate that to begin with appeals for topic, rule, and principle to Scripture that we should be able to demonstrate that fact. If the law of the Talmud of Babylonia derives from a long process of systematic exegesis, or if the sages of the Talmud of Babylonia expound the topic at hand through an essentially exegetical medium of thought, then that tractate above most others should demonstrate it. As to the second proposition, if it is the case that the Bavli talks about pretty much everything, then any tractate should be as suitable as any other to find out precisely the contours and character of a document of such a promiscuous topical program as to cover pretty much anything.

II. *Arakhin in Particular*

Let us now turn to Mishnah-tractate Arakhin in the context of the written Torah's statement of its topical program and of the facts that that program means to delineate. This protracted exercise lays out Mishnah-tractate Arakhin together with the counterpart materials of Tosefta-tractate Arakhin. We see that the Tosefta's treatment of the topic depends in every way upon the Mishnah's. The Tosefta in general contains materials of three kinds: direct citation and gloss of the Mishnah's sentences; exegesis, without direct citation, of the Mishnah's sentences, in discussions that are fully comprehensible only by reference to the Mishnah; and statements that deal with the subject-matter of the Mishnah but that are fully comprehensible without reference to the Mishnah. The first two types vastly predominate throughout the Tosefta's treatment of the Mishnah. The reason that the Tosefta is to be classified as a traditional document is simple. The Tosefta appeals for order, structure, and program to the Mishnah's tractate. It has no plan or agenda of its own. So the Tosefta's authorship sets forth nearly all of its materials in relationship to the Mishnah, and it has faithfully conformed to nearly the whole of a received agenda. Here is a case of close-to-absolute "tradition," within the pattern proposed just now.

The tractate opens in a way somewhat reminiscent of M. Hul. 1:1, stating that all may pledge the Valuation of themselves or someone else; all are subject to the valuation of others; all vow, or are subject to the vow, that their worth will be paid. This is made specific, which of course limits the force of the opening rule. Limitations then have to do with those whose Valuation is unclear, e.g., because their sexual traits are not certain; those who may be evaluated but may not pledge the Valuation of another,

because they are not deemed to possess the power of intention.
M. 1:2 presents a dispute on the status of the gentile. M. 1:3-4 –
the latter joined to the former but irrelevant to the chapter – deal
with the status of one who is about to die. The anonymous rule
(T.: Meir) maintains that such a person is not subject to a vow
that someone will pay his worth and is not subject to the pledge
that someone will pay his Valuation. Hananiah allows the latter,
because there is a fixed value, but concedes that in the former
case, a person about to die has no worth and therefore is not
subject to the stated vow.

1:1

    A.   All pledge the Valuation [of others] and are subject to the pledge
       of Valuation [by others],

    B.   vow [the worth of another] and are subject to the vow [of payment
       of their worth by another]:

    C.   priests and Levites and Israelites, women and slaves.

    D.   A person of doubtful sexual traits and a person who exhibits traits
       of both sexes vow [the worth of another] and are subject to the vow
       [of payment of their worth by another], pledge the Valuation [of
       others], but are not subject to the pledge of Valuation by others.

    E.   for evaluated is only one who is certainly a male or certainly a fe-
       male.

    F.   A deaf-mute, an imbecile, and a minor are subject to the vow [of
       payment of their worth by another], and are subject to the pledge
       of Valuation by others, but do not vow the worth, and do not
       pledge the Valuation, of others.

    G.   for they do not possess understanding.

    H.   One who is less than a month old is subject to the vow [of payment
       of worth by another], but is not subject to the pledge of Valuation.

M. 1:1

The pericope is in four parts, an introduction, A-B, which is limited at C, then three special cases, D, explained by E, F, explained
by G, and H. It is difficult to see the whole as other than a unitary construction. A speaks of paying the fixed Valuation specified at Lev. 27:1-8, and B, of vowing the estimated worth of
another, not under the rule of the fixed Valuation. C completes
the opening rule but, of course, also reverses the sense of A's
blanket statement that *all* effect and are subject to both forms of

donation. D then flows from C, also limiting the force of A, and
its reason is clear at E. One cannot ascertain the Valuation of one
who may be either male or female, since Scripture specifies a
different Valuation for each. F then excludes those who, for one
reason or another, are not deemed to exercise effective judgment.
H simply restates the Scriptural specification that Valuations apply to one more than a month old. It links M. 1:1 to M. 1:2,
building upon the distinction between M. 1:1A and B, the pledge
of a Valuation as against the vow of one's worth.

A. R. Meir says, "Greater is the applicability of the rule of being sub-
    ject to the pledge of Valuation than the applicability of the rule of
    pledging the Valuation of others.

B. "For: *A deaf-mute, an imbecile, and a minor are subject to the pledge of Val-
    uation by others, but do not pledge the Valuation of others* [M. Ar. 1:1F]."

C. R. Judah says, "Greater is the applicability of the rule of pledging
    the Valuation of others than the applicability of being subject to the
    pledge of Valuation [by others].

D. "For: *A person of doubtful sexual traits and a person who exhibits traits of both
    sexes pledge the Valuation [of others] but are not subjected to the pledge of Val-
    uation [[to be paid by others]* [M. Ar. 1:1D).

E. "Also: The Samaritan [MS Vienna, editio princeps: Gentile] should
    be subject to the rule of pledging the Valuation of others but should
    not be under the rule of being subject to the pledge of Valuation
    [by others]" [M. Ar. 1:2A, C].

                    T. 1:1 Z p. 543, Is. 11-13

A. Women and slaves vow [the worth of others] and are subject to vow
    [of payment of their worth by others], are subject to the pledge of
    Valuation [by others] and pledge the Valuation [of others] [M. Ar.
    1:1A-C].

B. If at this time they have [sufficient property], they collect from
    them. If not, they write a writ of indebtedness and collect it from
    them after some time.

C. Gentiles vow [to give the worth of others] and are subject to vow
    [that others will give their worth] [M. Ar. 1:2D].

D. Those missing limbs and afflicted by sores, even though they are not
    of worth, are subject to the pledge of Valuation.

                    T. 1:2 Z p. 543, Is. 13-16

T. 1:1 has Meir and Judah, then links M. 1:1D to Judah's position at M. 1:2A, C. T. 1:2D's point is that where there is a fixed
value, it does not rest on the condition of the one who is evaluated.

1:2

A. The gentile –
B. R. Meir says, "He is subject to the pledge of Valuation [by others], but he does not pledge the Valuation [of others]."
C. R. Judah says, "He pledges the Valuation [of others] but is not subject to the pledge of Valuation [by others]."
D. And this one and that one agree that they vow and are subject to the vow [of payment of worth].

M. 1:2

The dispute is perfectly balanced, with the point at issue expressed in the reversal of word order, B/C. Meir's position is that an Israelite may pledge the Valuation of a gentile, but a gentile may not pledge the Valuation either of himself or of anyone else. Judah's view is the opposite. Both parties have to figure out how the gentile is excluded from the law of Valuations (Lev. 17:1: *speak to the children of Israel*). In Meir's view, the matter rests upon the action of the person who takes upon himself to pay the Valuation; hence others may pledge the Valuation of the gentile, but the gentile may not pledge the Valuation of others. In Judah's view, the matter rests upon the status of that which is subject to Valuation. Hence the gentile may pledge the Valuation of an Israelite, but not of himself. Both parties agree that vows are permitted in all cases.

1:3-4

A. He who is on the point of death or he who goes forth to be put to death
B. is not subject to the vow [of payment of his worth by others] nor subject to the pledge of Valuation [by others].
C. R. Hananiah b. 'Aqabya says, "He is subject to the pledge of Valuation,
D. "because its {a Valuation's} price is fixed.
E. "But he is not subject to the vow [of payment of his worth by others],
F. "because its {a vow's} price is not fixed."
G. R. Yosé says, "he vows [the value of another] and declares something sanctified.
H. "And if he caused damage, he is liable to make restitution."

M. 1:3

A. The woman who goes forth to be put to death –
B. they do not postpone [the execution] for her until she will give birth.

C.   [If] she sat on the travailing stool, they postpone [the execution] for
     her until she will give birth.

D.   The woman who is executed – they derive benefit from her hair.

E.   A beast which is executed – it [the hair] is prohibited from bene-
     fit.

                                    M. 1:4

The pericope consists of a dispute, A-B *vs.* C-F; the form of the
second opinion, C-F, follows that of M. 1:1D-E, F-G, that is, the
specification of a reason for a rule. One who is about to die is
worth nothing, so too the one about to be executed. Therefore
he is not subject to the vow that others will pay his worth or to
the pledge of Valuation. Hananiah rejects this view for the stated reason. The pledge of Valuation certainly is fixed and payable; the worth to be paid by a vow is null. Yosé's saying is separate from the foregoing. The man's estate can be encumbered
by these vows or other obligations.

At M. 1:4 we have a pair of balanced rules, A-B (apocopated),
then C; and D-E. The rules are attached for obvious reasons, but
do not belong to our tractate.

A.   *"He who is on the point of death* and one who is eight days old *is not subject
     to the vow [of payment of his worth by others] nor subject to the pledge of Val-
     uation [by others[.*

B.   *"And he who goes forth to be put to death is not subject to the vow [of payment
     of his worth by others] nor subject to the pledge of Valuation [by others],"* the
     words of R. Meir [M.Ar. 1:3A-B].

C.   *R. Hanina b. Aqiba qq says, "He is subject to the pledge of Valuation, because
     its price is fixed. But he is not subject to the vow [of payment of his worth by
     others], because its price is not fixed"* [M. Ar. 1:3C-F].

D.   *R. Yosé says, "he vows [the value of another] and pledges a Valuation [of an-
     other] and declares something sanctified. And if he caused damage, he is liable to
     make restitution"* [M. Ar. 1:3G-H].

                        T. 1:3 Z p. 543, ls. 16-19

A.   A woman who goes forth to be put to death [M. Ar. 1:4A] –

B.   [if] the offspring put forth its hand, they postpone [the execution]
     for her until she will give birth.

C.   For if she had given birth, her offspring would have been stoned
     [see *TR* II, p. 275]].

D.   The woman who goes forth to be put to death –

E.   [if] she said, "Give my hair to my daughter," they give it to her.

F.   If she died without specifying [to whom the hair should be given],
     they do not give it to her [the daughter].

G.   For those that are dead are prohibited from the benefit [of any

possessions, hence cannot after death be supposed to have disposed
of property in this wise].
T. 1:4 Z p. 543, ls. 19-21

T. 1:3 cites M. 1:3. T. 1:4A-B then restate M. 1:4C. D-G augment M. 1:4D. Has the Tosefta shown us traits of a traditional
writing? It certainly has. The point then is clear: the Mishnah has
set the program of the Tosefta, and in our framework, the Tosefta
is a highly traditional document. That is not to say the Tosefta
does not contain autonomous writing as well, because it does. But
the Tosefta depends for its order, structure, and program of exposition upon the Mishnah. It cannot be read on its own; the
passage before us forms a vine to the trellis of the Mishnah. But
the Mishnah can be read on its own. Without the Tosefta our
knowledge of the halakhah is incomplete, but the Mishnah in its
own terms provides a self-interpreting document.

III. *The Selectivity of the Bavli*

How does the Bavli relate to the Mishnah? The answer, we shall
see, is that the Talmud takes over the Mishnah and subordinates
the document, its laws and formal traits, to the Bavli's own program. That is not the mark of a traditional writing but of a highly
selective body of authors, compilers, and editors. For one thing,
the Bavli implicitly criticizes the Mishnah by providing information that the Mishnah's framers do not deem urgent. Take proof-
texts for the laws of the Mishnah, for example. Everyone knows
that the Mishnah's framers omit proof-texts even when presenting scriptural law. The tractates, Pesahim and Yoma, for instance,
scarcely cite the pertinent verses of the Pentateuch and yet are
quite incomprehensible without constant reference to those verses.
But does Scripture define "the tradition," which is then carried
forward by the Talmud, which then dictates the program and the
character of the Talmud? To answer that question, let me cite M.
Arakhin 9:8 and its associated Talmud, 106B-107A:

9:8
A. **He who leases a field from his fellow**
B. **to sow barley in it**
C. **may not sow it with wheat.**
D. **[If he leased it to sow] wheat,**

E.   he may sow it with barley.

F.   Rabban Simeon b. Gamaliel prohibits [doing so].

G.   [If he leased it to sow] grain he may not sow it with pulse,

H.   [to sow] pulse, he may sow it with grain.

I.   Rabban Simeon b. Gamaliel prohibits [doing so].

I.1

A.   Said R. Hisda, "What is the scriptural basis for the ruling of R. Hisda? As it is written, 'The remnant of Israel shall not do iniquity nor speak lifes; neither shall a deceitful tongue be found in their mouth' (Zeph. 3:13)."

B.   An objection was raised [to the rule of M. 9:8D-F]: **The collection of alms for Purim must be distributed on Purim. And the collection of alms for a given town must be distributed in that town. They do not investigate too closely to see whether or not the poor are deserving. But they buy calves for the poor and slaughter them, and the poor consume them. And what is left over should not fall to the fund for charity. "Out of funds collected for Purim a poor person should not make a strap for his sandal, unless he so stipulated in the council of the citizens of that town," the words of R. Jacob stated in the name of R. Meir. But Rabban Simeon b. Gamaliel [107A] imposes a lenient ruling in this matter. [The passage continues: But they should be used only for food for the holiday." R. Meir says, "He who borrows money from his fellow to purchase produce with it should not purchase utensils with it. If he borrowed money for the purchaser of utensils, he should not buy produce with it, for he thereby deceives the lender." (T. Meg. 1:5A-K)]**

D.   *Said Abayye, "The reason of R. Simeon accords with the position of the master [Rabbah b. Nahmani], who has said, 'If one wishes to let his land become sterile, let him sow it one year with wheat, the next with barley, one year lengthwise, the next crosswise. [Freedman: Therefore if he leased it for wheat, he may not sow it with barley, in the opinion of R. Simeon b. Gamaliel, lest wheat have been sown there the previous year.]' But that is the case only if one does not plow after the harvest and again before sowing. If he does so, there is no harm."*

May we then say that a generative and precipitating interest of sages is in deriving from Scripture whatever there is to say about the Mishnah's rules? This passage does not suggest so. Once we distinguish, as we must, between a formality of adducing proof texts and a generative problematic deriving from Scripture and dictating the shape and structure of a sustained discussion, then those who answer that question affirmatively will find slight satisfaction in the numerous passages that are like the one just now cited. For what provokes the discussion at hand is not the prooftext that is cited, let alone the issue of whether, and how, Scripture has imposed the rule at hand. It is, rather, whether or not it is the fact that under all circumstances the assumed or stipulated conditions are to be observed; some say that is so, some deny it. Simeon b. Gamaliel denies it. Then the operative consideration turns out to be the practicalities of preserving the fertility of the soil or renewing it. Scripture does not stand behind this passage; the content of Scripture has not precipitated the thought that is set forth here; a variety of established truths has to be sorted out, and that is what the framer of the passage accomplishes. Accordingly, we have to differentiate formal appeal to proof-texts from the substantive formation of an exegetical program out of Scripture. If Scripture were to predominate, then the requirements of exegesis would be dictated by the program, the order, the details and propositions of Scripture. If Scripture does not predominate, then it takes a subordinated and essentially ancillary role in the pursuit of an inquiry that finds its generative problematic and its energy elsewhere.

IV. *What Does a Traditional Document Look Like? The Case of Sifra*

To show how the Bavli exercises selectivity, let us now turn, for a second contrast, beyond the Tosefta, to a document that depends upon a prior, received text for its program and character. It is Sifra, a systematic reading of the book of Leviticus. The passage in Scripture that is discussed in both Sifra and tractate Arakhin Chapter Seven is as follows:

> If a man dedicates to the Lord part of the land which is his by inheritance, [then your valuation shall be according to the seed for it; a sowing of a homer of barley shall be valued at fifty shekels of silver. If he dedicates his field from the year of jubilee, it shall stand at your full valuation. But if he dedicates his field after the jubilee, then the priest shall compute the money-value for it according to the years that remain until the year of jubilee, and a deduction shall be made from your valuation. And if he who dedicates the field wishes, redeeming, to redeem it, then he shall add a fifth of the valuation in money to it, and it shall remain his. But if he does not wish to redeem the field, or if he has sold the field to another man, it shall not be redeemed any more; but

the field, when it is released in the jubilee, shall be holy to the Lord, as a field that has been devoted; the priest shall be in possession of it. If he dedicates to the Lord a field which he has bought, which is not a part of his possession by inheritance, then the priest shall compute the valuation for it up to the year of jubilee, and the man shall give the amount of the valuation on that day as a holy thing to the Lord. In the year of jubilee the field shall return to him from whom it was bought, to whom the land belongs as a possession by inheritance. Every valuation shall be according to the shekel of the sanctuary; twenty gerahs shall make a shekel   (Lev. 27:16-25).

The reading of these lines in Sifra is in two chapters, given in sequence. First comes Sifra 273. Parashat Behuqotai. Pereq 10, which shows us what a document that takes as its problematic the exegesis of Scripture, its hermeneutic, its program, its problematic:

CCLXXIII:II.1.

   A. "If a man dedicates to the Lord part of the land which is his by inheritance:"
   B. I know only that the law covers a field received by inheritance from one's father.
   C. How do I know that it covers also a field received by inheritance from one's mother?
   D. Scripture says, "If a man dedicates...."

Here the statement of Scripture is clarified so as to encompass a field inherited on the maternal side. This too is covered by the law. Then the details of the law as given in Scripture are exemplary of a principle and general—a field inherited, whether from father or mother—and not prescriptive and specific—a field inherited only from the party named, the father.

2. A. "then your valuation shall be according to the seed for it:"
    B. not in accord with its dimensions [but rather, its productive capacity].
3. A. "a sowing of a homer of barley shall be valued at fifty shekels of silver:"
    B. Lo, this is by decree of the King [without further explanation]:
    C. All the same are he who sanctifies a field in the desert of Mahoz and he who sanctifies a field among the orchards of Sebaste:
    D. [If he wants to redeem it], he pays fifty sheqels of silver for every part of a field that suffices for the sow-

ing of a homer of barley [M. Arakhin 3:2B-C, 7:1].

4. A. How do we know that a person is not permitted to sanctify his field at the time of the Jubilee, though if one has done so, the field is sanctified?

B. Scripture says, "If he dedicates his field from the year of jubilee."

5. A. Why does Scripture say, "his field"?

B. How do you know that, **if in the field were crevices ten handbreadths deep or rocks ten handbreadths high, they are not measure with it [M. Arakhin 7:1G]?**

C. Scripture says, "his field," [and these are not reckoned as part of his field forming domains unto themselves].

6. A. "it shall stand at your full valuation:"

B. [For a Jubilee of fifty-nine years,] one pays forty-nine selas and forty-nine pundions [T. Arakhin 4:10B].

C. What is the value of this pondion?

D. It is at the rate of exchange of a pondion and some change [Hillel].

7. A. "[But if he dedicates his field] after the jubilee:"

B. Near the Jubilee.

C. How do we know the rule for the period some time after the Jubilee?

D. Scripture says, "But if he dedicates his field after the jubilee."

8. A. "his field:"

B. What is the point of Scripture here?

C. How do you know that, **if in the field were crevices ten handbreadths deep or rocks ten handbreadths high, they are not measure with it [M. Arakhin 7:1G]?**

D. Scripture says, "his field," [and these are not reckoned as part of his field forming domains unto themselves].

9. A. How do we know that **they do not declare a field of possession sanctified less than two years before the year of Jubilee nor do they redeem it less than a year after the year of Jubilee [M. Arakhin 7:1A-B]?**

B. Scripture says, "then the priest shall compute the money-value for it according to the years that remain until the year of jubilee." [Hence there must be at least two years].

C. Scripture says, "But if he dedicates his field after the jubilee, then the priest shall compute the money-value for it according to the years that remain until the year of jubilee" [T. Arakhin 4:8A-B].

10. A. And how do we know that **they do not reckon the months against the sanctuary, but the sanctuary reckons the months to its own advantage [M. Arakhin 7:1C-D]?**

B. Scripture says, "But if he dedicates his field after the jubilee, then the priest shall compute the money-value for it according to the years that remain until the year of jubilee."

11. A.   And how do we know that **if one said, "Lo, I shall pay for each year as it comes," they do not pay any attention to him, but he pays the whole at once [M. Arakhin 7:1J-K]**?

  B.   Scripture says, "But if he dedicates his field after the jubilee, then the priest shall compute the money-value for it according to the years that remain until the year of jubilee."

12. A.   "years that remain:"

  B.   years does one reckon,

  C.   and one does not reckon months.

13. A.   And how do we know that if the sanctuary wanted to treat the months as a year, it may do so?

  B.   Scripture says, "[the priest] shall compute."

14. A.   "until the year of jubilee:"

  B.   [But no part of the year of the Jubilee] shall enter the calculation.

15. A.   "and a deduction shall be made from your valuation:"

  B.   even from the sanctuary['s claim,]

  C.   so if the sanctuary had the usufruct for a year or two prior to the Jubilee, or did not exercise the right of usufruct but had access to it [cf. T. Arakhin 4:10B],

  D.   one deducts a sela and a pundion for each year.

16. A.   "And if he who dedicates the field wishes, redeeming, to redeem it:"

  B.   the duplicated verb serves to encompass a woman.

17. A.   "And if he who dedicates the field wishes, redeeming, to redeem it:"

  B.   the duplicated verb serves to encompass an heir.

18. A.   "the field:"

  B.   What is the point of Scripture here?

  C.   One might have thought that subject to the law is only one who sanctifies a field that can take a kor of seed.

  D.   How do I know that if one sanctified a field that can take a letekh of seed, a seah of seed, a qab of seed, the same rule applies?

  E.   Scripture says, "the field."

19. A.   "he shall add a fifth of the value in money to it, and it shall be his:"

  B.   If he paid the money, lo, it is his.

  C.   And if not, it is not his.

20. A.   "But if he does not wish to redeem the field:"

  B.   this refers to the owner.

21. A.   "or if he has sold the field to another man:"

  B.   this refers to the temple treasurer.

22. A.   "to another man:"

  B.   and not to his son.

  C.   May one say, "to another man"—and not to his brother?

  D.   When Scripture says, "man," it encompasses his brother.

  E.   How come you include the son but exclude the brother [in the present rule]?

F. After Scripture has used inclusionary language, it has gone and used exclusionary language.

G. I include the son, who takes the place of his father as to a betrothal of a bondwoman {Ex. 21:9: "And if he designated her for his son, he shall deal with her as is the practice with free maidens"], and as to control of a Hebrew slave [Ex. 21:6: "He shall then remain his slave for life"—but not the slave of his heir, meaning his brother (Hillel)].

H. But I exclude the brother, who does not take the place of the deceased brother either as to the betrothal of a bondwoman or as to control of a Hebrew slave.

23. A. "it shall not be redeemed any more:"

B. Might one suppose that one may not purchase it from the temple treasurer and it then will enter the status of a field that has been acquired through purchase [not inheritance]?

C. Scripture says, ""it shall not be redeemed any more:"

D. In its prior status, it will not be redeemed, but one may purchase it from the temple treasurer and it then will enter the status of a field that has been acquired through purchase [not inheritance].

The exposition is inclusionary, Nos. 1, 2. No. 3 begins a long sequence of passages, proceeding through No. 11, drawn from, or dependent upon, the language and the rules of the Mishnah and the Tosefta, as indicated. From No. 12 to the end we work out a familiar type of low-level exegesis, this, not that, or this, and also that. If we ask ourselves whether the passage at hand can have been composed without the Mishnah's rules, the answer is clear. Nos. 3-11 take for granted the rules of the Mishnah or Tosefta, which are cited verbatim and then given appropriate support in a cited verse. The issues of these compositions derive from the Mishnah and the Tosefta, because they concern the vindication of those document's formulations of the rules by appeal to Scripture. Then the authorship of Sifra in the cited compositions, and in the composite overall, responds to and draws for its generative conceptions upon the Mishnah and the Tosefta.

Overall, then, the framers of Sifra wish us to read the verses of Scripture clause by clause and to link to them, in a systematic way, whatever we find in the Mishnah that pertains to the rule or subject at hand. What we now ask is whether the authorship of the Bavli has adopted this same program, or a program that in some important ways concurs that the principal task is to follow the program and issues of Scripture—in form at least, but, if possible, in substance as well. Sifra assuredly provides a fine example of a

document that takes shape around Scripture and defines its program in response to the problem of showing how the law of Judaism is justified by, derives from, is vindicated within, Scripture.
That is why Scripture forms the organizing principle of the document and defines its order and its structure. But the Bavli does
not conform to this model, not at all, and as we shall now see,
even when we consider the same subject-matter as is before us,
we do not find a parallel interest in organizing discourse around,
and in response to, Scripture. Once more we remind ourselves
that at stake is not merely the formality of providing proof-texts
for the Mishnah's statements. It is the substantive exercise of framing entire discussions around Scripture and in response to the facts
as Scripture lays them out and the problems of the subject-matter as Scripture wishes to define them. That is something, we shall
now see, that the framers of the Bavli did not do, even here, where
they very well might have.

V. *What does a Selective Document Look Like? The Bavli's Reading of Sifra's Topic*

Does this unit's authorship concur with the authorship of Sifra
concerning what must predominate in our reading of the subject-
matter covered at Lev. 27:16-25 and treated by the Mishnah in
tractate Arakhin Chapter Seven?

7:1A-D [24A]

A. **They do not sanctify [a field of possession] less than two
years before the year of Jubilee.**
B. **And they do not redeem it less than a year after the year
of Jubilee.**
C. **[In redeeming the field] they do not reckon the months
against the sanctuary.**
D. **But the sanctuary reckons the months [to its own advan-
tage].**

I.

A. [To the rule at M. 7:1A-B, which states that an act of sanctification
of a field cannot take place within two years of the Jubilee year,]
the following objection was raised [from an authoritative teaching
that indicates one <u>may</u> do so]:

B. People may consecrate [fields] whether before or after the Jubilee year [without limit], but in the Jubilee year itself, one should not consecrate a field. And if one has declared a field to be consecrated, it is not regarded as consecrated. [There is a clear contradiction in the teaching at hand.]

C. Both Rab and Samuel said, ["The meaning of the Mishnah-passage is] people may not consecrate a field so that it is redeemed at a rate for less than two years. [No matter when the act of consecration takes place, the redemption fee covers two years of crops.]

D. "And since people may not so consecrate as to redeem a field for the going rate of less than two years, a person should be mindful of his property and not consecrate a field in a span of time less than two years [prior to the Jubilee]."

II.

A. It has been stated:

B. He who consecrates his field in the Jubilee year itself—

C. Rab said, "It is consecrated, and the man has to pay fifty [sheqels to redeem it]."

D. Samuel says, "It is not consecrated in any aspect."

E. R. Joseph raised the following objection, "Now in regards the matter of sale, in which Samuel differs from Rab, one may construct an argument _a fortiori_ [to support Samuel's view that one may not sell such a field, namely:] If a field that already has been sold reverts to its former owner [in the Jubilee year], a field that has not been sold—all the more so that it should not be subject to sale. [For if it were sold, it would simply revert automatically to the seller in the Jubilee year.]

F. "But as regards the present case [of consecrating the field], is it possible to construct an argument _a fortiori_? [No. For as we shall see, the field does not always revert to the former owner in the Jubilee year. If the owner does not redeem it, then the priests must redeem it. Accordingly, one cannot infer as Samuel does that a field dedicated during the Sabbatical year automatically reverts to the owner. On the contrary, the owner must redeem it.]

G. "For surely we have learned in the Mishnah: If the Jubilee year arrived and the field was not redeemed, 'The priests enter into possession of it but pay its price,' the words of R. Judah [M. 7:4A-B]. [So there is no argument _a fortiori_ at hand to sustain Samuel's position.]"

H. Samuel concurs with R. Simeon, who has said [in the same passage:] R. Simeon says, "They [priests] enter into possession of it but do not pay [the price of the field]." [Here, the field automatically, without any redemption, passes to the ownership of the priests. Therefore we may construct the following argument _a fortiori_: One that already has been consecrated automatically goes forth in the Jubilee year. One that has not already been consecrated—is it not an argument a fortiori that it should not be subject to consecration at all?!]

I.   [24B] And Rab reasons that, ultimately does not the field return to the owner? [Surely not.] It returns to the priests, and the priests acquire possession from the table of the Most High. [So an act of consecration is valid, even in the Jubilee year, and contrary to Simeon's view, Rab maintains that this is not really an alienation of the field from the sanctuary at all, since the field never ultimately reverts to the owner anyhow.]

J.   What is the scriptural basis for Rab's view [at C]?

K.   It is because Scripture has said, "If from the year of the Jubilee he shall sanctify his field" (Lev. 27:17)—inclusive of the Jubilee year.

L.   And Samuel [replies], "Is it written, 'And if in the year of the Jubilee...'? 'From the Jubilee year' is what is written, meaning, from the year after the Jubilee year."

M.   To be sure, in Rab's view, we find written, "If from the year of Jubilee" and also "and if after the Jubilee" (Lev. 27:17, 18). [Accordingly, if the field was consecrated in the Jubilee year, the full fifty sheqels are paid in the redemption price. If the redemption took place after the Jubilee year, then there is a reduction from the full price.]

N.   But in Samuel's view, what is the meaning of [the other verse:] "after the Jubilee"? It means, "After the year after the Jubilee" [thus accommodating his view of matters].

O.   An objection was raised [from I B]: People may consecrate fields whether before or after the Jubilee year without limit, but in the Jubilee year itself, one should not declare a field to be consecrated. And if one has declared a field to be consecrated, it is not regarded as consecrated. [This surely contradicts Rab at II C.]

P.   Rab will reply to you, "The meaning is that to be sure people may not consecrate a field so that it is redeemed at a rate governed by the rule of deduction. But the field indeed is holy so that one has to pay the full fifty sheqels [covering the entire fifty years]."

Q.   Does this then bear the inference that, if one consecrates the field before the Jubilee, it is sanctified so as to be redeemed at the deduction-rate? But lo, Rab and Samuel both have said [I C], "People may not consecrate a field so that it is redeemed at a [deduction-] rate for less than two years."

R.   Rab may reply to you, "Now who is represented here? It is the rabbis, but I follow the view of Rabbi, who has said, 'When we speak of 'first,' the first day is included, so too when we speak of 'seventh,' the seventh is included. Here too, when Scripture speaks of 'From the year,' the Jubilee year is included [just as was stated above, K]."

S.   But if this is rabbis' view, where does the pondion come in? [Jung, p. 144, n. 7: If Scripture refers to the second year after the Jubilee [as Rab maintains], so that fifty sheqels are payable for forty-eight years, the redeemer must add one <u>pondion</u> to each sheqel. But according to Rabbi, Scripture speaks of the year of Jubilee itself, so that fifty sheqels are payable for fifty years, i.e., just a <u>sela</u> per year. How then does the <u>pondion</u> come in at all?]

T. And if you wish to propose that [Rabbi] does not require [the <u>pondion</u>], have we not learned: If one has sanctified the field two or three years before the Jubilee year, Rabbi says, "I maintain that one pays a <u>sela</u> and a <u>pondion</u>" [Cf. M. 7:2I].

U. Rabbi accords with the principle of R. Judah, who has said, "The fiftieth year counts on both fifty-year cycles. [Thus there are forty-nine years for each of which the redeemer has to pay a sheqel and a <u>pondion</u>.]

V. Does it follow that Samuel [who maintains that it is only after the Jubilee year that the redemption at a reduction takes place] takes the view that Rabbi concurs with rabbis? [Jung, p. 145, n. 1: That the Jubilee year is not included in the cycle of forty-nine years, so that there are full forty-nine years between one Jubilee and another apart from the Jubilee year itself.]

W. For if [Rabbi's] view were to accord with that of R. Judah, he should read, "One <u>sela</u> and two <u>pondions</u>" [since we assign the year to both cycles, hence one <u>sela</u> covering the year, but a <u>pondion</u> for the preceding cycle and a <u>pondion</u> for the cycle now commencing].

X. Accordingly, we must conclude that, in Samuel's view, Rabbi [who demands only one <u>pondion</u>] concurs with rabbis [vis à vis Judah].

Y. Come and hear [reverting to II B-D]: <u>And they do not redeem it less than a year after the year of Jubilee [M. 7:1B].</u>

Z. Now that statement poses no problem to the view of Samuel [that an act of consecration in the Jubilee year itself is invalid], so, it follows, people do not redeem a field less than a year after the end of the Jubilee year, [since there would be no field subject to redemption prior to that point, there having been no valid act of consecration during the year itself.]

AA. But as to Rab, what can be the meaning of <u>Less than a year after the year of Jubilee?</u>

BB. Do you reason that the language means literally "after the Jubilee year"? What is the meaning of "after the Jubilee year"? [25A] It is "in the midst of the Jubilee, for so long as a year has not been completed, one does not deduct it [Jung, p. 145, n. 6: from the total of remaining years to the next Jubilee, and he who redeems must pay for the incomplete years a full sheqel with its <u>pondion</u>. The Mishnah thus means that after the Jubilee all redemptions must be made on the basis of complete years.]

CC. What then does he wish to tell us? Is it that they do not reckon with months so far as the sanctuary is concerned? But lo, that principle is explicitly expressed, as follows: <u>In redeeming the field they do not reckon the months against the sanctuary [M. 7:1C].</u>

DD. His intent is to indicate the reason for the rule. That is, what is the reason that <u>They do not redeem it less than a year after the year of Jubilee [M. 7:1B]</u>? It is because <u>in redeeming a field they do not reckon the months against the sanctuary [M. 7:1C]</u>.

<u>III.</u>

A. <u>In redeeming the field, they do not reckon the months etc. [M. 7:1C]</u>:

B. Our rabbis have taught on Tannaite authority: How do we know that <u>in redeeming the field they do not reckon the months against the sanctuary?</u>

C. As it is said, "Then the priest himself shall compute the money-value for it according to the years [that remain until the year of Jubilee]" (Lev. 27:18).

D. It is years that you compute, and you do not compute months.

E. And how do we know that if you wish to compute the months and treat them as a full year, you may do so?

(F. What would be an example of such a computation?

G. For instance, if one consecrated the field in the middle of the forty-eighth year?)

H. Scripture has said, "And the priest <u>himself</u> shall compute..." (Lev. 27:18)—in any way [advantageous to the Temple, along the lines of M. 7:1D].

The field of possession cannot be sanctified in the forty-eighth and forty-ninth year of the cycle, nor redeemed with a deduction in the first. Scripture speaks of years (Lev. 27:18), which must be at least two. If a person wants to redeem his field after the Jubilee, the reckoning in accord with the years remaining up to the Jubilee is made only at the end of a complete year. If he wants to redeem the field immediately following the jubilee, he pays the full fifty sheqels (Lev. 27:17). The payment required for redeeming the field of possession at the outset of the Jubilee-cycle thus is fifty sheqels for the specified area, that is, one sheqel per year (I). This sum then is diminished by one forty-ninth of the fifty sheqels as each year passes, one sheqel and one <u>pondion</u> (= 1/48th of a sheqel). The amount of money to be paid for redemption consists, therefore, of as many sheqels and <u>pondions</u> as the number of years up to the next Jubilee. The point of M. 7:1C-D is that two years and three months, for example, are not deemed as two years to the disadvantage of the Temple. One year and eleven months are reckoned as one year, not two full years. Units I and II form a single, continuous discussion, even though, as is clear, unit I may be read by itself. Since Unit II refers back to it, however, we have to regard the entire construction as a sustained and brilliant exercise. The principles of the Mishnah-paragraph are elucidated in all their complexity through the inquiry into the theories of the great Amoraic masters, Rab and Samuel. Unit III clarifies M. 7:1C-D's scriptural foundations. does this unit's authorship concur with the authorship of Sifra concerning what must predominate in our reading of the subject-matter covered at Lev. 27:16-25 and treated by the Mishnah in tractate Arakhin Chapter Seven? Unit I undertakes the comparison of the rule of the Mishnah with another rule on Tannaite authority. The issue is not pertinent to the verses of Scripture cited at the commencement of Chapter Six. The same is so at Unit II.

Only at the end of Unit II do we ask for a scriptural basis for Rab's view; that is hardly the centerpiece of the discussion. What is important is that both parties can show their principles derive from, or at least do not contradict, the law of Scripture. That is a quite different issue from the one that is raised by claims of a "proclivity," or allegations that discourse commences with the concern that everything be shown to flow from Scripture. Unit III does indeed ask "how do we know," cite Scripture, and then prove the point from Scripture. But has Scripture dictated the treatment of the Mishnah's topic, which derives from Scripture? The answer is entirely in the negative. It is one thing to maintain that authorities of the Talmud of Babylonia wish to show that a law of the Mishnah rests on Scriptural foundations. They are pleased to do so. Let me state what I conceive to be the decisive issue: *it is quite another thing to demonstrate that Scripture has dictated the shape, structure, and direction of the treatment of the topic of Scripture in the Talmud of Babylonia's reading of the Mishnah.* That is manifestly not the case here.

7:1E-K, 7:2

E. **He who sanctifies his field at the time of the Jubilee's [being in effect] [compare M. 8:1]**

F. **pays the fifty sheqels of silver [for every part of a field that suffices for] the sowing of a homer of barley.**

G. **[If] there were there crevices ten handbreadths deep or rocks ten handbreadths high, they are not measured with it.**

H. **[If they were in height] less than this, they are measured with it.**

I. **[If] one sanctified it two or three years before the Jubilee, he gives a sela and a pondion for each year.**

J. **If he said, "Lo, I shall pay for each year as it comes," they do not pay attention to him.**

K. **But he pays the whole at once.**

M. 7:1

A. **The same rule applies to the owner [of the field] and every [other] man [in regard to what is paid (M. 7-1I-K) for the redemption of the field].**

B. **What is the difference between the owner and every other man?**

C. **But: the owner pays the added fifth, and no other person pays the added fifth [M. 8:1].**

M. 7:2

I.

A. A Tanna taught [with reference to M. 7:1F]: A field that will take a <u>kor</u> of seed, not one that yield a <u>kor</u> of produce.

B. Seed sewn by hand, and not sewn by oxen.

C. Levi repeated [the following teaching:] "Not [sewn] too thick nor too thin but in an ordinary manner."

II.

A. <u>If there were there crevices ten handbreadths deep, etc. [M. 7:1G]:</u>

B. But let them be considered as sanctified as autonomous areas [of the field, since they are not regarded as part of the arable field for purposes of redemption, and let them be redeemed on their own].

C. And if you wish to propose that, since they do not take a <u>kor</u> of seed, they are not subject to consecration,

D. has it now been taught [to the contrary]: "A field..." (Lev. 27:16).

E. Why does Scripture say, "A field"?

F. Since it is said, "Fifty sheqels of silver for every part of a field that suffices for the sowing of a <u>homer</u> of barley" (Lev. 27:16), I know only that [the law applies] to a case such as is specified [in Scripture, that is, to a field of the specified size]. How do I know that the law encompasses a field suitable for sowing only a <u>letekh</u> of seed or a half <u>letekh</u>, a <u>seah</u> of seed or a <u>tirqab</u> or a half-<u>tirqab</u>?

G. Scripture says, "A field"—of any dimensions. [Accordingly, the question phrased at B is a valid one.]

H. Said Mar Uqba bar Hama, "Here we deal with crevices filled with water, which are not available for sowing seed anyhow. You may closely examine the language of the Mishnah to see that point, since it speaks of things that are similar to rocks.

I. That does indeed prove it.

J. But then, if that is the case, smaller [areas than ten handbreadths] should be subject to redemption as well.

K. They are called small clefts of the earth or spines of the earth [and are taken into account as part of the field].

III.

A. If one sanctified it two or three years before the Jubilee [M. 7:11:]

B. Our rabbis have taught: "And a deduction will be made from your valuation" (Lev. 27:18)—also from [the rate paid to the] sanctuary, so that, if the sanctuary had the usufruct of the field for a year or two years,

C. or, further, if it did not enjoy the usufruct but it was in [the Temple's] possession,

D. one deducts a sela and a pondion for a year.

IV.

A. If he said, "Lo, I shall pay, etc.... [M. 7:1J]:

B. Our rabbis have taught: How do we know that if the owners said, "Lo, we shall pay for each year as it comes," one pays no attention to them?

C. Scripture says, "The priest shall compute the money-value" (Lev. 27:18)—so that the money is all together.

V.

A. The same rule applies to the owner of the field and to every other man. What is the difference between the owner and every other man? But the owner pays the added fifth, and no other person pays the added fifth [M. 7:2].

M. 7:1E-F brings us to the measurement of the field sufficient for the sowing of a homer of barley. When the Jubilee-law is in force, the redemption-price is paid as just now specified. (When it is not in force it is paid in accord with the value of the field.) All E-F say is what is stated by Lev. 27:16-17. G-H's point is that ridges or crevices do not go into the measurement of the specified area. I goes over familiar ground. The fifty selas are paid for forty-nine years from one Jubilee to the next, a sela per year. The fiftieth sela is added, by having the forty-eight pondions of which it is made up divided among the forty-eight years. Thus the man pays a sela and a pondion per year, just as we have seen. J-K add the further qualification that the full sum must be paid at one time.

M. 7:2 restates the rule of Lev. 27:19: If he who dedicates the field wishes to redeem it, then he shall add a fifth of the valua-

tion in money to it. If, therefore, there are twenty years remaining in the Jubilee-cycle, the man pays twenty selas and twenty
pondions, plus five more of each, twenty-five selas and twenty-
five pondions in all. M. thus reads the verse to exclude the person who has not dedicated his own field but who wishes to redeem a field dedicated by someone else; he does not pay the
added fifth. The Talmud works its way through selected passages
of the Mishnah and consistently supplies proof-texts for the Mishnah's rules. Only unit II undertakes a substantial inquiry. Does
this unit's authorship concur with the authorship of Sifra concerning
what must predominate in our reading of the subject-matter covered at Lev. 27:16-25 and treated by the Mishnah in tractate
Arakhin Chapter Seven? Unit I's interest is in the clarification of
the language of the Mishnah, not Scripture.

Unit II tests the law of the Mishnah against the law of Scripture. The same is to be said of units III and IV. So the composite assuredly wishes to read the Mishnah, or the rule before us,
in dialogue with Scripture. Does this unit talk about "everything"
or some few things? Some few things. Can we explain why the
Talmud includes everything that is before us—and therefore can
we postulate that the authorship of the Bavli has excluded what
it found irrelevant and included only what served its purpose? Yes,
we can say, a limited program has guided the framing of the
passage, and that program in the main is the interplay between
the Mishnah and Scripture; whatever information that is adduced,
of the larger store in hand (as we know from Tosefta) has been
selected to respond to that one concern.

7:5

A. **He who purchases a field from his father, [if] his father
died, and afterward he sanctified it, lo, it is deemed a
field of possession (Lev. 27:16).**
B. **[If] he sanctified it and afterward his father died,**
C. **"lo, it is deemed in the status of a field which has been
bought," the words of R. Meir.**
D. **R. Judah and R. Simeon say, "it is deemed in the status
of a field of possession. "Since it is said, And if a field
which he has bought which is not a field of his possession (Lev. 27:22)—**
E. **"a field which is not destined to be a field of possession,**
F. **"which excludes this, which is destined to be a field of
possession [i.e., when his father dies]."**

G. A field which has been bought does not go forth to the priests in the Jubilee,

H. for a man does not declare sanctified something which is not his own.

I. Priests and Levites sanctify [their fields] at any time and redeem them at any time, whether before the Jubilee or after the Jubilee.

I.

A. Our rabbis have taught: "How do we know [from Scripture] that in the case of one who purchases a field from his father and who consecrated it, afterward whose father died, the field should be regarded as his as a field of possession [= M. 7:5D]?

B. "Scripture states, 'And if a field which he has bought, which is not a field of his possession' (Lev. 27:22),—a field which is not destined to be a field of possession, which excludes this field, which is destined to be a field of possession," the words of R. Judah and R. Simeon [M. 7:5D-F].

C. R. Meir says, "How do we know that in the case of one who purchases a field from his father, and whose father died, and who afterward consecrated the field, the field should be his as a field of possession?

D. "Scripture states, 'And if a field which he has bought, which is not a field of his possession' (Lev. 27:22)—a field which is not [at this moment] a field of possession, excluding this case, which indeed is a field of possession."

E. May we then propose that it is in this principle that the parties differ:

F. R. Meir maintains [C] the theory that the acquisition of the usufruct of the field is equivalent to the acquisition of the capital [the field itself].

G. R. Judah and R. Simeon [A-B] take the position that acquisition of the usufruct of the field is not in the category of the acquisition of the capital [the field itself].

H. Said R. Nahman bar Isaac, "In ordinary circumstances, in the view of R. Simeon and R. Judah, acquisition of the usufruct of the field is equivalent to acquisition of the capital [ownership of the field itself].

I. "But [27A] in the present case, there is a verse of Scripture at hand, which they have interpreted as follows:

J. "Scripture might as well state, 'If it is a field acquired by purchase which is not a field of his possession,' or it might also have written, 'which is not a field of possession.'

K. "What is the meaning of the explicit reference, to 'A field of his possession'? Not a field which is not going to become a field of possession under any circumstances.

L. "That usage excludes the present case, in which it is destined to enter the status of a field of possession [in due course]."

<u>II.</u>

A. <u>Priests and Levites sanctify their fields at any time [M. 7:5I]:</u>

B. It was assuredly necessary to make explicit reference to their right to redeem the field at any time, to distinguish them from Israelites, who may redeem [their fields] only up to the Jubilee year [but not afterward].

C. So we are informed that priests and Levites may redeem their fields at any time.

D. But what purpose was there to include the reference to the fact that priests and Levites may consecrate their fields at any time? Even Israelites also may do so.

E. And if you say that the reference is to the Jubilee year itself [that priests and Levites, but not Israelites, may consecrate their fields], then that thesis would pose no problem for Samuel, who has said that in the Jubilee year itself, a field may not be consecrated. So we would be informed that priests and Levites may consecrate their fields at all times [including the Jubilee year, when Israelites may not do so.]

F. But in the view of Rab, what purpose is there in including such a detail about priests and Levites? Even Israelites also may do so.

G. But, according to your own thinking, why should the framer of the passage have included the language, <u>whether before the Jubilee or after the Jubilee?</u> [In your reading of the passage], the meaning would then be that priests and Levites, but not Israelites, may consecrate fields before and after the Jubilee, but Israelites may not do so. [That reading is manifestly absurd.]

H. Rather, since the framer of the passage stated in the former case [namely, that of the Israelites, M. 7:13] <u>whether before the Jubilee or after the Jubilee</u>, he recorded the same formulation in the latter case [priests and Levites], <u>whether before or after the Jubilee.</u>

I. And since, along these same lines, he formulated the former case, <u>They may not consecrate... or redeem...,</u> he formulated the latter case in the same way, <u>They do consecrate... they do redeem.</u>

We recall (M. 3:2) that a field of possession differs from a field which has been purchased. The former is acquired by inheritance, the latter is bought. The former is subject to the fixed valuation of Lev. 27:16ff., the latter is evaluated in accord with its actual worth. The former if not redeemed by the Jubilee falls to the priests; the latter does not. Now we ask some secondary questions on the disposition of fields which may fall to one by inheritance but which also are purchased by the potential heir. A makes the basic point that if one purchases a field from his father but afterward will have inherited it in any case, then the field is deemed a field of possession. If after the father's death the man sanctifies the field, it

falls into the category of a field he has acquired through inheritance, not purchase. B then asks the more interesting question:
What if the man purchased it from the father and sanctified it.
He has not then inherited the field. But he is <u>going</u> to acquire by
inheritance what he already has acquired through purchase. Meir
does not treat that which is going to happen as if it already has
happened. Therefore if the man purchased the field and sanctified it before the death of the father, then at the time the field
was sanctified, it is in the status only of a field which has been
bought. Judah and Simeon take up the contrary position, for reasons
which are specified nicely at E-F. G-H then tells us what difference is made between the field of possession and the one of
purchase. Scripture, of course, states this same rule. I (= Lev.
25:32) is distinct from the foregoing construction. It excludes priests
and Levites from the Jubilee rule. They may redeem a field even
after the Jubilee year. I do not understand why it has been placed
here. Unit I, as usual, provides a scriptural foundation for the
positions of the authorities of the Mishnah-passage. Unit II investigates the implications of the formulation of the rule as the
Mishnah presents it.

   Does this unit's authorship concur with the authorship of Sifra
concerning what must predominate in our reading of the subject-
matter covered at Lev. 27:16-25 and treated by the Mishnah in
tractate Arakhin Chapter Seven? We start, unit I, with the inquiry
into the scriptural basis for a rule of the Mishnah. But if we examine the rule—one who purchases a field from his father and
who consecrated it, afterward whose father died, the field should
be regarded as his as a field of possession—we can hardly find in
Scripture reason to raise such a question to begin with. It must
follow that the question has originated elsewhere than in Scripture's
account of the topic before us. Answering the question by appeal
to Scripture is not the same thing as trying to justify every statement we make from Scripture; more to the point, a "proclivity"
toward reading a topic as Scripture does, rather than (e.g.,) as the
Mishnah does is hardly shown in this passage; the opposite "proclivity" is demonstrated. Unit II obviously works on a problem
that Scripture has not precipitated. Does this unit talk about "everything" or some few things? The program is as usual economical and rigorously disciplined. Can we explain why the Talmud
includes everything that is before us—and therefore can we pos-

tulate that the authorship of the Bavli has excluded what it found irrelevant and included only what served its purpose? The basis throughout is the same: the Mishnah's program. The Bavli represents an exercise in Mishnah-exegesis, and, while scriptural exegesis plays its role, the interest in linking the law (of the Mishnah) to Scripture must be judged subordinate. Does Sifra's sustained interest in Scripture-exegesis characterize the Talmud of Babylonia? No, the Talmud of Babylonia reads the Mishnah in the manner in which Sifra reads Scripture.

VI. *Tradition or Selectivity*

Do the principal documents of the Judaism of the dual Torah exhibit continuities from one to the next. If they do, then, on literary grounds alone, we may claim that the writings constitute sources that all together form a tradition, a set of documents making a single unitary, continuous, and, therefore, also cogent, statement. If they do not, then we shall have to seek other than documentary evidence for the traditional status and character imputed to these same writings by the theology and law of formative Judaism. Again to state with emphasis: I therefore want to know whether and how—again, in concrete, literary terms—a document makes its part of such a traditional statement, speaking, for its particular subject, in behalf of the entirety of the antecedent writings of the Judaic system at hand and standing in a relationship of continuity – not merely connection – with other such writings. The answer to that question will tell me how a traditional writing is formulated. If the question has no answer, and in the Bavli it does not, then it must follow that the Bavli is a document that has been framed through a process of not tradition but selection. And that is how I see the Bavli.

Let me expand on the question before us. How does the authorship of a corpus of writings that unfold on after another take up sources and turn them from traditions into a systematic and cogent statement. To answer the question, for obvious reasons I turned to the document universally assigned canonical and official status in Judaism from antiquity to the present day, the Talmud of Babylonia. In the centuries beyond the closure of the Bavli in ca. A.D. 600, people would universally turn to the Bavli as the starting point for all inquiry into any given topic, and rightly so. Since the Bavli made the first and enduringly definitive statement, we impute to the Bavli canonical status. If, therefore, we wish to ask about how a variety of sources turned into a tradition, that is to say, about the status as statements of a continuous tradition of documents of the formative age of the Judaism of the dual Torah, we inquire into the standing of a Bavli-tractate as testimony on its subject within the larger continuous system of which it is reputed to form a principal part. What we want to know about that testimony therefore is how the Bavli relates to prior documents. The reason is that we want to know whether or not the Bavli constitutes a statement of a set of such antecedent sources, therefore a step in an unfolding tradition, so Judaism constitutes a traditional religion, the result of a long sedimentary process. As is clear, the alternative and complementary issue is whether or not the Bavli makes its own statement and hence inaugurates a "new tradition" altogether (in that theological sense of tradition I introduced in the preface). In this case the Judaism defined by the Bavli is not traditional and the result of a sedimentary process but the very opposite: fresh, inventive, responsive to age succeeding age.

On any given topic, a tractate of the Bavli presents the final and authoritative statement that would emerge from the formative period of the Judaism of the dual Torah. That statement constituted not only an authoritative, but also an encompassing and complete account. That is what I mean by the making of a traditional statement on a subject: transforming in particular the received materials—whatever lay at hand—into a not-merely cogent but fixed and authoritative statement. What I wish to find out is the canonical status of the Bavli, insofar as the authorship of the Bavli transformed its antecedents, its sources, into traditions: the way things had been, are and must continue to be, in any given aspect of the life and world view of Israel, the Jewish people, as the Bavli's authorship understood the composition of that Israel. Accordingly, I mean to investigate how a principal authorship in Judaism has taken up whatever sources it had in hand and transformed them into the tradition of Judaism: the canonical statement, on a given subject, that would endure. To state the result of that work, which precipitated the interests that have been continued in this one, very simply:

What earlier authorships—represented by the Talmud of the Land of Israel—wished to investigate in the Mishnah, the points

they wished to prove by reference to verses of Scripture important in our tractate—these have little or nothing in common with
the points of special concern systematically worked out by the
authorship of the Bavli. The Bavli's authorship at ca. 600 approaches Mishnah-exegesis with a program distinct from that of
the Yerushalmi's authorship of ca. 400, and the Bavli's authorship reads a critical verse of Scripture within a set of considerations entirely separate from those of interest to the authorships
of Leviticus Rabbah and Pesiqta deRab Kahana of ca. 450 and
500. Any notion that the Bavli's authorship has taken as its principal task the restatement of received ideas on the Mishnah-top-
ics and Scripture-verses at hand derives no support to speak of
from the sample we shall examine.

To broaden the range of discourse, let me underline what I
conceive to be the results of that finding. So far as a process of
tradition takes over the formation of a cogent and sustained statement, considerations extraneous to rational inquiry, decided, not
demonstrated facts—these take over and divert the inexorable
processes of applied reason from their natural and logically necessary course. And the opposite is also the case. Where a cogent
statement forms the object of discourse, syllogistic argument and
the syntax of sustained thought dominate, obliterating the marks
of a sedimentary order of formation in favor of the single and
final, systematic one. So far as an authorship proposes to present
an account of a system, it will pay slight attention to preserving
the indicators of the origins of the detritus of historical tradition,
of which, as a matter of fact, the systemic statement itself may well
be composed.

The threads of the tapestry serve the artist's vision; the artist
does not weave so that the threads show up one by one. The
weavers of a tractate of the Bavli make ample use of available
yarn. But they weave their own tapestry of thought. And it is their
vision—and *not* the character of the threads in hand—that dictates the proportions and message of the tapestry. In that same
way, so far as processes of thought of a sustained and rigorous
character yield writing that makes a single, cogent statement, tradition and system cannot form a compatible unit. Where reason
governs, it reigns supreme and alone, revising the received materials and, through its own powerful and rigorous logic, restat-

ing into a compelling statement the entirety of the prior heritage of information and thought.

Why does it matter to my study of the formation of Judaism? The reason is that critical to that study are the correct classification and characterization of the Talmud of Babylonia. Is the story of the formation of Judaism in late antiquity the history of the sedimentary agglutination of a tradition? Or does the Judaism that through the Bavli comes out of late antiquity speak for some few people, who have formed a system pretty much within the outlines of their own plan? For whom, then, does the Judaism embodied in the Bavli speak, in what context, for what purpose, in response to what ineluctable problem, providing what self-evidently valid answer? Whether or not these questions are even to be addressed to the document depends upon whether we conceive the document to be traditional or systemic. That is why the issue of selectivity proves so preponderant: if choices, then who made the selections and why. If no choices, then for whom does the document speak, and why does it speak at all—as, by definition, it assuredly does?

While the writing appears to be "traditional," because of its perennial reference to received traditions, it in fact is highly selective. The reason that judgment matters is that, in interpreting the character of the system adumbrated by the Bavli, my first step is to classify the system as a whole, and, as is now clear, I classify that system as not traditional but autonomous, not received but composed with a plan and a program particular to its authorship. In my hermeneutics, I therefore contrast thought received as truth transmitted through a process of tradition against thought derived from active rationality. This I do by asking a simple question: does what is the most rigorously rational and compelling statement of applied reason known to me, the Talmud of Babylonia or Bavli, constitute a tradition and derive from a process of traditional formulation and transmission of an intellectual heritage, facts and thought alike? Or does that document make a statement of its own, cogent and defined within the requirements of an inner logic, proportion, and structure, imposing that essentially autonomous vision upon whatever materials its authorship has received from the past? My mode of asking that question in these pages, we recall, is to test allegations that yield a picture of a traditional document against the character of three documents themselves: Tosefta, which is traditional in relationship to the Mishnah, having no structure but the Mishnah's; Sifra, which is traditional in relationship to Scripture; and the Bavli, which to begin with selects what it wishes of the Mishnah (thirty-seven out of sixty-two usable tractates) and then imposes its plan and its questions upon the Mishnah. The first two are classified as traditional, the first as selective.

In contrasting selectivity with traditionality, quite clearly, I use tradition in a literary sense, as referring to a process by which writings of one kind and not another take shape. So let me then define what I mean by tradition and place into the context of Judaism the issue I have framed, to begin with, in such general terms. For if any noun follows the adjective, "Rabbinic," it is not "Judaism" but "tradition." And by "tradition" people mean two contradictory things.

First, when people speak of "tradition," they refer to the formative history of a piece of writing, specifically, an incremental and linear process that step by step transmits out of the past an essential and unchanging fundament of truth *preserved in writing*, by stages, with what one generation has contributed covered by the increment of the next in a sedimentary process, producing a literature that, because of its traditional history as the outcome of a linear and stage by stage process, exercises authority over future generations and therefore is nurtured for the future. In that sense, tradition is supposed to describe a *process* or a chain of transmission of received materials, refined and corrected but handed on not only unimpaired, but essentially intact. The opening sentence of tractate Abot, "Moses received Torah from Sinai and handed it on to Joshua," bears the implication of such a literary process, though, self-evidently, the remainder of that chapter hardly illustrates the type of process alleged at the outset.

The second meaning of tradition bears not upon process but upon content and structure. People sometimes use the word tradition to mean a fixed and unchanging essence deriving from an indeterminate past, a truth bearing its own stigmata of authority, e.g., from God at Sinai.

These two meanings of the same word coexist. But they are incompatible. For the first of the two places a document within an on-going, determinate historical process, the latter speaks of a single statement at the end of an indeterminate and undefined process, which can encompass revelation of a one-time sort. In this context I use only the first of the two meanings. When, therefore, I ask whether or not the Bavli is a traditional or a selective document, I want to know whether the present literary character of the Bavli suggests to us that the document emerges from a sedimentary process of tradition in the sense just now specified: an incremental, linear development, step by step, of law and theology from one generation to the next, coming to expression in documents arrayed in sequence, first to last. The alternative—which I believe has here once more proven the more likely of the two propositions—is that the Bavli originates as a cogent and proportioned statement through a process we may compare – continuing our geological metaphor – to the way in which igneous rock takes shape: through a grand eruption, all at once, then coalescence and solidification essentially forthwith. Either the Bavli will emerge in a series of layers, or it will appear to have formed suddenly, in a work of supererogatory and imposed rationality, all at once, perfect in its ultimate logic and structure.

When I maintain that the Bavli is not a traditional document, I issue a judgment as to its character viewed as literature in relationship to prior extant writings. Everyone of course must concur that, in a theological sense, the Bavli is a profoundly traditional document, laying forth in its authorship's terms and language the nature of the Judaic tradition, that is, Judaism, as that authorship wishes to read the tradition and have it read. But this second sense will not recur in the pages that follow. In framing the issue of tradition versus system, I sidestep a current view of the literature of formative Judaism. That view, specified presently, ignores the documentary character of each of the writings, viewing them all as essentially one and uniform, lacking all documentary definition.

What I have shown for Tosefta's and Sifra's relationship to the Bavli is a simple proposition. The prior writings were used when wanted, ignored when not; they provided valued, authoritative information; but they defined no program, provided no framework and order of inquiry, dictated no issues, determined no results. The heirs, in the Bavli, utilized these sources (or, materials later on collected and preserved therein) pretty much as they found them useful, meaning, for their reasons, in the realization of their program. With the Bavli as the literary realization of the system overall, we may then conclude that the Judaism of the dual

Torah knows not traditions to be recited and reviewed but merely sources, to be honored always but to be used only when pertinent to a quite independent program of thought. That is to say, the components of the Torah of that Judaism do not contribute equally and jointly to a single comprehensive statement, handed on from generation to generation *and from book to book,* all of them sources forming a tradition that constitutes the Torah.

Each has a particular message and make a distinctive statement. In literary terms, the various rabbinic documents commonly (and, from a theological perspective, quite correctly) are commonly represented as not merely autonomous and individual statements, or even connected here and there through shared passages, but in fact as continuous and and interrelated developments, one out of its predecessor, in a long line of canonical writings (to Sinai). The Talmud of Babylonia, or Bavli, takes pride of place – in this picture of "the rabbinic tradition" – as the final and complete statement of that incremental, linear tradition, and so is ubiquitously described as "*the* tradition," par excellence. In this concluding monograph I shall demonstrate that, vis-à-vis its sources, the Bavli represents an essentially autonomous, fresh, and original statement of its own. How so? Its authorship does not take over, rework, and repeat what it has received out of prior writings but makes its own statement, on its own program, in its own terms, and for its own purposes.

Every test I can devise for describing the relationship between the authorship of the Bavli and the prior and extant writings of the movement of which that authorship forms the climax and conclusion yields a single result. Unlike Sifra and Tosefta, the authorship of the Bavli does not pursue anyone else's program— even that of the Mishnah. The Bavli's authorship selected thirty-seven tractates and therefore bypassed twenty-five. How traditional is an authorship that has attended to a little more than half of its received and authoritative writing? No less than 40% of the tractates of the Mishnah are simply ignored by the Bavli. And however sustained its exegesis of the Mishnah-tractates that are taken up, the Bavli's authorship does not merely receive and refine writings concluded elsewhere. It takes over a substantial heritage and reworks the whole into its own sustained and internally cogent statement – and that forms not the outcome of a process of sedimentary tradition but the opposite: systematic statement of a cogent and logical order, made up in its authorship's rhetoric, attaining comprehensibility through the syntax of its authorship's logic, reviewing a received topical program in terms of the problematic and interests defined by its authorship's larger purposes and proposed message. The samples of the Bavli we reviewed—and any others I might have chosen!—constitute either composites of sustained, essentially syllogistic discourse, in which case they form the whole and comprehensive statement of a system, or increments of exegetical accumulation, in which case they constitute restatements, with minor improvements, of a continuous tradition. In my view, the reader is going to review sustained, directed, purposive syllogistic discourse, not wandering and essentially agglutinative collections of observations on this and that, made we know not when, for a purpose we cannot say, to an audience we can scarcely imagine, so as to deliver a message that, all together and in the aggregate, we cannot begin to recapitulate.

In its final, literary context defined by the documents or sources we can identify, the Bavli emerges as anything but the seal of "tradition" in the familiar sense. For it is not based on distinct and completed sources handed on from time immemorial, subserviently cited and glossed by its own authorship, and it does not focus upon the systematic representation of the materials of prior documents, faithfully copied and rehearsed and represented. We have, of course, to exclude the Mishnah, but this fundamental document is treated by the authorship of the Bavli in a wholly independent spirit. The upshot is that the Bavli does not derive from a process of tradition in the first sense stated above, although, as a faithful and practicing Jew, I believe that the Bavli truly constitutes "tradition" in that second, theological sense to which I referred: a new statement of its own making and a fresh address to issues of its own choosing. Viewed as literature, the Bavli is not a traditional document at all. It is not the result of an incremental and linear process; it does not review and restate what others have already said; its authorship does not regard itself as bound to the program and issues received from prior ages. By its selectivity, the Bavli's authorship shows us that their document constitutes a systemic and not a traditional statement.

True, the Talmud of Babylonia draws upon prior materials. It was not made up out of whole cloth by its penultimate and ultimate authorship, the generations that drew the whole together and placed it into the form in which it has come down from the seventh century to the present day. The Bavli's authorship both received out of the past a corpus of *sources*, and also stood in a line of *traditions* of sayings and stories, that is, fixed wordings of thought the formulation and transmission of which took place not in completed documents but in ad hoc and brief sentences or little narratives. These materials, deriving from an indeterminate past through a now-inaccessible process of literary history, constitute traditions in the sense defined in the preface: an incremental and linear process that step by step transmits out of the past an essential and unchanging fundament of truth and writing. The process of selectivity worked itself out in a review of these traditions. The document emerged out of those principles of selectivity that guided the choice. The next task in the description of the formation of Judaism therefore requires us to discover the principles that told people why this, not that. This distinction, then, between traditions and sources, between selectivity and tradition, has now to be spelled out.

Traditions: some of these prior materials never reached redaction in a distinct document and come down as sherds and remnants within the Bavli itself. These are the ones that may be called traditions, in the sense of materials formulated and transmitted from one generation to the next, but not given a place in a document of their own.

Sources: others had themselves reached closure prior to the work on the Bavli and are readily identified as autonomous writings. Scripture, to take an obvious example, the Mishnah, tractate Abot (the Fathers), the Tosefta (so we commonly suppose), Sifra, Sifré to Numbers, Sifré to Deuteronomy, Genesis Rabbah, Leviticus Rabbah, the Fathers according to Rabbi Nathan, Pesiqta deRab Kahana, Pesiqta Rabbati, possibly Lamentations Rabbah, not to mention the Siddur and Mahzor (order of daily and holy day prayer, respectively), and various other writings had assuredly concluded their processes of formation before the Bavli's authorship accomplished their work. These we call *sources* – more or less completed writings.

To conclude: in contrasting tradition and selectivity, tradition as against system, I really want to know the answer to one question: is a document that is received as authoritative (in theological terms, "canonical") essentially a restatement of what has gone before, or is a such a writing fresh and original? If the answer is that the Bavli restates a consensus formed through ages, then our conception of the literary definition of the canon of Judaism will take one form. I have shown once more that the Bavli's authorship makes an essentially new statement. When we know how that statement is—what I call "the Bavli's one voice"—and what statement is intended, we shall understand the final stage in the formation of Judaism. The Bavli in relationship to its sources is simply not a traditional document, in the plain sense that most of what it says in a cogent and coherent way expresses the well-crafted statement and viewpoint of its authorship. Its authorship exercised an on-going privilege of selectivity. Excluding, of course, the Mishnah, to which the Bavli devotes its sustained and systematic attention, little of what our authorship says derives cogency and force from a received statement, and most does not. The authorship of the Bavli selectively made up a tradition.

PART TWO

THE BAVLI'S FORMAL COGENCY

CHAPTER ONE

HOW THE TALMUD IS ORGANIZED

I. The Debate on Whether or Not the Talmud is Well-Organized, and Whether It Is Organized At All

Until now the Talmud's exegetes could debate the simple question of whether the Bavli followed a plan of organization for its materials, and, if it did, what that plan might be. Once I undertook an outline of the Bavli, start to finish, all thirty-seven tractates, I settled that question. The Bavli is exquisitely organized, once one discerns the principles of order and recognizes the problems the sages solved in adopting those principles. Just as the Bavli as a whole is cogent, doing some few things over and over again, so it follows a simple program, start to finish. Also, just as the Talmud conforms to a few simple rules of rhetoric, including choice of languages for discrete purposes, and that fact attests to the coherent viewpoint of the authorship at the end—the people who put it all together as we have it—because it speaks, over all, in a single way, in a uniform voice, so it exhibits traits of uniformity in program and exposition. The Talmud is not merely an encyclopaedia of information, but a sustained, remarkably protracted, uniform inquiry into the logical traits of passages of the Mishnah or of Scripture. Most of the Talmud deals with the exegesis and amplification of the Mishnah's rules or of passages of Scripture. Wherever we turn, that labor of exegesis and amplification, without differentiation in topics or tractates, conforms to a few simple rules in inquiry, repeatedly phrased, implicitly or explicitly, in a few simple rhetorical forms or patterns. Since a great many present the Bavli as disorganized, the burden of proof for the contrary view rests on its advocates, beginning here. First, in this chapter, I shall show that a tractate of the Bavli follows a simple and lucid outline, with nearly every composition and every composite given its place for a solid, considered reason. Then, in the chapter to follow, I shall explain how the compositions in the Bavli cohere, and how the composites hold together. Finally, in Chapter Three,

I turn to the Bavli's massive miscellanies, the rather strange, jerry-built composites that in most tractates appear to impede reasonable exposition of an established topic and that impart to the Bavli the appearance of disorganization. This demonstrates beyond any reasonable doubt that viewed whole, the Talmud is carefully and reasonably organized, and we are able to identify the principles of systematic arrangement that govern, once we decode the system and understand the redactional problems that faced the compilers of the documents.

II. *The Bavli's Structure and System*

By "structure" I mean, a clearly-articulated pattern that governs the location of fully-spelled out statements. By "system," I mean, a well-crafted and coherent set of ideas that explain the social order of the community addressed by the writers of a document, a social philosophy, a theory of the way of life, world view, and character of the social entity formed by a given social group. I see a collective, anonymous, and political document, such as the one before us, as a statement to, and about, the way in which people should organize their lives and govern their actions. At issue then in any document such as the remarkable one before us is simple: does this piece of writing present information or a program, facts to whom it may concern, or a philosophically and aesthetically cogent statement about how things should be?

The connection between structure and system is plain to see. From the way in which people consistently frame their thoughts, we move to the world that, in saying things one way rather than in some other, they wish to imagine the world in which they wish to live, to which they address these thoughts. For if the document exhibits structure and sets forth a system, then it is accessible to questions of rationality. We may ask about the statement that its framers or compilers wished to make by putting the document together as they did. But if we discern no structure and perceive no systematic inquiry or governing points of analysis, then all we find here is inert and miscellaneous information, facts but no propositions, arguments, viewpoints.

Now the Talmud commonly finds itself represented as lacking organization and exhibiting a certain episodic and notional character. That view moreover characterizes the reading and representation of the document by learned and experienced scholars, who have devoted their entire lives to Talmud study and exegesis. It must follow that upon the advocate of the contrary view—the one implicit in the representation of the document for academic analysis—rests the burden of proof. I set forth the allegation that the Talmud exhibits a structure and follows a system and therefore exhibits a commonly-intelligible rationality. The claim to write an academic commentary explicitly states that proposition. For the tractate before us, I have therefore to adduce evidence and argument.

I maintain that through the normal procedures of reasoned analysis we may discern in the tractate a well-crafted structure. I hold that the structure made manifest, we may further identify the purpose and perspective, the governing system of thought and argument, of those who collected and arranged the tractate's composites and put them together in the way in which we now have them. So to reca-pitulate, by "structure" I mean, how is a document organized? and by "system," what do the compilers of the document propose to accomplish in producing this complete, organized piece of writing? The answers to both questions derive from a simple outline of the tractate as a whole, underscoring the types of compositions and composites of which it is comprised. Such an outline tells us what is principal and what subordinate, and how each unit—composition formed into composites, composites formed into a complete state-ment—holds together and also fits with other units, fore and aft. The purpose of the outline then is to identify the character of each com-ponent of the whole, and to specify its purpose or statement. The former information permits us to describe the document's structure, the latter, its system.

The character of the outline dictates all further analytical initia-tives. Specifically, when we follow the layout of the whole, with its indentations successively indicating the secondary and tertiary am-plification of a primary point, we readily see the principles of orga-nization that govern. These same guidelines on organizing discourse point also to the character of what is organized: complete units of thought, with a beginning, middle, and end, often made up of smaller, equally complete units of thought. The former we know as compos-ites, the latter as compositions. Identifying and classifying the com-ponents of the tractate—the composites, the compositions of which they are made up—we see clearly how the document coheres: the plan and program worked out from beginning to end. When we define that plan and program, we identify the facts of a pattern that permit us to say in a specific and concrete way precisely what the compilers of the tractate intended to accomplish. The structure realizes the system, the program of analysis and thought that takes the form of the presentation we have before us. From what people do, meaning, the way in which they formulate their ideas and organize them into cogent statements, we discern what they proposed to do, meaning, the intellectual goals that they set for themselves.

These goals—the received document they wished to examine, the questions that they systematically and in an orderly manner brought to that document—realized in the layout and construction of their writing, dictate the points of uniformity and persistence that throughout come to the surface. How people lay out their ideas guides us into what they wished to find out and set forth in their writing, and that constitutes the system that defined the work they set out to accomplish. We move from how people speak to the system that the mode of discourse means to express, in the theory that modes of speech or writing convey modes of thought and inquiry. We move from the act of thought and its written result backward to the theory of thinking, which is, by definition, an act of social consequence. We therefore turn to the matter of intention that provokes reflection and produces a system of inquiry. That statement does not mean to imply I begin with the premise of order, which sustains the thesis of a prior system that defines the order. To the contrary, the possibility of forming a coherent outline out of the data we have examined defines the first test of whether or not the document exhibits a structure and realizes a system. So everything depends upon the possibility of outlining the writing, from which all else flows. If we can see the order and demonstrate that the allegation of order rests on ample evidence, then we may proceed to describe the structure that gives expression to the order, and the system that the structure sustains.

The experience of analyzing the document with the question of cogency and coherence in mind therefore yields a simple recognition. Viewed whole, any given tractate contains no gibberish but only completed units of thought, sentences formed into intelligible thought and self-contained, in that we require no further information to understand those sentences, beginning to end. The tractate organizes these statements as commentary to the Mishnah. But large tracts of the writing do not comment on the Mishnah in the way in which other, still larger tracts do. Then how the former fit together with the latter frames the single most urgent question of structure and system that I can identify.

What justifies my insistence that an outline of the document, resting on the premise that we deal with a Mishnah-commentary, governs all further description? To begin with, the very possibility of outlining Babylonian Talmud tractates derives from the simple fact that the framers have given to their document the form of a commentary to the Mishnah. It is in the structure of the Mishnah-tractate that they locate everything together that they wished to compile. We know that is the fact because the Mishnah-tractate defines the order of topics and the sequence of problems. Relationships to the Mishnah are readily discerned; a paragraph stands at the head of a unit of thought; even without the full citation of the paragraph, we should find our way back to the Mishnah because at the head of numerous compositions, laid out in sequence one to the next, clauses of the Mishnah-paragraph are cited in so many words or alluded to in an unmistakable way. So without printing the entire Mishnah-paragraph at the head, we should know that the received code formed the fundamental structure because so many compositions cite and gloss sentences of the Mishnah-paragraph and are set forth in sequence dictated by the order of sentences of said Mishnah-paragraph. Internal evidence alone suffices, then, to demonstrate that the structure of the tractate rests upon the Mishnah-tractate cited and discussed here. Not only so, but the sentences of the Mishnah-paragraphs of our tractate are discussed in no other place in the entire Talmud of Babylonia in the sequence and systematic exegetical framework in which they are set forth here; elsewhere we may find bits or pieces, but only here, the entirety of the tractate.

That statement requires one qualification, and that further leads us to the analytical task of our outline. While the entire Mishnah-tractate in any given instance is cited in the Talmud, the framers of the Talmud by no means find themselves required to say something about every word, every sentence, every paragraph. On the contrary, they discuss only what they choose to discuss, and glide without comment by large stretches of the tractate. A process of selectivity, which requires description and analysis, has told the compilers of the Talmud's composites and the authors of its compositions[1] what

---

[1] This statement requires refinement. I do not know that all available compo

demands attention, and what does not. Our outline has therefore to signal not only what passage of the Mishnah-tractate is discussed, but also what is not discussed, and we require a general theory to explain the principles of selection ("making connections, drawing conclusions" meaning, to begin with, making selections). For that purpose, in the outline, I reproduce the entirety of a Mishnah-paragraph that stands at the head of a Talmudic composite, and I underscore those sentences that are addressed, so highlighting also those that are not.

It follows that the same evidence that justifies identifying the Mishnah-tractate as the structure (therefore also the foundation of the system) of the Talmud-tractate before us also presents puzzles for considerable reflection. The exegesis of Mishnah-exegesis is only one of these. Another concerns the purpose of introducing into the document enormous compositions and composites that clearly hold together around a shared topic or proposition, e.g., my appendix on one theme or another, my elaborate footnote providing information that is not required but merely useful, and the like. My characterization in the next chapter of composites as appendices and footnotes signals the fact that the framers of the document chose a not-entirely-satisfactory way of setting out the materials they wished to include here, for large components of the tractate do not contribute to Mishnah-exegesis in any way at all. If these intrusions of other-than-exegetical compositions were proportionately modest, or

---

sitions have been reproduced, and that the work of authors of compositions of Mishnah-exegesis intended for a talmud is fully exposed in the document as we have it. That is not only something we cannot demonstrate—we do not have compositions that were not used, only the ones that were—but something that we must regard as unlikely on the face of matters. All we may say is positive: the character of the compositions that address Mishnah-exegesis tells us about the concerns of the writers of those compositions, but we cannot claim to outline all of their concerns, on the one side, or to explain why they chose not to work on other Mishnah-sentences besides the ones treated here. But as to the program of the compositors, that is another matter: from the choices that they made (out of a corpus we cannot begin to imagine or invent for ourselves) we may describe with great accuracy the kinds of materials they wished to include and the shape and structure they set forth out of those materials. We know what they did, and that permits us to investigate why they did what they did. What we cannot know is what they did not do, or why they chose not to do what they did not do. People familiar with the character of speculation and criticism in Talmudic studies will understand why I have to spell out these rather commonplace observations. I lay out an argument based on evidence, not on the silences of evidence, or on the absence of evidence—that alone.

of topical composites negligible in size, we might dismiss them as
appendages, not structural components that bear much of the weight
of the edifice as a whole. Indeed, the language that I chose for identifying and defining these composites—footnotes, appendices, and
the like—bore the implication that what is not Mishnah-commentary also is extrinsic to the Talmud's structure and system.

But that language served only for the occasion. In fact, the outline before us will show that the compositions are large and ambitious, the composites formidable and defining. Any description of
the tractate's structure that dismisses as mere accretions or intrusions so large a proportion of the whole misleads. Any notion that
"footnotes" and "appendices" impede exposition and disrupt thought,
contribute extraneous information or form tacked-on appendages—
any such notion begs the question: then why fill up so much space
with such purposeless information? The right way is to ask whether
the document's topical composites play a role in the re-presentation
of the Mishnah-tractate by the compilers of the Talmud. We have
therefore to test two hypotheses:

1) the topical composites ("appendices," "footnotes") do belong and
   serve the compilers' purpose; or:
2) the topical composites do not participate in the re-presentation
   of the Mishnah-tractate by the Talmud and do not belong because they add nothing and change nothing.

The two hypotheses may be tested against the evidence framed in
response to a single question: is this topical composite necessary? The
answer to that question lies in our asking, what happens to the reading of the Mishnah-tractate in light of the topical composites that
would not happen were we to read the same tractate without them?
The outline that follows systematically raises that question, with
results specified in due course. It suffices here to state the simple result
of our reading of the tractate, start to finish: the question of structure, therefore also that of system, rests upon the position we identify for that massive component of the tractate that comprises not
Mishnah-commentary but free-standing compositions and composites of compositions formed for a purpose other than Mishnah-commentary.

The principal rubrics are given in small caps. The outline takes
as its principal rubrics two large-scale organizing principles.

The first is the divisions of the Mishnah-tractate to which the
Talmud-tractate serves as a commentary. That simple fact validates

the claim that the tractate exhibits a fully-articulated structure. But the outline must also underscore that the Mishnah-tractate provides both more and less than the paramount outline of the Talmud-tractate. It is more because sentences in the Mishnah-tractate are not analyzed at all. These untreated Mishnah-sentences are given in bold face lower case caps, like the rest of the Mishnah, but then are specified by underlining and enclosure in square brackets.

Second, it is less because the structure of the tractate accommodates large composites that address topics not defined by the Mishnah-tractate. That brings us to the second of the two large-scale modes of holding together both sustained analytical exercises and also large sets of compositions formed into cogent composites. These are treated also as major units and are indicated by Roman numerals, alongside the Mishnah-paragraphs themselves; they are also signified in small caps. But the principal rubrics that do not focus on Mishnah-commentary but on free-standing topics or propositions or problems are not given in boldface type. Consequently, for the purposes of a coherent outline we have to identify as autonomous entries in our outline those important composites that treat themes or topics not contributed by the Mishnah-tractate.

III. *Outlining the Bavli*

The basis for the outline is the availability of an encompassing reference system, fully executed in outline-form for the entire Talmud. The work becomes possible because of my systematic commentary on the Bavli, which showed through graphics the main lines of not only order but structure, the divisions of cogent thought and how they are related to one another and to the framework in which all take their place. Having provided the Bavli with its first reference-system—dividing its contents into their constituent-units, I proceeded to identify principal, secondary, and tertiary components of its composition. This work was fully exposed in my *Talmud of Babylonia. An Academic Commentary*. It is what made possible, by its very nature, the orderly outlining of the document as a whole. My re-presentation of the Bavli in the academic commentary, through graphics making my comments on the structure and system of the document throughout, yielded for each of the thirty-seven tractates a systematic outline of the whole.

Accordingly, we are able for the first time to follow how the compilers of the document put things together. We can see what program of inquiry guided their work, how they decided what comes first and what takes second place, what types of materials they utilized, and, it must follow, what types of materials they did not introduce at all. In this way a variety of long-standing questions concerning the character of the Bavli are definitively settled. Not only so, but we are now able to identify the types of compositions and large-scale composites of which the Bavli's framers made use, and that permits us systematically to study the classifications of those types, e.g., Mishnah-commentary, other-than-Mishnah-commentary, to take the two most obvious classifications of all. Not by a repertoire of examples but by a complete catalogue of all items, therefore, we can now say precisely what types of materials are used, in what proportions, in what contexts, for what purposes, and the like. Before the presentation of this outline, we did not know how many is "many," or how much is "occasionally." From now on generalizations, accompanied by reasonably accurate statements of the numbers and proportions of exemplary data, take a probative role in all study of the character and definition of the Bavli.

In the prior Part of this account of how the Bavli works, I argued that the Bavli throughout speaks in a single, uniform voice, and that that voice is not only single but unique in the context of Rabbinic compilations of late antiquity. Now there can be no further argument on that point; the evidence of the uniformity of discourse is spread out here, in stupefying detail. Anyone who takes a contrary view will have to show that these outlines err, not in one detail or another, not in a matter of mere judgment, but fundamentally and essentially. And that is not going to be possible. Enough of the contents of the Bavli is supplied in these pages so that readers can judge for themselves precisely how the compilers of the Bavli have organized their composites, deciding whether or not I am correct in my insistence that a single program governs every tractate; and that we can define that program and show its presence in the thirty-seven tractates, line by line.

For me, the natural next step is a study of the composites that are formed around propositions other than those pertinent to the Mishnah or that take shape in response to analytical problems (exegetical, legal) that the Mishnah does not provoke or even accommodate. On the strength of this complete outline, I conceive that we may begin the systematic inquiry into types of writing that reached closure prior to the formation of the Bavli and for purposes other than those defined by the compilers of the Bavli. Until this time, studies of the problem of the pre-history of the document have proved episodic and unsystematic, therefore indeterminate in their results. In the foreseeable future we shall have a reliable account of precisely what compositions and composites in the Bavli attest to writing not carried out by the Bavli's compilers but drawn upon by them. So the history of the Bavli—the pre-history, really—now comes into view. We may proceed not with guess-work based on a few phrases here and there but with quite orderly and coherent analysis of the document viewed whole.

IV. *A Case in Point: The Structure of Bavli Tractate Horayot*

I have chosen as my exemplary case Bavli Horayot, because it is a brief tractate but bears within itself a fair component of composites, to be seen in context and explained there. I give the entire Mishnah-tractate and then summarize the character of the Talmud's treatment of the Mishnah-paragraphs, even isolated sentences, as we proceed.

I. MISHNAH-TRACTATE HORAYOT 1:1

A. [IF] THE COURT GAVE A DECISION TO TRANSGRESS ANY OR ALL OF THE COMMANDMENTS WHICH ARE STATED IN THE TORAH:
  1. I:1: The Talmud raises the question omitted by the Mishnah, which is, the liability of the court in such a situation.
  2. I:2: Reprise of the foregoing.

B. AND AN INDIVIDUAL WENT AND ACTED IN ACCORD WITH THEIR INSTRUCTIONS, [SO TRANSGRESSING] INADVERTENTLY:
  1. II:1: Why not formulate the Tannaite rule as, and an individual went and acted in accord with their instructions? What need do I have for the emphatic addition, inadvertently?

C. WHETHER THEY CARRIED OUT WHAT THEY SAID AND HE CARRIED OUT WHAT THEY SAID RIGHT ALONG WITH THEM, (2) OR WHETHER THEY CARRIED OUT WHAT THEY SAID AND HE CARRIED OUT WHAT THEY SAID AFTER THEY DID, (3) WHETHER THEY DID NOT CARRY OUT WHAT THEY SAID, BUT HE CARRIED OUT WHAT THEY SAID—HE IS EXEMPT, SINCE HE RELIED ON THE COURT:
  1. III:1: What need is there to cover in the Tannaite formulation all of these several cases?

D. [IF] THE COURT GAVE A DECISION, AND ONE OF THEM KNEW THAT THEY HAD ERRED, OR A DISCIPLE WHO IS WORTHY TO GIVE INSTRUCTION:

1.IV:1: What need do I have for both categories?

E. OR A DISCIPLE WHO IS WORTHY TO GIVE INSTRUCTION:
AND HE [WHO KNEW OF THE ERROR] WENT AND CARRIED OUT WHAT THEY SAID, WHETHER THEY CARRIED OUT WHAT THEY SAID AND HE CARRIED OUT WHAT THEY SAID RIGHT ALONG WITH THEM, WHETHER THEY CARRIED OUT WHAT THEY SAID AND HE CARRIED OUT WHAT THEY SAID AFTER THEY DID, WHETHER THEY DID NOT CARRY OUT WHAT THEY SAID, BUT HE CARRIED OUT WHAT THEY SAID—LO, THIS ONE IS LIABLE, SINCE HE [WHO KNEW THE LAW] DID NOT IN POINT OF FACT RELY UPON THE COURT:

1. V:1: Like whom? Simeon b. Azzai and Simeon b. Zoma.

F. THIS IS THE GOVERNING PRINCIPLE: HE WHO RELIES ON HIMSELF IS LIABLE:

1. VI:1: What case is encompassed by the governing principle beyond those already specified?

G. AND HE WHO RELIES ON THE COURT IS EXEMPT:

1. VII:1: What case is encompassed by the governing principle beyond those already specified?

2. VII:2: The governing principle represents the position of R. Judah, but sages say, "A private party who acted in accord with the instructions of a court [and inadvertently violated the law] is liable to present an offering."

3. VII:3: The governing principle represents the position of R. Meir, but sages said, "An individual who committed a transgression by following the instructions of the court is liable."

   a. VII:4: When reckoning what forms a majority, in the case of an erroneous decision by a court, the operative criterion is the greater part of the population of the entire land of Israel.

4. VII:5: With reference THE GOVERNING PRINCIPLE: HE WHO RELIES ON HIMSELF IS LIABLE, AND HE WHO RELIES ON THE COURT IS EXEMPT, we now turn to the dispute concerning the kind of offering required in various situations of public inadvertent sin involving court instruction, at M. 1:5, so that, when a majority violates the law by reason of the court's ruling, they make atonement through a communal offering of a bull, but if a minority does so, it is exempt since it relied upon the court, but what about a case in which before the offering is presented, the community's numbers diminish so that the ratio of transgressors to non-transgressors has changed? If the number of transgressors was a minority but through deaths in the interim became a majority of the community, what is the law?

5. VII:6: If the court gave the decision that suet is permitted , and a minority of the community went and acted in accord

with that decision, and then the court retracted and gave correct instructions, and the court once more gave the decision that suet is permitted, but now a different minority of the community acted, what is the law?

6. VII:7: If the court gave instructions that suet is permitted, and a minority of the community went and acted in accord with that instruction, and then that court died, but another court was appointed and they retracted, but then they issued a new instruction to the same effect, and another minority acted in accord with the new instruction of this new court, what is the law?

7. VII:8: In a case in which a hundred who went into session to give instruction, liability for judicial error is incurred only if all of them will give that instruction, as it is said, "And if all of the assembly shall err" (Lev. 4:13)—the court is exempt unless everyone of them errs, meaning, unless their instruction has permeated throughout the community of Israel.

    a. VII:9: When ten sit in judgment, the chain of responsibility is suspended on the necks of all of them.

        i. VII:10: R Huna: when he would go to court, he would bring with him from the school house ten Tannaite-tradition-memorizers, "so that each one of us may carry a chip of the beam."

        ii. VII:11: R. Ashi: same saying based on a different story.

II. MISHNAH-TRACTATE HORAYOT 1:2-3

A. [IF] THE COURT GAVE A DECISION AND REALIZED THAT IT HAD ERRED AND RETRACTED, WHETHER THEY BROUGHT THEIR ATONEMENT OFFERING OR DID NOT BRING THEIR ATONEMENT OFFERING, AND AN INDIVIDUAL DID IN ACCORD WITH THEIR INSTRUCTION— R. SIMEON DECLARES HIM EXEMPT. AND R. ELIEZER SAYS, "IT IS SUBJECT TO DOUBT."

1. I:1: What is the operative consideration behind the ruling of R. Simeon?

2. I:2: Tannaite version of the dispute and various opinions on the same matter as is treated in the Mishnah.

B. WHAT IS THE DOUBT? [IF] THE PERSON HAD STAYED HOME, HE IS LIABLE. [IF] HE HAD GONE OVERSEAS, HE IS EXEMPT. SAID R. AQIBA, "I CONCEDE IN THIS CASE THAT HE IS NIGH UNTO BEING EXEMPT FROM LIABILITY" SAID TO HIM BEN AZZAI, "WHAT IS THE DIFFERENCE BETWEEN THIS ONE AND ONE WHO STAYS HOME?" FOR THE ONE WHO STAYS HOME HAD THE POSSIBILITY OF HEARING [THAT THE COURT HAD ERRED AND RETRACTED], BUT THIS ONE DID NOT HAVE THE POSSIBILITY OF HEARING [WHAT HAD HAPPENED]:"

1. II:1: Did R. Aqiba make a valid statement to Ben Azzai?

C. [IF] A COURT GAVE A DECISION TO UPROOT THE WHOLE PRINCIPLE
    [OF THE TORAH],
    (1) [IF] THEY SAID, "[THE PROHIBITION AGAINST HAVING INTER-
    COURSE WITH] A MENSTRUATING WOMAN IS NOT IN THE TORAH
    [LEV. 15:19]." (2) "[THE PROHIBITION OF LABOR ON] THE SAB-
    BATH IS NOT IN THE TORAH." (3) "[THE PROHIBITION AGAINST]
    IDOLATRY IS NOT IN THE TORAH." LO, THESE ARE EXEMPT [FROM
    THE REQUIREMENT OF LEV. 4:14].
    1. III:1: Tannaite proof of the proposition on the basis of Scrip-
        ture.
        a. III:2: development of foregoing.
            ɪ. III:3: as above.
D. [IF] THEY GAVE INSTRUCTION TO NULLIFY PART AND TO CARRY
    OUT PART [OF A RULE OF THE TORAH], LO, THEY ARE LIABLE. HOW
    SO? [IF] THEY SAID, 'THE PRINCIPLE OF PROHIBITION OF SEXUAL
    RELATIONSHIPS WITH A MENSTRUATING WOMAN INDEED IS IN THE
    TORAH, BUT HE WHO HAS SEXUAL RELATIONS WITH A WOMAN
    AWAITING DAY AGAINST DAY IS EXEMPT." (2) "THE PRINCIPLE OF
    NOT WORKING ON THE SABBATH IS IN THE TORAH, BUT HE WHO
    TAKES OUT SOMETHING FROM PRIVATE DOMAIN TO PUBLIC DOMAIN
    IS EXEMPT." (3) "THE PRINCIPLE OF NOT WORSHIPPING IDOLS IS
    IN THE TORAH BUT HE WHO BOWS DOWN [TO AN IDOL] IS EX-
    EMPT."—LO, THESE ARE LIABLE, SINCE IT IS SAID, "IF SOMETHING
    BE HIDDEN" (LEV. 4:13)—SOMETHING, AND NOT EVERYTHING:
    1. IV:1: The court is liable only if it gives wrong instruction in
        a matter that the Sadducees do not accept as a matter of rev-
        elation [that is, the oral Torah]. But in a matter that the
        Sadducees too concede, the court is exempt.
    2. IV:2: If the court announced that there is no prohibition
        against ploughing on the Sabbath [vs. Ex. 34:21], what is the
        law?
    3. IV:3: If the court announced that there is no prohibition in
        the Torah against working on the Sabbath during the Sab-
        batical Year, what is the law?

          III. MISHNAH-TRACTATE HORAYOT 1:4A-G

A. (1) [IF] THE COURT GAVE A DECISION, AND ONE OF THE MEMBERS
    OF THE COURT REALIZED THAT THEY HAD ERRED AND SAID TO
    THEM, "YOU ARE IN ERROR,"
    OR (2) IF THE HEAD OF THE COURT WAS NOT THERE,
    OR (3) IF ONE OF THEM WAS A PROSELYTE, A MAMZER, A NETIN,
    OR AN ELDER WHO DID NOT HAVE CHILDREN—LO, THESE ARE EX-
    EMPT [FROM A PUBLIC OFFERING UNDER THE PROVISIONS OF LEV.
    4:14],
    1. I:1: how on the basis of Scripture do we know this fact?
B. SINCE "CONGREGATION" IS SAID HERE [LEV. 4:13], AND "CON-
    GREGATION" IS SAID LATER ON [NUM. 15:24]. JUST AS "CONGRE-

GATION" LATER ON APPLIES ONLY IN THE CASE IN WHICH ALL OF
THEM ARE SUITABLE FOR MAKING A DECISION, SO "CONGREGATION"
STATED HERE REFERS TO A CASE IN WHICH ALL OF THEM ARE SUIT-
ABLE FOR MAKING A DECISION:

1.   II:1: As to the locus classicus of the proof, how do we know
     that fact to begin with?

IV. Mishnah-Tractate Horayot 1:4H-L

A.   [IF] THE COURT GAVE AN INCORRECT DECISION INADVERTENTLY,
     AND THE ENTIRE COMMUNITY FOLLOWED THEIR INSTRUCTION [AND
     DID THE THING IN ERROR] INADVERTENTLY, THEY BRING A BUL-
     LOCK. [IF THE COURT GAVE AN INCORRECT DECISION] DELIBER-
     ATELY, BUT THE COMMUNITY, FOLLOWING THEIR INSTRUCTION, DID
     THE THING IN ERROR] INADVERTENTLY, THEY BRING A LAMB OR A
     GOAT (LEV. 4:32, 27).
     [IF THE COURT GAVE INCORRECT INSTRUCTION] INADVERTENTLY,
     AND [THE COMMUNITY FOLLOWED THEIR INSTRUCTION AND DID THE
     THING IN ERROR] DELIBERATELY, LO, THESE ARE EXEMPT [UNDER
     THE PROVISIONS OF LEV. 4:4].

1.   I:1: the one who inadvertently violated the law who is liable
     is equivalent to the one who intentionally violated the law
     in that both know the court to be in error yet only the latter
     does not present an atonement offering.

V. Mishnah-Tractate Horayot 1:5

A.   "[IF] THE COURT MADE AN [ERRONEOUS] DECISION, AND THE ENTIRE
     COMMUNITY, OR THE GREATER PART OF THE COMMUNITY, CARRIED
     OUT THEIR DECISION, THEY BRING A BULLOCK. IN THE CASE OF
     IDOLATRY, THEY BRING A BULLOCK AND A GOAT," THE WORDS OF
     R. MEIR. R. JUDAH SAYS, "TWELVE TRIBES BRING TWELVE BUL-
     LOCKS. AND IN THE CASE OF IDOLATRY, THEY BRING TWELVE BUL-
     LOCKS AND TWELVE GOATS." R. SIMEON SAYS, "THIRTEEN
     BULLOCKS, AND IN THE CASE OF IDOLATRY, THIRTEEN BULLOCKS
     AND THIRTEEN GOATS: A BULLOCK AND A GOAT FOR EACH AND
     EVERY TRIBE, AND [IN ADDITION] A BULLOCK AND A GOAT FOR
     THE COURT." "[IF] THE COURT GAVE AN [ERRONEOUS] DECISION,
     AND SEVEN TRIBES, OR THE GREATER PART OF SEVEN TRIBES,
     CARRIED OUT THEIR DECISION, THEY BRING A BULLOCK. IN THE
     CASE OF IDOLATRY, THEY BRING A BULLOCK AND A GOAT," THE
     WORDS OF R. MEIR. R. JUDAH SAYS, "SEVEN TRIBES WHICH COM-
     MITTED A SIN BRING SEVEN BULLOCKS. AND THE OTHER TRIBES,
     WHO COMMITTED NO SIN, BRING A BULLOCK IN THEIR BEHALF, FOR
     EVEN THOSE WHO DID NOT SIN BRING AN OFFERING ON ACCOUNT
     OF THE SINNERS." R. SIMEON SAYS, "EIGHT BULLOCKS, AND IN THE
     CASE OF IDOLATRY, EIGHT BULLOCKS AND EIGHT GOATS: A BUL-

LOCK AND A GOAT FOR EACH AND EVERY TRIBE, AND A BULLOCK
AND A GOAT FOR THE COURT."

1. I:1: Tannaite formulation of the matter.
   a. I:2: Who is the Tannaite authority who holds the position, Scripture says, "when the sin through which they incurred guilt becomes known,—not that the sinners should be made known?
   b. I:3: What is the scriptural basis for the positions of Judah, Simeon, and Meir of I:1?

B. "[IF] THE COURT OF ONE OF THE TRIBES GAVE AN [ERRONEOUS] DECISION, AND THAT TRIBE [ONLY] CARRIED OUT THEIR DECISION, THAT TRIBE IS LIABLE, AND ALL THE OTHER TRIBES ARE EXEMPT," THE WORDS OF R. JUDAH. AND SAGES SAY, "THEY ARE LIABLE ONLY BY REASON OF AN [ERRONEOUS] DECISION MADE BY THE HIGH COURT ALONE, AS IT IS SAID, 'AND IF THE WHOLE CONGREGATION OF ISRAEL SHALL ERR (LEV. 4:13)—AND NOT THE CONGREGATION OF THAT TRIBE [ALONE].'"

1. II:1: The question was raised: in R. Judah's opinion, if a single tribe commits a transgression on account of the instruction of the high court, do the rest of the tribes have to present offerings as well, or do they not have to do so?
2. II:2: The question was raised: in R. Simeon's opinion, if the law violation is done on the instructions of the high court, do they present an offering or not?
3. II:3: As to R. Judah and R. Simeon, who maintain that a single tribe may be classified as "the community," where in Scripture do they find proof for their position?
4. II:4: "They that had come from the captives of the exile offered up whole-offerings to the God of Israel, twelve bullocks for all Israel, ninety-nine rams, seventy-seven lambs, and, as a purification-offering, twelve he goats, all this as a burnt-offering for the Lord" (Ezra 8:35). In line with the Judah's, Simeon's, and Meir's positions at hand, how would we explain the requirement of these twelve bullocks?
5. II:5: If the court gave instructions in error but the members knew that they had erred and they retracted the ruling after the community had transgressed, but if one of the public has died before the offering was made, they are required to present it in any event. If one of the court died, they are exempt. Who is the Tannaite authority behind this ruling?

VI. MISHNAH-TRACTATE HORAYOT 2:1

A. [IF] AN ANOINTED [HIGH] PRIEST MADE A DECISION FOR HIMSELF [IN VIOLATION OF ANY OF THE COMMANDMENTS OF THE TORAH], DOING SO INADVERTENTLY, AND CARRYING OUT [HIS DECISION] INADVERTENTLY, HE BRINGS A BULLOCK (LEV. 4:3).

1. I:1:With what case do we deal? It is a case in which he gave instruction and forgot on what grounds he had given the instruction, and at the moment at which he erred, he said, 'Lo, I act on the basis of my instruction.' Now what might you have supposed? Since, if he realized the facts of the situation, he might have retracted, he is in the situation of one who acts deliberately and should not therefore be obligated under the present count. So we are informed that that is not the case.

B. [IF] HE [MADE AN ERRONEOUS DECISION] INADVERTENTLY, AND DELIBERATELY CARRIED IT OUT, DELIBERATELY [MADE AN ERRONEOUS DECISION] AND INADVERTENTLY CARRIED IT OUT, HE IS EXEMPT. FOR AN [ERRONEOUS] DECISION OF AN ANOINTED [HIGH] PRIEST FOR HIMSELF IS TANTAMOUNT TO AN [ERRONEOUS] DECISION OF A COURT FOR THE ENTIRE COMMUNITY.

1. II:1: What is the source in Scripture for this ruling?
    a. II:2: Amplification of the foregoing.

VII. MISHNAH-TRACTATE HORAYOT 2:2

A. [IF] HE MADE AN [ERRONEOUS] DECISION BY HIMSELF AND CARRIED IT OUT BY HIMSELF, HE EFFECTS ATONEMENT FOR HIMSELF BY HIMSELF.

1. I:1: What is the source of this ruling [that the anointed priest's atonement procedure is determined by the context of his error]?
2. I:2: How can we imagine a case of his doing so?
3. I:3: theoretical problem based on foregoing.

B. [IF] HE MADE [AN ERRONEOUS] DECISION WITH THE COMMUNITY AND CARRIED IT OUT WITH THE COMMUNITY, HE EFFECTS ATONEMENT FOR HIMSELF WITH THE COMMUNITY. FOR A COURT IS NOT LIABLE UNTIL IT WILL GIVE AN ERRONEOUS DECISION TO NULLIFY PART AND TO CARRY OUT PART [OF THE TEACHINGS OF THE TORAH]:

1. II:1: How on the basis of Scripture do we know it is the fact that a court is not liable until it will give an erroneous decision to nullify part and to carry out part [of the teachings of the Torah]?

C. AND SO IS THE RULE FOR AN ANOINTED [HIGH PRIEST]:

1. III:1: How on the basis of Scripture do we know this fact?

D. AND [THEY] ARE NOT [LIABLE] IN THE CASE OF IDOLATRY [SUBJECT TO AN ERRONEOUS DECISION] UNLESS THEY GIVE A DECISION TO NULLIFY IN PART AND TO SUSTAIN IN PART [THE REQUIREMENTS OF THE TORAH] [M. 1:3].

1. IV:1: How on the basis of Scripture do we know this fact?

VIII. Mishnah-Tractate Horayot 2:3A-C

A. **They are liable only on account of something's being hidden (Lev. 4:13) along with an act [of transgression] which is performed inadvertently:**
    1. I:1: What is the scriptural source of this rule?
B. **And so in the case of the anointed [high priest]**
    1. II:1: as above.
C. **And [they are] not [liable] in the case of idolatry except in the case of something's being hidden along with an act [of transgression] which is performed inadvertently:**
    1. III:1: as above.
    2. III:2: But the Tannaite formulation of the Mishnah-rule has omitted reference to the rule governing the anointed priest when it comes to idolatry. Who is the authority behind the Mishnah-rule? It is Rabbi.
        a. III:3: What is the scriptural basis for the position of Rabbi?
        b. III:4: continuation of foregoing.
        c. III:5: as above.

IX. Mishnah-Tractate Horayot 2:3D-F

A. **The court is liable only if they will give an erroneous decision in a matter, the deliberate commission of which is punishable by extirpation, and the inadvertent commission of which is punishable by a sin offering, and so in the case of the anointed [high priest],**
    1. I:1: how on the basis of Scripture do we know this fact?
B. **and [they are] not [liable] in the case of idolatry, except in the case in which they gave instruction in a matter the deliberate commission of which is punishable by extirpation, and the inadvertent commission of which is punishable by a sin offering.**
    1. II:1: How on the basis of Scripture do we know this fact concerning a case of idolatry?
    2. II:2: Continuation of foregoing.
    3. II:3: Continuation of foregoing.

X. Mishnah-Tractate Horayot 2:4

A. **They are not liable on account of [a decision inadvertently violating] a positive commandment or a negative commandment concerning the sanctuary, And they do not bring a suspensive guilt offering on account of [violation of] a positive commandment or a negative commandment concerning the sanctuary.**
    But they are liable for [violating] a positive command-

MENT OR A NEGATIVE COMMANDMENT INVOLVING A MENSTRUAT-
ING WOMAN. AND THEY DO BRING A SUSPENSIVE GUILT OFFERING
ON ACCOUNT OF [VIOLATION OF] A POSITIVE COMMANDMENT OR A
NEGATIVE COMMANDMENT CONCERNING A MENSTRUATING WOMAN.
WHAT IS A POSITIVE COMMANDMENT CONCERNING A MENSTRUAT-
ING WOMAN? TO KEEP SEPARATE FROM A MENSTRUATING WOMAN.
AND WHAT IS A NEGATIVE COMMANDMENT? NOT TO HAVE SEXUAL
RELATIONS WITH A MENSTRUATING WOMAN.

1. I:1: how on the basis of Scripture do we know that fact, that
   the community is not obligated to an offering in general, nor
   is the individual liable to a suspended built offering when it
   comes to imparting uncleanness to the Temple?

XI. MISHNAH-TRACTATE HORAYOT 2:5

A. THEY ARE NOT LIABLE [BECAUSE OF INADVERTENT VIOLATION OF
THE LAW] (1) CONCERNING HEARING THE VOICE OF ADJURATION
[LEV. 5:11, (2) A RASH OATH [LEV. 5:4], (3) OR IMPARTING UN-
CLEANNESS TO THE SANCTUARY AND TO ITS HOLY THINGS [LEV.
5:3]—
"AND THE RULER FOLLOWS SUIT," THE WORDS OF R. YOSÉ THE
GALILEAN.

1. I:1: What is the Scripture basis for the position of R. Yosé
   the Galilean?
   a. I:2: theoretical problem flowing from the facts of the fore-
      going. A ruler who was afflicted with the skin-ailment—
      what is the law that applies to him? The purification
      offering involves an offering of variable value, so Lev.
      14:10, 21, but as we see, he is not liable to present such
      an offering.

B. R. AQIBA SAYS, "THE RULER IS LIABLE IN THE CASE OF ALL OF
THEM, EXCEPT IN THE CASE OF HEARING THE VOICE OF ADJURA-
TION. FOR THE KING DOES NOT JUDGE AND OTHERS DO NOT JUDGE
HIM, DOES NOT GIVE TESTIMONY, AND OTHERS DO NOT GIVE TES-
TIMONY CONCERNING HIM:"

1. I:1: What is the Scriptural foundation for the ruling of R.
   Aqiba?

XII. MISHNAH-TRACTATE HORAYOT 2:6-7

A. IN THE CASE OF ALL THE COMMANDMENTS IN THE TORAH, ON AC-
COUNT OF WHICH THEY ARE LIABLE FOR DELIBERATE VIOLATION
TO EXTIRPATION, AND ON ACCOUNT OF INADVERTENT VIOLATION
TO A SIN OFFERING, AN INDIVIDUAL BRINGS A FEMALE LAMB OR A
FEMALE GOAT [LEV. 4:28, 32]. A RULER BRINGS A MALE GOAT [LEV.
4:23], AND AN ANOINTED [HIGH PRIEST] AND A COURT BRING A
BULLOCK [M. 1:5, 2:1]. BUT IN THE CASE OF IDOLATRY, THE
INDIVIDUAL, RULER, AND ANOINTED [HIGH PRIEST] BRING A FE-

MALE GOAT [NUM. 15:27]. AND THE COURT BRINGS A BULLOCK
AND A GOAT [M. 1:5], A BULLOCK FOR A WHOLE OFFERING AND
A GOAT FOR A SIN OFFERING. AS TO A SUSPENSIVE GUILT OFFER-
ING, AN INDIVIDUAL AND A RULER MAY BECOME LIABLE. BUT THE
ANOINTED [HIGH PRIEST] AND COURT DO NOT BECOME LIABLE. AS
TO AN UNCONDITIONAL GUILT OFFERING, AN INDIVIDUAL, A RULER,
AND AN ANOINTED [HIGH PRIEST] MAY BECOME LIABLE, BUT A
COURT IS EXEMPT. ON ACCOUNT OF HEARING THE VOICE OF AD-
JURATION, A RASH OATH, AND IMPARTING UNCLEANNESS TO THE
SANCTUARY AND ITS HOLY THINGS, A COURT IS EXEMPT, BUT AN
INDIVIDUAL, A RULER, AND AN ANOINTED [HIGH PRIEST] ARE LI-
ABLE.

1. I:1: In any case in which the individual is liable for a suspensive guilt offering, the ruler is in the same category, the
anointed priest and the court are exempt. And in any case
in which he is subject to an unconditional guilt offering, the
ruler and the anointed priest are in the same category, and
the court is exempt. As for violations involving not heeding
the call to testify, uttering a vain oath, and contamination of
the Temple and its Holy Things, the members of the court
are exempt from the offering of variable value, but the ruler
and the anointed priest are liable. Nonetheless, the ruler is
not liable for failure to heed the call nor is the anointed priest
for imparting uncleanness to the Temple and its Holy Things.
Whenever the individual presents an offering of variable
value, the rule is in his category, and the anointed priest and
the court are exempt.

B. "BUT A HIGH PRIEST IS NOT LIABLE FOR IMPARTING UNCLEANNESS
TO THE SANCTUARY AND ITS HOLY THINGS," THE WORDS OF R.
SIMEON.

1. II:1: What are the scriptural grounds for the position of R.
Simeon?

C. AND WHAT DO THEY BRING? AN OFFERING OF VARIABLE VALUE.
R. ELIEZER SAYS, "THE RULER BRINGS A GOAT OFFERING."

1. III:1: R. Eliezer made this statement only in connection with
imparting uncleanness to the sanctuary and its Holy Things,
since reference is made in that regard to extirpation at Num.
19:20 just as is the case for violations that require an offering of fixed value.

2. III:2: R. Eliezer concurs that the ruler need not present a
suspended guilt offering if he only suspects he has violated
the prohibition against imparting uncleanness to the Temple.

XIII. MISHNAH-TRACTATE HORAYOT 3:1-2

A. AN ANOINTED [HIGH] PRIEST WHO SINNED AND AFTERWARD PASSED
FROM HIS OFFICE AS ANOINTED HIGH PRIEST, AND SO A RULER WHO
SINNED AND AFTERWARD PASSED FROM HIS POSITION OF GREAT-

NESS—THE ANOINTED [HIGH] PRIEST BRINGS A BULLOCK, AND THE
PATRIARCH BRINGS A GOAT [M. 2:6].

1. I:1: Now there is good reason to specify An anointed [high]
priest who sinned and afterward passed from his office as
anointed high priest and sinned...brings a bullock, for it is
necessary to make explicit that the prior status governs his
liability for transgression after he leaves office. But why does
the Mishnah have to specify the case of an anointed high
priest who passed from his office as anointed high priest and
then sinned?

B. AN ANOINTED [HIGH] PRIEST WHO PASSED FROM HIS OFFICE AS
ANOINTED HIGH PRIEST AND THEN SINNED, AND SO A RULER WHO
PASSED FROM HIS POSITION OF GREATNESS AND THEN SINNED—A
HIGH PRIEST BRINGS A BULLOCK. BUT A RULER IS LIKE ANY ORDI-
NARY PERSON.

1. II:1: What is the source in Scripture for this distinction?

XIV. MISHNAH-TRACTATE HORAYOT 3:3

A. [IF] THEY SINNED BEFORE THEY WERE APPOINTED, AND THEN THEY
WERE APPOINTED, LO, THEY ARE IN THE STATUS OF ANY ORDINARY
PERSON.

1. I:1: How on the basis of Scripture do we know that if the
anointed priest sinned prior to appointment to office, he
presents the offering of an ordinary person?
2. I:2: Further exegesis of the same verses.
   a. I:3: Amplification of foregoing.

B. TO BE A RULER IS TO BE A SLAVE. THE RULER WHO SINS. "IN CASE
IT IS A CHIEFTAIN WHO INCURS GUILT BY DOING UNWITTINGLY ANY
OF THE THINGS WHICH BY THE COMMANDMENT OF THE LORD HIS GOD
OUGHT NOT TO BE DONE" (LEV. 4:22)

1. I:4: "In case it is a chieftain who incurs guilt by doing unwittingly any of the things which by the commandment of
the Lord his God ought not to be done" (Lev. 4:22)—excluding the one who is ill.
2. I:5: Happy is the generation, the ruler of which brings an
offering for sinning inadvertently. If the ruler brings an offering, do you have to ask about ordinary folk? And if he
brings an offering for an inadvertent sin, do you have to ask
what he will do in the case of one that he does deliberately?

C. REWARD AND PUNISHMENT IN THIS WORLD AND IN THE NEXT. THE
RIGHTEOUS AND THE WICKED

1. I:6: Happy are the righteous, for in this world they undergo
what in the world to come is assigned as recompense for the
deeds of the wicked, and woe is the wicked, for in this world
they enjoy the fruits of what is assigned in the world to come
to the deeds of the righteous.

D. The Case of Lot and Abraham

1. I:7: What is the meaning of the verse of Scripture, "For the paths of the Lord are straight, that the righteous shall pass along them, but the transgressors will stumble in them" (Hos. 14:10)? The matter may be compared to the case of two men who roasted their Passover offerings. One of them ate it for the sake of performing the religious duty, and the other one ate it to stuff himself with a big meal. Lot becomes the focus.

2. I:8: "'A brother offended the mighty city:' this refers to Lot, who took his leave from Abraham in order to sin with his daughters. 'and contention is like the bars of a castle:' by siring Moab and Ben Ammi with his daughters, Lot made contention between Israel and Amon, 'Neither an Amonite nor a Moabite shall come into the community of the Lord' (Dt. 23:4)."

3. I:9: "'To lust is a separatist drawn, and of any wisdom will be be contemptuous' (Prov. 18:1): 'To lust is a separatist drawn:' this refers to Lot, who took his leave from Abraham."

E. The Case of Tamar and Zimri

1. I:10: Tamar committed an act of prostitution, and Zimri committed an act of prostitution. Tamar committed an act of prostitution, and there went forth from her kings and prophets. Zimri committed an act of prostitution, and how many myriads of Israel fell in consequence.

F. The Importance of the Right Attitude

1. I:11: A transgression committed for its own sake, in a sincere spirit, is greater in value that a religious duty carried out not for its own sake, but in a spirit of insincerity.

2. I:12: A person should always be occupied in study of the Torah and in practice of the commandments, even if this is not for its own sake [but in a spirit of insincerity], for out of doing these things not for their own sake, a proper spirit of doing them for their own sake will emerge.

G. R. Simeon says, "If their sin became known to them before they were appointed, they are liable. But if it was after they were appointed, they are exempt:"

1. II:1: "...from among the populace:" excluding the chieftain. "...from among the populace:" excluding the anointed priest.

2. II:2: What is the law on the office of ruler's interrupting one's continuity of status, so that when he rises to office, he is no longer culpable for transgression?

3. II:3: If when he was an ordinary person, he ate something

that may or may not have been suet, and then he was appointed, and then the matter in doubt was discovered, what is the law?

4. II:4: What is the sense of the clause of Scripture, 'unwittingly incurs guilt by doing any of the things which by the Lord's commandments ought not to be done'? This refers to one who were he informed would simply refrain from carrying out the transgression, thus excluding an apostate, who were he informed would not refrain from carrying out the transgression. There can be no issue that such a one violating the law does not do so either unwittingly or by reason of the inappropriate instruction of the court.

    a.   II:5: What is the definition of an apostate.

        I.   II:6: Clarification of foregoing.

       II. II:7: Clarification of foregoing.

     III. II:8: Clarification of foregoing.

H. AND WHO IS A RULER? THIS IS THE KING, AS IT IS SAID, "AND DOES ANY ONE OF ALL THE THINGS WHICH THE LORD HIS GOD HAS COMMANDED NOT TO BE DONE" (LEV. 4:22)—A RULER WHO HAS NONE ABOVE HIM EXCEPT THE LORD HIS GOD:

1. III:1: Scriptural proof for the proposition of the Mishnah: "Let it remain with him and let him read in it all his life, so that he may learn to revere the Lord his God, to observe faithfully every word of this Torah as well as these laws" (Dt. 17:19). Just as "his God' stated in that passage refers to a chieftain above whom is the authority only of the Lord his God, so "his God" stated here refers to a chieftain above whom is the authority only of the Lord his God

2. III:2: Rabbi asked R. Hiyya, "What about me? Do I present a he-goat [as undisputed ruler]?"

XV. MISHNAH-TRACTATE HORAYOT 3:4

A. WHO IS THE ANOINTED [HIGH PRIEST]? IT IS THE ONE WHO IS ANOINTED WITH THE ANOINTING OIL, NOT THE ONE WHO IS DEDICATED BY MANY GARMENTS:

1. I:1: In the anointing oil that Moses made in the wilderness they would boil aromatic roots.

    a.   I:2: secondary expansion of the foregoing.

    b.   I:3: secondary expansion of the foregoing.

    c.   I:4: secondary expansion of the foregoing.

    d.   I:5: secondary expansion of the foregoing.

    e.   I:6: secondary expansion of the foregoing.

       I. I:7: secondary expansion of the foregoing.

    f.   I:8: secondary expansion of the foregoing.

       I. I:9: amplification of the foregoing.

      II. I:10: as above.

g.   I:11: secondary amplification of foregoing.

B.   ANOINTING KINGS

1.   I:12: The way in which the oil is applied to a king for the purpose of anointment.

   a.   I:13: gloss on foregoing.

2.   I:14: Further Tannaite statements on the same topic.

   a.   I:15: gloss of foregoing.

3.   I:16: Further Tannaite statements on the same topic.

   a.   I:17: gloss of foregoing.

      i.   I:18: More good advice in line with the foregoing.

4.   I:19: Conclusion of I:17.

C.   IT IS THE ONE WHO IS ANOINTED WITH THE ANOINTING OIL, NOT THE ONE WHO IS DEDICATED BY MANY GARMENTS:

1.   II:1: Tannaite proof from Scripture of the Mishnah's allegation.

   a.   II:2: Secondary amplification of the foregoing.

D.   THERE IS NO DIFFERENCE BETWEEN THE HIGH PRIEST WHO IS ANOINTED WITH ANOINTING OIL, AND THE ONE WHO IS DEDICATED WITH MANY GARMENTS, EXCEPT FOR [THE LATTER'S OBLIGATION TO BRING] THE BULLOCK WHICH IS BROUGHT BECAUSE OF THE [VIOLATION] OF ANY OF THE COMMANDMENTS.

THERE IS NO DIFFERENCE BETWEEN A [HIGH] PRIEST PRESENTLY IN SERVICE AND A PRIEST [WHO SERVED] IN THE PAST EXCEPT FOR THE [BRINGING OF] THE BULLOCK OF THE DAY OF ATONEMENT AND THE TENTH OF AN EPHAH. (1) THIS ONE AND THAT ONE ARE EQUIVALENT IN REGARD TO THE SERVICE ON THE DAY OF ATONEMENT. (2) AND THEY ARE COMMANDED CONCERNING [MARRYING] A VIRGIN. AND THEY ARE FORBIDDEN TO [MARRY] A WIDOW. (3) AND THEY ARE NOT TO CONTRACT CORPSE UNCLEANNESS ON ACCOUNT OF THE DEATH OF THEIR CLOSE RELATIVES. (4) NOR DO THEY MESS UP THEIR HAIR. (5) NOR DO THEY TEAR THEIR CLOTHES [ON THE OCCASION OF A DEATH IN THE FAMILY]. (6) AND [ON ACCOUNT OF THEIR DEATH] THEY BRING BACK A MANSLAYER.

1.   III:1: Identifying the named authority behind the anonymous statement of the Mishnah.

2.   III:2: What is the Scriptural basis for the position of R. Meir?

   a.   III:3: Secondary analysis of the key citation of the foregoing passage.

      i.   III:4: Gloss of the foregoing.

XVI. MISHNAH-TRACTATE HORAYOT 3:5

A.   A HIGH PRIEST [ON THE DEATH OF A CLOSE RELATIVE] TEARS HIS GARMENT BELOW, AND AN ORDINARY ONE, ABOVE.

A HIGH PRIEST MAKES AN OFFERING WHILE HE IS IN THE STATUS OF ONE WHO HAS YET TO BURY HIS DEAD, BUT HE MAY NOT EAT [THE PRIESTLY PORTION]. AND AN ORDINARY PRIEST NEITHER

MAKES THE OFFERING NOR EATS [THE PRIESTLY PORTION].

1. I:1: "The word 'below' is meant literally, and the word 'above' is meant literally."

XVII. MISHNAH-TRACTATE HORAYOT 3:6

A. [WHEN THE PRIEST FACES A CHOICE ON TENDING TO TWO OR MORE ANIMALS THAT HAVE BEEN DESIGNATED AS OFFERINGS, THEN:] WHATEVER IS OFFERED MORE REGULARLY THAN ITS FELLOW TAKES PRECEDENCE OVER ITS FELLOW:

1. I:1: What is the source in Scripture for this rule?

B. AND WHATEVER IS MORE HOLY THAN ITS FELLOW TAKES PRECEDENCE OVER ITS FELLOW.

1. II:1: How do we know this?

C. [IF] A BULLOCK OF AN ANOINTED PRIEST AND A BULLOCK OF THE CONGREGATION [M. 1:5] ARE STANDING [AWAITING SACRIFICE]— THE BULLOCK OF THE ANOINTED [HIGH PRIEST] TAKES PRECEDENCE OVER THE BULLOCK OF THE CONGREGATION IN ALL RITES PERTAINING TO IT.

1. III:1: How do we know this?
2. III:2: Tannaite formulation of the same rule on the strength of scriptural support.
3. III:3: Continuation of foregoing.

XVIII. MISHNAH-TRACTATE HORAYOT 3:7

A. THE MAN TAKES PRECEDENCE OVER THE WOMAN IN THE MATTER OF THE SAVING OF LIFE AND IN THE MATTER OF RETURNING LOST PROPERTY BUT A WOMAN TAKES PRECEDENCE OVER A MAN IN THE MATTER OF [PROVIDING] CLOTHING AND REDEMPTION FROM CAPTIVITY. WHEN BOTH OF THEM ARE STANDING IN DANGER OF DEFILEMENT, THE MAN TAKES PRECEDENCE OVER THE WOMAN.

1. I:1: Tannaite statement of the same matter.
2. I:2: In matters of uncleanness, with respect to the prefect of the priests and the priest anointed for battle, which takes precedence?

XIX. MISHNAH-TRACTATE HORAYOT 3:8

A. A PRIEST TAKES PRECEDENCE OVER A LEVITE"
1.I:1:Scriptural proof for that proposition.

B. A LEVITE OVER AN ISRAELITE:
1.II:1: Scriptural proof for that proposition.

C. AN ISRAELITE OVER A MAMZER:
1.III:1: The reason for that proposition.

D. A MAMZER OVER A NETIN:
1.IV:1: The reason for that proposition.

E. A NETIN OVER A PROSELYTE:

1.V:1: The reason for that proposition.

F.   A PROSELYTE OVER A FREED SLAVE"

1.VI:1: The reason for that proposition.

G.   UNDER WHAT CIRCUMSTANCES? WHEN ALL OF THEM ARE EQUIVA-
LENT. BUT IF THE MAMZER WAS A DISCIPLE OF A SAGE AND A HIGH
PRIEST WAS AN AM HAARES, THE MAMZER WHO IS A DISCIPLE OF
A SAGE TAKES PRECEDENCE OVER A HIGH PRIEST WHO IS AN AM
HAARES:

1.   VII:1: What is the source in Scripture for the proposition that
learning in the Torah takes precedence over all else?

2.   VII:2: Secondary consideration of the proposition that a proselyte takes precedence over a freed slave.

3.   VII:3: Continuation of foregoing. Tangential reference to forgetfulness accounts for the continuation at No. 4.

    a.   VII:4: Secondary expansion on a topic of the foregoing:
forgetfulness. Five things cause what one has learned to
be forgotten.

H.   THE HONOR THAT IS PAID TO A SAGE; THE TRAITS OF THE SAGE

1.   VII:5: Correct conduct when a sage enters the room.

    a.   VII:6: Gloss of foregoing.

    b.   VII:7: as above.

    c.   VII:8: as above.

        i.   VII:9: gloss of the foregoing.

2.   VII:10: The intellectual gifts. Erudition versus analytical skills.

3.   VII:11: Continuation of foregoing: story.

4.   VII:12: As above.

5.   VII:13: As above.

V. *The Results of the Outline*

We find ourselves able to outline most of the tractate simply by
referring to the Mishnah-tractate's principal statements. The larger
composites that do not define their purpose within Mishnah-commentary take up themes called for by the contents of the Mishnah.
I find nothing in the tractate that cannot be situated in relationship
to the program of the Mishnah.

As we review the outline of the tractate, we note that one way or
the other every principal allegation of Mishnah-tractate Horayot is
subjected to discussion, though at many points a process of selection has guided the framers of this tractate to one set of problems
rather than to some other. The main traits of mind that defined the
choices are readily inferred from the pattern of results consistently
attained. In general three sets of issues predominate: [1] the wording and sense of sentences in the Mishnah; [2] the foundations in

the written part of the Torah, or Scripture, and [3] implications of the Mishnah's rule, which may lead to investigating questions provoked but not addressed by the Mishnah, secondary theoretical issues, and other modes of extension and augmentation. The intellectual quest therefore finds its definition in Mishnah-exegesis.

The greater part of the Talmud's system comes to expression in the questions the framers of the Talmud's Mishnah-exegesis address to the Mishnah; what they wished to say, they stated, for the most part, through the questions they brought to a prior document. Since so much of their commentary appears to adhere closely to the main lines of the Mishnah's own statements, it is easy to conclude that the Talmud's system replicated the Mishnah's. But that is deceiving. Not only do the questions of the Talmud—clarify what the Mishnah's authors must have assumed was already clear, identify authority for the Mishnah that the Mishnah's authors did not find need to expose, say more than the Mishnah's authors found sufficient—subvert the Mishnah. Other than Mishnah-exegetical compositions and composites impart to the topic treated by the Mishnah a very different character altogether. The notion that, in the Talmud, we find pretty much what the Mishnah's statements mean but little else—the "plain meaning" in modern parlance, or the historically-determinate meaning initially intended by the Mishnah's writers—proves not only anachronistic but naive, even bordering on the disingenuous. Nothing in the writings before us compels us to imagine that the Talmud's compositions' and composites' writers conceived any meaning to inhere in the words before them except for the meaning they brought to those words—whatever it was.

The upshot is simply put: to the framers of the Talmud, a reasoned reading of the Mishnah defended the logical coherence of the document they proposed to compile. But then, the rationality proves formal, not substantive. But even at the level at which we work—large-scale aggregates and their formal testimonies—we may identify points of violence to the rationality of order and form, and, violating the structure established for the whole, these plunge us into issues of system. When large-scale composites take shape around topics or propositions not formed in response to statements in the Mishnah, the structure defined by the character of the document overall bears the weight of anomalies. I find these at XIV.B, C, D, E, F; XV.B, and XIX.H.

VI. *The System Revealed by the Outline*

Most of the paragraphs of the Mishnah are taken up in one way or another. I noted only a few that were not fully analyzed, and most of these turn out to be secondary expansions of the Mishnah's own generalizations. But we should not fail to note that even when the Talmud devotes itself to an analysis of the Mishnah's statements, it may well go its own way, beyond the limits of what Mishnah-exegesis requires, though still well within the limits of the Mishnah's topical program. This observation directs our attention to a gray area, between Mishnah-exegesis and the presentation of essentially autonomous discourse, such as is taken up in the next rubric. Here, where Mishnah-commentary spells over into free-ranging exploration of problems precipitated by the Mishnah's concerns but far transcending the Mishnah's own program, we enter the framework of independent thought given the form of subordinated commentary. A survey of the entirety of the document will allow a clearer focus upon this gray area. For the moment it suffices to note that in the Bavli's Mishnah-commentary are embedded the marks of much independent reflection.

Then we must ask, How do the topical composites fit into the Talmud-tractate Horayot and what do they contribute that the Mishnah-tractate of the same name would lack without them? Here is the critical test of whether a system of thought has guided the composition of the Bavli-tractate. Let us take the identified cases one by one.

The composite in Unit XIV is provoked by the allusion XIV.A to the transformation of a common person into a ruler or high priest. The change in status is marked—it is, after all, the critical focus of our tractate as a whole!—and it is at that point that the condition of the ruler enters in.

> XIV.B: the first point remarks upon the enviable society, the ruler of which acknowledges even inadvert transgression. That is the mark of good government, accounting also for how rare good government is.
>
> XIV.C: At the head of the next sequence is the contrast between the righteous and the wicked, with the certainty of reward and punishment in the world to come underscoring the justice of God in all things.
>
> XIV.D: The first contrast between the good ruler and the bad one

is Lot and Abraham, and the point is, the attitude of the ruler makes all the difference. People may do the same thing, but only if the motive is honorable is that deed consequential; if the motive is dishonorable, then the good that one does turns out to yield nothing. The same actions, e.g., Lot and his daughters, can be both good and bad, and the point of differentiation is the attitude of the ones who do said actions.

XIV.E: The same point, contrasting the good and the evil, emerges in the next example. Tamar and Zimri did the same thing, with very different results.

XIV.F: The key point of differentiation therefore is not the action but the attitude that infuses the action. And the right attitude is one of sincerity; this is stated in an extreme way, better the transgression done sincerely ("for its own sake") than the religious duty done insincerely ("not for its own sake"). But this same point is forthwith modulated: doing commandments and study of Torah in an insincere spirit (e.g., for personal gain) gives way to doing them in a sincere spirit.

XV.B: The composite on anointing kings does not vastly change the face of the unit in which it occurs; the Mishnah has dealt with anointing priests, and what the Talmud here contributes is simply a complement to the Mishnah's topic.

XIX.H: The point of the Mishnah, that the sagacity takes priority over hierarchical status, is not vastly transformed by the Talmud. The composite itself appears somewhat unfocused and diffuse; the unit on correct conduct when a sage enters the room and the secondary expansions and glosses thereof bears no proposition I can identify. The contrast between analytical skills and erudition, while interesting, really does not affect the main point, which is the hierarchical point that the Mishnah has stated in so many words. And yet, a second look suggests otherwise. Now we find ourselves deep within the concerns of the Talmud's sages with analytical capacities, not merely knowledge but the power to use knowledge to form fresh knowledge, and that lies beyond the imagination of the hierarchical program of the Mishnah's framers. By introducing the considerations of hierarchization where they do not pertain—learning vs. analytical abilities indeed!—the framers of the Talmud's concluding units place in a different light the very allegations about the status accorded to the sage; that status, while a given, proves only instrumental. It is what one can do with what one learns that makes the difference, and that is not a matter of status at all. In that same context the stories about Simeon b. Gamaliel and Judah the Patriarch

and their invocation of their political status in the setting
of the superior learning of the sages (also portrayed in an
unflattering light, to be sure), form a wry comment on the
sages' hierarchical superiority. That sages take precedence
in the Talmud proves less weighty than that, among sages, competition for power takes the diverse form of politics, personalities, and preferment.

Can we state what the compilers of this document propose to accomplish in producing this complete, organized piece of writing? The
key to Mishnah-tractate Horayot lies in its location, which is in the
Division of Damages, rather than in the Division of Holy Things.
Since the bulk of the problems finds resolution in whether a given
party is obligated to present an offering, and, if so, which offering
said party is required to present, the surface of the tractate is stud-
ded with issues typical of the fifth division, but rare in the fourth.
But the organizer of the Mishnah, laying out the divisions and as-
signing to them the tractates and therefore the topical expositions
they were to receive, had his reasons. The fourth division concerns
itself in significant part with the civil administration of the Jews in
the Land of Israel. Tractate Sanhedrin, with its account of the tri-
partite regime of high priest and Temple, king and army, sages and
court, set alongside the great pinnacle of the Mishnah, the thirty
chapters of Baba Qamma, Baba Mesia, and Baba Batra, with their
movement from the abnormal to the normal, form a sustained account of the life of government and secular relationships within the
politics of holy Israel. What we learn in Horayot concerns the er-
rors of the civil authorities, apportioning responsibility for the consequences of error, underscoring the obligation of the individual to
face the results of his own actions. The real problem of the tractate
as the Mishnah presents matters of government proves remarkably
contemporary: what does the private person do when the community's officials err.

Faced with an error on the part of the government, what can a
person do? If he knows the government errs, he may not find ex-
culpation in the plea that he has merely carried out orders. If the
government errs and the individual does not know better and therefore inadvertently has violated the law, then, but only then, the
possibility of atoning is raised. So we require, for the process of
remission to get underway, both political error and personal inadvertence. Since the issues derive from the right reading of the Torah, right instruction and right action are contrasted with wrong

instruction and inadvertent error. That is why the key language throughout invokes the twin criteria, [1] They are liable only on account of something's being hidden (Lev. 4:13) along with [2] an act [of transgression] which is performed inadvertently. The former concerns a misinterpretation or exegetical error in the law, and the latter involves the mitigating circumstance of a deed in violation of the law done without intent to break the law.

So the principal point of concern of the tractate is that the law be properly known and intentionally observed; if the law is set forth in error by the responsible authorities, the remissive provisions of the law take over. No wonder the tractate reaches its conclusion where it does, with its meditation on the hierarchical inversion accomplished by the sage. For everything in the end depends upon informed government over responsible, critical citizens (to use an anachronistic term). Israel may have its high priest and king, its castes from times of old. But Israel in the end depends upon the sage, whatever his caste, he who can be relied upon not to commit an error of misinterpretation, and who provides the model for those who would avoid inadvertent sin. That explains the order of the exposition of the topic.

The Mishnah's version of the halakhah of Horayot reaches its conclusion when it emerges from the complexities of responsibility for the public interest, the public's stake in the correct administration of law, and the subtle transformation that takes a private person and endows him with the status of embodiment of the community (what happens when one sins and then becomes high priest or ruler being one formulation of matters). Then, laying down the fundamental conviction that hierarchy in this world contrasts with the hierarchy established by the Torah, the Mishnah-tractate makes its final statement on issues of status and responsibility. That is specifically where we confront the Talmud's two striking additional points. Together they accomplish a surprise no less remarkable than the Mishnah-tractate's meditation on hierarchy.

The first treats as altogether null all questions of hierarchy, beginning to end, making the point that it is not the position one holds that matters, or even the acts that one performs in office, but the attitude that characterizes the office holder. This point is hammered home in the contrasts between Lot and Abraham, the two daughters of Noah, Zimri and Tamar, and in the elaborate essay on the centrality of right attitude. When all is said and done, then, we step aside from the Mishnah-tractate altogether, with its concern for error committed inadvertently, with oversight and misinterpretation of the law, by stating that what matters in the end is not what one does but the attitude that one brings to one's action. True, the Mishnah has invited that very point, by its insistence upon the criterion of inadvertence (inadvertently committing an act that is based upon an erroneous reading of the Torah). But inadvertence forms an invitation to the profound thinking on intentionality that the sizable composite the Talmud introduces places on display. The main point of the Mishnah concerns the consequences of inadvertent action, based upon the wrong decision of public authorities. The main point of the Talmud, where it speaks for itself and not in exegesis of the Mishnah, differentiates not actions at all, whether based upon improper government or uninformed sagacity, but rather attitudes by which one and the same action is carried out.

The second treats as null the datum of the tractate, that the sage forms a single and undifferentiated caste in the hierarchy of ruler and ruled, priests, Levites, Israelites, and on down. The sage stands at the apex by reason of learning; the caste of the sages requires no more sustained a process of differentiation than any other, than the priests (but for the high priest), than the Levites, than the Israelites. The main point of the Mishnah is that the sage disrupts all other established modes of hierarchization. The Talmud's treatment of that point subverts that celebration of the sage within the caste system by introducing those tensions of learning versus intellect, mastery of traditions versus power of logic and reason, that impose upon the status of sagacity those variables that the life of intellect generates. The status of "being a sage" no longer carries weight; various modes of sagacity impart complexity and subtle to the simplicities of the Mishnah's uncomplicated conception of hierarchization. Since no one can ultimately determine whether Sinai takes precedence over the one who can pierce mountains, the indeterminacy of intellect upsets all conceptions of hierarchization, and the sages move on into an altogether new and unpredictable plane of being. It would be difficult to point to a more complete, if subtle, subversion of a Mishnah-tractate than the one accomplished by the framers of the Bavli, who here present us with one of their (very many) intellectual masterpieces. For the rest, I point to my *The Talmud of Babylonia. An Academic Commentary*, where each tractate is analyzed along the

lines set forth here. The components of that project are listed in
Chapter Four of this book.

VII. *What the Outline Demonstrates*

Now to close with the main point: through the outline of the Bavli
I prove a few simple facts. First, because of the character of the
outline, we see that we may speak of a composition, not merely a
compilation. That is because, first, the Talmud's authors or authorship follow a few rules, which we can easily discern, in order to say
everything they wish. So the document is uniform and rhetorically
cogent. The highly orderly and systematic character of the Talmud
emerges, first of all, in the regularities of language. Second, the outline
shows in enormous detail how the Talmud speaks through one voice,
that voice of logic that with vast assurance reaches into our own
minds and by asking the logical and urgent next question tells us
what we should be thinking. So the Talmud's rhetoric seduces us
into joining its analytical inquiry, always raising precisely the question that should trouble us (and that would trouble us if we knew
all of the pertinent details as well as the Talmud does). The Talmud speaks about the Mishnah in essentially a single voice, about
fundamentally few things. Its mode of speech as much as of thought
is uniform throughout. Diverse topics produce slight differentiation
in modes of analysis. The same sorts of questions phrased in the same
rhetoric—a moving, or dialectical, argument, composed of questions
and answers—turn out to pertain equally well to every subject and
problem. The Talmud's discourse forms a closed system, in which
people say the same thing about everything. The fact that the Talmud speaks in a single voice supplies striking evidence (1) that the
Talmud does speak in particular for the age in which its units of
discourse took shape, and (2) that that work was done toward the
end of that long period of Mishnah-reception that began at the end
of the second century and came to an end at the conclusion of the
sixth century.

The outline shows in vast detail a single governing fact. It is that
in a given unit of discourse, the focus, the organizing principle, the
generative interest—these are defined solely by the issue at hand.
The argument moves from point to point, directed by the inner logic
of argument itself. A single plane of discourse is established. All things
are leveled out, so that the line of logic runs straight and true.

Accordingly, a single conception of the framing and formation of the unit of discourse stands prior to the spelling out of issues. More fundamental still, what people in general wanted was not to create topical anthologies—to put together instances of what this one said about that issue—but to exhibit the logic of that issue, viewed under the aspect of eternity. Under sustained inquiry we always find a theoretical issue, freed of all temporal considerations and the contingencies of politics and circumstance.

Once these elemental literary and structural facts make their full impression, everything else falls into place as well. Arguments such as the one we followed just now did not unfold over a long period of time, as one generation made its points, to be followed by the additions and revisions of another generation, in a process of gradual increment and agglutination running on for two hundred years. That theory of the formation of literature cannot account for the unity, stunning force and dynamism, of the Talmud's dialectical arguments. To the contrary, someone (or small group) at the end determined to reconstruct, so as to expose, the naked logic of a problem. For this purpose, oftentimes, it was found useful to cite sayings or positions in hand from earlier times. But these inherited materials underwent a process of reshaping, and, more aptly, refocusing. Whatever the original words—and we need not doubt that at times we have them—the point of everything in hand was defined and determined by the people who made it all up at the end. The whole shows a plan and program. Theirs are the minds behind the whole. In the nature of things, they did their work at the end, not at the outset. There are two possibilities. The first is that our document emerges out of a gradual increment of a sedimentary process. Or it emerges as the creation of single minded geniuses of applied logic and sustained analytical inquiry. But there is no intermediate possibility.

What is the result of this work? My complete outline of the Bavli demonstrates once for all that the whole—the unit of discourse as we know it—was put together at the end. At that point everything was in hand, so available for arrangement in accordance with a principle other than chronology, and in a rhetoric common to all sayings. That other principle will then have determined the arrangement, drawing in its wake resort to a single monotonous voice: "the Talmud." The principle is logical exposition, that is to say, the analysis and dissection of a problem into its conceptual components.

The dialectic of argument is framed not by considerations of the chronological sequence in which sayings were said but by attention to the requirements of reasonable exposition of the problem. That is what governs.

In this regard, then, the Talmud is like the Mishnah in its fundamental literary traits, therefore also in its history. The Mishnah was formulated in its rigid, patterned language and carefully organized and enumerated groups of formal-substantive cognitive units, in the very processes in which it also was redacted. Otherwise the correspondences between redactional program and formal and patterned mode of articulation of ideas cannot be explained, short of invoking the notion of a literary miracle. The Talmud too underwent a process of redaction, in which fixed and final units of discourse were organized and put together. The probably-antecedent work of framing and formulating these units of discourse appears to have gone on at a single period, among a relatively small number of sages working within a uniform set of literary conventions, at roughly the same time, and in approximately the same way. The end-product, the Talmud, like the Mishnah, is uniform and stylistically coherent, generally consistent in modes of thought and speech, wherever we turn. That accounts for the single voice that leads us through the dialectical and argumentative analysis of the Talmud. That voice is ubiquitous and insistent.

Units of discourse organized not in accordance with the requirements of cogent and dialectical argument exhibit one of two qualities. (1) They present an anthology of sayings on a single topic, without reworking these sayings into a coherent argument. (2) They present a sequence of related, short-term statements, zigzagging from point to point without evidence of an overall plan or purpose: this, then that. Stories, tales, and fables, by contrast, do exhibit the traits of unity and purpose so striking in the generality of units of discourse devoted to analysis of law. So the point of differentiation is not subject matter—law as against lore. Rather, it is the literary and conceptual history of the unit of discourse at hand. So we find very good reason to suppose that the text as we have it does speak about the limited context of the period of the actual framing of the text's principal building blocks. These building blocks give evidence of having been put together in a moment of deliberation, in accordance with a plan of exposition, and in response to a finite problem of logical analysis. The units of discourse in no way appear to have taken shape slowly, over a long period of time, in a process governed by the order in which sayings were framed, now and here, then and there, later and anywhere else (so to speak). Before us is the result of considered redaction, not protracted accretion, mindful construction, not sedimentary accretion.

CHAPTER TWO

THE BAVLI'S MASSIVE MISCELLANIES

I. *Defining a Miscellany*

The results of our analysis of how the Bavli is organized and of the two main types of writing—compositions and composites—now bring us to focus upon one of the two types of composite-making. One draws together information required to establish a single overriding proposition, so is purposeful and well-crafted. The other kind of composite, the kind that imparts to the Talmud traits of disorganization and haphazard assembly of odds and ends, is what I call "a massive miscellany." Here we pursue this third and final element of the document.

The Talmud of Babylonia makes use of two distinct principles for the formation of large-scale composites of distinct compositions, and the framers of the document very rarely set forth a composition on its own, standing without clear ties to a larger context. Ordinarily, they brought together distinct and free-standing compositions in the service of Mishnah-exegesis and amplification of law originating in a Mishnah-paragraph under analysis. For that purpose they would then draw upon already-written compositions, which would be adduced as cases, statements of principles, fully-exposed analyses, inclusive of debate and argument, in the service of that analysis. So all of the compositions in a given composite would serve the governing analytical or propositional purpose of the framer of the composite. Where a composition appears to shade over into a direction of its own, that very quickly is seen to serve as a footnote or even an appendix to the composite at hand.

Recognizing the orderly character of the Bavli, we may now turn to concentrate upon the agglutinative composites that do not conform to the norms of rhetorical form and logical cogency that impart to the Bavli its wonderful cogency. What are traits that we may discern in this kind of compilation? How are we to establish some sort of hypothesis concerning the rules, if any, that govern and so make the miscellany accessible and purposeful, within the framework of the Bavli? To answer these questions, let us turn to a sample of what I characterize as a miscellany. It is given in Bavli Baba Batra Chapter Five, starting at 72B, with the further page numbers signified in the text.

2. A. *Our rabbis have taught on Tannaite authority:*

   B. **He who sells a ship has sold the wooden implements and the water tank on it.**

   C. **R. Nathan says, "He who sells a ship has sold its rowboat."**

   D. **Sumkhos says, "He who has sold a ship has sold its lighter"** [T. B.B. 4:1A-C].

3. A. *Said Raba, "The rowboat and the lighter are pretty much the same thing. But R. Nathan, who was a Babylonian, uses the word familiar to him, as people use that word in Babylonia when referring to the rowboat that is used at the shallows, and Sumkhos, who was from the Land of Israel, used the word that is familiar to him, as people say in the verse,* 'And your residue shall be taken away in lighters' (Amos 4:2)."

4. A. *Said Rabbah, "Sailors told me, 'The wave that sinks a ship appears with a white froth of fire at the crest, and when stricken with clubs on which is incised,* "I am that I am, Yah, the Lord of Hosts, Amen, Amen, Selah," *it will subside [and not sink the ship].'"*

5. A. *Said Rabbah, "Sailors told me, 'Between one wave and another there is a distance of three hundred parasangs, and the height of the wave is the same three hundred parasangs. Once, when we were on a voyage, a wave lifted us up so high that we could see the resting place of the smallest star, and there was a flash, as if one shot forty arrows of iron; and if it had lifted us up any higher, we would have been burned by the heat. And one wave called to the next,* "Friend, have you left anything in the world that you did not wash away? I'll go and wipe it out." *And the other said,* "Go see the power of the master, by whose command I must not pass the sand of the shore by even so much as the breadth of a thread: 'Fear you not me? says the Lord? Will you not tremble at my presence, who have placed the sand for the bound of the sea, an everlasting ordinance, which it cannot pass' (Jer. 5:22).'"*

6. A. *Said Rabbah, "I personally saw Hormin, son of Lilith, running on the parapet of the wall of Mahoza, and a rider, galloping below on horseback, could not catch up with him. Once they put a saddle for him two mules, which* **[73B]** *stood on two bridges of the Rognag, and he jumped from one to the other, backward and forward, holding two cups of wine in his hands, pouring from one to the other without spilling a drop on the ground. It was a stormy day:* 'they that go down to the sea in ships mounted up to he heaven, they went down to the deeps' (Ps. 107:27). *Now when the state heard about this, they killed him."*

7. A. *Said Rabbah bar bar Hannah, "I personally saw a day-old antelope as big as Mount Tabor. How big is Mount Tabor? Four parasangs. Its neck was*

three parasangs long, and his head rested on a spot a parasang and a half. Its ball of shit blocked up the Jordan River."

8.   A.   *And said Rabbah bar bar Hannah, "I personally saw a frog as big as the Fort of Hagronia—how big is that? sixty houses!—and a snake came along and swallowed the frog; a raven came along and swallowed the snake; and perched on a tree. So you can just imagine how strong was the tree."*

     B.   *Said R. Pappa bar Samuel "If I weren't there on the spot, I would never have believed it!"*

9.   A.   *And said Rabbah bar bar Hannah, "Once we were traveling on a ship, and we saw a fish [whale] in the nostrils of which a mud-eater had entered. The water cast up the fish and threw it on the shore. Sixty towns were destroyed by it, sixty towns got their food from it, and sixty towns salted the remnants, and from one of its eyeballs three hundred kegs of oil were filled. Coming back twelve months later, we saw that they were cutting rafters from the skeleton and rebuilding the towns."*

10. A.   *And said Rabbah bar bar Hannah, "Once we were traveling on a ship, and we saw a fish the back of which was covered with sand out of which grass was growing. We thought it was dry land so we went up and baked and cooked on the back of the fish. When the back got hut, it rolled over, and if the ship hadn't been nearby, we would have drowned."*

11. A.   *And said Rabbah bar bar Hannah, "Once we were travelling on a ship, and the ship sailed between one fin of a fish and the other for three days and three nights; the fish was swimming upwards and we were floating downwards [with the wind]."*

     B.   *Now, should you suppose that the ship did not sail fast enough, when R. Dimi came, he said, "It covered sixty parasangs in the time that it takes to heat a kettle of water. And when a cavalryman shot an arrow, the ship outstripped the arrow."*

     C.   *R. Ashi said, "That was one of the small sea monsters, the ones that have only two fins."*

12. A.   *And said Rabbah bar bar Hannah, "Once we were travelling on a ship, and we saw a bird standing in the water only up to its ankles, with its head touching the sky. So we thought the water wasn't very deep, and we thought of going down to cool ourselves, but an echo called out, 'Don't go down into the water here, for a carpenter's axe dropped into this water seven years ago, and it hasn't yet reached the bottom.' And it was not only deep but also rapidly flowing."*

     B.   *Said R. Ashi, "The bird was the wild cock, for it is written,* 'And the wild cock is with me [with God in heaven]' (Ps 50:11).".

13. A.   *And said Rabbah bar bar Hannah, "Once we were travelling in the desert, and we saw geese whose feathers fell out because they were so fat, and streams of fat flowed under them. I said to them, 'May we have a share of your meat in the world to come? One of them lifted a wing, the other a leg [showing me what my portion would be]. When I came before R. Eleazar, he said to me,* 'Israel will be called to account on account of these geese.'"
     [Slotki: the protracted suffering of the geese caused by their growing fatness is due to Israel's sins, which delay the coming of the Messiah.]

14. A.   *And said Rabbah bar bar Hannah, "Once we were travelling in the desert,*
          and a Tai-Arab joined us, who could pick up sand and smell it and tell us
          which was the road to one place and which to another. We said to him,
          'How far are we from water?' He said to us, 'Give me sand.' We gave him
          some, and he said to us, 'Eight parasangs.' When we gave him some sand
          later, he told us that we were three parasangs off.' I had changed the sand,
          but I was not able to confuse him.

     B.   *"He said to me, 'Come on, and I'll show you the dead of the wilderness*
          [Num. 14:32ff.]. I went with him and saw them. They looked as though
          they were exhilarated. **[74A]** *They slept on their backs and the knee of one*
          of them was raised. The Arab merchant passed under the knee, riding on a
          camel with a spear on high and did not touch it. I cut off one corner of the
          purpose blue cloak of one of them, but we could not move away. He said to
          me, 'If you've taken something from them, return it, for we have a tradition
          that if anybody takes something from them, he cannot move away.' I went
          and returned it and then we could move away.

     C.   *"When I came before rabbis, they said to me, 'Every Abba is an ass, and*
          every son of Bar Hana is an idiot. What did you do that for? Was it to
          find out whether the law accords with the House of Shammai or the House
          of Hillel? You could have counted the threads and the joints [to find out the
          answer to your question].'

     D.   *"He said to me, 'Come and I will show you Mount Sinai.' I went and saw*
          scorpions surrounding it, and they stood like white asses. A heard an echo
          saying, 'Woe is me that I have taken an oath, and now that I have
          taken the oath, who will release me from it?' When I came before
          rabbis, they said to me, 'Every Abba is an ass, and every son of Bar Hana
          is an idiot. You should have said, 'It is released for you.' But I was think-
          ing that perhaps it was an oath in connection with the flood [which favored
          humanity]."

     E.   *And rabbis?*

     F.   If so, what need is there for the language, "woe is me"?

     G.   *"He said to me, 'Come and I will show you those who were associated with*
          Korah who were swallowed up [Num. 16:32ff.]. I saw two cracks that
          emitted smoke. I took a piece of clipped wool and soaked it in water, put it
          on the point of a spear, and pushed it in there. When I took it out, it was
          singed. He said to me, 'Listen closely to what you will hear.' and i heard
          them say, 'Moses and his Torah are truth, and we are liars.' He
          said to me, 'Every thirty days Gehenna causes them to turn over as one rotates
          meat in a pot, and this is what they say: "Moses and his Torah are
          truth and we are liars."'"

     H.   *"He said to me, 'Come and I will show you where heaven and earth meet.'*
          I took my basket it and put it in a window of heaven. When I finished
          saying my prayers, I looked for it but did not find it. I said to him, 'Are
          there thieves here?" He said to me, 'It is the result of the wheel of heaven
          turning, wait here until tomorrow, and you will find it.'"

15. A.   *R. Yohanan told this story: "Once we were traveling along on a ship, and*
          we saw a fish that raised its head from the sea. Its eyes were like two moons,

and water streamed from its nostrils like the two rivers of Sura."

16. A. *R. Safra told this story: "Once we were traveling along on a ship, and we saw a fish that raised its head from the sea. It had horns on which was engraved: 'I am a lesser creature of the sea. I am three hundred parasangs long, and I am going into the mouth of Leviathan.'"*

   B. *Said R. Ashi, "That was a sea goat that searches for food, and has horns."*

17. A. *R. Yohanan told this story: "Once we were traveling along on a ship, and we saw a chest in which were set jewels and peals, surrounded by a kind of fish called a Karisa-fish. A diver went down* **[74B]** *to bring up the chest, but the wished realized it and was about to wrench his thigh. He poured on it a bottle of vinegar, and it sank. An echo came forth, saying to us, 'What in the world have you got to do with the best of the wife of R. Hanina, b. Dosa, who is going to store in it the purple-blue for the righteous in the world to come.'"*

18. A. *R. Judah the Hindu told this story: "Once we were traveling along on a ship, and we saw a jewel with a snake wrapped around it. A diver went down to bring up the jewel. The snake drew near, to swallow the ship. A raven came and bit off its head. The waters turned to blood. Another snake and took the head of the snake and attached it to the body again, and it revived. The snake again came to swallow the ship. A bird again came and cut off its head. The diver seized the jewel and threw it into the ship. We had salted birds. We put the stone on them, and they took it up and flew away with it."*

19. A. *Our rabbis have taught on Tannaite authority:*

   B. There was the case involving R. Eliezer and R. Joshua, who were travelling on a ship. R. Eliezer was sleeping, and R. Joshua was awake. R. Joshua shuddered and R. Eliezer woke up. He said to him, "What's wrong, Joshua? How come you trembled?"

   C. He said to him, "I saw a great light on the sea."

   D. He said to him, "It might have been the eye of Leviathan that you saw, for it is written, 'His eyes are like the eyelids of the morning' (Is. 27:1)."

20. A. *Said R. Ashi, "Said to me Huna bar Nathan, 'Once we were traveling in the desert, and we had taken with us a leg of meat. We cut it open, picked out [what we are not allowed to eat] and put it on the grass. While we were going to get some wood, the leg returned to its original form, and we roasted it. When we came back after twelve months, we saw the coals still glowing. When I presented the matter to Amemar, he said to me, 'The grass was an herb that can unite severed parts, and the coals were broom [which burns a long time inside, while the surface is extinguished].'*

21. A. "And God created the great sea monsters" (Gen. 1:21):

   B. *Here this is interpreted, "the sea gazelles."*

   C. R. Yohanan said, "This refers to Leviathan, [Slotki:] the slant serpent, and Leviathan the tortuous serpent: 'In that day the Lord with his sore and great and strong sword will punish Leviathan the slant serpent and Leviathan the tortuous serpent' (Is. 27:1)."

22. A. Said R. Judah said Rab, "Whatever the Holy One, blessed be

he, created in his world did he create male and female, and so too, the Leviathan the slant serpent and Leviathan the tortuous serpent he created male and female, and if they had mated with one another, they would have destroyed the whole world.

B. "What did the Holy One, blessed be he, do? He castrated the male and killed the female and salted it for the righteous in the world to come: 'And he will slay the dragon that is in the sea' (Is. 27:1).

C. "And also Behemoth on a thousand hills [Ps. 50:10) he created male and female, and if they had mated with one another, they would have destroyed the whole world.

D. "What did the Holy One, blessed be he, do? He castrated the male and quick-froze the female and preserved her for the righteous in the world to come: 'Lo, now his strength is in his loins' (Job 40:16) speaks of the male, 'and his force is in the stays of his body' (Job 40:16) speaks of the female."

E. *In that other case, too, while castrating the male, why did he not simply quick-freeze the female [instead of killing it]?*

F. *Fish is dissolute [and cooling would not have sufficed].*

G. *Why not do it in reverse order?*

H. *If you wish, I shall say that the female fish preserved in salt tastes better, and if you wish, I shall say, "Because it is written, 'There is Leviathan whom you have formed to sport with' (Ps. 104;26), and with the female that would not be seemly.*

I. Here too, in the case of the Behemoth, why not preserve the female in salt?

J. *Salted fish tastes good, salted meat doesn't.*

23. A. And said R. Judah said Rab, "When the Holy One, blessed be he, proposed to create the world, he said to the prince of the sea, 'Open your mouth, and swallow all the water in the world.'

B. "He said to him, 'Lord of the world, it is enough that I stay in my own territory.'

C. "So on the spot he hit him with his foot and killed him: 'Hew stirs up the sea with his power and by his understanding he smites through Rahab' (Job 26:12)."

D. *Said R. Isaac, "That bears the implication that* the name of the prince of the sea is Rahab."

E. [Rab continues,] "And had the waters not covered him over, no creature could stand because of his stench: 'They shall not hurt nor destroy in all my holy mountain...as the waters cover the sea' (Is. 11:9). Do not read 'they cover the sea' but 'they cover the angel of the sea.'"

24. A. And said R. Judah said Rab, "The Jordan issues from the cave of Paneas."

B. *So too it has been taught on Tannaite authority:*

C. The Jordan issues from the cave of Paneas.

D. And it goes through the Lake of Sibkay and the Lake of Tiberias and rolls down into the great sea, and from there it rolls onward until it rushes into the mouth of Leviathan: "He is confident because the Jordan rushes forth to his mouth" (Job 40:23).

E. *Objected Raba bar Ulla, "This verse speaks of* Behemoth on a thousand hills."

F. Rather, said Raba bar Ulla, "When is Behemoth on a thousand years confident? When the Jordan rushes into the mouth of Leviathan." [Slotki: so long as Leviathan is alive, Behemoth also is safe.]

25. A. *When R. Dimi came, he said R. Yohanan said, "What is the meaning of the verse,* 'For he has founded it upon the seas and established it upon the floods' (Ps. 24:2)? This refers to the seven seas and four rivers that surround the land of Israel. And what are the seven seas? The sea of Tiberias, the sea of Sodom, the sea of Helath, the sea of Hiltha, the sea of Sibkay, the sea of Aspamia, and the Great sea. And what are the four rivers? The Jordan, the Yarmuk, the Keramyhon, and the Pigah."

26. A. *When R. Dimi came, he said R. Yohanan said,* "Gabriel is destined to organize a hunt **[75A]** for Leviathan: 'Can you draw out Leviathan with a fish hook, or press down his tongue with a cord' (Job 40:25). And if the Holy One, blessed be he, does not help him, he will never be able to prevail over him: 'He only that made him can make his sword approach him' (Job 40:19)."

27. A. *When R. Dimi came, he said R. Yohanan said,* "When Leviathan is hungry, he sends out fiery breath from his mouth and boils all the waters of the deep: 'He makes the deep to boil like a pot' (Job 41:23). And if he did not put his head into the Garden of Eden, no creature could endure his stench: 'he makes the sea like a spiced broth' (Job 41:23). And when he is thirsty, he makes the sea into furrows: 'He makes a path to shine after him' (Job 41:24)."

B. Said R. Aha bar Jacob, "The great deep does not recover its strength for seventy years: 'One thinks the deep to be hoary' (Job 41:24), and hoary old age takes seventy years."

28. A. Rabbah said R. Yohanan said, "The Holy One, blessed be he, is destined to make a banquet for the righteous out of the meat of Leviathan: 'Companions will make a banquet of it' (Job 40:30). The meaning of 'banquet' derives from the usage of the same word in the verse, 'And he prepared for them a great banquet and they ate and drank' (2 Kgs. 6:23).

B. "'Companions' can refer only to disciples of sages, in line with this usage: 'You that dwells in the gardens, the companions hearken for your voice, cause me to hear it' (Song 8:13). The rest of the creature will be cut up and sold in the markets of Jerusalem: 'They will part him among the Canaanites' (Job 40:30), and 'Canaanites' must be merchants, in line with this usage: 'As for the Canaanite, the balances of deceit are in his hand, he loves to oppress' (Hos. 12:8). If you prefer: 'Whose merchants are princes, whose traffickers are the honorable of the earth' (Is. 23:8)."

29. A. Rabbah said R. Yohanan said, "The Holy One, blessed be he, is destined to make a tabernacle for the righteous out of the hide of Leviathan: 'Can you fill tabernacles with his skin' (Job 40:31). If someone has sufficient merit, a tabernacle is made for him; if he does not have sufficient merit, a mere shade is made for him: 'And his head with a fish covering' (Job 40:31). If someone has sufficient merit, a shade is made for him, if not, then a mere necklace is made for him: 'And necklaces about your neck' (Prov. 1:9). If someone has sufficient merit, a necklace is made for him; if not, then an amulet: 'And you will bind him for your maidens' (Job 40:29).

B. "And the rest of the beast will the Holy One, blessed be he, spread over the walls of Jerusalem, and the glow will illuminate the world from one end to the other: 'And nations shall walk at your light, and kings at the brightness of your rising' (Is. 60:3)."

30. A. "And I will make your pinnacles of rubies" (Is. 54:12):

B. *Said R. Samuel bar Nahmani, "There is a dispute between two angels in the firmament, Gabriel and Michael, and some say, two Amoraim in the West, and who might they be? Judah and Hezekiah, sons of R. Hiyya.*

C. *"One said, 'The word translated rubies means onyx...'*

D. *"The other said, 'It means jasper.'*

E. *"Said to them the Holy One, blessed be he, 'Let it be in accord with both this opinion and that opinion.'"*

31. A. "And your gates of carbuncles" (Is. 60:3):

B. *That is in line with what what said when R. Yohanan went into session and expounded as follows:* "The Holy One, blessed be he, is destined to bring jewels and pearls that are thirty cubits by thirty and will cut out openings from them ten cubits by twenty, setting them up at the gates of Jerusalem."

C. A certain disciple ridiculed him, *"Well, jewels even the size of the egg of a dove are not available, so will jewels of such dimensions be found?"*

D. *After a while his ship went out to sea. He saw ministering angels engaged in cutting up jewels and pearls thirty cubits by thirty, on which were engravings ten by twenty. He said to him, "He said to him, "For whom are these?"*

E. *They said to him,* "The Holy One, blessed be he, is destined to set them up at the gates of Jerusalem."

F. *The man came before R. Yohanan. He said to him, "Give your exposition, my lord. It is truly fitting for you to give an exposition.* For just as you said, so I myself have seen."

G. He said to him, "Empty-headed idiot! If you had not seen, you would not have believed! So you ridicule the teachings of sages." He set his eye on him and the student turned into a heap of bones.

32. A. *An objection was raised:*

B. "And I will lead you upright" (Lev. 26:13)—

C. [Since the word for "upright" can be read to mean, at twice the normal height], R. Meir says, "That means, two hundred cubits, twice the height of the First Man."

D. R. Judah says, "A hundred cubits, the height of the temple and its walls: 'We whose sons are as plants grown up in their youth, whose daughters are as corner pillars carved after the fashion of the temple' (Ps. 144:12)." [Slotki: how then in view of their increase to a hundred cubits in height, requiring correspondingly high gates, can Yohanan say that the gates were only twenty cubits in height?]

E. *When R. Yohanan made that statement, it was with reference only to [Slotki:] ventilation windows.*

33. A. And said Rabbah said R. Yohanan, "The Holy One, blessed be he, is destined to make seven canopies for every righteous person: 'And the Lord will create over the whole habitation of Mount Zion and over her assemblies a cloud of smoke by day and the shining of a flaming fire by night, for over all the glory shall be a canopy' (Is. 4:5). This teaches that for every one will the Holy One create a canopy in accord with the honor that is due him."

B. Why is smoke needed for the canopy?

C. Said R. Hanina, "It is because everyone who treats disciples of sages in a niggardly way in this world will have his eyes filled with smoke in the world to come."

D. Why is fire needed in a canopy?

E. Said R. Hanina, "This teaches that each one will be burned by [envy for] the canopy of the other. Woe for the shame, woe for the reproach!"

34. A. Along these same lines you may say: "And you shall put some of your honor upon him" (Num. 27:20)—but not of your honor.

B. The elders of that generation said, "The face of Moses glows like the face of the sun, the face of Joshua like the face of the moon.

C. "Woe for the shame, woe for the reproach!"

35. A. Said R. Hama bar Hanina, "Ten canopies did the Holy One, blessed be he, make for the First Man in the garden of Eden: 'You were in Eden, the garden of God; every precious stone was your covering, the cornelian, the topaz, the emerald, the beryl, the onyx, the jasper, the sapphire, the carbuncle, and the emerald and gold' (Ez. 28:13)."

B. Mar Zutra said, "Eleven: 'every precious stone.'"

C. Said R. Yohanan, "The least of them all was gold, *since it was mentioned last.*"

36. A. *What is the meaning of* "by the work of your timbrels and holes" (Ez. 28:13)?

B. Said R. Judah said Rab, "Said the Holy One, blessed be he, to Hiram, king of Tyre, 'I looked at you [for your arrogance] when I created the excretory holes of human beings."

C.   *And some say that this is what he said to him,* "I looked at you **[75B]** when I decreed the death penalty against the first Man."

37. A.   *What is the meaning of* "and over her assemblies" (Is. 4:5)?

 B.   Said Rabbah said R. Yohanan, "Jerusalem in the age to come will not be like Jerusalem in this age. To Jerusalem in this age anyone who wants to go up may go up. But to Jerusalem in the age to come only those who are deemed worthy of coming will go up."

38. A.   And said Rabbah said R. Yohanan, "The righteous are destined to be called by the name of the Holy One, blessed be he: 'Every one that is called by my name, and whom I have created for my glory, I have formed him, yes, I have made him' (Is. 43:7)."

39. A.   Said R. Samuel bar Nahmani said R. Yohanan, "There are three who are called by the name of the Holy One, blessed be he, and these are they: the righteous, the Messiah, and Jerusalem.

 B.   "The righteous, as we have just said.

 C.   "The Messiah: 'And this is the name whereby he shall be called, the Lord is our righteousness' (Jer. 23:6).

 D.   "Jerusalem: 'It shall be eighteen thousand reeds round about, and the name of the city from that day shall be, "the Lord is there" (Ez. 48:35). Do not read 'there' but 'its name.'"

40. A.   Said R. Eleazar, "The time will come when 'holy' will be said before the name of the righteous as it is said before the name of the Holy One, blessed be he: 'And it shall come to pass that he that is left in Zion and he that remains in Jerusalem shall be called holy' (Is. 4:3)."

41. A.   And said Rabbah said R. Yohanan, "The Holy One, blessed be he, is destined to lift up Jerusalem to a height of three parasangs: 'And she shall be lifted up and be settled in her place' (Is. 4:3). '...in her place' means 'like her place' [Slotki: Jerusalem will be lifted up to a height equal to the extent of the space it occupies]."

42. A.   *So how do we know that the place that Jerusalem occupied was three parasangs?*

 B.   Said Rabbah, "Said to me a certain elder, 'I myself saw the original Jerusalem, and it filled up three parasangs.'"

43. A.   And lest you suppose that there will be pain in the ascension, Scripture states, "Who are these that fly as a cloud and as the doves to their cotes" (Is. 60:8).

 B.   *Said R. Pappa, "You may derive from that statement the fact that a cloud rises to a height of three parasangs."*

44. A.   Said R. Hanina bar Pappa, "The Holy One blessed be he wanted to give Jerusalem a fixed size: 'Then said I, Whither do you go? And he said to me, To measure Jerusalem, to see what is its breadth and what is its length' (Zech. 2:6).

 B.   "Said the ministering angels before the Holy One, blessed be he, 'Lord of the world, you have created in your world any number of cities for the nations of the earth, and you did not fix the measurements of their length or breadth. So are you going to fix measurements for Jerusalem, in the midst of which are your name, sanctuary, and the righteous?'

C.   "Then: 'an angel said to him, Run, speak to this young man, saying, Jerusalem shall be inhabited without walls, for the multitude of men and cattle therein' (Zech. 2:8)."

45. A.   Said R. Simeon b. Laqish, "The Holy One, blessed be he, is destined to add to Jerusalem [Slotki:] a thousand gardens, a thousand towers, a thousand palaces, a thousand mansions. And each one of these will be as vast as Sepphoris in its hour of prosperity."

46. A.   *It has been taught on Tannaite authority:*

B.   Said R. Yosé, "I saw Sepphoris in its hour of prosperity, and in it were one hundred and eighty thousand markets for those who sold pudding [alone]."

47. A.   "And the side chambers were one over another, three and thirty times" (Ez. 41:6):

B.   *What is the meaning of* three and thirty times?

C.   Said R. Pappi in the name of R. Joshua of Sikni, "If there will be three Jerusalems, each building will contain thirty dwellings piled up on top of one another; if there will be thirty Jerusalems, then each building will contain three apartments on top of one another."

From the viewpoint of the Bavli overall, the anomalous traits of the conglomerate are clear: once we have left behind us the Tannaite complement to the Mishnah, there is no clear purpose or point established in what follows, No. 3 provides a talmud to No. 2, that is to say, a well-crafted expansion, in this instance explaining the word-choices of the prior item. But then we have a sequence of units that have only the most tenuous connection to the fore-going. No. 2-3 have spoken of ships, and No. 4 speaks of a ship. No. 4 does not continue No. 3 (nor does any following unit); it is parachuted down because of a shared subject, that alone. But even the subject is not a substantial point in common, since No. 4 wants to talk about ships that sink and how God participates in the matter, and nothing could be further from the frame of reference of No. 3.

    What, then, are the units that do coalesce in the conglomerate that follows? Clearly, Nos. 4, 5 talk about the supernatural in connection with ships that founder at sea. No. 6 runs along the same lines, but its connection to No. 5 is not much tighter than that of No. 4 to No. 3. No. 7, however, is another matter; it shares the "I personally saw"-formula, and not only so, but what the master personally saw is a quite extraordinary thing. So we can see how the compositions at Nos. 6, 7, 8 were formed into a piece; obviously, there is no explanation for why one is prior, another later, in the sequence; but there is a tight connection among the three items. Another such set begins at No. 9: "once we were travelling and...," which is the recurrent formula through Nos. 10-18+19. Now why have Nos. 9-18+19 been linked to Nos., 6-8? No. 8 speaks of "I personally saw" a frog as big as..., and the next, "Once we were travelling and we saw a fish...as big as...." So the shift is from one rhetorical formula to another, but the subject matter remains the same. That strikes me as rather deft composite-making indeed. The following items, Nos. 10-12, conform to the same pattern, talking about wonders of nature that a sage saw. No. 13 then marks another shift, however, since while the wonders of nature go forward, the fat geese are not really of the same order as the amazingly huge fish; and the lesson is a different once, namely, "Israel will be called to account...."

That this is the commencement of a new topic, joined with the prior form, is shown at No. 14. Here we retain the "once we were traveling"-formula; but we drop the sustaining theme, big fish and the like, and instead, we pick up the new motif, which is, God's judgment of Israel, now: the dead raised by Ezekiel, No. 14; and the same story repeats the new motif, now the theme of God's judgment of Israel in connection with the oath of Sinai. What follows at No. 15 is yet another formula: "X told this story; once we were traveling...," and now we revert to the theme of the wonders of nature. Have we really lost the immediately-prior theme? Not at all, for now our natural wonders turn out to concern Leviathan, and, later on, that theme is explicitly joined to the judgment of Israel: the righteous will get invited to the banquet at which Leviathan will form the main course. So Nos. 15-17 (and much that follows) turn out to link the two distinct themes that have been joined, and, we see, the movement is quite deft. We have a rhetorical device to link a variety of compositions on a given subject, we retain that rhetorical device but shift the subject, then we shift the rhetorical device but retain the same subject, and, finally, we join the two distinct subjects. The theme of Leviathan holds together Nos., 21-22+23. No., 24 is tacked on because Leviathan plays a role, and the same is to be said for Nos. 30. The general interest in the restoration of Israel moves from the messianic meal to Jerusalem, Nos. 31-45+46, 47. So there is a clear topical program, and while we have a variety of subunits, these are put together in a way that we can explain without stretching.

To restate this analysis in outline form, let me now reproduce the outline of the entire composite, which shows still more clearly how matters fit together:

XL. MISHNAH-TRACTATE BABA BATRA 5:1A-D

A. HE WHO SELLS A SHIP HAS SOLD THE MAST:

1. I:1: this refers to the mast, and so Scripture says, "They have taken cedars from Lebanon to make masts for you" (Ezek. 27:5).

B. SAIL:

1. II:1: bears that meaning in line with this verse: "Of fine linen with richly woven work from Egypt was your sail, that it might to for you for an ensign" (Ezek. 27:7).

C. AND ANCHOR:

1. III:1: Repeated R. Hiyya as a Tannaite statement: "This refers to the anchors, in line with this verse: 'Would you tarry for them until they were grown? Would you shut yourselves off for them and have no husbands' (Ruth 1:13)."

D. AND WHATEVER STEERS IT:

1. IV:1: What is the source in Scripture for that statement? Said R. Abba, "This speaks of the oars: 'Of the oaks of Bashan have they made your oars' (Ezek. 27:6)."

2. IV:2: He who sells a ship has sold the wooden implements and the water tank on it. R. Nathan says, "He who sells a ship has sold its rowboat." Sumkhos says, "He who has sold a ship has sold its lighter" (T. B.B. 4:1A-C).

3. IV:3: Gloss of foregoing. Said Raba, "The rowboat and the lighter are pretty much the same thing. But R. Nathan, who was a Babylonian, uses the word familiar to him, as people use that word in Babylonia when referring to the rowboat that is used at the shallows, and Sumkhos, who was from the Land of Israel, used the word that is familiar to him, as people say in the verse, 'And your residue shall be taken away in lighters' (Amos 4:2).

E. COMPOSITE OF SEA-STORIES OF RABBAH BAR BAR HANNAH

1. IV:4: Said Rabbah, "Sailors told me, 'The wave that sinks a ship appears with a white froth of fire at the crest, and when stricken with clubs on which is incised, "I am that I am, Yah, the Lord of Hosts, Amen, Amen, Selah," it will subside and not sink the ship.'"

2. IV:5: Said Rabbah, "Sailors told me, 'Between one wave and another there is a distance of three hundred parasangs, and the height of the wave is the same three hundred parasangs...'"

3. IV:6: Said Rabbah, "I personally saw Hormin, son of Lilith, running on the parapet of the wall of Mahoza, and a rider, galloping below on horseback, could not catch up with him..."
    a. IV:7: Said Rabbah bar bar Hannah, "I personally saw a day-old antelope as big as Mount Tabor..."
    b. IV:8: And said Rabbah bar bar Hannah, "I personally saw a frog as big as the Fort of Hagronia..."
4. IV:9: And said Rabbah bar bar Hannah, "Once we were traveling on a ship, and we saw a fish whale in the nostrils of which a mud eater had entered. The water cast up the fish and threw it on the shore..."
5. IV:10: And said Rabbah bar bar Hannah, "Once we were traveling on a ship, and we saw a fish the back of which was covered with sand out of which grass was growing..."
6. IV:11: And said Rabbah bar bar Hannah, "Once we were traveling on a ship, and the ship sailed between one fin of a fish and the other for three days and three nights; the fish was swimming upwards and we were floating downwards with the wind."
7. IV:12: And said Rabbah bar bar Hannah, "Once we were traveling on a ship, and we saw a bird standing in the water only up to its ankles, with its head touching the sky."
    a. IV:13: And said Rabbah bar bar Hannah, "Once we were traveling in the desert, and we saw geese whose feathers fell out because they were so fat, and streams of fat flowed under them."
    b. IV:14: And said Rabbah bar bar Hannah, "Once we were traveling in the desert, and a Tai-Arab joined us, who could pick up sand and smell it and tell us which was the road to one place and which to another."

F. OTHER TRAVELLERS' TALES
1. IV:15: R. Yohanan told this story: "Once we were traveling along on a ship, and we saw a fish that raised its head from the sea. Its eyes were like two moons, and water streamed from its nostrils like the two rivers of Sura."
2. IV:16: R. Safra told this story: "Once we were traveling along on a ship, and we saw a fish that raised its head from the sea. It had horns on which was engraved: 'I am a lesser creature of the sea. I am three hundred parasangs long, and I am going into the mouth of Leviathan.'"
3. IV:17: R. Yohanan told this story: "Once we were traveling along on a ship, and we saw a chest in which were set jewels and pearls, surrounded by a kind of fish called a Karisa-fish. A diver went down to bring up the chest, but the fish realized it and was about to wrench his thigh. He poured on it a bottle of vinegar, and it sank. An echo came forth, saying to us, 'What in the world have you got to do with the chest

of the wife of R. Hanina b. Dosa, who is going to store in it the purple-blue for the righteous in the world to come.'

4.   IV:18: R. Judah the Hindu told this story: "Once we were traveling along on a ship, and we saw a jewel with a snake wrapped around it. A diver went down to bring up the jewel. The snake drew near, to swallow the ship. A raven came and bit off its head. The waters turned to blood. Another snake and took the head of the snake and attached it to the body again, and it revived. The snake again came to swallow the ship. A bird again came and cut off its head. The diver seized the jewel and threw it into the ship. We had salted birds. We put the stone on them, and they took it up and flew away with it."

5.   IV:19: There was the case involving R. Eliezer and R. Joshua, who were traveling on a ship. R. Eliezer was sleeping, and R. Joshua was awake. R. Joshua shuddered and R. Eliezer woke up. He said to him, "What's wrong, Joshua? How come you trembled?"

6.   IV:20: Said R. Ashi, "Said to me Huna bar Nathan, 'Once we were traveling in the desert, and we had taken with us a leg of meat. We cut it open, picked out what we are not allowed to eat and put it on the grass. While we were going to get some wood, the leg returned to its original form, and we roasted it. When we came back after twelve months, we saw the coals still glowing. When I presented the matter to Amemar, he said to me, "The grass was an herb that can unite severed parts, and the coals were broom which burns a long time inside, while the surface is extinguished."'"

G.   LEVIATHAN

1.   IV:21: "And God created the great sea monsters" (Gen. 1:21): Here this is interpreted, "the sea gazelles."

2.   IV:22: Said R. Judah said Rab, "Whatever the Holy One, blessed be He, created in his world did he create male and female, and so, too, Leviathan the slant serpent and Leviathan the tortuous serpent he created male and female, and if they had mated with one another, they would have destroyed the whole world...."

H.   WATER: CHARACTER AND SOURCES

1.   IV:23: And said R. Judah said Rab, "When the Holy One, blessed be He, proposed to create the world, he said to the prince of the sea, 'Open your mouth, and swallow all the water in the world.'"

2.   IV:24: And said R. Judah said Rab, "The Jordan issues from the cave of Paneas....And it goes through the Lake of Sibkay and the Lake of Tiberias and rolls down into the great sea, and from there it rolls onward until it rushes into the mouth

of Leviathan: 'He is confident because the Jordan rushes forth to his mouth' (Job 40:23)."

Objected Raba bar Ulla, "This verse speaks of Behemoth on a thousand hills."

     a.   IV:25: When R. Dimi came, he said R. Yohanan said, "What is the meaning of the verse, 'For he has founded it upon the seas and established it upon the floods' (Ps. 24:2)? This refers to the seven seas and four rivers that surround the land of Israel. And what are the seven seas? The sea of Tiberias, the sea of Sodom, the sea of Helath, the sea of Hiltha, the sea of Sibkay, the sea of Aspamia, and the Great sea. And what are the four rivers? The Jordan, the Yarmuk, the Keramyhon, and the Pigah."

I.   LEVIATHAN AGAIN

     1.   IV:26: When R. Dimi came, he said R. Yohanan said, "Gabriel is destined to organize a hunt for Leviathan: 'Can you draw out Leviathan with a fish hook, or press down his tongue with a cord' (Job 40:25). And if the Holy One, blessed be He, does not help him, he will never be able to prevail over him: 'He only that made him can make his sword approach him' (Job 40:19)."

     2.   IV:27: When R. Dimi came, he said R. Yohanan said, "When Leviathan is hungry, he sends out fiery breath from his mouth and boils all the waters of the deep: 'He makes the deep to boil like a pot' (Job 41:23). And if he did not put his head into the Garden of Eden, no creature could endure his stench: 'He makes the sea like a spiced broth' (Job 41:23). And when he is thirsty, he makes the sea into furrows: 'He makes a path to shine after him' (Job 41:24)."

     3.   IV:28: Rabbah said R. Yohanan said, "The Holy One, blessed be He, is destined to make a banquet for the righteous out of the meat of Leviathan: 'Companions will make a banquet of it' (Job 40:30). The meaning of 'banquet' derives from the usage of the same word in the verse, 'And he prepared for them a great banquet and they ate and drank' (2 Kgs. 6:23)."

     4.   IV:29: Rabbah said R. Yohanan said, "The Holy One, blessed be He, is destined to make a tabernacle for the righteous out of the hide of Leviathan: 'Can you fill tabernacles with his skin' (Job 40:31). If someone has sufficient merit, a tabernacle is made for him; if he does not have sufficient merit, a mere shade is made for him: 'And his head with a fish covering' (Job 40:31). If someone has sufficient merit, a shade is made for him, if not, then a mere necklace is made for him: 'And necklaces about your neck' (Prov. 1:9). If someone has sufficient merit, a necklace is made for him; if not, then an amulet: 'And you will bind him for your maidens' (Job 40:29).

J.   OTHER STATEMENTS CONCERNING THE TIME OF THE MESSIAH

1. IV:30: "And I will make your pinnacles of rubies" (Isa. 54:12).
2. IV:31: "And your gates of carbuncles" (Isa. 60:3).
3. IV:32: Continuation of the foregoing.
4. IV:33: And said Rabbah said R. Yohanan, "The Holy One, blessed be He, is destined to make seven canopies for every righteous person: 'And the Lord will create over the whole habitation of Mount Zion and over her assemblies a cloud of smoke by day and the shining of a flaming fire by night, for over all the glory shall be a canopy' (Isa. 4:5). This teaches that for every one will the Holy One create a canopy in accord with the honor that is due him."

    a. IV:34: Supplement to the foregoing.

5. IV:35: Said R. Hama bar Hanina, "Ten canopies did the Holy One, blessed be He, make for the First Man in the garden of Eden: 'You were in Eden, the garden of God; every precious stone was your covering, the cornelian, the topaz, the emerald, the beryl, the onyx, the jasper, the sapphire, the carbuncle, and the emerald and gold' (Ezek. 28:13)."

    a. IV:36: Exegesis of proof-text used in the foregoing.

6. IV:37: Said Rabbah said R. Yohanan, "Jerusalem in the age to come will not be like Jerusalem in this age. To Jerusalem in this age anyone who wants to go up may go up. But to Jerusalem in the age to come only those who are deemed worthy of coming will go up."

7. IV:38: And said Rabbah said R. Yohanan, "The righteous are destined to be called by the name of the Holy One, blessed be He: 'Every one that is called by my name, and whom I have created for my glory, I have formed him, yes, I have made him' (Isa. 43:7)."

8. IV:39: Said R. Samuel bar Nahmani said R. Yohanan, "There are three who are called by the name of the Holy One, blessed be He, and these are they: the righteous, the Messiah, and Jerusalem."

9. IV:40: Said R. Eleazar, "The time will come when 'holy' will be said before the name of the righteous as it is said before the name of the Holy One, blessed be He: 'And it shall come to pass that he that is left in Zion and he that remains in Jerusalem shall be called holy' (Isa. 4:3)."

10. IV:41: And said Rabbah said R. Yohanan, "The Holy One, blessed be He, is destined to lift up Jerusalem to a height of three parasangs: 'And she shall be lifted up and be settled in her place' (Isa. 4:3). '...In her place' means 'like her place' Jerusalem will be lifted up to a height equal to the extent of the space it occupies."

    a. IV:42: Further as to Jerusalem in time to come.

    b. IV:43: As above.

  c. IV:44: As above.

  d. IV:45: As above.

   I. IV:46: Footnote to foregoing.

  e. IV:47: As above.

K. PURCHASE OF A SHIP: TRANSFER OF TITLE

 1. IV:48: As to the transfer of title to a ship—
Rab said, "Once the purchaser has dragged it any distance at all,
he has acquired title of possession to the ship."

  a. IV:49: Said R. Pappa, "One who sells a bond to someone else has to give him the following document in
writing in addition: 'Acquire it and everything that is in-
dentured within its terms.'"

  b. IV:50: Said Amemar, "The decided law is that letters
are acquired by an act of delivery and there is no need
to write a bill of sale as well, in accord therefore with
the position of Rabbi."

What we see is how the massive miscellany has been parachuted
down, whole, into the systematic exegesis of the Mishnah and the
halakhah—and we also can see why, as a topical appendix, the compiler found the composite pertinent. Readers already understand that,
in our setting, we should place this information in footnotes or in
an appendix at the end of the book, alternatives that were not tech-
nically available to the compilers of the Talmud, or, indeed, until
the invention of printing. What medieval writers did was add their
notes around the sides of the received text; only from the sixteenth
century, and indeed, much later, did the possibility of situating extraneous but useful information in footnotes and appendices arise.

But have we conceded too rapidly that we deal with a mere
miscellany, lacking all traits of rational organization, even of a topical character? Abbreviating appropriately, let me now repeat the
entire composite, this time clearly distinguishing not the rhetorical
but the topical (even propositional) components. I simply set forth
in a single column everything I take to form a single large scale
composite, distinct from everything fore and aft thereof. Now I shall
show that, in so grand and random a composite indeed, a clear
principle of organization governs, and in graphic terms, I shall indicate it.

4. A. *Said Rabbah, "Sailors told me,*
    'The wave that sinks a ship
    appears with a white froth of
    fire at the crest, and when
    stricken with clubs on which is

incised, "I am that I am, Yah, the Lord of Hosts, Amen, Amen, Selah," it will subside [and not sink the ship].'"

5. A. *Said Rabbah, "Sailors told me, 'Between one wave and another there is a distance of three hundred parasangs, and the height of the wave is the same three hundred parasangs. Once, when we were on a voyage, a wave lifted us up so high that we could see the resting place of the smallest star, and there was a flash, as if one shot forty arrows of iron; and if it had lifted us up any higher, we would have been burned by the heat. And one wave called to the next, "Friend, have you left anything in the world that you did not wash away? I'll go and wipe it out." And the other said, "Go see the power of the master, by whose command I must not pass the sand of the shore by even so much as the breadth of a thread:* 'Fear you not me? says the Lord? Will you not tremble at my presence, who have placed the sand for the bound of the sea, an everlasting ordinance, which it cannot pass' (Jer. 5:22).'"'*

6. A. *Said Rabbah, "I personally saw Hormin, son of Lilith, running on the parapet of the wall of Mahoza, and a rider, galloping below on horseback, could not catch up with him. Once they put a saddle for him two mules, which* **[73B]** *stood on two bridges of the Rognag, and he jumped from*

one to the other, backward and forward, holding two cups of wine in his hands, pouring from one to the other without spilling a drop on the ground. It was a stormy day: 'they that go down to the sea in ships mounted up to he heaven, they went down to the deeps' (Ps. 107:27). *Now when the state heard about this, they killed him."*

7.   A.   *Said Rabbah bar bar Hannah, "I personally saw a day-old antelope as big as Mount Tabor. How big is Mount Tabor? Four parasangs. Its neck was three parasangs long, and his head rested on a spot a parasang and a half. Its ball of shit blocked up the Jordan River."*

8.   A.   *And said Rabbah bar bar Hannah, "I personally saw a frog as big as the Fort of Hagronia—how big is that? sixty houses!—and a snake came along and swallowed the frog; a raven came along and swallowed the snake; and perched on a tree. So you can just imagine how strong was the tree."*

9.   A.   *And said Rabbah bar bar Hannah, "Once we were traveling on a ship, and we saw a fish [whale] in the nostrils of which a mud-eater had entered. The water cast up the fish and threw it on the shore. Sixty towns were destroyed by it, sixty towns got their food from it, and sixty towns salted the remnants, and from one of its eyeballs three hundred kegs of oil were filled. Coming back twelve months later,*

we saw that they were cutting rafters from the skeleton and rebuilding the towns."

10. A. *And said Rabbah bar bar Hannah, "Once we were traveling on a ship, and we saw a fish the back of which was covered with sand out of which grass was growing. We thought it was dry land so we went up and baked and cooked on the back of the fish. When the back got hut, it rolled over, and if the ship hadn't been nearby, we would have drowned."*

11. A. *And said Rabbah bar bar Hannah, "Once we were travelling on a ship, and the ship sailed between one fin of a fish and the other for three days and three nights; the fish was swimming upwards and we were floating downwards [with the wind]."*

12. A. *And said Rabbah bar bar Hannah, "Once we were travelling on a ship, and we saw a bird standing in the water only up to its ankles, with its head touching the sky. So we thought the water wasn't very deep, and we thought of going down to cool ourselves, but an echo called out, 'Don't go down into the water here, for a carpenter's axe dropped into this water seven years ago, and it hasn't yet reached the bottom.' And it was not only deep but also rapidly flowing."*

13. A. *And said Rabbah bar bar Hannah, "Once we were travelling in the desert, and we saw geese whose feathers fell out because they were so fat, and streams of fat flowed under them. I said to them, 'May we have a share of your meat in the world to come?' One of them lifted a wing, the*

other a leg [showing me what my portion would
be]. When I came before R. Eleazar, he said to
me, 'Israel will be called to account on account of these geese.'" [Slotki: the protracted suffering of the geese caused ᵇ
their growing fatness is due to Israel's siᵣ
which delay the coming of the Messiah.]

14. A. *And said Rabbah bar bar Hannah, "Once we
were travelling in the desert, and a Tai-Arab
joined us, who could pick up sand and smell it
and tell us which was the road to one place and
which to another. We said to him, 'How far are
we from water?' He said to us, 'Give me sand.'
We gave him some, and he said to us, 'Eight
parasangs.' When we gave him some sand later,
he told us that we were three parasangs off.' I
had changed the sand, but I was not able to
confuse him.*

15. A. *R. Yohanan told this story: "Once we were traveling along on a ship, and we saw a fish that
raised its head from the sea. Its eyes were like
two moons, and water streamed from its nostrils
like the two rivers of Sura."*

16. A. *R. Safra told this story: "Once we were traveling along on a ship, and we saw a fish that raised
its head from the sea. It had horns on which was
engraved: 'I am a lesser creature of the sea. I am
three hundred parasangs long, and I am going into
the mouth of Leviathan.'"*

17. A. *R. Yohanan told this story: "Once we were traveling along on a ship, and we saw a chest in
which were set jewels and peals, surrounded by
a kind of fish called a Karisa-fish. A diver went
down* **[74B]** *to bring up the chest, but the wished
realized it and was about to wrench his thigh.
He poured on it a bottle of vinegar, and it sank.
An echo came forth, saying to us, 'What in the
world have you got to do with the best of the wife
of R. Hanina, b. Dosa, who is going to store in
it the purple-blue for the righteous in the world
to come.'"*

18. A. *R. Judah the Hindu told this story: "Once we
were traveling along on a ship, and we saw a
jewel with a snake wrapped around it. A diver
went down to bring up the jewel. The snake drew
near, to swallow the ship. A raven came and bit
off its head. The waters turned to blood. Anoth-*

er snake and took the head of the snake and attached it to the body again, and it revived. The snake again came to swallow the ship. A bird again came and cut off its head. The diver seized the jewel and threw it into the ship. We had salted birds. We put the stone on them, and they took it up and flew away with it."

19. A. *Our rabbis have taught on Tannaite authority:*

    B. There was the case involving R. Eliezer and R. Joshua, who were travelling on a ship. R. Eliezer was sleeping, and R. Joshua was awake. R. Joshua shuddered and R. Eliezer woke up. He said to him, "What's wrong, Joshua? How come you trembled?"

20. A. *Said R. Ashi, "Said to me Huna bar Nathan, 'Once we were traveling in the desert, and we had taken with us a leg of meat. We cut it open, picked out [what we are not allowed to eat] and put it on the grass. While we were going to get some wood, the leg returned to its original form, and we roasted it. When we came back after twelve months, we saw the coals still glowing. When I presented the matter to Amemar, he said to me, 'The grass was an herb that can unite severed parts, and the coals were broom [which burns a long time inside, while the surface is extinguished].'*

21. A. "And God created the great sea monsters" (Gen. 1:21): R. Yohanan said, "This refers to Leviathan, [Slotki:] the slant serpent, and Leviathan the tortuous serpent: 'In that day the Lord with his sore and great and strong sword will punish Leviathan the slant serpent and Leviathan the tortuous serpent' (Is. 27:1)."

22. A. Said R. Judah said Rab, "Whatever the Holy One, blessed be he, created in his world did he create male and female, and so too, the Leviathan the slant serpent and Leviathan the tortuous serpent he created male and female, and if they had mated with one another, they would have destroyed the whole world.

23. A. And said R. Judah said Rab, "When the Holy One, blessed be he, proposed to create the world, he said to the prince of

the sea, 'Open your mouth, and swallow all the water in the world.'

24. A.   And said R. Judah said Rab, "The
Jordan issues from the cave of Paneas."

25. A.   *When R. Dimi came, he said R. Yohanan*
said, "What is the meaning of the verse, 'For
he has founded it upon the seas and
established it upon the floods' (Ps.
24:2)? This refers to the seven seas and
four rivers that surround the land of
Israel. And what are the seven seas?
The sea of Tiberias, the sea of Sodom, the sea of Helath, the sea of
Hiltha, the sea of Sibkay, the sea of
Aspamia, and the Great sea. And what
are the four rivers? The Jordan, the
Yarmuk, the Keramyhon, and the Pigah."

26. A.   *When R. Dimi came, he said R. Yohanan*
said, "Gabriel is destined to organize
a hunt **[75A]** for Leviathan: 'Can you
draw out Leviathan with a fish hook,
or press down his tongue with a cord'
(Job 40:25). And if the Holy One,
blessed be he, does not help him, he
will never be able to prevail over him:
'He only that made him can make his
sword approach him' (Job 40:19)."

27. A.   *When R. Dimi came, he said R. Yohanan*
said, "When Leviathan is hungry, he
sends out fiery breath from his mouth
and boils all the waters of the deep:
'He makes the deep to boil like a pot'
(Job 41:23). And if he did not put his
head into the Garden of Eden, no
creature could endure his stench: 'he
makes the sea like a spiced broth' (Job
41:23). And when he is thirsty, he
makes the sea into furrows: 'He makes
a path to shine after him' (Job 41:24)."

28. A.   Rabbah said R. Yohanan said, "The
Holy One, blessed be he, is destined
to make a banquet for the righteous
out of the meat of Leviathan: 'Companions will make a banquet of it' (Job
40:30). The meaning of 'banquet' de-

rives from the usage of the same word in the verse, 'And he prepared for them a great banquet and they ate and drank' (2 Kgs. 6:23).

29. A. Rabbah said R. Yohanan said, "The Holy One, blessed be he, is destined to make a tabernacle for the righteous out of the hide of Leviathan: 'Can you fill tabernacles with his skin' (Job 40:31). If someone has sufficient merit, a tabernacle is made for him; if he does not have sufficient merit, a mere shade is made for him: 'And his head with a fish covering' (Job 40:31). If someone has sufficient merit, a shade is made for him, if not, then a mere necklace is made for him: 'And necklaces about your neck' (Prov. 1:9). If someone has sufficient merit, a necklace is made for him; if not, then an amulet: 'And you will bind him for your maidens' (Job 40:29).

30. A. "And I will make your pinnacles of rubies" (Is. 54:12):

C. *"One said, 'The word translated rubies means onyx...'*

D. *"The other said, 'It means jasper.'*

E. *"Said to them the Holy One, blessed be he, 'Let it be in accord with both this opinion and that opinion.'"*

31. A. "And your gates of carbuncles" (Is. 60:3):

B. *That is in line with what what said when R. Yohanan went into session and expounded as follows:* "The Holy One, blessed be he, is destined to bring jewels and pearls that are thirty cubits by thirty and will cut out openings from them ten cubits by twenty, setting them up at the gates of Jerusalem."

32. A. *An objection was raised:*

B.   "And I will lead you upright" (Lev. 26:13)—

C.   [Since the word for "upright" can be read to
mean, at twice the normal
height], R. Meir says,
"That means, two hundred
cubits, twice the height of
the First Man."

33.   A.   And said Rabbah said R.
Yohanan, "The Holy One,
blessed be he, is destined to
make seven canopies for
every righteous person:
'And the Lord will create
over the whole habitation
of Mount Zion and over
her assemblies a cloud of
smoke by day and the shining of a flaming fire by
night, for over all the glory shall be a canopy' (Is.
4:5). This teaches that for
every one will the Holy
One create a canopy in accord with the honor that is
due him."

34.   A.   Along these same lines you
may say: "And you shall
put some of your honor
upon him" (Num. 27:20)—
but not of your honor.

B.   The elders of that generation said, "The face of
Moses glows like the face
of the sun, the face of
Joshua like the face of the
moon.

35.   A.   Said R. Hama bar Hanina,
"Ten canopies did the
Holy One, blessed be he,
make for the First Man in
the garden of Eden: 'You
were in Eden, the garden
of God; every precious
stone was your covering,
the cornelian, the topaz,

the emerald, the beryl, the onyx, the jasper, the sapphire, the carbuncle, and the emerald and gold' (Ez. 28:13)."

36. A. *What is the meaning of* "by the work of your timbrels and holes" (Ez. 28:13)?

B. Said R. Judah said Rab, "Said the Holy One, blessed be he, to Hiram, king of Tyre, 'I looked at you [for your arrogance] when I created the excretory holes of human beings."

C. *And some say that this is what he said to him,* "I looked at you **[75B]** when I decreed the death penalty against the first Man."

37. A. *What is the meaning of* "and over her assemblies" (Is. 4:5)?

B. Said Rabbah said R. Yohanan, "Jerusalem in the age to come will not be like Jerusalem in this age. To Jerusalem in this age anyone who wants to go up may go up. But to Jerusalem in the age to come only those who are deemed worthy of coming will go up."

38. A. And said Rabbah said R. Yohanan, "The righteous are destined to be called by the name of the Holy One, blessed be he: 'Every one that is called by my name, and whom I have created for my glory, I have formed him, yes, I have made him' (Is. 43:7)."

39. A. Said R. Samuel bar Nahmani said R. Yohanan,

"There are three who are
called by the name of the
Holy One, blessed be he,
and these are they: the
righteous, the Messiah,
and Jerusalem.

B.   "The righteous, as we have
just said.

C.   "The Messiah: 'And this is
the name whereby he shall
be called, the Lord is our
righteousness' (Jer. 23:6).

D.   "Jerusalem: 'It shall be
eighteen thousand reeds
round about, and the
name of the city from that
day shall be, "the Lord is
there" (Ez. 48:35). Do not
read 'there' but 'its
name.'"

40.   A.   Said R. Eleazar, "The time
will come when 'holy' will
be said before the name of
the righteous as it is said
before the name of the
Holy One, blessed be he:
'And it shall come to pass
that he that is left in Zion
and he that remains in
Jerusalem shall be called
holy' (Is. 4:3)."

41.   A.   And said Rabbah said R.
Yohanan, "The Holy One,
blessed be he, is destined to
lift up Jerusalem to a
height of three parasangs:
'And she shall be lifted up
and be settled in her place'
(Is. 4:3). '...in her place'
means 'like her place'
[Slotki: Jerusalem will be
lifted up to a height equal
to the extent of the space
it occupies]."

42.   A.   *So how do we know that the
place that Jerusalem occupied
was three parasangs?*

B. Said Rabbah, "Said to me a certain elder, 'I myself saw the original Jerusalem, and it filled up three parasangs.'"

43. A. And lest you suppose that there will be pain in the ascension, Scripture states, "Who are these that fly as a cloud and as the doves to their cotes" (Is. 60:8).

44. A. Said R. Hanina bar Pappa, "The Holy One blessed be he wanted to give Jerusalem a fixed size: 'Then said I, Whither do you go? And he said to me, To measure Jerusalem, to see what is its breadth and what is its length' (Zech. 2:6).

    B. "Said the ministering angels before the Holy One, blessed be he, 'Lord of the world, you have created in your world any number of cities for the nations of the earth, and you did not fix the measurements of their length or breadth. So are you going to fix measurements for Jerusalem, in the midst of which are your name, sanctuary, and the righteous?'

45. A. Said R. Simeon b. Laqish, "The Holy One, blessed be he, is destined to add to Jerusalem [Slotki:] a thousand gardens, a thousand towers, a thousand palaces, a thousand mansions. And each one of these will be as vast as Sepphoris in its hour of prosperity."

46. A. *It has been taught on Tannaite authority:*

    B. Said R. Yosé, "I saw Sepphoris in its hour of prosperity, and in it were one hundred and eighty thousand markets for those who sold pudding [alone]."

47. A. "And the side chambers were one over another, three and thirty times" (Ez. 41:6):

B. *What is the meaning of* three and thirty times?

C. Said R. Pappi in the name of R. Joshua of Sikni, "If there will be three Jerusalems, each building will contain thirty dwellings piled up on top of one another; if there will be thirty Jerusalems, then each building will contain three apartments on top of one another."

There is a very clear and simple topical program before us. We treat three subjects, and the order in which they are treated is the only possible order. By that I mean, had we dealt with the third topic first, it would have had no context nor would it have supplied a context to the first and second. The same is to be said with respect to the second; if it came first, then the first sequence would have made no sense at all. So the first sequence prepares the way for the second, the second, for the third. Within each set of compositions, there are some clear points of connection and not mere intersection, let alone formal coherence through a shared topic. Obviously, the triptych can be represented as propositional in only the most general terms. But, equally obviously, we have much more than just this, that, and the other thing, all thrown together: a miscellany. What we have, rather, is a different mode of agglutination of compositions into composites, and small composites into big composites, from the mode that is familiar to us throughout approximately 85-90% of the Bavli.

II. *Propositions for General Consideration*

These conclusions concerning the massive miscellany now stand firm:

1. In the miscellany before us, do we identify the first-class, cogent exposition of a proposition? Not at all. Is there the sustained consideration of a given problem? No again.
2. But is it a mere miscellany—disorganized, pointless, a scrap book of one thing and another? Hardly. Do principles of organization emerge? They certainly do.

Well, then, if not exactly a miscellany, but also not a composite of the kind the predominates in the Bavli in its exposition of the Mishnah, then what do we have? This brief account has raised more questions than it has settled. The main point must not be lost. The Bavli contains important composites that differ in their redactional, rhetorical, topical, and logical traits from its paramount composites. Compared to the dominant type of composite, the one that serves as Mishnah-commentary and amplification, these other composites exhibit a miscellaneous quality. The real issue is whether or not before us are anomalies, and for that purpose, we shall have to ask not only whether we deal with miscellanies, viewed in their own terms, but whether or not we confront anomalies, viewed in the context of the chapters that contain them. So let us examine three important composites and see [1] how they hold together, and [2] what place they make for themselves in the context of the chapters in which they occur, and [3] how, if at all, the composites or miscellaneous type of composite proposes to expand our understanding of the Mishnah.

In addition to propositional and even analytical composites, the framers of the Bavli also formed compositions into thematic composites, and on the face of it, this second type of composite presents the appearance of a miscellany. But far from forming a mere rubbish heap of this and that, this other type of composite proves not at all miscellaneous. Clear, governing, and entirely predictable principles allow us to explain how one composition is joined to another. Ordinarily, a sizable miscellany will tell us more about a subject that the Mishnah addresses or richly illustrate a principle that the Mishnah means to set forth through its cases and examples. In that sense, the miscellaneous kind of composite is set forth as Mishnah-commentary of a particular kind. As we have seen, an agglutinative composite may be formed by appeal to a common theme, ordinarily stated by the Mishnah or at least suggested by its contents, and several closely-related themes will then come under exposition in a massive miscellany. One common theme will be a passage of Scripture, systematically examined. A subordinate principle of agglutination will join composites attributed to the same authority or tradent, though it would be unusual for the compositions so joined to deal with entirely unrelated topics. So the principal point of differentiation between propositional composites and agglutinative ones is that the form analyze a problem, the latter illustrate a theme or even a proposition.

It follows that two modes of forming composites serve the framers of the Bavli, the paramount, propositional and analytical mode, and the subordinate, agglutinative sort. The one joins together a variety of distinct compositions into a propositional statement, commonly enriched with analytical initiatives, and frequently bearing a burden of footnotes and appendices. The other combines distinct compositions into a thematic composite, the proposition of which is ordinarily rather general and commonplace. A second principle of agglutinative composite-making appeals to common attributions, though when two or more compositions are joined into a composite because they are assigned to the same authority or tradental chain, they very likely will also bear in common an interest in a single theme, if not in a uniform proposition in connection with that theme.

III. *Genres of Aggadah and Halakhah and the Massive Miscellany*

Since all of the miscellanies we have examined concern theological or exegetical subjects, none focusing upon a problem of law, we should be tempted to propose that agglutinative discourse governs the treatment of one type of subject matter, theology or exegesis, but not another, the more prominent, and generally held, normative one, of law. To demonstrate that the distinction between lore and law (*aggadah* and *halakhah*) makes no difference in whether or not compositions will be linked into composites by appeal to propositional-analytical or merely agglutinative principles of formation, let me give a fine example of an agglutinative legal ("halakhic") passage, which shows beyond any doubt that there is no important point of distinction, so far as agglutinative discourse is concerned, between compositions and sub-composites of one kind and of the other. We find in both types of subject-matter precisely the same literary traits of composite-making. Here the compositions are joined agglutinatively, by reference to a common subject-matter; but the composite that results does not make a point, e.g. of proposition, analysis, or argument. Rather, it serves to illustrate a theme. We deal with Bavli Baba Batra chapter Five.

Mishnah/Bavli-tractate Baba Batra 5:11

A. **Said Rabban Simeon b. Gamaliel, "Under what circumstances?**

B. **"In the case of liquid measures.**

C. **"But in the case of dry measures, it is not necessary"**

D. [88B] **And [a shopkeeper] is liable to let the scales go down by a handbreadth [to the buyer's advantage].**

E. **[If] he was measuring out for him exactly, he has to give him an overweight—**

F. **one part in ten for liquid measure,**

G. **one part in twenty for dry measure.**

H. **In a place in which they are accustomed to measure with small measures, one must not measure with large measures;**

I. **with large ones, one must not measure with small;**

J. **[in a place in which it is customary] to smooth down [what is in the measure], one should not heap it up;**

K. **to heap it up, one should not smooth it down.**

III.1

A. **In a place in which they are accustomed to measure with small measures, one must not measure with large measures; with large ones, one must not measure with small; in a place in which it is customary to smooth down what is in the measure, one should not heap it up; to heap it up, one should not smooth it down:**

B. *Our rabbis have taught on Tannaite authority:*

C. How on the basis of Scripture do we know that **in a place in which it is customary to smooth down what is in the measure, one should not heap it up; to heap it up, one should not smooth it down**? Scripture says, "A perfect measure" (Dt. 25:15). [Slotki: deviating from the usual practice the buyer or the seller may defraud or mislead others.]

D. And how do we know that if one said, "Lo, where it is customary to heap up, I will level it off, and reduce the price,' or, in a place where they level, I will heap it up, and raise the price," they do not listen to him [he may not do so]?

E. Scripture says, "A perfect and just measure you shall have" (Dt. 25:15).

2. A. *Our rabbis have taught on Tannaite authority:*
   B. How on the basis of Scripture do we know that in a place where the practice is to allow an overweight, they do not give the exact weight, and in a place in which they give an exact weight, they do not give an overweight?
   C. Scripture says, "A perfect weight" (Dt. 25:15).
   D. And how on the basis of Scripture do we know that if one said in a place in which they give an overweight, "Lo, I shall give an exact weight and charge him less," or in a place in which they give an exact weight, "Lo, I shall give him an overweight and add to the price," they do not listen to him?
   E. Scripture says, "A perfect weight and a just one" (Dt. 25:15).
   F. Said R. Judah of Sura, "'You shall not have anything in your house' (Dt. 25:14). Why? Because of your 'diverse weights' (Dt. 25:13). But if you keep 'a perfect and just weight,' you shall have' (Dt. 25:15) things, 'if a perfect and just measure, you shall have....'"

There is no problem in explaining why No. 2 is tacked on to No. 1. The proposition is the same, so is the form. But what follows is another matter, since we are now going to entertain a different proposition altogether.

3. A. *Our rabbis have taught on Tannaite authority:*
   B. "You shall have...:" this teaches that they appoint market supervisors to oversee measures, but they do not appoint market supervisors to control prices.

No. 4 will now illustrate the foregoing.

4. A. *The household of the patriarch appointed market supervisors to oversee measures and to control prices. Said Samuel to Qarna, "Go, repeat the Tannaite rule to them:* they appoint market supervisors to oversee measures, but they do not appoint market supervisors to control prices.
   B. *He went out and instructed them:* "They appoint market supervisors to oversee measures and to control prices."
   C. *He said to him, "What do they call you? Qarna [horn]? Let a horn grow out of your eye." A horn grew out of his eye.*
   D. *And as for Qarna, in accord with what authority did he reach this conclusion?*
   E. *It was in accord with what Rammi bar Hama said R. Isaac said,* "They appoint market supervisors to oversee measures and to control prices, on account of crooks."

Now we have a miscellany, meaning, a set of compositions, each standing on its own foundation, all making clearly-articulated points, none related except in a shared theme to what stands fore or aft. What we shall also observe is sub-sets, clearly joined to one another, but connected to the larger context only by the general theme. These subsets do not require explicit specification, being obvious on the face of it.

5.   A.   *Our rabbis have taught on Tannaite authority:*
     B.   If somebody ordered a litra, he should measure out a litra; if he ordered a half-litra, he should measure out for him a half litra; a quarter-litra, he should measure out a quarter.
     C.   *So what does that passage tell us?*
     D.   *It is that we provide weights in these denominations.*
6.   A.   *Our rabbis have taught on Tannaite authority:*
     B.   If someone ordered three quarters of a litra, he should not say to him, "Weigh out for me three quarters of a litra one by one," but he should say to him, "Weight out a litra for me but leave out a quarter-litra with the meat" [Slotki: on the other scale].
7   A.   *Our rabbis have taught on Tannaite authority:*
     B.   If someone wanted to order ten litras, he should not say to him, "Weigh them out for me one by one and allow an overweight for each," but all of them are weighed together, with one overweight covering the whole order [cf. T. B.B. 5:9B-I]
8.   A.   *Our rabbis have taught on Tannaite authority:*
     B.   [Slotki:] The hollow handle in which the tongue of the balance rests must be suspended in the air three handbreadths [removed from the roof from which the balance hangs], and it must be three handbreadths above the ground.
     C.   The beam and the rope that goes with it should be twelve handbreadths, and the balances of wool dealers and glass ware dealers must be suspended two handbreadths in the air from the ceiling and two above the ground. The beams and ropes that go with them must be nine handbreadths in length. The balance of a shopkeeper and a householder must be suspended a handbreadth in the air from above and a handbreadth above the ground. The beam and ropes that go with them must be six handbreadths. A gold balance must be suspended three fingerbreadths in the air from above and three above the ground. I don't know the length of the beam and the cords.
     D.   *What kind of balance is the one mentioned first [before the specific rulings for those of the wool dealers, glass ware dealers, and so on]?*
     E.   **[89B]** *Said R. Pappa, "The one used for heavy pieces of metal."*
9.   A.   Said R. Mani bar Patish, "Just as they have specified certain restrictions with regard to disqualifying balances for commercial purposes, so they have laid down disqualifications with regard to their constituting utensils for the purpose of receiving cultic uncleanness."

B.   *What does he tell us that we do not learn from the following:* **The cord of the scales of the storekeepers and [or] of household-ers—[to be susceptible to uncleanness must be in length at least] a handbreadth. A handle of the ax at its front—a handbreadth. The projection of the shaft of a pair of compasses—a handbreadth. The shaft of a stone-mason's chisel—a handbreadth A cord of the balances of wool dealers and of glass weighers—two hand-breadths. The shaft of a millstone chisel—two hand-breadths. The battle ax of the legions—two handbreadths. The goldsmith's hammer—two hand-breadths. And of the carpenters—three handbreadths]** **[M. Kel. 29:5-6]**/ [Slotki: since this restriction has been applied to one kind of balance, are not the other kinds of balance to be implied?]

C.   The statement that he made is necessary to deal with the sizes of the beam and cords [that are not dealt with at the parallel].

A subset now follows, Nos. 10-13, glossed by No. 14.

10. A.   *Our rabbis have taught on Tannaite authority:*
    B.   They make weights out of neither tin or led or alloy but of stone or glass.

11. A.   *Our rabbis have taught on Tannaite authority:*
    B.   They make the strike not out of a board, because it is light, nor out of metal, because it is heavy, but out of olive, nut, sycamore, or box wood.

12. A.   *Our rabbis have taught on Tannaite authority:*
    B.   They do not make the strike thick on one side and thin on the other.
    C.   They do not make the strike with a single quick movement, be-cause striking in that way brings loss to the seller and advantage to the buyer, nor very slowly, since this is a loss to the buyer but a benefit to the seller.
    D.   In regard to all of these shady practices, said Rabban Yohanan b. Zakkai, "Woe is me if I speak, woe is me if I do not speak. If I speak, then sharpies will learn from me, and if I don't speak, then the sharpies will say, 'The disciples of sages haven't got the slightest idea what we are doing.'"

13. A.   *The question was raised: "So did he speak of them or didn't he?"*
    B.   Said R. Samuel bar R. Isaac, "He did speak of them: 'For the ways of the Lord are right, and the just walk in them; but trans-gressors stumble therein' (Hos. 14:10)."

14. A.   *Our rabbis have taught on Tannaite authority:*
    B.   "You shall do no unrighteousness in judgment, in surveying, weight, or in measure" (Lev. 19:35):
    C.   "in surveying:" these refers to surveying the real estate, mean-

ing, one should not measure for one party in the dry season and another in the rainy season.

D. "weight:" one should not keep one's weights in salt.

E. "in measure" (Lev. 19:35): one should not make the liquid form a head.

F. And that yields an argument a fortiori: if with reference to a mere "measure" [Lev. 19:35), which is merely one sixth of a log, the Torah demanded meticulous attention, how much the more so must one give meticulous case in measuring out a hin, half a hin, a third of a hin, a quarter of a hin, a log, a half a log, a quarter of a log, a toman, half a toman, and an uqla.

15. A. Said R. Judah said Rab, "It is forbidden for someone to keep in his house a measure that is either smaller or larger than the norm, even for the purpose of a piss pot."

B. *Said R. Pappa, "But we have stated that rule only in a place where measures are not properly marked with a seal, but where they are properly sealed, they are permitted, since, if the purchaser sees no mark, he is not going to accept their use. And even in a place where measures are not properly marked with a seal, we have stated that rule only in a case in which they are not supervised [by administrative officers of the market], but if they are ordinarily supervised, we should have no objection."*

C. *But that is not the case, for sometimes the buyer may come by at twilight and may happen to take a faulty measure. And so too that has been taught on Tannaite authority:* It is forbidden for someone to keep in his house a measure that is either smaller or larger than the norm, even for the purpose of a piss pot. But he may make a seah measure, a tarqab, a half tarqab, a qab, a half qab, a quarter qab, a toman, **[90B]** and an ukla measure. How much is an uqla-measure? It is a fifth of a quarter of a qab. In the case of liquid measures, one may make a hin, a half hin, third hin, quarter hin, log, half log, quarter log, eighth log, and eight of an eighth, which is a qortob.

D. *So why shouldn't someone also make a double-qab measure?*

E. *It might be confused with a tarqab.*

F. *Therefore people may err by as much as a third.*

G. *If so, then a qab also people should not make, since they might confused it with a half-tarqab. Rather, as to a double qab, this is the reason that one is not to make it, specifically, that one will confused it with a half tarqab.*

H. *And this proves that one may err by a quarter.*

I. *If so, a half toman and an ukla measure are things people should not make.* [Slotki: the difference between a half toman, a sixteen qab, and an ukla, a twentieth qab, is only one eightieth of a qab, which is a fifth of the half toman, less than a quarter, so that these two measures could certainly be mistaken for one another.]

J. *Said R. Pappa, "With small measures people are quite expert."*

K. *What about a third of a hin and a fourth of a hin—shouldn't people be forbidden to make these?*

L. *Since these were utilized in the sanctuary, rabbis made no decree in their regard.*

M. *Well, shouldn't there be a precautionary decree with respect to the sanctuary?*

N. *The priests are meticulous in their work.*

16. A. Said Samuel, "They may not increase the size of the measures [whether or not people concur] by more than a sixth, nor the coins by more than a sixth, and he who makes a profit must not profit by more than a sixth."

B. What is the operative consideration for the first of these three rulings?

C. *If we say that it is because the market prices will rise, then for that same consideration, it should not be permitted to increase the size of the measures even by a sixth. And if the operative consideration is overreaching, so that the transaction should not have to be annulled, did not* Raba say, "One can retract from an agreement that involves fraud in measure, weight, or number, even though it is less than the standard, a sixth, of overreaching." *And if the operative consideration is that the dealer may not incur any loss, then is the whole purpose of the law to guard him from loss? Is he not entitled to make a profit? But "buy and sell at no profit, merely to be called a merchant!"*

D. *Rather, said R. Hisda, "Samuel identified a verse of Scripture and interpreted it,* 'And the shekel shall be twenty gerahs, twenty sheqels, twenty-five sheqels, ten and five sheqels shall be your maneh' (Ez. 45:12). **[90B]** *Now was the maneh to be two hundred forty denars?* [But it is supposed to be twenty five sheqels or a hundred denars (Cashdan).] *But three facts are to be inferred from this statement:* [1] the maneh used in the sanctuary is worth double what the maneh is usually worth; [2] they may not increase the size of the measures [whether or not people concur] by more than a sixth, and [3] the sixth is added over and above the original [so to add a sixth, the original is divided into five parts and another part of equal value, making a sixth one, then is added to it, so the maneh consisted of 240 denars (Cashdan, *Menahot*)]."

17. A. *R. Pappa bar Samuel ordained a measure of three qepizi. They said to him,* "Lo, said Samuel, 'They may not increase the size of the measures [whether or not people concur] by more than a sixth'!"

B. *He said to them, "What I am ordaining is an entirely new measure." He sent it to Pumbedita, and they did not adopt it. He sent it to Papunia and they adopted it, naming it the Pappa-measure.*

Any doubt that we are dealing with a miscellany is removed by what follows, which in no way pertains to the foregoing in any detail. And yet it is introduced for a very clear purpose, which is to make a point about a common theme and proposition: fair-dealing in the market, giving and getting true value.

18. A. *Our rabbis have taught on Tannaite authority:*

B. Concerning those who store up produce, lend money on usury, falsify measures, and price-gouge, Scripture says, "Saying, when will the new moon be gone, that we may sell grain, and the Sabbath, that we may set forth grain? Making the ephah small and the shekel great and falsifying the balances of deceit" (Amos 8:5). And in their regard, Scripture states, "The Lord has sworn by the pride of Jacob, surely I will never forget any of their works" (Amos 8:7).

C. *What would be an example of those who store up produce?*

D. *Said R. Yohanan, "Like Shabbetai the produce-hoarder."*

19. A. *The father of Samuel would sell produce at the early market price when the early market price prevailed [that is, cheap, so keeping prices down through the year (Slotki)]. Samuel his son held the produce back and sold it when the late market prices prevailed, but at the early market price.*

F. *They sent word from there, "The father is better than the son. How come? Prices that have been held down remain down."*

20. A. Said Rab, "Someone may store up his own produce" [but may not hoard for trading purposes (Slotki)].

B. *So too it has been taught on Tannaite authority:*

C. **[Following Tosefta's version:] They do not hoard in the Land of Israel things upon which life depends, for example, wine, oil, fine flour, and produce. But things upon which life does not depend, for instance, cummin and spice, lo, this is permitted. And they put things in storage for three years, the eve of the seventh year, the seventh year itself, and the year after the seventh year.**

D. **Under what circumstances.**

E. **In the case of that which one purchases in the market.**

F. **But in the case of what one puts aside from what he himself has grown, even for a period of ten years it is permitted.**

G. **But in a year of famine even a qab of carobs one should not put into storage, because he brings a curse on the prices [by forcing them upward through artificial demand] [T. A.Z. 4:1A-G].**

21. A. *Said R. Yosé b. R. Hanina to Puga his servant, "Go, store up fruit for me for the next three years: the eve of the Sabbatical year, the Sabbatical year, and the year after the Sabbatical year."*

22. A. *Our rabbis have taught on Tannaite authority:*

B. **They do not export from the Land of Israel to Syria things upon which life depends, for example, wine, oil, and fine flour.**

C. **R. Judah b. Batera says, "I say that they export wine to Syria, because in doing so, one diminishes silliness [in the Land of Israel]."**

D. Just as they do not export to Syria, so they do not export from one hyparchy to another.

E. And R. Judah permits doing so [91A] from one hyparchy to another [T. A.Z. 4:2].

23. A. *Our rabbis have taught on Tannaite authority:*

B. **They are not to make a profit in the land of Israel from the necessities of life, for instance, wine, oil, and flour.**

C. **They said concerning R. Eleazar b. Azariah that he would make a profit from wine and oil all his life [T. A.Z. 4:1H-J].**

D. *In the matter of wine, he concurred with the view of R. Judah [b. Batera], and in the matter of oil, as it happens, in the place where R. Eleazar b. Azariah lived, oil was abundant.*

24. A. *Our rabbis have taught on Tannaite authority:*

B. People are not to profit from eggs twice.

C. *Said Mari bar Mari, "There was a dispute between Rab and Samuel. One says, 'Two for one' [selling for two what was bought for one], and the other said, 'Selling by a dealer to a dealer' [making two profits on the same object]."*

25. A. *Our rabbis have taught on Tannaite authority:*

B. They sound the alarm on account of a collapse in the market in trading goods even on the Sabbath.

C. Said R. Yohanan, "For instance, linen clothing in Babylonia and wine and oil in the Land of Israel."

D. *Said R. Joseph, "But that is the case when these are so cheap that ten go for the price of six."*

26. A. *Our rabbis have taught on Tannaite authority:*

B. **A person is not allowed to emigrate from the Land of Israel unless wheat goes at the price of two seahs for a sela.**

C. **Said R. Simeon, "Under what circumstances? Only in a case in which he does not find any to buy even at that price. But if he finds some to buy at that price, even if a seah of grain goes for a sela, he should not emigrate."**

D. **And so did R. Simeon bar Yohai say, "Elimelech, Machlon and Kilion were the great men of his time, and one of those who sustained the generation. But because he went abroad, he and his sons died in famine. But all the Israelites were able to survive on their own land, as it is said, 'and when they came to Bethlehem, the whole town was stirred because of them' (Ruth 1:19). This teaches that all of the town had survived, but he and his sons had died in the famine" [T. A.Z. 4:4A-H].**

27. A. "and when they came to Bethlehem, the whole town was stirred because of them, and the women said, 'Is this Naomi'" (Ruth 1:19):

B. *What is the meaning of the phrase, "Is this Naomi"?*

C. Said R. Isaac, "They said, 'Did you see what happened to Naomi, who emigrated from the Land for a foreign country?'"

28. A. And said R. Isaac, "The day that Ruth the Moabite emigrated from the Land to a foreign land,the wife of Boaz died. *That is in line with what people say: 'Before a person dies, his successor as master of the house is appointed.'*"

29. A. Said Rabbah bar R. Huna said Rab, "Isban is the same as Boaz."

B. *So what in the world does that mean?*

C. *It is in line with what Rabbah b. R. Huna further said, for* said Rabbah bar R. Huna said Rab, "Boaz made for his sons a hundred and twenty wedding banquets: 'And Isban had thirty sons and thirty daughters he sent abroad, and thirty daughters he brought from abroad for his sons, and he judged Israel seven years' (Judges 12:9). For each one of them he made two wedding feasts, one in the household of the father, the other in the household of the father in law. But to none of them did he invite Manoah, for he said, *'How will that barren mule ever repay my hospitality?'* And all of them died in his lifetime. That is in line with what people say, *'In your lifetime you begot sixty? What good are the sixty? Marry again and get another one, brighter than all sixty.'*"

30. A. Said R. Hanan bar Raba said Rab, "Elimelech and Salmon and 'such a one' [Ruth 4:1] and the father of Naomi were all sons of Nahshon b. Amminadab [Ex. 6:23, Num. 10:14]."

B. *So what in the world does that mean?*

C. It is that even one who has a substantial store of unearned merit gained from his answers, it will serve him no good when he emigrates from the Land to a foreign land."

31. A. And said R. Hanan bar Raba said Rab, *"The mother of Abraham was named Amathelai, daughter of Karnebo; the name of the mother of Haman was Amatehilai, daughter of Orabti; and the mnemonic will be, 'unclean to the unclean, clean to the clean.' The mother of David was Nizbeth daughter of Adael, the mother of Samson was Zlelponit, and his sister was Nasyan."*

B. *So what?*

C. For answering heretics.

32. A. And said R. Hanan bar Raba said Rab, "For ten years our father, Abraham, was kept in prison, three in Kuta, seven in Kardu."

B. *And R. Dimi of Nehardea repeats the matter in reverse order.*

C. *Said R. Hisda, "The lesser Kuta is the same as Ur of the Chaldees [Gen. 11:31]."*

33. A. And said R. Hanan bar Raba said Rab, "The day on which our father, Abraham, died, all of the principal authorities of the nations of the world formed a line and said, 'Woe is the world that has lost **[91B]** its leader, woe to the ship that has lost its helmsman.'"

34. A. "And you are exalted as head above all" (1 Chr. 29:11):

B. *Said R. Hanan bar Raba said Rab, "Even the superintendent of the water supply is appointed by Heaven."*

35. A. Said R. Hiyya bar Abin said R. Joshua b. Qorhah, "God forbid! Even if [Elimelech and his family] had found bran, they would never have emigrated. So why were they punished? Because they should have besought mercy for their generation but failed to do so: 'When you cry, let them that you have gathered deliver you' (Is. 57:13)."

36. A. Said Rabbah bar bar Hannah said R. Yohanan, "This [prohibition against emigration] has been taught only when money is cheap [and abundant] and produce expensive, but when money is expensive [and not to be found, there being no capital], even if four seahs cost only a sela, it is permitted to emigrate."

B. *Said R. Yohanan, "I remember when four seahs of grain cost a sela and many died of starvation in Tiberias, not having an issar for bread."*

C. *And said R. Yohanan, "I remember when workmen wouldn't agree to work on the east side of town, where workers were dying because of the scent of bread [which they could not afford to buy]."*

37. A. *And said R. Yohanan, "I remember when a child would break open a carob pod and a line of honey would run over both his arms."*

B. *And said R. Eleazar, "I remember when a raven would grab a piece of meat and a line of oil would run down from the top of the wall to the ground."*

C. *And said R. Yohanan, "I remember when boys and girls would promenade in the market at the age of sixteen or seventeen and not sin."*

D. *And said R. Yohanan, "I remember when they would say in the house of study, 'Who agrees with them falls into their power, who trusts in them—what is his becomes theirs."*

38. A. It is written, "Mahlon and Chilion" (Ruth 1:2) and it is written "Joash and Saraph" (1 Chr. 4:22)!

B. Rab and Samuel—

C. One said, "Their names really were Mahlon and Chilion, and why were they called Joash? Because they despaired hope of redemption [the words for Joash and despair using the same letters], and Saraph? because they become liable by the decree of the Omnipresent to be burned."

D. And the other said, "Their names really were Joash and Saraph, but they were called Mahlon and Chilion, Mahlon, because they profaned their bodies [the words for Mahlon and profane using the same letters], and Chilion, because they were condemned by the Omnipresent to destruction [the words for destruction and Chilion using the same letters]."

E. *It has been taught on Tannaite authority in accord with the view of him who said that their names really were Mahlon and Chilion. For it has been taught on Tannaite authority:* What is the meaning of the verse, "And Jokim and the men of Cozeba and Joash and Saraph, who had dominion in Moab, and Jashubilehem, and the things are ancient"?1 Chr. 4:22)?

F. "Jokim:" this refers to Joshua, who kept his oath to the men of Gibeon [Josh. 9:15, 26].

G. "and the men of Cozeba:" these are the men of Gibeon who lied to Joshua [the words for lie and Cozeba using the same letters] [Josh. 9:4].

H. "and Joash and Saraph:" Their names really were Mahlon and Chilion, and why were they called Joash? Because they despaired hope of redemption [the words for Joash and despair using the same letters], and Saraph? because they become liable by the decree of the Omnipresent to be burned.

I. "who had dominion in Moab:" they married wives of the women of Moab.

J. "and Jashubilehem:" this refers to Ruth of Moab, who had returned [using letters that are shared with Jashub] and remained in Bethlehem of Judah.

K. "and the things are ancient:" these things were stated by the Ancient of Days.

39. A. "These were the potters and those that dwelt among plantations and hedges; there they dwelt occupied in the kings work" (1 Chr. 4:23):

B. "These were the potters:" this refers to the sons of Jonadab, son of Rahab, who kept the oath of their father [Jer. 35:6].

C. "and those that dwelt among plantations:" this speaks of Solomon, who in his rule was like a fecund plant.

D. "and hedges:" this refers to the Sanhedrin, who hedged in the breaches in Israel.

E. "there they dwelt occupied in the kings work:" this speaks of Ruth of Moab, who lived to see the rule of Solomon, her grandson's grandson: "And Solomon caused a throne to be set up for the king's mother" (1 Kgs. 2:19), in which connection R. Eleazar said, "For the mother of the dynasty."

40. A. *Our rabbis have taught on Tannaite authority:*

B. "And you shall eat of the produce, the old store" (Lev. 25:22)—without requiring preservatives.

C. *What is the meaning of* without requiring preservatives?

D. R. Nahman said, "Without grain worms."

E. And R. Sheshet said, "Without blast."

F. *It has been taught on Tannaite authority in accord with the view of R. Sheshet, and it has been taught on Tannaite authority in accord with the view of R. Nahman.*

G. *It has been taught on Tannaite authority in accord with the view of R. Nahman:*

H. "And you shall eat the old store" (Lev. 25:22)—might one suppose that the sense is that the Israelites will be eager for the new produce because last year's has been destroyed [by the grain worm]? Scripture says, "until her produce came in," that is, until

the produce will come on its own [without an early, forced harvest (Slotki)].

I.   *It has been taught on Tannaite authority in accord with the view of R. Sheshet:*

J.   "And you shall eat of the produce, the old store" (Lev. 25:22)—
     might one suppose that the sense is that the Israelites will be ea-
     ger for the new produce because last year's has been spoiled
     [Slotki: by the blast]? Scripture states, "until her produce came
     in," that is, until the new crop will come in the natural way.

41. A.   *Our rabbis have taught on Tannaite authority:*

     B.   "And you shall eat old store long kept" (Lev. 26:10)—whatever
          is of an older vintage than its fellow is better in quality than its
          fellow.

     C.   I know that that is so only of things that are ordinarily aged. What
          about things that are not ordinarily aged?

     D.   Scripture is explicit: "old store long kept" (Lev. 26:10)—in all
          cases.

42. A.   "And you shall bring forth the old from before the new" (Lev.
          26:10)—

     B.   this teaches that the storehouses will be full of last year's crop,
          and the threshing floors, this year's crop, and the Israelites will
          say, "How are we going to remove the one before the other?"

     C.   *Said R. Pappa, "Everything is better when aged, except for dates, beer, and
          fish-hash."*

III.1, 2 provide a scriptural basis for the rule and principle of the
Mishnah. The key-verse of No. 2 accounts for the inclusion of No.
3, which carries in its wake No. 4. Further Tannaite thematic supplements are at Nos. 5-8. No. 8 is glossed by No. 9, and then Nos.
10-12+13, 14 continue the Tannaite supplement. Carrying forward
the general theme at hand, Nos. 15-42 form a miscellany built around
the general theme before us. To show graphically the place of each
composition within the larger composite at hand, let me now reproduce the outline of the entire passage:

D.   IN A PLACE IN WHICH THEY ARE ACCUSTOMED TO MEASURE WITH
     SMALL MEASURES, ONE MUST NOT MEASURE WITH LARGE MEASURES;
     WITH LARGE ONES, ONE MUST NOT MEASURE WITH SMALL; IN A
     PLACE IN WHICH IT IS CUSTOMARY TO SMOOTH DOWN WHAT IS IN
     THE MEASURE, ONE SHOULD NOT HEAP IT UP; TO HEAP IT UP, ONE
     SHOULD NOT SMOOTH IT DOWN.

     1.   III:1: How on the basis of Scripture do we know that in a
          place in which it is customary to smooth down what is in the
          measure, one should not heap it up; to heap it up, one should
          not smooth it down? Scripture says, "A perfect measure"
          (Deut. 25:15). Deviating from the usual practice the buyer
          or the seller may defraud or mislead others.

2. III:2: How on the basis of Scripture do we know that in a place where the practice is to allow an overweight, they do not give the exact weight, and in a place in which they give an exact weight, they do not give an overweight?
    a. III:3: "You shall have...": this teaches that they appoint market supervisors to oversee measures, but they do not appoint market supervisors to control prices.
    b. III:4: The household of the patriarch appointed market supervisors to oversee measures and to control prices. Said Samuel to Qarna, "Go, repeat the Tannaite rule to them: They appoint market supervisors to oversee measures, but they do not appoint market supervisors to control prices.
3. III:5: If somebody ordered a litra, he should measure out a litra; if he ordered a half-litra, he should measure out for him a half-litra; a quarter-litra, he should measure out a quarter.
4. III:6: If someone ordered three-quarters of a litra, he should not say to him, "Weigh out for me three-quarters of a litra one by one," but he should say to him, "Weight out a litra for me but leave out a quarter-litra with the meat" on the other scale.
5. III:7: If someone wanted to order ten litras, he should not say to him, "Weigh them out for me one by one and allow an overweight for each," but all of them are weighed together, with one overweight covering the whole order cf. T. B.B. 5:9B-I.

E. THE CORRECT WEIGHTS AND MEASURES: DEFINITIONS

1. III:8: The hollow handle in which the tongue of the balance rests must be suspended in the air three handbreadths removed from the roof from which the balance hangs, and it must be three handbreadths above the ground.
2. III:9: Said R. Mani bar Patish, "Just as they have specified certain restrictions with regard to disqualifying balances for commercial purposes, so they have laid down disqualifications with regard to their constituting utensils for the purpose of receiving cultic uncleanness."
3. III:10: They make weights out of neither tin or lead or alloy but of stone or glass.
4. III:11: They make the strike not out of a board, because it is light, nor out of metal, because it is heavy, but out of olive, nut, sycamore, or box wood.
5. III:12: They do not make the strike thick on one side and thin on the other.
    a. III:13: Gloss of foregoing.

F.   FALSIFYING WEIGHTS AND MEASURES

1.   III:14: "You shall do no unrighteousness in judgment, in sur-
     veying, weight, or in measure" (Lev. 19:35): "In surveying":
     these refers to surveying the real estate, meaning, one should
     not measure for one party in the dry season and another in
     the rainy season. "Weight": one should not keep one's weights
     in salt.

2.   III:15: Said R. Judah said Rab, "It is forbidden for someone
     to keep in his house a measure that is either smaller or larger
     than the norm, even for the purpose of a piss pot."

3.   III:16: Said Samuel, "They may not increase the size of the
     measures whether or not people concur by more than a sixth,
     nor the coins by more than a sixth, and he who makes a profit
     must not profit by more than a sixth."

     a.   III:17: R. Pappa bar Samuel ordained a measure of three
          qepizi. They said to him, "Lo, said Samuel, 'They may
          not increase the size of the measures whether or not
          people concur by more than a sixth'!"

G.   HOARDING; MANIPULATING THE MARKET PRICES

1.   III:18: Concerning those who store up produce, lend money
     on usury, falsify measures, and price gouge, Scripture says,
     "Saying, when will the new moon be gone, that we may sell
     grain, and the Sabbath, that we may set forth grain? Mak-
     ing the ephah small and the sheqel great and falsifying the
     balances of deceit" (Amos 8:5). And in their regard, Scrip-
     ture states, "The Lord has sworn by the pride of Jacob, surely
     I will never forget any of their works" (Amos 8:7).

     a.   III:19: The father of Samuel would sell produce at the
          early market price when the early market price prevailed
          that is, cheap, so keeping prices down through the year.
          Samuel his son held the produce back and sold it when
          the late market prices prevailed, but at the early mar-
          ket price.

2.   III:20: Said Rab, "Someone may store up his own produce"
     but may not hoard for trading purposes."

     a.   III:21: Said R. Yosé b. R. Hanina to Puga his servant,
          "Go, store up fruit for me for the next three years: the
          eve of the Sabbatical Year, the Sabbatical Year, and the
          year after the Sabbatical Year."

3.   III:22: They do not export from the Land of Israel to Syria
     things upon which life depends, for example, wine, oil, and
     fine flour.

4.   III:23 They are not to make a profit in the Land of Israel
     from the necessities of life, for instance, wine, oil, and flour.

5.   III:24: People are not to profit from eggs twice.

6. III:25: They sound the alarm on account of a collapse in the market in trading goods even on the Sabbath.

H. MIGRATION FROM THE LAND OF ISRAEL BY REASON OF FAMINE. THE CASE OF RUTH'S FAMILY

1. III:26: A person is not allowed to emigrate from the Land of Israel unless wheat goes at the price of two seahs for a sela.

2. III:27: "And when they came to Bethlehem, the whole town was stirred because of them, and the women said, 'Is this Naomi'" (Ruth 1:19): What is the meaning of the phrase, "Is this Naomi"?

3. III:28: And said R. Isaac, "The day that Ruth the Moabite emigrated from the Land to a foreign land, the wife of Boaz died. That is in line with what people say: 'Before a person dies, his successor as master of the house is appointed.'"

4. III:29: Said Rabbah bar R. Huna said Rab, "Isban is the same as Boaz."

5. III:30: Said R. Hanan bar Raba said Rab, "Elimelech and Salmon and 'such a one' (Ruth 4:1) and the father of Naomi were all sons of Nahshon b. Amminadab (Ex. 6:23, Num. 10:14)."

   a. III:31: And said R. Hanan bar Raba said Rab, "The mother of Abraham was named Amathelai, daughter of Karnebo; the name of the mother of Haman was Amatehilai, daughter of Orabti; and the mnemonic will be, 'unclean to the unclean, clean to the clean.' The mother of David was Nizbeth daughter of Adael, the mother of Samson was Zlelponit, and his sister was Nasyan."

   b. III:32: And said R. Hanan bar Raba said Rab, "For ten years our father, Abraham, was kept in prison, three in Kuta, seven in Kardu."

   c. III:33: And said R. Hanan bar Raba said Rab, "The day on which our father, Abraham, died, all of the principal authorities of the nations of the world formed a line and said, 'Woe is the world that has lost its leader, woe to the ship that has lost its helmsman.'"

   d. III:34: "And you are exalted as head above all" (1 Chr. 29:11): Said R. Hanan bar Raba said Rab, "Even the superintendent of the water supply is appointed by Heaven."

6. III:35: Said R. Hiyya bar Abin said R. Joshua b. Qorhah, "God forbid! Even if Elimelech and his family had found bran, they would never have emigrated. So why were they punished? Because they should have besought mercy for their generation but failed to do so: 'When you cry, let them that you have gathered deliver you' (Isa. 57:13)."

7.   III:36: Said Rabbah bar bar Hannah said R. Yohanan, "This prohibition against emigration has been taught only when money is cheap and abundant and produce expensive, but when money is expensive and not to be found, there being no capital, even if four seahs cost only a sela, it is permitted to emigration."

    a.   III:37: And said R. Yohanan, "I remember when a child would break open a carob pod and a line of honey would run over both his arms."

8.   III:38: It is written, "Mahlon and Chilion" (Ruth 1:2) and it is written "Joash and Saraph" (1 Chr. 4:22)! Rab and Samuel— One said, "Their names really were Mahlon and Chilion, and why were they called Joash? Because they despaired hope of redemption the words for Joash and despair using the same letters, and Saraph? Because they become liable by the decree of the Omnipresent to be burned."

9.   III:39: "These were the potters and those that dwelt among plantations and hedges; there they dwelt occupied in the king's work" (1 Chr. 4:23): "These were the potters": this refers to the sons of Jonadab, son of Rahab, who kept the oath of their father (Jer. 35:6).

I.   THE BLESSINGS OF PLENTY

1.   III:40: "And you shall eat of the produce, the old store" (Lev. 25:22)—without requiring preservatives.

2.   III:41: "And you shall eat old store long kept" (Lev. 26:10)— whatever is of an older vintage than its fellow is better in quality than its fellow.

3.   III:42: "And you shall bring forth the old from before the new" (Lev. 26:10)—This teaches that the storehouses will be full of last year's crop, and the threshing floors, this year's crop, and the Israelites will say, "How are we going to remove the one before the other?"

The outline tells the whole story: why each component, each composition, joined to its neighbors into a composite, is situated where it is, and what contribution everyone of them makes to the statement of the entire construction. Once more we are able to understand why the compilers of the passage have arranged matters as they have, what, in their minds, which do communicate with ours, they saw as the principle(s) of organization.

I see no formal differences between the miscellany at hand and those we have already examined. The only difference is subject-matter—but not *classification of subject-matter*. Is it possible, then, to state the propositions of the subsets of the miscellany? These seem to me to state the paramount proposals:

1. People are to employ honest measures and when selling, to give accurate and honest measures: Nos. 5-17.
2. People are not to take advantage of shortages nor create shortages: Nos. 18-25.
3. If there are shortages, people are to try to remain in the Land of Israel if they possibly can: Nos. 26-28+29-36, 37-40.

One might argue that the combination of the set yields the syllogism that honesty in buying and selling the necessities of life is what makes possible Israel's possession of the Holy Land, but that does not seem to me a plausible proposal. I see here only a thematic composite, all the numbered items addressed to that single theme, perhaps, furthermore, with a number of cogent propositions joining some of compositions as well.

IV. *Conclusion*

We have now formed a hypothesis that quite random compositions, each with its own focus, will be formed into a composite on the basis of one of three theories of linkage: [1] topic (sometimes propositional, sometimes merely thematic, in delination), [2] attribution, or [3] sequence of verses of a passage of Scripture. The agglutination of topically-coherent compositions predominates. And this leads to a further theory on the miscellany. The conglomerates of random compositions formed into topical composites ordinarily serve as an amplification of a topic treated in the Mishnah, or are joined to a composite that serves in that way, so that, over all, the miscellanies are made to extend and amplify the statements of the Mishnah, as much as, though in a different way from, the commonplace propositional, analytical, and syllogistic composite.

The Bavli contains no important or sizable sequences of compositions that are entirely unrelated to one another, that is, nothing we should classify as a mere miscellany—a hodgepodge—at all. Faced with three massive miscellanies, we have come to the conclusion that what appears to be a random hodgepodge of this and that and the other thing in fact forms a considered and even crafted composite, the agglutinative principles of which we may readily discern. In fact what we have in the miscellany is nothing more than a Mishnah-commentary of a peculiar sort, itself extended and spun out, as the more conventional Mishnah-commentaries of the Bavli tend to be extended and spun out. The miscellany may be defined, therefore, in a very simple way: it is, specifically, a composite that has been compiled so as to present for the Mishnah a commentary intending to provide information on topics introduced by the Mishnah,—that, and not much more than that. True, the miscellany is not propositional, and it is certainly not analytical. But it is very much a composite in the sense in which I have defined that literary structure in the present context: purposeful, coherent, and I think, elegant. What appears to be odd, incoherent, pointless, rambling, to the contrary attests in its own way to the single and definitive program of the Bavli's framers. Whatever those framers wished to say on their own account they insisted on setting forth within the framework of that received document upon the structure of which they made everything to depend. All the more reason to admire the remarkable originality and genuinely fresh perspective—and statement—that, in the guise of a commentary, the Bavli was to make.

CHAPTER THREE

RATIONALITY AND STRUCTURE

I. *Self-Evidence*

When we know what a body of writing accepts as self-evident, we penetrate into the deepest layers of the order and the structure that sustain that entire corpus at its foundation but that are rarely articulated. The mark of self-evidence answers this question: what native category "obviously" joins with what other one, and what does not? When we can outline the principles of constructing groups of categories into intelligible combinations, we find in those principles the main lines of theological order and structure. When we can state what emerges as self-evident when we join two other-wise distinct topics, we gain insight into the established laws of meaning and order that govern a system of coherent thought. So in examining the rules for joining native categories, we identify those indicators of correct usage that point toward the logic pervading the whole.

To appeal to the metaphor of language is easy. Certain words in a language, as certain native categories in the documents of the Oral Torah, properly join together, forming intelligible clusters of meaning and even complete thoughts. Other words or native categories, when joined, jar. They yield gibberish. When we know which words may join with which others, and which not, formulating the theological counterpart to the rules of syntax of a language, we know the inner logic of the system: how to set forth statements that make sense. We may even explain why in context they make sense. Native categories such as "God," "Israel," "Sinai," "Torah," for example, combine and recombine. While meanings may well shift in context, within a prescribed range of possibilities, "God," ""gentiles," "idolatry" and "love," rarely join, and when "Sinai," "Torah, and "gentiles" do, the negative (e.g., "why did the gentiles *not* accept...?") must make its appearance early and prominently.

So too, linking words that theological syntax deems unconnected and unavailable for connection—the (unthinkable) pairs, "the wicked

Mordecai," "the good Haman," for instance—produce, for language, gibberish, and for theology, error, even blasphemy. Constructions of native categories that are not capable of locking together make no sense. When we know which words never join which others in cogent combinations—"an idol of God" or "a gentile who worships God alone," for instance—we may spell out the substrate of theological truths. These then dictate the details and map out the system as a whole. So too in grammar, violating syntactic rules yields what is unintelligible and beyond all rationality. And the theological connections and constructions—media of joining native categories into clusters of meaning—of the Oral Torah identify for us the counterpart to the rules of syntax of the grammar of a language. Learning from the details how to frame the governing rules of order and the laws of proper arrangement of native categories, equivalent to forming words into sentences, we gain access to the principles of thought that surface only in detail.

But how are we to locate those rules of thought and their necessary consequences in the established propositions of theological truth? The answer is, we pursue the question of the self-evidence of intersections—this category and that. We ask, what are the connections between one native category and another that documents deem self-evidently consequential? Why do the documents take for granted that when a given topic intersects with another, a specific conclusion is mandatory? The answers to questions of that order outline a part of the theological substrate of the documents. That is because like a word-association exercise, what is deemed intuitive or self-evident leads us into the deepest structures of structure and system, what is not articulated but everywhere operates.

II. *Making Connections and Drawing Conclusions*

The composite documents of the Oral Torah encompass points at which the extensive treatment of an extraneous topic interrupts the flow of exposition and even argument. Then we are made to wonder what one thing has to do with another. In some instances, the sole answer we may identify is, nothing. But in numerous others the insertion of the disruptive item redefines its own context and recasts the on-going discourse at hand. Then, it is clear, the intrusion represents a constructive initiative, an intended reshaping of the exposition altogether. When we ask, what has this to do with that, and when we attempt a response, we find time and again that at the foundations of the jarring juxtaposition or not-to-be-predicted connection is a self-evident proposition. It follows that, by "connections" I mean, points of self-evident meaning that are yielded in the (redactional) intersection between and among composites devoted to distinct topics, cases in which subjects are joined in the premise that they illuminate one another. And, within the same premise, they do so in an obvious way, yielding an inexorable result of theological truth. So far as, in a grammar of a language, syntax sets forth rules rules of turning words into combinations, we find in these points of self-evidence the theological counterpart to syntax: these join to allow us to say that—but they do not join for any other purpose.

The framers of the Bavli not only composed exegetical exercises in clarification of the Mishnah and related law as well as systematic exegetical compositions on specific passages of the Written Torah, or drew upon available compositions assembled for that. purpose. They also accommodated within their exposition enormous, free-standing compositions and even large-scale composites devoted to particular topics. These form autonomous statements, not dependent for form or meaning upon the exegetical program of the document—exegesis of the Mishnah and of Scripture—as a whole. Now, in some settings, the large-scale, free-standing composite belongs for formal reasons, e.g., as a composite of facts that supplement the discussion at hand, constituting the equivalent of a long footnote or even an appendix.

But in some instances these topical composites are so situated as to form a gloss upon the exegesis of law or theology that the exposition of the Mishnah in its own terms has provoked—a topical gloss that changes everything. And here we find access to the self-evident connections that permit us to join what on the surface ought not to intersect with the base-exposition at hand. That is where we ask, what has this to do with that—and find an illuminating answer to the question. For us the jarring juxtapositions function like a word-association-test, telling us that topic A triggers an association with topic B, furthermore pointing to a new meaning gained by topic A (and even by topic B in its own framework) from said association. Thus, to the compilers of the Bavli a clear rationality guided the inclusion of the exposition a topical intersection, this and that, so no one has to ask, what has this to do with that. What appears to impede the work—the topical appendices tend to run on, and the composites prove disruptive and tedious in places—enriches the Talmud's comprehensive statement. It is for us to identify these anomalous constructions and ask about what is taken for granted in the topical intersection that they bring about.

The way to follow the unfolding of the Talmud's structure and rationality is to outline a tractate, start to finish, and to see what units fit into the program of exposition of the Mishnah, and what units seem to take up an unrelated subject. Then one has to ask, is there a point that registers by reason of the juxtaposition of the anticipated—the topical exposition of the Mishnah's program—and the unanticipated? In such coherent study by means of an outline, two important traits of the writing prove blatant. The first is the presence of large composites that do not serve the purpose of commenting on the Mishnah, and the second, the intrusion of such composites into the very heart of the work of Mishnah-exegesis. These miscellaneous composites of materials on a given topic, lacking all argument and proposition, not only intrude but disrupt. Not only so, but it is not always easy to explain why a given composite is inserted where it is; juxtapositions of Mishnah-exegesis and a topical miscellany—a composite of materials on a given subject that the Mishnah, for its part, has not introduced, or of materials that vastly exceed what is required for the explanation of a reference in the Mishnah—prove jarring. What has one thing to do with another— wheat with straw, so to speak? From the study of these jarring juxtapositions emerges another set of rules that correspond to syntax in language: a theory of rational connection. The counterpart to syntax in a language, when it comes to the insert of topical composites, is an explanation of why they are inserted where they are, and what the framer of the document accomplished in including in his exposition of the Mishnah and its law rather formidable topical composites that bear no obvious relationship to the tasks of Mishnah-commentary.

Juxtapositions—the making of connections—that jar and disrupt turn out to bear an entirely pertinent, even urgent, message for the larger discourse in which they take their place. Indeed, these topical composites themselves commonly constitute a comment upon the paramount subject of the Mishnah-tractate at the very point at which they find their position—if only by highlighting what belongs but has been omitted. Properly understood, the topical miscellanies do not jar and do not violate the document's prevailing rationality.

What we shall see is that juxtapositions that jar and disrupt turn out to bear an entirely pertinent, even urgent, message for the larger discourse in which they take their place. That message is taken for granted, not demonstrated but rather insinuated as a given. Indeed, these topical composites themselves commonly constitute a comment upon the paramount subject of the Mishnah-tractate at the very point at which they find their position—if only by highlighting what belongs but has been omitted. Properly understood, the topical miscellanies do not jar and do not violate the document's prevailing rationality: what it takes for granted as self-evident.

III. *How to Proceed*

To the compilers of the Bavli a clear rationality guided the inclusion of the exposition a topical. What appears to impede the work enriches it, and an account of the structure of the Talmud, its sequence of exegetical problems and its palpable requirement of supplementary topical information, shows the rationality of inserting discussions of topics not required by the labor of Mishnah-exposition. To sustain the case that the Talmud of Babylonia adheres to a governing rationality, that defined by the logic of Mishnah-exegesis and amplification, I have to identify these anomalous constructions and propose a theory of why they are inserted where they are, and what the framer of the document accomplished in including in his exposition of the Mishnah and its law rather formidable topical composites that bear no obvious relationship to the tasks of Mishnah-commentary. How the whole holds together at any one passage then is what requires explanation. And that means, what has one thing got to do with some other.

The question, what has this to do with that, finds its answer here in these pages for every point in the Talmud at which—so my outline of the Bavli shows—the subject takes an unexpected turn. Juxtapositions that jar and disrupt turn out to bear an entirely pertinent, even urgent, message for the larger discourse in which they take their place. Indeed, these topical composites themselves commonly constitute a comment upon the paramount subject of the Mishnah-tractate at the very point at which they find their position—if only by highlighting what belongs but has been omitted. Properly understood, the topical miscellanies do not jar and do not violate the document's prevailing rationality.

How to set forth the evidence and argument that sustains my proposition? Through my analytical outlines of the Talmud I claim to have penetrated into that rationality that made this fit very well with that, and that rationality that at the same time excluded the other thing. When we know the principles of association, of making connections and drawing conclusions, then we can define the logic, the rationality, that governs throughout. That takes shape in the (to the compilers of the document) self-evident principle of coherence that holds the whole together, even (or especially) where the sequence of completed cogent discourses appears to disintegrate into a haphazard and incoherent collection of unrelated sayings and stories about nothing in particular.

IV. *Describing the Construction of a Tractate and Explaining Its Rationality*

No mere arguments joined to examples can suffice to overcome a prevailing attitude toward a widely-studied document. That is why I do not offer general arguments but detailed treatments of data. Specifically, in my *Academic Commentary* to the Bavli (and the Yerushalmi), I systematically addressed issues of coherence. There I defined the Talmud's definitive character as a commentary, through visual signals portraying the whole in a process of large-scale description, analysis, and interpretation. I further identified and defined the components, beyond Mishnah-commentary. The path I took carried me through a detailed, line by line rereading of the document, with a uniform program of questions always guiding our progress. Since Mishnah-exegesis defines the Talmud's purpose, though not its character, I identified, then frame my discussion around, the Talmud's definitive units of discourse, which are those organized around Mishnah-paragraphs. The commentary on the Talmud's structure then asked how the Mishnah-paragraph before us has been analyzed, and whether that analysis has then dictated the introduction of further discussion. The question of structural cogency is answered by the information produced by a description of the Talmud as Mishnah-commentary. But the Talmud commonly moves beyond the limits of the Mishnah-paragraph that defines the starting point of its discussion.

The essential work of that academic commentary—showing how things cohere, when they do, or pointing out their incoherence, when they do not hold together—thus came into view, yielding the problem taken up here. In the commentary, after I had set forth the tractates, I made a complete outline of the whole, showing how the successive clauses of the Mishnah formed the main beams of structure and system for the document, then pointing up both the points of coherence and also the various anomalies. My task then was to explain where that further discussion that the Bavli introduces has led us and, if we can, also to account for the cogency of the result. For the critical issue of structure centers upon coherence and cogency: the whole that is made up of the parts, and that, in this context, exceeds the sum of the parts. If, as I said at the outset, we can explain how connections are made, then we can describe, also, those principles of reasoning that lead us to link this to that, but not to the other thing. And when we can define the principles of making selections and imputing connections, we also can identify bases for drawing the coherent conclusions from selecting those connections. That is to say, through the uniformities of selection, connection, and conclusion, we may define that governing system that the structure's cogency both supports and also expresses in formal language. The results of that inquiry are recapitulated here.

This produced a very systematic and comprehensive examination of the Bavli's massive miscellanies. In my outlines I accounted for each completed unit of discourse in the tractate, showing its relationship either to the requirement of Mishnah-exegesis or to the needs of secondary expansion and generalization of the law portrayed by the Mishnah. That outline, in each case, then focused attention upon the large-scale composites that provide information on a topic but do not propose to clarify a rule of the Mishnah; these I called topical appendices, or topical miscellanies (as the case required). At the end of the outline of the tractate, I raised questions: of structure and system, and this I did in the same manner for all tractates. The questions I pursued are spelled out at tractate Moed Qatan, my starting point, roughly in the following way (revised to remove what is particular to that tractate). Let me spell out the outline of analysis, which serves in this chapter to present the data that point to the Talmud's structure and its rationality. First come the points of structure, the questions I brought to bear on each tractate:

Points of Structure

1) *Does the Babylonian Talmud-tractate that is under study follow a coherent outline governed by a consistent rules?*
The answer to that question consistently demonstrated that the Talmud-tractate follows a coherent outline—that supplied by the Mishnah-chapters at their successive paragraphs; at remarkably few points was I unable to account for the position and purpose of a complete composition, one with a beginning, middle, and end. I could identify few, if any, such compositions that do not relate to the composite of which they form a part, and I can point to not a single composite without a clear purpose in the tractate's large-scale constructions. The outline I was able to construct from one tractate to the next ordinarily followed a simple order: topic sentence, ordinarily a sentence of the Mishnah-tractate, at some points a subject or proposition not supplied by it; analytical discussion of the topic-sentence; propositions generated by the topic-sentences. Where the compilers wish to provide both analysis and illustrative cases, the order is, first, analysis, then illustration.

2) *What are the salient traits of its structure?*
The outline of the Talmud-tractate follows the outline of the Mishnah-tractate, but extends beyond the Mishnah-tractate in two ways. First, important statements of the Mishnah-tractate are not analyzed at all. Second, important propositions not set forth in the Mishnah-tractate are examined, and significant topical composites are inserted without regard to the Mishnah-tractate's program but in addition to it. The rules that the outline reveals present no surprises. In examining any sentence of the Mishnah or of a comparable Tannaite document, [1] the compilers first discuss the formulation, authorities, or scriptural foundations for the Mishnah's or other Tannaite document's statement. Then [2] secondary augmentation will begin, whether through an extension of the rule to other cases, or an investigation of the implicit principle of the rule and its intersection with other types of cases altogether. Following comes [3] the consideration of Tannaite formulations of rules that pertain in theme or problem or principle, and these will be subjected to the same sequence and type of analytical questions that have already been brought to bear upon the Mishnah.

3) *What is the Rationality of the structure?*

We proceed from the particular—the Mishnah's rule—to the general. We first deal with the details of the particular, then we move outward to theoretical considerations. We deal with rules accorded Tannaite origin or sponsorship, first found in the Mishnah, then found in the Tosefta (not so firm a rule), and finally given a signal of Tannaite status but not found in a compilation of Tannaite statements now in our hands (e. g., Tenno rabbanon, Tanné and the like). These procedures emerged inductively, through an account of one tractate after another, and, within the tractates, the successive chapters. I did not give a few examples and a broad generalization, I did the exact opposite: every detail, start to finish, and from the details, the claim to set forth the rationality of the document found its sustaining validation.

4) *Where are the points of irrationality in the structure?*

Here we reach the issue of this chapter: the compositions and composites that violate the document's principles of structure. The foregoing account of the orderly structure of the Talmud-tractate under study then requires attention to those composites that violated the demonstrated structure and therefore contradict its rationality—that is, in context, irrational intrusions. With only the Mishnah-tractate in hand, we should have no basis for predicting the topics of the composites that provide other than Mishnah-exegesis, augmentation, and extension. Only when we ask why a given topical composite, extrinsic to the Mishnah-tractate, has been positioned where it is, and whether or not said composite can have occupied a position elsewhere in the Talmud-tractate or have been omitted with a significant loss of meaning.

The answers to these four questions then led me, tractate by tractate, to the inquiry into the system of said tractate. By "system" ("rationality" or "logic" would serve as well) in this context I mean, how does the Talmud's reading of the Mishnah-tractate impost upon the Mishnah-tractate a viewpoint or a logic of its own: do we understand the Mishnah-tractate under study in a different way from the way we should without the Talmud's commentary? The inquiry into where and how the Talmud's own system, its logic, has reshaped the presentation of the topic to which the Mishnah-tractate is devoted takes the form of asking another set of questions, three in all. These are as follows.

Points of System

1) *Does the Babylonian Talmud-tractate that is under study serve only as a re-presentation of the Mishnah-tractate of the same name?*
For negative and positive reasons, the answer to this question in general, though not always, is one-sidedly negative. The negative reason is that Talmud-tractate does not re-present Mishnah-tractate that is under study, because it omits consideration of sizable passages of the Mishnah-tractate. I can conceive of no way to predict what the Talmud-tractate's framers will omit; I see no pattern, nor can I explain why, in the same set of sentences, a given sentence will attract extensive consideration and another will not. But it suffices to say that the Talmud-tractate in no way pretends to cover every clause of the Mishnah. I further have formed the subjective impression that at no point do the framers of compositions concerning clauses of the Mishnah strain to find something to fill up space where they have nothing to say. I can rarely point to a passage that strikes me as extraneous or fabricated for the occasion. That subjective impression gains a measure of objective standing when we observe that the same types of discussion accorded to a given Mishnah-clause recur throughout. A coherent and cogent program of Mishnah-exegesis governs everywhere. That seems to me to bear the implication that the framers of the Talmud-tractate do not acknowledge the task of filling up space by making statements where they have nothing interesting to say. My tentative hypothesis is that where a sentence of the Mishnah attracts no analytical inquiry, it is because it contains nothing that the framers of our Talmud-tractate found problematic; where they say nothing, it is because they have nothing to say. But to test that hypothesis we should have to pursue the question of the sources of the Talmud-tractate, that is, the resources upon which the compilers of composites drew, or the authors of compositions devoted to Mishnah-exegesis wrote up. That is not a question that concerns me here, since the answer tells us nothing about structure and system, explaining what we do not have, not what we do.

The positive reason is that the Talmud-tractate that is under study includes presentation of topics and principles and propositions that the Mishnah-tractate does not present. These I then catalogued. The proportion of the tractate represented by the freestanding topical composites is accurately estimated only by a word count, that is, the number of words in the listed composites as against the number of words in the tractate as a whole. Without making such a word-count, I believe readers will concur in the simple judgment that the important topical composites extrinsic to Mishnah-exegesis and yet primary in the Talmud-tractate form a substantial component of the whole. These extrinsic composites and compositions take shape around their own subjects or propositions or problems, and they do not respond to those of the Mishnah-tractate. But, as we shall now see, they do change the re-presentation of the Mishnah-tractate in important ways, to which we now turn.

2) *How do the topical composites fit into the Talmud-tractate under study and what do they contribute that the Mishnah-tractate of the same name would lack without them?*
Here we come to the crux of the matter: how the Talmud recasts the Mishnah's treatment of the Mishnah's own topic. That is done by introducing systematic presentations of topics beyond those covered by the Mishnah but in the context of the exposition of those of the Mishnah. To answer this question, I examined each composite and asked how it fit into the tractate under study. The topical composites fit in in two distinct ways. First, some of them greatly expand the scope of the Mishnah-rule, introducing a level of abstraction that Mishnah-exegesis does not require. Mishnah-exegesis is made to set the stage for a much broader consideration of principles that transcend cases and recast rules into representations of underlying conceptions of a high order of generalization. In this first type of topical composite, the Mishnah's rule is re-presented as an indicator of a deeper, compelling problem of thought, often of a philosophical, rather than a narrowly-legal character.

Second, and more strikingly, the larger number of the topical composite change the face of the Mishnah-tractate by raising to prominence subjects treated by the Mishnah only incidentally and in a subordinate status.

3) *Can we state what the compilers of this document propose to accomplish in producing this complete, organized piece of writing that we now have (that is, my thesis that in our hands we possess the best of all possible Talmuds?*
The answer to this question lies in explaining the connection between topics laid out by the Mishnah-tractate and those introduced by the Talmud's insertion of topical composites or miscellanies. I asked, What made sages conceive that the latter should find a comfortable and capacious place amid the former? This lead to system-

atic discussions on the connections between topics that sages found
self-evident—and that, in the nature of things, a merely topical
program of exegesis must find jarring. Once we ask, what has one
thing to do with the other—the Mishnah's topic with the Talmud's
insertion of an extraneous, therefore anomalous topic—the issue of
making connections and drawing conclusions—the self-evidence of
list-making—comes to the fore. A substantive, ultimately theological, explanation is required, and it is contained in the answer to a
simple question. Precisely what has this topic unheralded by the
Mishnah to do with that topic that the Mishnah has assigned for
exegesis? The principal mode of thought of the Mishnah is that of
comparison and contrast. Something is like something else, therefore follows its rule; or unlike, therefore follows the opposite of the
rule governing the something else.

So as a matter of hypothesis, let us assume that the framers of
Talmud-tractate that is under study found self-evidently valid the
modes of thought that they learned from the Mishnah and so made
connections between things that were alike, on the one side, or things
that were opposite, on the other. Then, if the contrast proves obvious, the point of comparison—how are these things similar, and what
rule pertains to both—emerges with equal facility. So in establishing the connection, through treating the categories as equivalent and
counterpart to one another, what have our sages in Talmud-tractate
that is under study said in their own behalf, not about the Mishnah
but through their re-presentation of the Mishnah? They make the
connection between the one and the other. When we can explain
that connection, we are also able to account for the character of the
Talmud—not only its systematic commentary to the Mishnah, which
imparts to the whole the character of coherence and cogency—but
also its jarring juxtapositions. In the structure that the outline reveals, we discern a rationality that makes juxtapositions logical and
rational—and deeply meaningful.

We take up four representative and important tractates and show
why and how jarring juxtapositions in fact reveal the rationality of
the Bavli's structure, its exposition of what makes certain connections self-evident: Yoma, Moed Qatan, Abodah Zarah, and Makkot.

V. *The Structure and Rationality of Babylonian Talmud Yoma*

Points of Structure

1) *Does Babylonian Talmud-tractate Yoma follow a coherent outline governed by a consistent rules?*
The Mishnah-tractate dictates the Talmud's treatment of its topic, and seen whole, the Bavli-tractate belongs in the classification of a commentary. The order of topics demonstrates that fact, since at only a very few points are we unable to relate a large-scale composite to the topical program of Mishnah-tractate Yoma. And, as those who have reviewed the tractates now in print will have noted, other tractates do not even demand that we recognize exceptions of any kind. Indeed, this tractate derives much of its power from its elaborate presentations of topics that in the Mishnah receive only a little attention, or none at all. But for that same reason it proves exceptional when compared to the tractates that address only the Mishnah's propositions, or the Mishnah's topics seen as themes, rather than as the occasion for propositional exercises at all.

2) *What are the salient traits of its structure?*
Overall, we find two distinct components of the structure of the Talmud-tractate: comments on the Mishnah, generally episodic if also systematic, and also large-scale composites.

3) *What is the Rationality of the structure?*
The rationality of the document finds its definition in the principles of Mishnah-exegesis, on the one side, and the program of Mishnah-representation on the other. That is to say, if we were to remove all of the compositions and composites not linked to Mishnah-amplification in one form or the other, we should find little left of the tractate as we know it.

4) *Where are the points of irrationality in the structure?*
I identify these asymptomatic entries: I.A, B, E, G, VII.D, VIII.A, XII.G, XIV.B, D, XV.E, XVIII.F, XIX.C, E, XX.B, XXXV.B, C, D, E, G, XXXVI.B, C, H, I, XL.C, XLI.D, H. Now the issue is, how have these entries changed the face of the Bavli-tractate's representation of the Mishnah-tractate?

Points of System

1) *Does the Babylonian Talmud-tractate Yoma serve only as a re-presentation of the Mishnah-tractate of the same name?*
This question finds its answer in two facts. First, how many compositions of the Mishnah-tractate altogether lack Talmud-discussions? The answer is, few, and these prove episodic. We cannot predict which Mishnah-paragraphs will lack Talmud-compositions or propose a theory on the traits that would characterize the Mishnah-sentences that are treated or those that are not. The matter appears to me to be random. Second, and perhaps of greater interest, how many composites in the Talmud stand completely out of relationship with the Mishnah? That question is answered in the next rubric.

2) *How do the topical composites fit into the Talmud-tractate Yoma and what do they contribute that the Mishnah-tractate of the same name would lack without them?*
The tractate is formidable in size, and it carries with it a large and important component of free-standing composites, some of which intersect with the Mishnah in topic, others of which bear upon the theme of the tractate but make no contribution to the amplification of anything that the Mishnah-tractate has to say about that theme. We know that the compilers undertake an initiative of weight when we find jarring juxtapositions. We may suppose that the compilers mean only to provide information, not an occasion for reflection through startling points of intersection, when a topic introduced in the Mishnah in a tangential way is given an exposition lacking all argument or coherent point. The difference then is the mixing of things ordinarily kept distinct as against the provision of information on a subject. This becomes clear in the exposition that follows.

I.A: The framers begin with a remarkable conception, which is to compare the rite of the Day of Atonement with another rite, so placing Leviticus Sixteen into relationship with other systematic Pentateuchal expositions of the most distinguish offerings of the cultic calendar. In selecting another rite for comparison, what guided them? I see three distinct considerations. First is the formal one, which is articulated: rites that demand that the high priest prepare for a week in advance. But there are more than formal considerations. For, second, the compilers surely reflected on critical cultic occasions that brought the cult outside the walls of the Temple. Since a major step in the order of service here is to send forth the scapegoat, it is quite natural to take up a comparable occasion on which a sacrifice is made outside of the Temple. For that purpose, the rite of burning the red cow to produce ashes for purification water, in line with the rite described at Numbers Chapter Nineteen, comes to mind; that offering is not in the Temple but on Mount of Olives. What draws these two offerings into alignment is a third quality. The scapegoat carries with it the sins of the people; the purification-water bears the classification of *hat'at*, translated both purification- and sin. In the present context, therefore, by raising the question of how rites compare, two rites of atonement, one for uncleanness, the other for sin, are drawn into alignment for purposes of comparison and contrast. But having moved beyond the limits of the Talmud's presentation, I note at the end the formal consideration obviously governs, even though the substantive effect—introducing the notion of rites that take up conduct outside of the cult—is to direct attention from the inner to the outer dimensions of the Day. This initiative at the formal level finds its counterpart in substantive ways, as we shall see, when the Talmud insists in its re-presentation of the topic of the Day of Atonement upon asking about considerations external to the Temple and its cult but critical to the life of Israel and its sanctification and salvation.

I.B: The initiative at the opening composite is carried forward on a still larger scale at I.B: what makes the requirement of the Day of Atonement unique, and how we relate the rules governing that day with those governing another comparable occasion, the consecration of the Tent of Meeting. The upshot is that in the majestic opening reading, the Mishnah's simple, factual account is left behind, as the topic, the rite of the Day of Atonement, is addressed in its own, much larger setting of comparable rites, first, the burning of the red cow, second, the consecration of the tent of meeting. Only at I.C, D, do we come back to the high priesthood.

I.E: As if I.A, B, did not suffice to draw attention from the
Mishnah's facts to the context, I.E really revises the entire matter, and the composite does so in a dramatic way.
Now the entire face of the presentation by the Mishnah
changes. From purification of sin and uncleanness, on
the one side, and the formation of the tabernacle/
Temple, on the other, we proceed to what is always the
critical issue in the Rabbinic system, the destruction of
the Temple. This is now set forth as the result of the
corruption of the priesthood, particularly the high priesthood. So the Day of Atonement calls to mind [1] sin,
[2] the Temple and its cult, and [3] the power of sin to
destroy the Temple and its cult. The treatment of the
third theme seems to me miscellaneous, and the upshot
is, what we have is the theme alone, not an exposition
that makes some stunning point in the way that I.A, and
B do. The upshot, however, is the same, and that is,
the definition of an entirely fresh context in which the
theme of the Mishnah-tractate, the Day of Atonement,
is going to be expounded. Indeed, once we have worked
our way through I.A and B, we can scarcely see as definitive for the topic the Mishnah-tractate's identification of its program of exposition—Leviticus Chapter Sixteen, point by point. What the Mishnah-tractate's authors found important about the Day of Atonement the
Bavli-tractate's compilers chose to treat as subsidiary and
incidental to the points they wished to register at the
very beginning of their tractate.

I.G: Why should the topic of the councillors' chamber, I.F,
should call to mind the requirement of putting a
mezuzah on the doorposts of all Israelites' houses—gates
of houses, courts, provinces, cities? The juxtaposition of
subjects is jarring. But if we remember where we
started—finding contexts in which to interpret the order of service of the Day of Atonement—the answer
presents itself quite readily. We begin by moving from
the Temple outward: rites comparable in that preparation outside of the cult (the high priest's separation)
and beyond the limits of the Temple (the scapegoat, the

red cow). We proceeded to a clear statement that the reason the Temple was destroyed was the sins of the priesthood and of Israel. Now we treat as comparable the sanctity of the dwellings of all Israel and the sanctity of the Temple and its chambers. The mezuzah marks off Israel's dwellings as holy, a counterpart to the Temple's very walls and hangings. The presentation, by contrast with the topic, proves once more miscellaneous; I see no point at which anything is said, beyond the introduction of the topic itself, that bears meaning, let alone a clear and relevant proposition.

VII.D: Saul is introduced because he violated the prohibition of taking a census; but then he provides the occasion to underscore the power of sin, however small, to yield weighty consequences. Still, it seems to me this topical appendix does not vastly change the face of the setting in which it is presented.

VIII.A: The exposition of the general procedure of the lottery simply spells out details of the Mishnah's topic.

XII.G: The secondary amplification of facts and rules relevant to the Mishnah's topic seems to me inert.

XIV.B: The wonderful composite at XIV.B really clarifies the presentation of the Mishnah's topic; it does not introduce an unanticipated topic, let alone a problem out of alignment with the Mishnah's, but only works in its own way through the very information that the Mishnah has already given. The improvement upon the Mishnah's presentation nonetheless is particularly talmudic: a more systematic and orderly account of what has already been laid out in a systematic manner.

XIV.D: The richly glossed account of the proper order of the daily priestly rites—by contrast to that of the Day of Atonement—enriches in a factual way the Mishnah's own presentation. I do not discern a single point at which a not-to-be-predicted subject makes an appearance.

XV.E: Now we come to a small but important insertion. We have been told that priests could spend their own money on enhancing the rites. Now we are told, in a huge composition of obvious artistic merit, how riches and poverty and good looks are fundamentally irrelevant to Torah-study. Whether one is rich or poor, handsome or ugly, all are obligated to Torah-study. This composition forms a subtle but powerful comment on the topic of the Mishnah-composite before us, the kind of editorial insertion that changes the face of the whole.

XVIII.F: Once more, we have a startling juxtaposition, one that the Mishnah-composite accommodates but hardly requires. That is, the exposition of the Mishnah-composition is complete in its own terms. Then we have a massive composite on the righteous and the wicked in general. But while in the Mishnah, attention focuses upon those who contributed to the cult or refused to do so, here we deal with issues of personal morality, on the one side, and the power of the righteous to save the world, on the other. The conduct in the cult now recedes into the background, and conduct in the social order of holy Israel comes to the fore. The comment made by placing this remarkable composite here is then unmistakable. Virtue in everyday affairs forms the primary consideration, and Israelites who wish to do what is right take priority over those whose virtue involves only cultic activities. Since the Mishnah has cited Prov. 10:7 in the setting of those who were remembered favorably or unfavorably for their activities in the Temple, while the Talmud wishes to read the same verse in the setting of Israel's everyday life, the intent is obvious. Here is a fine example of how the Talmud's compositors make their statement through the juxtaposition of distinct composites, and the comparison and contrast of those composites' themes or even propositions, respectively.

XIX.C: I see this entry as topical; nothing is jarring here, since we have dealt with the outcome of the lottery, and the composite on Simeon begins with that subject. The composite has been assembled for its own purpose, which is to present Simeon the Righteous, but fits in quite well as a supplement to the Mishnah's rule, nothing more.

XIX.E: The question of whether the rite under discussion is essential or merely recommended in no way changes the

Mishnah's presentation of the subject.

XX.B: Here we find a reprise of the opening exercise in comparison of the rite of the Day of Atonement, the rite of burning the Red Cow, and other, cognate rituals, now the purification rite involving thread. The composite is a very sizable one, but I am unable to identify in it any proposition, or even a theme, that leads us to take up a position outside of the framework of the factual repertoire of the Mishnah. Here is a lost occasion for theological reflection, sharpening by contrast the quite remarkable character of the juxtapositions that make their own, fresh statement.

[XXII.C: *We note a substantial composite of questions raised by Pappa, C.4ff.; but these fit well into the topical program of XXII.C and in no way form a distinct composite with its own principle of selection and coherence.]*

XXXV.B: The topic of the Mishnah—the high priest's garments—accounts for the inclusion of this composite.

XXXV.C: The same goes for this composite. But the next items change the picture.

XXXV.D: We move from rules on the disposition of the sacred objects to moral lessons to be drawn from verses that deal with the utensils and furniture of the Temple. The moral lessons are commonplaces; what is interesting is only that at this point a set of sayings is introduced to impart to the Mishnah's topic a set of meanings that the Mishnah does not require.

XXXV.E: Here we find the jarring juxtaposition that bears the Talmud's statement upon the Mishnah's topic or proposition, not only the Talmud's re-statement thereof. We move from moral lessons deriving from Scripture's account of the Temple's appurtenances to Torah-study sayings pertinent to those same matters. The moral sayings now are recast as lessons for disciples of sages, and the important lesson is that the sage's disciple must be sincere in his convictions and conduct, his inside corresponding to his outside.

XXXV.G: Here we have a topical composite to supplement the Mishnah's exposition.

XXXVI.B: Now we come to Talmud's most remarkable theologi-

cal statement. We begin with a preparatory composite
on the affliction of souls through fasting. This is important because it introduces the theme of hunger as affliction. And that raises to the surface a question that
invites the stunning juxtaposition of the next entry.

XXXVI.C: A verse invites our interest in manna, which is, "Who
fed you in the wilderness with manna...that he might
afflict you" (Dt. 8:16). So we turn to a huge and coherent exposition of manna as a form of affliction, on the
one side, but grace, on the other. What happens when
the subject of manna is introduced? The issue of fasting for Heaven is given its counterpart: Heaven feed-
ing Israel. So the topic, fasting on the Day of Atonement, is given a new dimension of meaning, we give to
Heaven, but Heaven has fed us, and feeds us, so the
transaction is reciprocal. When humanity fasts and shows
its humility and contrition, Heaven responds with the
realization of grace that is provided through supernatural
food. Fasting, a deed in the natural world, evokes in
Heaven a supernatural response. Now the activities of
the Day of Atonement are set into a fresh context and
recast in cosmic dimensions. The cultic program for the
Day recedes in consequence; the activities of the private person take over. God's interest and response address what all Israel does. Nothing in the Mishnah's presentation of the holy day, it goes without saying, has prepared us for such an amazing interjection of a theme
that is at once unanticipated and alien, and, once introduced, also quite natural.

XXXVI.H: What we have here is a repertoire of relevant facts.

XXXVI.I: The same is so here. The face of the Mishnah is unaffected.

XL.C: This brief appendix treats the topic of the Mishnah.

XLI.D: The composite on repentance carries forward the
Mishnah's theme; I see here nothing that will have
surprised the Mishnah's own framers in context. Nor
do I find any proposition that vastly revises the standard picture of the subject. We therefore see how critical to the making of the Talmud's own statement is the
intrusion of the unanticipated topic—that principally,

possible even, that alone.

XLI.H: This composite stands out of all relationship to the Mishnah-paragraph that stands at the head of its Talmud-unit. It is rare in the Talmud to come across a discussion so out of phase with the Mishnah-context as the present item. The real question is, why has the compositor of XVI.D not included the composite in his presentation of the high priest's confession. If I were making the Talmud over, that is the point to which I would move XLI.H. As it is, it is not only out of place but also fails to make the point that, in the right position, it can have made. It suffices to observe that, in the dozen and a half tractates to date, I have found no other composite that both stands out of relationship to its larger context, whether Mishnaic or Talmudic, and also fails to make the contribution that it ought to have made in its proper context, in the way that this one does. That exception to the rule of brilliant composition forms a mark of the Talmud's compositors' amazing intellectual rigor.

3) Can we state what the compilers of this document propose to accomplish in producing this complete, organized piece of writing?

To understand what our compilers have accomplished, we have to call to mind the fundamental program of the Mishnah-tractate. Even a simple glance at the Mishnah-tractate suffices to show that all chapters but the final one are devoted to an exposition of the Temple rite on the Day of Atonement. Only the last chapter of the Mishnah-tractate addresses the situation of the individual Israelite, not in the Temple cult, and how he observes the occasion. The Mishnah-tractate therefore closely follows the presentation of the Day of Atonement at Leviticus Chapter Sixteen, which carefully catalogues the activities of the high priest on the holy day, but in a sentence or two suffices to tell ordinary folk how they are to conduct themselves. The challenge facing the Talmud-tractate framers, therefore, is to place the facts of the Mishnah's first seven chapters into a framework that accords proportion and balance to the re-presentation of the Mishnah-tractate. That is to say, along with the exposition of the facts of Leviticus Chapter Sixteen as the Mishnah lays them out and complements them, the meaning of the Day of Atonement in the holy life of Israel the people has to be set forth.

Now, when the compilers of the Bavli address the Mishnah, they define for themselves three tasks. First and paramount, they identify what they deemed to be the Mishnah's problematic, that is, what the Mishnah states that they deem to require amplification. So they clarify the Mishnah's words and phrases; they find Scriptural bases for the Mishnah's rules; they ask about the authority behind an anonymous ruling and make an effort to show that rulings belonging to a given authority may be accepted even by those who oppose his position on a parallel matter. Second, they add some sizable complexes of materials that address a topic of the Mishnah, rather than the problematic thereof, and as we now have seen, they organize sizable compositions into composites that supplement the Mishnah's inclusion of a topic with more information about that topic. These composites so far as I can see lack any proposition and accomplish little more than the recapitulation of marginally interesting facts. They fill space, they do not impart structure or add sense. And, third, as we now have seen, the Bavli's framers make us see the Mishnah's topic in a very different way from the way that we would understand that topic absent their work. This they do at critical points in the tractate.

Let us quickly review the main points that we derive from the massive composites that stand wholly outside of the exposition of our Mishnah-tractate and even of our Mishnah-tractate's topic:

1) the rites of the Day of Atonement fall into the larger framework of Israel's rites of purification and atonement for sin; these take place outside of the cult, as much as inside the Temple; they require of the high priest a higher level of sanctification through purification than the Temple's internal cult requires

2) the rite of sanctification of the tent of meeting—also in the world beyond the Temple walls—is comparable to the rite of the Day of Atonement

3) the world intruded on the Temple by reason of Israel's (unatoned-for) sin, which brought about the destruction of the Temple and the cessation of its cult—all the more reason to atone for sin on the Day of Atonement

4) the Temple's points of domestic sanctity, its special chambers, are comparable in their holiness to Israel's points of sanctity, its homes, towns, and cities, all of which are encompassed in the signs of sanctification that apply both in the holy place and also in the homes and towns of holy Israel

5) the Temple requires high priests who can invest their own funds in its rites; the study of Torah is obligatory on all Israel equally, without regard to wealth or poverty, beauty or ugliness

6) Righteous people in this world strengthen their capacity to do what is right; they can avoid the influence of wicked neighbors; even on account of a single righteous man is the world created; a righteous man does not take his leave from the world before another righteous man like him is created the Holy One, blessed be he, saw that the righteous are few. He went and planted some of them in every generation; even for the sake of a single righteous man the world endures; when a man has lived out the better part of his years and has not sinned, he will not likely sin again. And we are responsible for what we make of ourselves, specifically: if someone comes to make himself unclean, they open the way to him, but if he comes to purify himself, they assist him, but transgression dulls the heart of man.; if a person makes himself a bit unclean, he is made very unclean; if someone sanctifies himself a bit, he is made abundantly sanctified.

7) The propositions prominent in the exposition of the theme of the manna treats the manna as Heaven's response to self-affliction for sin. Thus "Who fed you in the wilderness with manna...that he might afflict you" (Dt. 8:16): Just as the prophet told the Israelites what was to be found in clefts or holes, so manna would reveal to Israelites what was in the clefts and holes. Meat, for which they asked not in the right way, was given to them at the wrong time. Bread, for which they asked in the right way, was given to them at the right time. "While the meat was yet between their teeth" (Num. 11:33). And it is written, "But a whole month" (Num. 11:20)—The middling folk died on the spot, the wicked suffered pain for a whole month. When the righteous eat the quail, it is at ease, but when the wicked eat it, it is like thorns for them. "Man did eat the bread of the mighty" (Ps. 78:25)—"It is the bread that the ministering angels eat." The manna marked Israel as supernatural—and so does its fasting.

These important additions, in the form of large-scale composites, introduce into the representation of the theme of the Day of Atonement conceptions and considerations of which the Mishnah scarcely takes cognizance. While the conception of Heaven's response to

afflicting oneself by fasting is providing manna in the wilderness—
the bread that the angels eat!—strikes me as the single most remarkable initiative, the other propositions before us prove equally striking.
Seen as a group, they yield the following proposition: the Day of
Atonement, which the Torah lays out as principally a Temple occasion, overspreads the world. That is not a merely-moral statement
but one of cultic consequence, since we see the rite itself as one
affecting the world beyond the Temple walls in the way in which
the one analogous in its careful concern for the high priest's purification, the burning of the red cow, does. Israel's sin in the world
intrudes into the cult, because the Temple, the mark of divine favor, was lost on account of Israel's sin. But Israel's virtue, the virtue of self-affliction through fasting, can win Heaven's cordial
response, analogous to the provision of manna in the wilderness. That
is because Israel's ordinary life compares with the Temple's sanctification; even as the Temple space is sanctified, so Israel's space is
marked off by signs of the holy. Just as the Temple's priests display
their riches in the ample cult, so Israel's sages display their resources
of virtue and intellect in the service of the mind and heart, study of
the Torah. And, it must follow, the righteousness represented by a
life fearful of sin and rich in repentance, which comes to its climax
on the Day of Atonement, infuses the entire people of Israel, not
only the priesthood in the Temple on that same holy day.

The upshot is, the Mishnah's presentation of the Day of Atonement, its recapitulation of the themes of Leviticus Chapter Sixteen
in the proportions of Scripture's treatment of that topic, is both
replicated and revised. What for Leviticus and Mishnah-tractate
Yoma forms a cultic occasion, in which Israel participates as bystand-
ers, emerges in Bavli-tractate Yoma as an event in the life of holy
Israel, in which all Israel bears tasks of the weight and consequence
that, on that holy day, the High Priest uniquely carries out. On the
Day of Atonement, holy Israel joins the high priest in the Holy of
Holies; this they do on that day by afflicting themselves through
fasting and other forms of abstinence, recalling how with Heaven's
favor they would eat the bread of angels; this they do on the other
days of the year by entering into the disciplines of the Torah; this
they do through their lives of virtue. The Day of Atonement, the
occasion on which the high priest conducts the rite in the privacy
of the Holy of Holies, emerges transformed: the rites are private,
but the event is public; the liturgy is conducted in the holy Temple,

with sins sent forth through the scapegoat, but the event bears its consequences in holy Israel, where sins are atoned for in the setting of the everyday and and the here and now. What is singular and distinct—the rites of atonement on the holiest day of the year in the holiest place in the world—now makes its statement about what takes place on every day of the year in the ordinary life of holy Israel.

And that is how the Day of Atonement would make its way through time, not the sacrificial rite of the high priest in the Temple, but the atonement-celebration of all Israel in the world. What mattered to the compilers of Leviticus and the Mishnah alike was the timeless rite of atonement through the bloody rites of the Temple What captured the attention of the framers of the Bavli-tractate, by contrast, was the personal discipline of atonement through repentance on the Day of Atonement and a life of virtue and Torah-learning on the rest of the days of the year. They took out of the Holy of Holies and brought into the homes and streets of the holy people that very mysterious rite of atonement that the Day of Atonement called forth. When the compilers of our Talmud moved beyond the limits of the Mishnah-tractate, they transformed the presentation the day and its meaning, transcending its cultic limits. And it was their vision, and not the vision of Leviticus Sixteen and the Mishnah's tractate, that would prove definitive.

The irony comes to expression in the fact that, from antiquity to our own day, the Day of Atonement would enjoy the loyalty of holy Israel come what may, and everywhere, gaining the standing of Judaism's single most widely observed occasion. That fact attests to the power of the distinctive ideas set forth by the framers of the Bavli to transform a sacerdotal narrative into a medium of the inner, moral sanctification for Israel, the holy people in utopia entering into the status of the holy priest and the locus of the Temple's inner sanctum. But that reframing of the rite defines the Bavli-tractate's compilers intent, since, after all, it turns out to form the very first point that the framers of the Bavli make when they commence their exposition of the Mishnah-tractate. The opening composite turns out to bear the entire message, just as it should.

VI. *The Structure and Rationality of Babylonian Talmud Moed Qatan*

Points of Structure

1) *Does Babylonian Talmud-tractate Moed Qatan follow a coherent outline governed by a consistent rules?*
The Talmud-tractate follows a coherent outline; at remarkably few points were we unable to account for the position and purpose of a complete composition, one with a beginning, middle, and end. I can identify few, if any, such compositions that do not relate to the composite of which they form a part, and I can point to not a single composite without a clear purpose in the tractate's large-scale constructions. The outline I was able to construct followed a simple order: topic sentence, ordinarily a sentence of the Mishnah-tractate, at some points a subject or proposition not supplied by it; analytical discussion of the topic-sentence; propositions generated by the topic-sentences. Where the compilers wish to provide both analysis and illustrative cases, the order is, first, analysis, then illustration.

2) *What are the salient traits of its structure?*
The outline of the Talmud-tractate follows the outline of the Mishnah-tractate, but extends beyond the Mishnah-tractate in two ways. First, important statements of the Mishnah-tractate are not analyzed at all. Second, important propositions not set forth in the Mishnah-tractate are examined, and significant topical composites are inserted without regard to the Mishnah-tractate's program but in addition to it. The rules that the outline reveals present no surprises. In examining any sentence of the Mishnah or of a comparable Tannaite document, [1] the compilers first discuss the formulation, authorities, or scriptural foundations for the Mishnah's or other Tannaite document's statement. Then [2] secondary augmentation will begin, whether through an extension of the rule to other cases, or an investigation of the implicit principle of the rule and its intersection with other types of cases altogether. Following comes [3] the consideration of Tannaite formulations of rules that pertain in theme or problem or principle, and these will be subjected to the same sequence and type of analytical questions that have already been brought to bear upon the Mishnah.

3) *What is the Rationality of the structure?*
We proceed from the particular—the Mishnah's rule—to the general. We first deal with the details of the particular, then we move

outward to theoretical considerations. We deal with rules accorded Tannaite origin or sponsorship, first found in the Mishnah, then found in the Tosefta (not so firm a rule), and finally given a signal of Tannaite but not found in a compilation of Tannaite statements now in our hands (e. g., Tenno rabbanon, Tanné and the like).

4) *Where are the points of irrationality in the structure?*
The foregoing account of the orderly structure of the Talmud-tractate Moed Qatan contains no explanation of the introduction of large-scale composites that we find as principle subdivisions of the divisions of the outline, I-XXI. With only the Mishnah-tractate in hand, we should have no basis for predicting the topics of the composites that provide other than Mishnah-exegesis, augmentation, and extension. Only when we ask why a given topical composite, extrinsic to the Mishnah-tractate, has been positioned where it is, and whether or not said composite can have occupied a position elsewhere in the Talmud-tractate or have been omitted with a significant loss of meaning, which we do at Points of System No. 2, will the topical composites be shown to participate in the rationality of the Talmud-tractate.

Points of System

1) *Does the Babylonian Talmud-tractate Moed Qatan serve only as a re-presentation of the Mishnah-tractate of the same name?*
For negative and positive reasons, the answer to this question is one-sidedly negative. The negative reason is that Talmud-tractate does not re-present Mishnah-tractate Moed Qatan, because it omits consideration of sizable passages of the Mishnah-tractate. I can conceive of no way to predict what the Talmud-tractate's framers will omit; I see no pattern, nor can I explain why, in the same set of sentences, a given sentence will attract extensive consideration and another will not. But it suffices to say that the Talmud-tractate in no way pretends to cover every clause of the Mishnah. I further have formed the subjective impression that at no point do the framers of compositions concerning clauses of the Mishnah strain to find something to fill up space where they have nothing to say. I cannot point to a passage that strikes me as extraneous or fabricated for the occasion. That subjective impression gains a measure of objective standing when we observe that the same types of discussion accorded to a given Mishnah-clause recur throughout. A coherent and cogent

program of Mishnah-exegesis governs everywhere. That seems to me
to bear the implication that the framers of the Talmud-tractate do
not acknowledge the task of filling up space by making statements
where they have nothing interesting to say. My tentative hypothesis
is that where a sentence of the Mishnah attracts no analytical inquiry, it is because it contains nothing that the framers of our Talmud-tractate found problematic; where they say nothing, it is because
they have nothing to say. But to test that hypothesis we should have
to pursue the question of the sources of the Talmud-tractate, that
is, the resources upon which the compilers of composites drew, or
the authors of compositions devoted to Mishnah-exegesis wrote up.
That is not a question that concerns me here, since the answer tells
us nothing about structure and system, explaining what we do not
have, not what we do.

The positive reason is that the Talmud-tractate Moed Qatan
includes presentation of topics and principles and propositions that
the Mishnah-tractate does not present. Because of the inclusion of
large-scale topical composites at I.B, II.B, VII.B, C, IV.B, C, X.B,
C, XV.C, D E, XVIII.B, C, D, E, F, G, I, XIX.B, C, D, F, XX.C,
E, F, XXI. B, C. The proportion of the tractate represented by the
freestanding topical composites is accurately estimated only by a word
count, that is, the number of words in the listed composites as against
the number of words in the tractate as a whole. Without making such
a word-count, I believe readers will concur in the simple judgment
that the important topical composites extrinsic to Mishnah-exegesis
and yet primary in the Talmud-tractate form a substantial component of the whole. These extrinsic composites and compositions take
shape around their own subjects or propositions or problems, and
they do not respond to those of the Mishnah-tractate. But, as we
shall now see, they do change the re-presentation of the Mishnah-
tractate in important ways, to which we now turn.

2) *How do the topical composites fit into the Talmud-tractate Moed Qatan and
what do they contribute that the Mishnah-tractate of the same name would lack
without them?*

I.B: The comparison of the Sabbatical Year's rules with those
              governing the intermediate days of the festival: this com-
              posite imposes the study of the relationship between two
              species of the single genus, occasions on which, by rea-
              son of a lesser degree of sanctification, limitations less
              drastic than those governing the Sabbath or the festi-

val day are placed on acts of labor. The Mishnah has introduced the comparison of the two occasions, the Sabbatical Year and the intermediate days of the festival, and the Talmud-composite has taken up that comparison in its own terms, not for the purpose of Mishnah-exegesis, as an examination of I.B shows. This composite could not have made sense anywhere else in the tractate and had to be situated exactly where it is. It is therefore intrinsic to the exposition of the Mishnah, and what it does is redefine our perspective upon the Mishnah by insisting on a broader, comparative framework for reflection on the law.

II.B: This composite simply pursues the Mishnah's topic. It can have been introduced only here.

VII.B, C: What this freestanding composition and its appended composite contributes is the theme, taking leave of the master. The Mishnah-rule covers taking wives and the conduct of a woman on the occasion of a wedding. I see no direct connection to the Mishnah-topic. Introducing disciples' relationships with the master and their coming and going calls to mind the comparability of the familial relationship (here: marriage) and the supernatural relationship of master-disciple. I cannot point to any other appropriate setting in our tractate for this topic. What is contributed is the consideration of that other relationship, the supernatural one. But how the occasion—intermediate days of the festival—plays a role I cannot say. Since the composite continues the theme introduced in VII.A.1.c.2, I am inclined to think the reason for introducing it derives from the needs of expounding the composite to which it is attached, rather than the tractate into which the whole is inserted.

IX.B, C: The general theme of the composite is the conduct of workers, using workers to do work that Israelites may at the same span of time not carry out, contracting for work to be done on the intermediate days of the festival and the like. The composite serves very well in context and cannot have found a comfortable location any where else in the tractate. It expands the case of the Mishnah into the consideration of the principle of contracting—whether with gentile or with Israelite workers—to perform various acts of labor. The net effect is vastly to expand the scope of the Mishnah, transforming the case into a rule, the rule into a broad and ubiquitously relevant principle.

X.B: Here we compare two sets of laws that have in common the same status, namely, laws that apply to interstitial cases. The intermediate days of the festival are not the festival, but also not secular; the Samaritan is not an Israelite, but is also not a gentile. Once more, if we look back at the Mishnah-rule, X.A, we find ourselves in a comparable situation, namely, an interstitial case, involving a situation that has come about by accident and that can cause great loss, and how we contend with it; the way we deal with a middle-range situation—two rules in conflict—frames the problem throughout. Then the net effect again is to recast the Mishnah-rule in a much broader framework and to highlight the deeper conflict at hand.

X.C: The issue here is limits on labor performed on the intermediate days of the festival in connection with observance of the festival—another kind of interstitiality. Now, there are limits, just as pertain in general to the intermediate days of the festival. But there also is a reason to extend those limits, since the acts of labor now pertain to the festival itself. Once more, the composite cannot serve elsewhere in the tractate, and it makes a formidable contribution to the examination of the Mishnah in a broader context than suggested by the Mishnah-rule itself.

XV.C, D, E: Here is the point at which the framers of the Talmud have made a statement that is entirely their own, reshaping the topic of the Mishnah in ways that the Mishnah-tractate cannot have led us to anticipate in any way. The set of composites takes up the rules governing the mourner on the intermediate days of the festival, and this shades over into a systematic presentation of the rules of mourning in their own terms. Then, E, others who are comparable to the mourner in their status—not permitted to conduct themselves in ordinary society in accord with the rules that otherwise govern uniformly—are introduced. The net effect is to transform the re-presentation of the Mishnah-tractate by introducing a topic that the Mishnah-tractate scarcely touches.

XVIII.B, C, D, E, F, G, I: The topic of mourning is once more treated in its own terms, out of all relationship to the Mishnah-tractates interest in it. Here again, we have what amounts to a small tractate on mourning, a range of general rules, special problems, and then the inevitable case of the sage produced in this context as in many others now carrying us far beyond the limits of the Mishnah-tractate.

XIX.B, C, D, F: The topic of mourning for sages, the death of sages, and the like, along with further comments on mourning rites, predominates once more. Here again, the Mishnah-tractate in a tangential way has introduced a topic in the contest of the Mishnah-tractate's program. Then the Talmud-composite treats the topic in terms not to be predicted out of the way in which the Mishnah-tractate has introduced said topic. Now the topic takes on a life of its own.

XX.C, E, F: Forms of lamentation take over, and the matter of the intermediate days of the festival falls by the way. Once more the result is the same. The essay shades over from mourning to death: dying suddenly, the angel of death, and the angel of death and sages.

XXI. B, C, D: Not surprisingly, the freestanding composite pursues its own interest, which is [1] rules of mourning with [2] special interest in sages. It is hardly surprising that D ends with the condition of sages in the world to come, that is, after death.

The topical composites fit in in two distinct ways. First, some of them—represented by I.B, IX.B, C, and X. B (a very subtle entry indeed)—greatly expand the scope of the Mishnah-rule, introducing a level of abstraction that Mishnah-exegesis does not require. Mishnah-exegesis is made to set the stage for a much broader consideration of principles that transcend cases and recast rules into representations of underlying conceptions of a high order of generalization. In this first type of topical composite, the Mishnah's rule is re-presented as an indicator of a deeper, compelling problem of thought, often of a philosophical, rather than a narrowly-legal character.

Second, and more strikingly, the larger number of the topical composites—represented by the composites from XV.C-E to the end!—change the face of the Mishnah-tractate by raising to prominence subjects treated by the Mishnah only incidentally and in a subordinate status. A tractate on conduct on the intermediate days of the festival has been turned into one on that subject and on another as well.

3) *Can we state what the compilers of this document propose to accomplish in producing this complete, organized piece of writing?*
The answer to this question lies in explaining the connection between rites of mourning and the rules governing conduct on the intermediate days of the festival. What made sages conceive that the latter should find a comfortable and capacious place amid the former—even to the extent of extensively and promiscuously interspersing rules of mourning in expositions of intermediate days of the festival? True, the Mishnah-tractate introduces the mourner, along with other classes of persons in a special situation on the intermediate days of the festival. But the Talmud has not then given us large-scale discussions of the person released from prison or others who appear on the same lists as the mourner. So the formal explanation—the topic is introduced by the Mishnah, so it is discussed in its own terms in the Talmud—begs the question.

Rather, a substantive explanation is required, and it is contained in the answer to a simple question. Precisely what has death to do with the intermediate days of the festival? The principal mode of thought of the Mishnah is that of comparison and contrast. Something is like something else, therefore follows its rule; or unlike, therefore follows the opposite of the rule governing the something else. So as a matter of hypothesis, let us assume that the framers of Talmud-tractate Moed Qatan found self-evidently valid the modes of thought that they learned from the Mishnah and so made connections between things that were alike, on the one side, or things that were opposite, on the other. How do death and mourning compare to the intermediate days of the festival? The point of opposition—the contrastive part of the equation—then proves blatant. Death is the opposite of the celebration of the festival. The one brings mourning, the other, joy. And the Mishnah's inclusion of the mourner on its list of those whose special situation must be taken into account then precipitates thought about the item on the list—the mourner—that most clearly embodies the special circumstance of all items on the list.

But if the contrast proves obvious, the point of comparison—how are these things similar, and what rule pertains to both—emerges with equal facility. Extremes of emotion—mourning, rejoicing—come together in the normal cycle of life and the passage of time. Each takes its place on a continuum with the other, whether from the perspective of the passage of time in nature or the passage of life, also in nature; whether from the perspective of the sacred or from the standpoint of uncleanness. The natural rhythm of the year brings Passover and Tabernacles, the celebration of the first full moon after the vernal and autumnal equinoxes, respectively. The natural rhythm of life brings its moments of intense emotion too. But death and the festival also form moments of a single continuum, one of uncleanness yielding to its polar opposite, sanctification, sanctification yielding to uncleanness. Death, we must not forget, also serves as a principal source of uncleanness, the festival, the occasion for sanctification beginning with the removal of cultic uncleanness and the entry into a state of cultic cleanness. These opposites also take their place on a single continuum of being.

So in establishing the connection, through treating the categories as equivalent and counterpart to one another, between death and the festival's intermediate days, what have our sages in Talmud-tractate Moed Qatan said in their own behalf, not about the Mishnah but through their re-presentation of the Mishnah? They make the connection between the one and the other—death and the festival's intermediate days—so as to yield a conclusion concerning the everyday and the here and now. These are neither permanently sanctified nor definitively unclean, neither wholly the occasion for rejoicing without restriction as to acts of labor nor entirely the occasion of common ventures without restriction as to attitudes of exaltation. The days between festivals, like ordinary life, after birth but before death—these are to be seen as sanctified but not wholly so, just as life forms the realm of the angel of death, but only for a while. The festival comes—and so does the resurrection of the dead and the life of the world to come, of which the festival, like the Sabbath, gives us a foretaste.

VII. *The Structure and Rationality of Babylonian Talmud Abodah Zarah*

Points of Structure

1) *Does Babylonian Talmud-tractate Abodah Zarah follow a coherent outline governed by a consistent rules?*
In general, our tractate is organized around the Mishnah-tractate of the same name. But as we shall note, it contains numerous, enormous, and important free-standing compositions and composites, which in no way comment on the Mishnah.

2) *What are the salient traits of its structure?*
Where the Tractate focuses upon the Mishnah, it takes up, ordinarily in this order, the meanings of words and phrases, the scriptural basis for Mishnah-rules, and the name of the authority behind an anonymous passage. It will then proceed to questions of a secondary order, e.g., implications of a statement, possible contradictions, in rule or in principle, between two distinct statements in the Mishnah or in other Tannaite compilations, and, then may come essays on the principle of law or the theme of law of the subject.

3) *What is the Rationality of the structure?*
The focus upon Mishnah-commentary tells us what enters into the composite, and why one item takes priority over another.

4) *Where are the points of irrationality in the structure?*
We have to distinguish among the large composites that do not directly address the amplification of the Mishnah between two types. The first is the composite that is tacked on for formal reasons, e.g., more sayings that bear the same attributive formula as the saying that has served the Mishnah, or more information on a subject that the Mishnah treats. The second is the composite that in no way relates to the Mishnah's rules, principles, or authorities. I place the former in parentheses, and catalogue the latter, which then are treated in the proper context: the question of how the intruded ("irrational") composites have affected and drastically changed the re-presentation of the Mishnah-tractate.

These are the composites that diverge from Mishnah-commentary: I.B, C, D,E, F, G, H; I.N (other rulings of Joshua b. Qorha); II.C (other rulings of Nahum the Mede); III.C, E; III.H (other festivals of idolatry); VIII.C, D, E, F, G; IX.B; XIII.B (Appendix on the Symptoms of Various Ailments and their Cures).

Points of System

1) *Does the Babylonian Talmud-tractate Abodah Zarah serve only as a re-presentation of the Mishnah-tractate of the same name?*
The Bavli tractate serves not only but mainly as a re-presentation of the Mishnah-tractate of the same name. That is to say, the Bavli-tractate presents the Mishnah-tractate but imparts to the received statement a vast, additional message of its own, one that puts into perspective and imparts depth and significance to the Mishnah-tractate's rules. The full meaning of that statement becomes clear presently.

2) *How do the topical composites fit into the Talmud-tractate Abodah Zarah and what do they contribute that the Mishnah-tractate of the same name would lack without them?*
Our task is now to survey those large-scale composites that accomplish a task other than that of Mishnah-exegesis. I have already catalogued them above. I omit reference to those items that are mere topical appendices or compilations of sayings in the name of an authority who figures in a Mishnah-comment. These are specified above. The remainder are as follows:

I.B: A Theology of Gentile Idolatry: Its Origins and its Implications for Holy Israel: Why the gentiles rejected the Torah. It was offered to each of them, but they were too much absorbed by their own matters to accept God's will. They did not even carry out the seven commandments of the children of Noah.

I.C: The Critical Importance of Torah-Study for the Salvation of Israel, Individually and Collectively: Why are human beings compared to fish of the sea? To tell you, just as fish in the sea, when they come up on dry land, forthwith begin to die, so with human beings, when they take their leave of teachings of the Torah and religious deeds, forthwith they begin to die.

I.D: God Favors Holy Israel over the Gentiles, Because the Former Accept, Study, and Carry Out the Torah and the Latter Do Not. Therefore at the End of Days God Will Save Israel and Destroy Idolatry: R. Hinena bar Pappa contrasted verses of Scripture: "It is written, 'As to the almighty, we do not find him exercising plenteous power' (Job 37:23), but by contrast, 'Great is our Lord and of abundant power' (Ps. 147:5), and further, 'Your right hand, Lord, is glorious in power' (Ex. 15:6). But there is no contradiction between the first and second and third statements, for the former speaks of the time of judgment when justice is tempered with mercy, so God does not do what he could and the latter two statements refer to a time of war of God against his enemies."

I.E: GOD'S JUDGMENT AND WRATH, GOD'S MERCY AND FORGIVENESS FOR ISRAEL: "It is written, 'You only have I known among all the families of the earth; therefore I will visit upon you all your iniquities' (Amos 3:2). If one is angry, does he vent it on someone he loves?" He said to them, "I shall tell you a parable. To what is the matter comparable? To the case of a man who lent money to two people, one a friend, the other an enemy. From the friend he collects the money little by little, from the enemy he collects all at once."

I.F: BALAAM, THE PROPHET OF THE GENTILES, AND ISRAEL; GOD'S ANGER WITH THE GENTILES BUT NOT WITH ISRAEL: The prophet of the gentiles was a fool, but he did have the power to curse; Israel was saved by God. Said R. Eleazar, "Said the Holy One, blessed be He, to Israel, 'My people, see how many acts of righteousness I carried out with you, for I did not grow angry with you during all those perilous days, for if I had grown angry with you, there would not have remained from Israel a remnant or a survivor.'"

I.G: THE TIME OF GOD'S ANGER IN RELATIONSHIP TO THE GENTILES AND TO ISRAEL; THE ROLE OF IDOLATRY IN GOD'S WRATH AGAINST THE NATIONS: That time at which God gets angry comes when the kings put on their crowns on their heads and prostrate themselves to the sun. Forthwith the Holy One, blessed be He, grows angry.

I.H: THE SINFUL ANCESTOR OF THE MESSIAH AND GOD'S FORGIVENESS OF HIM AND OF ISRAEL: God's forgiveness of David is the archetype of God's forgiveness of Israel. If an individual has sinned, they say to him, 'Go to the individual such as David, and follow his example, and if the community as a whole has sinned, they say to them, 'Go to the community such as Israel. TORAH-STUDY IS THE ANTIDOTE TO SIN: "What is the meaning of the verse of Scripture, 'Happy are you who sow beside all waters, that send forth the feet of the ox and the ass' (Isa. 32:20)? 'Happy are you, O Israel, when you are devoted to the Torah and to doing deeds of grace, then their inclination to do evil is handed over to them, and they are not handed over into the power of their inclination to do evil."

III.C: THE DIVISIONS OF ISRAEL'S HISTORY; THE HISTORY OF THE WORLD IN ITS PERIODS: here we deal with the history of Israel by its periods, with special attention to Israel's relationships with Rome, on the one side, and the point at which the Messiah will come, on the other, ca. 468: When four hundred years have passed from the destruction of the Temple, if someone says to you, 'Buy this field that is worth a thousand denars for a single denar, don't buy it.

III.E: COLLECTION OF STORIES ABOUT RABBI AND ANTIGONUS: Rabbi maintained cordial relationships with the Emperor, in which Rabbi gave the sage advice, and the emperor took it.

VIII.C: THE TRIAL OF ELIEZER B. HYRCANUS. IN THE MATTER OF MINUT: Reference to the idolators' judges' tribunal, scaffold, and stadium, calls to mind the trial of the sage by reason of the charge of Minut, or, in context, Christianity. It is no different in its workings from the state: "the two daughters who cry out from Gehenna, saying to this world, 'Bring, bring.' And who are they? They are Minut and the government."

VIII.D: IDOLATRY AND LEWDNESS: the antidote is Torah-study.
VIII.E: ROMAN JUSTICE, JEWISH MARTYRDOM: Hanina, my brother, don't you know that from Heaven have they endowed this nation Rome with dominion? For Rome has destroyed his house, burned his Temple, slain his pious ones, and annihilated his very best—and yet endures! And yet I have heard about you that you go into session and devote yourself to the Torah and even

call assemblies in public, with a scroll lying before you in your bosom.

VIII.F: THE STADIUM, THE CIRCUS, THE THEATER: He who goes to a stadium or to a camp to see the performances of sorcerers and enchanters or of various kinds of clowns, mimics, buffoons, and the like—lo, this is a seat of the scoffers, as it is said, "Happy is the man who has not walked in the counsel of the wicked...nor sat in the seat of the scoffers. But his delight is in the Torah of the Lord" (Ps. 1:12). Lo, you thereby learn that these things cause a man to neglect the study of the Torah.

VIII.G: HAPPY IS THE MAN WHO HAS NOT WALKED IN THE COUN-SEL OF THE WICKED, NOR STOOD IN THE WAY OF SINNERS, NOR SAT IN THE SEAT OF THE SCORNFUL. "'Happy is the man who has not walked'—to theaters and circuses of gentiles; 'nor stood in the way of sinners'—he does not attend contests of wild beasts..."

IX.B: COMPOSITE ON THE PROHIBITION OF STARING IN A LAS-CIVIOUS OR OTHERWISE IMPROPER MANNER

3) *Can we state what the compilers of this document propose to accomplish in producing this complete, organized piece of writing?*
Clearly, the sages have made a massive and governing transforma-tion of the tractate. We know that is the fact because the topic, idolatry, that emerges from the Bavli is presented in a quite differ-ent way from the manner in which the Mishnah has portrayed it. And the shift takes place in the extraneous composites. In this tractate, strikingly, the real re-presentation of the topic takes place in the opening pages, as though the framers wished to make certain we would address the subject of idolatry in the proper context. Here is a fine case of what one may call "re-contextualization."

Specifically, the large and fundamental composites that accom-plish other than the exegesis of the Mishnah, many of them stand-ing at the very head of the tractate, place the subject, idolatry, into an entirely new framework, a historical one. Everything is recast in light of our sages' perception of matters, their definition of the con-text in which we are to discuss this particular subject. Consequently, I doubt that any other tractate has been so thoroughly or profoundly recast into the image, after the likeness, of sages' Judaic system than this one. These strong judgments require ample demonstration, which I shall now provide.

A full grasp of what our sages have accomplished in this tractate requires that we compare the foregoing outline with the outline of the topic as it is set forth in the Mishnah-tractate. The first point to note is that the Mishnah-tractate restates the Written Torah's theology of idolatry and imparts to it a practical and concrete character. We have therefore to examine the three principal stages in the unfolding of the Torah's teachings on idolatry, the Written one, the oral one, and the authoritative re-presentation of the oral one, for Scripture, the Mishnah, and the Talmud, respectively. First comes the relationship of the Mishnah to Scripture.

A. *Scripture*

The tractate devoted to idolatry illustrates that relationship between Mishnah and Scripture in which Mishnah makes concrete and everyday the general conceptions of Scripture. Specifically, what our tractate does is to supply rules and regulations to carry out the fundamental Scriptural commandments about the destruction of idols and all things having to do with idolatry. It follows that while our tractate deals with facts and relies upon suppositions which Scripture has not supplied, its basic viewpoint and the problem it seeks to solve in fact derive from the Mosaic code. Before proceeding, we had best review those general statements which Scripture does make:

> *Ex. 23:13*
> "Take heed to all that I have said to you; and make no mention of the names of other gods, nor let such be heard out of your mouth."
>
> *Ex. 23:24*
> "When my angel goes before you, and brings you in to the Amorites, and the Hittites, and the Perizzites, and the Canaanites, the Hivites, and the Jebusites, and I blot them out, you shall not bow down into their gods, nor serve them, nor do according to their work, but you shall utterly overthrow them and break their pillars in pieces."
>
> *Ex. 23:32-33*
> "You shall make no covenant with them or with their gods. They shall not dwell in your land, lest they make you sin against me; for if you serve their gods, it will surely be a snare to you."
>
> *Ex. 34:12-16*
> The Lord said to Moses, "Come up to me on the mountain, and wait there; and I will give you the tables of stone, with the law and the commandment, which I have written for their instruction." So Moses rose with his servant Joshua, and Moses went up into the mountain of God. And he said to the elders, "Tarry here for us, until we come

to you again; and, behold Aaron and Hur are with you; whoever has a cause, let him go to them."

Then Moses went up on the mountain, and the cloud covered the mountain. The glory of the Lord settled on Mount Sinai, and the cloud covered it six days; and on the seventh day he called to Moses out of the midst of the cloud.

Deut. 7:1-5

"When the Lord your God brings you into the land which you are entering to take possession of it, and clears away many nations before you, the Hittites, the Girgashites, the Amorites, the Canaanites, the Perizzites, the Hivites, and the Jebusites, seven nations greater and mightier than yourselves, and when the Lord your God gives them over to you, and you defeat them; then you must utterly destroy them; show no mercy to them. You shall not make marriages with them, giving your daughters to their sons or taking their daughters for your sons. For they would turn away your sons from following me, to serve other gods; then the anger of the Lord would be kindled against you, and he would destroy you quickly. But thus shall you deal with them: you shall break down their altars, and dash in pieces their pillars, and hew down their Asherim, and burn their graven images with fire."

Deut. 7:25-26

"The graven images of their gods you shall burn with fire; you shall not covet the silver or the gold that is on them, or take it for yourselves, lest you be ensnared by it; for it is an abomination to the Lord your God. And you shall not bring an abominable thing into your house, and become accursed like it; you shall utterly detest and abhor it; for it is an accursed thing."

Deut. 12:2-3

"You shall surely destroy all the places where the nations whom you shall dispossess served their gods, upon the high mountains and upon the hills and under every green tree; you shall tear down their altars, and dash in pieces their pillars, and burn their Asherim with fire; you shall hew down the graven images of their gods, and destroy their name out of that place."

B. *From Scripture to the Mishnah*

The tractate which proposes to realize these commandments in ordinary life is in three parts, moving form the general to the specific. It turns, first, to commercial relationships, second, to matters pertaining to idols, and, finally, to the very urgent issue of the prohibition of wine, part of which has served as a libation to an idol. There are a number of unstated principles before us. What a gentile is not likely to use for the worship of an idol is not going to be prohibited. What may serve not as part of idolatry but as an appurtenance thereto is prohibited for Israelite use but permitted for Israelite commerce. What serves for idolatry is prohibited for use and for benefit. Certain further assumptions about gentiles, not pertinent specifically to idolatry, are expressed. Gentiles are assumed routinely to practice bestiality, bloodshed, and fornication, without limit or restriction. This negative image of the gentile finds expression in the laws before us. The outline of the tractate follows.

I.	**Commercial relationships with gentiles. 1:1-2:7**
A.	**Festivals and fairs. 1:1-4**
1:1	For three days before gentile festivals it is forbidden to do business with them.
1:2	Ishmael: Three days afterward also.
1:3	These are the festivals of gentiles.
1:4	A city in which there is an idol—in the area outside of it, it is permitted to do business.
B.	**Objects prohibited even in commerce. 1:5-2:2**
1:5	These are things which it is forbidden to sell to gentiles.
1:6	In a place in which they are accustomed to sell small cattle to gentiles, they sell them (the consideration being use of the beasts for sacrifices to idols).
1:7	They do not sell them bears, lions, or anything which is a public danger. They do not help build with them a basilica, scaffold, stadium, or judges' tribunal.
1:8-9	They do not make ornaments for an idol, sell them produce which is not yet harvested, sell them land in the Holy Land.
2:1	They do not leave cattle in gentiles' inns, because they are suspect in regard to bestiality.
2:2	They accept healing for property (e.g., animals) but not for a person.
C.	**Objects prohibited for use but permitted in trade. 2:3-7**
2:3	These things belonging to gentiles are prohibited, and the prohibition concerning them extends to deriving any benefit from them at all: wine, vinegar, earthenware which absorbs wine, and hides pierced at the heart.
2:4	Skins of gentiles and their jars, with Israelite wine collected in them—they are prohibited, the prohibition extends to deriving benefit, so Meir. Sages: Not to deriving benefit.
2:5	On what account did they prohibit cheese made by gentiles?
2:6-7	These are things of gentiles which are prohibited, but the prohibition does not extend to deriving benefit from them. Milk, bread, oil, etc.

2:7	These are things which to begin with are permitted for Israelite consumption.
II.	**Idols. 3:1-4:7**
A.	**General Principles. 3:1-7**
3:1	All images are prohibited, because they are worshipped once a year, so Meir, Sages: Prohibited is only one which has an emblem of authority.
3:2-3	He who finds the shreds of images—lo, these are permitted.
3:4	Gamaliel: What gentiles treat as a god is prohibited.
3:5	Gentiles who worship hills and valleys—the hills or valleys are permitted, but what is on them is forbidden.
3:6	If one's house-wall served also as the wall of a Temple and it fell down, one may not rebuild it.
3.7	There are three states in regard to idolatry: what is built for idolatrous purposes is forbidden. What is improved is forbidden until the improvement is removed. What merely happens to be used for an idol is permitted once the idol is removed.
B.	**The Asherah. 3:7-10**
3:7	What is an asherah?
3:8-9	Use of an asherah-tree.
3:10	Desecrating an asherah-tree.
C.	**The Merkolis. 4:1-2**
4:1-2	Three stones beside a Merkolis (= Hermes) are forbidden, so Ishmael.
D.	**Nullifying an idol. 4:3-7**
4:3	An idol which had a garden or bathhouse.
4:4-6	An idol belonging to a gentile is prohibited forthwith. One belonging to an Israelite is forbidden only once it has been worshipped. How one nullifies an idol.
4:7	If God does not favor idolatry, why does he not wipe it away?
III.	**Libation-wine. 4:8-5:12**
4:8	They purchase from gentiles the contents of a winepress which has already been trodden out, for it is not the sort of wine which gentiles use for a libation until it has dripped down into the vat.
4:9	Israelites tread a winepress with a gentile, but they do not gather grapes with him.
4:10	A gentile who is found standing beside a cistern of wine—if he had a lien on the vat, it is prohibited. If he had no lien on it, it is permitted.
4:11	He who prepares the wine belonging to a gentile in a condition of cleanness and leaves it in his domain.
5:1	He who hires an Israelite worker to work with him in the

preparation of libation-wine—the Israelite's salary is forbidden.

5:2   Libation-wine which fell on grapes—one may rinse them off, and they are permitted. If the grapes were split and absorbed wine, they are prohibited.

5:3-4   A gentile who with an Israelite was moving jars of wine from place to place—if the wine is assumed to be watched, it is permitted. If the Israelite told the gentile he was going away for any length of time, the wine is prohibited.

5:5   The same point, now in the context of eating at the same table.

5:6   A band of gentile raiders which entered a town peacefully—open jars are forbidden, closed ones permitted.

5:7   Israelite craftsmen, to whom a gentile sent a jar of libation-wine as salary, may ask him to pay in money instead, only if this is before the wine has entered their possession. Afterward it is forbidden.

5:8-9   Libation-wine is forbidden and imparts a prohibition on wine with which it is mixed in any measure at all. If it is wine poured into water, it is forbidden only if it imparts a flavor.

5:10   Libation-wine which fell into a vat—the whole of the vat is forbidden for benefit. Simeon b. Gamaliel: All of it may be sold except the value of the volume of libation-wine which is in it.

5:11-12   A stone winepress which a gentile covered with pitch—one dries it off, and it is clean. One of wood, one of earthenware.

The opening unit unfolds in a fairly orderly way, from a prologue on the special problems of fairs, to the general matter of things Israelites may not even buy or sell, as against things they may not use but may trade, I.B, C. The second unit lays down some general principles about images, then presents special ones on two specific kinds of idols, II.B, C, and at the end asks the logical necessary question about how one nullifies an idol entirely. The third unit is a very long essay about libation-wine and its effect upon Israelite-gentile commerce. I do not see any coherent subdivisions of this sizable discussion, which goes over the same ground time and again.

C. *From the Mishnah to the Talmud*

From its initial insertion of a massive account of gentile idolatry, the Talmud reframes issues. The Mishnah asks not a single question of history or theology. it deals only with 1 commercial relationships with

gentiles, so far as these are affected by idolatry, 2 idols, and 3 libation wine. So the topic at hand is treated in a routine and commonplace manner. The Talmud transforms and transcends the topic. It
transforms it by reframing the issue of idolatry so that at stake is no
longer relationships between Israel and idolatrous nations but rather,
those between idolatrous nations and God. It then transcends the
topic by introducing the antidote to idolatry, which is the Torah.
So Israel differs from idolatrous nations by reason of the Torah, and
that imparts a special character to all of Israel's everyday conduct,
not only its abstinence from idol-worship. In fact, the Talmud makes
this tractate into an occasion for reflection on the problem of Israel
and the nations.

Predictably, the sages invoke the one matter that they deem critical
to all else: the Torah. Israel differs from the gentiles not for the merely
negative reason that it does not worship idols but only an invisible
God. It differs from them for the positive reason that the Torah that
defines Israel's life was explicitly rejected by the gentiles. Every one
of them had its chance at the Torah, and all of them rejected it.
When the gentiles try to justify themselves to God by appealing to
their forthcoming relationships to Israel, that is dismissed as self-
serving. The gentiles could not even observe the seven commandments assigned to the Noahides. From that point, the composite that
stands at the head of the tractate and imparts its sense to all that
will follow proceeds to the next question, that is, from the downfall
of the gentiles by reason of their idolatry and rejection of the Torah to the salvation of Israel through the Torah.

Lest we miss the point, the reason for God's favor is made explicit: God favors Israel because Israel keeps the Torah. God therefore is strict with the gentiles but merciful to Israel. This is forthwith
assigned a specific illustration: Balaam, the gentiles' prophet, presents the occasion to underscore God's anger toward the gentiles and
his mercy to Israel. Bringing us back to the beginning, we then are
shown how God's anger for the gentiles comes to the fore when the
gentiles worship idols: when the kings who rule the world worship
nature rather than nature's Creator. How God forgives Israel is then
shown in respect to David's sin, and Torah-study as the antidote to
sin once more is introduced. It is difficult to conclude other than
that the framers of the Talmud have added to the presentation of
the topic the results of profound thought on idolatry as a force in
the history of humanity and of Israel. They thus have re-presented

the Mishnah's topic in a far more profound framework of reflection than the Mishnah, with its rather petty interests in details of this and that, would have lead us to anticipate.

The next set of free-standing composites present episodic portraits of the matters introduced at the outset. The first involves world history and its periods, divided, it goes without saying, in relationship to the history of Israel, which stands at the center of world history. Rome defines the counterpart, and Israel's and Rome's relationships, culminating in the coming of the Messiah, are introduced. The next two collections form a point and counterpoint. On the one side, we have the tale of how Rabbi and the Roman Emperor formed a close relationship, with Rabbi the wise counsellor, the ruler behind the throne. So whatever good happens in Rome happens by reason of our sages' wisdom, deriving as it does from the Torah, on which the stories predictably are going to harp. Then comes as explicit a judgment upon Christianity in the framework of world-history as I think we are likely to find in the Talmud. The set of stories involves Eliezer b. Hyrcanus and how he was tried for Minut, which the story leaves no doubt stands for Christianity. Now "Minut" and the Roman government are treated as twin-sources of condemnation. And it is in that very context that the stories of Roman justice and Jewish martyrdom, by reason of Torah-study, are introduced. Not only so, but—should we miss the contrast the compilers wish to draw—the very same setting sets forth the counterpart and opposite: the stadium, circus, and theater, place for scoffers and buffoons, as against the sages' study-center, where people avoid the seat of the scornful but instead study the Torah.

The Talmud's associations with idolatry then compare and contrast these opposites: Israel and Rome; martyrdom and wantonness; Torah and lewdness and other forms of sin; probity and dignity and buffoonery; and on and on. The Mishnah finds no reason to introduce into the consideration of idolatry either the matter of the Torah or the issue of world history. The Talmud cannot deal with the details of conduct with gentiles without asking the profound questions of divine intentionality and human culpability that idolatry in the world provokes. And yet, if we revert to the Mishnah's fabricated debates with the philosophers, we see the issue introduced and explored. What the Mishnah lacks is not a philosophy of monotheism in contrast with polytheism and its idols, but a theology of history and a theodicy of Israel's destiny, a salvific theory. These the Talmud introduces, with enormous effect. And, we note, once these propositions have been inserted, the Talmud allows the systematic exposition of the Mishnah to go forward without theological intrusion of any kind. The point has been made.

Now, we wonder, where have our sages learned to interpret the issue of idolatry in a historical and theological framework, rather than in a merely practical and reasonable one, such as the Mishnah's authorship provides? A glance at the verses of Scripture given earlier answers the question. Idolatry explains the fate of the nations, Israel's covenant through the Torah, Israel's. But the verses of Scripture cited earlier hardly serve as source for the reflections on Israel and Rome, the ages of human history, the power of God to forgive, and, above all, the glory of the Torah as the mediating source of God's love and forgiveness. All of this the sages themselves formulated and contributed. Scripture provided important data, the Mishnah, the occasion, but for the theology of history formed around the center of the Torah, we look to our sages for the occasion and the source. And sages' success in meeting the challenge of the topic at hand explains why no tractate more successfully demonstrates how the Talmud's framers' massive insertions transform the Mishnah's statement into one of considerably enhanced dimensions and depth. None more admirably matched their capacities of deep reflection on the inner structure of Israel's history with the promise and potential of a subject of absolutely primary urgency.

VIII. *The Structure and Rationality of Babylonian Talmud Makkot*

Points of Structure

1) *Does Babylonian Talmud-tractate Makkot follow a coherent outline governed by a consistent rules?*
The outline given above serves for nearly the whole of the tractate. That is to say, if we start with the principles of a topical outline, with the conception that a topic-sentence governs what is to be said in the sequence of paragraphs that follow, then with the paragraphs laid out as secondary expositions and expansions of the topic or proposition, with a new topic-sentence signalling a new set of expositions and expansions relevant to that, and so on down, we can outline nearly every line of the tractate. The Mishnah's statements serve as the topic sentences in the outline I have worked out. The

secondary expositions, bearing capital letters as their marks, then form a succession of close and logically-sequential expositions of the topic-sentences that the Mishnah has provided and the Talmud's framers have selected. These are the exceptions: III.A, B, IX D, XVI B, C, XVI F, G, H, XXII D, XXX C. It follows that Bavli-tractate Makkot does follow a coherent outline, and we may inductively define the rules that govern throughout.

2) *What are the salient traits of its structure?*
The of a Talmud-composite had in hand completed compositions deriving from an indeterminate past. What he then did was to follow a simple outline. He laid out the Mishnah-tractate, making a decision on which passages of the tractate he wished to expound. I have no clear theory of the criteria that instructed him on the matter, because a theory on why given paragraphs of the Mishnah were not treated must await the examination of a much larger sample than the tractates that at this moment are in hand. In any event we cannot show that the framer picked and chose among a large corpus of available Mishnah-comments; we cannot show that he included everything to which he had access; we cannot show that he made up pretty much everything he had to say; and we cannot show that he limited himself to the utilization of received materials. What we cannot show, we do not know. So the first salient trait of the structure of the tractate is, the formulation of a systematic exegesis for (parts of) tractate Makkot.

A fixed order of exposition governed: [1] the scriptural foundations of, or links to, rules of the Mishnah; [2] the explanation of words or phrases in the Mishnah; [3] the introduction of Tannaite complements to the Mishnah, meaning, compositions (or even composites) bearing the marks of origin among the official, Tannaite memorizers. Afterward, so far as exegesis of a given Mishnah-sentence or paragraph was underway, [4] theoretical problems would be introduced, refinements of the law, interstitial cases in which two principles intersected and produced unclarity, and the like. That order is not a matter of hypothesis, so far as this tractate is concerned, it is demonstrated beyond doubt, beginning to end. That is, if all four types of material are set forth in the exposition of a given Mishnah-sentence or paragraph, the specified order governs. The third or fourth types will appear first in order only when the first and second types are not introduced at all. That seems to me ample evidence that a well-defined structural program governed. Other components of the program, e.g., cases, tangential discussions, not to mention the free-standing composites that in no way bear upon Mishnah-exegesis, all are organized in a logical way as well, but have to be dealt with in their own terms.

3) *What is the Rationality of the structure?*

The rationality of Bavli-tractate Makkot may be defined very simply. The framers of the tractate undertook to examine and analyze Mishnah-tractate Makkot so as to clarify its contents, on the one side, and to show the logical coherence and cogency of the diverse rules of the tractate, on the other. The principles of cogency were two. First, the discrete rules of the Mishnah relate to the received, written Torah of Sinai, and they gain cogency not because they spin out a single logical proposition, or even because they work out in an orderly way the components of a topic and explain each component in its place. Rather, they gain cogency because all of the discrete statements derive from a single, prior source, which is, the written Torah. The first principle of rationality then concerns the coherence of discrete and free-standing statements, e.g., this Mishnah-paragraph, that Mishnah-rule, and coherence is imposed by a common derivation in the Torah. The first principle of cogency therefore is formal.

But a second principle of cogency plays an equally important role, and that concerns the substance of matters. The Mishnah-rules cohere not only because all of them derive from the same prior source, but because each of them takes up its position in the exposition of a topic. The orderly presentation of the tractate, line by line, defines a rationality that insists upon the principle that subjects themselves exhibit an inner logic; hold together by reason of the fit of the parts thereof. That accounts for the principle of organization that lays out the tractate as a commentary to the Mishnah, itself a topical formulation of the law, rather than as a commentary to those passages of Scripture to which the Mishnah-rules relate. That that alternative rationality of structure can have governed hardly can be doubted, since we do have systematic expositions of topics in accord with their appearance in Scripture, not the Mishnah, in Mekhilta, Sifra, and the two Sifrés.

It follows that two principles of cogency intersect, the scriptural and the topical, and the topical takes pride of place. That is the meaning of the Bavli's presentation of its ideas in the form of a commentary to the Mishnah.

4) *Where are the points of irrationality in the structure?*
If rationality derives from the interplay of form and substance, as just now spelled out, then rationality defines, also, its counterpart and opposite, irrationality. Where does Mishnah-exposition break down? There we find the points of irrationality. Then the answer is simple: at the listed passages, III.A, B, IX D, XVI B, C, XVI F, G, H, XXII D, XXX C, where Mishnah-exegesis does not define the focus of a composite, but where some other principle does. The point of irrationality on the surface is structural. But in that aspect, it also conflicts with both the scriptural and the topical principles of coherent discourse; neither Scripture's relevant passages nor the Mishnah's topical program governs, and at some interesting points in this tractate, a completely different theory of the composition of an exposition of the law, and not the Talmud's theory, takes over. Had this other theory prevailed, we should have law, but not the Talmud; and we should have exegesis, but not the Midrash-compilations as we know them.

Points of System

1) *Does the Babylonian Talmud-tractate Makkot serve only as a re-presentation of the Mishnah-tractate of the same name?*
This Bavli-tractate serves mainly as a re-presentation of the Talmud-tractate of the same name, in that the structure of the document finds its definition therein. But, as we recognize, large tracts of Mishnah-tractate Makkot are ignored or given the most routine exposition. When we realize that a fair measure of the Mishnah-exposition follows a repeated formula over the discussion of several Mishnah-paragraphs, the routine character of the re-presentation becomes striking. But since the framers obviously picked and chose, we must say that their system rests only asymmetrically upon that of the Mishnah. But, I hasten to add, in this tractate as in most others, where the authors of a composition do expound the meaning of a sentence or paragraph of the Mishnah, I cannot point to a single passage in which, it seems to me, they have brought a program of their own such that they have recast the Mishnah-sentence or paragraph into a different framework of meaning from that defined by the Mishnah's authors or framers. That seems to me a consistent, and very important, result of our examination of this tractate.

2) *How do the topical composites fit into the Talmud-tractate Makkot and what do they contribute that the Mishnah-tractate of the same name would lack without them?*

An answer composed of generalizations contributes nothing. We turn directly to each specific item.

III.A and B: The entire composition goes its own way, and if this kind of composition predominated, we should have nothing resembling a talmud, such as the Talmuds that we know. The law of Judaism would have reached us in a completely different form from the form—the applied reason and practical logic given dynamism by dialectics—that we know. And the history of Judaism, so far as the intellectual life of the faith defines that history, would have taken a different course from the one that it took.

The composite at 1:1L-N, from beginning to end, shows a different theory of composite-making from the one that predominates in the Talmud overall. In this theory we collect statements attributed by a principal authority to a founder of the tradition in Babylonia, Rab or Samuel; these statements cover a variety of topics and express no single cogent principle; nor do they take up one problem in a variety of forms. And since the composite does not take shape around a problem of Mishnah-exegesis or of the analysis of a problem of law, exegesis of Scripture, or theology, it follows that the theory of composite-making is different from the theory that produced the Talmud's composites as we know them. Had the present theory prevailed, we should have no Talmud—systematic exposition of the Mishnah, with additions—but rather collections of sayings joined by the formality of common source in a given authority's school. These collections then will have yielded something other than a coherent statement of the law of the Mishnah, properly expanded. They will have given us the same law, but in very different form.

And yet, we notice, the character of the discussion of the components of the composite that sets forth the formulation of Judah in Samuel's or in Rab's name in no way differs from the character of the discussion of our conventional Talmud. I take that fact to mean people subjected to the same sort of sustained analytical discussion diverse types of composites, not only the types that yielded the Talmud as we know it. So in circulation were composites built on various principles, analyzed in a uniform manner. Then, it must follow, those who made the Talmud as we know it picked the kinds of materials they wanted for their Talmud and, in general, omitted such other kinds as did not serve their purpose. And one of the important other kinds is the one before us: compilations of masters' sayings, organized around other than topical-programmatic lines.

This composite does not change the face of our tractate, because it has no bearing upon the re-presentation of the tractate's topical program. The composite rather shows us a different face of the law, one that, had it predominated, would have ignored the structure of the Mishnah altogether and re-formed the law into a set of rulings assigned to this authority or that one, to this set of verses of Scripture or that one, to this formulary pattern or that one. Then the topical organization of the law would have given way to a mode of presentation bearing a different rationality altogether. The figure of the authority, the tradition of his school, would have predominated; the law would then have consisted of what the authority taught, and search for the rule in a given case or concerning a given problem would have involved finding which authority dealt with the topic. Along with the orderly presentation of topics, the analytical and dialectical discussion of them would never have gotten under way, since dialectics as we know them depend upon not personality or authority but reason and the governing, objective logic that inheres in a given topic. From our perspective, the one contribution this composite makes to our tractate is to show us how things might have been, and to underscore the reasons for admiring the way in which the framers of the Talmud laid matters out.

IX D: This item introduces the complication of the suitability of testimony of witnesses. It may be that the intent is to carry forward the introduction of the rules of testimony into the matter at hand, but that is not a compelling consideration.

XVI B: The introduction of the matter of relationships of disciples and masters—a general point, of enormous interest—into the rules governing going into exile reshapes the topic by adding a profound observation. It is that while someone may go into exile from his home town and family, the Torah never leaves him; if his master goes into exile, he goes along; if he goes into exile, his master goes along. The point then is that exile affects the natural relationships, but not supernatural ones. In a case of manslaughter, God knows that there has been no murder and does not inflict the penalty of separation from the Torah upon the surviving party to a tragic accident. The Torah legislates for this world, allowing for a penalty to manslaughter, since, after all, the victim has died; but the Torah also distinguishes this world's penalties, which are painful but can be endured, from those of Heaven. Exile from the Torah would be a penalty that cannot be endured and may not be inflicted. So XVI.B recasts the rules at hand into a very original point.

XVI C: In light of the foregoing, we cannot find surprising the explicit statement of what is implicit, which is, the Torah is the sole source of authentic, enduring wealth. This world's rewards are transient; Torah-study with a multitude of disciples forms the reward of eternity. So XVI.C forms an essential step in a carefully-wrought statement. Then the topic, exile, provides the occasion for making a statement that the framers of the Talmud wish to make, not only in its own terms, therefore abstractly, but also in terms of one topic after another, and so in a very concrete way.

XVI F: Since an "elder" is a sage, the addition here makes the same point once more: a city that lacks elders, or sages, is not a suitable city of refuge. This addition is now predictable: the dimension of Torah-learning, which is supernatural, completely recasts our perception of the topic, its issues, and its messages.

XVI G: While this composition does not expound a clause of the Mishnah, it fits into the context of those that do.

XVI H: This passage is built on the following structure:

> On the verse, "And Joshua wrote these words in the book of the Torah of God" (Josh. 24:26), *there was a difference of opinion between R. Judah and R. Nehemiah.*
> As to the suitability of a scroll of the Torah, the parchment skins of which are sewn together with thread of flax, *there was a difference of opinion between R. Judah and R. Meir.*

The principle of composition then is obvious: disputes between Judah and someone else; and the principle of inclusion is beyond comprehension within the rationality of our Talmud—and of the Mishnah.

XXII D: The curse of a sage takes effect even when it is not justified. The passage to which this propositional composite is attached concerns the curse of the mother of the manslayer. Once more, therefore, we know why the passage has been included: it is to recast the topic in a new dimension, one in which the supernatural enters in. The mother's curse may not take effect; the sage's curse will.

XXX C: Here we find a systematic set of reflections on Israel's history, which make a striking point. A quick review of the reflections shows us what that point is. To restate the main propositions laid out in sequence: The statement maintains that [1] the sage succeeds to prophecy, because now the sage, through master of the Torah, can convey Heaven's statement to Israel; [2] the Holy Spirit appears to Israel, but the upshot is the same as that of Torah-learning; and Moses our rabbi made decrees, but sages annulled them. This last point yields the proposition that the sage is the master of prophecy, because the sages know how to read prophecy in the correct way.

3) *Can we state what the compilers of this document propose to accomplish in producing this complete, organized piece of writing?*
With the sole exception of IX.D, we can account for the intruded compositions and composites in one of two ways. One set of materials portrays legal topics by organizing teachings of named masters. Then the named master, not the topic, forms the source of coherence. The other set of materials portrays the topic of our tractate in a quite fresh way, by introducing a dimension of all law that the Mishnah ordinarily does not portray, namely, how the intrusion of the sage imparts a supernatural character to the affairs of this world. [1] The Torah does not abandon a person, but accompanies the disciple into exile; that means the supernatural family of master and disciples forms a unit subject to the judgment of the law; the Torah is the sole enduring and reliable form of wealth; a city without "elders," that is, sages, cannot afford the refuge that the Torah has provided for the manslayer; the sage is the heir to prophecy, has direct access through his powers of analytical learning, to Heaven's wishes, and disposes of prophecy much as the prophets were able to dispose of even the teachings of Moses.

The Mishnah-tractate that concerns flogging and exile has been transformed into a statement about the glory of the Torah as represented by the sage, who may be subject to flogging and exile, but who always represents that transcendent reality that the Torah conveys in this world. The topic is now seen from a different perspective altogether, and though the Mishnah has been faithfully set forth, through the introduction of topics not required for Mishnah-exegesis, and through the juxtaposition of those topical presentations with the exposition of the Mishnah, all things have changed. It is probably extending matters beyond the limits to observe that in a

tractate bearing such a message, the presentation of composites
formed around the names of sages delivers the message of the priority of the sage over prophecy, as much as the power of the sage
to transcend exile and the power of the Torah to secure a permanent endowment, that other intruded compositions and composites
deliver as well. That observation about the appropriateness even of
what is least coherent in the most definitive and formal traits must,
for the moment, form a mere footnote. But the text and its message
leave no grounds for doubt on how the Talmud-tractate has recast
the Mishnah-tractate and made the Mishnah-tractate into a medium
for the message that the Talmud's system, and not the Mishnah's,
wishes to set forth.

IX. *Conclusion*

All thirty-seven tractates of the Bavli yield their points of interest
and show us the self-evident connections that their compilers, on their
own, in response to the Mishnah, or in the tradition of the Mishnah,
establish.[2] This insistence of mine upon the rationality of jarring
juxtapositions runs counter to the view of the Talmud that prevails
even among those who claim to know the document well, and that
is because of the way in which it is studied. The Talmud up to now
has been understood within the processes of philological inquiry and
phrase by phrase exegesis conducted in other than academic settings,
yeshivas and Jewish seminaries for example. In recent times, the
Talmud is not studied in its own terms at all, but texts selected by
reason of their common topic will be studied in their own framework. So students do not even master the Talmud in the way in which
its framers and compilers created it. Whether people study isolated
passages, losing track of the whole, or whether to begin with they
ignore the whole for congruent parts, the result is the same: the
impression that the document is just a collection of this and that,
not a purposive and well-crafted piece of writing to be mastered
through its own disciplines—a mere scrapbook.

---

[2] These are spelled out completely in *Rationality and Structure: The Bavli's Anomalous Juxtapositions*. Atlanta, 1997: Scholars Press for South Florida Studies in the
History of Judaism.

Questions of coherence, order, rationality of discourse under such conditions do not command attention, for if people concentrate on words and phrases and small, whole units out of all larger context, they are unlikely to ask, what has this to do with that? In that setting the Talmud serves as a source of information, opinion, authoritative fact out of all context, but it is rarely perceived as a cogent and systematic (and I argue, systemic) statement overall. Issues of detail overwhelm concerns of structure and order. The received exegetical tradition, essential in its theological and political setting of faith and useful also in the academic one, yields a mass of detail, but no coherent account formed of the details. People quote sayings but grasp little of their broader intellectual context. Setting forth bits and pieces while never gaining sight of the whole (and in recent times even saying there is no whole, only parts to be detached and reassembled as one likes), the received exegetical and philological tradition addresses few questions of serious academic concern. But it forms the basis for this next step in a centuries-old labor of mediation. On its successes, we build. Responding to questions it did not address, we move forward.

CHAPTER FOUR

WHERE THE TALMUD COMES FROM

I. *Where the Talmud Comes from: The Present-Tense Question of Origins*

The Talmud (a.k.a., the Talmud of Babylonia, the Bavli) is principally—an estimated 90% in its total volume—a systematic exegesis
of the Mishnah and amplification of its law. We therefore know where
it originates. The Talmud comes from those who compiled it as a
massive exegesis and amplification of the Mishnah. Whether that
work took a month, a year or a century, at every point the Talmud
is formally coherent and intellectually cogent, and responsibility for
those who made it so belongs to the ones who made and carried
out the Talmud's rules of formulation and composition, on the one
side, and its protocol of thought and analysis, on the other. The
writers of Mishnah-exegetical compositions and compilers of
Mishnah-exegetical composites guaranteed the persistence of formalization, by utilizing a limited repertoire of forms. The character of
the Mishnah itself and the acuity of its Talmudic exegetes produced
the latter trait, its prevailing, intellectual cogency. We may therefore define the Talmud and identify its indicative formal and intellectual traits—hence the traits its compilers imparted to it. But that
fact raises a question about that small part of the Talmud that does
not conform to the document's framers' plan.

Specifically, what about the elements of the Talmud that do not
carry out its primary task—where do they come from? I refer to two
types of writing, the smallest whole units of thought ("cognitive units")
that can stand entirely on their own and do not depend upon a larger
documentary context for meaning; and, second and principally, the
sizable but wholly coherent compositions that the Talmud contains
but does not require for its framers to accomplish the paramount
goal of Mishnah-exegesis. These are the two kinds of constituents
of the Talmud that stand autonomous of the document's main construction. They stand autonomous of their present documentary
setting—hence, free-standing.

Mishnah-commentary and amplification dictate the character of the greatest part of the document: its organization, its order of discourse, from logically-necessary start to the sole rational point of conclusion, its selection of topics for discussion and appropriate illustrative materials, its elaboration and amplification of issues. Since, I have shown, the Talmud's generative structure defines its purpose as a systematic commentary to the Mishnah, the writing set forth to accomplish the Talmud's task may readily be distinguished from that put down for some other task. The criterion of distinguishing completed pieces of writing that accomplish the document's framers' purpose from those that carry out some other purpose (perhaps even one lacking all bearing upon the formation of a complete document) therefore finds definition in quite objective and formal terms. So we turn to materials that the compilers of the Talmud utilized but that they did not necessarily make up.

The other-than-Mishnah-exegetical compositions and composites that the Bavli utilizes but that the Bavli's primary framers and compilers did not produce in their work of Talmud-making, then, illuminate a considerable question. Specifically, they will tell us where that part of the document comes from, outside of the circles of its primary writers and compilers, the Mishnah-exegetes who composed the Talmud from beginning to end. We seek to identify the building blocks of Talmudic discourse that advance a redactional program other than that of the Talmud overall, in its paramount components. These are then defined as the completed units of thought that took shape around a task other than that of Mishnah-exegesis and can find for themselves a comfortable place in some other document than the one before us, or in many other documents, for that matter. Once we know how to identify the irreducible minima of discourse other than that that sets the norm in the Talmud, we can take up the analysis of the Talmud's extra-talmudic component.

These two types of writings lead us to the world of those who stand outside of the Talmud's main center and focus:

1) the smallest cognitive units that can stand on their own, ignore the rules of documentary composition and may appear in any document, not only this one; and also therefore speak out of a context other than the Talmud's primary one, and
2) cogent compositions autonomous of context; these compositions (and the composites that they comprise) likewise respond to a program other than that which governed the writing of the Talmud's

principal and preponderant compositions and composites; they may or may not have found a place in some other document, but they certainly ignore the rules that define this one.

Each type accordingly encompasses sets of words that hold together and that on the face of it make a complete statement on their own, without depending upon any other sentence(s) for context or meaning. They afford access to what people were thinking outside of the framework of those who set forth the Talmud within its definitive limits. In the Introduction I spell out the sense of that definition of the work. The second of the two types of free-standing components, the autonomous compositions and composites, rapidly take the center-stage here. What data come under consideration?

First come free-standing sentences, those that convey sense and meaning on their own and not within the limits of a larger composition. These episodic units may serve a variety of secondary purposes but, removed from context, on their own are able to sustain clarity and meaning. How do we know them, and how important a place do they take?

Second are those sizable, autonomous and coherent topical compositions that, as I shall explain, do not serve the Talmud's primary purpose of Mishnah-commentary and amplification and clearly have not been assembled in response to that exegetical task at all. For whom do they speak and what message do they convey?

The former convey statements that do not depend upon the Talmud's context for their meaning; the latter set forth entire sets of coherent statements, compositions worked out for a purpose other than that which governs through the Talmud overall.

To what indicative data do I appeal in quest of the components of the Talmud that stand independent of the Talmud and therefore come from some source other than the writers of the materials particular to the Talmud? The criteria, as already indicated, are two. First, defining the Talmud as a systematic commentary to the Mishnah, I treat as native to the Talmud all writing that clearly depends for context and meaning upon the work of Mishnah-exegesis and amplification. Those components of the Talmud cannot be classified as writings that come from somewhere else—and that is by definition. They come from the people who made the Talmud, since by the definition imposed through the Talmud itself, it is writing these compositions and compiling these composites that defined their task; it is what they did to make the Talmud.

Second, in asking, where did the Talmud come from? I immediately set aside those formidable proportions of the document that both define the character, constitute the greatest part, of the document and cannot be said, phenomenologically, to come from some other source but only from the circles that made the document itself. Now, if the whole of the Talmud were made up of writings classified as Mishnah-commentary and amplification (together with secondary articulation and topical appendices), then on the foundations of phenomenology we should not require more than a single answer to the question, where did the Talmud come from? It would be, from people who wrote Mishnah-exegetical compositions and compiled Mishnah-exegetical composites. But that is not the fact, and that leads us to the second, and paramount, class of writing that the Talmud preserves: writing, whether [1] free-standing sayings or [2] larger compositions or even entire composites. That is coherent writing that in no way carries out the Talmud's documentary program. Here we identify the pertinent evidence, that is, the writing that leads us beyond the Talmud's own structure and system and opens the way to an account of what the framers of the Talmud utilized but did not (necessarily) make up on their own.

When I refer to the sources upon which the compilers of the Talmud draw, I do not mean those obvious and always-acknowledged sources, Scripture, the Mishnah, the Tosefta, tractate Abot, Sifra, the two Sifrés, and the like. The Talmud's compilers certainly utilized known sources and accomplished their goals by supplying a talmud to abstracts taken from them. Theirs is a wholly intratextual canon. No one has ever had reason to doubt that fact (even those who argue in favor of the intertextuality of the Rabbinic literature), because the Talmud always signals its utilization of completed documents outside of its own framework.

II. *Historical Formulations of the Question of the Talmud's Original Components*

A historical formulation of the problem would propose differentiation on the basis of not only tangible and formal traits of composition, but also substantive allegations as to fact made in said composition. But to undertake that other mode of description and explanation that converts a text's allegations into fact, we should have to know how to do so, that is, differentiate opinion or allegation from demonstrable fact, subject to tests of falsification and validation. For this other, historical mode of framing the question is one that settles questions of time and temporal sequence; that formulation would take up questions of origins in an other-than-formal framework, for it would provide a temporal and spatial narrative of origins. The "where" (of "where does the Talmud come from") then would speak of schools and persons, not a formal repertoire of literary traits, inclusive of forms. We should then propose to correlate the answer—the *where* in the form of *whence,* and that would mean, when, from whom, and why—with historical circumstance, time, and place. A history of the document would then yield an account of the sequence in the stages of its formation, on the one side, and the correlation of that sequence with social or economic or political or theological events, on the other—a satisfying and complete answer to the question of origins of the document.

But given the questions the historical mode of description, analysis, and interpretation takes up, such historical study by its own claim and self-definition then requires data that attest to matters of time, sequence, order, and synchronicity; place and personality; specificities of circumstance. But in its present form, these the Talmud does not supply. Our first physical evidence of the writing reaches us from long after we suppose the writing itself took shape and reached closure. No references in contemporary writings speak of the document or mention the names of its principal authorities. And about them we know therefore only what the Talmud tells us. If the document assigns a saying to a named authority, we have no way of determining whether that person, at that particular time, said what is assigned to him. Replicable tests of validation and falsification have yet to be devised.

Not only so, but most of the assigned statements bear little consequence beyond their particular legal or theological context, so even if we knew that a given figure really said what is attributed to him, we should not on that account attain a richer historical understanding of context and circumstance and sequence and the specificities of temporal order, such as history promises to provide. Further, we do not know when the document reached closure or under whose auspices; we have only allegations on those matters coming long after the fact. We do not know anything about the time and circumstance of the preparation of materials that may have served the compilers. We readily distinguish among the various types of writing in the document—that is the purpose of this phenomenology—but no concrete evidence allows us to indicate what particular compositions, or even types of compositions, came first, what later on.

Obviously, if we had reliable historical data, we could use historical language in formulating and answering the question of origins. And, as a matter of fact, we do address a question that in historical, rather than phenomenological, form has occupied scholarship for two hundred years: where does the Talmud come from, and how did it all begin? The use of the past tense in framing these questions of an essentially literary character conforms to the convention that now prevails. Many others, whose work I have systematically examined over the past quarter-century, have asked in historical terms the question addressed in these pages concerning the sources utilized by the compilers of the Talmud. In a volume I edited more than two decades ago, with my graduate students of that period I surveyed the principal approaches to the question.

III. *Defining the Smallest Whole Units of Discourse*

Let me spell out the criteria for identifying the free-standing units of cognition (whether single sentences or whole compositions that cannot be deconstructed without a complete collapse of cogency and sense). What distinguishes these free-standing cognitive units from the setting in which they now are found is that we can remove them from their larger context with no loss in the sense or meaning that inheres in the units seen on their own. If we can take a cognitive unit, defined as such solely by appeal to the rules of grammar that govern throughout, and find in that unit a full and exhaustive statement of its own, on its own, then we may identify that cognitive unit as free-standing.

We may further postulate that that unit can have existed in its free-standing form before being utilized for the further purposes of the author of the composition in which it occurs (or even the composite in which said composition occurs). In this way I point to what is original, that is, from the viewpoint of the final document, read within the defining boundaries of its formal traits, what is the starting point of a given composition (or even composite). When I have set forth a complete repertoire of these original constitutive elements, I should expect to be able to systematize the results and investigate the prior components of the document (in historical language, its "pre-history") whether formal or substantive, so far as the original cognitive units coalesce into a coherent picture.

Since the Talmud comprises diverse kinds of writing, it also is made up of more than a single sort of irreducible minima of comprehensible statement, and, it follows, the answer to the question raised here will take plural form: the Talmud comes from circles or persons whose primary cognitive units of thought reach literary, permanent form in the document in these several, distinct ways, rather than in some other(s). It further follows that the sole point at issue is the original units of cognitive discourse that the the framers of the Talmud utilize, and not some theoretical—but now not extant—pre-literary forms or formulas. Since we do not know what we cannot show, we can go only so far as the document itself permits. Since, for us, the document's literary origins form a present tense question, all else follows: the documentary evidence serves to answer our question, but also to set the boundaries of the reliable and factual answer presented in this study. Let me therefore set forth with emphasis the definition of the class of data that I propose to identify:

> These original cognitive units available to the framers of the document or of its constitutive composites and the compositions of which they are made up and not (necessarily) fabricated by those writers in their work of composition or composite-construction constitute those sets of words that hold together and that on the face of it make a complete statement on their own, without depending upon any other sentence(s) for context or meaning.

Clearly, everything depends upon how we determine what are the irreducible sense-statements or cognitive units, those that are used to form larger aggregates but themselves utilize no ready-made formulas bearing distinctive and comprehensible meaning on their own. Judgments concerning the irreducibility of a coherent set of words (a.k.a., a sentence) appeal to a few simple considerations, to be fully exposed, and do not vary by reason of subjective considerations (e.g., what sounds right here but not there). We shall have to take a sample passage and consider, point by point, what components (groups of words that objective, prevalent grammar indicates fit together and if deconstructed lose all sense and meaning within the operative rules of grammar of the document) can stand on their own. This judgment then lifts the cognitive unit outside of the context of discourse in which it is now used in a given composition. The exercise thus requires explaining why (a reasonable person would concede) these components bear a full and exhaustive thought, now set forth in one way rather than in some other for formalization and transmission.

It rapidly will become clear that the Talmud is made up of more than one type of irreducible units of irreducible whole units of discourse. Indeed, the purpose of this initial probe is to establish the types of irreducible whole units of discourse or cognitive units. Once we can identify the various types of such units we move on to the settings that contain them—and identify also those that do not. Then we shall see that these different types of writing (themselves classified by the native categories of the Talmud's own discourse) yield diverse results, with one type of irreducible cognitive unit occurring in one class of discourse, another type in a different class of discourse. On that account, as the work unfolds, time and again form-analysis must intersect with the classification of types of discourse, hence, my formulation: forms and types define the governing criteria. All this yields my picture of whence the Talmud. That is, In the end, my answer to the question of where the Talmud comes from uses the present tense, deriving as it does from the traits (forms and types) of those designated phenomena that in my view answer the question of origins: here, no further, hence the (phenomenological) point of origination.

IV. *An Example of a Composite of Free-Standing Cognitive Units*

The Talmud comes from those who formulate its smallest whole units of discourse; these stand for the document's starting point in the form in which the document now is known. The Talmud is made up of composites, which themselves hold together autonomous compositions, which comprise sets of thoughts that are complete in themselves, fully formulated, the thought completely exposed. When we define the repertoire of these smallest whole units of discourse, we set forth the original and generative constituents of the whole.

The question, what is the character of the materials that comprise these compositions? requires me to identify the forms and types of the smallest whole units of thought or, as I call them elsewhere, "cognitive units." I refer to the irreducible minima, the diverse, completely worded, formulations of coherent thought that the framers of the Talmud's compositions and the compositors of the Talmud's composites used for building blocks. When we can define the traits of these irreducible cognitive units, we know whatever is to be known about where the Talmud comes from, that is, the starting point and the origin of the document. These traits permit us to describe the document's components; they constitute that corpus of indicative phenomena the structure and composition of which I propose to spell out, the entire rationality or logos of which the word "phenomenology" contains.

To explain: a composition is a complete and coherent statement, containing everything the writers maintain we need to understand the intent of the author(s). A composition may consist of a single sentence that is entirely intelligible in its own terms. Such a sentence may take on nuance or even meaning when set side by side with another or several others, but taken out of that context, the sentence still makes an intelligible statement. But a composition also may draw together two or more components that standing alone mean nothing but juxtaposed make a coherent statement. A composite is a construction of two or more compositions, in which the formation and juxtaposition of completed thoughts serve to hold together a variety of propositions in a single coherent statement. Once we know the character of the whole, we naturally proceed to ask about the traits—the types and the forms—of the parts.

As a matter of fact, all documents, with only one exception, produced by Rabbinic Judaism in late antiquity draw together cognitive units into compositions that impose dimensions of meaning upon those constituents that is not contained within them. By juxtaposing two or more originally independent statements, the generality of authors of compositions made a whole that vastly transcended the sum of the parts. To show the rule, let me introduce an example of the sole exception, a document important parts of which consist of catalogues of unrelated sayings, all of them completely and exhaustively clear on their own, none of them placed into a context of sense or meaning that transcends itself. I refer to the catalogues of sayings in tractate Abot, typified by the following. What I mean by cognitive units that are free-standing and in no way related to a larger context—hence the irreducible minimum of coherent thought—is illustrated in each of the units of tractate Abot that I mark with a Roman numeral, set off from my already-complete reference system, which I reproduce. I give ten items (twelve, really), to provide a full sample.

I.   3:2 A. R. Hananiah, Prefect of the Priests, says, "Pray for the welfare of the government.

II.

B. "For if it were not for fear of it, one man would swallow his fellow alive."

C. R. Hananiah b. Teradion says, "[If] two sit together and between them do not pass teachings of Torah, lo, this is a seat of the scornful, as it is said, Nor sits in the seat of the scornful (Ps. 1:1).

E. "But two who are sitting, and words of Torah do pass between them—the Presence is with them,

F "as it is said, Then they that feared the Lord spoke with one another, and the Lord hearkened and heard, and a book of remembrance was written before him, for them that feared the Lord and gave thought to His name (Mal. 3:16)."

G. I know that this applies to two.

H. How do I know that even if a single person sits and works on Torah, the Holy One, blessed be he, sets aside a reward for him?

I. As it is said, Let him sit alone and keep silent, because he hay laid it upon him (Lam. 3:28).

III. 3:3 A. R. Simeon says, "Three who ate at a single table and did not talk about teachings of Torah while at that table are as though they ate from dead sacrifices (Ps, 106:28),

B. "as it is said, For all tables are full of vomit and filthiness [if they are] without God (Ps. 106:28).

C. "But three who ate at a single table and did talk about teachings of Torah while at that table are as if they ate at the table of the Omnipresent, blessed is he,

D. "as it is said, And he said to me, This is the table that is before the Lord (Ez. 41:22)."

IV. 3:4 A. R. Hananiah b. Hakhinai says, "(1) He who gets up at night, and (2) he who walks around by himself, and (3) he who turns his desire to emptiness-lo, this person is liable for his life."

3:5 A. R. Nehunya b. Haqqaneh says, "From whoever accepts upon himself the yoke of Torah do they remove the yoke of the state and the yoke of hard labor.

B. "And upon whoever removes from himself the yoke of the Torah do they lay the yoke of the state and the yoke of hard labor."

V. 3:6 A. R. Halafta of Kefar Hananiah says, "Among ten who sit and work hard on Torah the Presence comes to rest,

B. "as it is said, God stands in the congregation of God (Ps. 82:1).

C. "And how do we know that the same is so even of five? For it is said, And he has founded his group upon the earth (Am. 9:6).

D. "And how do we know that this is so even of three? Since it is said, And he judges among the judges (Ps. 82:1).

E. "And how do we know that this is so even of two? Because it is said, Then they that feared the Lord spoke with one another, and the Lord hearkened and heard (Mal. 3:16).

F "And how do we know that this is so even of one? Since it is said, In every place where I record my name I will come to you and I will bless you (Ex. 20:24)."

VI. 3:7 A. R. Eleazar of Bartota says, "Give him what is his, for you and yours are his.

B. "For so does it say about David, For all things come of you, and of your own have we given you (I Chron. 29:14)."

C. R. Simeon says, "He who is going along the way and repeating [his Torah tradition] but interrupts his repetition and says, 'How beautiful is that tree! How beautiful is that ploughed field!'-Scripture reckons it to him as if he has become liable for his life."

VII. 3:8 A. R. Dosetai b. R. Yannai in the name of R. Meir says, "Whoever forgets a single thing from what he has learned-Scripture reckons it to him as if he has become liable for his life,

B. "as it is said, Only take heed to yourself and keep your soul diligently, lest You forget the words which your eyes saw (Dt. 4:9)."

C. Is it possible that this is so even if his learning became too much for him?

D. Scripture says, Lest they depart from your heart all the days of your life.

E. Thus he becomes liable for his life only when he will sit down and actually remove [his learning] from his own heart,

VIII.A 3:9 A. R. Haninah b. Dosa says, "For anyone whose fear of sin takes precedence over his wisdom, his wisdom will endure,

B. "And for anyone whose wisdom takes precedence over his fear of sin, his wisdom will not endure."

VIII.B C. He would say, "Anyone whose deeds are more than his wisdom-his wisdom will endure.

D. "And anyone whose wisdom is more than his deeds-his wisdom will not endure."

VIII.C 3:10 A. He would say, "Anyone from whom people take pleasure-the Omnipresent takes pleasure.

B. "And anyone from whom people do not take pleasure, the Omnipresent does not take pleasure."

IX. C. R. Dosa b. Harkinas says, "(1) Sleeping late in the morning, (2) drinking wine at noon, (3) chatting with children,

and (4) attending the synagogues of the ignorant drive a
man out of the world."

X. 3:11 A. R. Eleazar the Modite says, "(1) He who treats Holy
Things as secular, and (2) he who defiles the appointed
times, (3) he who humiliates his fellow in public, (4) he
who removes the signs of the covenant of Abraham, our
father, (may he rest in peace), and (5) he who exposes aspects of the Torah not in accord with the law,

B. "even though he has in hand learning in Torah and good
deeds, will have no share in the world to come."

What demonstrates that each of the ten units is free-standing and
produced outside of any larger program of compilation? First, and
obviously, any of the signified units can stand on its own; separated
from the items set forth fore and after, none loses any meaning
whatsoever.

There is a second and less obvious, but deeply probative, fact. If
the units were set forth in any other order but that now prevailing,
the first last, the second fifth, for instance. the composite would make
no more, or no less, sense than it now does, and none of the free-
standing units—each a composition on its own—would gain or lose
intelligibility. That by itself proves the autonomy of each entry, and
points to the compilers' basic indifference to utilizing the several
statements to make of the whole something more than the sum of
the parts (or, for that matter, something less!). The three items of
VIII do not violate the rule; giving the attributive (X says) in place
of "he would say" yields the same result as we see elsewhere. Not
only so, but if we reorganized the discrete statements in some other
order, the composite would make neither more nor less sense, read
start to finish, than it does now.

V. *An Initial Probe*

Definitions having been set forth and placed in context, let us now
proceed to the main problem: how do we know these supposedly-
irreducible minima of thought, these smallest whole cognitive units?
To answer the question, I turn directly to a passage of the Talmud
and work my way through to substantive claims as to what I maintain are the components of the whole that stand on their own with
no loss of sense or meaning—those items that can form the ready-
made, available statements that the framers of a composition used
but did not (necessarily) make up for themselves.

For the present purpose, we turn to the opening composite of Bavli-tractate Moed Qatan. I reproduce the version set forth in my Academic Commentary, signifying the secondary and tertiary developments through a system of successive indentations. This is so that we may readily see the point at which a free-standing cognitive unit intrudes, the kind of discourse that affords that sort of writing a comfortable place. We further are able to identify the context in which a free-standing composition or composite finds its place. Further, I reproduce my original explanation of the intellectual cogency of the Talmud, showing in detail how the passage follows a highly rational program. That underscores the basic hermeneutics of the Talmud, read as a coherent commentary to, and amplification of the law of, the Mishnah. Once we see the order and continuity of the reading of a given Mishnah-paragraph, we grasp the fully disciplined character of the document overall. That is why it is important to explain the sense and order of the reading of the Mishnah, step by step.

This interest in context allows us to form some hypotheses on the matter. I have now to identify the smallest free-standing cognitive units that the Talmud's Mishnah-exegetical composite contains. I underline those smallest-whole cognitive units that seem to me to stand on their own and to convey a cogent statement entirely independent of the enveloping formal or redactional context. The result is quite surprising.

Mishnah Moed Qatan 1:1A

A. **They water an irrigated field on the intermediate days of a festival and in the Sabbatical Year [when many forms of agricultural labor are forbidden],**

I.1

A. **[They water an irrigated field on the intermediate days of a festival and in the Sabbatical Year, whether from a spring that first flows at that time, or from a spring that does not first flow at that time:]** *since it is explicitly stated that they may water a field from a spring that flows for the first time, which may damage the soil by erosion [making necessary immediate repair of the damage during the intermediate days of the festival], is it necessary to specify that they may water from a spring that does not first flow at that time, which is not going to cause erosion?*

B. *One may say that it is necessary to include both the latter and the former, for if the Tannaite framer had given the rule only covering a spring that first flows on the intermediate days of the festival, it is in that case in particular*

> *in which it is permitted to work on an irrigated field, but not for a rain-watered field, because the water is going to cause erosion, but in the case of a spring that does not first flow on the intermediate days, which is unlikely to cause erosion, I might have said that even a rain-watered field may be watered. So by specifying both cases the framer of the Mishnah-paragraph informs us that there is no distinction between a spring that flows for the first time and one that does not flow for the first time. The rule is the same for both: an irrigated plot may be watered from it, but a rain-watered plot may not be watered from [either a new or an available spring].*

Mishnah-criticism presupposes that the document says only what is necessary, but does not set forth in so many words rules that one may infer on the basis of what is made explicit. The solution demonstrates that without making the rule articulate, the Mishnah's formulation left room for misconstruction. Specifically, we can have concluded that a consideration present in one case but not in the other accounts for the lenient ruling accorded only that case. This is amply spelled out.

2. A. *And on what basis is it inferred that the meaning of the words* **"irrigated field"** *is, a thirsty field [which has to be irrigated]?*
    B. *It is in line with that which is written:* "When you were faint and weary" (Dt. 25:18), *and the Hebrew word for weary is represented in Aramaic by the word that means, "exhausted."*
    C. *And how do we know that the words translated rain-watered field refers to a well-fucked field?*
    D. "For as a man has sexual relations with a maiden, so shall your sons be as husbands unto you" (Is. 62:5), *and the word in Aramaic is rendered, "Behold, as a boy fucks a girl, so your sons shall get laid in your midst."*

Mishnah-criticism proceeds from the analysis of the wording—looking for flaws—to the correct rendition of the meaning of the code's words. The third step, now taken, identify the authority behind the Mishnah's anonymous, therefore normative, rule. The premise of the Talmud is that a rule that is anonymous stands for the consensus of sages and is the law, while one that bears a name is schismatic and is not the law. At stake, once we know the authority behind the law, is whether other rulings in the name of that same authority, intersecting if not in detail then in principle, are consistent with this one. If they are not, then the decided law shows flaws of coherence, and these have to be identified and worked out.

3. A. *Who is the Tannaite authority who takes the position that work on the intermediate days of a festival is permitted if it is to prevent loss, but if it*

is to add to gain it is not permitted, and, further, even to prevent loss, really heavy labor is forbidden?

The premise of the Mishnah's rule is now made explicit. The cases yield the rule that on the intermediate days of a festival one may carry out those acts of labor that prevent loss but not those that produce gain. And that leniency is further limited by the consideration that even to prevent loss, heavy labor is forbidden.

B. *Said R. Huna, "It is R. Eliezer b. Jacob, for we have learned in the Mishnah:* **R. Eliezer b. Jacob says, 'They lead water from one tree to another, on condition that one not water the entire field. Seeds which have not been watered before the festival one should not water on the intermediate days of the festival' [M. 1:3].** *"*

Watering the entire field is forbidden, since it merely hastens the maturing process. But seeds that have not begun their growth-processes may not be watered at all; that would be work not to prevent loss but to secure gain. Neither however concerns preventing loss. That question now arises.

C. *Well, I might concede that there is a representation of R. Eliezer's position that he prohibits work to add to one's gain, but have you heard a tradition that he disallows work in a situation in which otherwise loss will result?*

D. *Rather, said R. Pappa, "Who is the authority behind this rule? It is R. Judah, for it has been taught on Tannaite authority:* **'From a spring that first flows on the intermediate days of a festival they irrigate even a rain watered field,' the words of R. Meir. And sages [=Judah vis à vis Meir] say, 'They irrigate from it only a field that depends upon irrigation, which has gone dry.' R. Eleazar b. Azariah says, "Not this nor that, [[but they do not irrigate a field from it [namely, a field the spring of which has gone dry] even in the case of an irrigated field]' [T. Moed 1:1A-C].** *Even further, said R. Judah, 'A person should not clean out a water channel and with the dredging on the intermediate days of a festival water his garden or seed bed.'"*

E. *Now what is the meaning of "that has gone dry"? If you say that it really has dried up, then what is going to be accomplished by watering it?*

F. *Said Abbayye, "The point is that this former water source has gone dry and another has just emerged."*

Judah's ruling at D clearly pertains to preventing loss; the field depends on irrigation, so its crop is in danger. That reading is challenged at E: how does this prevent loss? The answer is, the earlier spring has gone dry, a new spring has begun to flow. Judah maintains the farmer may use that. We now proceed to a gloss on the cited passage that has no bearing upon our problem.

The free-standing statement <u>as underlined </u>in fact derives from another document, to the program of which said statement conforms. Here we have nothing like an autonomous cognitive unit, and I shall not call attention to further instances of the same phenomenon. As we shall now see, I cannot point to another example of a smallest whole cognitive unit in the entire protracted composite.

> G. **R. Eleazar b. Azariah says, "Not this nor that:"** *there is no difference between the case of an old spring that has gone dry or that has not gone dry, in any event a spring that has just flowed may not be utilized on the intermediate days of the festival.*

We revert to our task, showing the authority behind the anonymous rule. Our interpretation of the cited passage has yielded the attribution to Judah. But another interpretation of the same passage, based on a different premise, produces a different result.

> H. *And how to you know [that it is Judah in particular who takes the position that work on the intermediate days of a festival is permitted if it is to prevent loss, but if it is to add to gain it is not permitted, and, further, even to prevent loss, really heavy labor is forbidden]? Perhaps R. Judah takes the position that he does, that is, that it is permitted to use the water for an irrigated field but not for a field that depends on rain, only in the case of a spring that has just now begun to flow,* **[2B]** *since it may cause erosion, [hence, that may cause damage, as stipulated], but in the case of a spring that has not just now begun to flow and will not cause erosion, such a spring might be permitted for use even on a field that depends on rain?*

Then Judaism will permit watering a field from a spring that has not just emerged, even in a field that depends on rain; but the Mishnah's anonymous rule says that in the case of a spring that has not emerged for the first time, the water may be used for irrigation only for a field that depends on irrigation but not for a field that depends on rain water, in which case Judah and the Mishnah's anonymous rule take contradictory positions.

> I. *If so, then in accord with which authority will you assign our Mishnah-paragraph? For in fact, in R. Judah's view, there is no distinction between a spring that has just now flowed and one that has not just now flowed; in either case, an irrigated field may be watered, while one that depends on rain may not. And the reason that the passage specifies the spring that has just now flowed is only to show the extend to which R. Meir was prepared to go, even a spring that has just now flowed may be used, and that is, even for a field that depends upon rain.*

The solution is to insist that Judah does not make the proposed distinction, and that yields a rule in his name that is consistent with the Mishnah's. The language that is supposed to have yielded the distinction for Judah is to be read in the context of Meir's position, which is still more lenient than Judah's, as the language before us explains. We have now completed the exposition of the Mishnah.

The next unit, which is a free-standing discussion pursuing its own interest and in no way a formal comment on our Mishnah-paragraph, cites our Mishnah-paragraph in the context of its pursuit of a solution to its problem. That formally accounts for the introduction of the passage into the amplification of our Mishnah-paragraph. But, as I shall explain at the end, introducing the composition into our composite serving M. 1:1 profoundly deepens our grasp of the law, not just the case and ruling, before us. Our concern in the Mishnah-paragraph before us has been to specify those interstitial acts that are neither heavy labor nor optional, but of moderate difficulty and necessary to preserve the value of the crop. Much then has to do with the character of the act. This yields an interest in the character and classification of agricultural labor: how hard, and for what purpose, is the work done. In what follows, we take up a free-standing composition that analyzes the classification of agricultural labor, once more with special reference to watering the field. Since what follows is a free-standing discussion that does not pursue the program of Mishnah-exegesis or continue the secondary implications of that program, and indeed does not even intersect with the law or principle before us, I indent the passage. The citation, later on, of a sentence of our Mishnah-passage provides the formal explanation for the inclusion of the following composition, but, as I shall propose at the end, reading the Mishnah-paragraph in light of what follows yields a profound grasp of the law, not only the rule, to which the Mishnah-paragraph's statement points. This is how the compositors of the Talmud move our vision from the rule to the laws, and from the laws to law.

4.   A.   *It has been stated:*
        B.   He who on the Sabbath weeds a field or waters his seedlings—*on what count is he to be admonished [not to do so]?*
        C.   Rabbah said, "On the count of plowing."
        D.   R. Joseph said, "On the count of sowing."

One who violates the law of the Sabbath is admonished that he is violating the law, being told specifically what law he is violating, and on what count. Here the act or weeding or watering is classified among the classes of forbidden labor. Is watering an act of plowing or of sowing? The point of intersection is now clear. Our Mishnah-paragraph has dealt with irrigating a field, which is a marginal activity; under some conditions it may be performed on the intermediate days of the festival. Can we sow? Certainly not. Can we plow? As we shall now see, there is an aspect of plowing that pertains to the intermediate days of the festival, namely, softening the soil.

> E. *S aid Rabbah, "It is more reasonable to see matters as I do. For what is the purpose of plowing, if not to loosen the soil, and, here too, he loosens the soil."*
>
> F. *Said R. Joseph, "It is more reasonable to see matters as I do. For what is the purpose of sowing? It is to make produce sprout up. And here too, he makes produce sprout up."*

Here is a point of intersection with our rule, since we recall we may save the crop but not enhance its growth. Joseph's thinking, then, intersects with the problem before us, when he introduces the notion that plowing is forbidden on the count of enhancing the crop's growth. But how will Rabbah differ, since plowing a crop enhances its growth by aerating the roots. Keeping in mind that we deal with a free-standing composition, we cannot find surprising the systematic analysis of the dispute just now introduced:

> G. *Said Abbayye to Rabbah, "There is a problem in your position, and there also is a problem in the position of R. Joseph.*
>
> H. *"There is a problem in your position: does this act come only under the classification of plowing and not sowing?*
>
> I. *"And there also is a problem in the position of R. Joseph: does this act come only under the classification of sowing and not plowing?*

We are now on quite familiar ground, namely, the area where we deem a given action to fall into two distinct classifications. Yet, if the issue is crop-enhancement, then distinguishing one position from the other produces a distinction that makes slight difference.

> J. *"And should you say that in any place in which an act may be classified under two taxa, one is subject to liability on only one count, has not* R. Kahana *said, 'If one pruned his tree but requires the wood for fuel, he is liable on two counts, one on the count of planting, the other on the count of harvesting'?"*
>
> K. *That's a problem.*
>
> L. Objected R. Joseph to Rabbah, "**He who weeds or covers with dirt diverse seeds is flogged. R. Aqiba says, 'Also one who preserves them'** [T. Kil. 1:15A-B]. *Now*

from my perspective, in that I hold that one is liable on the count of sowing, that explains the penalty, since sowing is forbidden in connection with mixed seeds in the vineyard; but from your perspective, in that you say that the count is plowing, is there any prohibition of plowing in connection with mixed seeds?"

If plowing is classified as crop-enhancing, then on what basis is it forbidden to plow when the taboo against mixed seeds has been violated? That is an easy question to answer. Preserving the crop is a form of enhancing it.

M. *He said to him, "The count is that he has preserved them."*

N. *"But lo, since the concluding clause states,* **R. Aqiba says, 'Also one who preserves them,'** *it must follow that the initial Tannaite authority maintains that the count for sanction is not that of preserving the crop of mixed seeds!"*

O. *"The whole of the statement represents the position of R. Aqiba, and the sense of the passage is to explain the operative consideration, specifically: what is the reason that* **he who weeds or covers with dirt diverse seeds is flogged***? It is because one is thereby preserving them, since* **R. Aqiba says, 'Also one who preserves them.'** *"*

P. *What is the basis in Scripture for the position of R. Aqiba?*

Q. *It is in line with that which has been taught on Tannaite authority:*

R. "You shall not sow your field with two kinds of seed" (Lev. 19:19)—

S. I know only that sowing is forbidden. How do we know that preserving the sown seed is forbidden?

T. Scripture says, "Mixed seeds in your field not....," [meaning: it is the mixing of seeds that is emphatically forbidden, and you may have no share by your action in producing such a situation (Lazarus)].

We revert to the discussion broken off at U. We continue our interest in the intersecting issues, first, grounds for prohibiting watering a field—plowing vs sowing; and, second, the matter of the sanctification expressed through prohibition of labor on the Sabbath and the Festival day, as against the sanctification expressed through that same prohibition on days that are comparable to the Sabbath and the Festival but of a diminished level of sanctification. For that purpose, we revert to our Mishnah-paragraph. And that in a formal sense accounts for the inclusion here of the entire, massive composition, together with its inserted and appended supplements. But, as I shall explain at the end, the result of the insertion of the discussion is greatly to deepen our understanding of the context in which the law of our Mishnah-paragraph finds its place. So we grasp not merely the rule, but the law, when we have read our Mishnah-paragraph as part of a larger essay of thinking about labor, sanctification, the Sabbath and Festivals, and spells of time that are comparable to the Festival or to the Sabbath. Since we have dealt with the intermediate days of festivals, comparable to the Festival day, we turn now to the Sabbatical Year, that is to say, the seventh year of a seven-year cycle, which, as its name states, is comparable to the Sabbath, in bearing prohibitions as to acts of labor by reason of Sabbath rest, but at the same time is subject to a lesser degree of sanctification than the Sabbath. This excellent composition in no way qualifies as a free-standing entry.

U.   *We have learned in the Mishnah:* **They water an irrigated field on the intermediate days of a festival and in the Sabbatical Year [M. 1:1A}:**

V.   [With respect to the inclusion of **in the Sabbatical Year**:] *Now there is no difficulty understanding the rule concerning the intermediate days of the festival, which pertains to a situation in which there is substantial loss, on account of which rabbis have permitted irrigation.* [We simply repeat the result of the opening exegetical discussion, without citing it verbatim. Our passage's author need not have known Nos. 1-3 above. Now reference is made to the present composition's important question, now linked to the Mishnah-rule before us:] *But as to the Sabbatical Year, whether one holds that watering is classified as sowing or that watering is classified as plowing, is it permitted either to sow or to plow in the Sabbatical Year [that it should be permitted to water the field]?* [On what basis have we treated the intermediate days of the festival as comparable to the Sabbatical Year, even though they share the classification of spans of time that are comparable to the *Sabbath or Festival day but at a diminished level of sanctification.]*

The question is a powerful one and brings to the surface the premises of our entire discussion, which are, we compare days that are comparable to the Sabbath or Festival, therefore we invoke the rule governing the one for the law that prevails on the other, here, intermediate days of the festival, there, the Sabbatical Year. Once we have asked the question in this way, the answer is obvious, and Abbayye can be relied upon, as always, to see it:

W.   Said Abbayye, "It is concerning the Sabbatical Year at this time that the rule speaks, and the rule represents the position of Rabbi."

X.   *For it has been taught on Tannaite authority:*

Y.   Rabbi says, "'This is the manner of release: release [by every creditor of that which he has lent his neighbor' (Dt. 15:2)—it is of two different acts of release that Scripture speaks, one, the release of lands, the other, the release of debts. When you release lands you release debts, and when you do not release lands, you do not release debts." [The prohibition of agricultural labor in the Sabbatical Year now that the Temple is destroyed is merely by reason of rabbinical authority, and that prohibition is not enforced where loss is involved (Lazarus). Therefore, from our perspective, the lenient ruling for the intermediate days of the festival applies also to the Sabbatical Year in the present age.]

Z.   *Raba said, "You may even maintain that the rule before us represents the position of rabbis [vis à vis Rabbi]. It is the generative categories of labor that the All-Merciful has prohibited,* **[3A]** *but the subsidiary classes of labor* [such as the ones we are considering as analogous to the generative category, that is, watering is either in the class of plowing or in the class of sowing] *have not been forbidden. For it is written, 'But in the seventh year shall be a Sabbath of solemn rest for the land...you shall neither sow your field nor prune your vineyard. That which grows of itself of your harvest you shall not reap and the grapes of your undressed vine you shall not gather' (Lev. 25:4-5). Since pruning falls within the generative category of sowing, and grape gathering falls within the generative category of reaping, for what concrete legal purpose did the All-Merciful make written reference to these items? It is to present the inference that it is to these particular derivative classes of generative categories of labor that liability pertains, but to all others, there is no liability."*

AA. *So they don't, don't they? But has it not been taught on Tannaite authority:*

We now adduce evidence that the subsidiary acts of labor do fall under the same restrictions as the generative acts of labor, and this is explicit. The evidence is from Sifra and is marked as Tannaite in attribution. Spelling out the evidence is not critical to the exposition and I treat it as a footnote or appendix. The concluding sentence disposes of the whole, as we shall see presently.

BB. **["The Lord said to Moses on Mount Sinai, Say to the people of Israel, When you come into the land which I give you, the land shall keep a Sabbath to the Lord. Six years you shall sow your field, and six years you shall prune your vineyard and gather in its fruits; but in the seventh year there shall be a Sabbath of solemn**

rest for the land, a Sabbath to the Lord; you
shall not sow your field or prune your vineyard.
What grows of itself in your harvest you shall
not reap, and the grapes of your undressed vine
you shall not gather; it shall be a year of solemn rest for the land. The Sabbath of the land
shall provide food for you, for yourself and for
your male and female slaves and for your hired
servant and the sojourner who lives with you;
for your cattle also and for the beasts that are
in your land all its yield shall be for food" (Lev.
25:1-7):] "you shall not sow your field or prune
your vineyard:"

CC.   the Torah forbids me only to sow or prune,
DD.   And how do we know that farmers may not fer-
      tilize, prune trees, smoke the leaves or cover
      over with powder for fertilizer?
EE.   Scripture says, "your field you shall not...."—
      no manner of work in your field, no manner of
      work in your vineyard, shall you do.
FF.   And how do we know that farmers may not trim
      trees, nip off dry shoots, trim trees?
GG.   Scripture says, "your field you shall not...."—
      no manner of work in your field, no manner of
      work in your vineyard, shall you do.
HH.   And how do we know that one may not manure,
      remove stones, dust the flower of sulphur, or
      fumigate?
II.   Scripture says, "your field you shall not...."—
      no manner of work in your field, no manner of
      work in your vineyard, shall you do.
JJ.   Since Scripture says, "you shall not sow your
      field or prune your vineyard,"
KK.   might one suppose that the farmer also may not
      hoe under the olive trees, fill in the holes un-
      der the olives trees, or dig between one tree and
      the next?
LL.   Scripture says, "you shall not sow your field or
      prune your vineyard"—
MM.   sowing and pruning were subject to the gener-
      al prohibition of field labor. Whey then were
      they singled out?
NN.   It was to build an analogy through them, as fol-
      lows:
OO.   what is distinctive in sowing and pruning is that
      they are forms of labor carried on on the ground
      or on a tree.

PP.   **So I know that subject to the prohibition are also other forms of labor that are carried on on the ground or on a tree, [excluding from the prohibition, therefore, the types of labor listed] [Sifra CCXLV:I.3-6].**

QQ.   *What we have here is a rule made by rabbinical authority, for which support is adduced from Scripture.*

The solution to the problem at QQ is a simple one. The prohibition derives from rabbis, who then can release it on their own; the role of Scripture is not to declare the rule but only to provide support for rabbis' opinion. We have now completed our exposition. The foregoing insertion has alleged at KK-LL that it is permitted in the Sabbatical Year to aerate the soil under an olive tree. That matter is now treated on its own; the composition that follows is then an appendix to an appendix. The indentation is meant to show the relationship of the following composition to the foregoing.

5.   A.   *And is it permitted to stir the soil under an olive tree in the Sabbatical Year? Has it not been taught on Tannaite authority:*

   B.   *Now it is permitted to hoe [in the Sabbatical Year]? And has it not been written, "*

   C.   "But the seventh year you shall let [the land] rest and lie still" (Ex. 23:11).

   D.   "You shall let it rest" from hoeing,

   E.   "and lie still" from having stones removed.

   F.   *Said R. Uqba bar Hama, "There are two kinds of hoeing. In one kind one closes up the holes [around the roots of a tree], and in the other, he aerates the soil [around the roots of a tree].*

   G.   *"Aerating the soil is forbidden, closing up the holes is permitted [since the former serves the roots of the tree, the latter merely protects the tree]."*

Yet another free-standing composition is appended. We have dealt with plowing and sowing on the intermediate days of the festival, which we have treated as comparable to the Sabbatical Year. So it is natural to pursue the rules of the Sabbatical year as these have been introduced. Is it then permitted at all to plow in the Sabbatical Year? The next appendix follows.

6.   A.   *It has been stated:*

   B.   He who plows in the Sabbatical Year—

   C.   R. Yohanan and R. Eleazar—

   D.   One said, "He is flogged."

   E.   The other said, "He is not flogged."

Clearly, there is debate on the matter, and the premise of our discussion, comparing the two types of diminished sanctification, depends upon the opinion of the one who says he is not flogged. Were
we to conclude here, we should have an ample presentation of our
free-standing composition, as well as its secondary accretions. But
we proceed to expand upon the expansion, in fresh commentary to
what has just preceded. It answers, specifically, the question, hence
the basis for the division? At stake for us is a rational reading of the
law; we wish to show that both parties to a dispute have ample basis
for their opinions, and, ideally, the basis for the dispute will be a
deeper, more systematic conflict on how, exactly, we interpret Scripture. The issue in its own terms has been set forth. What is the basis
in a more encompassing reading of matters? What underlies the
dispute is now spelled out, in an appended commentary on the
dispute itself.

> 7. A.   *May we say that the dispute concerns that which R. Abin
> said R. Ilaa said, for* said R. Abin said R. Ilaa, "In
> any passage in which you find a generalization con-
> cerning an affirmative action, followed by a qual-
> ification expressing a negative commandment, peo-
> ple are not to construct on that basis an argument
> resting on the notion of a general proposition fol-
> lowed by a concrete exemplification only the sub-
> stance of the concrete exemplification." [Freedman,
> *Sanhedrin*, p. 777-8, n. 8: The rule in such a case is:
> the general proposition includes only what is enu-
> merated in the particular specification. But when
> one is thrown into the form of a positive command
> and the other stated as a negative injunction this
> does not apply.]
>
> B.   *By this theory of what is at issue, one who says he is flogged
> does not concur with what R. Abin said R. Ilai said, and
> one who said, "He is not flogged," concurs with what R.
> Abin said.* [Lazarus: The general rule in positive
> terms: "The land shall keep a Sabbath..." (Lev. 25:2-
> 5); the particulars in negative terms, "You shall nei-
> ther sow..." (Lev. 25:4-5); the general rule again in
> positive form, "It shall be a year of solemn rest...."
> Then the particulars are considered typical as illus-
> trations, serving to include in the general rule all
> such items as are similar to the particulars. If the
> particulars are typical of the general rule, one who
> does any of these would break the law. In the case
> of the former, he takes sowing, pruning, reaping,

and gleaning as typical illustrative instances, and
plowing is covered and is punishable. In the case
of the latter, plowing is not included among the
forbidden processes and is not punishable.]

C. *No, all parties reject the position stated by R. Abin in R.
Ilai's name. One who says he is flogged has no problems
anyhow.*

D. *The one who says he is not flogged may reply in this way:*

E. *Since pruning falls within the generative category of sowing,
and grape gathering falls within the generative category of
reaping, for what concrete legal purpose did the All-Merciful make written reference to these items? It is to present the
inference that it is to these particular derivative classes of
generative categories of labor that liability pertains, but to
all others, there is no liability."*

Following the printed text, we now go over the previously-introduced
demonstration that for the purposes of the Sabbatical Year we treat
as uniform, under the same law and penalty, an entire class of acts
of labor.

F. *So they don't, don't they? But has it not been taught on
Tannaite authority:*

G. **["The Lord said to Moses on Mount Sinai,
Say to the people of Israel, When you come
into the land which I give you, the land shall
keep a Sabbath to the Lord. Six years you
shall sow your field, and six years you shall
prune your vineyard and gather in its fruits;
but in the seventh year there shall be a Sabbath of solemn rest for the land, a Sabbath
to the Lord; you shall not sow your field or
prune your vineyard. What grows of itself
in your harvest you shall not reap, and the
grapes of your undressed vine you shall not
gather; it shall be a year of solemn rest for
the land. The Sabbath of the land shall provide food for you, for yourself and for your
male and female slaves and for your hired
servant and the sojourner who lives with
you; for your cattle also and for the beasts
that are in your land all its yield shall be
for food" (Lev. 25:1-7):] "you shall not sow
your field or prune your vineyard:"**

H. **the Torah forbids me only to sow or prune,**

I. **And how do we know that farmers may not
fertilize, prune trees, smoke the leaves or**

cover over with powder for fertilizer?

J.   Scripture says, "your field you shall not...."—no manner of work in your field, no manner of work in your vineyard, shall you do.

K.   And how do we know that farmers may not trim trees, nip off dry shoots, trim trees?

L.   Scripture says, "your field you shall not...."—no manner of work in your field, no manner of work in your vineyard, shall you do.

M.   And how do we know that one may not manure, remove stones, dust the flower of sulphur, or fumigate?

N.   Scripture says, "your field you shall not...."—no manner of work in your field, no manner of work in your vineyard, shall you do.

O.   Since Scripture says, "you shall not sow your field or prune your vineyard,"

P.   might one suppose that the farmer also may not hoe under the olive trees, fill in the holes under the olives trees, or dig between one tree and the next?

Q.   Scripture says, "you shall not sow your field or prune your vineyard"—

R.   sowing and pruning were subject to the general prohibition of field labor. Whey then were they singled out?

S.   It was to build an analogy through them, as follows:

T.   what is distinctive in sowing and pruning is that they are forms of labor carried on on the ground or on a tree.

U.   So I know that subject to the prohibition are also other forms of labor that are carried on on the ground or on a tree, [excluding from the prohibition, therefore, the types of labor listed] [Sifra CCXLV:I.3-6].

V.   *What we have here is a rule made by rabbinical authority, for which support is adduced from Scripture.*

We proceed to a further refinement on the proposition at hand. The Sabbatical Year is augmented by a month fore and aft, during which prohibitions of a diminished order are introduced, on the one side, and continued, on the other. This protects the sanctity of the Sabbatical Year by training the farmers to observe the taboos before the advent of the year, and making certain they continue to observe them for a bit of time after the year has terminated, so that they do not cut the year short. So we ask whether the result just now adduced pertains to these still-less sanctified spells, and that is a gloss upon an appendix, and is so marked:

W. **[3B]** *When R. Dimi came, he said, "Might one suppose that one is flogged even for doing so during the additional time that has been added to the Sabbatical Year [fore and aft]? But the discussion resolved in favor of exempting one who worked during the addition to the Sabbatical Year."*

X. *But I don't know what is this "discussion" and to what reference is made under the category, "addition"!*

Y. *R. Eleazar said, "Reference is made to plowing, and this is the sense of the statement: might one suppose that one is flogged on account of plowing in the Sabbatical Year? For that conclusion would derive from a reading of the relevant verses under the principle of a generalization followed by a particularization of the foregoing followed by another generalization. And the discussion resolved in favor of exempting one who worked during the addition to the Sabbatical Year in the following way: if the flogging were in order, then what is the sense of the many particularizations that the text contains?"*

Z. *R. Yohanan said, "Reference is made to* the days that sages added to the Sabbatical Year prior to the advent of the New Year that marks the commencement of the Sabbatical Year proper, *and this is the sense of the statement: might one suppose that one is flogged on account of plowing on the days that sages added to the Sabbatical Year prior to the advent of the New Year that marks the commencement of the Sabbatical Year proper? For that conclusion would derive from the following:* 'In plowing time and in reaping time you shall rest' (Ex. 34:21). *And the discussion resolved in favor of exempting one who did so,"* as we shall have to explain below.

AA. *To what is reference made in the allusion to* the days that sages added to the Sabbatical Year prior to the advent of the New Year that marks the commencement of the Sabbatical Year proper?

We now proceed to a secondary development of the statement that has just been made. Were we to stop before what follows, we should suffer no less of sense or meaning. The discussion that follows moreover goes off in its own direction.

BB. *That is in line with what we have learned in the Mishnah:* **Until what time do they plow an orchard during the year preceding the Sabbatical Year? The House of Shammai say, "As long as [the plowing] continues to benefit the produce [of the Sixth Year. Until that year's fruit ripens and is harvested]." But the House of Hillel say, "Until Pentecost." And the opinion of the one is close to the opinion of the other [M. Sheb. 1:1]. Until what time do they plow in a field of grain (lit.: a white field) during the year preceding the Sabbatical Year? Until the moisture [in the ground] is gone As long as people plow in order to plant chatemelons and gourds. Said R. Simeon, "You have put the law into the hands of each individual. Rather, [one may plow] in a field of grain until Passover [when Israelites offer the first sheaf of new grain at the Temple; cf. Lev. 23:10] and [one may plow] in an orchard until Pentecost [when they present the firstfruits] [M. Sheb. 2:1]."**

CC. And said R. Simeon b. Pazzi said R. Joshua b. Levi in the name of Bar Qappara, "Rabban Gamaliel and his court took a vote concerning these two spells and annulled them." [It was permitted to till down to the New Year itself (Lazarus).]

DD.   *Said R. Zira to R. Abbahu, and some say, R. Simeon b. Laqish to R. Yohanan, "How could Rabban Gamaliel and his court have annulled an ordinance made by the House of Shammai and the House of Hillel? And lo, we have learned in the Mishnah:* **[And why do they record the opinion of an individual along with that of the majority, since the law follows the opinion of the majority? So that, if a court should prefer the opinion of the individual, it may decide to rely upon it.] For a court has not got the power to nullify the opinion of another court unless it is greater than it in wisdom and in numbers. [If] it was greater than the other in wisdom but not in numbers, in numbers but not in wisdom, it has not got the power to nullify its opinion—unless it is greater than it in both wisdom and numbers [M. Ed. 1:5]***!"*

EE.   *For a moment he was stupefied, but then he said to him, "I say,* this is what they stipulated among themselves: whoever wants to nullify the rule may come along and nullify it."

FF.   *Well, did that measure really be-*

long to them? Was it not a law revealed by God to Moses at Mount Sinai? For that is in line with what R. Assi said R. Yohanan said in the name of R. Nehunia of the Valley of Bet Hauran, "The rules covering ten saplings, [**As regards ten saplings which are spread out within a seah space—they plow the entire seah space for the saplings' sake until the New Year of the Sabbatical Year (M. Sheb. 1:6A-B)**], the willow [carried around the altar during the festival], and the water offering are laws revealed to Moses at Sinai."

GG. Said R. Isaac, "When we received as a tradition the law adding additional restricted time to the Sabbatical Year as a law revealed to Moses at Sinai, it was only concerning the thirty days prior to the New Year. The House of Shammai and Hillel came along and ordained that work should cease from Passover [for the grain field] and from Pentecost [for an orchard], and, at the same time, they made the stipulation with regard to what they said that, whoever might afterward come along and want to nullify those spells of restricted time may come along and nullify them."

HH. But are these specified spells of time merely law? Are they not based in fact on explicit verses of Scripture? For has it not been taught on Tannaite authority:

II. "Six days you shall work but on the seventh day you shall rest, in plowing time and in harvest you shall rest" (Ex. 34:21) [whatever the need, plowing and reaping may not be done on the Sabbath or the Sabbatical Year]—

JJ. R. Aqiba says, "The reference to plowing and reaping is not required to indicate that these actions are forbidden in the Sabbatical Year itself, for that is explicitly covered when Scripture says, 'neither shall you sow your field or prune your vineyard' (Lev. 25:4-5). Rather, the purpose is to impose the restriction of plowing even in the year prior to the Sabbatical Year **[4A]** when the effect of the plowing will extend into the Sabbatical Year, and it is to restrict harvesting produce partly grown in the Sabbatical Year but reaped in the year following the Sabbatical Year."

KK. R. Ishmael says, "Just as plowing is optional, so reaping is optional. Excluded from the prohibition of work on the Sabbath then is the reaping of the first sheaf of barley for the sheaf to be waved, which is a religious duty [and may be done on the Sabbath]."

LL. *Rather, said R. Nahman bar Isaac, "When the law was handed on as a tradition [concerning the time prior to the Sabbatical Year], this concerned permitting tilling to benefit saplings, while the cited verses of Scripture concern prohibiting tilling around old trees."*

MM. *Well, if it was necessary to ap-*

peal to a traditional low to al-
low tilling around saplings up to
the advent of the New Year, is it
not self-evident that doing so
around old trees is going to be
forbidden?

NN. *Rather, when the traditional law*
was handed down as a prohibi-
tion, it was required only from the
view of R. Ishmael, while the
verses of Scripture form the ba-
sis of the position of R. Aqiba.

OO. *R. Yohanan said, Rabban*
Gamaliel and his court nullified
the restrictions on the authority of
the Torah."

PP. *What is the scriptural basis for*
their position?

QQ. *They formed a verbal analogy*
based on the use of the word
"Sabbath" with reverence to both
the Sabbatical Year, called the
Sabbatical Year, and also the
Sabbath of Creation, along these
lines:

RR. Just as in the case of the
Sabbath of Creation, prohibitions pertain to the holy
day but not to the time beforehand or afterward, so in
the case of the Sabbatical
Year, prohibitions pertain
to the year but not to the
time beforehand or after-
ward.

SS. *Objected R. Ashi, "On the view*
of one who maintains that the re-
striction is a traditional law, can
an argument based on verbal
analogy come along and nullify
a traditional law? And if one
says that it is based on a verse
of Scripture, along these same
lines, can an argument formed of
a verbal analogy come along and
nullify the result of the reading
of a verse of Scripture?"

TT. *Rather, said R. Ashi, "Rabban
     Gamaliel and his court adopted
     the reasoning of R. Ishmael, who
     said, 'The prohibitions of tilling
     on the spell prior to the actual
     advent of the Sabbatical Year
     derives from a traditional law.
     And to what span of time did
     that traditional law pertain? It
     was during the time that the
     Temple was standing, just as the
     rule of the water libation [which
     likewise derived from a tradi-
     tional law] pertained only dur-
     ing the time that the Temple was
     standing. But when the Temple
     is no longer standing, the law
     received by tradition does not
     apply.'"*

The final entry clearly serves as a massive appendix; it is intelligently situated for that purpose at the end, since it does not impede the presentation of the whole. In contemporary scholarship we should situate in an appendix at the end of a chapter or of a book such a discussion, only tangentially relevant to the main point. One of the marks of the conclusion of a systematic and cogent presentation of a point is the insertion of such sizable complexes of supplementary data. Whoever wrote up the composition had his own focus and in no way evinces knowledge of the ultimate location of his writing; and whoever inserted the composition selected it for the sake of completeness, even recognizing how the insertion would impart to his composite a discursive character. He has paid a heavy price for his decision, since the Talmud before us loses cogency before it has run its course even half way. Then what lesson did he propose to teach by the composition as we have it, in which the opening units pursue a single line of thought, and everything else wanders off hither and yon?

To frame the question more concretely: we have now completed the presentation of the entire treatment of M. 1:1A. The run-on effect of the whole proves blatant. Had we stopped at No. 3, we should have found a fairly ample exposition of the Mishnah-passage. Not only so, but Nos. 4-6 really do not address the Mishnah-rule at all; they go their own way, with a focus upon the Sabbatical Year, not

the intermediate days of the festival. But the Sabbatical Year in the
Mishnah-rule is subordinate, introduced by reason of an analogy that
is not spelled out. Any allegation that the Talmud is coherent and
well-drafted must address the challenge of the sizable and meandering
composite before us. The secondary expansion, No. 4, drawing in
its wake the appended, also free-standing discussions at Nos. 5 and
6, bearing their extensions and accretions, obviously has taken up
most of our attention. Together with its enormous amplification in
successive appendices, the consideration of that matter has defined
the context in which the Talmud wishes us to read the Mishnah-
paragraph at hand.

Now to the main point of this survey: I maintain that the entire
Talmudic passage—a sequence of compositions and composites—
has been put together in a considered and thoughtful way to amplify our grasp of the Mishnah's statement. To show that that is the
fact, I have now to ask, What has the framer accomplished in introducing the passage into the context of our Mishnah-paragraph?
First, he has raised the issue of the Sabbath and its categories of
prohibited labor, and therefore he has introduced a complication
into our consideration of the Mishnah-passage. We deal here with
watering. Watering on the Festival is forbidden, since all acts of labor
but cooking that are forbidden on the Sabbath are forbidden on the
Festival. Then we forthwith deal with the prohibition of watering
on the Sabbath and ask by what reason it is forbidden, with implications for the considerations operative in our Mishnah-rule governing the diminished sanctity of the intermediate days of the festival.
In doing so, the compositor who took a free-standing discussion and
deposited it here has accomplished a second matter in the exegesis
of the theme before us. He has settled the paramount issue of our
tractate: to what do we compare the intermediate days of the festival? Are they comparable to the Festival and the Sabbath, only
subject to diminished restrictions? Or are they comparable to week-
days, but subject to some restrictions rather than none?

Juxtaposing the exposition of M. 1:1 with a rule concerning the
Sabbath (therefore also: the Festival taboo against labor), introducing a case comparable to the Mishnah's, namely, watering the field,
the compiler of the set has underscored the theoretical issue that must
engage us. It is, in substance, the governing analogy, Sabbath-Festival or ordinary week day, that generates the specific rulings at hand.
Since I maintain that the juxtaposition makes a point directly per-

tinent to the theoretical problem our Mishnah states in concrete terms, let me spell out the connections I see to join to the exposition of our Mishnah-rule an otherwise utterly irrelevant passage. That brings us to the substance of the comment on the Mishnah-passage that is effected by the compositor simply by introducing the present free-standing composition. It is to introduce the complications of classifications of acts of labor into the simple matter at hand. Our Mishnah-paragraph has made the point that we may keep a crop alive through irrigating it, but we may not go to great effort to water the crop, and we may also not do more than keep it alive; that is, we may do nothing to enhance the growth. That point is made explicit in the language, *"work on the intermediate days of a festival is permitted if it is to prevent loss, but if it is to add to gain it is not permitted."*

The free-standing composition then goes over the same ground in a different setting. Why? Because the free-standing composition addresses the matter of crop enhancement on the Sabbath; the Festival day is comparable to the Sabbath in every prohibition but that concerning food-preparation. Hence the issue of the Sabbath and the Festival, so far as crop-enhancement is the governing consideration, pertains here. We then draw the contrast between crop-enhancement—watering the crop, the same act the Mishnah-rule has introduced—on the Sabbath or Festival and on the intermediate days of the festival. What we simply may not do on the former occasion we may or may not be permitted to do on the latter. Introducing this discussion has served to remind us that while we deal with the intermediate days of the festival, the diminished sanctity that pertains must be protected, and the very same considerations that govern on the Sabbath (here: crop-enhancement) govern also on the intermediate days of the festival, but in a different way.

The operative principle then is underscored: loss is prevented, gain is not permitted. And that means, what may not be done on the Sabbath or Festival also may not be done on the intermediate days of the festival. By introducing the rule for the Sabbath and producing the explanation that the operative consideration behind the rule is the prohibition against crop-enhancement, the framer has made his main point: the intermediate days of the festival are comparable not to ordinary days, but subject to some restrictions, but to the Festival or Sabbath, and are subject to formidable restrictions. The governing analogy is the Sabbath and Festival, their restrictions diminished only for very special reasons, and not the everyday practices of the unconsecrated week, subject to a few special limitations. If this juxtaposition expresses the point I have spelled out—the priority of the Sabbath-Festival in defining the governing metaphor—then we should have a sustained interest in showing how the intermediate days of the festival really are comparable to the Festival itself, and are not comparable to, and do not follow the rules that pertain on, the ordinary days of the secular calendar.

The upshot is that, in introducing an independent composition, with its own focus, the compositor has asked us to read the Mishnah-rule in a more complex way and so made us understand the rule as part of a larger web of law on the comparison of sacred and this-worldly matters. We then form a preliminary hypothesis that the key to the selection-process is an interest in comparison and contrast of like classes of things, e.g., spans of time that are not sanctified like the Sabbath and Festival but that are in a diminished level of sanctification. Within that category falls each class of data we have worked on. Then the connections that are made yield the conclusions that are drawn, and, inclusive of the supplementary appendices, the whole holds together and imparts a lesson that on their own the parts do not convey. In this way the Talmud vastly transcends the labor of Mishnah-commentary and also enriches our grasp of the law that the Mishnah conveys through detail.

VI. *Do Cognitive Units Supply Free-Standing Building Blocks of Talmudic Discourse?*

The smallest whole units of discourse, the cognitive ones, prove remarkably few and lacking all influence. If we look for statements along the lines of those in tractate Abot, examined earlier, we find, so far as I can see, a single one. The treatment of the Mishnah-passage dealt with here is carried out in compositions and still larger composites, and the work reaches its goals without the intrusion of free-standing cognitive units. But it requires and presupposes the introduction of compositions and, all the more so, composites. It follows that this systematic exposition of the Talmud as a commentary to the Mishnah leaves no doubt whatsoever on two matters.

1) Remarkably few quite-free-standing cognitive units make their appearance; I see only one.
2) A contrary generalization covers the whole, namely: it is wholly

in response to the Mishnah's statement that the Talmud is carefully set forth, and every item is in its proper place to accomplish the goals of the compiler.

Our sample points toward one hypothesis alone: cognitive units do not supply free-standing building blocks of Talmudic discourse. The sample indicates the opposite; cognitive units that can stand alone and yield reasonably good sense in fact do not stand on their own but form part of compositions that impart still better sense. We can take some statements out of the framework of the compositions in which they occur, but we quickly realize that, when we do, even though they make sense, they lose context and meaning.

A number of compositions are utilized in the formation of the large-scale composite; a variety of available texts are drawn upon. But if we want to know how the Talmud uses not available writing from other documents but writing that freely moves from document to document, unaffected by the requirements of any one of its places of settlement, we shall have to look elsewhere than to the present passage. For here we simply find no evidence at all. So the Talmud does not come from the collection and arrangement of sayings of various sages. It comes from a systematic effort at composition of a cogent statement, to the purposes of which free-standing sayings always are subordinated. Nearly everything before us takes on sense and meaning in its larger documentary context, whether the document be the Talmud, the Tosefta, Sifra, or a compilation of Tannaite formulations.

VII. *Compositions: The Free-Standing Building Blocks of Talmudic Discourse*

By composition I mean a coherent, systematic, and complex construction of thought, in which a number of sentences are joined and attain meaning only in their union. A composition makes a single point, all elements of its statement being required to make that point, none of them standing on its own in any consequential manner (except as borrowed from some other context for purposes of citation or proof). The Talmud draws heavily upon compositions written to serve a purpose other than the work of Mishnah-exegesis that for the Talmud defines the documentary logic. Producing only a single plausible candidate for classification as an autonomous cognitive unit, the sample provided a number of quite sizable pieces of writing drawn together for purposes other than those defined by the Talmud's particular purpose. These are the ones that conform either to the requirements of other documents besides this one or to the theoretical ones of no document now in hand. To pursue our inquiry, we have now to define the traits of a free-standing composition and then to reexamine our sample data.

By "a composition" in the present context I mean a presentation of a coherent proposition, fully set forth, standing on its own, not dependent upon materials fore or aft for internal coherence, cogently argued, amply sustained with the requisite probative evidence, proof-texts, cases, or statements of acknowledged authorities. An alternative word would be "paragraph" or "syllogism" or "small chapter" or some other formulation besides composition, but such a merely formal usage would obfuscate rather than clarify matters. In line with the rules of documentary phenomenology, a composition may serve the purpose of the document in which it occurs or that of some other document or that of no document known to us. In my reference system, I use an Arabic numeral to signify a complete composition, cogent in its own terms. And, it is self-evident, by "composite" I mean, a collection of such compositions. Ordinarily, I signify a composite by a Roman numeral, but my usage varies according to context; in any event, at issue here is the composition, not the composite, and, in work on the other-than-Mishnah-exegetical compositions and composites, the reason I see a composite, holding together a number of coherent compositions, is invariably self-evident.

To illustrate what I mean by a composition from the opening lines, all devoted to Mishnah-exegesis, I review three compositions, each exhibiting the definitive traits:

I.1

A.   **[They water an irrigated field on the intermediate days of a festival and in the Sabbatical Year, whether from a spring that first flows at that time, or from a spring that does not first flow at that time:]** *since it is explicitly stated that they may water a field from a spring that flows for the first time, which may damage the soil by erosion [making necessary immediate repair of the damage during the intermediate days of the festival], is it necessary to specify that they may water from a spring that does not first flow at that time, which is not going to cause erosion?*

B.   *One may say that it is necessary to include both the latter and the former, for if the Tannaite framer had given the rule only covering a spring that first flows on the intermediate days of the festival, it is in that case in particular in which it is permitted to work on an irrigated field, but not for a rain-watered field, because the water is going to cause erosion, but in the case of a spring that does not first flow on the intermediate days, which is unlikely to cause erosion, I might have said that even a rain-watered field may be watered. So by specifying both cases the framer of the Mishnah-paragraph informs us that there is no distinction between a spring that flows for the first time and one that does not flow for the first time. The rule is the same for both: an irrigated plot may be watered from it, but a rain-watered plot may not be watered from [either a new or an available spring].*

2. A. *And on what basis is it inferred that the meaning of the words* **"irrigated field"** *is, a thirsty field [which has to be irrigated]?*

    B. *It is in line with that which is written:* "When you were faint and weary" (Dt. 25:18), *and the Hebrew word for weary is represented in Aramaic by the word that means, "exhausted."*

    C. *And how do we know that the words translated rain-watered field refers to a well-fucked field?*

    D. "For as a man has sexual relations with a maiden, so shall your sons be as husbands unto you" (Is. 62:5), *and the word in Aramaic is rendered, "Behold, as a boy fucks a girl, so your sons shall get laid in your midst."*

3. A. *Who is the Tannaite authority who takes the position that work on the intermediate days of a festival is permitted if it is to prevent loss, but if it is to add to gain it is not per*Mishnah *mitted, and, further, even to prevent loss, really heavy labor is forbidden?*

The premise of the Mishnah's rule is now made explicit. The cases yield the rule that on the intermediate days of a festival one may carry out those acts of labor that prevent loss but not those that produce gain. And that leniency is further limited by the consideration that even to prevent loss, heavy labor is forbidden.

    B. *Said R. Huna, "It is R. Eliezer b. Jacob, for we have learned in the Mishnah:* **R. Eliezer b. Jacob says, 'They lead water from one tree to another, on condition that one not water the entire field. Seeds which have not been watered before the festival one should not water on the intermediate days of the festival' [M. 1:3].** "

Watering the entire field is forbidden, since it merely hastens the maturing process. But seeds that have not begun their growth-processes may not be watered at all; that would be work not to prevent loss but to secure gain. Neither however concerns preventing loss. That question now arises.

    C. *Well, I might concede that there is a representation of R. Eliezer's position that he prohibits work to add to one's gain, but have you heard a tradition that he disallows work in a situation in which otherwise loss will result?*

    D. *Rather, said R. Pappa, "Who is the authority behind this rule? It is R. Judah, for it has been taught on Tannaite authority:* **'From a spring that first flows on the intermediate days of a festival**

they irrigate even a rain watered field,' the words of
R. Meir. And sages [=Judah vis à vis Meir] say, 'They
irrigate from it only a field that depends upon irriga-
tion, which has gone dry.' R. Eleazar b. Azariah says,
"Not this nor that, [[but they do not irrigate a field from
it [namely, a field the spring of which has gone dry]
even in the case of an irrigated field]' [T. Moed 1:1A-
C]. Even further, said R. Judah, 'A person should not clean out
a water channel and with the dredging on the intermediate days
of a festival water his garden or seed bed.'"

E.   *Now what is the meaning of* "that has gone dry"*? If you say that it really*
     has dried up, then what is going to be accomplished by watering it?

F.   *Said Abbayye, "The point is that this former water source has gone dry and*
     another has just emerged."

The cogent statement of No. 1 then explains why each case of the
Mishnah-statement is absolutely required, showing none is redundant; No. 2 makes the point that a given word bears the meaning
assigned to it because of evidence that sustains that proposition; No.
3 specifies the implicit premise contained within the law and proceeds to identify the authority behind that premise—and so throughout. None of the compositions depends upon the others, fore or aft,
for sense, context, or cogency. That is proved by the fact that the
order of inquiry can have been reversed with no loss of sense or
meaning, so the three sets of sentences constitute three free-standing compositions, but, of course, they meet at the Mishnah.

The composition ordinarily forms the Talmud's smallest whole
unit of coherent discourse, though from time to time we may identify a free-standing sentence that defines an irreducible minimum
of meaning. In general, however, if we were to remove a sentence
from a composition, the sentence would lose all sense, and the composition would disintegrate as well. That test of deconstruction ordinarily yields a demonstration that the composition defines that
smallest whole unit of coherent discourse that defines the building
blocks of the Talmud. And, to recapitulate, those compositions that
do not serve the Talmud's definitive purpose then come from outside of the framework of the document's authors and compilers. They
define where the Talmud comes from—so far as it does not come
from its own circles.

The compositions supply all of the data a reader (or listener)
requires to understand the point that the framer of that composition wishes to make. The compositions very often coalesce into

composites, and the document overall is made up of large-scale composites—sets of compositions that themselves are cogent, completed units of discourse, with a beginning, middle, and end. The composite then ordinarily takes a number of compositions and forms them into a still larger and more encompassing statement.

The compositions commonly take their place within larger composites, just as, one may argue, Nos. 1, 2, and 3, given above, all form elements of a composite organized around the requirements of Mishnah-exegesis. A composite commonly draws upon available compositions either formed in response to, or made available [1] in part by, prior and completed documents and their exegesis, such as Scripture, the Mishnah, the Tosefta; and [2] in part by compositions worked out entirely within their own limits. Most of the compositions and composites in the Talmud serve the task of Mishnah-exegesis and amplification, and that is the case in the sample was have examined. But some serve other purposes than those defined by the document in which they now find their home. The formal requirements of both types of composites are the same, and the role of compositions within them is uniform.

Commonly, compositions take a position within a large composite. We have then to ask, are these to be classified within the large composite, or as free-standing and autonomous items on their own? In my judgment, what is subordinate to a large-scale composite is to be classified entirely within the rubric in which that composite finds its place. The reason is that the subordinated composition serves a purpose beyond itself, therefore has been selected by the framer of the composite to accomplish a goal not in the mind of the (original) author of said composition.

The Talmud contains compositions and composites that in their formation do not serve its governing purpose of Mishnah-exegesis but hold together in some other fashion altogether—but are introduced to serve the purpose of Mishnah-exegesis. These compositions and composites then took shape for some purpose other than that of Mishnah-exegesis and were made to serve a secondary, to their framers subordinate, purpose. Indeed, such free-standing compositions and composites may not even pertain to the Mishnah at all, and, as a matter of fact, the Talmud contains a small number of compositions and composites that in no way intersect with the Mishnah. In my *Academic Commentary* I provisionally called these "topical appendices" and I gave each one its own subhead. I treated them as major rubrics of the whole but set in plain type their theme or proposition, rather than in the bold face type reserved for the major rubrics that the Mishnah-paragraphs themselves laid out. Both were expedients meant to postpone consideration of the Talmud's other-than-Mishnah-exegetical compositions and composites; now they demand attention in their own right.

We ordinarily can explain why the compilers included these free-standing composites and the compositions that they hold together. A variety of explanations serve, to be sure. But, in general, I see the free-standing composite or composition as intended to provide information tangential to the main point but useful in fully exposing said point. To explain: the Talmud of Babylonia in contemporary terms would be presented heavy with footnotes and appendices. That is, in our mode of setting forth our ideas and the documentation for them, we include in our text the main points of proposition, evidence, and argument; we relegate to footnotes the sources upon which we draw; we place in appendices substantial bodies of secondary material, relevant to the main body of our text only tangentially, yet required for a full presentation of what we wish to say. The authorship of the Talmud of Babylonia accomplishes, within the technical limitations that governed its formulation of its proposition, evidence, and argument, what we work out through footnotes and appendices.

VIII. *Composites: The Principal Building Blocks of Talmudic Discourse. A Demonstration from Bavli Tractate Abodah Zarah to Mishnah-Tractate Abodah Zarah 1:1*

From the viewpoint of the Bavli, the composite is the basic building block of thought. From the viewpoint of identifying where the Bavli comes from, besides the authors of the Mishnah-exegesis and amplification who produced most of the document, the free-standing composition defines the smallest whole unit of thought. These definitions appear to conflict, but in fact explain data from two distinct perspectives.

First, why insist that a composite—and not the several compositions that may find their redactional location within a given composite—forms the basic building block of thought, and the irreducible minimum of discourse, of the Bavli? The reason is that only when we grasp how a variety of materials, some of them already completed compositions, are drawn together into a single sustained and comprehensive statement, we shall understand the work of the compiler. The Bavli is a work of purposive compilation, and when we understand the rules of composition in the twin-sense—the writing of compositions, the formation of composites—we shall have a clear picture of what the framers of the Bavli did.

Why (paradoxically) insist that the compositions, with special reference to those that do not address the work of Mishnah-exegesis, *also* form irreducible minima of thought? The answer derives from a proposition already introduced: the importance of recognizing that some pieces of writing were composed to serve the purposes of the formation of a particular document in which they occur, others to serve the purposes of some other document than one we now have, and still others to serve the purposes of a document that we now cannot even imagine, in the present context then is clear. When we want to know how a given document took shape, we need to know how its compilers did their share of the writing; we have also to explain how and why they were able also to make use of writing done for some document, or purpose, other than, different from, the requirements of their document and its distinctive purpose. And once we undertake such an explanation—as I have done for all thirty-seven tractates' free-standing "topical appendices"—we concede that these pieces of writing come from somewhere else.

To illustrate these theoretical remarks, I have chosen to reproduce part of a sustained passage, which allows us to distinguish one composite from another, and, within a composite, the compositions that comprise the whole. What we shall now see with great clarity is how the entirety of the vast, run-on and continuous passage in fact forms [1] a single entity, a composite made up of [2] available compositions in part. And some of these compositions were made up with a purpose other than that of Mishnah-exegesis, and, as we proceed, we shall see very clearly not only the point the author of the composite wished to make, but also the kind of document that author had in mind for the ultimate destination of his writing.

Because each composition is linked to the others, fore and aft, we must classify the whole—**I.1** with its footnote at **I.2,** and then with that footnotes extended notes, glosses, appendices and the like, through to **I.32**—as a single, sustained composite, to be classified whole and all together. And in point of fact, even attention to the subject-matter—the theme and recurrent propositions—justifies treating all thirty-two compositions as a single cogent composite. For the whole of the composite when seen all together addresses only the single issue introduced by the Mishnah and addressed in the exercise of text-criticism of I.1: gentile idolatry, Israelite service of God but also Israelite sin, and the punishment to be exacted on some one day—the day of judgment—from the gentiles for their idolatry, and from Israel for its perfidy. Then we recognize how a single, sustained program or problem, which we can readily identify, has guided the compositor in writing up his complete statement—footnotes, appendices, and all. I give only a small segment of the whole.

Most of what is before us is comprised by compositions, laid out in majestic array as footnotes and appendices, secondary developments, expansions and clarifications, information fully spelled out to which, in a prior statement, allusion is made—a pedantic exercise of high consequence, in which everything we require is provided, and perhaps rather more than by our tastes we might have inserted. Each composition, as I explained, is inserted whole and complete, but given a (to the framers, natural and logical) position well integrated into a single running discussion. True, the whole looks run-on—all the more reason to treat all thirty-two compositions as a single composite and to classify that composite in some one way: a main point (and its enormous accretion of secondary material) on the problem, Mishnah-text-criticism. I now mean to show how one rule of composition has told the framer of the composite how to put things together—what to include, what to cover, after his fashion, as footnotes, what to tack on, again after his fashion, as appendices. In light of this explanation of the constitutive rules of composition—composition meaning, the making of cogent and coherent composites!—my claim that I know the rules of composition and can specify what they are may be evaluated.

The graphic way in which I show what I conceive to be a footnote is to indent a discussion that seems to me secondary, e.g., filling out what is stated in a prior matter. As I proceed I shall explain why I represent matters as I do, and then at the end is a summary of the whole. In this way I show that a composite in fact forms a single, continuous, and, properly read, coherent and cogent, even economical statement, a statement formulated in large part out of ready-made compositions. With this passage in hand, readers will grasp why I identify the composition as the Talmud's basic building block and, as indicated, why the ready-made compositions that do not conduct Mishnah-exegesis come from somewhere else—where the Talmud comes from, beyond its own framework.

1:1

A. [2A] **Before the festivals of gentiles for three days it is forbidden to do business with them.**

B. **(1) to lend anything to them or to borrow anything from them.**

C. **(2) to lend money to them or to borrow money from them.**

D. **(3) to repay them or to be repaid by them.**

E. **R. Judah says, "They accept repayment from them, because it is distressing to him."**

F. **They said to him, "Even though it is distressing to him now, he will be happy about it later."**

Mishnah 1:1.I.1

A. **[2A]** Rab and Samuel [in dealing with the reading of the key-word of the Mishnah, translated festival, the letters of which are 'aleph daled, rather than 'ayin daled, which means, calamity]:

B. *one repeated the formulation of the Mishnah as, "their festivals."*

C. *And the other repeated the formulation of the Mishnah as "their calamities."*

D. *The one who repeated the formulation of the Mishnah as "their festivals" made no mistake, and the one who repeated the formulation of the Mishnah as "their calamities" made no mistake.*

E. *For it is written, "For the day of their calamity is at hand" (Dt. 32:15).*

F. *The one who repeated the formulation of the Mishnah as "their festivals" made no mistake,, for it is written, "Let them bring their testimonies that they may be justified" (Is. 43:9).*

G. *And as to the position of him who repeats the formulation of the Mishnah as "their festivals," on what account does he not repeat the formulation of the Mishnah to yield, "their calamities"?*

H. *He will say to you, "'Calamity' is preferable [as the word choice when speaking of idolatry]."*

I. *And as to the position of whim who repeats the formulation of the Mishnah as "their calamities," on what account does he not repeat the formulation of the Mishnah to yield "their festivals"?*

J. *He will say to you, "What causes the calamity that befalls them if not their testimony, so testimony is preferable!"*

K. *And as to the verse, "Let them bring their testimonies that they may be justified" (Is. 43:9), is this written with reference to gentiles? Lo, it is written in regard to Israel.*

L. For said R. Joshua b. Levi, "All of the religious duties that Israelites carry out in this world come and give testimony in their behalf in the world to come: 'Let them bring their witnesses that they may be justified' (Is. 43:9), that is, Israel; 'and let them hear and say, It is truth' (Is. 43:9)—this refers to gentiles."

M.   Rather, said R. Huna b. R. Joshua, "He who formulates the
Mishnah to refer to their calamities derives the reading from this
verse: 'They that fashion a graven image are all of them vanity,
and their delectable things shall not profit, and their own witnesses
see not nor know' (Is. 44:9)."

The foregoing, we see clearly, presents a beautifully balanced dispute-form, and the form is used to provide a medium for presenting Mishnah-text criticism: how are we to read the text of the
paragraph before us. That classification presents no problems. We
must now enter a much more difficult question because I maintain
that, along with the classification of I.1, everything that is attached
to I.1 in a continuous and ongoing manner goes along as a single
composite, the whole put together in its own terms, but then utilized by the framer of the Talmud before us—folios 2A-5B—as a
continuous (if in our perspective rather run-on) statement. It is
obviously a composite. But I classify the entire composite all together
and all at once, because it is more than a composite: it also is a
composition. And the reason I see it as a coherent and cogent composition is that every item fits together with its predecessor and leads
us without interruption to its successor, from the starting lines of **I.1**
to the concluding ones of **I.32**. When I have made that claim stick,
I shall have justified my insistence on seeing the whole as a coherent composition, to be classified in its entirety in a single entry, within
a single rubric. And that is what is at stake in this long and detailed
examination of four folios, eight pages, of the Talmud.

No. 1 has referred us to gentile idolatry and Israelite loyalty to
the religious duties assigned to them by God. We now have a long
exposition of the theme of gentile idolatry and perfidy. Everything
that follows in **I.2** serves as a play on the theme of **I.1**.L-M! The
unity of the whole of I.2 will be readily apparent because of the insets
of gloss and expansion, and the further insets of the appendices to
the gloss and expansion.

I.2

A.   R. Hanina bar Pappa, and some say, R. Simlai, gave the following exposition [of the verse,"They that fashion a graven image
are all of them vanity, and their delectable things shall not profit, and their own witnesses see not nor know" (Is. 44:9)]: "In the
age to come the Holy One, blessed be he, will bring a scroll of
the Torah and hold it in his bosom and say, 'Let him who has
kept himself busy with it come and take his reward.' Then all the

gentiles will crowd together: 'All of the nations are gathered together' (Is. 43:9). The Holy One, blessed be he, will say to them,
'Do not crowd together before me in a mob. But let each nation
enter together with **[2B]** its scribes, 'and let the peoples be gathered together' (Is. 43:9), and the word 'people' means 'kingdom:'
'and one kingdom shall be stronger than the other' (Gen. 25:23)."

B.   *But can there be a mob-scene before the Holy One, blessed be he? Rather,*
     it is so that from their perspective they not form a mob, so that they
     will be able to hear what he says to them.

C.   [Resuming the narrative of A:] "The kingdom of Rome comes
     in first."

     D.   *How come? Because they are the most important. How do we know*
          on the basis of Scripture they are the most important? Because it
          is written, "And he shall devour the whole earth and shall
          tread it down and break it into pieces" (Gen. 25:23), and
          said R. Yohanan, "This Rome is answerable, for its
          definition [of matters] has gone forth to the entire world
          [Mishcon: 'this refers to Rome, whose power is known
          to the whole world']."

     E.   *And how do we know that the one who is most important*
          comes in first? It is in accord with that which R. Hisda
          said.

     F.   For said R. Hisda, "When the king and the com-
          munity [await judgment], the king enters in first for
          judgment: 'That he maintain the case of his servant
          [Solomon] and [then] the cause of his people Isra-
          el' (1 Kgs. 8:59)."

     G.   *And how come? If you wish, I shall say it is not appropri-*
          ate to keep the king sitting outside. And if you wish, I shall
          say that [the king is allowed to plea his case] before the anger
          of the Holy One is aroused."

H.   [Resuming the narrative of C:] "The Holy One, blessed be
     he, will say to them, 'How have defined your chief occupa-
     tion?'

I.   "They will say before him, 'Lord of the world, a vast num-
     ber of marketplaces have we set up, a vast number of bath
     houses we have made, a vast amount of silver and gold have
     we accumulated. And all of these things we have done only
     in behalf of Israel, so that they may define as their chief
     occupation the study of the Torah.'

J.   "The Holy One, blessed be he, will say to them, 'You com-
     plete idiots! Whatever you have done has been for your own
     convenience. You have set up a vast number of marketplac-
     es to be sure, but that was so as to set up whore-houses in
     them. The bath-houses were for your own pleasure. Silver
     and gold belong to me anyhow: "Mine is the silver and mine
     is the gold, says the Lord of hosts" (Hag. 2:8). Are there any

among you who have been telling of "this," and "this" is only the Torah: "And this is the Torah that Moses set before the children of Israel' (Dt. 4:44)." So they will make their exit, humiliated.

K. "When the kingdom of Rome has made its exit, the kingdom of Persia enters afterward."

   L. *How come? Because they are second in importance. And how do we know it on the basis of Scripture? Because it is written,* "And behold, another beast, a second, like a bear" (Dan. 7:5), *and in this connection R. Joseph repeated as a Tannaite formulation,* "This refers to the Persians, who eat and drink like a bear, are obese like a bear, are shaggy like a bear, and are restless like a bear."

M. "The Holy One, blessed be he, will say to them, 'How have defined your chief occupation?'

N. "They will say before him, 'Lord of the world, We have thrown up a vast number of bridges, we have conquered a vast number of towns, we have made a vast number of wars, and all of them we did only for Israel, so that they may define as their chief occupation the study of the Torah.'

O. "The Holy One, blessed be he, will say to them, 'Whatever you have done has been for your own convenience. You have thrown up a vast number of bridges, to collect tolls, you have conquered a vast number of towns, to collect the corvée, and, as to making a vast number of wars, I am the one who makes wars: "The Lord is a man of war" (Ex. 19:17). Are there any among you who have been telling of "this," and "this" is only the Torah: "And this is the Torah that Moses set before the children of Israel" (Dt. 4:44).' So they will make their exit, humiliated.

   P. *But if the kingdom of Persia has seen that such a claim issued by the kingdom of Rome did no good whatsoever, how come they go in at all?*

   Q. *They will say to themselves, "These are the ones who destroyed the house of the sanctuary, but we are the ones who built it."*

R. "And so it will go with each and every nation."

   S. *But if each one of them has seen that such a claim issued by the others did no good whatsoever, how come they go in at all?*

   T. *They will say to themselves, "Those two subjugated Israel, but we never subjugated Israel."*

   U. *And how come the two conquering nations are singled out as important and the others are not?*

   V. *It is because the rule of these will continue until the Messiah comes.*

W. "They will say to him, 'Lord of the world, in point of fact, did you actually give it to us and we did not accept it?'"

   X. *But how can they present such an argument, since it is written,* "The Lord came from Sinai and rose from Seir to them, he shined forth from Mount Paran" (Dt. 33:2), *and fur-*

ther, "God comes from Teman" (Hab. 3:3). *Now what in the world did he want in Seir, and what was he looking for in Paran?* Said R. Yohanan, "This teaches that the Holy One, blessed be he, made the rounds of each and every nation and language and none accepted it, until he came to Israel, and they accepted it."

Y. *Rather, this is what they say,* "Did we accept it but then not carry it out?"

Z. *But to this the rejoinder must be,* "Why did you not accept it anyhow!"

AA. Rather, "this is what they say before him, 'Lord of the world, Did you hold a mountain over us like a cask and then we refused to accept it as you did to Israel, as it is written, "And they stood beneath the mountain" (Ex. 19:17).'"

BB. And [in connection with the verse, "And they stood beneath the mountain" (Ex. 19:17),] said R. Dimi bar Hama, "This teaches that the Holy One, blessed be he, held the mountain over Israel like a cask and said to them, 'If you accept the Torah, well and good, and if not, then there is where your grave will be.'"

CC. "Then the Holy One, blessed be he, will say to them, 'Let us make known what happened first: "Let them announce to us former things" (Is. 43:9). As to the seven religious duties that you did accept, where have you actually carried them out?'"

DD. *And how do we know on the basis of Scripture that they did not carry them out? R. Joseph formulated as a Tannaite statement,* "'He stands and shakes the earth, he sees and makes the nations tremble' (Hab. 3:6): what did he see? He saw the seven religious duties that the children of Noah accepted upon themselves as obligations but never actually carried them out. Since they did not carry out those obligations, he went and remitted their obligation."

EE. *But then they benefited—so it pays to sin!*

FF. Said Mar b. Rabina, **[3A]** "What this really proves is that even they they carry out those religious duties, they get no reward on that account."

GG. *And they don't, don't they? But has it not been taught on Tannaite authority:* R. Meir would say, "How on the basis of Scripture do we know that, even if it is a gentile, if he goes and takes up the study of the Torah as his occupation, he is equivalent to the high priest? Scripture states, 'You shall therefore keep my statues and my ordinances, which, if a human being does them, one shall gain life through them' (Lev. 18:5). What is written is not 'priests' or 'Levites' or 'Israelites,' but rather, 'a human being.' So you have learned the fact that, even if it is a gentile, if he goes and takes up the study of the Torah as his occupation, he is equivalent to the high priest."

HH. Rather, what you learn from this [DD] is that they will not receive that reward that is coming to those who are commanded to do them and who carry them out, but rather, the reward that they receive will be like that coming to the one who is not commanded to do them and who carries them out anyhow.

II. For said R. Hanina, "Greater is the one who is commanded and who carries out the religious obligations than the one who is not commanded but nonetheless carries out religious obligations."

JJ. [Reverting to AA:] "this is what the gentiles say before him, 'Lord of the world, Israel, who accepted it—where in the world have they actually carried it out?'

KK. "The Holy One, blessed be he, will say to them, 'I shall bear witness concerning them, that they have carried out the whole of the Torah!'

LL. "They will say before him, 'Lord of the world, is there a father who is permitted to give testimony concerning his son? For it is written, "Israel is my son, my firstborn" (Ex. 4:22).'

MM. "The Holy One, blessed be he, will say to them, 'The heaven and the earth will give testimony in their behalf that they have carried out the entirety of the Torah.'

NN. "They will say before him, 'Lord of the world, The heaven and earth have a selfish interest in the testimony that they give: 'If not for my covenant with day and with night, I should not have appointed the ordinances of heaven and earth' (Jer. 33:25).'"

OO. *For said R. Simeon b. Laqish, "What is the meaning of the verse of Scripture,* 'And there was evening, and there was morning, the sixth day' (Gen. 1:31)? This teaches that the Holy One, blessed be he, made a stipulation with all of the works of creation, saying to them, 'If Israel accepts my Torah, well and good, but if not, I shall return you to chaos and void.' *That is in line with what is written:* 'You did cause sentence to be heard from heaven, the earth trembled and was still' (Ps. 76:9). If 'trembling' then where is the stillness, and if stillness, then where is the trembling? Rather, to begin with, trembling, but at the end, stillness."

PP. [Reverting to MM-NN:] "The Holy One, blessed be he, will say to them, 'Some of them may well come and give testimony concerning Israel that they have observed the entirety of the Torah. Let Nimrod come and give testimony in behalf of Abraham that he never worshipped idols. Let Laban come and give testimony in behalf of Jacob, that he never was suspect of thievery. Let the wife of Potiphar come and give testimony in behalf of Joseph, that he was never suspect of 'sin.' Let Nebuchadnessar come and give testimony in behalf of Hananiah, Mishael, and Azariah, that they never bowed down to the idol. Let Darius come and give testimony in behalf of Daniel, that he did not neglect even the optional prayers. Let Bildad the Shuhite and Zophar the Naamatite and Eliphaz the Temanite and Elihu son of Barachel the Buzite come and testify in behalf of Israel that they have observed the entirety of the Torah: "Let the nations bring their own witnesses, that they may be justified" (Is. 43:9).'

PP.   "They will say before him, 'Lord of the world, Give it to us to begin with, and let us carry it out.'

QQ. "The Holy One, blessed be he, will say to them, 'World-class idiots! He who took the trouble to prepare on the eve of the Sabbath [Friday] will eat on the Sabbath, but he who took no trouble on the eve of the Sabbath—what in the world is he going to eat on the Sabbath! Still, [I'll give you another chance.] I have a rather simple religious duty, which is called "the tabernacle." Go and do that one.'"

RR.   *But can you say any such thing? Lo, R. Joshua b. Levi has said, "What is the meaning of the verse of Scripture, 'The ordinances that I command you this day to do them' (Dt. 7:11)? Today is the day to do them, but not tomorrow; they are not to be done tomorrow; today is the day to do them, but not the day on which to receive a reward for doing them."*

SS.   Rather, it is that the Holy One, blessed be he, does not exercise tyranny over his creatures.

TT.   *And why does he refer to it as a simple religious duty? Because it does not involve enormous expense [to carry out that religious duty].*

UU.   "Forthwith every one of them will take up the task and go and make a tabernacle on his roof. But then the Holy, One, blessed be he, will come and make the sun blaze over them as at the summer solstice, and every one of them will knock down his tabernacle and go his way: 'Let us break their bands asunder and cast away their cords from us' (Ps. 23:3)."

VV.   But lo, you have just said, "it is that the Holy One, blessed be he, does not exercise tyranny over his creatures"!

WW. *It is because the Israelites too—sometimes* **[3B]** *the*

summer solstice goes on to the Festival of Tabernacles,
and therefore they are bothered by the heat!

XX. But has not Raba stated, "One who is bothered
[by the heat] is exempt from the obligation of
dwelling in the tabernacle"?

YY. *Granting that one may be exempt from the duty, is he*
going to go and tear the thing down?

ZZ. [Continuing from UU:] "Then the Holy One, blessed
be he, goes into session and laughs at them: 'He who
sits in heaven laughs' (Ps. 2:4)."

AAA. Said R. Isaac, "Laughter before the Holy One,
blessed be he, takes place only on that day
alone."

BBB. *There are those who repeat as a Tannaite ver-*
sion this statement of R. Isaac in respect to that
which has been taught on Tannaite authority:

CCC. R. Yosé says, "In the coming age gentiles will come and convert."

DDD. *But will they be accepted? Has it not been taught*
on Tannaite authority: Converts will not be
accepted in the days of the Messiah, just
as they did not accept proselytes either
in the time of David or in the time of
Solomon?

EEE. Rather, "they will make themselves converts, and they will put on phylacteries
on their heads and arms and fringes on
their garments and a mezuzah on their
doors. But when they witness the war of
Gog and Magog, he will say to them,
'How come you have come?' They will
say, "'Against the Lord and against his
Messiah.'" For so it is said, 'Why are the
nations in an uproar and why do the
peoples mutter in vain' (Ps. 2:1). Then
each one of them will rid himself of his
religious duty and go his way: 'Let us
break their bands asunder' (Ps. 2:3).
Then the Holy One, blessed be he, goes
into session and laughs at them: 'He who
sits in heaven laughs' (Ps. 2:4)."

FFF. Said R. Isaac, "Laughter before the Holy
One, blessed be he, takes place only on
that day alone."

GGG. But is this really so? And has not R.
Judah said Rab said, "The day is made
up of twelve hours. In the first three the

Holy One, blessed be he, goes into session and engages in study of the Torah;
in the second he goes into session and
judges the entire world. When he realizes that the world is liable to annihilation, he arises from the throne of justice
and takes up a seat on the throne of
mercy. In the third period he goes into
session and nourishes the whole world
from the horned buffalo to the brood of
vermin. During the fourth quarter he
laughs [and plays] with leviathan: 'There
is leviathan, whom you have formed to
play with' (Ps. 104:26)." [This proves
that God does laugh more than on that
one day alone.]

HHH. Said R. Nahman bar Isaac, "With his
creatures he laughs [everyday], but at his
creatures he laughs only on that day
alone."

The composition, No. 2, constitutes a single, well-crafted essay,
bearing its own glosses. When the continuing discussion set forth by
Hanina bar Pappa or Simlai is interrupted with a gloss, that is readily
apparent. To show how that glossing process in our terms would form
a footnote, I indent what I conceive to be footnotes. The interesting point comes at BBB, where we have an appendix to AAA. That
is to say, the footnote, AAA, completes the foregoing statement, ZZ.
Then the additional information is added not to the basic text but
to the gloss; it is not filler, the information is valued. But the insertion clearly adds nothing to the basic text—hence it is relegated to
an appendix, which, in our technical age, we should simply place
at the end of a book. But then GGG forms a footnote to an appendix, therefore is indented still further. The composition in no way
pretends to provide an exegesis of the Mishnah, the specific allegations of which do not provoke, or even relate to, the proposition
before us. This is an example, then, of that free-standing composition that the Talmud utilizes, but that the framers of the composites and compositions of the Talmud did not make up within their
work on the Talmud.

The next passages, to the end of this entire composition, go their
own way. In order to justify my decision to classify the entirety of
I.2—which is to say, **I.2-I.32**, in a single way, I have to show that
the entire composite is connected to I.2, and that the whole forms

a secondary formation, brought together for the purpose of giving
a full and complete exposition of the statement of I.2 and of the
materials included within that statement. Time and again in what
follows we shall see clear-cut reference, to something stated in I.2,
not merely allusion to a theme or some other aspect of
"intertextuality." The initial composition, I.2, is quoted, not merely
referred to, and the entirety of what follows then serves that initial
passage. Since I conceive everything that follows to form either a
footnote to I.2 or an appendix to a footnote to I.2, I have set the
whole into wider margins than the foregoing. This underlines the
fact that the whole augments a principal and primary statement.

3.   A.   Said R. Aha to R. Nahman bar Isaac, "From the day on which
the house of the sanctuary, the Holy One blessed be he has had
no laughter.

   B.   *"And how on the basis of Scripture do we know that he has had none? If
we say that it is because it is written,* 'And on that day did the Lord,
the god of hosts, call to weeping and lamentation' (Is. 22:12), *that
verse refers to that day in particular. Shall we then say that that fact derives
from the verse,* 'If I forget you, Jerusalem, let my right hand forget
her cunning, let my tongue cleave to the roof of my mouth if I
do not remember you' (Ps. 137:5-6)? *That refers to forgetfulness, not
laughter. Rather, the fact derives from this verse:* 'I have long held my
peace, I have been still, I have kept in, now I will cry' (Is. 42:14)."

The reference to God's laughing at FFF accounts for the addition
of No. 3. Then we proceed to No. 4, a further reference to an item
at No. 2. Nos. 5, 6 address the general theme of Torah-study. Because these compositions introduce the theme of this world and the
world to come, punishment now, reward then, or recompense then
for evil deeds done now, we find secondary developments on these
themes at Nos. 7, 8, 9, 10, 11, 12, 13, 14.

4.   A.   [Referring to the statement that during the fourth quarter he
laughs [and plays] with leviathan,] *[nowadays] what does he do in
the fourth quarter of the day?*

   B.   He sits and teaches Torah to kindergarten students: "Whom shall
one teach knowledge, and whom shall one make understand the
message? Those who are weaned from the milk?" (Is. 28:19).

   C.   *And to begin with [prior to the destruction of the Temple, which ended his
spending his time playing with leviathan], who taught them?*

   D.   *If you wish, I shall say it was Metatron, and if you wish, I shall say that
he did both [but now does only one].*

   E.   And at night what does he do?

   F.   *If you wish, I shall say that it is the sort of thing he does by day;*

G. *and if you wish, I shall say,* he rides his light cherub and floats through eighteen thousand worlds: "The chariots of God are myriads, even thousands and thousands [shinan] (Ps. 68:48). Read the letters translated as thousands, shinan, as though they were written, she-enan, meaning, that are not [thus: "the chariots are twice ten thousand less two thousand, eighteen thousand (Mishcon)].

H. *And if you wish, I shall say,* he sits and listens to the song of the Living Creatures [hayyot]: "By the day the Lord will command his loving-kindness and in the night his song shall be with me" (Ps. 42:9).

5. A. Said R. Levi, "To whoever stops studying the words of the Torah and instead takes up words of mere chatter they feed glowing coals of juniper: 'They pluck salt-wort with wormwood and the roots of juniper are their food' (Job 30:4)."

B. Said R. Simeon b. Laqish, "For whoever engages in study of the Torah by night—the Holy One, blessed be he, draws out the thread of grace by day: 'By day the Lord will command his loving-kindness, and in the night his song shall be with me' (Ps. 42:9). Why is it that 'By day the Lord will command his loving-kindness'? Because 'in the night his song shall be with me.'"

C. *Some say,* said R. Simeon b. Laqish, "For whoever engages in study of the Torah in this world, which is like the night,—the Holy One, blessed be he, draws out the thread of grace in the world to come, which is like the day: 'By day the Lord will command his loving-kindness, and in the night his song shall be with me' (Ps. 42:9). [Supply: Why is it that 'By day the Lord will command his loving-kindness'? Because 'in the night his song shall be with me.']"

6. A. Said R. Judah said Samuel, *"What is the meaning of the verse of Scripture,* 'And you make man as the fish of the sea and as the creeping things, that have no ruler over them' (Hab. 1:14)? Why are human beings compared to fish of the sea? To tell you, just as fish in the sea, when they come up on dry land, forthwith begin to die, so with human beings, when they take their leave of teachings of the Torah and religious deeds, forthwith they begin to die.

B. "Another matter: just as the fish of the sea, as soon as dried by the sun, die, so human beings, when struck by the sun, die."

C. *If you want, this refers to this world, and if you want, this refers to the world to come.*

D. *If you want, this refers to this world,,* in line with that which R. Hanina *[said],* for said R. Hanina, "Everything is in the hands of Heaven except cold and heat: 'colds and heat boils are in the way of the froward, he who keeps his soul holds himself far from them' (Prov. 22:5)."

E. *and if you want, this refers to the world to come, in accord with that which was stated by R. Simeon b. Laqish.* For said R. Simeon b. Laqish,

"In the world to come, there is no Gehenna, but rather, the Holy One, blessed be he, brings the sun out of its sheathe and he heats the wicked but heals the righteous through it. The wicked are brought to judgment by **[4A]** it: 'For behold, the day comes, it burns as a furnace, and all the proud and all who do wicked things shall be stubble, and the day that comes shall set them ablaze, says the Lord of hosts, that it shall leave them neither root nor branch' (Mal. 3:19).

F.   "'it shall leave them neither root'—in this world; 'nor branch'—in the world to come.

G.   "but heals the righteous through it:' 'But to you that fear my name shall the sun of righteousness arise with healing in its wings' (Mal. 3:19). They will revel in it: 'And you shall go forth and gambol as calves of the stall' (Mal. 3:20)."

H.   [Continuing C, above:] "Another matter: just as with the fish of the sea, whoever is bigger than his fellow swallows his fellow, so in the case of human beings, were it not for fear of the government, whoever is bigger than his fellow would swallow his fellow."

I.   *That is in line with what we have learned in the Mishnah:* **R. Hananiah, Prefect of the Priests, says, "Pray for the welfare of the government. For if it were not for fear of it, one man would swallow his fellow alive" [M. Abot 3:2A-B].**

7.   A.   *R. Hinena bar Pappa contrasted verses of Scripture: "It is written,* 'As to the almighty, we do not find him exercising plenteous power' (Job 37:23), but by contrast, 'Great is our Lord and of abundant power' (Ps. 147:5), and further, 'Your right hand, Lord, is glorious in power' (Ex. 15:6).

      B.   "But there is no contradiction between the first and second and third statements, for the former speaks of the time of judgment [when justice is tempered with mercy, so God does not do what he could] and the latter two statements refer to a time of war [of God against his enemies]."

8.   A.   *R. Hama bar Hanina contrasted verses of Scripture: "it is written,* 'Fury is not in me' (Is. 27:4) but also 'The Lord revenges and is furious' (Nah. 1:2).

      B.   *"But there is no contradiction between the first and second statements,* for the former speaks of Israel, the latter of the gentiles."

      C.   R. Hinena bar Pappa said, "'Fury is not in me' (Is. 54:9), for I have already taken an oath: 'would that I had not so vowed, then as the briars and thorns in flame would I with one step burn it altogether' (Is. 54:9)."

9.   A.   *That is in line with what R. Alexandri said, "What is the meaning of the verse,* 'And it shall come to pass on that day that I will seek to destroy all the nations' (Zech. 12:9)—

B. "'seek'—seek permission from whom?

C. "Said the Holy One, blessed be he, 'I shall seek in the records that deal with them, to see whether there is a cause of merit, on account of which I shall redeem them, but if not, I shall destroy them.'"

10. A. *That is in line with what Raba said, "What is the meaning of the verse,* 'Howbeit he will not stretch out a hand for a ruinous neap though they cry in his destruction' (Job 30:24)?

B. "Said the Holy One, blessed be he, to Israel, 'When I judge Israel, I shall not judge them as I do the gentiles, for it is written, "I will overturn, overturn, overturn it" (Ez. 21:32), rather, I shall exact punishment from them as a hen pecks.'

C. "Another matter: 'Even if the Israelites do not carry out a religious duty before me more than a hen pecking at a rubbish heap, I shall join together [all the little pecks] into a great sum: "although they pick little they are saved" (Job 30:24).'

D. "Another matter: 'As a reward for their crying out to me, I shall help them' (Job 30:24)."

11. A. *That is in line with what R. Abba said, "What is the meaning of the verse,* 'Though I would redeem them, yet they have spoken lies against me' (Hos. 7:23)? 'I said that I would redeem them through [inflicting a penalty] on their property in this world, so that they might have the merit of enjoying the world to come, "yet they have spoken lies against me" (Hos. 7:23).'"

12. A. *That is in line with what R. Pappi in the name of Raba said, "What is the meaning of the verse,* 'Though I have trained [and] strengthened their arms, yet they imagine mischief against me' (Hos. 7:15)?

B. Said the Holy One, blessed be he, I thought that I would punish them with suffering in this world, so that their arm might be strengthened in the world to come, "yet they have spoken lies against me" (Hos. 7:23).'"

13. A. *R. Abbahu praised R. Safra to the* minim [in context: Christian authorities of Caesarea], *saying that he was* a highly accomplished authority. *They therefore remitted his taxes for thirteen years.*

B. *One day they came upon him and said to him, "It is written, 'You only have I known among all the families of the earth; therefore I will visit upon you all your iniquities' (Amos 3:2). If one is angry, does he vent it on someone he loves?"*

C. *He fell silent and said nothing at all. They wrapped a scarf around his neck and tortured him. R. Abbahu came along and found them. He said to them, "Why are you torturing him?"*

D. *They said to him, "Didn't you tell us that he is* a highly accomplished authority, *but he does not know how to explain this verse!"*

E. *He said to them, "True enough, I told you that he was a master of Tannaite statements, but did I say anything at all to you about his knowledge of Scripture?"*

F. *They said to him, "So how come you know?"*

G. *He said to them, "Since we, for our part, spend a lot of time with you, we have taken the task of studying it thoroughly, while others [in Babylonia, Safra's place of origin] do not study [Scripture] that carefully."*

H. *They said to him, "So tell us."*

I. He said to them, "I shall tell you a parable. To what is the matter comparable? To the case of a man who lent money to two people, one a friend, the other an enemy. From the friend he collects the money little by little, from the enemy he collects all at once."

14. A. *Said R. Abba bar Kahana, "What is the meaning of the following verse of Scripture:* 'Far be it from you to do after this manner, to slay the righteous with the wicked' (Gen. 18:25).

    B. "Said Abraham before the Holy One, blessed be he, 'Lord of the world! It is a profanation to act in such a way [a play on the Hebrew letters, shared by the words 'far be it' and 'profanation'], 'to slay the righteous with the wicked' (Gen. 18:25)."

    C. But is it not [so that God might do just that]? And is it not written, "And I will cut off from you the righteous and the wicked" (Ez. 21:8)?

    D. That speaks of one who is not completely righteous, but not of one who is completely righteous.

    E. And will he not do so to one who is completely righteous? And is it not written, "And begin the slaughter with my sanctuary" (Ez. 9:6), in which connection R. Joseph repeated as a Tannaite version, "Read not 'with my sanctuary' but rather, 'with those who are holy to me,' namely, the ones who carried out the Torah beginning to end."

    F. *There too,* since they had the power to protest against the wickedness of the others and did not do so, they were not regarded as completely righteous at all.

The preceding composite, made up of connected compositions, has made reference to God's forgiveness but also God's anger. So we now address, as a tertiary augmentation, the issue of God's anger: when it happens, how it affects judgment, why it is important to avoid God's wrath and the like. The whole is an appendix to an appendix, a strung-together set of compositions, all of them related fore and aft, so that, in following the chain from the end to the beginning, we can always account for why a given composition has been made part of the composite before us. So we can account for the movement from one to the next, beginning at No. 15:

15.   A.   *R. Pappa contrasted verses of Scripture: "It is written,* 'God is angry every day' (Ps. 7:12) but also 'who could stand before his anger' (Nah. 1:6).

B.   *"But there is no contradiction between the first and second statements,* for the former speaks of the individual, the latter of the community."

16.   A.   *Our rabbis have taught on Tannaite authority:*

B.   "God is angry every day" (Ps. 7:12), and how long is his anger? It is for a moment. And how long is a moment? The portion 1/53,848th of an hour is a moment.

C.   And no creature can determine that moment, except for Balaam that wicked man, of whom it is written, **[5A]** "who knew the knowledge of the Most High" (Num. 24:16).

D.   How can it be that a man who did not know the mind of his animal could have known the mind of the Most High?

17.   A.   *And what is the meaning of the statement that* he did not know the mind of his animal?

B.   *When they saw him riding on his ass, they said to him, "How come you're not riding on a horse?"*

C.   *He said to them, "I sent it to the meadow."*

D.   Forthwith: "The ass said, Am I not your ass" (Num. 22:30).

E.   *He said to it, "Just as a beast of burden in general."*

F.   *She said to him,* "Upon whom you have ridden" (Num. 22:30).

G.   *He said to it, "Only from time to time."*

H.   *She said to him,* "ever since I was yours {Num. 22:30). And not only so, but I serve you for riding by day and fucking by night."

I.   For here the word "I was wont" is used, and the same letters bear the meaning of bed mate: "...and she served him as a bed-mate" (1 Kings 1:2).

18.   A.   *And what is the meaning of the statement that* he could have known the mind of the Most High?

B.   For he knew precisely that moment at which the Holy One, blessed be he, was angry.

C.   *That is in line with what the prophet had said to them,* "O my people, remember now what Balak king of Moab consulted and what Balaam son of Beor answered him from Shittim to Gilgal, that you may know the righteousness of the Lord" (Mic. 6:5).

19.   A.   ["O my people, remember now what Balak king of Moab consulted and what Balaam son of Beor answered him from Shittim to Gilgal, that you may

know the righteousness of the Lord" (Mic 6:5)]:

B.   Said R. Eleazar, "Said R. Eleazar, "Said the Holy one blessed be he to Israel, 'My people, see how many acts of righteousness I carried out with you, for I did not grow angry with you during all those [perilous] days, for if I had grown angry with you, there would not have remained from Israel a remnant or a survivor.'

C.   "And that is in line with what Balaam says: 'How can I curse seeing that God does not curse, and how can I be wrathful, seeing that the Lord has not been wrathful' (Num. 23:8)."

20. A.   And how long is his wrath? It is for a moment. And how long is a moment? The portion 1/53,848th of an hour is a moment.

B.   And how long is a moment?

C.   Said Amemar—others say, Rabina—"So long as it takes to say the word 'moment.'"

D.   *And how on the basis of Scripture do we know that his wrath lasts for only a moment?*

E.   *As it is written,* "For his anger is for a moment, his favor is for a lifetime" (Ps. 30:6).

F.   *If you prefer:* "Hide yourself for a brief moment, until the wrath be past" (Is. 26:20).

21. A.   *When is he angry?*

B.   *Said Abayye, "In the first three hours of the day, when the comb of the cock is white."*

C.   *Isn't it white all the rest of the day?*

D.   *At other times it has red streaks, but then it has none.*

22. A.   *R. Joshua b. Levi—a certain* min *would bother him about verses of Scripture. Once he took a chicken and put it between the legs of the bed and watched it. He reasoned, "When that hour comes, I shall curse him."*

B.   *But when that hour came, he was dozing. He said, "What you learn from this experience is that it is not correct to act in such a way:* 'His tender mercies are over all his works' (Ps. 145:9), 'Neither is it good for the righteous to inflict punishment' (Prov. 17:26)."

23. A.   *It was taught as a Tannaite version in the name of R. Meir,* "[That time at which God gets angry comes] when the kings put on their crowns on their heads and prostrate themselves to the sun. Forthwith the Holy One, blessed be he, grows angry."

24. A.   *Said R. Joseph, "A person should not recite the Prayer of the Additional Service for the first day of the New Year [the Day of Judgment] during the first three hours of the day or*

B. *in private, lest, since that is the time of judgment, his deeds may be examined, and his prayer rejected.*"

B. *If so, then the prayer of the community also should not be recited at that time?*

C. *The merit [accruing to the community as a whole] is greater.*

D. *If so, then that of the Morning Service also should not be recited in private?*

E. *Since at that time the community also will be engaged in reciting the Morning Prayer, the individual's recitation of the Prayer will not be rejected.*

F. *But have you not said,* "In the first three the Holy One, blessed be he, goes into session and engages in study of the Torah; in the second he goes into session and judges the entire world"*?*

G. *Reverse the order.*

H. *Or, if you prefer, actually do not reverse the order.* For when God is occupied with study of the Torah, called by Scripture "truth" as in "buy the truth and do not sell it" (Prov. 23:23), the Holy One, blessed be he, in any event will not violate the strict rule of justice. But when engaged in judgment, which is not called "truth" by Scripture, the Holy One, blessed be he, may step across the line of strict justice [towards mercy].

The long process of glossing the glosses has come to an end, so we now refer back to another statement of No. 2, which we shall develop. That covers Nos. 25, -27:

25. A. Reverting to the body of the prior text:

B. *R. Joshua b. Levi has said, "What is the meaning of the verse of Scripture,* 'The ordinances that I command you this day to do them' (Dt. 7:11)? Today is the day to do them, but not tomorrow; they are not to be done tomorrow; today is the day to do them, but today is not the day on which to receive a reward for doing them:"

C. Said R. Joshua b. Levi, "All the religious duties that Israelites do in this world come and give evidence in their behalf in the world to come: 'Let them bring their witnesses that they may be justified, let them hear and say it is truth."

D. "Let them bring their witnesses that they may be justified:" this is Israel.

E. "let them hear and say it is truth:" this refers to the gentiles.

F. And said R. Joshua b. Levi, "All the religious duties that Israelites do in this world come and flap about the faces of gentiles in the world to come: 'Keep therefore and do them, for this, your wisdom and understanding, will be in the eyes of the peoples' (Dt. 4:6).

G. "What is stated here is not 'in the presence of the peoples' but 'in the eyes of the peoples,' which teaches you that they will come and flap about the faces of gentiles in the world to come."

H. And said R. Joshua b. Levi, "The Israelites made the golden calf only to give an opening to penitents: 'O that they had such a heart as this always, to fear me and keep my commandments' (Dt. 5:26)."

26. A. That is in line with what R. Yohanan said in the name of R. Simeon b. Yohai: "David was really not so unfit as to do such a deed [as he did with Beth Sheva]: 'My heart is slain within me' (Ps. 109:22) [Mishcon: David's inclinations had been completely conquered by himself]. And the Israelites were hardly the kind of people to commit such an act: "O that they had such a heart as this always, to fear me and keep my commandments' (Dt. 5:26). So why did they do it?

B. "**[5B]** It was to show you that if an individual has sinned, they say to him, 'Go to the individual [such as David, and follow his example], and if the community as a whole has sinned, they say to them, 'Go to the community [such as Israel].'

C. *And it was necessary to give both examples. For had we been given the rule governing the individual, that might have been supposed to be because his personal sins were not broadly known, but in the case of the community, the sins of which will be broadly known, I might have said that that is not the case.*

D. *And if we had been given the rule governing the community, that might have been supposed to be the case because they enjoy greater mercy, but an individual, who has not got such powerful zekhut, might have been thought not subject to the rule.*

E. *So both cases had to be made explicit.*

27. A. *That is in line with what R. Samuel bar. Nahmani said R. Jonathan said, "What is the meaning of the verse of Scripture, 'The saying of David, son of Jesse, and the saying of the man raised on high' (2 Sam. 23:1)?*

B. "It means, 'The saying of David, son of Jesse, the man who raised up the yoke of repentance.'"

Now that the expansion of the passage at No. 2 has been completed, we proceed to the extension of that expansion. The reward for the religious duty, the punishment for the sin—these themes are developed at No. 28, which makes the point, critical in No. 2 as well, that our accomplishment of religious duties is acknowledged, so too, what sins we have done.

28. A. Said R. Samuel bar Nahmani said R. Jonathan, "Whoever does a religious duty in this world—that deed goes before him to the world to come, as it is said, 'And your righteousness shall go before you' (Is. 58:8).

B. "And whoever commits a transgression in this world—that act turns aside from him and goes before him on the Day of Judgment, as it is said, 'The paths of their way are turned aside, they go up into the waste and perish' (Job 6:18)."

C. R. Eliezer says, "It attaches to him like a dog, as it is said, 'He did not listen to her to lie by her or to be with her' (Gen. 39:10).

D. "'To lie by her' in this world

E. "'Or to be with her' in the world to come."

No. 29 forms a gloss to No. 28, though, obviously, it also is free-standing and makes its own autonomous point. What we now are given is an account of the result of sin, which, in this world, is death, a sustained and well-argued proposition, the whole an appendix to the general theme of No. 2 but to the particular statements of No. 28: sin and punishment, on the day of judgment.

29. A. Said R. Simeon b. Laqish, "Come and let us express our gratitude to our ancestors, for if it were not for their having sinned, we for our part should never have been able to come into the world: 'I said you are gods and all of you sons of the Most High' (Ps. 82:6). Now that you have ruined things by what you have done: 'you shall indeed die like mortals' (Ps. 82:6)."

B. *Does that statement then bear the implication, therefore, that if they had not sinned, they would not have propagated? But has it not been written,* "And you, be fruitful and multiply" (Gen. 9:7)?

C. *That applies up to Sinai.*

D. *But in connection with Sinai it also is written,* "Go say to them, Go back to your tents" (Ex. 19:15), meaning, to marital relationships. *And is it not also written,* "that it might be well with them and with their children" (Dt. 5:26)?

E. That speaks only to those who were actually present at Mount Sinai.

F. *But has not R. Simeon b. Laqish stated, "What is the meaning of that which is written:* 'This is the book of the generations of Adam' (Gen. 5:1)? Now did the first Adam have a book? The statement, rather, teaches that the Holy One, blessed be he, showed to the first Adam each

generation and its authoritative expositors,
each generations and its sages, each generation and those that administered its affairs.
When he came to the generation of R. Aqiba,
he rejoiced in the master's Torah but he was
saddened by the master's death.

G.   "He said, 'How precious are your thoughts to
     me, O God' (Ps. 139:17)."

H.   And said R. Yosé, "The son of David will come only
     when all of the souls that are stored up in the body
     will be used up: 'For I will not contend for ever,
     neither will I be always angry, for the spirit should
     fall before me and the spirits which I have made'
     (Is. 57:16)." [Mishcon: in the face of the foregoing
     teachings, how could it be stated that had it not
     been for the sin of the golden calf, we should not
     have come into the world?]

I.   *Do not, therefore, imagine that the sense of the statement is,*
     we should have not come into the world [if our
     ancestors had not sinned], *but rather,* it would have
     been as though we had not come into the world.

J.   *Does that then bear the implication that, if they had not
     sinned, they would never have died? But not been written
     the passages that deal with the deceased childless brother's
     widow and the chapters about inheritances [which take for
     granted that people die]?*

K.   These passages are written conditionally [meaning,
     if people sin and so die, then the rules take effect,
     but it is not necessary that they take effect unless
     that stipulation is fulfilled].

L.   *And are there then any verses of Scripture that are stated
     conditionally?*

M.   *Indeed so, for said R. Simeon b. Laqish, "What is the
     meaning of that which has been written,* 'And it was
     evening and it was morning, the sixth day' (Gen.
     1:31)? This teaches that the Holy One, blessed be
     he, made a stipulation with the works of creation
     and said, 'If the Israelites accept the Torah, well
     and good, but if not, I shall send you back to the
     condition of formlessness and void."

N.   *An objection was raised:* "O that they had such a heart
     as this always, to fear me and keep my command-
     ments, that it may be well with them and their
     children" (Dt. 5:26): it is not possible to maintain
     that the meaning here is that he would take away
     the angel of death from them, for the decree had
     already been made. It means that the Israelites
     accepted the Torah only so that no nation or tongue

would rule over them: "that it might be well with them and their children after them" [Mishcon: how could R. Simeon b. Laqish hold that but for the golden calf worship Israel would have enjoyed physical deathlessness?]

O. *[R. Simeon b. Laqish] made his statement in accord with the position of this Tannaite authority, for it has been taught on Tannaite authority:*

P. R. Yosé says, "The Israelites accepted the Torah only so that the angel of death should not have power over them: 'I said you are gods and all of you sons of the Most High. Now that you have ruined things by what you have done 'you shall indeed die like mortals' (Ps. 82:6)."

Q. *But to R. Yosé also must be addressed the question, has it not been written,* "O that they had such a heart as this always, to fear me and keep my commandments, that it may be well with them and their children" (Dt. 5:26)? *Goodness is what is promised, but there still will be death!*

R. *R. Yosé will say to you, "If there is no death, what greater goodness can there ever be?"*

S. *And the other Tannaite authority—how does he read the phrase,* "You shall indeed die"?

T. *The sense of* "death" *here is* "poverty," *for a master has said,* "Four classifications of persons are equivalent to corpses, and these are they: the poor man, the blind man, the person afflicted with the skin disease [of Lev. 13], and the person who has no children.

U. "The poor man, as it is written: 'for all the men are dead who sought your life' (Ex. 4:129). *Now who were they? This refers to Dathan and Abiram, and they were certainly not then dead,* they had only lost all their money.

V. "The blind man, as it is written: 'He has made me dwell in darkness as those that have been long dead' (Lam. 3:6).

W. "The person afflicted with the skin disease, as it is written: 'Let her, I pray you, not be as one who is dead' (Num. 12;12).

X. "And the person who has no children, as it is written: 'Give me children or else I die' (Gen. 30:1)."

What follows, at Nos. 30, and following is an appendix to the foregoing. I see no tight bonds that link No. 30 to No. 29, though Nos.

30, 31, 32, and 33 present a continuous discussion of their own. I treat the whole as an appendix, therefore, tacked on to a prior appendix. No. 32 clearly glosses No. 31.

30. A. *Our rabbis have taught on Tannaite authority:*
    B. "If you walk in my statutes" (Lev. 26:3)— the word "if" is used in the sense of supplication, as in the verse, O that my people would hearken to me, that Israel would walk in my ways...I should soon subdue their enemies" (Ps. 81:14-15); "O that you had listened to my commandments, then my peace would have been as a river, your seed also would have been as the sand" (Is. 48:18).

31. A. *Our rabbis have taught on Tannaite authority:*
    B. "O that they had such a heart as this always, to fear me and keep my commandments, that it may be well with them and their children" (Dt. 5:26)
    C. Said Moses to the Israelites, "You are a bunch of ingrates, children of ingrates. When the Holy One, blessed be he, said to you, 'O that they had such a heart as this always, to fear me and keep my commandments, that it may be well with them and their children' (Dt. 5:26), they should have said, 'You give it.'
    D. "They were ingrates, since it is written, 'Our soul loathes **[5B]** this light bread' (Num. 21:5).
    E. "...the children of ingrates: 'The woman whom you gave to be with me, she gave me of the fruit of the tree and I ate it' (Gen. 3:12).
    F. "So our rabbi, Moses, gave an indication of that fact to the Israelites only after forty years: 'And I have led you forty years in the wilderness...but the Lord has not give you a heart to know and eyes to see and ears to hear unto this day' (Dt. 29:3, 4)."
       32. A. ["And I have led you forty years in the wilderness...but the Lord has not given you a heart to know and eyes to see and ears to hear unto this day" (Dt. 29:3, 4):]

> B. Said Raba, "This proves that a person will fully grasp the mind of his master only after forty years have passed."

If I were responsible to choose a suitable conclusion to this mass of material, one that would both say something fresh but also present a reprise of the entire thematic conglomerate that has gone before, I doubt I could make a better choice than the following, which we must, therefore, see as a deliberate sign that we have come to the end of an enormous, but continuous and sustained, discussion of the general theme of Israel's loyalty and gentiles' idolatry. I center the passage to signal its function, which is, to write the word *finis*.

> 33. A. *Said R. Yohanan in the name of R. Benaah, "What is the meaning of the verse of Scripture,* 'Happy are you who sow beside all waters, that send forth the feet of the ox and the ass' (Is. 32:20)? 'Happy are you, O Israel, when you are devoted to the Torah and to doing deeds of grace, then their inclination to do evil is handed over to them, and they are not handed over into the power of their inclination to do evil.
>   B. "For it is said, 'Happy are you who sow beside all waters.' For what does the word 'sowing' mean, if not 'doing deeds of grace,' in line with the use of the word in this verse: 'Sow for yourselves in righteousness, reap according to mercy' (Hos. 10:12), and what is the meaning of 'water' if not Torah: 'Oh you who are thirsty, come to the water' (Is. 55:1)."
>   C. As to the phrase, "that send forth the feet of the ox and the ass:"
>   D. it has been taught by the Tannaite authority of the household of Elijah:
>   E. "A person should always place upon himself the work of studying the Torah as an ox accepts the yoke, and as an ass, its burden."

Let me now summarize what we have before us. **I.1** begins with a systematic inquiry into the correct reading of the Mishnah's word-choices. The dispute is fully articulated in balance, beginning to end. **I.2** then forms a footnote to No. 1. No. 3 then provides a footnote to the leitmotif of No. 2, the conception of God's not laughing. and No. 4 returns us to the exposition of No. 2, at III. Nos. 5, 6 are tacked on—a Torah-study anthology—because they continue the general

theme of Torah-study every day, which formed the main motif of
No. 2—the gentiles did not accept the Torah, study it, or carry it
out. So that theme accounts for the accumulation of sayings on
Torah-study in general, a kind of appendix on the theme. Then—
so far as I can see, because of the reference to God's power—No.
7 begins with a complement to 6.I. The compositions, Nos. 7, 8, then
are strung together because of a point that is deemed to link each
to its predecessor. No. 7 is linked to the foregoing because of the
theme of God's power; but it also intersects with 2.III and complements that reference; the entire sequence beyond No. 2 then in one
way or another relates to either No. 2, theme or proposition, or to
an item that is tacked on to No. 2 as a complement. Thus No. 8 is
joined to No. 7 because of the shared method of contrasting verses.
Then No. 9 is tacked on because it continues the proposition of
No. 8.

No. 10 continues the foregoing. No. 11 is tacked on to No. 10
for the reason made explicit: it continues what has gone before. The
same is so for No. 12. No. 13 continues the theme, but not the form
or the proposition, of the prior compositions, namely, punishment
little by little, e.g., in this world, in exchange for a great reward later
on. The established theme then is divine punishment and how it is
inflicted: gently to Israel, harshly to the gentiles; the preferred form
is the contrast among two verses. That overall principle of conglom-
eration—form & theme—explains the inclusion of Nos. 14, 15+16,
which is tacked on to 15. But then the introduction of Balaam, taken
as the prototype for the min, accounts for the inclusion of a variety
of further sayings on the same theme, specifically, No. 17, a gloss
on the foregoing; No. 18, a continuation of the foregoing process of
glossing, No. 19, an amplification on the now-dominant theme; No.
20, a reversion to No. 16; No. 21, a story on the theme of how difficult
it is to define precisely the matter dealt with in the foregoing. No.
21, 22, 23 complete the discussion of that particular time at which
God is angry, a brief moment but one that is marked by a just cause.
No. 23 then introduces the theme of choosing the right time—that
is not the moment of divine wrath—for prayer. This seems to me a
rather miscellaneous item, and it marks the conclusion of the systematic expansion begun much earlier. That that is the fact is shown
by the character of No. 24, which cites 2.HHH, and by No. 25, which
explicitly reverts to 2.RR, which justifies my insistence that the entire
corpus of materials that follow No. 2 simply amplify and augment

No. 2, and that is done in a very systematic way.

Some of the sets, as we have seen, were formed into conglomerates prior to insertion here, but once we recognize that all of the sets serve the single task at hand, we see the coherent of what on the surface appears to be run on and miscellaneous. So these materials serve No. 2, some as footnotes, some as appendices, and some as footnotes or appendices to footnotes or appendices. No. 26 is a fine case in point. It complements 25.H, and is tacked on for that reason. Then No. 27 complements No. 26's statements concerning David. Bearing a formal tie to No. 27, with the same authority, No. 28 fits in also because it reverts to the theme of No. 25, the power of the religious duties that one carries out. No. 29 continues the theme of No. 28, that is, death and the day of judgment. Simeon's statement defines the center of gravity of the passage, which obviously was complete prior to its inclusion here. The reason it has been added is its general congruence to the discussions of sin, penitence, death and forgiveness. No. 30 is attached to No. 31, and No. 31 is tacked on because it refers to the proof-text in the prior composition. No. 32 takes up the proof-text of No. 31. No. 33 writes a solid conclusion to the whole, addressing as it does the basic theme that Israel's actions define their fate, and that study of the Torah is what determines everything else. That is a thematic conclusion to a composite largely devoted, one way or another, to that one theme.

Lest we lose sight of the purpose of this rather protracted analysis of the connections between and among compositions, connections that make well-knit composites out of a selection of compositions, I remind the reader of what is at stake. It is not merely to show that a composite of compositions in fact forms a single literary entity, a complete and whole, and within the conventions of these authors, cogent and coherent statement. It is to justify my classifying the whole as a single unit, for purposes of setting forth the rules of composition: of making composites, of writing whole and complete statements, both. I maintain, as I said in the opening lines, that the whole of **I.1-32** form a single, continuous and uninterrupted statement, the entirety of which is to be classified within a single rubric.

IX. *Conclusion*

The Talmud comes from circles of Mishnah-exegetes. To compile the document, the Talmud's framers further drew upon ready-made and available, free-standing building blocks of discourse concerning topics other than the Mishnah and its law. These form a negligible part of the whole, but, a sustained examination will show, they also constitute an important component of the Judaism—the system of religious belief and behavior—that the Talmud sets forth. The other-than-Mishnah-exegetical compositions and composites of the Talmud demand examination in their own terms. But they tell us little about where the Talmud comes from, only about what those responsible for the document as we know it utilized in their work.

CHAPTER FIVE

A REFERENCE SYSTEM FOR
THE TALMUD

I. *Providing a New Reference System*

In light of the theories of how the Bavli is organized set forth in the preceding chapter, readers will understand why I have provided the Bavli, along with all of the other documents of Rabbinic Judaism in its formative age, with a new reference system. It is one that aims at supplying information not only concerning the location of a given sentence (or paragraph, or composition, or composite) but also concerning the character of the passage, its classification and place in the ordinal unfolding of a sustained presentation. Let me explain.

A reference-system may simply provide a convenient means to refer to a given sentence, e.g., the chapter and the place within the chapter of said sentence. That is the conventional way of identifying passages in Scripture. It may also refer to the page and the line on the page, once more for reference purposes. The Bavli's received reference-system consists of the tractate name, and the page on which a sentence occurs, that is, Bavli Abodah Zarah 2a points us to Bavli-tractate Abodah Zarah p. 2 the obverse side of the page—and not to a particular place on the page; sometimes a helpful bit of information will be added, "in the middle." Clearly, when I began my analytical work, I required a more helpful means to refer to passages.

I determined to devise a system that would supply still more information, however, not only the chapter and the position of the sentence there in, but a signal as to the character of the passage. For the Bavli, I use the double-system, the received one, page and side of the page, and also something like this: Bavli Abodah Zarah 1:1 I:1.A. That is to say, the Bavli's treatment of the opening paragraph of the Mishnah of a given chapter, thus 1:1; then the first paragraph of the first chapter; thus 1:1 then the first completed composite (sometimes: composition), thus I, then the first composition thereof, thus :1, then the first sentence thereof, thus A. As soon as I see the reference-entry, I know precisely where I am, not only in the text, but also in the formal repertoire and arrangement of the text. For analytical purposes, e.g., comparing and contrasting compositions and even whole composites, the system proves quite serviceable.

In making my translations of the canon of the Judaism of the dual Torah—Mishnah, Tosefta, two Talmuds, various Midrash-compilations—I supply to the canonical writings a systematic and uniform reference-system, corresponding, in the Bible, to the use of numbers for chapters and verses, e.g., Gen. 1:12. Because of the failure of all prior translators as well as editors of critical versions of the received classics to provide a reference system, I found it necessary to re-translate all canonical writings of the Judaism of the dual Torah that already had been presented in English, as well as to translate for the first time those many documents that were not in English. The reason, as I shall show here, is simply that no analytical work of any kind is possible without a reference-system that identifies the parts of a large passage. Not only so, but in a bilingual document, readers must be told what language the original authors used. But until very recently, no translation differentiated one language from the other. Since, it is clear, colleagues engaged in the same work of translation of rabbinic canonical writings do not yet grasp why an analytical reference system of some kind is required, recent works in German and Spanish,[3] for instance, at best numbering paragraphs, but, ordinarily, not doing even that, I propose to show what is at stake in a very simple exercise.

The problem goes beyond translation. No Hebrew-language re-printing of the Talmud has ever made possible any sort of large-scale analytical work at all. Not only so, but I do not believe that any Hebrew edition, e.g., a critical text, at which Israel colleagues think they excel, attends to that minimum task. Giving page and line references hardly suffices, since these supply no signals, let alone visual evidence, on what is before us. Not only so, but—perhaps it was deemed more "authentic" because "traditional"—every current translation into various European languages fails to provide even the most minimal sigla, e.g., indications of the smallest whole units of thought, sentences, paragraphs, completed expositions of a single idea, components of larger presentations of propositions, and the like—nothing, except page and line references (if that). No wonder the Bavli (among all writings) is (mis)represented as utterly confused, a hodge-

podge of this and that, when, in fact, it is an orderly and well-dis-
ciplined construction. Accordingly, the whole of rabbinic literature
has had to be retranslated in such a way as to indicate the individual
components of a composition, e.g., sentences, paragraphs, chapters
or completed whole presentations of propositions. I have accomplished most of that task, out of an interest in not philology, let alone
text-criticism, but history of religion.

II. *Signalling Traits for Analytical Consideration*

Only if the reader first meets an undifferentiated text, merely translated fairly literally, but in no way re-presented within the extant
technology by which we organize information in a purpose manner,
will the necessity of a differentiated text become self-evident. That
is why, in what follows, I first present, without comment, a sizable
abstract, marking each sentence off from the others only for the
purpose of allowing the reader some sort of minimal access to what
is said. I do not differentiate between Hebrew and Aramaic, and
I do not include any signals on how a given sentence relates to what
has gone before or to what is to follow. So I omit the signals that
I have devised to ease the reader's progress through the document,
that is, not highlighting what the intended audience automatically
will have grasped from shifts in language and other signals, articulated or implicit, in the flow of language. To facilitate some mini-

---

[3] Spanish, for one example: *Midrás Exodo Rabbah I,* by Luis-Fernando Girón
Blanc. Biblioteca Midrásica, 8. Valencia, Spain: Institución San Jerónimo, 1989.
Pp. vi+190. But the critical Hebrew text, of Exodus Rabbah used by the Spanish
translation, that of A. Shinan, also has no analytical reference system that anyone
can use. Not one [!] German "scientific" translation—Wewers's translation of the
Talmud of the Land of Israel, for example—has recognized the requirement of a
reference-system to make possible further study of the translated documents, with
the result that all we have in German is the contents of the Hebrew, but not the
construction or indications of the composition. Analytical scholarship on these
documents is possible only within my, or some counterpart, reference system. Translators may maintain that analysis is not part of their work. But as soon as we who
translate supply periods, commas, and quotation marks, we state what we conceive to be the elements of construction and composition. Then why not mark the
sentences, one by one, so people can refer to them? And why not say what we
conceive the "chapters" to be as well? I have done nothing more "radical" than
was done by the printers who originally presented the Bible in printed form and
added chapter and verse numbers. But, as is clear, I have had to do this work for
the entirety of rabbinical literature of late antiquity.

mal intelligibility, to be sure, I do include quotation-marks; many
of the "modern, scientific" translations do not give even that mark.

Then, immediately afterward, I re-represent the entire passage,
this time showing it as a differentiated set of citations and quota-
tions from various sources (now, the passages of the Mishnah and
Tosefta will be in bold face type). By giving Hebrew in plain type
and Aramaic in italics, further, I differentiate the two languages and
so drawing upon the signals that language-choice delivers. I also
display in indentation—further and further to the right hand column, as an item glosses a gloss, or provides an appendix to a gloss,
or footnotes a footnote—what I conceive to be the secondary or
subordinated discussions. As to the body of the materials, I differentiate what I conceive to be the smallest whole units of thought
("sentences")) paragraph by paragraph, marking each with a letter
for ready reference. I then identify what I conceive to be complete
propositional formulations ("paragraphs") by marking a set of let-
tered "sentences" with Arabic numerals. Finally, I mark what I
maintain are fully and exhaustively presented composites of propositions ("chapters") by a Roman number. Working from the whole
to the parts, I move from a complete statement through the components of that statement to the smallest whole units of thought of
which that statement is comprised.[4] A variety of issues are at stake
in providing such an analytical reference system, inclusive of the
signification of secondary and tertiary discourses by progressive
indentation. In the present context, my discussion will then show
how in presenting a vast corpus of material, and in fully providing
the apparatus of information, not only the main points of proposition, evidence, and argument, the framers have followed a few simple
rules, which a sensitive reader will have grasped after only minimal
study.

III. *Two Approaches to the Representation of the Same Text*

To show what is at stake in providing a new reference system, let
me now compare the old and the new. We revert to a passage already treated earlier, and for my system I give only a sample of how
I parse the passage. I have chosen by far the best English translation, that of Soncino, which has the merit of giving us a fully-natu-
ralized English rendition of the Talmud. That is to say, Soncino's
translators, the great pioneers in rendering Rabbinic writings acces-

sible to the English-speaking world, give us a fully-native version, rendering clauses into whole phrases, phrases into sentences, sentences into paragraphs, all in line with the requirements of the reader of our language. They therefore sacrifice a literal rendition of the diction and syntax of the Aramaic in favor of a representation in ordinary and correct English. That is to say, we cannot work our way back from the English to the Hebrew or Aramaic, as the case may be. But through their taste and judgment, through their provision of language the Talmud does not contain to provide access to the message of the Talmud, through their solutions to a very wide variety of problems even of counterpart-vocabulary, the Soncino translators accomplished their goal, a worthy one indeed. My retranslation of the Bavli (and other documents) and first-time translation of the Yerushalmi, Sifra (and other compilations) responded to different goals from theirs, to a program of analysis of the character of the writings that required information of another sort, a choice of voice, timber, and language of a different kind, from the selections that guided the Soncino scholars. The new reference system is the result, and in passages throughout this *Reader's Guide*, its use for the development of charts, e.g., concerning the order of types of forms of compositions in the Bavli, will have shown why it serves my purposes.

Presenting the opening Mishnah-paragraph and following Talmud of Babylonian Talmud tractate Abodah Zarah, pp. 2A-3B, I first offer the whole, differentiated only by periods, sentence by sentence. All translations of all documents of rabbinic literature except for mine, wherever and whenever made, will follow this format (a glance at the fine translation published by Soncino Press, London, will validate my claim on how translations represent the original of these pages):[5]

> **Mishnah:** Before the festivals of gentiles for three days it is forbidden to do business with them, to lend anything to them or to borrow anything from them, to lend money to them or to borrow money from them, to repay them or to be repaid by them. R. Judah says, "They accept repayment from them, because it is distressing to him." They

---

[4] I invented this reference system originally for my translation of the Mishnah, explaining its terms and categories in a work that to my knowledge, received not a single review: *A History of the Mishnaic Law of Purities*. Leiden, 1977: Brill. XXI. *The Redaction and Formulation of the Order of Purities in the Mishnah and Tosefta*.

said to him, "Even though it is distressing to him now, he will be happy about it later." **Gemara:** Before the festivals of gentiles for three days it is forbidden to do business with them. to lend anything to them or to borrow anything from them, to lend money to them or to borrow money from them. to repay them or to be repaid by them. R. Judah says, "They accept repayment from them, because it is distressing to him." They said to him, "Even though it is distressing to him now, he will be happy about it later." Rab and Samuel [in dealing with the reading of the key-word of the Mishnah, translated festival, the letters of which are 'aleph daled, rather than 'ayin daled, which means, calamity]: one repeated the formulation of the Mishnah as, "their festivals." And the other repeated the formulation of the Mishnah as "their calamities." The one who repeated the formulation of the Mishnah as "their festivals" made no mistake, and the one who repeated the formulation of the Mishnah as "their calamities" made no mistake. For it is written, "For the day of their calamity is at hand" (Dt. 32:15). The one who repeated the formulation of the Mishnah as "their festivals" made no mistake,, for it is written, "Let them bring their testimonies that they may be justified" (Is. 43:9). And as to the position of him who repeats the formulation of the Mishnah as "their festivals," on what account does he not repeat the formulation of the Mishnah to yield, "their calamities"? He will say to you, "'Calamity' is preferable [as the word choice when speaking of idolatry]." And as to the position of whim who repeats the formulation of the Mishnah as "their calamities," on what account does he not repeat the formulation of the Mishnah to yield "their festivals"? He will say to you, "What causes the calamity that befalls them if not their testimony, so testimony is preferable!" And as to the verse, "Let them bring their testimonies that they may be justified" (Is. 43:9), is this written with reference to gentiles? Lo, it is written in regard to Israel. For said R. Joshua b. Levi, "All of the religious duties that Israelites carry out in this world come and give testimony in their behalf in the world to come: 'Let them bring their witnesses that they may be justified' (Is. 43:9), that is, Israel; 'and let them hear and say, It is truth' (Is. 43:9)—this refers to gentiles." Rather, said R. Huna b. R. Joshua, "He who formulates the Mishnah to refer to their calamities derives the reading from this verse: 'They that fashion a graven image are all of them vanity, and their delectable things shall not profit, and their own witnesses see not nor know' (Is. 44:9)." As to the exposition [of the verse,"They that fashion a graven image are all of them vanity, and their delectable things shall not profit, and their own witnesses see not nor know" (Is.

---

[5] Other contemporary translations into English, in the names of "the Steinsaltz Talmud" and the Artscroll Talmud, organize the page around extensive notes and reproduce the effect of the Romm Talmud in Hebrew/Aramaic. Neither one indicates the components of the discussion and how they fit together, and no effort is made there, any more than in Soncino's pioneering and still paramount trans-

44:9)]: "In the age to come the Holy One, blessed be he, will bring a scroll of the Torah and hold it in his bosom and say, 'Let him who has kept himself busy with it come and take his reward.' Then all the gentiles will crowd together: 'All of the nations are gathered together' (Is. 43:9). The Holy One, blessed be he, will say to them, 'Do not crowd together before me in a mob. But let each nation enter together with **[2B]** its scribes, 'and let the peoples be gathered together' (Is. 43:9), and the word 'people' means 'kingdom:' 'and one kingdom shall be stronger than the other' (Gen. 25:23)." But can there be a mob-scene before the Holy One, blessed be he? Rather, it is so that from their perspective they not form a mob, so that they will be able to hear what he says to them. "The kingdom of Rome comes in first." How come? Because they are the most important. How do we know on the basis of Scripture they are the most important? Because it is written, "And he shall devour the whole earth and shall tread it down and break it into pieces" (Gen. 25:23), and said R. Yohanan, "This Rome is answerable, for its definition [of matters] has gone forth to the entire world [Mishcon: 'this refers to Rome, whose power is known to the whole world']." And how do we know that the one who is most important comes in first? It is in accord with that which R. Hisda said. For said R. Hisda, "When the king and the community [await judgment], the king enters in first for judgment: 'That he maintain the cause of his servant [Solomon] and [then] the cause of his people Israel' (1 Kgs. 8:59)." And how come? If you wish, I shall say it is not appropriate to keep the king sitting outside. And if you wish, I shall say that [the king is allowed to plea his case] before the anger of the Holy One is aroused." "The Holy One, blessed be he, will say to them, 'How have defined your chief occupation?' They will say before him, 'Lord of the world, a vast number of marketplaces have we set up, a vast number of bath houses we have made, a vast among the silver and gold have we accumulated. And all of these things we have done only in behalf of Israel, so that they may define as their chief occupation the study of the Torah.' The Holy One, blessed be he, will say to them, 'You complete idiots! Whatever you have done has been for your own convenience. You have set up a vast number of marketplaces to be sure, but that was so as to set up whore-houses in them. The bath-houses were for your own pleasure. Silver and gold belong to me anyhow: "Mine is the silver and mine is the gold, says the Lord of hosts" (Hag.

---

lation, to show visually how the Talmud works. They serve a different purpose and speak to a different cultural milieu. Between the two, I prefer the Artscroll, which preserves all the advantages of the received representation of the text in the greatest printed Talmuds in the original language. Steinsaltz tried to preserve the "traditional" page but to add "scholarly" data and produced only chaos. The great printers of the Talmud were better educators than Steinsaltz, having a clearer picture of their pedagogical goals, and Artscroll preserves their genius in our language, with the original text.

2:8). Are there any among you who have been telling of "this," and "this" is only the Torah: "And this is the Torah that Moses set before the children of Israel' (Dt. 4:44)." So they will make their exit, humiliated. When the kingdom of Rome has made its exit, the kingdom of Persia enters afterward." How come? Because they are second in importance. And how do we know it on the basis of Scripture? Because it is written, "And behold, another beast, a second, like a bear" (Dan. 7:5), and in this connection R. Joseph repeated as a Tannaite formulation, "This refers to the Persians, who eat and drink like a bear, are obese like a bear, are shaggy like a bear, and are restless like a bear." The Holy One, blessed be he, will say to them, 'How have defined your chief occupation?' hey will say before him, 'Lord of the world, We have thrown up a vast number of bridges, we have conquered a vast number of towns, we have made a vast number of wars, and all of them we did only for Israel, so that they may define as their chief occupation the study of the Torah.' The Holy One, blessed be he, will say to them, 'Whatever you have done has been for your own convenience. You have thrown up a vast number of bridges, to collect tolls, you have conquered a vast number of towns, to collect the corvée, and, as to making a vast number of wars, I am the one who makes wars: "The Lord is a man of war" (Ex. 19:17). Are there any among you who have been telling of "this," and "this" is only the Torah: "And this is the Torah that Moses set before the children of Israel" (Dt. 4:44).' So they will make their exit, humiliated. But if the kingdom of Persia has seen that such a claim issued by the kingdom of Rome did no good whatsoever, how come they go in at all? They will say to themselves, "These are the ones who destroyed the house of the sanctuary, but we are the ones who built it." And so it will go with each and every nation." But if each one of them has seen that such a claim issued by the others did no good whatsoever, how come they go in at all? They will say to themselves, "Those two subjugated Israel, but we never subjugated Israel." And how come the two conquering nations are singled out as important and the others are not? It is because the rule of these will continue until the Messiah comes. "They will say to him, 'Lord of the world, in point of fact, did you actually give it to us and we did not accept it?'" But how can they present such an argument, since it is written, "The Lord came from Sinai and rose from Seir to them, he shined forth from Mount Paran" (Dt. 33:2), and further, "God comes from Teman" (Hab. 3:3). Now what in the world did he want in Seir, and what was he looking for in Paran? Said R. Yohanan, "This teaches that the Holy One, blessed be he, made the rounds of each and every nation and language and none accepted it, until he came to Israel, and they accepted it." Rather, this is what they say, "Did we accept it but then not carry it out?" But to this the rejoinder must be, "Why did you not accept it anyhow!" Rather, "this is what they say before him, 'Lord of the world, Did you hold a mountain over us like a cask and then we refused to accept it as you did to Israel, as it is written,

"And they stood beneath the mountain" (Ex. 19:17).'" And [in connection with the verse, "And they stood beneath the mountain" (Ex. 19:17),] said R. Dimi bar Hama, "This teaches that the Holy One, blessed be he, held the mountain over Israel like a cask and said to them, 'If you accept the Torah, well and good, and if not, then there is where your grave will be.'" "Then the Holy One, blessed be he, will say to them, 'Let us make known what happened first: "Let them announce to us former things" (Is. 43:9). As to the seven religious duties that you did accept, where have you actually carried them out?'" And how do we know on the basis of Scripture that they did not carry them out? R. Joseph formulated as a Tannaite statement, "'He stands and shakes the earth, he sees and makes the nations tremble' (Hab. 3:6): what did he see? He saw the seven religious duties that the children of Noah accepted upon themselves as obligations but never actually carried them out. Since they did not carry out those obligations, he went and remitted their obligation." But then they benefited—so it pays to sin! Said Mar b. Rabina, **[3A]** "What this really proves is that even they they carry out those religious duties, they get no reward on that account." And they don't, don't they? But has it not been taught on Tannaite authority: R. Meir would say, "How on the basis of Scripture do we know that, even if it is a gentile, if he goes and takes up the study of the Torah as his occupation, he is equivalent to the high priest? Scripture states, 'You shall therefore keep my statues and my ordinances, which, if a human being does them, one shall gain life through them' (Lev. 18:5). What is written is not 'priests' or 'Levites' or 'Israelites,' but rather, 'a human being.' So you have learned the fact that, even if it is a gentile, if he goes and takes up the study of the Torah as his occupation, he is equivalent to the high priest." Rather, what you learn from this is that they will not receive that reward that is coming to those who are commanded to do them and who carry them out, but rather, the reward that they receive will be like that coming to the one who is not commanded to do them and who carries them out anyhow. For said R. Hanina, "Greater is the one who is commanded and who carries out the religious obligations than the one who is not commanded but nonetheless carries out religious obligations." "this is what the gentiles say before him, 'Lord of the world, Israel, who accepted it—where in the world have they actually carried it out?' "The Holy One, blessed be he, will say to them, 'I shall bear witness concerning them, that they have carried out the whole of the Torah!' "They will say before him, 'Lord of the world, is there a father who is permitted to give testimony concerning his son? For it is written, "Israel is my son, my firstborn" (Ex. 4:22).' The Holy One, blessed be he, will say to them, 'The heaven and the earth will give testimony in their behalf that they have carried out the entirety of the Torah.' They will say before him, 'Lord of the world, The heaven and earth have a selfish interest in the testimony that they give: 'If not for my covenant with day and with night, I should not have appointed

the ordinances of heaven and earth' (Jer. 33:25).'" For said R. Simeon
b. Laqish, "What is the meaning of the verse of Scripture, 'And there
was evening, and there was morning, the sixth day' (Gen. 1:31)? This
teaches that the Holy One, blessed be he, made a stipulation with all
of the works of creation, saying to them, 'If Israel accepts my Torah,
well and good, but if not, I shall return you to chaos and void.' That
is in line with what is written: 'You did cause sentence to be heard
from heaven, the earth trembled and was still' (Ps. 76:9). If 'trembling'
then where is the stillness, and if stillness, then where is the trembling?
Rather, to begin with, trembling, but at the end, stillness." "The Holy
One, blessed be he, will say to them, 'Some of them may well come
and give testimony concerning Israel that they have observed the entirety of the Torah. Let Nimrod come and give testimony in behalf of
Abraham that he never worshipped idols. Let Laban come and give
testimony in behalf of Jacob, that he never was suspect of thievery.
Let the wife of Potiphar come and give testimony in behalf of Joseph,
that he was never suspect of 'sin.' Let Nebuchadnessar come and give
testimony in behalf of Hananiah, Mishael, and Azariah, that they never
bowed down to the idol. Let Darius come and give testimony in behalf of Daniel, that he did not neglect even the optional prayers. Let
Bildad the Shuhite and Zophar the Naamatite and Eliphaz the Temanite
and Elihu son of Barachel the Buzite come and testify in behalf of Israel
that they have observed the entirety of the Torah: "Let the nations
bring their own witnesses, that they may be justified" (Is. 43:9).' They
will say to him, "Then give it to us to begin with, and let us carry it
out.' The Holy One, blessed be he, will say to them, 'World-class idiots!
He who took the trouble to prepare on the eve of the Sabbath [Fri-
day] will eat on the Sabbath, but he who took no trouble on the even
of the Sabbath—what in the world is he going to eat on the Sabbath!
Still, [I'll give you another chance.] I have a rather simple religious
duty, which is called "the tabernacle." Go and do that one.'" But can
you say any such thing? Lo, R. Joshua b. Levi has said, "What is the
meaning of the verse of Scripture, 'The ordinances that I command
you this day to do them' (Dt. 7:11)? Today is the day to do them, but
not tomorrow; they are not to be done tomorrow; today is the day to
do them, but not the day on which to receive a reward for doing them."
Rather, it is that the Holy One, blessed be he, does not exercise tyranny over his creatures. And why does he refer to it as a simple religious duty? Because it does not involve enormous expense [to carry
out that religious duty]. Forthwith every one of them will take up the
task and go and make a tabernacle on his roof. But then the Holy,
One, blessed be he, will come and make the sun blaze over them as
at the summer solstice, and every one of them will knock down his
tabernacle and go his way: 'Let us break their bands asunder and cast
away their cords from us' (Ps. 23:3)." But lo, you have just said, "it is
that the Holy One, blessed be he, does not exercise tyranny over his
creatures"! It is because the Israelites too—sometimes **[3B]** the sum-

mer solstice goes on to the Festival of Tabernacles, and therefore they are bothered by the heat! But has not Raba stated, "One who is bothered [by the heat] is exempt from the obligation of dwelling in the tabernacle"? Granting that one may be exempt from the duty, is he going to go and tear the thing down? "Then the Holy One, blessed be he, goes into session and laughs at them: 'He who sits in heaven laughs' (Ps. 2:4)." Said R. Isaac, "Laughter before the Holy One, blessed be he, takes place only on that day alone." There are those who repeat as a Tannaite version this statement of R. Isaac in respect to that which has been taught on Tannaite authority: R. Yosé says, "In the coming age gentiles will come and convert." But will they be accepted? Has it not been taught on Tannaite authority: Converts will not be accepted in the days of the Messiah, just as they did not accept proselytes either in the time of David or in the time of Solomon? Rather, "they will make themselves converts, and they will put on phylacteries on their heads and arms and fringes on their garments and a mezuzah on their doors. But when they witness the war of Gog and Magog, he will say to them, 'How come you have come?' They will say, "'Against the Lord and against his Messiah.'" For so it is said, 'Why are the nations in an uproar and why do the peoples mutter in vain' (Ps. 2:1). Then each one of them will rid himself of his religious duty and go his way: 'Let us break their bands asunder' (Ps. 2:3). Then the Holy One, blessed be he, goes into session and laughs at them: 'He who sits in heaven laughs' (Ps. 2:4)." Said R. Isaac, "Laughter before the Holy One, blessed be he, takes place only on that day alone." But is this really so? And has not R. Judah said Rab said, "The day is made up of twelve hours. In the first three the Holy One, blessed be he, goes into session and engages in study of the Torah; in the second he goes into session and judges the entire world. When he realizes that the world is liable to annihilation, he arises from the throne of justice and takes up a seat on the throne of mercy. In the third period he goes into session and nourishes the whole world from the horned buffalo to the brood of vermin. During the fourth quarter he laughs [and plays] with leviathan: 'There is leviathan, whom you have formed to play with' (Ps. 104:26)." [This proves that God does laugh more than on that one day alone.] Said R. Nahman bar Isaac, "With his creatures he laughs [everyday], but at his creatures he laughs only on that day alone."

That is what the page, without markings other than commas, periods and quotation marks yields. I argue that a proper reference-system displays the cogency and well-crafted character of this piece of writing. But, at this point, anyone with the patience to have read the entire passage will by now have found utterly implausible my allegation that that page is at all coherent. And even were I to paragraph the column of words as the Soncino translation does, it

would make little different to that judgment. Long columns of undifferentiated words simply cannot be analyzed in any manner at
all; the absence of a reference system renders the translation gibberish: we understand the sentences, but composition that they form.

Without further ado, we reconsider part of the passage, now differentiating the composites by Roman numerals, the compositions
that form the components of the composites by Arabic numerals,
the constitutive parts of the compositions by letters; the sources—
Mishnah, Tosefta from everything else—by different type faces; the
two languages, Hebrew and Aramaic, by regular type and italics,
respectively; and the text—the principal discourse—from footnotes
and appendices by indenting and double and triple indenting the
latter. In this way—through a simple and visually easily understood
reference-system—we see precisely what is in play in the page; my
comments then will explain what our authors have done to give us
everything they thought we had to know. We see that they followed
a few simple rules, which we can discern and which guide us in
reading their writing. I give only part of the passage, which is fully
worked out earlier in this part of the project. In my *The Talmud of
Babylonia. An Academic Commentary*, I have presented the entire Bavli
in this same way; the counterpart work for the Yerushalmi is complete; the outlines of both Talmuds for the divisions served by the
two of them together are complete; and the comparison of the two
Talmuds in line with those outlines is complete. I have also done
the same work for the principal Midrash-compilations, a full "academic commentary" along with an outline for each of the documents.
All of these are listed in the appendix to this chapter.

Mishnah/Bavli Abodah Zarah
1:1

A.   [2A] **Before the festivals of gentiles for three days it is
     forbidden to do business with them.**
B.   **(1) to lend anything to them or to borrow anything from
     them.**
C.   **(2) to lend money to them or to borrow money from
     them.**
D.   **(3) to repay them or to be repaid by them.**
E.   **R. Judah says, "They accept repayment from them,
     because it is distressing to him."**
F.   **They said to him, "Even though it is distressing to him
     now, he will be happy about it later."**

Mishnah 1:1.I.1

A.   **[2A]** Rab and Samuel [in dealing with the reading of the key-word of the Mishnah, translated festival, the letters of which are 'aleph daled, rather than 'ayin daled, which means, calamity]:

B.   *one repeated the formulation of the Mishnah as, "their festivals."*

C.   *And the other repeated the formulation of the Mishnah as "their calamities."*

D.   *The one who repeated the formulation of the Mishnah as "their festivals" made no mistake, and the one who repeated the formulation of the Mishnah as "their calamities" made no mistake.*

E.   *For it is written,* "For the day of their calamity is at hand" (Dt. 32:15).

F.   *The one who repeated the formulation of the Mishnah as "their festivals" made no mistake,, for it is written,* "Let them bring their testimonies that they may be justified" (Is. 43:9).

G.   *And as to the position of him who repeats the formulation of the Mishnah as "their festivals," on what account does he not repeat the formulation of the Mishnah to yield, "their calamities"?*

H.   *He will say to you, "'Calamity' is preferable [as the word choice when speaking of idolatry]."*

I.   *And as to the position of whim who repeats the formulation of the Mishnah as "their calamities," on what account does he not repeat the formulation of the Mishnah to yield "their festivals"?*

J.   *He will say to you, "What causes the calamity that befalls them if not their testimony, so testimony is preferable!"*

K.   *And as to the verse,* "Let them bring their testimonies that they may be justified" (Is. 43:9), *is this written with reference to gentiles? Lo, it is written in regard to Israel.*

L.   For said R. Joshua b. Levi, "All of the religious duties that Israelites carry out in this world come and give testimony in their behalf in the world to come: 'Let them bring their witnesses that they may be justified' (Is. 43:9), that is, Israel; 'and let them hear and say, It is truth' (Is. 43:9)—this refers to gentiles."

M.   Rather, said R. Huna b. R. Joshua, "He who formulates the Mishnah to refer to their calamities derives the reading from this verse: 'They that fashion a graven image are all of them vanity, and their delectable things shall not profit, and their own witnesses see not nor know' (Is. 44:9)."

The foregoing, we see clearly, presents a beautifully balanced dispute-form, and the form is used to provide a medium for presenting Mishnah-text criticism: how are we to read the text of the paragraph before us. That classification presents no problems. We must now enter a much more difficult question because I maintain that, along with the classification of I.1, everything that is attached to I.1 in a continuous and ongoing manner goes along as a single composite, the whole put together in its own terms, but then utilized by the framer of the Talmud before us—folios 2A-5B—as a continuous (if in our perspective rather run-on) statement. It is obviously a composite. But for reasons spelled out earlier, I classify the entire composite all together and all at once, because it is more than a composite: it also is a composition. And the reason I see it as a coherent and cogent composition is that every item fits together with its predecessor and leads us without interruption to its successor, from the starting lines of **I.1** to the concluding ones of **I.32**.

No. 1 has referred us to gentile idolatry and Israelite loyalty to the religious duties assigned to them by God. We now have a long exposition of the theme of gentile idolatry and perfidy. Everything that follows in **I.2** serves as a play on the theme of **I.1**.L-M! The unity of the whole of I.2 will be readily apparent because of the insets of gloss and expansion, and the further insets of the appendices to the gloss and expansion. We saw, through the device of indentations, how much in the expansion of the foregoing in fact serves as gloss, footnote, and appendix; recognizing that fact we see a rather well-crafted and cogent composite, made up of a principal composition—extending to the far left-hand margin—and a variety of subordinated compositions, moving off to the right in progressive indentations. And what we can see, visually, any well-endowed disciple of the document will readily have understood through his thoughtful reading of the document: this is primary, that is secondary and subordinate. In ages past the disciples will not have called what I indent "footnotes" or even "appendices." But they also will not have found confusing the glosses and supplements that, all together, give a full and rich account of any subject introduced in the primary discussion.

True, this is not how Plato and Aristotle set out their ideas; but the great philosophers also did not choose as the medium for writing down their ideas a commentary on a received text, in constant dialogue with yet another received text (the Mishnah, Scripture), with persistent attention to a variety of other received data, all to be provided in a complete and purposeful argument on a point of fundamental importance. They simply set forth a complete and purposeful argument in behalf of a proposition; the evidence and argument were recast by the philosophers into the language required for the proposition they wished to argue, whether in dialogue or in dialectical form. The character of the Judaic sages' system—the inheritance of revelation with which they proposed to enter dialogue—called forth a form that, in itself, expressed the character of the nurturing culture beyond.

INDEX OF SUBJECTS

INDEX OF SCRIPTURE AND RABBINICAL WORKS

THE BRILL REFERENCE LIBRARY

OF

ANCIENT JUDAISM

The Brill Reference Library of Ancient Judaism *presents research on fundamental problems in the study of the authoritative texts, beliefs and practices, events and ideas, of the Judaic religious world from the sixth century B.C.E. to the sixth century C.E. Systematic accounts of principal phenomena, characteristics of Judaic life, works of a theoretical character, accounts of movements and trends, diverse expressions of the faith, new translations and commentaries of classical texts — all will find a place in the* Library.

ISSN 1566-1237